The Women's Travel Guide
25 American Cities

The Women's Travel Guide

25 American Cities

Jane E. Lasky
and
Brenda Fine

G.K.HALL &CO.

70 LINCOLN STREET, BOSTON, MASS.

To
Gerry and Burt
Audrey, Michael, and Rachel

Copyright 1986 by Jane E. Lasky and Brenda Fine.
All rights reserved.

Library of Congress Cataloging-in-Publication Data

Lasky, Jane E.
    The women's travel guide.

    1. United States—Description and travel—
1981-   —Guide-books.   2. Women travelers—
United States—Guide-books.   3. Business travel—
United States—Guide-books.   I. Fine, Brenda.
II. Title.
E158.L26   1986   917.3'04927   86-4751
ISBN 0-8161-8735-5
ISBN 0-8161-9053-4 (pbk.)

Copyedited under the supervision of Michael Sims.
Designed and produced by John Amburg.
Set in 9/11 Optima Medium by Modern Graphics, Inc.

CONTRIBUTORS

Mimi Baer
Deborah M. Bernstein
Kay Brown
Laurie Glenn Buckle
Ellen Carver
Joan Dames
Nancy E. Diggins
Ginna Dukehart
Susan Farewell
Audrey Fine
Kay Fine
Cathy Fiscus
Gail Forman
Nancy Jo Friedman
Susie Fuhrman
Jennifer Gavin
Jan Harrison
Elizabeth Harryman
Lynn O'Rourke Hayes
Laurel Herman
Mary Hickey
Florence Hiedovitz
Barbara Horngren
Mary Jane Horton
Vicki Houston
Joyce Johnson
Lynda Johnson
Deborah Jurkowitz
M. J. Kaplan
Madeline Lee
Pamela Lechtman
Lois Levin
Lanny Lewis
Sharon Litwin

Sue Lynn
Catherine Lord
Sally McElwreath
Michelle Mancini
Maribeth Mellin
Yvonne Middleton
Jessica Miller
Jeanine Moss
Jody Murphy
Peggy Orenstein
Rosemarie O'Sullivan
Paula Panich
Vangie Philo-Sorensen
Janet Podolak
Susan R. Pollack
Celeste Reid
Katherine Rodeghier
Judith L. Rowcliffe
Leona Rubin
Candy Sagon
Melisa Sanders
Sandy Sheehy
Diane Siskin
Lois Smith
Connie S. Sokoloff
Marilyn Dorn Staats
Shifra Stein
Janet Steinberg
Jan Talley
Marie L. Tibor
Nancy E. Vaughan
Sandra Weiner
Ann M. Woolman
Helena Zukowski

CONTENTS

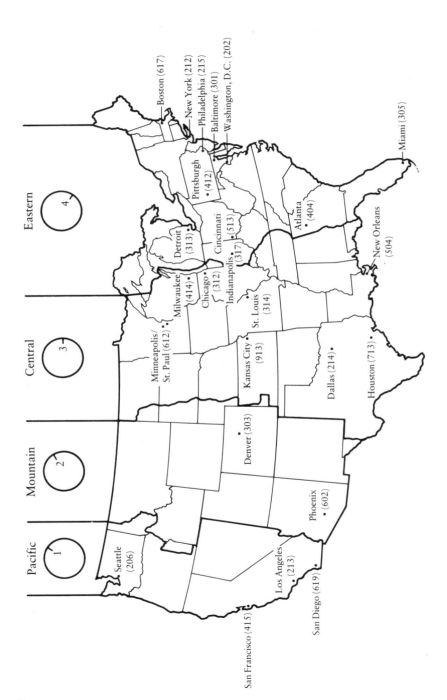

Pacific

Mountain

Central

Eastern

1

2

3

4

Seattle (206)

San Francisco (415)

Los Angeles (213)

San Diego (619)

Phoenix (602)

Denver (303)

Minneapolis/ St. Paul (612)

Milwaukee (414)

Chicago (312)

Detroit (313)

Indianapolis (317)

Cincinnati (513)

Kansas City (913)

St. Louis (314)

Dallas (214)

Houston (713)

Pittsburgh (412)

Atlanta (404)

New Orleans (504)

Boston (617)

New York (212)

Philadelphia (215)

Baltimore (301)

Washington, D.C. (202)

Miami (305)

INTRODUCTION

You've just learned you're being sent on business to an unfamiliar city. The problem: you have never visited this particular destination, and you don't know a soul there. There's no one you can call on who has a finger on the city's pulse, so you're facing the usual questions.

What do local businesswomen wear during the day?
Where do top executives entertain clients?
What is the safest, most conveniently located hotel?
Do you really need a rental car to get around town?

It's perplexing. In order to operate in an efficient, businesslike manner, you need the whole picture, but where do you get it?

Well, relax.

Open this book and become an instant expert on the local ins and outs of twenty-five urban business destinations. You'll quickly discover that *The Women's Travel Guide* ignores the usual glowing, press-release kind of approach so typical of ordinary guide books. And you won't find any of those impersonal, telephone book sort of hotel and restaurant listings, either (you know, the ones that leave you thinking, "Fine, but how can I find out the *real* story before I make a big mistake?").

This book gives you the real story—why the "best hotel" in town may not be so great for women traveling alone and why the most popular restaurant may not be the most suitable place to hold a business lunch. It also tells you the unvarnished truth about places and areas of town that local women have learned to enjoy or to avoid.

In short, we've edited out the puff and fluff to provide the true inside story of each city. You'll find our insights are highly personal, representing both our own experiences and those of the hundreds of women we conferred with who live in or travel frequently to each city covered.

You'll probably also notice we use the word *we* frequently. That's because we, Jane and Brenda, personalize everything we recommend. If we feel, for example, that a certain hotel continues to discriminate, even subtly, against women traveling alone, we tell you so. And we're equally up-front about praising those places that are savvy enough to cater to women. We feel that they deserve our business because they're trying harder to please.

And just who are "we" to tell you what we think? We are journalists who travel for a living. We stay in these hotels, eat in these restaurants, dash through these airports, and deal with these corporate communities—these and hundreds of others all over the country—on a regular basis. So it's only natural that we've formed some strong opinions, opinions that we're certain other traveling women will find helpful.

But we haven't just relied on our own decades of experience, we've verified our own good and bad experiences with women nationwide—all of whom travel extensively themselves. Consequently, each city portrait reflects the firsthand knowledge both of women who live and work in these major cities and, most important, of women who travel to these destinations frequently.

Speaking of which, there are some facts you should know about yourself if travel is part of your job. You have tremendous clout in the travel industry. Hotels, airlines, and restaurants are all scrambling to woo and please you because of vital statistics like these: in 1970 women who traveled on business represented a mere 1 percent of all business travelers; by 1983 we had grown to a hefty 33 percent, and we're still surging ahead. Projections are that by the year 2000 we will make up at least half of the entire traveling work force. That's a lot of woman power on the loose.

This means we can expect—even demand—a lot more than our "foremothers" back in the seventies could have dreamed of, those pioneer women travelers who had to put up with unsafe accommodations, undesirable tables in restaurants, patronizing or downright hostile male executives in offices, and all the other indignities that used to come with the territory.

Fortunately for us, times are changing. But there's still lots of room for improvement on a nationwide basis. And that's where this book will come in handy. We've provided you with the basic groundwork for each city, eliminating a lot of the guesswork by telling the true story of what you can expect to find. You may not agree with all our decisions, but at least you won't have to contend with faceless, generic listings of what's in town to guess where you might find the best bets. (And, if you don't agree with us, we hope you'll write to us c/o the G.K. Hall Reference Division and let us know. We welcome input from all women travelers.)

A word about absolutes. We've often quoted prices throughout this book, prices that were up-to-the-minute at press time. We hope you'll remember inflation when you refer to them, and regard them as guidelines, indicators for comparison on the relative price scale of a particular market area. We also ask your indulgence in the matter of addresses and phone numbers. Restaurants, even top-of-the-line establishments, have an exasperating habit of changing names, addresses, and phone numbers as they change management. And some even have the temerity to go out of business. We hope you won't be too inconvenienced if this happens with some place we've recommended. We've given you the most up-to-date information available.

PER DIEMS

The following list tells what you can expect a typical day to cost for the basics: meals (breakfast, lunch, dinner), and a single room, all in first-class establishments. Totals shown include tips, as well.

Atlanta	$119	Milwaukee	$ 90
Baltimore	96	Minneapolis/St. Paul	98
Boston	137	New Orleans	100
Chicago	151	New York	202
Cincinnati	89	Philadelphia	112
Dallas	122	Phoenix	85
Denver	113	Pittsburgh	113
Detroit	110	St. Louis	92
Houston	112	San Diego	139
Indianapolis	95	San Francisco	133
Kansas City (Missouri)	101	Seattle	97
Los Angeles	148	Washington, D.C.	157
Miami	96		

These figures are for the fourth quarter of 1985.* While we can logically expect the figures to change from quarter to quarter, keep in mind that the relativity of costs between the cities can be expected to remain fairly constant. Thus, New York City's per diem will probably always be higher than Cincinnati's.

TRAVEL TRENDS

In the past decade, the travel industry has shifted, adjusted, and up-graded its services to keep up with the increasing number of women taking to the road. A number of trends have emerged that make travel a much more enjoyable pursuit than it once was.

AMERICAN CONCIERGES. Once found only in European and Asian hostelries and always the friend of Americans traveling abroad,

*Figures are supplied by Runzheimer, a management consulting firm that specializes in travel and living costs. To learn more about the services this firm offers, or to subscribe to its quarterly information newsletter, call 800/558-1702, or write to Runzheimer International, Rochester, WI 53167.

concierges are now being added to the staffs of U.S. hotels as well. These enterprising hotel employees will fulfill just about any request, difficult or otherwise, put to them by their guests. If you need help making appointments for business meetings or getting tickets to a popular sporting event, seek out the hotel's concierge, usually available at desks in the lobbies of larger, deluxe hotels across the nation. With increasing frequency American concierges are women, while in other countries the profession is still dominated by men. If you choose a small hotel that doesn't include the services of a concierge, request help from guest services at the reception desk and you'll usually be able to get the assistance you seek.

EXECUTIVE FLOORS.   Because businesswomen (and men, too, for that matter) often require special services of the hotels in which they are staying, many hotels now offer what is known in the travel industry as an executive floor. Guest rooms on these floors are designed to enable business travelers to entertain clients and hold meetings in special lounges or in their rooms, which often have been structured to seem more like boardrooms than bedrooms. Security is often more stringent on these floors, too, with features like key-access elevators and a second concierge on duty on the floor.

AIRPORT HOTELS.   Once suitable only for a few hours' snooze between flights, hotels operated near metropolitan airports are now becoming sensible—even chic—places to stay even if your trip is for more than one night. These properties often include all the services you'd expect to find in a downtown facility, with the added advantage that they are conveniently located, making a quick exit a snap once business is finished.

WEEKEND PACKAGES.   With hotels often filling to capacity on weekdays because of increased corporate traffic, many find themselves with rooms to spare once the weekend rolls around. In an effort to keep bookings up, many hotels offer weekend packages on Friday, Saturday, and Sunday nights. The lure? Lower rates and extra free amenities, like a bottle of champagne or a free meal, to keep you interested.

BUSINESS CENTERS.   On the road with lots of work to do? Don't despair. Auxiliary work stations have started to spring up all over—in airports (for the really transient); in standard office buildings away from your own; and, in an increasing number of cases, right in your hotel. These handy offices-away-from-home offer equipment and services like those you'd find in your usual workplace, such as computers, photocopiers, and a full range of secretarial support.

AIRLINE CLUBS.   Once the preserve of the privileged, special airport lounges are becoming havens for harried business travelers. Their softly lit, plush-carpeted, living-room atmospheres with telephones and conference rooms have turned these formerly first-class hideaways into necessities for every frequent flyer. All are good values at yearly memberships ranging from about $45 to $85, sometimes coupled with a $15 to $60 initiation fee. While some have become a bit too crowded for their own good, they still represent an enticing alternative to plastic chairs, fluorescent glare, and mobs clamoring in main concourses.

HOW TO USE THIS BOOK

For easy reference, each of the twenty-five cities we profile in this book is presented in similar format. We begin at the beginning of your trip (an introduction to what makes the city tick) and follow through every phase of your stay.

CITY MAPS. To assist you in selecting the most convenient hotel before departure or for a quick orientation upon arrival, we introduce each city with a schematic map locating recommended hotels and key landmarks. Note that the distances shown are not to scale, so you'll need to pick up a more detailed city plan from your concierge.

GETTING YOUR BEARINGS. In this get-acquainted essay we offer you a sense of place as well as a personal evaluation of each city. Don't look for a history lesson here—unless specific past events relate directly to current happenings. Rather, take this orientation for what it is: an insider's look that fills you in on how business is conducted in that city today.

WHAT TO WEAR. We've taken the guesswork out of packing for this trip. You may not want to change your style, but it's always nice—and wise, too—to fit into a business situation, so we fill you in on how local businesswomen tend to dress for work.

WEATHER WATCH. To make packing easier, we look at the weather picture, too, commenting on the city's idiosyncrasies.

GETTING THERE. Here we let you in on what to expect at the airport, ways you can best cover the miles from the airport to your hotel, and what car rentals are available.

GETTING AROUND. During your stay will you be better off taking the bus, walking, or driving a rental car? Here is where we evaluate the best and most efficient ways to get around town.

GETTING FAMILIAR. It's not a bad idea to glean as much information as you can, beforehand, about the city you'll be visiting. Learn where to go or who to write for vital information. Learn, too, the top publications in town for both business and general news.

QUICK CALLS. Local telephone numbers for the correct time, weather, and emergencies are here, as well as the city's area code. (We don't repeat those three digits before every phone listing in the chapter.)

AT YOUR SERVICE.   Our choices for the hotels that best suit the needs of the traveling businesswoman are listed in this section. These are neither the most nor the least expensive—they're simply the best for women. With each entry we have tried to convey a sense of hotel ambience, along with its physical location, special amenities, and on-premises dining facilities.

An accompanying chart lets you see at a glance the range of services offered by all of the chosen hotels, including such services as:

Concierge: Is there a special staff member on duty to see to your special requests?

Executive Floor: Does the hotel operate a special floor (sometimes also referred to as a concierge floor or business floor) that offers special amenities and services to business travelers?

No-Smoking Rooms: Are there rooms set aside for nonsmokers and those who don't enjoy staying in rooms previously occupied by smokers? (Some hotel chains even offer entire no-smoking floors.)

Fitness Facilities: Does the hotel offer in-house exercise rooms or health spa facilities? We don't note those hotels that offer an arrangement with nearby health clubs *off* the premises.

Pool: Is there a pool—either indoor or outdoor—on the premises?

24-Hour Room Service: Can you expect room service around the clock?

Restaurant for Client Entertaining: Which restaurant best suits those who prefer to host business meals in the hotel?

Extra Special Amenities: Can you expect to find deluxe amenities like hair dryers, bathroom scales, terry robes, and makeup mirrors provided by the hotel?

Electronic Key System: Does the hotel use reprogrammable computer key cards, or conventional keys for the guest rooms?

Business/Secretarial Services: Is the hotel equipped with business amenities like copying and telex machines, translation and secretarial services for its guests' use?

Check-Out Time: By what hour must you check out before being charged for an extra day?

Frequent Guest Program: Is there an incentive program for regular guests that allows them to earn free or reduced rates, upgrades, or other rewards?

Business Traveler Program: Does the hotel have a program that offers special treatment like no-stop check in and check out, and corporate rates? Be sure to request corporate rates when booking. You may not qualify, but it doesn't hurt to ask, as each hotel has its own policies.

Average Single Rate: What are the average room rates for a single traveler? Often several will apply: the regular rate, the corporate rate, and those—slightly higher—for singles on the executive floor. Some hotels that offer corporate rates decline to quote them for publication. Be sure to explore all options when booking.

ON A BUDGET. While every city has low-priced accommodations, not all are appropriate for a woman traveling alone. We've selected at least one place—and sometimes two or three—in each city that combines savory surroundings with reasonable rates. Note that budget hotels appear on the maps but not on the charts.

Also in this section are economical places to eat. Often, these are also the most fun places in town. Whenever possible we've also included thrifty entertainment possibilities like free concerts, outdoor performances, even half-price movies.

DINING OUT. This section offers a selection of our favorite restaurants, including suggestions of where to dine for power business meals, where you'll feel most comfortable dining alone, and those places considered by locals to be the best in town. In urban-sprawl cities we've grouped restaurants by neighborhoods to help in your selections.

CITY BY DAY. Have a few leisure hours? We give you a well-rounded selection of museums, historical attractions, and other sites, usually beginning with the best vantage point from which to get an overview of the city.

CITY BY NIGHT. Want to take in the ballet, the opera, or a theater event while you're in town? In this section we fill you in on the city's cultural activities.

LATE NIGHT IN THE CITY. Here we give you some idea of the city's after-hours tempo—which clubs and bars are suitable for a woman on her own and which ones should be avoided.

AT LEISURE. Here's where we suggest you take advantage of those economical hotel weekend packages, stay over a few days before or after your business trip, and enjoy the local attractions you won't have time for during the work week. **Day-Tripping** suggests those places outside the city that merit your attention. **In Town** lists activities you might want to enjoy at a more leisurely pace. And **Sunday Customs** lets you in on how the locals like to spend their day of rest. For the sports-minded we've included an array of athletic diversions both **Active** and **Spectator**.

The UNIQUELY section can crop up anywhere in a chapter and can cover almost anything—from Kansas City jazz to New York bargains to Atlanta's *Gone with the Wind* traditions—whatever the special aspect of that city might be, to give you an additional insight into what helps to make it unique.

TRAVEL SAVVY

Business travel is sufficiently stress-filled without your having to put up with unnecessary pressures on the road. Here are some suggestions to help make things a bit easier on yourself.

GUARANTEE RESERVATIONS whenever you can. Just give your credit card number over the phone when you make your reservation. You will then have the peace of mind of knowing that your room will be held for you no matter how late you check in. Your only obligation is to be sure to cancel if you won't be arriving—otherwise they'll charge you anyway.

TOLL-FREE NUMBERS are a great boon to anyone's budget. Use them for comparing prices, making reservations, and gathering travel information. Because they change so frequently, we've listed very few in this book. But we urge you to call the information number, 800/555-1212 to get the current toll-free numbers for car-rental agencies, hotels, and airlines.

TIPS ON TIPPING. Deciding who gets how much stumps all of us at one time or another. Here are some general rules to remember:

Bellman or Porter—50¢ to $1 per bag. A minimum of $1 for a single bag.

Chambermaid—$1 for each day.

Room Service—15 percent of the bill (not including tax) if there's no service charge.

Concierge—7 to 10 percent of the daily room rate for services beyond the usual. It's wise to give a portion of this up-front to guarantee super service.

Restaurant dining—The general rule is to tip 15 to 20 percent of the total (before taxes) if there are no service charges. If you pay with a credit card sometimes the charge slip will break down the service into categories. In this event merely divide the total of the tip, allotting one-quarter for the captain and three-quarters for the waiter. For the maître d', a cash tip of $5 to $10 is appropriate if he was helpful, or if you plan to return to this restaurant and want to be greeted like visiting royalty.

IN-HOTEL SAFETY requires some work on your part, as well as a savvy hotel management. The basics, as you well know, include insisting that the room meet your personal standards, and making sure the desk clerk doesn't announce your room number to the lobby at large. You should also:

• Have whoever escorts you to your room check the safety features— smoke detector, door locks—before he leaves.
• Avoid rooms on the ground floor.
• Always keep all doors locked. This includes the sliding door onto the balcony, if you have one.
• Don't admit anyone you're not expecting. If someone knocks and says he's from housekeeping or maintenance, call that department to confirm before opening the door.
• When taking out your key in the elevator, be sure not to display the room number on it.

- Don't hang the "Make up My Room" sign outside the door. It announces to the world that you're not in the room.
- Check the location of the nearest fire exit. To fix it in your mind, go into the hall and actually count the number of steps from your door to the exit. It could save your life in a smoke-filled emergency.

We discuss general safety tactics in each chapter as they apply in the individual city. While some cities pride themselves on their low crime rates and "safe" environments, we err on the side of caution, suggesting that city strolls be confined to daylight hours and that cabs make the most sensible after-dark transportation. We also strongly recommend you check with the hotel's concierge or other staff member about the safest jogging routes for your early-morning or evening exercise.

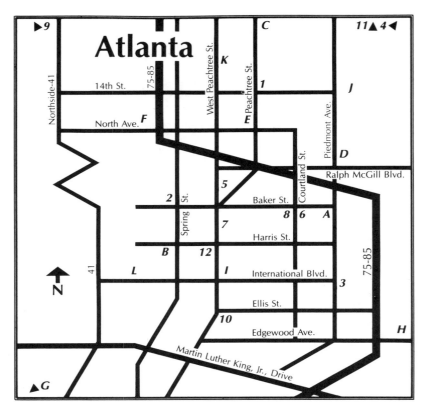

HOTELS

1 Colony Square
2 Days Inn
3 Downtown Holiday Inn
4 Guest Quarters
5 Habersham
6 Hilton & Towers
7 Hyatt Regency
8 Marriott Marquis
9 Pickett
10 Ritz-Carlton Atlanta
11 Ritz-Carlton Buckhead
12 Westin Peachtree Plaza

LANDMARKS

A Atlanta Center
B Atlanta Market Center
C Buckhead
D Civic Center
E Fox Theatre
F Georgia Tech
G Hartsfield International Airport
H Martin Luther King Historic District
I Peachtree Center
J Piedmont Park
K Woodruff Arts Center
L World Congress Center

ATLANTA

GETTING YOUR BEARINGS

Atlanta is a city of the future that remains fiercely proud of its heritage; for every high-tech building there's an antebellum mansion. And you're never too far away from a heartfelt rendition of "Dixie" or a Confederate flag waving from a passing car. There are also plenty of folks here who take offense at any title other than the War between the States. They believed in the motto, "The South Shall Rise Again"—and indeed it has.

Atlanta is a great sprawl of a city, the southern hub for 439 of the Fortune 500 industrial firms, 50 of the largest life insurance companies, and countless commercial banking, health care, and financial companies. The city's vast commercial focus is nicely balanced by its easygoing heritage. The quality of life is very important to people here—the suburbs and residential areas are among the most beautiful anywhere, cultural activities and events are world-class, leisure time is highly prized, and good manners are a virtue second only to godliness.

If you've never experienced the legendary southern hospitality before, Atlanta is a great city for an introduction to this honored tradition. They'll "ma'am" you at every turn, compete to see who can open your door, light your cigarette, and pay your tab. But don't be lulled into believing these easygoing charmers are less than laser-sharp. Beneath those chivalrous exteriors lurk good-old-boy mentalities. They have, and always have had, their network—and you're not part of it.

Women doing business in Atlanta report that the macho attitude is very much alive. Businessmen here are very conservative—and expect women to be even more so.

Atlanta offers about a million square feet of exhibition space, and this doesn't take into account the thousands of square feet of meeting spaces in hotels. Statistics show that Atlanta is relatively inexpensive for visiting business travelers.

Most businesses have offices in the downtown area; the hotels are there, too, along with some strategic meeting and cultural facilities. However, this area is *dead* at night. We have driven along Peachtree Street (the main drag) at night and not seen a single person walking anywhere.

The up-and-coming area of Atlanta is Buckhead, a beautiful area just a bit north of downtown. It began as a wealthy suburb, started adding some lovely restaurants, stores, and clubs, and is currently blossoming into a business center to rival the downtown area. Buckhead definitely does not close down at night—this is where all the action takes place.

A word about Peachtree: this word appears in dozens of guises at every turn in Atlanta. You'll see Peachtree roads, streets, drives, plazas, circles, and avenues in dizzying sequence. Before you get confused, remember only this: Peachtree Street is the main thoroughfare. It runs north-south, and as it heads north of downtown and into Buckhead, it becomes Peachtree Road. For most logistical problems, that's all the Peachtree information you'll need.

WHAT TO WEAR

Keeping the southern gentleman businessman in mind, you'll do best to bow to local customs and adopt protective coloring. Be conservative, even a bit on the down-side of conservative: wear blouses and skirts and suits rather than dresses. In summer, bright cottons are fine.

WEATHER WATCH

Even though this is Dixie, the winters can be freezing. Summers, as you might expect, are equally brutal with temperatures in the high 90s. Spring and fall make it all worthwhile. April is the very best month of all. With masses of dogwood and azaleas and other flowering trees and shrubs in full bloom, the entire area is extraordinarily beautiful.

GETTING THERE

Hartsfield International is the second busiest airport in the country. It is highly efficient—with moving sidewalks and a high-speed internal subway system—and ranks high with travelers, who rated it third in their top-ten favorite airports, according to a poll by *Ad Age.* (This despite all the jokes about the inevitability of having to pass through Atlanta no matter *where* your destination.)

Hartsfield is served by about 22 carriers. The number for general airport information is 530-6600.

It is about nine miles into downtown Atlanta, a drive that can take anywhere from 15 to 30 minutes, depending on traffic. Because a cab ride into town runs about $15, and the airport limo costs only about $6 per person, it's not difficult to see why most women prefer the limo (Airline Airport Shuttle: 766-5312). The only free hotel/airport services in

Atlanta are to airport hotels, not to those in the downtown or outlying areas.

Car Rentals

Avis	530-2700
Budget	659-3200
Hertz	659-3000
National	530-2800

GETTING AROUND

The need for a rental car will depend on where you want to go while you're in town. If everything—hotel, business meetings, contacts—is within the downtown area, you're better off using cabs and MARTA, the rapid rail system. On-street parking is scarce and regulations are strictly enforced.

Much of the metro area is spread out, however, and you'll definitely need a car if you plan to see any of it, or if you decide on a minivacation (see "At Leisure").

Local cabs don't enjoy the best of reputations. Many riders complain of their inefficiency and of drivers who don't know their way around town. Fares are metered: $1.70 on the drop and 80 cents per mile thereafter. Be sure to negotiate a flat rate to and from the airport. In the downtown area you can hail a cruising cab, or you can call ahead. We recommend these two companies: Atlanta Million, 688-9292, and Yellow Cab, 522-0200.

Atlanta's MARTA system is good news: clean, new, and super-safe with closed-circuit monitors and lots of police, both plainclothes and uniformed. While it's the greatest way to get from downtown to Lenox Square, for example, it doesn't go everywhere as yet. There's a connecting bus system that helps link more destinations. Call 522-4711 for helpful commuting directions. You may want to buy the $5 TourCard for one week's worth of unlimited MARTA travel. (Each one-way ride is 60 cents.) Pick up one when you get to town, or if you want to plan ahead, write MARTA, 2200 Peachtree Summit, 401 W. Peachtree Street, NE, Atlanta, GA 30365.

GETTING FAMILIAR

Atlanta Convention and Visitors Bureau
233 Peachtree Street, NE   521-6600
Atlanta, GA 30303
There is no toll-free number. Foreign-language visitors can use a special number: 577-2248.

Among the city's many convention centers:

Georgia World Congress Center
285 International Boulevard, NW   656-7676
Atlanta, GA 30313

Atlanta Market Center
240 Peachtree Street, NW   658-5683
Atlanta, GA 30303

Southern Conference Center
14th and Peachtree Streets   892-6000
Atlanta, GA 30361

The *Atlanta Constitution* is a daily morning paper. The *Atlanta Journal* is an evening daily. Check the *Journal's* Saturday "Weekend" section and the *Constitution's* "Dixie Living and Entertainment" section for current happenings, reviews, and other up-to-the-minute tips. *Atlanta* is a glossy monthly magazine with trendy features, listings, reviews of restaurants, and cultural and entertainment events.

——— *Quick Calls* ———

AREA CODE 404   Weather 455-7141
Time 936-8550   Police 911

AT YOUR SERVICE

Atlanta Marriott Marquis
265 Peachtree Center Avenue   Toll-free reservations: 800/228-9290
Atlanta, GA 30303   Local number: 521-0000
                                   Telex: 5106001069
This new giant, the largest hotel in the South, opened in the summer of 1985 to replace its older sister as the best Marriott in town. Its 46-story interior atrium is also a local record holder; it's the most towering atrium in town. Bubble elevators and lots of original works by contemporary artists complete the new-look decor. The upper six floors are executive floors (called Concierge Floors by this hotel). Executive Business Service is an on-demand service providing everything from instant business cards to audiovisuals for tomorrow's meeting. An in-house health club includes indoor and outdoor pools, exercise equipment, steam room, sauna, and juice bar.

There are five restaurants: **J.W.'s** for serious dining, **La Fuente** for Mexican cuisine, **Pompano's** for seafood, **Atrium Cafe** for French cuisine, and the **Arbor,** a coffee shop.

Ritz-Carlton Buckhead
3434 Peachtree Road, NE
Atlanta, GA 30326

Toll-free reservations: 800/241-3333
Local number: 237-2700
Telex: 549521

In this city of hotels, this one is considered Atlanta's most fashionable. It succeeds in combining traditional European service with southern hospitality—a winning combination. Even the neighborhood is right: Buckhead's the current in place to be. The 573 rooms are furnished with art and authentic antiques, and outfitted with extras like hair dryers and terry robes. The Club Level, for business travelers, goes even further with amenities like TVs in the bathrooms. There is a complete in-house fitness center.

The dining rooms and lounges are all excellent and fine for entertaining clients or being alone.

Ritz-Carlton Atlanta
181 Peachtree Street, NE
Atlanta, GA 30303

Toll-free reservations: 800/241-3333
Local number: 659-0400
Telex: 543291

An exceptional new hotel, elegant and clublike, in the heart of Atlanta's business district and near the Georgia World Congress Center. A superb collection of eighteenth- and nineteenth-century art works graces the public rooms. The 454 guest rooms are beautifully decorated and boast special amenities. The rooms on the Club Level (executive floors) offer traditional extras in services and luxuries.

Hotel restaurants are excellent, there's live entertainment in the **Cafe** off the main lobby. An elegant Continental breakfast is served in the lobby lounge each morning.

Atlanta Hilton and Towers
255 Courtland Street, NE
Atlanta, GA 30043

Toll-free reservations: 800/445-8667
Local number: 659-2000
Telex: 804370

A 30-story building (1,250 rooms) with several courtyards, built around a seven-story atrium. The result is airy and open, despite the massive size. The top three floors of the towers make up the executive level. A very popular hotel. Location is handy to downtown businesses.

Some excellent restaurants: **Nikolai's Roof** is so in even hotel guests have to make reservations well in advance. Let the concierge pull some strings for you (see "Dining Out"). **Cafe de la Paix** serves buffet dinners and very popular Sunday brunches; **Trader Vic's** is exactly what you would expect it to be. The two lounges, **Casablanca** and **Acapulco,** are thematic and just fine for solo women. The disco, **Another World,** is a hot spot (see "Late-Night Atlanta").

	Concierge	Executive Floor	No-Smoking Rooms	Fitness Facilities	Pool	24-Hour Room Service	Restaurant for Client Entertaining	Extra-Special Amenities	Electronic Key System	Business/Secretarial Services	Checkout Time	Frequent Guest Program	Business Traveler Program	Average Single Rate
Colony Square	●	●		●	●	●	Toulouse			●	1 p.m.	V.I.S. Very Imp. Services		$ 90 / $ 75
Guest Quarters (all suites)	●			●	●	●	Lark and Dove	●		●	2 p.m.			$166 / $150
Hilton & Towers	●		●	●	●		Nikolai's Roof				1 p.m.			$ 82 / $130
Hyatt Regency	●	●	●	●	●	●	Hugo's	●		●	12 noon	Gold Passport		$ 95 / $ 92
Marriott Marquis	●	●		●	●		J.W.'s		●	●		Honored Guest Club Marquis	Exec. Business Service	$109 / $ 99
Pickett (all suites)				●	●		Pralines	●	●	●	12 noon			$102 / $ 96
Ritz Carlton Atlanta	●	●				●	The Restaurant	●		●	12 noon	Executive Reservation Service		$105 / $120
Ritz Carlton Buckhead	●	●	●	●	●	●	The Dining Room			●	1 p.m.	Executive Reservation Service		$105 / $120
Westin Peachtree Plaza	●		●	●	●	●	Sundial		●	●	1 p.m.		Guaranteed Corp. Rate	$115 / $ 92

Hyatt Regency Atlanta

265 Peachtree Street, NE   Toll-free reservations: 800/228-8000
(Peachtree Center)   Local number: 577-1234
Atlanta, GA 30303   Telex: 542485

This is where it all began—all those towering Hyatt atriums, those glass-walled interior elevators, all those masses of green plants—right here in the heart of downtown Atlanta. Opened in 1967, this one remains popular with both vacationers and business travelers. The executive level, Regency Club, has excellent security (key-access elevator) and incorporates rooms "especially for women"—flowers and other feminine amenities.

The restaurants are excellent: **Polaris,** for both dining and drinking, revolves to give great views of the city; **Hugo's,** Hyatt's signature fine-dining restaurant; plus several wonderful ethnic-theme cafes at lobby level. The **Club Atlantis** is a supper club with name entertainment; **Ampersand Lounge** has a live piano bar.

Westin Peachtree Plaza

International Boulevard at Peachtree   Toll-free reservations: 800/228-3000
   Street   Local number: 659-1400
Atlanta, GA 30343   Telex: 804323

The South's tallest building (70 stories), this hotel has lots of wide-open spaces, including a half-acre lake in the lobby, and cramped guest rooms. Some women love it, especially those with business at the next-door Merchandise and Apparel Mart; others report feeling confused and uncomfortable in such a vast place. There are 1,100 rooms, with no special executive floor designation. General security includes a 24-hour security force and a doorman.

Sundial is a revolving restaurant on top of the hotel featuring Continental cuisine; **Savannah Fish Company** gets good reviews. The **Inner Circle Show Lounge** features live entertainment.

Colony Square Hotel

Peachtree Street at 14th Street   Toll-free reservations: 800/323-7500
Atlanta, GA 30361   Local number: 892-6000
                                  Telex: 543681

A midtown hotel, located across from the Atlanta Memorial Arts Center, about a $3 cab ride from downtown. The Southern Conference Center is on the premises, and the hotel is part of the Colony Square Shopping Mall. You're in the heart of a shopping/cultural scene in this hotel. Ask for one of the rooms with a sitting area. Most rooms have such amenities as alarm clocks and shoe buffers.

Restaurants include **Toulouse,** a two-star French restaurant that serves a before-theater menu (great for when you're dashing across the street to the theater) and the **Crown Room,** usually available only for private parties or meetings, but open to the public on Sundays between 10 A.M. and 2:30 P.M. for their famous "blue-jean brunch." The **Verandah** is a wine-tasting bar in the lobby.

Outside the Downtown Area

There are several new all-suites hotels in the area around Atlanta. These convenient accommodations include one- and two-bedroom suites with kitchens, which can be rented for a single night or on a long-term basis. Here are some of the ones we like best.

Guest Quarters
111 Perimeter Center West   Local number: 396-6800
(Ashford-Dunwoody area)
Atlanta, GA 30346

and

7000 Roswell Road   Local number: 394-6300
(Sandy Springs area)   Toll-free reservations for both: 800/424-
Atlanta, GA 30328   2900

Pickett Suite Hotel
2999 Windy Hill   Toll-free reservations: 800/742-5388
Marietta, GA   Local number: 956-9999

ON A BUDGET

Hotels

Days Inn
300 Spring Street NW   Toll-free reservations: 800/325-2525
Atlanta, GA 30308   Local number: 523-1144
Near the Merchandise and Apparel Mart. Rate for a single is about $59, regardless of season.

Habersham Hotel
330 Peachtree Street NE   Local number: 577-1980
Atlanta, GA 30308   Toll-free reservations: 800/241-4288
A small (93 rooms) hotel with some nice personal touches like morning juice and coffee delivered to your room, afternoon tea, turn-down service, wet bar and fridge in room. Free parking. Single rates: $59–$62.

Atlanta Downtown Holiday Inn
175 Piedmont Avenue, NE   Toll-free reservations: 800/465-4329
Atlanta, GA 30303   Local number: 659-2727
You couldn't ask for a more central location. Nothing fancy, but clean and well kept. Outdoor pool. Singles start at $80.

Restaurants

Some local favorites for when your palate craves something different—but your wallet craves a break:

Joe Dale's Cajun spread includes all your favorites: blackened red fish, jambalaya, shrimp creole. Prices range from $9 to $15 (with free side dishes including Dirty Rice). 3340 Peachtree Road (facing Piedmont). 261-2741.

Rio Bravo Cantina is new, clean, and authentically Mexican. Portions are huge—enough for your meal and a take-home, too. Interesting touch: the strolling guitarists are women. 3172 Roswell Road, NW. 262-7431.

Country Gourmet serves heaps of fresh vegetables and southern down-home cooking the way you'd like it to be. Three locations, all near Buckhead: 3525 Piedmont Road and 975 Johnson Ferry Road serve only breakfast and lunch; 3115 Buford Highway serves all three meals. Lunches about $3.50; dinners from $3.95 to $5.95. 262-9813.

Like something out of a fifties movie set, **The Varsity**—the world's biggest drive-in restaurant—throbs with energy. They've been serving Atlantans their hot dogs and fries for over 50 years. Open late every night. Inexpensive. 61 North Avenue, NW (across from Georgia Tech). 881-1706.

Entertainment

Matinee tickets to any performances—movies, Civic Center events, the symphony—are all temptingly discounted.

DINING OUT

Locals will tell you that most of the action in town takes place in Buckhead. This includes dining as well, both gourmet and trendy spots. However, there are a few notable exceptions. We've included what we believe to be among the best in all locations, especially for client entertaining. We call moderate those restaurants offering dinners for $15 to $30. Expensive is $35 to $75 (or even higher); inexpensive is under $15.

Buckhead Area

La Grotta Ristorante Italiano is all candlelight and terrace view. Expensive northern Italian cuisine served in elegant surroundings. Dinners only. Closed Sundays. 2637 Peachtree Road, NE. 231-1368. (There's another location in Roswell.)

Hedgerose Heights features Continental—French, German,

Swiss—favorites. Popular with locals and business people. Expensive. Closed Sundays. 490 East Paces Ferry Road, NE 233-7673

Bone's Steak and Seafood serves steakhouse fare in a clubby atmosphere some patrons describe as "sophisticated down-home," others as "charming old-time atmosphere." Very popular with advertising and media people; great place for late Sunday night dinner. Expensive. Open for dinner seven days; weekdays only for lunch. 3130 Piedmont Road. 237-2663.

Trotter's is another stylish Buckhead place with a harness racing theme. Northern Italian cuisine, great homemade pasta and seafood combinations. Country club atmosphere with excellent service and trendy clientele. Dinner served until midnight on weekends. Sunday brunch. 3215 Peachtree Road, NE. 237-5988.

Pano and Paul's may fool you at first. The exterior doesn't give a clue to the beautiful decor you'll find inside. A favorite hang-out of bankers and lawyers, this restaurant serves dinners only. Expensive Continental and American cuisine. West Paces Ferry Shopping Center. 261-3662.

103 West (same owners as Pano and Paul's) is also opulent and expensive. Miles of brocade, plush, and crystal. Continental cuisine. Closed Saturday lunch and all day Sunday. 103 West Paces Ferry Road, NW. 233-5993.

Coach and Six is a big favorite with frequent visitors as well as with locals. (Make your reservations well in advance.) Good steaks; try the hearty black bean soup. Menu is in seven languages. Why? Ask them. Expensive. Open for Sunday dinner. 1776 Peachtree Road, NW. 872-6666.

Maison Robert is a Swiss patisserie that spells sheer heaven for sweets lovers. Closed Sundays and Mondays. Inexpensive. No reservations. 3867 Peachtree Road. 237-3675.

Downtown/Midtown Area

Nikolai's Roof is so popular it's almost impossible to get a reservation. Classic Russian specialties are served in opulent czarist style. Open daily; two seatings, 6 and 9 P.M. Expensive. Roof of Atlanta Hilton Hotel. 659-2000.

Pentimento Cafe offers a creative cuisine in a lovely patio environment in the heart of the Memorial Arts Center. Perfect for museum-day lunches, or before- or after-theater dinners. Both the menu and restaurant hours are seasonal; best to call ahead for specifics. Moderate prices. 1280 Peachtree Street. 875-6665.

The Peasant Group—especially **The Pleasant Peasant**—specializes in moderately priced, innovative American and Continental cuisine served in trendy bistro setting. No reservations. 555 Peachtree Street. 874-3223

The Abbey plays its ecclesiastical theme to the hilt: harpist in the choir loft; waiters in monks' habits. Despite this (or maybe because of this), it's a very popular place in town. Cuisine is French country. On the last Friday of every month you can order an eight-course dinner in the wine cellar. Expensive. 163 Ponce de Leon Avenue, NE. 876-8532.

Pittypat's Porch. You remember dotty, lovable old Aunt Pittypat. Her Old South hospitality here includes seven-course meals, an "endless appetizer," and lots of charm. Service is family style and there are rocking chairs on the interior balconies. More than worth the moderate prices—it's a lot of fun. 25 International Boulevard, NW. 525-8228.

Mary Mac's Tea Room is where you should head if you want to mix with real Atlanta for some authentic southern food. This place has been a local favorite since 1935. The food here is great: southern home cooking, plentiful, and inexpensive. Dinners only. Closed on weekends. No credit cards. 224 Ponce de Leon Avenue, NE. 876-6604.

ATLANTA BY DAY

The face of Atlanta may be modern, but her spirit is deeply rooted in her history. For a helpful overview of this historical heritage, take in the giant **Cyclorama** depicting Atlanta's darkest day, July 22, 1864, the Battle of Atlanta. Narrations explain this unique 360-degree canvas that stands 50 feet high and measures 400 feet around. Open seven days. In Grant Park (southeast section of town). 800 Cherokee Avenue, SE. 624-1071.

High Museum of Art is a $20 million building housing an invaluable collection of art ranging from Renaissance and baroque to impressionist works. Paintings, sculpture, and decorative pieces by European and American artists. The building, an architectural masterpiece in its own right, presents a distinctive high-gloss enamel white exterior, six levels, and a four-story skylit atrium. Closed Mondays. Peachtree and 16th streets. The Memorial Arts Center. 892-3600.

Nearby is the **Robert W. Woodruff Arts Center,** which contains Atlanta's cultural heart: **Symphony Hall,** the **Alliance Theater, Atlanta Children's Theater,** and the **Atlanta College of Art.** Together, these two buildings constitute the Atlanta Arts Alliance. For information, call 892-3600. There's also an information hot line: 892-4444.

For another one-step look at Atlanta's history, both wealthy and dirt-poor, visit the Historical Society's two restored properties: Swan House and the Tullie Smith House—both on 22 acres of landscaped preserve. 3103 Andrews Drive, NW. 261-1837. **Swan House,** a 1928 Palladian revival building, represents some of Atlanta's highest high society; it belonged to a prominent Georgia family. There are beautiful European and Oriental furnishings and objects; formal gardens and fountains. The trick here is to try to spot the swan motif in furnishings and decor as you tour the house. The **Tullie Smith House** is an authentic 1840s "plantation plain" Georgia farmhouse, which the society moved here—lock, stock, and attached buildings—from Decatur. Tours of both houses are available every day. Call 261-1837.

The **Swan Coach House,** the former coach house of the Swan House, is now a restaurant, gift shop, and gallery. Very popular with local women (and with visiting women in-the-know). You can make reservations for groups of more than ten; larger groups rate a private dining room. Open seven days. Art gallery closed on Sunday. 261-0636.

You may have heard talk about **Underground Atlanta.** This old section of downtown (below the present level) has fallen into disrepair. Plans now include a purported $120 million restoration by the Rouse Company that would spiff everything up, add entertainment, food, and retail stores. No target date as yet.

UNIQUELY ATLANTA

Alas, you Rhett and Scarlett fans, *GWTW* is all but gone from Atlanta. Don't plan on pigging out on your favorite book/movie while you're in town—what's here is hard to locate and mainly reserved for large groups.

Out at Lovejoy, for example, Mrs. Jane Talmadge displays her 1836 antebellum plantation (said to have inspired the design of the Wilkes mansion, Twelve Oaks) and the facade of the movie-set Tara along with other *GWTW* memorabilia—but only for special large groups. 478-6807. Some tour companies like Gray Line run excursions out to Madison and Covington where Tara-style mansions grow like tract houses. Not the real thing, but you can pretend. The **Public Library** has a small collection— some Margaret Mitchell, some *GWTW*. She researched the book here. Peachtree and Forsyth streets. 688-4034. And if you're in luck, your visit will coincide with one of the frequent showings of the film in the splendid **Fox Theater.** 660 Peachtree, NE. 881-1977.

THE SHOPPING SCENE

Atlanta is a shopper's heaven—stores everywhere you turn, and a vast international variety of selections.

Downtown, the two retail giants, **Rich's** and **Davison's,** reign supreme. Both are full service, offering some designer and avant-garde fashions along with mid-priced ready-to-wear. Both have many branch operations around town in the various malls. There's only one mall downtown—**Peachtree Center,** three levels of shops, services, cafes. 231 Peachtree Street, NE. 659-0800.

We may get differing opinions on this, but we believe *the* ultimate shopping experience can be found at the corner of Peachtree and Lenox roads in Buckhead (about eight miles north of downtown) where Lenox Square and Phipps Plaza meet. Between these two shopping meccas, we can't imagine any dedicated shopper not finding whatever she desires. **Lenox Square** is a long-standing trendsetter, with branches of

Rich's, Davison's, and Neiman-Marcus as well as over 200 boutiques and specialty stores in an enclosed mall. Open Sundays. 3393 Peachtree Road, NE. 233-8084. **Phipps Plaza** features the heavy-duty fashion names: Gucci, Tiffany, Saks Fifth Avenue, Lord & Taylor, along with designer boutiques. Lots of restaurants, theaters, services. 3500 Peachtree Road, NE. 261-7910.

There are, literally, dozens of other malls—some more specialized, others not as exciting—around metro Atlanta. One such specialty mall is **Outlet Square,** an entire mall of off-price stores, including Burlington Coat Factory, Marshall's, and dozens of shops discounting everything from accessories to home furnishings. At the intersection of Clairmont Road and Buford Highway (take exit 25 off I-285). 633-2566. There's also a **Loehmann's** not too far away (3299 Buford Highway, near I-285 and Druid Hills Road) for major bargains on ready-to-wear and some designer samples.

Little Five Points is a historic area as well as a trendy place to browse. Dating back to the 1920s, this site includes antebellum and Confederate buildings. The Old South rises here. 524-8629.

ATLANTA BY NIGHT

Again we stress: the downtown area is *dead* at night. If you go there, be sure to cab in and out. Local women report that no matter how tempting the production, they hesitate to go to either the Theatrical Outfit or the Academy Theater—the neighborhoods are just too iffy.

We used to get them confused. Just so you won't: the Civic Center hosts only cultural-type events (musicals, ballet, classical concerts); the World Congress Center is more like Madison Square Garden (the circus, rock concerts). You can pick up advance tickets to any kind of performance at any **SEATS Outlet** (at Turtle Record stores and other locations). Call 577-2626.

The fabulous **Fox Theater** is Atlanta's 1920s pleasure palace, built to pamper and impress audiences back when movies reigned supreme. Now a national landmark, the theater's Byzantine/Moorish splendor should be seen just for itself as well as for the performances it showcases. 660 Peachtree Street, NE. 881-1977.

Civic Center is where you'll find resident ballet and symphony companies, as well as such visitors as New York's Metropolitan Opera. 395 Piedmont Avenue.

 Atlanta Symphony 873-5811
  (Winter Pops series)
 Atlanta Ballet 873-5811
 Atlanta Chamber Players 892-2414
 Metropolitan Opera 262-2161

The **Robert W. Woodruff Arts Center** is home to the Atlanta Symphony, directed by Robert Shaw; the **Alliance Theater; Atlanta Children's**

Theater; and the **Atlanta College of Art.** Check local listings for schedules. Call 892-2414 for information. We've found a delightful place for both lunches as well as before and after theater dinners: **Pentimento Cafe.** It's right in the Memorial Arts Center (see "Dining Out").

The movie theaters in the Buckhead shopping centers are safe enough and well attended: **Theaters I and II** in Lenox Square, Phipps Plaza **Theater Tower.**

LATE-NIGHT ATLANTA

There's definitely a nightlife out there—you just have to be picky about what you choose. As in any city, the lounges in your hotel are probably the safest bet. Some of them—like the cafe-bar in the Buckhead Ritz-Carlton which features entertainment by Nat "King" Cole's brother—are outstanding.

FOR JAZZ FANS
        Dante's Down the Hatch features award-winning jazz in an 18th-century sailing-vessel motif. Thirteen interconnecting levels with jazz, folk, even classical music. Open late all week. 3380 Peachtree Road (across from Lenox Square). 266-1600.
        Carlos McGee's attracts the under-30s fun seekers—jazz and disco. 3035 Peachtree Road. 231-7979.
        Walter Mitty's Jazz Cafe presents live performers of both contemporary and progressive jazz. Open late all week. 816 N. Highland Avenue, NE. 876-7115.

STRICTLY DISCO
        Limelight. Said to be the model the other Limelights in New York and Chicago are based on, this one has all the vitals: VIP room, screening rooms, shows, restaurant, and, of course, disco. 3330 Piedmont Road, NE (Buckhead). 231-3520.
        Elan, out near the Perimeter Mall, features top-40 sounds. There's also a restaurant serving lunch and dinner. 4505 Ashford-Dunwoody Road. 393-1333.
        Another World is flash and dazzle high atop the Atlanta Hilton. 255 Courtland Street. 659-2000.

COFFEE HOUSE ATMOSPHERE
        Cafe Intermezzo is quite elegant. Great for pastries, coffees, light meals. In the Park Place Mall. 396-1344.
        Capo's Cafe has very good food, reasonable prices. Neighborhood could be better. 992 Virginia Avenue, NE. 876-5655.
        Harrison's is trendy, favored by the foreign car set. Two locations: 2110 Peachtree Road, NE (351-7596); Galleria (952-0004).
        Zasu's is an art deco environment with late-night coffees and bar drinks. Dinner served until 2:30 A.M. 1923 Peachtree Street, NE. 352-3052.

AT LEISURE

Because Atlanta is so spread out, you can't possibly see everything of interest during one business trip. If you can attach a few days to either end of your official trip for a minivacation, we have some great recommendations. Start with this one: check around the various hotels to find the best deal on weekend packages.

Day-Tripping

Stone Mountain Park is one of the area's must-see places. A huge 3,200-acre recreational/educational park with such features as the world's largest granite carving—Confederate Memorial Carving (called Mount Rushmore South by locals); paddlewheel riverboats; a laser show; wildlife trails; even a 90-room historic guest inn. You name it—it's probably there. Open daily. Admission charge (under $5). Sixteen miles east of town. MARTA bus service available from downtown. 469-9831.

Lake Lanier Island and **Pinelsle Resort:** 60 square miles of wooded lands and lakes. An outdoor person's paradise with riding, fishing, camping, golf, and tennis. The hotel is a good one (four stars from Mobil). Thirty-five miles northeast of town, about a 45-minute drive. Call 945-6701 for general information; 945-8921 for hotel reservations.

Kennesaw Mountain National Battlefield Park, site of a crucial encounter in 1864 before General Sherman began his siege of Atlanta and his march to the sea. This 2,800-acre park includes a Civil War Museum and tower with overview of battlefield. Ten-minute slide show. Free admission. Twenty miles north of town on Old Route 41 in Marietta. 427-4686.

White-water rafting and floating are possible in varying degrees of realism and difficulty. For the white-water variety, take on the Chattooga and Ocoee rivers. (Call Southeastern Expeditions: 329-0433). For milder floats, try the Chattahoochee River (call 955-6931), or the Chattahoochee River Park, which is more a theme-park version. Highway 41 in northwest Atlanta. 952-0184.

The **Smith House** is in Dahlonega, Georgia, the gold-rush capital of this state. Visit the gold museum and lunch at the Smith House for family-style southern cooking. 266-1781.

In Town

The **Atlanta Flea Market and Antique Center** features some 140 merchants selling anything you could possibly want or imagine, and a couple of food facilities. Open weekends from noon until 7 or 8 P.M. 5360 Peachtree Industrial Boulevard in Chamblee (four miles north of Lenox Square).

Roswell is a beautiful suburb of Atlanta filled with antebellum homes that were once part of a historical society founded in 1830. Today, most have been carefully restored and are occupied by their owners. The entire village is delightful, a lovely place to stroll, browse, and shop. You'll also find **Bulloch Hall,** the ancestral home of President Theodore Roosevelt, in this suburb.

The **Atlanta Preservation Center** conducts guided walking tours of four in-town historic districts. There are two tours each Saturday and two on Sunday. Each lasts about two hours and costs $3. Call 522-4345 for times and information.

If you're here in the spring, treat yourself to one of nature's glories: the flowering of Atlanta's suburbs. Drive along Habersham, Blackland, Tuxedo, and West Paces Ferry roads and marvel at the beauty that people and nature can create when they work in harmony.

Sunday Customs

In this corner of the world, which is famous for its hospitality, brunch is a civilized Sunday tradition where the array of foods can be enough to last the entire day. Listed here are some we especially like.

The **Ritz-Carlton Atlanta** offers a sumptuous buffet that includes golden and black Beluga caviar—and a very elite clientele. 10 A.M. to 2:30 P.M. 934-9700.

Bugatti, in the Omni Hotel, serves an interesting northern Italian brunch. 659-0000.

The **Waverly Hotel** offers a bit of everything in elegant surroundings. 11 A.M. to 3 P.M. Galleria Parkway. 953-4500.

Cafe de la Paix is the spot for a French-style brunch. Very attractive atmosphere. Hilton Hotel. 10 A.M. to 3 P.M. 659-2000.

The Mansion serves its elegant brunch in a garden setting. Favorite of many locals. 11:30 A.M. to 2:30 P.M. 179 Ponce de Leon Avenue, NE. 876-0727.

Lickskillet Farm's brunch is typical of the attention to historical detail the village of Roswell prides itself on. 11 A.M. to 3 P.M. 475-6484.

If you're not up to a full-scale brunch, join many trendy locals at **Katz' Deli Restaurant** (a very in place to be seen on a Sunday morning as you munch your bagel and read the Sunday papers). 2205 Cheshire Bridge Road, NE. 321-7444. Not quite the real thing but similar is **Boychik's** in the Georgetown Shopping Center on Chamblee-Dunwoody Road. 452-0516.

Spectator Sports

The **Atlanta Braves** play baseball in the Atlanta–Fulton County Stadium from April to October. (This stadium is known as the "launching pad" because so many home runs are hit here.) Seats $4 to $8.50. Take the MARTA shuttle bus or drive. 577-9100.

The NFL **Falcons,** an average football team, play in the NFC's Western Division. Games are also at Atlanta–Fulton County Stadium.

The NBA **Hawks** play basketball in the Omni. Also an average team, they play in the Central Division.

Active Sports

Call the **Atlanta Track Club** for the best advice on where to jog. 231-9064.

Want to play polo? Call the **Atlanta Polo Club:** they'll rent you some ponies and the rest is up to you. 252-5712.

Piedmont Park, three miles northeast of downtown, is a great municipal park with free tennis courts, swimming, good jogging trails, and a botanical gardens.

Baltimore

Biddle St.

Chase St.

Franklin St.

Pleasant St.

Fayette St.

Lombard St.

Pratt St.

LITTLE ITALY

Eastern Ave.

INNER HARBOR

St. Paul St.

Charles St.

Light St.

Hopkins Pl.

Central Ave.

Broadway

N

HOTELS

1 Canterbury
2 Four Seasons
3 Grand
4 Hay Adams
5 Holiday Inn—Capitol Hill
6 Jefferson
7 Phoenix-Park
8 Quality Inn—Capitol Hill
9 Vista International
10 Washington
11 Watergate

LANDMARKS

A Baltimore-Washington
  International (BWI)
B Charles Center
C Civic Center
D Convention Center
E Federal Hill
F Fells Point
G Harborplace
H Joseph Meyerhoff
  Symphony Hall

I Lexington Market
J National Aquarium
K Office of Promotion and
  Tourism
L Pennsylvania Station
M Walters Art Gallery
N Washington Monument
O World Trade Center

BALTIMORE

GETTING YOUR BEARINGS

Baltimore is likely to surprise you. This city seems to march to its own drummer, usually personified by the energetic William Donald Schaefer, mayor of Baltimore past, present, and future (unless he decides to run for governor—which is not unlikely, according to insiders).

Now a figure almost larger than life, Schaefer began his career as mayor by taking on the challenge of the old Baltimore, a sinking ship of urban blight, and creating what is, today, a squeaky-clean, prosperous city with a universal civic pride that even we, as visitors, can feel. Walk the downtown area and you'll be hard put to find a street free of new building construction. Entire neighborhoods, saved by his ingenious one-dollar-per-house restoration plans, are now models of city residence at its best. It is a city on the way up with a flourishing downtown, a tourist-pleasing harbor attraction, a thriving international port, and a wealth of educational and health care institutions.

For visitors, the compact downtown area is especially handy. Most businesses maintain offices there, and good hotel facilities exist nearby, as do restaurants and places of entertainment. Most are in locations that are safe to visit after dark. Also within walking distance of the downtown hotels is the 400,000-square-foot Baltimore Convention Center with meeting rooms accommodating 50 to 1,600 people.

Baltimore has some delightful ethnic and historic neighborhoods, too, such as Little Italy, Federal Hill, and Fells Point. Like much of the downtown area, they can be strolled and sampled as safely at night as during daylight hours.

Hosting business lunches or dinners in Baltimore is stress-free for women. Local restaurants, while offering sophisticated cuisines, are still small-town enough to make an effort to cater to their customers. And this includes a gracious presentation of the check to the host whether male or female, as requested.

WHAT TO WEAR

Businesswomen in Baltimore dress similarly to women in nearby Washington, D.C. Conservative dressing goes with the conservative industries;

19

the trendier professions call for more fashion-conscious clothes. But the stress is always on business. Save the casual wear for leisure times along the Inner Harbor or evenings over a plate of delicious—but messy—Chesapeake Bay crabs.

WEATHER WATCH

The proximity to water dictates Baltimore's weather, which is, in a word, unpredictable. Expect rain at any time during the spring, windy or cold winters, hot and humid summers. Best to consult temperatures in your local paper several days before leaving for an up-to-date look at what's in store.

GETTING THERE

Baltimore-Washington International (BWI) scored as the ninth favorite U.S. airport among frequent travelers polled by *Ad Age.* For BWI general information, call 859-7111.

BWI is ten miles by expressway from town, about 15 minutes driving time. Taxi fare is about $14; the airport limo costs $6. The problem with the limo service is its availability. For the return trip home, be sure to reserve your spot in the limo far in advance; otherwise there might not be room for you. The BWI airport cab number is 859-1100; the airport limo service, 859-7545.

Amtrak goes to Pennsylvania Station in 15 minutes. Take a cab to your hotel from there. Amtrak's number is 539-2112.

Car Rentals

Ajax	796-2202
Avis	859-1680
Budget	859-0850
Hertz	859-3600
National	859-8860
Sears	859-0910
Thrifty	769-4900

GETTING AROUND

You may find you need a car, particularly if you are staying downtown and your business is out at one of the hospitals in the area.

Downtown on-street parking is extremely limited. Go for the parking garages, which are numerous and reasonably priced.

You can hail a cruising cab, or call ahead for one (allow about ten minutes in good weather). Distances are metered. Sharing is allowed, but there's no fare reduction. Cab companies include Yellow Cab, 685-1212; Diamond Cab, 947-3333; and Sun Cab, 235-0300.

Buses run only along the main streets. Exact change of 75 cents is required.

A charming way to travel, if you have the time, is on the **Baltimore Trolley,** an old-fashioned model updated to travel several routes. Drivers and guides are also entertainers, so you get a bit of showmanship along with your ride—all for 25 cents. Trolleys run along Charles Street and St. Paul Street, and on weekends and holidays, you'll find them in the Inner Harbor.

At press time, extensions are being added to the subway system. The fare is 75 cents.

GETTING FAMILIAR

Baltimore Office of Promotion and Tourism
34 Market Place   837-INFO
Suite 310
Baltimore, MD 21202
Write for information and other materials, particularly their excellent newspaper, *Baltimore Good Times,* which is issued seasonally. Or visit the BOPT at the Inner Harbor Information Center for literature or assistance. You should also take time to watch their 16-minute video of the city.

Baltimore Convention Center
1 W. Pratt Street   659-7000
Baltimore, MD 21201

Local newspapers include the *Baltimore Sun* (morning), the *Baltimore Evening Sun* (afternoon), and the *Baltimore News American* (morning). *Baltimore* magazine is a glossy monthly that includes restaurant and entertainment guides, as well as listings of special events, lectures, exhibits, and attractions. Some interesting editorial features, too. *Baltimore Scene* magazine is a give-away, available in your hotel.

Quick Calls

AREA CODE 301	Time 844-1212
Weather 936-1212	Police 222-3333

	Concierge	Executive Floor	No-Smoking Rooms	Fitness Facilities	Pool	24-Hour Room Service	Restaurant for Client Entertaining	Extra-Special Amenities	Electronic Key System	Business/Secretarial Services	Checkout Time	Frequent Guest Program	Business Traveler Program	Average Single Rate
Admiral Fell Inn (37 Rooms)	Front desk		•				Admiral Fell Restaurant			•	11 a.m.		Corp. rates	$ 90 / $ 75 corp.
Belvedere	•			•	•		John Eager Howard			•	12 noon	1300 Club	Corp. rate including room up-grade	$ 65 / $ 59 corp.
Hyatt Regency	•	Regency Club •		•	•	•	Trellis Garden	•		•	12 noon	Gold Passport	Corp. rates	$ 92
Omni International	•	•	•	•	•	•	Jacqueline's	•	•	•	12 noon	ESP		$ 84
Society Hill (15 rooms)							Society Hill Restaurant							$ 65
Tremont Hotel	•			•			8 East	•		•	11 a.m.	•	•	$85
Tremont Plaza	•	•	•	•	•	•	Tug's	•		•	11 a.m.	•	•	$65

AT YOUR SERVICE

Belvedere Hotel

1 E. Chase Street
Baltimore, MD 21202

Toll-free reservations: 800/692-2700
Local number: 332-1000
Telex: 8745801

Located in a quiet, residential neighborhood known as Mt. Vernon, this 182-room hotel offers both services and proximity to the cultural part of town. A 1903 structure, it was renovated in 1982 with traditional decor. Attracts visiting theater people; no conventions. Health Club, run by the YWCA, is open to guests for a nominal fee. The hotel operates a shuttle bus service for guests to and from theater and symphony performances.

The **John Eager Howard Room** is their fine dining restaurant, serving American food in a lovely setting. The **Owl Bar,** open until 1 A.M. attracts a sophisticated crowd, serves light snacks. The **13th Floor Lounge** offers a panoramic view of the city and live entertainment. Comfortable for women alone.

Tremont Hotel

8 E. Pleasant Street
Baltimore, MD 21202

Toll-free reservations: 800/638-6266
Local number: 576-1200

There are two Tremonts in town; this is the smaller, all-suites Tremont. Luxury and space are key words here; the suites are equipped with just about every amenity, including a kitchen loaded with such gadgets as microwaves and grinders for the canisters of fresh coffee beans. Management will stock the larder to your specification if you let them know in advance. The lobby is small, and security very personal; no one merely walks past the desk.

Their gourmet restaurant, **8 East,** is an excellent choice for business entertaining; **8 East Lounge** is small and quiet, mostly hotel guests. Very comfortable for women alone.

Tremont Plaza

222 St. Paul Street
Baltimore, MD 21202

Toll-free reservations: 800/638-6266
Local number: 727-2222

This is the larger Tremont—235 suites. Housed in an existing building, the hotel has undergone an $18 million contemporary updating. Location of both Tremonts is near the Inner Harbor in the heart of the business district.

Tug's Restaurant focuses on American seafood in an oak-and-etched-glass setting. **Tug's Lounge** attracts an older professional crowd.

Omni International

101 W. Fayette Street
Baltimore, MD 21201

Toll-free reservations: 800/THE-OMNI
Local number: 752-1100
Telex: 87464

The ambitious $15 million renovation of this Omni earned a "best comeback" award in *Baltimore* magazine. It's a big, 750-room hotel with all the services and activities you would expect. Big convention business. Convenient to Civic Center and Convention Center. Connects to Inner Harbor via an elevated walkway. Hotel design includes two towers: the top 12 floors of the south tower are executive floors.

     Jacqueline's is the gourmet restaurant. **Miller Brothers,** an old-time restaurant, also serves Sunday brunch

Hyatt Regency

300 Light Street	Toll-free reservations: 800/228-9000
Baltimore, MD 21202	Local number: 528-1234
	Telex: 87577

Connected to Harbor Place and the Convention Center by Skywalks, this 490-room Hyatt combines a superb waterfront location with all the comforts a large hotel can offer.

     The lobby is signature Hyatt with lots of plants, a soaring atrium, and glass-enclosed elevators.

     On the 12th floor is a series of rooms that have been designed with women in mind, equipped with hair dryers and lighted makeup mirrors. The Regency Club is the concierge floor, with the usual special perks that include free breakfasts, snacks, and drinks, as well as key-operated elevators for increased security.

     The **Trellis Gardens** is the formal dining room with its specialty seafood menu; **Cascades** is the coffee shop; and **Skylights** is the bar, which has a nice, comfortable atmosphere that is welcoming to women alone.

Society Hill Hotel

58 W. Biddle Street	Local number: 837-3630
Baltimore, MD 21201	

A 15-room jewel, this urban inn combines the best of a bed-and-breakfast with country inn ambience. No two rooms are the same, and each is decorated in turn-of-the-century antiques. Soft colors, personal accents, big scented towels, potpourri in bowls. Security is personal and excellent. Guests are issued front-door keys. New arrivals check in downstairs at the restaurant. The hotel is located in the heart of the cultural center, across the street from the Joseph Meyerhoff Symphony Hall.

     The restaurant and bar downstairs are considered among Baltimore's best. The atmosphere is upscale, the food is excellent, and so is the jazz in the bar.

Admiral Fell Inn

888 S. Broadway	Toll-free reservations: 800/BXB-INNS
Market Square at Thames Street	Local number: 522-7377
Baltimore, MD 21231	

There are 37 rooms in this authentic 1800s inn, each one dedicated to a historic resident of note, each different from the others, each a charming blend of soft colors, fireplaces, and authentic period pieces.

     The inn is warm and personal. Guests gather in the library,

noting their drinks on an honor-system chit. Each of the four floors has its own quiet gathering area with comfortable chairs, a card table, and a closetful of games.

Located in Fells Point, one of Baltimore's earliest waterfront communities, the inn is one of dozens of historic buildings that now house thriving businesses—restaurants, pubs, and shops. The area is cobblestoned, lovingly preserved, and fun to stroll or browse in. Although this area is completely safe, we advise caution in the immediate surrounding areas.

The inn has available a free shuttle bus service into town or to the nearby hospital locations for its guests.

ON A BUDGET

Hotels

Days Inn
100 Hopkins Place (at Lombard Street)   Toll-free reservations: 800/325-2525
Baltimore, MD 21201   Local number: 685-3500
Ideal location, about five blocks from Inner Harbor, across from Civic Center. Has 251 rooms, a no-smoking floor, restaurant, meeting/banquet rooms, small outdoor pool with food service. Airport shuttle. Singles for $69.00.

Holiday Inn Inner Harbor
301 W. Lombard Street   Toll-free reservations: 800/HOLIDAY
Baltimore, MD 21201   Local number: 685-3500
This is one block from Convention Center, three blocks from the Inner Harbor (but on the edge of a seedy neighborhood). Good services, including an enclosed pool, hair salon, restaurant, airport shuttle. Singles from $49 to $74.

Comfort Inn
24 W. Franklin Street   Toll-free reservations: 800/228-5150
Baltimore, MD 21201   Local number: 576-8400
This inn has 200 rooms, some of which are two-level suites, some designated nonsmoking. Excellent range of services. The location is farther away from the Inner Harbor than the first two, which puts you closer to the cultural section of town. Singles from $53.

Restaurants

Connolly's, at the end of Pier 5, is one of the mayor's favorite restaurants. Lunch and dinner menus are the same. Huge sandwiches for $3 to $4. Good seafood, reasonably priced. 701 E. Pratt Street. 837-6400.

Burke's is a popular lunch spot for good burgers, onion rings, and chicken. Business crowd here at lunchtime. Light and Lombard streets. 752-4189.

Entertainment

The song says, the best things in life are free—and Baltimore's **Inner Harbor** makes it seem almost true. You *will* need green stuff for food and shopping, but the street theater, the floating showboat with its concerts, the strolling mimes and magicians are all free. Not to mention the view—which is merely spectacular.

DINING OUT

In food circles the word *Baltimore* is almost synonymous with the word *crab*—fresh from Chesapeake Bay and always delicious. Served locally on brown paper (newspapers are no longer used—too unsanitary) and cracked with wooden mallets, the crabs are definitely a feast for casual dining. Leave your good silk dress in the closet, and get down and get into this marvelous culinary tradition.

For Baltimore, we've designated as moderate any meal up to $10 for lunch and from $20 to $30 for dinner. Above that is expensive; below, inexpensive.

Neighborhood Dining

Harborplace has a large choice of spots in a safe, enclosed building overlooking the harbor (see "Baltimore by Day"). Among the best places to eat:

Taverna Athena, 547-8900
Mariner's Pier One, 962-5050
Jean Claude's Cafe, 332-0950
Tandoor, 547-0575
Bamboo House—voted best Chinese restaurant in town by *Baltimore* magazine—625-1191
American Cafe—same as in D.C.—962-8800
Phillips, 685-6600
Gianni's, 837-1130

Little Italy

Da Mimmo is modern and elegant. 217 S. High Street. 727-6876.
Capriccio serves northern Italian cuisine in a quiet atmosphere. High and Fawn streets. 685-2710.
Chiapparelli's is lively and noisy. 237 High Street. 837-0309.

Sabatino's, is a politicians' favorite. 901 Fawn Street. 727-9414.
Trattoria Petrucci is small and quiet. 300 S. High Street. 752-4515.
Velleggia's serves southern Italian specialties. 204 S. High Street. 685-2620.

"Restaurant Row" is how locals refer to **Charles Street.** This corridor of restaurants runs roughly from the Belvedere Hotel to the Washington Monument and includes the following:

Brass Elephant is an elegant northern Italian restaurant in a restored 1861 townhouse. Good for business dinners and Sunday brunch. Dressy. Moderate to expensive. 924 N. Charles Street. 547-8480.

Tony Cheng's Szechuan is also housed in an elegant old townhouse. Good for business entertaining. Moderate. 801 N. Charles Street. 539-6666.

Shogun serves authentic traditional dishes. Excellent sushi bar. Moderate. 316 N. Charles Street. 962-1130.

Pacifica is trendy. Mesquite-grilled fish and meats, light cuisine. Also features a raw bar. Moderate. 326 N. Charles Street. 727-8264.

Peabody Bookstore is delightful—an old bookstore with an antique bar. Nightly live entertainment. Light menu, sandwiches, steaks. Inexpensive to moderate. 913 N. Charles Street. 539-9201.

All around Town

Peerce's Downtown consistently wins high honors in local polls. An extensive menu of American and Continental dishes. Excellent for business lunches. Neighborhood becomes deserted after business hours; best to skip dinner here. Moderate. 225 N. Liberty Street. 727-0910.

Haussner's is a Baltimore legend, as much for its antique-crammed decor as for its food. Everything here has been around for ages, even the waitresses! German/seafood cuisine. Moderate. 3242 Eastern Avenue. 327-8365.

Tio Pepe is another of the locals' favorites. Spanish-style atmosphere. Very popular; very hard to get reservations. Expensive. 10 E. Franklin Street. 539-4675.

Society Hill Hotel offers nouvelle cuisine in a charming urban inn setting. Popular for symphony-goers; Meyerhoff Hall is just across the street. Moderate. 58 W. Biddle Street. 837-3630.

Danny's is another Baltimore institution. Serves beef and seafood in elegant surroundings. Good wine list. Prix-fixe early dinner from 5 to 7 P.M. Moderate. 217 S. High Street. 727-6876.

Rusty Scupper is recommended for those times you'd like your seafood with a view. Good business crowd here; great view of the harbor. Moderate. 402 Key Highway. 727-3678.

Milton Inn is a 1740 inn considered one of America's finest for food and atmosphere. Continental cuisine. Expensive. York Road, Sparks (note: this is quite a distance from downtown—three miles north of Hunt Valley). 771-4366.

Bertha's is one of Fells Point's new/old landmarks. Her green bumper stickers, "Eat Bertha's Mussels," have been spotted in all 50 states. You don't have to eat mussels; try other seafood dishes or the English specialties. Moderate. 734 Broadway. 327-5795.

Dinner at Sea

Lunch or dinner cruises aboard the **Lady Baltimore** can be fun if you have a buddy. There's live music and dancing, and with 600 passengers, maybe you don't need a buddy after all. Meet people, feast, and sightsee all at the same time. Reservations: 727-3113.

BALTIMORE BY DAY

To see Baltimore spread out beneath you, and to get a fix on the relationship of city to harbor, we recommend the following:

World Trade Center's **Top of the World observatory** on the 27th floor of this I. M. Pei–designed building. Well-defined viewing maps at each window. Open 10 A.M. to 5 P.M. Nominal admission charge. 401 E. Pratt Street (Inner Harbor).

Washington Monument, the nation's first formal architectural monument to George Washington (July 4, 1815), where 25 cents and climbing 228 steps will give you a 178-foot-high overview of the city. 700 Block of N. Charles Street. Open Friday through Tuesday.

Without question, the biggest attraction in town is the **Inner Harbor.** This sparkling clean showplace is also a working harbor, complete with all manner of pleasure craft—some of which are for hire. **Harborplace,** the focus of the showplace, is a Rouse Company project and one of the best. You can easily spend one day or several browsing the stores, sampling endless foods—from fast to chic—enjoying the free street theater, and watching the changing harbor.

On the don't-miss list here:

The **National Aquarium,** which is actually more water-world environment than traditional aquarium. Designed to move you upward through levels of water-worlds, into and above an actual rain forest. Over 8,000 creatures along the way. Admission about $6. Pier 3, Inner Harbor. 576-3800.

Tall ships lie at anchor along the harbor. Climb aboard the three-masted *U.S. Frigate Constellation* (open seven days, nominal admission), or the *Lightship Chesapeake,* a 1930s beauty now listed in the National Register of Historic Places. Open seven days a week in summer. Nominal admission.

Do-it-yourself **boating** on the Inner Harbor includes everything from paddleboats ($4.25 for 30 minutes) and tiny electric boats ($9 for 30 minutes) to harbor sails of up to two hours. There's even a water taxi service if you're too tired to walk another step around the promenade. And there are dinner cruises, too (see "Dining Out").

Footnotes offers walking tours of both the harbor and ethnic neighborhoods. Tours last about 90 minutes each, and leave from Pratt Street Pavilion in Harborplace. About $7.50. Call 764-8067.

Outside the Harbor

Charles Center, considered the cornerstone of the downtown renaissance, consists of Center Plaza and Hopkins Plaza. Here you'll find the Morris A. Mechanic Theater, the Federal Building, restaurants, and shops. The public square is great for people-watching. Often there are daytime as well as evening concerts and festivals.

Fells Point is a historic area dating back to 1730 and is still a working harbor. It is currently enjoying a rebirth and has been designated a historic district. It is also great fun to visit, strolling the cobbled streets and dropping in on any of the casual restaurants and pubs. The Broadway market is here, too. Have dinner at Bertha's (see "Dining Out") or any of the many other eating places you'll pass, each in an original period building. The area is safe day or night. But be sure to taxi in or out after dark.

Lexington Market has been operating continuously for more than 200 years. This historic landmark has 150 stalls selling baked goods, candy, cheeses, produce, meats, and more. Snack on ethnic foods, fried chicken, steamed crabs. Or try Faidley's famous raw bar.

Baltimore Museum of Art houses the prestigious collection of the Cone sisters. Friends of Gertrude Stein, these women bought impressionists' works early on—Monet, Cezanne, Matisse, and Picasso—some say, the best from each artist. The museum also features a lovely sculpture garden and cafe. Tuesday through Friday, 10 A.M. to 4 P.M.; Saturday and Sunday, 11 A.M. to 6 P.M.

Walters Art Gallery houses this family's remarkable collection of fine arts. Everything from Chinese porcelains and Middle Eastern art to 19th-century paintings. The 1908 building replicates the 16th-century Palazzo Bianco in Genoa. Tuesday through Saturday, 11 A.M. to 5 P.M. Wednesdays, free admission. Closed Monday. Charles and Center streets. 547-9000.

Federal Hill is a quaint historic district currently undergoing urban renewal. Lots of craft shops, bookstores, antique shops to browse. Also, a sweeping view of the Port of Baltimore and central city.

Fort McHenry is the star-shaped fort where Francis Scott Key was inspired to write the "Star-Spangled Banner." Don't miss the film depicting the fort's colorful history. Open daily 9 A.M. to 5 P.M. (until 8 P.M. in summer). Foot of E. Fort Avenue. 962-4290.

Star-Spangled Banner House was the home of Mary Pickersgill who sewed the flag that was Key's inspiration. 844 E. Pratt Street.

THE SHOPPING SCENE

Baltimore is not a particularly distinguished shopping town. Many local women drive to the **White Flint Mall** in Rockville, Maryland, north of Washington, D.C., to shop Bloomingdale's, Lord & Taylor, and I. Magnin.

The **Cross Keys Village Square,** while not quite in the same league, does feature some lovely shops, notably Jones & Jones, Nettle Creek, and Irresistibles. Thirty shops and services in all just ten minutes from downtown. Take the #10 MTA bus, or drive north on Falls Road.

In town, the most interesting shops are at **Harborplace** and along **Charles Street.**

Harborplace, Pratt Street Pavilion, has some 40 retail shops, among them, Laura Ashley, Crabtree & Evelyn, Pappagallo, Jones & Jones (boutique fashions and accessories).

Antiques Row, along Howard Street, will test your abilities to tell class from kitsch.

Vintage clothing galore on **Read Street** and **South Charles Street.**

Local department stores are Hecht's and Hutzler's. Both are fairly small by big-city standards; both concentrate mainly on clothing.

BALTIMORE BY NIGHT

Baltimore Box Office offers one-stop ticket service to all performing arts and sporting events. Occasionally they also have half-price tickets available. Pier 4, Inner Harbor. 576-9333. In general, it is not necessary to buy tickets ahead of your arrival.

Joseph Meyerhoff Symphony Hall is a beautiful new home for the Baltimore Symphony. Tickets run from $8.50 to $25. 1212 Cathedral Street. 837-5691

Lyric Opera House recalls the European splendor of the Leipzig Music Hall. Home to both the Baltimore Opera and large Broadway musicals. 1404 Maryland Avenue. 685-5086.

Morris A. Mechanic Theater hosts road shows of Broadway hits and other theater greats. Baltimore and Charles streets. 752-1407.

Center Stage offers repertory and classics as well as contemporary theater. 700 N. Calvert Street. 332-0033.

Pier Six Concert Pavilion is a 3,200-seat theater in the Inner Harbor. Sit under a fabric roof of billowing sails or on the lawn. From July to Labor Day. 727-5580 for concert information.

Insomniac's Tour of Baltimore begins at 1:30 A.M. and concludes at Edgar Allan Poe's gravesite in Westminster Presbyterian Church cemetery. 653-2998.

The few movie theaters in downtown are not places you'd want to frequent alone. Check out the **Baltimore Film Forum** at the Baltimore Museum of Art, which shows films in repertoire. 685-4170. Also the **Enoch**

Pratt Library shows free films in the Wheeler Auditorium. 400 Cathedral Street. 396-4616. Look for the brand-new movie complex with nine cinemas in the Inner Harbor.

LATE-NIGHT BALTIMORE

Baltimore, despite its clean-up success, still harbors something known locally as "the Block." This area, the 400 block of East Baltimore Street, is spiked with sex shops, questionable lounges, and prostitutes. A great place to avoid.

Several hotels have attractive and safe bars and lounges. Among them:

Omni International's **Baltimore 100** and the **Rendezvous.**

Hyatt Regency's **Constellation Foyer** (live music, popular for after-theater) and **Skylights** on the top floor—excellent views.

Belvedere Hotel's **Thirteenth Floor**—another lounge with a good city view—or the **Owl Bar,** a popular bar and restaurant.

Society Hill Hotel's jazz piano bar, which attracts celebrities (it's across from the Joseph Meyerhoff Symphony Hall) and an upscale crowd.

In Harborplace, a no-worry, safe place at night, there are:

Mariner's Pier One in the Pratt Street Pavilion, which has live piano nightly and draws a 25-to-40s crowd; and **Phillips,** in the Light Street Pavilion, which attracts slightly younger people. The **American Cafe** features the area's top jazz groups; the 20-to-30s crowd. 962-8800.

A sophisticated clientele swears by **Danny's,** at 1201 N. Charles Street.

AT LEISURE

If you want to tack a few days of leisure onto your work week, Baltimore has some interesting possibilities both in town and in the surrounding countryside. Be sure to investigate the weekend package deals offered by all local hotels before making your reservations.

Day-Tripping

Tour **Colonial Annapolis,** which is just 45 minutes away by car or 2 hours by boat. Contact the Tourism Council of Annapolis, 171 Conduit Street. 268-7676. Year-around cruises: 727-3113.

Washington, D.C., is one hour away by car or by Amtrak (about $10 one way). See the chapter on Washington, D.C., for suggestions on how to enjoy your leisure time in the capital.

Sail the famous **Chesapeake Bay,** between May and October, aboard American Cruise Lines. 800/243-6755.

In Town

Again, the leisure-time focus is on the harbor. There seem to be endless variations on the boating theme in this town (see "Baltimore by Day" for information on self-driven boat rentals). Cruise to Fort McHenry and Fells Point with Defender and Guardian tours. They leave from Inner Harbor every half hour from 11 A.M. to 5:30 P.M. 752-1515.

Historic walking tours are offered, without charge, by the Women's Civic League. Reservations are required. Tours range from one to two hours, and begin at 9 Front Street. 837-5424.

In February, don't miss the **Winter Crafts Market.** Check local publications for details.

Sunday Customs

To mingle with the local in–crowds, make your brunch reservations at any of the following places (see "Dining Out" for addresses and phone numbers): Brass Elephant, John Eager Howard Room, Owl Bar, Society Hill Hotel, Tony Cheng's.

Spectator Sports

Be the ultimate spectator at the **Babe Ruth Birthplace Museum** and Maryland **Baseball Hall of Fame Museum.** You'll find life-sized, animated, and talking figures of the Babe in this official Orioles museum center—a row house that was rescued from demolition by loyal local fans. 216 Emory Street. 727-1539.

To say that Baltimorians take their Orioles seriously would be the sports understatement of all times. They are rabid sports fans, fiercely devoted to their team. The American League East **Orioles** play baseball in Memorial Stadium, 33d and Ellerslie Avenue, from April through October. 338-1300

The USFL **Stars** play football in Memorial Stadium. 576-STAR.

After Baltimore lost their NFL Colts to Indianapolis, diehard football fans cheer on the **Washington Redskins** in RFK Stadium one hour's drive away in Landover, Maryland. 350-3400.

Similarly, hockey and basketball fans share their enthusiasm with D.C. fans as the **Washington Capitals** (NHL hockey) and the **Washington Bullets** (NBA basketball) play in Capital Centre in Landover, Maryland.

Baltimore calls itself the **lacrosse** capital of the world. And their Johns Hopkins team is, indeed, world-class. 235-6882. The **Lacrosse Hall of Fame** is at the Johns Hopkins University. 235-6882.

In mid-May, the **Preakness,** the second leg of horseracing's Triple Crown, is run at Pimlico Race Course. The annual prerace party is huge and lots of fun. Park Heights and Belvedere avenues. 542-9400.

Active Sports

The **Downtown Athletic Club** offers a full range of indoor facilities—pool, jogging track, racketball court, and so on—to visitors. Your hotel key entitles you to a guest membership fee of $15. 210 E. Centre Street. 332-0966.

Tennis courts, free and operated by the city, are at both Clifton Park (east of downtown) and Patterson Park (in central area). At Clifton, pick up free permit at the Mansion House (between Hartford and Blair streets). 243-3500. At Patterson, pick up free permit at Bath House (near Linwood Avenue). 396-8256.

Golfers can head out about 30 minutes north of the city to play Pine Ridge, ranked one of the top 50 courses in the United States. Nominal fee. 252-2011. Another course, Mount Pleasant, is in the northern section of the city. 254-5100.

The ideal **jogging** place is around the promenade at Inner Harbor. But because of year-round crowds, this is really possible only very early in the morning. Forget those after-work jogs here.

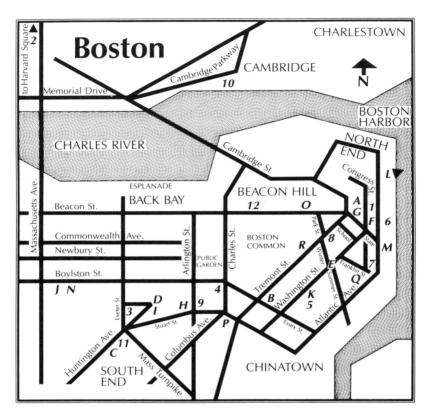

Boston

to Harvard Square **2**

CHARLESTOWN

Cambridge Parkway

CAMBRIDGE

10

N

Memorial Drive

BOSTON HARBOR

CHARLES RIVER

Cambridge St.

NORTH END

Congress St.

L

ESPLANADE

BEACON HILL

12

O

Beacon St.

BACK BAY

Massachusetts Ave.

Commonwealth Ave.

Newbury St.

Arlington St.

Charles St.

BOSTON COMMON

PUBLIC GARDEN

A

G

1

F

6

Park St.

School St.

State St.

M

Boylston St.

R

8

Winter St.

7

J N

4

Tremont St.

Washington St.

B

Franklin St.

E

Q

Exeter St.

D
I

H

9

3

Stuart St.

P

K
5

Essex St.

Atlantic Ave.

Summer St.

Huntington Ave.

11

C

Columbus Ave.

Mass Turnpike

SOUTH END

CHINATOWN

HOTELS

- **1** Bostonian
- **2** Charles
- **3** Copley Square Hotel
- **4** Four Seasons Hotel
- **5** Lafayette
- **6** Marriott Long Wharf
- **7** Meridien
- **8** Parker House
- **9** Park Plaza and Towers
- **10** Royal Sonesta
- **11** Westin
- **12** Women's City Club

LANDMARKS

- **A** City Hall
- **B** Combat Zone
- **C** Copley Place
- **D** Copley Square
- **E** Downtown Crossing
- **F** Faneuil Hall / Quincy Market
- **G** Government Center
- **H** Greyhound Bus Terminal
- **I** John Hancock Observatory Tower

- **J** Hynes Auditorium
- **K** Lafayette Place
- **L** Logan International Airport
- **M** New England Aquarium
- **N** Prudential Center
- **O** State House
- **P** Theatre District
- **Q** Trailways Bus Terminal
- **R** Visitor's Information Center

BOSTON

GETTING YOUR BEARINGS

This city's reputation of quintessential New England conservatism is so well entrenched we tend to cringe at our social gaffes, like speaking too loudly or not wearing white gloves.

But that's just hype.

Underneath all that proper-Bostonian facade beats an urban heart that's vital and vigorous; a city that understands the avant-garde as well as the buttoned-down conservative. Sleek glass skyscrapers share space with historic brick-and-stone churches; nuclear-age universities like Harvard and MIT coexist with neighborhoods like the North End where third-generation Italian-Americans still speak no English and have never ventured more than six blocks beyond their home territory. A city of many facets and much diversity.

Among the dozens of neighborhoods that make up Greater Boston, the ones we return to most often when we're in town on business are:

Downtown, where most financial and legal business is centered, as well as the JFK Federal Building, City Hall, Downtown Crossing–Washington Street shopping, and Quincy Market. If work takes you to this section of town, don't fret about appointment overload; everything is close by, so it's feasible to schedule meetings allowing only 15 to 20 minutes in between.

Back Bay, an area that was once under water but, thanks to deft planning, has emerged as a section that boasts Boston's only logical grid of streets. Here you'll find the majority of insurance companies and agencies. Here, too, is a stretch of green space known as the Public Garden. Taxi here from Downtown unless you have half an hour to walk. For a visual crash course on the city's diversity, check out the action in the Public Garden: locals usually take over the grasslands in the adjacent Boston Common for athletics; visitors opt for the swan boats; and senior citizens stake out the best people-watching benches to view the passing parade that includes everything from rockers with technicolor hair to bejeweled Brahmin matrons. A bit of incidental information: Fannie Farmer's original Boston Cooking School operated in Back Bay.

Beacon Hill, prestigious "village" in the heart of the city most often compared to the posher sections of London, is an enclave of immaculately preserved brownstones. Among famous former residents: Louisa May Alcott, Jenny Lind, and Alice Brown who founded the Women's Rest Tour Association which was dedicated to assisting women travelers. The Women's City Club is here, too. Part of the fun of wandering the narrow, cobblestone streets is searching for the tiny architectural jewels everywhere: iron bootscrapers, fanlight doorways, gaslights.

North End if you are passionate about pasta. Here in a few blocks is a wealth of Italian cuisines to pamper your love of great food. It's also regarded as one of Boston's safest neighborhoods for walking—day or night. It's not all Italian, though. Rose Kennedy was born here in 1890; Paul Revere's home on North Street is a popular place to visit; and today young people drawn by the neighborhood action are buying up lofts for apartment conversion.

The Charles River, as much a psychological as a physical divider, liberates the relaxed and intellectual city of Cambridge from Boston proper on the other side. Cambridge is home to MIT, Radcliffe, "Hahvahd"—a bucolic focal point of the nation's oldest university dating back to 1636— and the Square, a prototypical student hangout replete with art-film theaters, trendy boutiques, and more bookstores per block than anywhere else in the country. We keep returning to this side of the river— which now also boasts some of Boston's newest and nicest hotels—to explore, to check out what's happening, to learn what's influencing the next generation of professionals.

For your nonbusiness leisure time in Boston, the city is remarkably easy to figure out. Most sights you'll want to see are located close to one another. Here we stress: Boston is definitely a walking city. You'll quickly discover that two factors combine to make this true: one, it's easy to walk—almost everything is just a short stroll away, and, two, it's almost impossible to drive—the one-way streets, diabolical and illogical, seem to conspire against the out-of-town driver and parking is scarce.

We should point out, however, that walking is recommended only as a daytime activity. Boston is, after all, a large city with its fair share of urban crime areas. Local women back us up in our insistence on cabs after dark, even in the so-called safe areas. Be particularly careful in the theater district, warns one businesswoman who visits often, and avoid Boston Common—fairly safe during the day but unpleasant in spots.

WHAT TO WEAR

Bostonians, male and female alike, agree that for doing business *conservative* is the byword. Any time we're heading here, we pack our most impeccably tailored suits and classic pumps. (Note: we do not hesitate, however, to join in the local custom of stowing those heels and donning our Nikes en route between meetings. Boston cobblestones are charming, but murder on the ankles and feet.)

Jewelry is best kept simple and to a minimum; you can't go wrong with a single strand of pearls and unobtrusive earrings. The exceptions to this ultraconservative dress code are mostly found in the advertising/public relations/retailing/design fields, whose businesswomen dress on the cutting edge of fashion.

Pants are appropriate only when work takes place outside, and then only if you are not a supervisor.

WEATHER WATCH

Bostonians seem to take perverse Yankee pride in their ability to accept whatever their weather dishes out. Summers and winters tend to go overboard in the extremes, making most visitors wish they'd brought more defensive clothing. Boots are essential to any winter wardrobe; raincoats with zip-out linings are always a safe bet.

One weather note of note: Boston is extraordinarily windy. Blame it on the tall buildings' wind-tunnel effect; blame it on the proximity to the Atlantic. Whatever the culprit, be prepared to lose your perm, if not your balance, when a nor'easter hits town.

Because temperatures everywhere have been at odds with regular norms, we recommend you study listings in your local paper several days before packing for your Boston trip.

GETTING THERE

Unlike most international airports, **Logan International** is actually *in* Boston, a scant three miles northeast of downtown. Logan is served by 38 international and domestic carriers. Eastern (800/327-8376, 617/262-3700), People's Express (617/523-0820), and New York Air (800/221-9300; 617/569-8400) run hourly shuttle flights to New York. For information at Logan International Airport, call 561-1818.

Local businesswomen rave about the speed and efficiency of taking the subway's Blue Line (part of the MBTA subway-and-trolley system, known locally as the T) from the airport into town. One frequent visitor says she can't deal with the trauma of under-harbor tunnel traffic in and out so she relies completely on the Blue Line. A free shuttle bus to the station, 60 cents for the subway (buy tokens at any T stop)—and you're in town in 15 minutes.

Others opt for cab or car service and hope for the best with the traffic. Peak-hour congestion can dramatically slow your trip despite the proximity of the airport to downtown hotels.

Cabs line up outside the terminal; fare into the city should run under $10. Sharing is common practice; just don't let the meter stop if you are continuing on to another hotel. Many hotels offer shuttle bus service for under $5. For luxury transportation, we recommend Commonwealth Limousine 787-5575.

For a special view of Boston, take the water taxi to or from the airport. Departs from Atlantic Avenue and whisks you to Logan in 15 minutes to connect with terminal shuttle buses. Costs $4. Call Massport at 973-5500 for details of the schedule.

GETTING AROUND

If your business transpires within Boston's city center, a car is not necessary. As we said, streets are a confusion of one-way mazes; parking is all but nonexistent. Besides, it's easier and more enjoyable to walk. One word of warning: Boston drivers more often than not ignore stop signs, so pedestrians should check twice to be sure the coast is clear before crossing the street.

With that in mind, it's safe to set out on foot anywhere at almost any time of day, with the exception of the "Combat Zone" on lower Washington Street. Cabs are imperative after dark no matter what the destination. Taxis: Boston Cab, 536-5010; Checker Cab, 536-7000; and Red Cab, 734-5000.

We have found cabs or the T to be reasonable alternatives when walking just doesn't make sense—say, from downtown to Back Bay. It's usually no problem to hail a taxi in the business district or call one from a restaurant or office. Be advised: many Boston cabbies will ask you how to get to your destination and the cabs are not always spic and span.

The T operates four lines: Green, Red, Orange, and Blue. We've been told by local women, however, that it's unwise to use the Orange Line south of Washington Street at any time. Pick up a T map at the information booth at Logan or at any depot. Exact 60-cent fare required. Trains run 5 to 20 minutes apart. Although some women swear the system is safe in the evenings for mid-town destinations, we always feel safer—and smarter—taking cabs at night. For bus and subway information: 772-3200 or 772-5000; Massport: 973-5500.

Car Rentals

If company business is on the outskirts of town along Route 128 (Boston's version of Silicon Valley), or if you insist on a car, we consider these companies reliable:

Avis	424-0800
Budget	569-4000
Hertz	569-7272
National	569-6700

GETTING FAMILIAR

Greater Boston Convention and Visitors Bureau
Prudential Plaza   267-6446
Box 490
Boston, MA 02199
Open daily from 9 A.M. to 5 P.M. Drop in or write ahead for their Official
Guide to Boston kit, which includes maps, walk guides, and lots of truly
helpful information. **Visitors Information** is also located on Tremont Street
at the Boston Common.

     Hynes Auditorium, Boston's convention center, is undergoing a
total revamping. Meanwhile, conventioneers gather at the area's many
new hotels and at the **Bayside Expo Center,** located on the harbor in nearby
Dorchester and easily reached via the Red Line, U Mass/JFK stop. Call
825-5151 for information.

     The **Boston Chamber of Commerce** can also answer quick ques-
tions. Call 367-9275.

The *Boston Globe* (daily, morning and afternoon) is the paper of record.
The *Boston Herald* (daily, morning) is the more sensational, folksy one.
The Thursday edition of the *Globe* includes a pull-out "Calendar" section
with complete entertainment listings and information. *Boston Magazine,*
a monthly publication, is trendy, opinionated, and controversial (trans-
lation: fun to read). Also includes dining and entertainment guides. Its
"Best of Boston" recommendations are safe choices for everything from
ice cream to ice skating. *Boston By-Week* is a seasonal guide, distributed
at tourist centers. It's free. Recommended reading: *Hassle-Free Boston:
A Manual for Women.* This 212-page paperback gives you a woman's
Boston—all aspects filtered through a woman's point of view. By Mary
Maynard and Mary-Lou Maynard Dow. Lewis Publishing Company. $7.95.

     For your local paper, national or international, try the Out-of-
Town Newsstand—a newspaper and magazine kiosk right at the Harvard
Square subway station. 354-7777.

— *Quick Calls* —

AREA CODE 617	Weather 936-1234
Time 637-1234	All emergencies 911

AT YOUR SERVICE

While most hotels try to cater to their guests' wishes, we all know that
some succeed better than others. We feel that the following hotels not

Hotel	Concierge	Executive Floor	No-Smoking Rooms	Fitness Facilities	Pool	24-Hour Room Service	Restaurant for Client Entertaining	Special In-Room Amenities	Electronic Key System	Business/Secretarial Services	Checkout Time	Frequent Guest Program	Business Traveler Program	Average Single Rate
Bostonian	●		●			●	Seasons	●		●	1 p.m.		W.T.A.	$150
Charles	●	●	●	●	●	●	Rarities	●	●		1 p.m.			$150
Four Seasons	●			●	●	●	Aujourd'hui Le Matin Le Soir	●		●	1 p.m.	guest history		$160
Lafayette	●			●	●	●	Le Marquis de Lafayette	●	●	●	1 p.m.		Club Suisse	$125 reg. $110 corp.
Marriott Long Wharf	●	●		●	●		Harbor Terrace			●	12 noon	Honored Guest		$165 ex. floor $149 other
Meridien	●			●	●	●	Julien	●	●	●	1 p.m.	in-room amenities	RSVP	$140
Park Plaza and Towers	●	●		●		●	Fox and Hounds	●		●	1 p.m.		Corporate Connection	$75 (hotel) $100 (Towers)
Parker House	●		●			●	Parker's	●	●	●	12 noon	Select Guest	Executive Service Plan	$155 (if E.S.P. $125)
Royal Sonesta	●	●		●	●		Rib Room	●	●	●	12 noon			$125
Westin	●		●	●	●	●	Turner Fisheries			●	1 p.m.	guest history		$125

only go the extra mile but also can be relied on to provide particularly thoughtful service and a sense of security to women traveling alone.

Bostonian Hotel

Faneuil Hall Marketplace   Toll-free reservations: 800/343-0922
Boston, MA 02109   Local number: 523-3600
                                  Telex: 948159

Overlooking historic Faneuil Hall and Quincy Market adjacent to Government Center, and a cobblestone's throw from the North End, this 154-room hotel—Boston's smallest of the deluxe—offers both convenience and privacy. The feeling here is residential, with an emphasis on personal service. Some rooms have fireplaces, Jacuzzis, and balconies. A special program, WTA (Women Traveling Alone), ensures that you'll encounter both a savvy staff and rooms outfitted with handy extras.

Light meals and drinks in the **Atrium Cafe,** but the major food focus is on their **Seasons Restaurant,** for award-winning cuisine and client-perfect ambience (see "Dining Out").

Charles

One Bennett and Eliot Street   Toll-free reservations: 800/882-1818
Cambridge, MA 02138   Local number: 864-1200
                                   Telex: 857417

If business takes you to the Cambridge side of the river, this new hotel offers upscale accommodations as well as convenience. Although new (opened in January 1985), it's loaded with such old-fashioned charms as red oak furniture and down quilts. Each room features a small sitting room adjacent to the bedroom—perfect for business meetings. Other newfangled touches are a full-service health club, electronic key system, and the next-door convenience of the Charles Square shopping complex.

Rarities is their gourmet restaurant, romantic, expensive, and dressy. Try the **Courtyard Cafe** for casual meals, the **Regatta Bar** for nightly jazz.

Four Seasons Hotel

200 Boylston Street   Toll-free reservations: 800/268-6282
Boston, MA 02116   Local number: 338-4400
                                   Telex: 853349

Located on Boston Common and handy to the State House, this newest Four Seasons Hotel continues a tradition of excellent service with special attention to women traveling alone. Of 288 rooms, a good number conform to the unique Four Seasons Room design, an arrangement that cleverly separates the work area from the bedroom. In our experience, any Four Seasons hotel can be counted on for flawless service and unparalleled security.

Aujourd'hui Restaurant is their gourmet room (see "Dining Out"); **Bristol Court** serves casual meals, tea, late-night snacks. **Bristol Lounge** is cozy with live piano music and a roaring fire in the wintertime.

Lafayette

1 Avenue de Lafayette   Toll-free reservations: 800/992-0124
Boston, MA 02111   Local number: 451-2600
                               Telex: 853840

Centrally located in Downtown Crossing, this 22-story Swissotel takes full advantage of the new Lafayette Place shopping complex of restaurants, shops, and services to complement its own array of amenities. The hotel's unique design of four atriums allows for a feeling of privacy and helps ensure tight security. Opened in March 1985, this European-flavored hotel stresses fine furnishings and quiet elegance. Private lobbies in each atrium serve as semiprivate living rooms for guests' meetings. Conveniently located adjacent to Jordan Marsh and the boutiques of newly opened Lafayette Place for last-minute shopping or lunchtime browsing.

Cafe Suisse is their informal, three-meal restaurant. **The Lounge** offers drinks and live piano, as well as afternoon tea. **Restaurant Le Marquis de Lafayette** is for serious gourmet dining—creative cuisine by a French chef favored by Michelin.

Marriott Hotel Long Wharf

296 State Street   Toll free reservations: 800/228-9290
Boston, MA 02109   Local number: 227-0800
                               Telex: 928065

Looking much like a docked ocean liner, this 400-room hotel hugs historic Long Wharf at the foot of State Street. Nearby are Faneuil Hall, historic sites, the downtown area. Busy business travelers may want to book a room on their seventh floor since it offers extra perks for those on the go, including room outfitted with a dining table that doubles as a work area. Housekeeping will quickly produce essentials like irons and hair dryers on request.

Harbour Terrace specializes in reasonably priced seafood. The **Palm Garden** is open for casual meals all day, including a popular Sunday brunch. The local in-crowd favors **Rachael's** with its complimentary hors d'oeuvres and a deejay to blend top-40 sounds for dancing.

Hotel Meridien

250 Franklin Street   Toll-free reservations: 800/543-4300
Boston, MA 02110   Local number: 451-1900
                               Telex: 940194

A luxury hotel in Boston's financial district, the French-flavored Meridien occupies what was originally the Federal Reserve Bank Building. Old World architectural opulence now complements state-of-the-art guest services. Guest rooms were designed to fit into existing architectural spaces to retain the structure's authenticity. The result: no two of the 328 rooms are alike. Some are even duplexes (loft bedrooms with downstairs living rooms)—great for business meetings. Ask questions and be specific when making your reservations. You'll find all the deluxe touches you would expect from a luxury hotel, including a classically helpful concierge. (Remember the French invented the concierge concept.)

Julien is the Meridien's serious French restaurant housed in what was originally the Federal Reserve members' court. (see "Dining Out"). The lively **Julien Lounge,** with its piano bar and original N. C. Wyeth murals is an after-work favorite of local businesspeople. **Cafe Fleuri,** a typical French bistro, is fine for casual all-day dining, including one of Boston's most popular Sunday brunches, and a weekday buffet (September to May) that's amazingly reasonable at about $15.00.

Boston Park Plaza and Towers

Arlington Street at Park Plaza
Boston, MA 02117

Toll-free reservations: 800/225-2008
Local number: 426-2000
Telex: 940107

Good location by day—overlooking the Public Garden and its swan boats, close to downtown sites—but a bit deserted after dark (although the area is currently benefiting from a gentrification program to improve both security and aesthetics). A 1,000-room, business-geared hotel that offers office services and fitness and beauty facilities, along with moderate prices. Best for women is the Towers, an 82-room concierge floor with all the extras, including the Club Suite Lounge.

There is a branch of **Legal Sea Foods** in the hotel, along with several choices of dining: **Fox and Hounds,** a fine Edwardian dining room; **Cafe Rouge,** an all-meals casual room; **Swan's,** a cheery lobby lounge with live piano starting at 3 P.M.; **Terrace Room** featuring *Forbidden Broadway,* a cabaret spoof of sacred theater hits.

Parker House

60 School Street
Boston, MA 02107

Toll free reservations: 800/328-4488
Local number: 227-8600
Telex: 7103216707

As Boston as—yes, Parker House rolls—this landmark hotel continues to refurbish and keep up with the times. Its financial district location makes it central to all downtown businesses. No cookie-cutter rooms here; some have separate work areas, some come with dressing rooms, some have showers but no tubs. Be sure to specify your preferences. As part of the Omni-Dunfey group, Parker House offers ESP (Executive Service Plan) to ensure an automatic reduction in room rates. (Your call gets a $155 room for $125.) Other benefits include the extra in-room amenities like digital clocks and bathroom scales.

Dine in the hotel at the **Cafe Tremont,** a popular place for breakfast meetings and a comfortable spot for women on their own. Good wines by the glass and afternoon hors d'oeuvres. Live it up at the **Last Hurrah,** a turn-of-the century saloon where Boston's young professionals meet and dance to the Bo Winiker Band, especially during their swinging Sunday brunch. Elegant, formal dining upstairs at **Parker's.**

Royal Sonesta Hotel

5 Cambridge Parkway   Toll-free reservations: 800/343-7170
Cambridge, MA 02142   Local number: 491-3600
                             Telex: 275293

On the banks of the Charles River in the East Cambridge waterfront section, the 400-room Royal Sonesta provides easy access to Harvard, MIT, and Massachusetts General Hospital, as well as offering spectacular views of the city. Free transportation provided (7 A.M. to 9:30 P.M.) by courtesy van to sites in Cambridge and downtown Boston. Original contemporary art is the personal love and trademark of the Sonnabend family, which operates the hotel. So your room, as well as every public space, will showcase the best current works of international artists. The ninth and tenth floors of the West Tower belong to the Royal Club, Sonesta's executive sections. Expect all the upscale services and amenities.

The **Rib Room** is a romantic dining experience complete with live harp music and dramatic views of Boston. **Toffs Restaurant** is a less formal art deco setting with nightly entertainment and outdoor dining when the weather cooperates. The **Greenhouse Cafe** for daily meals; **Lobby Lounge** for light snacks.

Westin Hotel

Copley Place   Toll-free reservations: 800/228-3000
10 Huntington Avenue   Local number: 262-9600
Boston, MA 02116   Telex: 948286

Everything is fashionable here—from the location (prestigious Back Bay) to the architectural elegance of this new 36-story beauty. You can expect top-of-the-line service, security, and luxuries in this giant 804-room hotel. Just next door is Copley Place, considered by some local businesswomen as Boston's best shopping complex (see "The Shopping Scene" for details).

In the hotel is **Turner Fisheries Bar and Restaurant,** a multi-award-winning operation serving some of the best seafood in this seafood town. Live entertainment in the bar nightly. **Ten Huntington** is Westin's elegant dining restaurant, with a wine bar that offers dozens of vintages by the glass. **The Brasserie** for cheerful, informal meals all day; the **Lobby Lounge,** amidst pink marbled waterfalls, offers some of the best people-watching in the city.

ON A BUDGET

Hotels

Copley Square Hotel

47 Huntington Avenue-   Local number: 536-9000
Boston, MA 02116

A smallish (153-room) hotel in a terrific location for a good price. A stone's throw from Copley Place, this Back Bay hotel has been garnering kudos for its European ambience and comfortable service. Rates $69 to $79.

Pop's Place serves light meals all day. There is a convenient lobby lounge, and the award-winning **Cafe Budapest** serves up Hungarian specialties in the basement.

Women's City Club

40 Beacon Street   Local number: 277-3550
Boston, MA 02108

If you are in town on the second Friday of any month, try and reserve a spot at the Prospective Member's Luncheon at the Women's City Club. Members have reciprocal privileges in some 50 clubs in the United States and abroad. They're also able to stay in the guest rooms and use the three dining rooms—not to mention attending those prestigious Literary Hours with famous-name speakers—all on Beacon Hill.

Restaurants

Harvard Bookstore Cafe is not in Harvard Square, but it is a lovely, low-key spot to snack while you browse the stacks. They serve three meals daily, are closed on Sunday. 190 Newbury Street. 536-0095.

Athens Olympia Cafe is acceptable for a modest business lunch and convenient for before-theater suppers. Try the appetizer platter and the spinach pie. Cab there after dark, as it's on the fringe of the Combat Zone. 51 Stuart Street. 426-6236.

In the financial district, try **Truffles.** Adjacent to the more elegant Gallagher's, this comfortable spot, popular with young executives, has a large, reasonably priced menu with excellent specials. 55 Congress Street. 523-6080.

Nosh and nibble your way through **Quincy Market.** The ethnic scene ranges from clam bars to knockwurst to sushi. While we're partial to **Seaside, Crickets,** and **Cityside,** it's fun to just wander and sample as you go.

DINING OUT

One New York executive who frequents Boston is disappointed with the standard of the city's restaurants, claiming "they're not too hot so I always stick to the fun kinds of places." We don't agree. We feel the quality is there, as is the variety: everything from al fresco snacking in Quincy Market to Old World serious dining in tradition-shrouded Locke-Ober. Boston is also on the cutting edge of the nation's newest dining trend: the reemergence of the excellent hotel dining room.

You can eat for just about any amount of money in Boston. For a guideline, we've defined lunch in the $20 to $30 range and dinners in the $25 to $35 range as expensive; mid-ranges of $10 to $22 as moderate; and anything below that as inexpensive.

Seasons, a glass-enclosed, rooftop haven in the Bostonian Hotel offers American cuisine selections that change with the seasons. Executive chef Lydia Shire is an award winner for her culinary excellence. Described by Marian Burros of the *New York Times* as offering "some of the best food served in any hotel in the country." Reservations a must. Expensive. 523-3600

Julien can be a bit stuffy and formal, but the food is worth it. Classic nouvelle French (this is the Meridien's haute cuisine restaurant) served in suitably luxe surroundings. Reservations. Expensive. 451-1900.

Restaurant Jasper on the waterfront at 240 Commercial. Modern American cuisine—try the duck, pecan and cranberry salad. Chef Jasper White also makes his own pastas. Closed Sundays. Reservations. Expensive. 523-1126.

Aujourd'hui Restaurant (in the Four Seasons Hotel) takes full advantage of its spectacular view of the Public Garden, a pastoral setting for its classic menu. Good news for business functions: Le Matin and Le Soir are two private dining rooms that can be reserved for parties of 8 to 12. Expensive. 338-4400.

Cafe Budapest offers Old World serenity (including violin and piano music in the lounge during dinner) with classic Hungarian cuisine. Busy on Saturday nights when no reservations are accepted. Best savored during the more leisurely week nights. Expensive. 90 Exeter Street. 734-3388.

Tigerlilies on Beacon Hill (23 Joy Street). The food is American nouvelle and very good, but the setting is the clincher. An old brick townhouse with courtyard and fireplace. Very cozy. Lunch and brunch; dinner only on Saturdays. Reservations. Moderate. 523-0609.

The Harvest Restaurant in Harvard Square is a favorite with the Cambridge crowd for its unusual dishes and is perfect for signing up a Harvard author. Comfortable lounge/bar is popular with academics and computer whizzes around the Square. Good selection of beer and wine. Courtyard tables when the weather cooperates. 44 Brattle Street. 492-1115.

Turner Fisheries Bar and Restaurant is another seafood winner—won "best clam chowder in Boston" award in 1984. Has an oyster bar, live jazz, and a seafood buffet after 5 P.M. In Westin Hotel, Copley Place. Moderate. 262-9600

One Boston businesswoman tells us when she and associates go out to eat, they always debate, "Do you want to go to Cornucopia, or shall we go to Cornucopia?" **Cornucopia,** near Lafayette Place, deserves this kind of loyalty. The setting is art deco, three floors keep noise levels low, and the menu, which is American nouvelle, is changed every two weeks. They make their own ice cream, pâté, and sorbet. If you're eating light it's OK to combine two appetizers as an entrée. Good for after-theater dinner. 15 West Street. Moderate. 338-4608.

The **North End,** as we keep discovering, is almost as good to the palate as a trip to Italy. Just wander the streets (they're supersafe—this is a real old-time *neighborhood*), follow your nose, and *mangia!* We've always had good luck with these:

Joe Tecce's Restaurant has a huge menu including fresh calamari and "Mrs. Tecce's Ravioli." Family-run place that has grown without losing its charm. Closed Sundays. Reservations. Moderate. 53 N. Washington Street. 742-6210.

Cafe Paradiso. Award-winning northern Italian cuisine. Separate downstairs cafe serves pastries and gelatos. Reservations. Moderate. 235-255 Hanover Street. 742-1768.

Mamma Maria, perhaps the North End's most elegant Italian restaurant (and the winner of *Boston Magazine's* award as the best Italian restaurant in the North End), serves northern Italian specialties with imagination. Moderate to expensive. 3 North Square. 523-0077.

Ristorante Lucia features dishes from the Abbruzzi as well as classic Italian fare. Closed Sundays. Moderate. 415 Hanover Street. 367-2353.

BEST FOR POWER BREAKFAST

The Ritz Cafe is *the* place where early morning business is conducted in Boston. In the Ritz-Carlton Hotel. 15 Arlington Street. 536-5700.

BEST FOR POWER LUNCH

Grille 23 & Bar (Berkley and Stuart streets, 542-2255) and **Locke-Ober Cafe** (3 Winter Place, 542-1340) are both males-only-style bastions where women now pick up checks with the best of them. (At Locke-Ober, be sure to reserve far enough in advance to assure a table in the prestigious downstairs section.) Either is an excellent choice for hosting any male associates, although the status gained will likely be far better than the food at Locke-Ober.

BOSTON BY DAY

Because we believe that an overview is the best way to begin to understand the layout of a new city, we recommend these two:

John Hancock Observatory Tower for an eagle's-eye view of Boston and its landmarks as seen from 740 feet up. Particularly enlightening are a voice-over skywalk of the city (on a clear day you can see New Hampshire), and two special multimedia presentations: "1775" and "Uncommonly Boston," designed to familiarize visitors with recent and past history. In Copley Square in the Back Bay. 247-1976.

"Where's Boston" is a multimedia quadraphonic essay of modern-day Boston that gives an up-to-the-minute handle on this complex city. Shows hourly from 10 A.M. to 5 P.M. Sack Theaters at Copley Place. 267-4949.

Rather like Dorothy in Oz, you can follow the red brick line along the **Freedom Trail.** It leads you through Boston's colonial history on a three-mile route in the heart of the city that covers 15 historic sites, including the State House, Granary Burying Ground, Boston Massacre site, Paul Revere House, *Old Ironsides,* and Bunker Hill Monument. Maps are available through hotel concierges or at visitor information booths along the route. Or strap on your tape recorder and try "Boston Walkabout," an informational walking tour on tape. Available in most hotel gift shops. If your schedule is too crowded for the three-hour-plus walk, there are bus tours of the trail. Call Hub Buslines (776-0630), Gray Line (426-8805), or Brush Hill (436-4100), or ride the Old Town Trolley (269-7010) for a nostalgic tour.

Wander **Quincy Market** (home of historic Faneuil Hall), a Rouse Company restoration of Boston's 19th-century marketplace near the waterfront. Three vast warehouses frame an area that literally vibrates with activity and energy. You'll probably visit more than once—for nibbling dozens of different cuisines, for shopping, and for people-watching. Visit the old Haymarket nearby on Friday or Saturday for a glimpse of the traditional market scene, Boston-style.

Museum of Fine Arts with its I.M. Pei–designed West Wing deserves one whole afternoon at the very least. It is second only to New York's Metropolitan in size and scope. Its Egyptian collection alone is among the country's best. Frequent special exhibits are mounted so be sure to ask. Terrific gift shop and restaurants. Open late on Wednesdays the West Wing is open late on Thursday and Friday. Closed Mondays. Free Saturday A.M. 465 Huntington Avenue near Fenway Park. 267-9377.

Near the Fine Arts Museum, the **Isabella Stewart Gardner Museum** is actually more a dazzling Venetian palazzo than a museum. Shipped here in pieces and rebuilt by Mrs. Gardner as a sumptuous setting for her extraordinary personal collection of Old Masters (Rembrandt, Raphael, Botticelli, and Rubens, to name a few), this mansion bewitches the eye at every turn. You may be lucky and your visit will coincide with one of the frequent chamber music concerts performed in the Tapestry Room. And don't miss the portrait of the lady herself as painted by her friend John Singer Sargent; its frank sensuality created quite a scandal in Victorian-era Boston. Closed Monday. 280 Fenway. 566-1401.

The Gallery of Museum Shops on the mezzanine level of Copley Place shopping complex offers some of the best in reproductions of paintings in seven of the nation's leading museums, including New York's Metropolitan and Boston's Fine Arts. Also on display are posters and information on various special displays and events. 100 Huntington Avenue. 267-6223.

The New England Aquarium on Central Wharf is known worldwide for its educational displays of 2,000 species of sharks, sea turtles, and exotic fish. Seasonal hours, so check. 742-8870.

Also well worth a visit are:

Boston Tea Party Ship and Museum. In December, there's a reenactment of the famous "tea party" and everyone is welcome to join in.

Refreshments, including hot tea, of course. The Congress Street Bridge. 388-1773.

> **Bunker Hill Pavilion.** 55 Constitution Road. 241-7575.

> **John F. Kennedy Library.** Columbia Point on Dorchester Bay, Dorchester. 929-4523.

> **Museum of Science.** Science Park. 742-6088.

> **USS *Constitution* Museum.** In the National Museum Park, Charlestown Navy Yard. 242-0543.

> Boston Events, a recording of the latest happenings. 267-6446.

UNIQUELY BOSTON

As we said, this is a great city for walking. To capture the spirit of old Boston, take a stroll through the cobblestoned streets of **Beacon Hill** (do wear flat-heeled shoes). Admire stately **Louisburg Square** with its purple-paned windows and take a peek at tiny, gas-lit Acorn Street. For an enthusiastic commentary, connect with one of the Boston by Foot tours (367-2345) and explore the **Hill, Back Bay,** the **North End,** or the heart of the **Freedom Trail.** Complete your tour with a walk through the **Public Garden,** lovely in any season but a treat in the spring when the **swan boats** are in operation ($1.00 for adults). Peanuts are extra! And if all that walking has given you an appetite, cross the street to the **Ritz** for an authentic afternoon tea.

Discover the real secrets of Harvard Square with an intimate walking tour of Old Cambridge. For details call Cambridge Discovery (491-6278). Don't miss the **Blacksmith House Bakery** on Brattle Street now popular for its European pastries, and the haunt of local literati.

THE SHOPPING SCENE

If there's no time for a systematic check of what's in-store in Boston, don't despair. Shopping is easy in this city. Almost everything is grouped into areas, each centrally located and within walking distance of most hotel and business addresses.

We find using the Boston Doubledecker (739-0100), a shopper's shuttle that connects Prudential Center to Quincy Market, to be convenient if we want to cover a lot of ground. Red London-style buses operate at 15-minute intervals, starting at 10 A.M. and stopping at 6 P.M. It operates on a continuous route, making 25 stops along the way. Starting point for the bus is on the Prudential Center side of Boylston Street where Gloucester intersects (near Hunter's Pub) and at the foot of the staircase leading to Government Center on State Street (for boarding) and at the corner of Congress and State streets for disembarking. Fare is 50 cents.

Quincy Market (also known as Faneuil Hall Marketplace) combines a bit of history with the mass appeal of trendy food outlets, but it's worthwhile for shopping addicts, too. Lots of stores and lots of atmosphere. You'll find yourself returning for snacks, as well as a shopping blitz at Ann Taylor.

Back Bay, an area bounded by Boylston and Newbury streets, offers haute couture European selections. (Newbury, in fact, is often dubbed Boston's Fifth Avenue.) High-fashion designer boutiques on Boylston. The Prudential Shopping Plaza—referred to locally as the Pru—is at 800 Boylston. Good only for Saks and Lord & Taylor. Better to visit Copley Place nearby, which many say could become Bostonians' favorite mall. Expensive but wonderful, Copley (pronounced Cop-Lee) Place opened in 1984 and connects the Westin and Marriott hotels; it boasts restaurants, theaters, and Neiman-Marcus. You'll also find Rive Gauche, Tiffany, Williams-Sonoma, and other prestigious names. Perfect for window shopping and small indulgences.

Downtown Crossing on Washington Street is home to New England's two retail giants: **Filene's** and **Jordan Marsh.** No matter how much you may hate crowds and confusion, do not allow yourself to leave Boston without at least one visit to Filene's Basement. Its particular challenge gives new meaning to the word *bargain.* Everyone has a favorite basement story: the Galanos gown snatched up for $100, the Italian suede jacket for $79. Our best tip: she who hesitates loses the bargain. Delay, and it will surely be gone when you return. Adapt guerrilla shopping tactics and be prepared to try on your favorites in the open as there are no dressing rooms. (Pros wear leotards.) Call 357-2978 for hours.

Filene's (upstairs) and Jordan Marsh are regular full-service department stores.

Just across Washington Street is **De Scenza,** a below-retail showplace for jewelry and gift items. Shop here if you need a status gift for your Boston hostess's dinner party. Or visit the Women's Educational and Industrial Union (356 Boylston Street) for unusual, moderately priced gifts with a Boston flavor.

If your clothes just don't seem to meet Boston standards, zip into **Designers Clothing Limited** (161 Devonshire Street) for an excellent selection of dress-for-success name labels at lower than retail prices. Sales help is actually helpful; the prices, a welcome surprise.

Not so conveniently located (but if you're a serious shopper, no obstacle is too great) is the **Outlet Center** on Route 9 outside town. Look for **Loehmann's, Ava Boutelle,** and the **Coat Store.** (You'll need a car to get out this far.) In town, scout out the bargains at **John Barry Ltd.,** 75 Kneeland Street in the heart of Chinatown.

If antiques are your passion, wander the shops along Charles Street between Back Bay and Beacon Hill, stopping for great coffee at the **Coffee Connection** or an Italian ice at **Il Doce Momento.** Hunting for the hottest novel or an unusual art book, hop on the T to Harvard Square, home of the Harvard Coop and, some say, "more bookstores than any other U.S. city."

BOSTON BY NIGHT

It comes as no big surprise that Boston is a major cultural center, home of first-rate theater, music, and dance. Because of such dedication to the arts, tickets can be a problem. We always alert our hotel's concierge in advance of arrival for tickets to performances we'd like to attend. There's also **Ticketron** (720-3400) for regularly priced tickets plus a surcharge, or **BOSTIX** at Quincy Market for same-day, half-price tickets and full-price advance sales. (Be forewarned that because of the savings, buying tickets at BOSTIX may be a time-consuming proposition; lines are usually very long.) Also check BOSTIX recorded messages (723-5181) for up-to-date entertainment information.

As Boston is also a major try-out town for shows en route to Broadway, we like to second-guess the critics and see a hit-in-training as it strives to become a legend. Try-out tickets are about $10 less than you'd pay on Broadway. Boston's theater district, an area roughly bounded by Washington, Tremont, and Boylston streets, includes the **Wilbur** (423-4008), **Shubert** (426-4520), and **Colonial** theaters (426-9366), and the **Charles Playhouse** (426-6912).

The nearby **Wang Center for the Performing Arts** (542-3600) is where you'll find touring companies of recent and classic Broadway shows. It also presents performances by visiting ballet and opera companies and the larger one-person shows.

Neither of us minds going to the theater alone, but we do have one rule: we always arrive and depart via cab. As the theater district is adjacent to the Combat Zone, this isn't the most savory part of town.

Boston Symphony Orchestra, a Boston hallmark now in its second century of performing excellence, performs at Symphony Hall, 251 Huntington Avenue, when it is not in its summer quarters at Tanglewood. The Friday afternoon series is a unique local tradition, worthwhile if your schedule permits. 266-1492.

Symphony Hall is home, too, to the beloved **Boston Pops,** when they're not at Tanglewood or performing in the Hatch Shell on the banks of the Charles River. Call 266-1492 to find out where they'll be while you're in town.

The **Opera Company of Boston** has an erratic season, but it's worth investigating for Sarah Caldwell's adventurous productions at the Opera House. The Opera House also presents performers from the popular music field. 539 Washington Street. 426-5300.

Other venues:

Boston Concert Opera. 111 West Concord Street. Rear. 536-1166.
Boston Shakespeare Company. 52 St. Botolph Street. 267-5600.
Boston Ballet. 553 Tremont Street. 542-3945.
Charles Playhouse, Stage II. 74 Warrenton Street. (*Shear Madness*, a whodunit comedy, has been running there for years.) 426-5225.
Huntington Theater Company. 264 Huntington Avenue. 266-3913.

Water Music. Evening cruises featuring jazz, folk, classical during warm-weather months. Cruises leave Long Wharf and tickets range from $9.50 to $22.50. 876-8742.

LATE-NIGHT BOSTON

Although proper Bostonians will tell you the city shuts up like a bay clam after 10 P.M., those so inclined will have no problem discovering a lively night scene that includes everything from jazz clubs to discos and even sing-along bars.

A safe and convenient way to get an idea of the late-night action is to board the **Boston Night Life** double-decker show bus and leave the driving to them. The brainchild of Bettyann Bernstein, this service provides newcomers an introduction to what's happening after hours in Boston. There's even entertainment on board this swinging bus as it heads on to the next club. Reserve ahead through your hotel's concierge, or call 566-2296. Cost: about $36.

Two ideas for those who want to try the sing-along bar scene are **Lily's Bar** in Quincy Market (227-4242), attracting a lively crowd, ranging from students to yuppie executives; and **Diamond Jim's** (536-2200) at the Lenox Hotel, a local favorite.

The **Last Hurrah** at the Parker House (lower level) features dancing with Bo Winiker's 16-piece dance band every night of the week except Sunday. Lots of history in this turn-of-the-century bar, an old hang-out of the Kennedys and the Fitzgeralds.

For Irish entertainment, try the **Black Rose,** 160 State Street, adjacent to Fanueil Hall. 742-2286.

The clublike art deco atmosphere of **Jason's** upscale Back Bay restaurant and bar is perfect for dancing or backgammon. Piano bar, live entertainment. 131 Clarendon Street. 262-9000.

Dancing and music reminiscent of *The Big Chill* is the scene at the **Juke Box** at the Hotel Bradford in the theater district. Attracts a fun-seeking crowd that dances to sixties and seventies music. Not in one of the city's better neighborhoods, so stay alert.

A very New York flavor in the disco area is the **Metro.** Reasonable cover of $10 on weekends. Attracts a varied clientele. 262-2424.

By contrast, the **Bay Tower Room** (723-1666), overlooking the waterfront from the 33d floor of 60 State Street, has a small dance floor, lots of class, and relaxing easy music. Safe for single women, no hassles. Live entertainment. Go for drinks and the view, not the food; locals report it is expensive and mediocre.

A fun alternative is to take in *Forbidden Broadway,* parodies of favorite shows from the Great White Way and their star performers. At the Boston Park Plaza Hotel's Terrace Room. Make reservations. 426-2000.

For what some say is the best jazz in town, go to **Ryles** in Cambridge. Live music, 9 P.M. to 2 A.M. Downstairs is where you'll hear the best sounds. Open Sunday through Thursday until 1 A.M.; Fridays and Saturdays until 2 A.M. If that's not enough, try their Sunday jazz brunch, noon to 4 P.M. 212 Hampshire Street. 876-9330.

AT LEISURE

If it's at all possible to work it out so that business in Boston ends as the weekend begins, do so. This is one city where you'll want to spend some extra time. Many diverse day trips are possible, and the changing seasons offer a whole spectrum of activities: fall foliage, winter skiing, summer beaching. Be sure to check with your hotel for special weekend packages and rates.

DAY-TRIPPING

Lexington and Concord, just outside the city, are steeped in our nation's history. In April of 1775 a few local farmers confronted the British Redcoats on the Lexington Green. The rest, as they say, is history. The old buildings still stand, like the Hancock-Clarke House where Samuel Adams and John Hancock were awakened by Paul Revere.

Neighboring **Concord** was once home to Louisa May Alcott, Nathaniel Hawthorne, and Ralph Waldo Emerson, all of whose homes are open to visitors. Refresh your soul with a walk around Thoreau's Walden Pond. Further information: Lexington Chamber of Commerce, 862-1450. Concord Chamber of Commerce, 369-3120.

Heading north from town along Route 1, you'll visit the town of **Salem,** known for its witchcraft hysteria in 1690. The House of the Seven Gables is also here. Further up the coast is **Gloucester** (pronounced Gloss-ter), a historic seaport that was also the setting for Kipling's *Captains Courageous.*

Here you will also find quaint **Rockport,** home of Motif #1 (now rebuilt after the blizzard of '78) and the charming but crowded artists' colony of Bearskin Neck. Worth a visit, especially out of season, to gallery hop, shop for souvenirs, and sample the seafood.

Just beyond is **Ipswich,** famous for both its clams and the miles of beautiful Crane's beach, and **Newburyport,** with its stately sea captains' homes and renovated waterfront.

Head south from Boston, and you're en route to **Cape Cod.** Have a day or two at leisure? Take the ferry from Falmouth/Woods Hole over to **Martha's Vineyard** or **Nantucket.** Farther south, but along an inland route is **Newport, Rhode Island,** with its castlelike mansions and a marina crowded with ocean-going yachts.

In-Town

For up-to-the-minute information on what's happening around town, send ahead for the Official Visitor Information Kit, which includes a seasonal calendar of events as well as a city guidebook, a well-organized city map, and a guide to the Freedom Trail. All yours for $3. Greater Boston Convention & Visitors Bureau, Box 490, Boston, MA 02199. Or call 536-4100.

Sunday Customs

Bostonians snuggle down to read the *Globe* and enjoy a second cup of coffee on Sunday mornings. But we find them out in force in the afternoons, browsing through Quincy Market or enjoying the outdoors at one of the parks, jogging along the river or brunching.

Brunch is a beloved Sunday ritual. Although everyone has a favorite, here are some of the most popular scenes:

T.G.I Fridays, corner of Exeter and Newbury streets in Back Bay. Boisterous and fun, waiters in crazy hats, a real meeting place. 266-9040.

St. Botolph Restaurant, 99 St. Botolph Street in the South End, behind the Colonnade Hotel. Wonderfully atmospheric old brownstone. Creative brunch menu as well as traditional favorites. We enjoy eating dinner here as well. 266-3030.

Parkers, 60 School Street in the Parker House Hotel. Very elegant, leisurely atmosphere with live harp music setting the mood. Each woman is presented with a long-stemmed rose. Extensive buffet gets an A plus. 227-8600.

Ritz Cafe, Ritz-Carlton Hotel. Eighty buffet selections, caviar, and champagne—all for $25. *The* place to be seen. 536-5700.

Spectator Sports

If your inclination isn't very energetic, take advantage of Boston's big-league teams for some spectator sporting.

The **Celtics** (basketball) and **Bruins** (hockey) battle in Boston Garden (227-3200); the **Red Sox** (baseball) play in Fenway Park (267-8661); and the New England **Patriots** (football) lock horns at Sullivan Stadium (543-7911) in Foxboro, about 40 miles south of Boston.

Active Sports

If the weather is warm, active weekenders head for the **Esplanade** along the Charles River to stroll, jog (round-trip from Harvard Bridge to Hatch Shell is 1½ miles), skate, bike, or just watch the scullers on the river.

Bikes: Community Bike (542-8623), at 490 Tremont Street, near South End police station, rents for $10 a day.

Skates: Beacon Hill Skate (523-9513), at 45 Charles Street, rents skates and knee-guards at $7 for 24 hours. Driver's license and credit card are required as deposit.

Boats: Boston Harbor Sailing Club (523-2619) maintains a fleet of 70 boats ranging from 25-foot Mako power boats to 30-foot Scampis. Ask about their private tours of Boston Harbor for up to six people. Cost: $35.00.

Chicago

HOTELS

1 Ambassador East
2 Drake
3 Hilton & Towers
4 Hyatt Regency
5 Knickerbocker
6 Marriott
7 Mayfair Regent
8 Palmer House & Towers
9 Park Hyatt
10 Richmont
11 Ritz-Carlton
12 Sheraton-Plaza
13 Tremont
14 Westin

LANDMARKS

A Art Institute of Chicago
B Daley Plaza (Civic Center)
C John Hancock Bldg.
D Marshall Field
E Merchandise Mart/Apparel
  Center

F Navy Pier
G O'Hare International Airport
H Orchestra Hall
I Sears Tower
J Water Tower

CHICAGO

GETTING YOUR BEARINGS

Carl Sandburg called his hometown Chicago, "City of the Big Shoulders." "Stormy, husky, brawling" were his words for the muscular, masculine feel of this earthy Midwest metropolis. The recent roughriding reign of feisty Jane Byrne as Chicago's first woman mayor showed that only a tough woman can run the place.

Yet Chicago's brawny image can be misleading.

Despite its heavy industry and heady stockyards, its former gun-toting gangsters and an earlier cigar-chomping mayor, Chicago is one of the easiest towns for a woman to do business in. We find that the key to success is to think and act as a Chicagoan: straightforward, to the point, open and frank.

Chicago's psyche lies west of New York and east of California. The city is more genuinely friendly than the former but not as casually emotive as the latter. You probably won't get kissed on the cheek here, but neither need you fear knives in the back. Handshakes are hearty, smiles sincere.

Welcome to the Midwest.

Behavior that may be admired as strong and assertive in the East can come off as brassy or pushy here. Showy image making that's good one-upmanship in the West may be perceived as shallow and self-centered in Chicago. In short, when in Chicago, say what you mean and mean what you say — don't play games.

About 3 million people live within Chicago's city limits and more than 7 million reside in the entire metropolitan area — the nation's third largest.

White-collar business districts are found in the northern, western, and northwestern suburbs as well as around O'Hare International Airport on the city's northwestern boundary.

The village of Rosemont, next to O'Hare, has an exposition facility that hosts about 60 trade shows a year. Chicago's convention and exposition center, McCormick Place, is on the lakefront south of the downtown business districts.

The Chicago River divides downtown Chicago roughly in half.

The Loop, south of the river, is named for the elevated train tracks that encircle Chicago's old downtown. Government buildings and the city's financial district are located here. Upper Michigan Avenue, north of the river, refers to North Michigan Avenue (the Magnificent Mile) and side streets. A number of advertising and public relations firms have addresses here and most of the city's best hotels and restaurants are located in this upper-crust neighborhood.

Chicago's come a long way. In the early 1800s, this was Indian territory and became urbanized as a jumping-off point for the Northwest Territories and the Plains. Some 300,000 people had made the city home by 1871 when Mrs. O'Leary's cow kicked over a kerosene lantern to set the town on fire. Most of what is now downtown went up in flames, but that tragedy provided the chance for America's finest architects to build, or rather rebuild, a major city from scratch.

Today, we find bold and beautiful architecture, a hallmark of Chicago. Besides the world's tallest building, the Sears Tower, other memorable edifices are the Richard J. Daley Center dominated by a Picasso sculpture. Helmut Jahn designed the State of Illinois Building, which is three-sided and done in pastels. And, across the way, Gothic columns and classic lines mark the 1920s-style city and county buildings. Frank Lloyd Wright did his bit in Chicago, too, with a smattering of mansions in the Hutchinson district. In all, there's an impressive assemblage of some of the country's best architecture.

We sometimes wonder why Chicago isn't the nation's focal point. And as far as this town wearing the tag Second City—no way.

WHAT TO WEAR

The home of the Merchandise Mart and the Apparel Center is blossoming as a fashion design center, but businesswomen in Chicago continue to dress traditionally. Business suits are standard — and practical, given the bitter cold winter weather. We find that the most effective professional look in Chicago is to be smart but subdued, not trendy or knock 'em dead.

WEATHER WATCH

Seasonal temperatures swing from an average high of 81 in July to an average low of 18 in January. Summers are hot and humid, winters harsh with blizzards. The downtown lakefront is often five or ten degrees warmer in winter and cooler in summer than the "official" Chicago temperatures you may read before arrival. Those are taken at O'Hare Airport.

GETTING THERE

Three airports serve Chicago, though, ironically, the two most convenient to the city are the least known and used.

O'Hare International Airport is still the world's busiest. This massive complex is about 20 miles northwest of the central business district — 45 minutes away in good traffic, an hour at peak traffic times, and $25 to $30 by cab.

In addition to serving most of America's major airlines, O'Hare welcomes the world via Air Canada, Air France, British Airways, Japan Air Lines, KLM, Lufthansa, Mexicana, SAS, and Swissair. Regional carriers feeding in from other midwestern points include Air Wisconsin, Mississippi Valley Airlines, and Britt (see Britt under Meigs Field, too).

Transportation from O'Hare, other than taxis, includes Carey Limousine (663-1220), about $45 to downtown; Continental Air Transport motorcoaches (454-7800), $7.50 one-way, $12.25 round-trip to most downtown hotels; and Chicago Transit Authority (CTA, 664-7200), a part-elevated, part-subway line boarded directly below the O'Hare baggage claim area and connecting to the Loop (Dearborn Station at the Daley Center) in 35 minutes for 90 cents. Cautions: the CTA line has no luggage racks and can be crowded with commuters from stops on the city's northwest side. Women traveling alone should not ride the train after dark. Otherwise, this is the best bargain for your time and money.

The quickest way to the lakefront from O'Hare (or Midway) is via Crescent Helicopter (800/247-7070). The service lands at Meig's Field, a five-minute cab ride from most downtown hotels. The flight, less than 10 minutes from either airport, costs $44 from O'Hare, $35 from Midway.

Midway Airport is 15 miles southwest of downtown Chicago and 30 minutes ($15 to $20) by cab. This airport is much less congested and far more convenient than O'Hare. Carriers flying in and out of Midway include Northwest Orient, Southwest, and Midway.

In addition to taxis, motorcoaches of Continental Air Transport serve Midway for $6 one-way, $12 round-trip to most downtown hotels. For Crescent Helicopter's fares, see O'Hare.

Meigs Field is a small airstrip on the lakefront used mostly for helicopter transfers from the major airports and for midwestern intercity hops by Britt. Popular for its connections to Springfield, the state capital.

Chicago is also served by frequent connections between other U.S. and Canadian cities by Amtrak, (558-1075) Greyhound, (781-2900) and Trailways (726-9500).

Car Rentals

Avis	694-5600 (O'Hare); 471-4495 (Midway)
Budget	686-4950 (O'Hare); 471-3595 (Midway)

Dollar	671-5100 (O'Hare)
Hertz	686-7272 (O'Hare); 735-7272 (Midway)
National	694-4640 (O'Hare); 471-3450 (Midway)

GETTING AROUND

Unless you have business appointments in the suburbs, renting a car is not practical. On-street parking is scarce, and downtown garages expensive. Given good weather, walking is the best way to negotiate central Chicago: from State Street in the heart of the Loop to Water Tower Place, center of the Upper Michigan Avenue district, takes about 30 minutes on foot. If you do drive, the best parking rates downtown are at the Monroe Street and Grant Park underground garages just east of Michigan Avenue and the Loop. $3.25 all day.

Taxis are easy to flag in downtown, especially on Michigan Avenue and LaSalle Street. The fare is $1 on entering the cab and 90 cents a mile thereafter. Cabs with an orange shared-ride pennant will carry two to three passengers to either airport ($12 O'Hare; $8 Midway). The two largest operators are Checker (666-3700) and Yellow Cab (829-4222).

The Chicago Transit Authority (CTA, not the rock group) and the Regional Transit Authority (836-7000) are the city-run systems that operate Chicago's buses, elevated and subway trains, and commuter rail lines. Bus and train fare is 90 cents on most routes with exact change required on buses. Avoid riding buses downtown at night, but rest easy and ride by day.

GETTING FAMILIAR

Chicago Convention & Tourism Bureau

McCormick Place on the Lake   225-5000
Chicago, IL 60616
Provides tourist and business traveler information from 8:30 A.M. to 5 P.M. weekdays. Also operates the **Water Tower Visitor Information Center** in the historic Water Tower at Michigan and Chicago avenues, daily 9 A.M. to 5 P.M.

Travel Information Center

310 S. Michigan Avenue   793-2094
Chicago, IL 60604
Operated by the state of Illinois's tourism division; provides information on Chicago and nearby state attractions from 9 A.M. to 5 P.M. weekdays. Also operates an information booth in Sears Tower, 233 S. Wacker and at O'Hare Airport.

The city's daily newspapers include the *Chicago Tribune* (morning, afternoon, evening editions), which features a Friday tabloid of weekend entertainment, and the *Chicago Sun-Times* (afternoon and evening editions). Other useful periodicals are *Crain's Chicago Business,* a weekly newspaper published on Mondays; *Chicago,* a monthly magazine with extensive dining and entertainment listings and reviews; and *This Week in Chicago, GuestInformant,* and *Where,* all in-room magazines listing local events and attractions.

Quick Calls

AREA CODE 312	**Weather 976-1212**
Time 976-1616	Travelers Aid 686-7562

AT YOUR SERVICE

Business hotels in downtown Chicago are clustered around the Upper Michigan Avenue neighborhood with a few south of the Chicago River in and around the Loop. We describe what we believe are among the best of the downtown hotels catering to working women.

Tremont

100 E. Chestnut Street	Toll-free reservations: 800/621-8133
Chicago, IL 60611	Local number: 751-1900
	Telex: 255157

Possibly the best hotel in the city for the traveling career woman, the Tremont offers personalized service in the setting of a small, European-style luxury hotel. In 1984, the Tremont's management set out to capture the female business traveler's attention under the direction of general manager Karen Komo. They came up with the Reserved Executive Service program. Now, upon check-in, women guests are issued a request form allowing a selection of personal items—makeup mirrors, hair dryers, shampoo, disposable razors, and the like—to be made available during the stay. The list is kept on file, and items are automatically placed in the guest's room on subsequent visits. Repeat guests are rewarded not only with these personal touches but with upgraded accommodations (a suite at no extra charge for every five nights spent at the Tremont within a 12-month period.)

Dining here includes **Cricket's,** serving Continental cuisine and open for breakfast (**Cricket's Hearth**), lunch, dinner. Clubby atmosphere. Business attire required. **Cricket's Bar** is a classy Upper Michigan Avenue gathering spot.

Hotel	Concierge	Executive Floor	No-Smoking Rooms	Fitness Facilities	Pool	24-Hour Room Service	Restaurant for Client Entertaining	Extra-Special Amenities	Electronic Key System	Business/Secretarial Services	Checkout Time	Frequent Guest Program	Business Traveler Program	Average Single Rate
Ambassador East	●	●	●			●	The Pump Room	●		●	1 p.m.		Executive Service	$140 / $129 corp.
Drake	●	●	●	●	●	●	Cape Cod Room, Oak Terrace	●		●	1 p.m.		Executive Business Service	$115 / $105 corp. / $165–$185 exec. floor
Chicago Hilton & Towers	●	●	●			●	Buckingham's	●	●	●	12 noon		Key Accounts Program	$ 90–$140 / $ 95 Towers
Hyatt Regency Chicago	●	●	●			●	Scampi	●		●	12 noon		Gold Passport	$107–$137 / $117 corp. / $153 regency
Knickerbocker	●					●	Prince of Wales			●	1 p.m.		Knickerbocker Preferred	$114–$130 / $110 corp. / $ 84 Knickerbocker preferred

62

Chicago Marriott	●	●	●	●	●		JW's	●		●	12 noon		Honored Guest Program	$114–$137 $141 concierge $114–$123 corp.
Mayfair Regent	●					●	Ciel Bleu	●		●	1 p.m.			$160
Palmer House & Towers	●	●		●	●		Empire Room, Trader Vic's			●	1 p.m.		Executive Business Service	$ 85–$135 $105–$155 Tower $105 corp.
Park Hyatt	●		●			●	La Tour	●		●	12 noon	Private Line	Corporate Rate	$155–$185 $160 corp.
Ritz-Carlton	●		●	●	●	●	The Dining Room	●		●	1 p.m.	Return Guest Program		$155–$190 $175 corp.
Sheraton-Plaza	●	●			●		Bentley's	●		●	1 p.m.		Sheraton Executive Traveler	$105–$135 $ 92 corp.
Tremont	●		●			●	Cricket's	●		●	1 p.m.	TBA—planned start-up in '86		$130–$160
Westin	●	●	●	●		●	Chelsea	●		●	1 p.m.	Mileage Plus	Westin Preferred	$115–$190 $190 ex. floor $120 corp.

Mayfair Regent
181 E. Lake Shore Drive   Toll-free reservations: 800/545-4000
Chicago, IL 60611   Local number: 787-8500
                                 Telex: 256266
Understated elegance is in evidence throughout the Mayfair Regent, located on one of the city's most elite residential streets overlooking Lake Michigan just off the Magnificent Mile. Personalized service (guests are escorted to rooms by an assistant manager) makes women feel not only welcome but secure. The lobby is small and unpretentious, and service is excellent.

The **Ciel Bleu Restaurant** is one of the city's finest and ideal for business dining. Overlooks the lake and offers French cuisine at all three meals. The **Palm Restaurant**—like its New York City and Los Angeles counterparts—specializes in steak and lobster; it's good for lunch or dinner. Cocktails and afternoon tea in the lobby lounge.

Park Hyatt
800 N. Michigan   Toll-free reservations: 800/228-9000
Chicago, IL 60611   Local number: 280-2222
                                 Telex: 256216
One of Chicago's poshest, most expensive hotels, the Park Hyatt is a prototype for Hyatt's small, European-style hotels. No huge ballrooms and convention groups here. Just excellent service, luxurious accommodations and amenities. VIPs and high-ranking corporate decision makers stay here where female guests are pampered. Located behind historic Water Tower Place shopping mall.

For dining, **La Tour** is elegant and expensive, specializing in new American cuisine, which changes seasonally. Three meals daily; suitable for entertaining business associates. The private dining room, **Rousseau,** seats up to 12. High tea and cocktails in **The Salon** (lobby lounge) where on weeknights caviar and hor d'oeuvres are served. Cocktails also in La Tour's **Grand Marque Lounge.**

Drake
140 E. Walton   Toll-free reservations: 800/445-8667
Chicago, IL 60611   Local number: 787-2200
                                 Telex: 270278
One of Hilton's fine Vista International Hotels, the Drake has been a Chicago institution since 1920. Situated at the head of the Magnificent Mile and overlooking Oak Street Beach, the hotel is near Michigan Avenue shopping and business addresses. Though a large property, the Drake has an elegant, Old World feel. Service and amenities, particularly for female guests, are top-notch and include camera security and bellman escort to rooms.

For dining, the **Oak Terrace** is open for three meals and a good place to talk business. The **Cape Cod Room** specializes in seafood and is well known locally. Appropriate for business lunch or dinner. **Coq d'Or** is an intimate lounge for light lunches or suppers and cocktails. Afternoon tea and cocktails are served in the plush **Palm Court lobby.**

Ambassador East

1301 N. State Parkway	Toll-free reservations: 800/843-6664
Chicago, IL 60610	Local number: 787-7200
	Telex: 9102212120

An Omni Classic hotel, the Ambassador East is a Chicago classic as well. It dates back to 1930 when the rich and famous crisscrossed the country by railroad. Often, they would spend the night in Chicago between trains and the Ambassador East was their local address. Bogey and Bacall honeymooned here. Located in the heart of the elite Gold Coast residential neighborhood and removed but still accessible by cab to Upper Michigan Avenue, a pleasant 15-minute walk (safe during daylight).

For dining, the **Pump Room** serves Continental cuisine at three meals daily; dressy attire for dinner. Many a celebrity has occupied the famed Booth One of this restaurant. Cocktails in **Pump Room Bar** and in **Byfield's,** a popular cabaret.

Ritz-Carlton

160 E. Pearson	Toll-free reservations: in Illinois 800/
Chicago, IL 60611	828-1188; outside Illinois 800/621-6906
	Local number: 266-1000
	Telex: 206014

Managed by Four Seasons Hotels, Chicago's Ritz-Carlton is a chic hotel in a superb location, occupying floors 10 through 31 of Water Tower Place with shopping, restaurants, parking, entertainment all under one roof. Excellent security system. Service oriented, with attention to detail and a sensitivity toward needs of women business travelers.

Those of us who always seem to be on a diet will appreciate the **Dining Room** for its low-calorie, low-sodium, low-cholesterol French meals. Appropriate for business lunch or dinner. The **Cafe** serves breakfast, casual lunch, dinner, and late snacks. The **Greenhouse** serves light lunches, afternoon tea, with a piano bar in the evenings. A nice place for a quiet dessert. Cocktails served in the **Bar** with live entertainment and dancing five nights a week.

Palmer House and Towers

17 E. Monroe	Toll-free reservations: 800/445-8667
Chicago, IL 60690	Local number: 346-2772
	Telex: 382182

The best choice for accommodations in the Loop itself, the Palmer House and Towers is one of Chicago's grand old hotels (built in 1927), which just completed a structural and philosophical face-lift. Impressive second-floor lobby sets the tone. This is a nice hotel in which to hold a small meeting, not a massive convention. Executive floor and frequent traveler perks.

To tempt the palate, there's **Trader Vic's** for lunch and dinner.

The menu's Polynesian and so is the decor. An okay place for client meals. So is the **Steak House,** serving steak and seafood, although the atmosphere is masculine. Open for lunch and dinner. The **Empire Room** for lunch and Sunday brunch—with a jazz trio—has a Continental menu. Worth a visit if just to get a glimpse of the regal, empire-style decor. The **French Quarter** has breakfast and lunch buffets as well as an à la carte menu. A coffee shop serves breakfast and lunch, and a drugstore luncheonette serves three meals in a casual atmosphere with counter service. **Molly's Parlor** is an English pub open from 3 to 10 P.M. with daily specials and complimentary hors d'oeuvres. The **Den** on the lobby level serves light lunches and evening cocktails with complimentary hors d'oeuvres. **Gaslight Club** is private, open only to members and hotel guests.

Chicago Marriott

540 N. Michigan Avenue	Toll-free reservations: 800/228-9290
Chicago, IL 60611	Local number: 836-0100
	Telex: 9102211360

Convenient Michigan Avenue location makes this a good, full-service choice for business travelers calling on clients downtown. Its 1,100 rooms make this hotel a frequent host to large convention groups.

Breakfast is served in **Allie's Bakery,** a coffee shop, and is well suited for business talk. **La Plaza Dining Room** and **JW's** serve Continental cuisine; good for business lunch or dinner. Cocktails in **Upper Avenue Lounge, Fourth Edition,** and **Lobby Lounge.**

Hyatt Regency Chicago

151 E. Wacker Drive	Toll-free reservations: 800/228-9000
Chicago, IL 60601	Local number: 565-1234
	Telex: 256237

Chicago's largest hotel and the largest Hyatt in the world, this hotel was built in 1975 and renovated a decade later. Has 2,033 rooms and more than 200 suites, plus 24-hour services on a comparably grand scale. Located just east of Michigan Avenue and south of the Chicago River between Upper Michigan Avenue and the Loop. Convenient to business in both areas.

The hotel has eleven restaurants and lounges including **Scampi,** open 24 hours and serving American cuisine; **Stetson's,** serving grilled steaks and seafood at lunch and dinner; **Skyway,** serving light soups, salads, and sandwiches for lunch, also serves breakfast; **Mrs. O'Leary's,** serving American favorites in turn-of-the-century atmosphere for lunch or dinner; **Captain Streeters,** serving a luncheon buffet. Cocktails served in **Rumours** overlooking the lobby; the **Center** nightclub with dancing; the **Plaza Bar** in the lobby; **Stetson's** and **Mrs. O'Leary's** saloon.

Sheraton-Plaza

160 E. Huron	Toll-free reservations: 800/325-3535
Chicago, IL 60611	Local number: 787-2900

Because it's a small hotel, the Sheraton-Plaza can and does offer personalized services and attention to guests' needs. Its location, just off North Michigan Avenue, is convenient to business appointments, restaurants, and shops. A pool on the rooftop gives a good city overview. Three meals a day and Sunday brunch are served in **Bentley's**, appropriate for business entertaining as well as for women dining alone. At dinner, the accent is on beef and seafood with a veal and lamb selection also available. Low-calorie meals offered all day. Cocktails in **Tiff's Lounge** as well as sandwiches, chili, and salads. **Rooftop Terrace Garden Cafe**—open during the summer—serves cocktails, salads, and sandwiches at poolside.

Knickerbocker

163 E. Walton	Toll-free reservations: 800/621-8140
Chicago, IL 60611	Local number: 751-8100
	Telex: 206719

A 1980s reincarnation of the old 1920s Knickerbocker, this elegant property still reflects that splendid era, right down to a glass dance floor in the Grand Ballroom. Located near the north end of Upper Michigan Avenue, convenient to shops, restaurants, and entertainment as well as business appointments.

For informal dining, breakfast and lunch, try the **Piccadilly Inn.** The **Prince of Wales** serves Continental cuisine at dinner to the soft strains of harp music. Cocktails and nightly entertainment in **Limehouse Pub.**

Chicago Hilton and Towers

720 S. Michigan Avenue	Toll-free reservations: 800/445-8667
Chicago, IL 60605	Local number: 922-4400

The venerable Conrad Hilton, flagship of the Hilton chain, closed in 1984–85 for a $150 million renovation. The aging giant on South Michigan Avenue was then transformed into the Chicago Hilton and Towers, an upgraded facility—complete with computerized business center—designed to meet today's business travelers' needs. Located south of the Loop and facing Grant Park and the lakefront beyond, the hotel is a short cab ride to either McCormick Place to the south or Upper Michigan Avenue to the north. Free bus to shopping and business districts.

For fine dining, make a reservation at **Buckingham's. Fast Lane Deli** serves New York–style deli sandwiches. **Pavilion** is a 24-hour cafe and buffet. Cocktails in **Lakeside Green**, a two-story atrium lounge with entertainment.

Westin Hotel

909 N. Michigan Avenue	Toll-free reservations: 800/228-3000
Chicago, IL 60611	Local number: 943-7200
	Telex: 206593

This very visible Upper Michigan Avenue hotel next to Hancock Center has upgraded facilities. Convenient to shops, restaurants, and business appointments.

For breakfast, lunch, and dinner in a casual atmosphere, try **Chelsea:** American cuisine, appropriate venue for business discussions. **Lion Bar** serves soup-and-sandwich lunches weekdays and complimentary hors d'ouevres weekdays; jazz entertainment Tuesday through Saturday nights. Cocktails also in the lobby bar.

ON A BUDGET

There are ways to beat Chicago's big-city prices and still be in the heart of things. "Chicago by Day" and "Chicago by Night" include free and half-price attractions and activities for leisure hours. Here we spotlight a hotel and a handful of restaurant finds, which, although they are not inexpensive, we still appreciate when the expense account is tight.

Hotel

Richmont

162 E. Ontario   Toll-free reservations: 800/621-8055
Chicago, IL 60611   Local number: 787-3580

For our money, this is the best buy in Chicago hotel accommodations—the sort of cozy, European-style hotel you hear others whispering is their secret find. Located just off Upper Michigan Avenue, the Richmont is close to business, restaurants, and shopping for well under $100 a night. All it lacks in terms of luxury extras is a concierge and room service. The Richmont has 136 standard rooms with queen-sized beds, 28 with two double beds, 13 parlors, and 13 suites. Single, $70 to $97; double, $82 to 109; parlor, $107; suite, $120. Checkout time is noon. Security is good: round-the-clock doorman and security staff, room numbers held in confidence, dead-bolt locks, smoke detectors, and room sprinklers.

Members of the Richmont Club—a club for frequent travelers with a membership fee attached—are guaranteed a room even with last-minute reservations. Those who join are entitled to complimentary local phone service and photocopies, room upgrades, check-cashing privileges, preferred reservation service, and express registration. The hotel's pamphlet, "Perks and Per-Diems," is an insider's guide to Chicago for business travelers. All this and complimentary Continental breakfast each morning. Sorry, there's currently no room service.

Its **Rue St. Clair** is an American bistro offering a varied lunch and dinner menu; a bar adjoins the eatery.

Restaurants

For dining without spending an entire week's budget in one day, try **L'Escargot's** petit dinner. This unpretentious restaurant, often overlooked for lunch or dinner and good with or without client in tow, offers a fixed-price menu Monday through Friday, from 5 to 6:15 and from 9:30 until 10:30, at $14.50. Small, subdued dining room is served by waiters whose main goal is to attend to your needs, not to flex their egos. Owner Lucette Verge oversees the day-to-day operation. Regular lunch ranges from $8 to $13; dinner from $19 to $26, still not overly steep for a fine Chicago restaurant. Tucked away off the second floor lobby of the Allerton Hotel. 701 N. Michigan. 337-1717.

For dining alone where you won't pay an arm and a leg and yet you'll feel comfortable, visit the **Szechwan House.** Hot and sour soup and spicy snails good choices here. A buffet lunch is set up from 11:30 to 2 on weekdays, and Sunday brunch is served from 11:30 to 2:30. Dinner daily. 600 N. Michigan. 642-3900.

DINING OUT

Naturally, a city built on the beefy shoulders of stockyards is going to serve steaks and roasts in the best all-American ways. But the stockyards have moved to Omaha and Kansas City, and waves of immigrants have redefined Chicago's eating habits.

Cosmopolitan elegance has come to Chicago dining, and for business purposes, that is where we will focus. But do not fail to miss the fun sides of Chicago cuisine, especially the deep-dish pizza now catching on as a national alternative to the thin crispy kind (especially good at **Bacinos** in three locations: 2204 N. Lincoln Avenue, 472-7400; 75 E. Wacker Drive, 263-0070; and 240 Skokie Boulevard in Northbrook, 272-5222). Another must try is the Polish sausages found in the largest Polish community this side of Warsaw.

Power breakfasts are becoming popular in Chicago. Most hotels serve them. **Bentley's** in the Sheraton Plaza is one. 160 E. Huron. 787-2900.

Another is **Allie's Bakery** in the Marriott. From 6:30 to 11:15. 540 N. Michigan. 836-0100.

The **Cafe in the Greenhouse** in the Ritz Carlton also serves a good business breakfast, from 7:30 to 9:30, but it's open only when the hotel is full, so call a day or so ahead. 160 E. Pearson. 266-1000.

Our choice for the most elegant business breakfast goes to the **Ciel Bleu** In the Mayfair Regent. The cuisine is French and the view of the lakefront is fabulous. 181 E. Lake Shore Drive. 951-2864.

If you're the grumpy sort who'd rather not face the world at breakfast, let alone a business contact, slide into a booth or table in the **Oak Terrace** off the lobby of the Drake Hotel. Breakfast is served from 7 to 11:30. You can sip your coffee while gazing out on Lake Michigan, a painless way to wake up. 140 E. Walton. 787-2200.

If you've got to make some business calls during lunch, eat at

Nick's Fishmarket. During the midday meal, customers can call from their tables. They even get the courtesy of a free five-minute call anywhere in the continental United States. Popular place for stockbrokers, lawyers, and traveling fish connoisseurs. Plush atmosphere. Private booths with dimmer switches for menu reading. Reservations a must. Expensive. In the First National Bank of Chicago at the corner of Monroe and Dearborn streets in the heart of Chicago's Loop. 621-0200.

A favorite spot for a business lunch or dinner is **Don Roth's River Plaza** on the Chicago River. Convenient to the Loop as well as Upper Michigan Avenue hotels and offices. Fish and steak are standard items on a no-nonsense American menu. Moderate. 405 N. Wabash. 527-3100.

Another of our picks, and practically an institution in Chicago, is the **Cape Cod Room** in the Drake Hotel, where seafood has been a specialty for generations. Take a client here for a low-key business meeting. Decor is rustic and nautical, not pretentious; service is attentive. Expensive. 140 E. Walton. 787-2200.

Your good taste shows when you entertain a client at **Avanzare,** a stylish northern Italian restaurant that's a bit pricey and worth it. Service is attentive starting with Nader, the maitre d', who will make you feel comfortable when dining alone and important when you're picking up the check with a client. Expensive. 161 E. Huron. 337-8056.

La Strada Ristorante also specializes in northern Italian cuisine but features the food of other regions of Italy as well. The maitre d' and the rest of the staff make a woman feel comfortable dining alone here, yet the cuisine and atmosphere are also conducive to business lunches and dinners. The location, at Randolph and Michigan, is convenient both to the Loop and to hotels north of the Chicago River on Upper Michigan Avenue. Moderate to expensive. 155 N. Michigan. 565-2200.

Bentley's in the Sheraton Plaza has a small dining room and is therefore comfortable for women who dine alone and don't wish to stand out in a crowd. Continental cuisine; moderate prices. 160 E. Huron. 787-2900.

Carlucci is a sophisticated yet comfortable restaurant serving traditional Italian dishes. Located on the newly defined Restaurant Row just north of downtown, the decor here creates a European cafe feel with arched faux marbre ceilings and a tiled entry. Great place to be decadent is the restaurant's 16-seat Galerteria for cannoli, eclairs, and cappucino. Moderate. 2215 N. Halsted Street. 281-1220.

Gordon Restaurant is a stylish place to dine when your aim is to eat light. Fare is simple, changing with the four seasons and spotlighting fresh seafood and natural sauces. Many herbs used in the preparation of the restaurant's Continental cuisine are grown in the restaurant and snipped when needed. Fine wine list with selections from California, France, Germany, and Italy. Reservations recommended. Moderate to expensive. 500 N. Clark Street. 467-9780.

CHICAGO BY DAY

For spectacular overviews of the city, two venues tell it all. Weather permitting, of course. The **John Hancock Center's observation deck** is open from 9 A.M. to midnight, daily. Charge is $2.50. 875 N. Michigan. 751-3681.

The **Sears Tower,** being the world's tallest building, offers its own distinctive view from the top. Also open from 9 A.M. to midnight. Charge is $2.00. 233 S. Wacker. 875-9696.

For a comprehensive capsule view of Chicago's many faces, take in **Here's Chicago,** a multimedia show in the historic Water Tower Pumping Station. 163 E. Pearson. 467-7114.

Chicago Historical Society has exhibits—including Lincoln memorabilia—plus film and slide shows that relay the Chicago story. In Lincoln Park, Clark Street at North Avenue. 642-4600.

We found the free peek into the financial world of the **Chicago Board of Trade** fascinating. It lets you know tons about grains, precious metals, and Treasury bonds. In the visitor's gallery, an eight-minute film explains the role of commodities futures. 141 W. Jackson. 435-3590.

The **Chicago Mercantile Exchange and International Monetary Market** deals in agricultural meats and foreign currencies. 444 W. Jackson. 930-8200.

Stop by the **Art Institute of Chicago,** if only to see its noted collection of French impressionist and postimpressionist art. One of the nation's leading art museums. Michigan at Adams. 443-3600.

The **Museum of Contemporary Art,** besides boasting seven galleries of permanent and changing exhibits, offers video and film festivals. Call for current happenings. 237 E. Ontario. 280-2660.

Three museums, clustered together on the lakefront, can be visited in one outing: the **Field Museum of Natural History** with mummies and dinosaur bones among its collection (Roosevelt Road at Lake Shore Drive, 922-9410); the **John G. Shedd Aquarium,** world's largest indoor aquarium (1200 S. Lake Shore Drive, 939-2438); and the **Adler Planetarium** with its multimedia sky show (1300 S. Lake Shore Drive, 322-0300).

Farther south on the lakefront is the **Museum of Science and Industry,** Chicago's most visited attraction. Among its 13 acres of exhibits (allow a full day here) are a working coal mine, a German U-boat, and a walk-through model of the human heart. 57th Street and Lake Shore Drive. 684-1414.

The **Chicago Academy of Sciences** has exhibits on the ecology and natural history of the Great Lakes region. 2001 N. Clark Street. 549-0606.

Hull House is what remains of the settlement founded by social pioneer Jane Addams in 1889. Exhibits on women's history, ethnic groups in Chicago and the city's neighborhoods. 800 S. Halsted on University of Illinois campus. 996-2793.

Chicago has dozens of small **special interest museums** devoted to surgical science, holographs, telephone and satellite communications, the peace movement, and the cultures of Germany, Poland, Lithuania, black America, and other ethnic groups. Check local listings.

THE SHOPPING SCENE

Situated at the head of the Corn Belt, on the edge of the prairie, and at the foot of the Great Lakes, Chicago may seem like a big country town likely to shop by catalog. But the richness of rural America has made Chicago the grandest shopping hub between the East Coast and the West. Foreign fashion has found its way here as quickly as international airlines have filled up O'Hare, and we find fine goods plus friendly midwestern service make shopping here a joy.

Downtown

Two major shopping areas highlight the city center. State Street Mall in the Loop encompasses the classic and colorful, hustling and bustling heart of big-city shopping. North Michigan Avenue, including Water Tower Place, offers the more elegant and upscale environment.

State Street Mall, a nine-block section of street closed to vehicle traffic, is a montage of flower carts, food vendors, sculpture, dime stores, specialty shops, and department stores. More moderately priced merchandise than Upper Michigan Avenue.

Field's State Street store is one of the largest in the nation. You've probably heard of it as **Marshall Field & Co.,** but Chicagoans just call it Field's. The store's clock at the corner of State and Washington is a landmark meeting spot for shoppers. 111 N. State. 781-1000.

Carson Pirie Scott & Co. (Carson's for short) sports an art nouveau ironwork facade designed by Louis Sullivan. Its corporate level on the ground floor carries fashions and accessories especially for career women. One South Street. 744-2000.

Most State Street shops are open from 10 A.M. to 5 P.M. Monday through Saturday and closed on Sundays. Carson's is open on Sundays; Field's is open the first Sunday of every month.

North Michigan Avenue, one of the finest shopping streets in the world, is an enclave of the rich and famous. It includes such shops as Gucci, Tiffany, Bally, Burberry, and Elizabeth Arden with major chain stores like Saks Fifth Avenue, Neiman-Marcus, I. Magnin, Bonwit Teller, and, to come, Bloomingdale's. Start at the 600 block and head north.

Water Tower Place in the 800 block is anchored by Lord & Taylor and Marshall Field & Co. This is a seven-story vertical mall of shops, restaurants, and cinemas featuring such renowned retailers as Laura Ashley, Courreges, Rodier of Paris, Godiva Chocolatier, and F.A.O. Schwarz.

Oak Street, just west of Michigan Avenue, houses a row of New York-style boutiques in rehabbed brownstones.

Most shops in Upper Michigan Avenue district are open daily from 10 A.M. to 5 P.M. (large department stores are open evenings) and noon to 5 P.M. on Sunday.

The Suburbs

The concentration of corporate headquarters and businesses in Chicago's northwest suburbs may give you cause to pause at two outlying shopping areas.

Woodfield Mall, one of the world's largest enclosed shopping malls (231 stores), stands at Golf Road and Route 53 in Schaumburg. 882-0220.

Oakbrook Centre is an established mall with a lively new section of fine specialty shops catering to an upscale clientele at 22d Street and Route 83 in Oak Brook. 654-0250.

CHICAGO BY NIGHT

Chicago nightlife has flourished in the town's Second City status behind New York. Actually, innovation in theater here may be even more notable than in New York. Broadway shows come here, but it is the Off-Loop theater companies that have won critical acclaim and national recognition. Use taxis to see what they have to offer and stick with the crowds and the main streets.

If your heart is set on seeing a Broadway hit, book in advance of your visit. The traveling shows are often sold out weeks, even months, in advance, and tickets can cost up to $40.

The **Goodman Theater** offers the town's repertory theater through the Art Institute of Chicago. There are no aisles in this house, so rows seem to never end. Be picky on seating. 200 S. Columbus. 443-3800.

Among major theaters in town are the **Artie Crown** (McCormick Place, 791-6000), the **Blackstone Theater** (60 E. Balbo, 346-0270), the **Mayfair Theater** (636 S. Michigan, 786-9120), and the **Shubert Theatre** (22 W. Monroe, 977-1700).

For Off-Loop theater, with tickets ranging from $10 to $20 per performance, consider the **Steppenwolf** (2851 N. Halsted, 472-4141), **Wisdom Bridge** (1559 W. Howard, 743-6442), the **Body Politic** (2261 N. Lincoln, 871-3000), **Organic** (3319 N. Clark, 327-5588), and **Victory Gardens Theatre** (2257 N. Lincoln, 549-5788).

The **Chicago Symphony Orchestra** performs from December through June in Orchestra Hall. 220 S. Michigan. 435-8111.

The **Lyric Opera** season is from September to December. In the Civic Opera House. 20 N. Wacker. 332-2244.

Look for **Chicago City Ballet** (943-1315) and **Hubbard Street Dance Company** (663-0853) in various locations around the city.

For tickets for any of the above, call the **League of Chicago Theaters,** 853-0505, between 10 A.M. and 8 P.M. (You must have a major credit card to purchase tickets by phone.) Or stop by the League's **Hot Tix** booth between 10 A.M. and 5 P.M. (except Sundays). Half-price tickets can be purchased on the day of the event in person at the booth. Sunday tickets are sold on Saturday. In the State Street Mall. 24 South State.

Curtain Call is a 24-hour information line telling what's up with Chicago arts events. 977-1755.

If a movie is what strikes your fancy, a word of warning: avoid the movie theaters along State Street as they attract an unsavory and possibly unsafe crowd. On the Loop, stop in at the **Fine Arts Theater** (418 S. Michigan, 939-3700), or **Facets Multimedia** (1517 W. Fullerton, 281-4114).

For the cinemas in Water Tower Place, purchase Saturday night tickets in advance. Theaters include the **Esquire** (58 E. Oak, 337-1117), the **Carnegie** (1026 N. Rush, 944-2966), **McClurg Court** (330 E. Ohio, 642-0723), and **Water Tower Place** (845 N. Michigan, 649-5790).

Of special note: John Dillinger, Public Enemy Number One during the gangster-ridden Roaring Twenties and depression-riddled 1930s, was gunned down in the **Biograph Theater.** Don't worry, it's a safe place today! 2433 N. Lincoln (in the north side neighborhood of Lincoln Park). 348-1350.

LATE-NIGHT CHICAGO

Chicago's leading nightlife area is around **Rush and Division streets,** drawing singles and conventioneers to the area's bars, discos, and trendy restaurants. It can get congested here, and as the evening wears on (some bars are open until 4 A.M.), the crowd can get unruly. However, the area is heavily patrolled by Chicago's finest, so it's relatively safe for the self-assured woman who's feeling adventurous.

Do not wander west of LaSalle Street, where the neighborhood changes dramatically for the worse. Among the hot spots in the Rush and Division area are **Bootleggers** (11 W. Division, 266-0944), the **Snuggery** (15 W. Division, 337-4349) and **Butch McGuire's** (20 W. Division, 337-9080). All combine libations, libido, music, and dance.

Other night spots that are relatively safe for women alone after the midnight hour include the following:

Byfield's in the Ambassador East Hotel is one of Chicago's leading cabarets booking the best of local talent with occasional national acts. Comedy and music. Most shows 8 P.M. with late shows on weekends. Elite Gold Coast neighborhood bordering on the Division Street area. Walk from Upper Michigan Avenue early in the evening. Take a cab late at night. 1301 N. State. 787-6433.

Park West is a club hosting a mixed bag of touring national acts. Hours vary. Trendy near-north-side neighborhood. Five-minute cab ride from Upper Michigan Avenue hotels. 322 W. Armitage. 929-1322.

Second City is the famous comedy club that launched the careers of John Belushi, Bill Murray, Valerie Harper, and many others. Improvisional comedy and comedy skits and revues. Most shows 8:30 or 9 P.M. Old-town neighborhood on the near north side borders on sleazy. Take a cab and don't walk west of Wells Street. 1616 N. Wells. 337-3992.

Blues is a small but popular blues club. Cover charge. Best after 8 P.M. Lincoln Park north-side residential neighborhood of rehabs and young urban professionals. Five- to ten-minute cab ride from Upper Michigan Avenue hotels. 2519 N. Halsted. 528-1012.

Holsteins is one of the city's best folk music clubs. Cover charge. Best after 8 P.M. Also in the Lincoln Park residential neighborhood. 2464 N. Lincoln. 327-3331.

Rich's Cafe Americain in the Holiday Inn Lakeshore is a classy jazz club often booking big-name acts. Times and covers vary. On the lake, walk east from Upper Michigan Avenue in the early evening. Cab it back late at night. East Ontario at Lake Shore Drive. 943-9200.

AT LEISURE

Proof of Chicago's greatness as a city is the lack of a major Friday afternoon exodus to anywhere else. Although there are numerous fascinating day-trips possible, the pleasure of extending a business trip here may well be in doing Chicago itself. The lakefront city relaxes on weekends, and you should, too. Combining convenient day-trips with pampering weekend packages is our favorite way.

Day-Tripping

Oak Park, an upscale suburb 10 miles (20 minutes) west of the city on I-290, is actually a historic district dominated by the spirit and immortal architecture of **Frank Lloyd Wright.** In a half-day trip you can see his home and studio (Chicago and Forest avenues, 848-1978), which has daily guided tours ($3). The **Oak Park Visitors Center** (Lake Street and Forest Avenue, 848-1976) has guidebooks and walking tours of the area encompassing 25 structures designed by Wright (10 A.M. to 5 P.M. daily, March to November). The CTA's Lake Street elevated train (90 cents) connects the Loop with the Visitor Center (one block north, two blocks east of the Harlem Avenue Station). However, the train makes several stops in Chicago's depressed and unsafe west-side neighborhoods; use discretion.

The **Pullman Historic District,** a south-side model community built in the 1880s for workers of the George M. Pullman Palace Car

Company, is one of the last company towns still standing in America. For a leap back into the last century, start at the **Historic Pullman Center** (614 E. 113th Street, 785-8181). Guided tours lasting 90 minutes are given on the first Sunday of the month, May through October, 12:30 and 1:30 P.M. ($3.50). Take the Illinois Central Railroad south to the 111th Street station and walk four blocks north. Board trains at Michigan and Randolph just east of the Loop ($2.30 one-way). Call the Illinois Central for schedules, 565-1600.

For a visit to authentic Victoriana, an overnight trip to **Galena,** a quaint northwest corner of Illinois (175 miles, about four hours from downtown Chicago), is a genuine charmer. Most structures in this town of 19th century antiques and architecture predate the Civil War. In those years, Galena was one of the largest commercial centers of the Northwest Territory because of the lead mines nearby (long since depleted). Contact the Galena Chamber of Commerce, 101 Bouthillier Street, Galena, IL 61036, telephone 800/892-9299 in Illinois or 815/777-0203 outside the state for information on accommodations, tours, antique shops, historic exhibits, and annual events.

Around Town

A weekend in town is a perfect time for activities you didn't have time for during your business week. Chicago is at its best when it slows down, and Chicagoans will tell you the place to head is the lake—either to the museums along its shore or to boats that look back on the stunning skyline.

Nearly all downtown hotels offer attractive weekend packages, the price and features of which may vary with the season. For example, the **Ambassador East,** (1300 N. State Parkway, 787-7200) offers a Classic Weekend that includes a credit toward dinner in its famed Pump Room restaurant, second cocktail at its Byfield's cabaret, and discounts and passes for a variety of attractions and events. The downtown **Marriott** (540 N. Michigan, 836-0100) offers Super Saver weekends on the Magnificent Mile that package reduced weekend rates with meals and recreation. **Richmont's** (162 E. Ontario, 787-3580) includes a champagne and hors d'oeuvres reception with the general manager on Saturdays. Several hotels offer theater packages that include tickets to current stage productions. The **Drake's** (140 E. Walton, 782-2200) Two on the Aisle package features an evening of theater beginning with pretheater dinner in the hotel.

One good reason for a woman business traveler to stay an extra day in Chicago is to experience the beauty regimen at **Elizabeth Arden** (717 N. Michigan, 266-5750). Elizabeth Arden's five-and-one-half-hour Maine Chance Day includes exercise class, steam-cabinet treatment, massage, haircut and styling, manicure and pedicure, face treatment, makeup, and light lunch ($182 with gratuity, $160 without). Three- and four-hour plans are also available. Appointments should be made several weeks in advance, especially for Saturday. No treatments are given on Sundays or Mondays.

For a full week or weekend of spa treatments, check into the **Heartland** in Gilman, Illinois, about an hour-and-a-half (80 miles) south of Chicago, or **Olympia Resort and Spa** in Oconomowoc, Wisconsin, about two-and-a-half-hours (135 miles) northwest of Chicago (a half-hour west of Milwaukee). The Heartland is a health and fitness retreat on a 31-acre rural estate in farm country near Kankakee, Illinois (business office in Chicago, 180 N. Michigan, 236-2050). The weekend rate is $300 double, $450 single, including transportation from Chicago, meals, two nights accommodations, and use of facilities (beauty treatments extra). The spa facilities at Olympia are on the ground floor of the resort's main building and include Roman pools, Grecian shower, eucalyptus room, steam and sauna, exercise rooms, whirlpools, herbal wrap room, loofa room, massage and facial rooms. The weekend Spa Sampler package is $194 and includes two nights accommodations, meals, use of spa facilities, a massage, facial, and two exercise classes per day. Phone for brochure and directions (1350 Royal Mile Road, Oconomowoc, Wis. 800/588-9573).

Chicago has been noted for innovation in architecture since before the turn of the century when the city began rebuilding the Loop after the Chicago Fire. The **Chicago Architecture Foundation** holds a variety of walking, bike, bus, and boat tours of Chicago architecture. Many tours start from the foundation's downtown **ArchiCenter** (330 S. Dearborn, 782-1776), which contains exhibits and books on Chicago architecture. A guided two-hour walking tour ($4, daily, times vary) takes participants past landmarks in the Loop.

Other highlights of escorted and do-it-yourself walking tours of the Loop are the many works of art in public plazas. Among them are Pablo Picasso's untitled sculpture in the Richard J. Daley Center Plaza (Washington and Dearborn), Joan Miro's sculpture *Chicago* (69 W. Washington), Alexander Calder's stabile *Flamingo* (Adams and Dearborn), Marc Chagall's mosaic *Four Seasons* in the First National Bank Plaza (Monroe and Dearborn), and Jean Dubuffet's sculpture *Monument with Standing Beast* at the State of Illinois Center (100 W. Randolph).

Crescent Helicopters operates a "flightseeing" service in addition to its regular commuter service at Meig's Field, S. Lake Shore Drive at 15th Street. A ten-minute ride in a four-passenger helicopter costs $25 per person and takes passengers over the Loop, Wrigley Field, Lincoln Park, and the Gold Coast, and then out over the lake for an aerial view of the lakefront and city skyline. Tours are available from noon to 4 P.M. and other times by appointment. Special arrangements can be made for groups. Helicopters of various sizes are available for charter. Information and reservations: 800/247-7070 locally, or 219/944-2301 out-of-state.

A variety of vessels offer sightseeing cruises of Chicago from Lake Michigan and the Chicago River from late spring through early autumn:

The *Star of Chicago* seats 375 passengers on two decks for three-hour dinner ($39.50) and two-and-a-half-hour lunch and Sunday brunch cruises ($21). Service is buffet style with a table of cold salads and appetizers, a hot buffet table with a selection of entrées and vegetables, and a pastry table. Breakfast items are added to the buffet for weekend brunch cruises, which also feature live jazz music. Cocktails and wine are available at additional charge. Decks are enclosed and air-conditioned, and there's a band and dance floor on the second deck. On two-hour TGIF (Thank Goodness It's Friday) cruises and Saturday moonlight cruises, cocktails are served with complimentary hors d'oeuvres ($14). The ship departs from Navy Pier, Grand Avenue, and the lake. Reservations: 644-5914 or 800/782-7827.

Wendella Sightseeing operates cruises on two vessels docked on the Chicago River at the foot of the Wrigley Building, 400 N. Michigan. Cruises range from one to two hours and are priced from $4.50 to $7.50. The boats cruise inland on the river past the Merchandise Mart and the Sears Tower and then maneuver through the locks onto Lake Michigan where they cruise past Buckingham Fountain and the Adler Planetarium. Departures are scheduled at 10 and 11:30 A.M., 1:15, 3:15, and 7:30 P.M. Reservations: 337-1446.

Mercury Sightseeing, docked opposite Wendella on the Chicago River at Michigan and Wacker, operates one-and-a-half-hour sightseeing cruises at 10 and 11:30 A.M. and 1:15 and 3:15 P.M. ($6), and two-hour cruises at 7:30 P.M. ($7.50). One-hour cruises run on a nonscheduled basis. Reservations: 381-5192.

Shoreline Marine operates two vessels from docks at the Adler Planetarium and Shedd Aquarium (1200 S. Lake Shore Drive). One-hour tours ($3.50) depart hourly, beginning at 12:20 P.M. Reservations: 427-2900.

Chicago from the Lake cruises the Chicago River and the lake. A one-and-a-half-hour cruise, departing at 10 A.M., features Chicago architecture and is cosponsored by the Chicago Architecture Foundation. The charge is $10 including Continental breakfast on board. For information on other cruises, phone 922-4020.

Sunday Customs

Brunch and a casual excursion make a perfect Sunday here where striking architecture, elegant shopping, rich museums, and beautiful parks offer choices galore.

One of the most sumptuous Sunday brunches in town, and one of the most expensive, is served from 10:30 until 2:30 at **La Tour** in the Park Hyatt (800 N. Michigan, 280-2222). The $25 fixed-price meal includes all the champagne you can drink plus more conventional breakfast beverages such as coffee and juice. Three buffet tables groan under the weight of cold hors d'oeuvres such as salmon and pâté, warm platters of lamb and roast beef, and an array of two dozen desserts. New American cuisine. This is one of the toniest spots in town, so dress accordingly.

While brunching at the **Ciel Bleu** atop the Mayfair Regent Hotel (181 E. Lake Shore Drive, 951-2864), you can feast your eyes on the view as you feast on the French and Continental dishes from the buffet. Sit near a north window for a striking look at the lakefront. The fixed-price brunch is served 11:30 to 1:30; $22.50 including champagne. Dress in your Sunday best.

A bit more casual, though no less filling brunch, is served in the **Dining Room** of the Ritz-Carlton Hotel (160 E. Pearson, 266-1000, ext. 4223). The Grand Buffet Brunch features four islands—seafood and salads; quiche, crepes, and veggies; omelets made to order; fruit and desserts— and seatings are at 10:30, 11, 1, and 1:30. Dress ranges from casual sportswear to business attire.

An inexpensive and convenient way to take in Chicago sights on Sundays during the summer months is aboard the **Culture Buses** operated by the Chicago Transit Authority (836-7000). Three routes begin and end at the Art Institute (Michigan at Adams), and buses run every half hour from 10:30 A.M. to 4:45 P.M. (Sundays and holidays only, Memorial Day weekend through September). Pay one fare ($2) per route and get on and off the bus at will. The south route travels down the lakefront with stops at the Field Museum, Adler Planetarium, Shedd Aquarium, and Museum of Science and Industry. The north route heads up North Michigan Avenue and through Lincoln Park with stops at the Lincoln Park Zoo, Museum of Contemporary Art, and Chicago Historical Society. The west route travels through a rather rough neighborhood with stops at small ethnic museums.

Lincoln Park Zoo (2200 N. Cannon Drive, 294-4660) is an idyllic place to spend a Sunday at any time of the year (open daily, 9 to 5; free admission). The red barn and outbuildings of the zoo's Farm in the Zoo is in striking contrast to the skyscrapers and high rises of Upper Michigan Avenue and the Gold Coast. The polar bear exhibit contains a pool with windows where viewers can watch the bears' underwater antics. The great ape house contains one of world's best collections of gorillas.

Lincoln Park itself is ideal for a Sunday stroll (on the lakefront north of North Avenue). There are picnic grounds, a lagoon, and paddleboats for rent (2045 N. Lincoln Park West, 975-7559). The **Lincoln Park Conservatory** (2400 N. Stockton, 294-4770) has four glassed-in exhibit houses containing permanent botanical exhibits and seasonal flower shows (9 to 5 daily; during shows, 10 to 6 Saturday through Thursday, 9 to 9 Friday; free admission).

Water Tower Place (835 N. Michigan Avenue, 440-3165) is alive with activity every Sunday from noon until 5. Department stores, boutiques, and specialty shops share space with cinemas, delicatessens, and restaurants. It's a good place to people-watch, too.

A double-decker bus operated by Carson, Pirie Scott & Co. connects Water Tower Place with Carson's State Street store in the Loop. The bus runs every half hour, 11 to 5, and is free.

During the summer, Sunday evenings on the lakefront can be spent listening to **music under the stars.** Free concerts begin at 7 in Grant Park (June through August) at the Petrillo Music Shell (Jackson Boulevard and Columbus Drive, 294-2420). Selections range from classics to pop music. Bring a bottle of wine and a chunk of cheese, and enjoy.

Tours of Chicago architecture are given year round on Sundays by the Chicago Architecture Foundation. Two-hour walking tours of the Loop depart at 2 P.M. from the ArchiCenter (330 S. Dearborn, 782-1776). For a recorded message on other weekend tours in downtown Chicago and outlying areas, call 922-3433.

Most major museums and galleries in Chicago are open Sundays as are the observation decks of the Sears Tower and the John Hancock Center (see "Chicago by Day").

Spectator Sports

Among the professional sports teams in Chicago are:

BASEBALL
   Chicago Cubs. Wrigley Field. 1060 W. Addison, 281-5050.
   Chicago White Sox. Comiskey Park. 35th and Dan Ryan. 924-1000.

BASKETBALL
   Chicago Bulls. Chicago Stadium. 1800 W. Madison. 346-1122.

FOOTBALL
   Chicago Bears. Soldier Field. McFetridge Drive and S. Lake Shore Drive. 663-5408.

HOCKEY
   Chicago Blackhawks. Chicago Stadium. 1800 W. Madison. 733-5300.

SOCCER
   Chicago Sting. Chicago Stadium. 1800 W. Madison. 558-5425.

Active Sports

The Chicago Park District (294-2333) maintains 31 bathing beaches and 20 miles of jogging and bike paths along the lakefront and in its parks. One of the most popular places to jog (safe in daylight) is through Lincoln Park on the lakefront north of North Avenue. You can jog through Lincoln Park Zoo (free admission) and past Lincoln Park's floral conservatory. A Parcours runners exercise station is located in the park just north of Fullerton Avenue. The best beaches for sunbathing are Oak Street Beach and North Avenue Beach, which are within walking distance of many Upper Michigan Avenue hotels. Beaches are open mid-June to Labor Day (no fee).

Golfers can practice their technique at a driving range maintained by the Park District in Lincoln Park near Diversey Avenue ($2.50 for a large bucket of balls, 8 A.M. to 10 P.M.) before trying out the nine-hole Waveland Golf Course (3600 N. Lake Shore Drive, 294-2274) on the lakefront a few blocks north (open April to September, dawn to dusk; $4 weekends, $3.50 weekdays).

Tennis players can keep up their game on outdoor lighted courts just east of the Loop: Grant Park Tennis Courts (9th and Columbus, 294-2307; $2 per day per person) and Daley Bicentennial Plaza Courts (Randolph Street and Lake Shore Drive, 294-4792; $5 per hour per court).

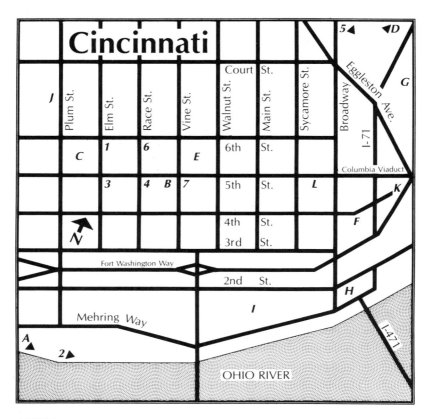

Cincinnati

HOTELS

1 Clarion
2 Drawbridge Inn
   & Convention Center
3 Hyatt Regency
4 Omni Netherland Plaza
5 Quality Inn Central
6 Terrace Hilton
7 Westin at Fountain Square

LANDMARKS

A Airport
B Carew Tower
C Convention Center
D Eden Park
E Fountain Square
F Lytle Park
G Mount Adams
H Riverfront Coliseum
I Riverfront Stadium
J St. Peter's Cathedral
K Taft Museum
L Taft Theatre

CINCINNATI

GETTING YOUR BEARINGS

Granted, you've heard it before—about how the city is in transition, how it's a city on the way up. But few cities actually demonstrate this as graphically as Cincinnati. When we first visited, back in the mid-seventies, it looked like a stage set for a W.W. II movie—old drug stores, movie houses with vintage marquees—everything had the look of a city in a time warp, bypassed by modern times.

Today, Cincinnati's urban revitalization is in full flower: everything either is in the process of being torn down to make way for state-of-the-art architecture or is being lovingly renovated to preserve its valuable authenticity. A get-acquainted walk through downtown will show you the contrasts: like the spiffy P&G installation, model of urban beautification, starring next door to a relic sadly awaiting the wrecker's ball.

This is truly a business city, drawing ever-increasing numbers of young professionals into the industrial, merchandising, manufacturing complexes that shape its daytime face.

For the visitor, Cincinnati's unique and superconvenient downtown layout is ideal. There is a Skywalk, a series of enclosed, above-ground walkways, that interconnects an area of four square blocks and encompasses all the primary hotels, the convention center, major department stores, and numerous small shops and restaurants. In bad weather you can walk, in carpeted comfort, from meetings to meals to your hotel without ever having to drag along your heavy coat. One word of caution: although the local PR folks will say it isn't so, we maintain that the Skywalk is not 100 percent safe at night. Truth is, we feel safer walking the short distances along the Fountain Square area—outdoors and on the streets after dark.

Downtown is compact—about ten square blocks—and extremely easy to navigate. Newcomers use the mnemonic device "Big, strong men will very rarely eat pork chops" to remember the order of streets in the downtown area (Broadway, Sycamore, Main, Walnut, Vine, Race, Elm, Plum, Central). Armed with this handy code and the knowledge that almost all business is conducted within these nine streets, you are ready to conquer the Cincinnati business world.

There are, however, some intangibles you should be aware of, insights not necessarily apparent to the uninformed observer—like the widely circulated myth that Cincinnatians consider their Kentucky neighbors just across the river to be the "south side of Cincinnati." This is just that—a myth. Most locals will admit that, while they do enjoy occasional jaunts to the old-money and horsey-set enclaves of Louisville and Lexington, they consider most of Kentucky to be déclassé and resent being lumped together with it.

Another bit of local snobbery you won't find written anywhere but should be aware of is the invisible line that divides the city into east and west. All the right stuff is east—Mt. Adams, Hyde Park, Indian Hill where the old money lives—while the west side is largely ignored, an unchic never-never land.

Several landmark neighborhoods you will hear constant references to are: Mt. Adams, a sort of local San Francisco, all hilly and charmingly crooked streets, with dozens of yuppie bars and restaurants, each with spectacular views of the city and the river; Eden Park is up here, where you'll find the art museum, theaters, Natural History Museum, and the Krohn Conservatory; and Lytle Park, at the eastern end of Fourth Street (downtown), an oasis of greenery, flowers, and historic buildings. The Taft Museum is here, free to all comers; Riverside Historic District is across the river in Covington, Kentucky, with Old South mansions and Confederate lore galore.

And, of course, there's Fountain Square, the traditional focal point of Cincinnati. Something is always going on here, whether it's a folk festival, free concert, or just the passing parade of residents and visitors. Erected in 1871, Fountain Square is a symbol of civic pride and local tradition. For the most part, Cincinnati streets are safe. And those around Fountain Square are safe even at night.

WHAT TO WEAR

Again, that fashion byword: conservative. Remember that you are not only in the Midwest, but also bordering on the Old South—a lethal combination for anything that might resemble trend-setting. Stick to the classics of well-tailored suits in accepted colors, minimal jewelry, and quiet accessories. If your stay will be within Skywalk's protection, you won't need much winter gear. Summers can be hot and muggy.

WEATHER WATCH

Because of the proximity of the river, temperatures in Cincinnati tend to be moderate. Winters hover around the freezing point and summers range in the mid-70s. Expect rain in the spring and fall. And be sure to check the temperatures listed in your hometown paper before packing for the trip.

GETTING THERE

Don't be alarmed when your flight to Cincinnati lands you in Kentucky. Although the **Greater Cincinnati Airport** is 12 miles south of the city in Covington, Kentucky, you're only a 20-minute cab ride from downtown. The fare should run about $15. An airport shuttle bus, which transfers between the terminal and downtown hotels, costs about $6.50.

Cincinnati's business district is very compact and you will have no need for a car if all your appointments are within this area. However, if you must travel to meetings, or if you plan to see some of the outlying area in your free time (see "At Leisure"), you will want to rent your own car:

Car Rentals

Avis	283-3773
Cheap & Cheerful	621-7368
Budget	283-1166
Hertz	283-3535
National	621-0202

GETTING AROUND

Taxis generally are plentiful, lined up outside the major hotels. Pick one up here, or call ahead—don't try to hail a cruising cab on the street. Two companies we've found to be reliable: Skyline, 251-7733; and Radio Cab Co., 681-5100.

If you're driving, be prepared to pay for parking; on-street spaces are scarce. Hotel valet parking should run about $8, and you can do it yourself for about $4.

Vital information for drivers:

Some exit ramps off the Cincinnati expressways turn off from the *left side of the highway.* If you forget this bit of local freeway eccentricity, it could be very dangerous.

Thanks to highway I-275, which circles the metropolitan area, inner-city traffic has been lightened. Several interstates—I-71, I-74, and I-75—also cut through the city. In short, driving is no problem here. As one local woman said, "Getting from one place to another is a cinch. The only problem we have is in staying under sixty miles per hour."

The Metro, as Cincinnati's bus system is called, covers the area quite well. Fare downtown is 10 cents. There is no subway system.

GETTING FAMILIAR

Greater Cincinnati Convention & Visitors Bureau

200 W. Fifth Street	Toll-free: 800/543-2613
Cincinnati, OH 45202	Local number: 621-2142
	Recorded bulletin board: 421-INFO

Northern Kentucky Convention & Visitors Bureau
605 Philadelphia Street   606/261-4677
Covington, KY 41011
You may find you need information or help from this neighbor, known locally as "the south side of Cincinnati," because of its proximity.

Cincinnati Convention Center
525 Elm Street   352-3750
Cincinnati, OH 45202
Located on the west end of the Skywalk.

Cincinnati Chamber of Commerce
579-3100

The Community Chest Information Center, 621-5000, has a list of all the help agencies in town.

There are two daily newspapers: the *Enquirer*, which is a morning paper, and the evening *Post*. *Cincinnati Magazine* is a monthly publication similar to all the glossy city magazines that provide interesting features with their listings of events, shows, and other timely information.

———— *Quick Calls* ————

AREA CODE 513	Weather 936-4850
Northern Kentucky 606	All emergencies 911
Time 721-1700	

AT YOUR SERVICE

Because of Cincinnati's unique, and extremely convenient Skywalk system, we are breaking our own rule and are recommending hotels concentrated in one area—the covered, aboveground Skywalk complex. Each is connected to the city's major shopping areas and to the convention center, as well as to each other (although access to one, the Westin, is sometimes handier at street level than along Skywalk). Also, these *are* the major hotels in town, and each has its own style and safety features to recommend it.

Clarion Hotel

141 W. Sixth Street   Toll-free reservations: 800/CLARION
Cincinnati, OH 45202   Local number: 352-2100

Because it is the closest hotel to the convention center, and because it is the largest in town (900 rooms), the Clarion is where you'll usually find the convention crowds. Despite its awesome size, you can find an oasis of privacy on the two-floor "manager's quarters" section. Otherwise, the regular guest rooms are nothing to write home about. Excellent health facilities include a heated outdoor pool and spa privileges. Free parking for hotel guests.

Hyatt Regency

151 W. Fifth Street   Toll-free reservations: 800/228-9000
Cincinnati, OH 45202   Local number: 579-1234
                                        Telex: 206672

Cincinnati's newest major hotel (June 1984) has utilized an interesting tie-in: Hyatt and Saks Fifth Avenue, which feed directly into each other. We believe that we, the guests, are the ones who benefit most from this symbiotic relationship—in addition to the obvious shopping proximity, there's also Saks's "Fifth Avenue Club" for personal shopping and its hair salon, which is great in a pinch. This Hyatt has the signature high-rise lobby atrium and an abundance of restaurants and bars for all moods. Guest rooms are small and not practical for any sort of business meeting. Even the Regency Club rooms, while deluxe, are not overly large. You might want to consider requesting a junior suite (about $118, but well equipped with work space) if you need to hold in-room meetings.

Omni Netherland Plaza

Fifth & Race streets   Toll-free reservations: 800-THE-OMNI
Cincinnati, OH 45202   Local number: 421-9100

Careful and costly ($25 million) renovation has restored this aging beauty to her former 1930s French opulence. Lavish touches of art deco, Victoriana, and Old World style and gentility offer a fantasy retreat from the hard-edge world around us. Each of the 624 rooms has been designed with an emphasis on elegant residential ambience. Meeting rooms, including the Versailles-like Hall of Mirrors, have a combined capacity of 1,200, enough to accommodate overflow from the convention center at the end of Skywalk.

The Palm Court complex is perhaps the single most impressively beautiful spot in the entire hotel. **Orchids at Palm Court** is the formal restaurant; **The Cafe at the Palm Court** offers a more casual atmosphere (see "Dining Out").

Terrace Hilton

15 W. Sixth Street   Toll-free reservations: 800/445-8667
Cincinnati, OH 45202   Local number: 381-4000

	Concierge	Executive Floor	No-Smoking Rooms	Fitness Facilities	Pool	24-Hour Room Service	Restaurant for Client Entertaining	Extra-Special Amenities	Electronic Key System	Business/Secretarial Services	Checkout Time	Frequent Guest Program	Business Traveler Program	Average Single Rate
Clarion	●	●		●	●	●	Top of the Crown				12 noon	One of a Kind Club		$ 76 reg. $ 66 corp.
Hyatt Regency	●	●	●	●	●	●	Champs			●	12 noon	Gold Passport		$110 $ 94
Omni Netherland Plaza	●		●				Orchids at Palm Court			●	12 noon	Select Guests		$105 $ 90
Terrace Hilton		●		●			The Gourmet Room				1 p.m.	Executive Business Service (E.B.S.)		$ 84 $ 68
Westin at Fountain Square		●		●	●	●	Delmonico's				3 p.m.			$115 $ 95

A high-rise hotel with 350 guest rooms, this Hilton also houses one of the best views and best restaurants in town—the **Gourmet Room** from which you can enjoy a panoramic view of the city, dine on haute cuisine, and entertain important clients, all within the convenience of your own hotel. There's nothing out of the ordinary here for women guests, however—no special services, outstanding decor, or architectural style-setting, not even a great health club. Just good, solid, urban hotel amenities.

Westin at Fountain Square
Cincinnati, OH 45202   Toll-free reservations: 800/228-3000
                              Local number: 621-7700
                              Telex: 241496

A bright, fairly new (1982) hotel with 460 guest rooms. The lobby is located on the fourth story of the atrium, a sunny space filled with plants and the sounds of live piano music. Ask for a room facing Fountain Square—you'll have a window on just about everything that's happening in town. Lots of in-house shopping here as well as Skywalk access to all the big stores. Nice additions to their health facilities are the coed exercise rooms with exercise tapes available. Facilities are also very secure, with cameras and intercoms. In fact, the entire hotel's security received the highest rating awarded by the International Loss Control Institute.

The main floor restaurant, **Fifth Street Market,** with its casual American regional dining menu, is where local people gather. Open for breakfast meetings, all meals, and late-night snacks. **Delmonico's** is one of the city's finest (see "Dining Out"). **Patterns** is where local single people come to dance, listen to music, and relax. You can feel safe and welcome here.

ON A BUDGET

Hotels

Some of the hotels and motels in northern Kentucky are closer to downtown Cincinnati than those in the Ohio suburbs are. Among those we feel offer a good deal are these:

Drawbridge Inn & Convention Center
I-75 and Buttermilk Pk.   Local number: 606/341-2800
Ft. Mitchell, KY 41017
Large (490 rooms) and sprawling, with indoor and outdoor pools. Singles from $37.

Quality Inn Central
4747 Montgomery Road   Local number: 351-6000
Cincinnati, OH 45212

North of downtown. Comfortable surroundings, with a very good restaurant, 151 rooms, outdoor pool. Singles from $44.

Restaurant

For reasons lost in history, Cincinnati considers itself the chili capitol of the country. And here in chili country, **The Skyline** is *the* undisputed chili restaurant. There are other chili places, to be sure, but Skyline is where local chili lovers go to get their fix of hot, hotter, hottest. Downtown. 381-4244.

Entertainment

In summertime, Cincinnati hosts a fair number of free concerts in the park and other public entertainment events. Several of the museums around town—the **Taft**, the **Krohn Conservatory**, the **Museum of Natural History**—have free days.

Also, we should put things into perspective: Cincinnati is not Los Angeles or New York in terms of overinflated ticket prices. It is possible to get good tickets to just about any top performance in town—ballet, symphony, stage show—for under $10.

DINING OUT

This city has an abundance of fine restaurants for its size. The top four—The Maisonette, Orchids, Delmonico's, and Celestial—also happen to be the most expensive. Happily not as expensive as other cities, Cincinnati's price scale fixes "expensive" as anything between $25 and $50 for dinner. The hands-down winner of "best place for power lunch" is the Maisonette. As one veteran of the power-dining circuit says, "The Maisonette is a ten; everything else would be grouped together as a one." Benjamin's is the place to be seen power-breakfasting.

Downtown (including Mt. Adams)

The Maisonette is *the* restaurant. You should not visit Cincinnati without experiencing its special charms. In the Comisar family for three generations, it has received Mobil's five-star award for 21 consecutive years. The cuisine is classic French; the wine cellar is outstanding. Reserve far in advance. Expensive. 114 E. Sixth Street. 721-2260.

Celestial (Mt. Adams), one of the city's best, has recently been renovated. Beautiful views out over the city and river valley while you dine. Continental cuisine. Expensive, although new policy stresses weeknight specials. 1071 Celestial Street. 241-4455.

Delmonico's overlooks Fountain Square, the town's lovely centerpiece. The award-winning cuisine is showcased in beautiful surroundings that include a harpist at dinner. Expensive. In the Westin Hotel. 241-3663.

Orchids at the Omni Netherland Plaza serves gourmet cuisine in elegant, Old World surroundings. Posh banquettes and beautiful flowers make anyone feel pampered. As *Town & Country* wrote, "The elegant service and beautiful surroundings are past compare." Expensive. 421-9100.

The **Gourmet Room** is still another French cuisine award winner. Here, the view from the 20th floor is also worthy of some awards. Expensive. Terrace Hilton. 15 W. Sixth Street. 381-4000.

Pigall's is a relative newcomer, offering four-star French fare in an elegant setting. Very popular with businesspeople for lunch. Expensive. 127 W. Fourth Street. 721-1345.

Top of the Crown is, literally, the top dining spot—32 floors above the city. Great views from this revolving restaurant. Continental cuisine. Expensive. Clarion Hotel, 141 W. Sixth Street. 352-2100.

Bacchus serves what has been dubbed the city's most innovative menu. All in a delightfully art nouveau atmosphere, with comfy booths or tables for people-watching. Moderate. 1401 Elm Street, across from Music Hall. 421-8314.

Benjamin's lets you in on the action as they charbroil fish and chops over their special mix of hardwood chips in an open-view kitchen. Relaxed atmosphere. Moderate. Two Garfield Place (between 8th and 9th on Vine). 621-2225.

Champs, as in champions, celebrates Cincinnati's beloved sports teams. The sporting motif carries throughout the room. Beef and fish specialties. Moderate. Hyatt Regency, 151 W. Fifth Street. 579-1234.

Edward's is the city's finest Italian restaurant. The decor is charming—turn-of-the-century mahogany and marble—and the food is wonderful. (Downstairs is Under the Fifth—see "Late-Night Cincinnati"). Moderate. Edwards Manufacturing Building, 2d floor, 529 E. Fifth Street. 381-2030.

Gano Alley Bar and Grill is the place to go for true grill-room dining. Known for its dry aged beef, fresh seafood from Louisiana and New England grilled over mesquite. East Sixth Street at One Bowen Place. 381-6200.

La Normandie Taverne & Chop House is what you'd expect a classically convivial "olde English taverne" to be. Lots of good cheer; daily specials listed on a blackboard. Moderate. 118 E. Sixth Street. 721-2761.

Grammer's is located in the heart of Cincinnati's most historic area, called "Over the Rhine." Features a traditional Old World German cuisine. It's best to take a cab in and out of this neighborhood. Moderate. 1440 Walnut Street. 721-6570.

The Diner is sheer reminiscence—a real diner setting: high-tech art deco with lots of Americana favorites on the menu. A new dining concept in Cincinnati. Moderate. 1203 Sycamore Street. 721-1212.

Mike Fink's is touristy—dining aboard a paddlewheeler riverboat—but so what. You *are* a tourist, and this *is* riverboat country, and besides, it's fun. The food is plentiful, there's a wonderful raw bar, and the 1936 boat is authentic (it's listed in the National Register of Historic Places). About a ten-minute cab ride from downtown. Moderate. Docked at the foot of Greenup Street. 606/261-4212.

East

The Precinct is a high-spirited place with macho-jock overtones; it's owned by the folks who own the NFL Bengals. There's good food ("the best steak in town"), dancing to the deejay's choice sounds. In all, a great place to bring a male associate or client. Be sure to reserve well in advance—and then be prepared to wait anyway. A five-minute cab ride from downtown. Expensive. Delta and Columbia Parkway. 321-5454.

The Heritage pioneered nouvelle cuisine in Cincinnati; now also embraces American regional cooking. Located in a historic manor house with seven distinctively different dining rooms. 7664 Wooster Pike. 561-9300.

Jay's Restaurant specializes in French cafe foods and ambience. Located in the elegant Regency Apartments where everyone's mother lives; the lunch scene is often a sea of blue-haired ladies. Moderate prices. 2444 Madison Road. 871-2888.

Laura O'Bryon's Restaurant & Pub features American cuisine in a historic 150-year-old home. Favorites are the hearty soups and homemade desserts. Moderate. 2038 Madison Road. 321-3443.

Milcroft Inn for American cuisine in 18th-century Federal decor. Garden dining in summer, fireside during the winter. Moderate. 203 Mill Street, Milford.

North

Chester's Roadhouse was originally a farmhouse-greenhouse. Now it utilizes lots of plants under a high sky-lit ceiling to showcase a menu of moderately priced fresh specials. Includes a do-it-your-way salad bar. 9678 Montgomery Road. 793-8700.

The **Golden Lamb Inn** is Ohio's oldest inn, dating back to 1803. And authentic American foods are king here: Shaker Ohio lemon pie, old-fashioned bread pudding, black-bottom pie, Butler County turkey. In operation for 179 years. 27 S. Broadway. Lebanon. 932-5065.

South

Coach & Four is warm, friendly, and inviting. Fine wines and foods. Best for steaks and fresh fish. Moderate. 214 Scott Street, Covington, Kentucky. 431-6700.

CINCINNATI BY DAY

This is a town with some spectacular overviews of its surrounding hills, the river and valley, even neighboring Kentucky—many of them from atop Mt. Adams. From downtown, try the **observatory** in the **Carew Tower** at 5th and Vine. It's open 9 to 5 P.M. Tuesday through Sunday, all year. Admission is nominal.

Cincinnati Art Museum, founded in 1881, houses over 100 galleries focusing on the great civilizations of the past 5,000 years. Outstanding Near and Far East collections; superb collection of musical instruments. Here, too, the society matrons of Cincinnati gather to volunteer their time and talents, many serving as docents. (This makes for an interesting way to observe old-money Cincinnati at work.) Closed Mondays; free admission on Saturdays. Eden Park, Mt. Adams. 721-5204.

Taft Museum is the 1820 Federal-style home of President W. H. Taft's half-brother, Charles Phelps Taft. It was from this porch that Taft declared his intention to run for president. You see the porch—and the house and its furnishings, some of them Duncan Phyfe pieces—as they were then. Open Monday through Saturday, 10 to 5 P.M.; Sundays, 2 to 5 P.M. 316 Pike Street, downtown. 241-0343.

Cincinnati Museum of Natural History and Planetarium is one of the oldest and most highly regarded in the country. The many permanent exhibits include South Seas, insect gallery, Audubon collection, and a walk-through cavern with stalagtites, stalagmites, and a 30-foot underground waterfall. The Planetarium offers four or five different programs a year. Closed Mondays; daily 9 to 5 P.M.; Sundays 1 to 5 P.M. 1720 Gilbert Avenue, Eden Park. 621-3889.

Krohn Conservatory is a glass-enclosed botanical garden filled with thousands of plants, all labeled, which are changed seasonally. The hands-down favorite is the Christmas display with a real stable populated with live baby animals. Free admission. Eden Park, Mt. Adams. 352-4086.

Cincinnati Zoo is the second oldest zoo in the country (1873), but remains one of the best. More than 2,500 animals, including the famous white Bengal tiger. (Which came first—the tiger or the team?) Open seven days a week, year round. 3400 Vine Street. 281-4700.

Because this is river country, don't miss out on some of the river cruises. Best bet: **BB Riverboats** with cruises year round for every whim. Choose from daily one-hour sightseeing, lunch, dinner, cocktail, or moonlight cruises. There are even private charters available in case you want to host a bang-up company party. Reservations are a must, whatever the choice (261-8500). Boats leave from the foot of Greenup Street.

All Cincinnati's art is not behind museum walls, as you will quickly discover as you walk around town. Of all the outdoor sculpture that abounds, perhaps the two most interesting are the **urban walls** project, huge paintings by local artists that cover the exterior walls of buildings—a privately funded civic project; and the **Circumspect,** a kinetic sculpture by Stuart Fink that allows spectators to become participants as they walk through, sit down, and shape the existing piece. A personal favorite is "The Nevelson," as the piece, **Sky Landscape Number 2,** is more familiarly known. This work, by sculptor Louise Nevelson, is an ever-changing delight to behold—and right out there for all to enjoy.

THE SHOPPING SCENE

While not exactly a shopper's haven, Cincinnati has enough browsing and buying possibilities to satisfy most of those shopaholic cravings.

Downtown, most of the stores are concentrated in the Fountain Square area. **Saks,** with its handy two-floor feed into the Hyatt, is on the ball with special services for busy women. Their Saks Fifth Avenue Club is basically a personal shopping arrangement that adds speedy in-hotel delivery to its list of services. **L. S. Ayres** is a full-service department store, also part of the Skywalk complex. Here's where you can try out the much-publicized "Magic Mirror"—the computerized system that lets you "try on" dozens of outfits without having to get undressed. This nifty little invention projects an image of you as you would look in each selection. Their Epicure Shop, with its wide range of exotic ingredients from around the world, is worth your visit. There are several branches of Ayres in the area. **Shillito Rikes** is another popular Cincinnati department store.

Gidding-Jenny is famous in these parts as an excellent specialty shop for top designer clothes and accessories. (There's a separate men's shop, as well.) 18 W. Fourth Street. 421-6400.

For concentrated boutique shopping, grab a cab to Hyde Park (about 15 minutes away). Around a square with a fountain in its center are branch stores of the downtown giants as well as eclectic independents. The favorites among these:

Dance Center for upbeat workout and jazzercise clothes and accessories. 321-7767.

Gattle's Incorporated is a store that recalls the days when gentlefolk appreciated such niceties as bed trays with lace doilies, monogrammed blanket covers, and real-linen linens. They're all there—along with some ultra eighties-style satin lingerie. 871-4050.

Lilly Pulitzer and **Carroll Reed** also have shops in Hyde Park.

Markets International houses over 50 shops, restaurants, craft stores, and food purveyors under one roof. Open every day. 123 Merchant Street, Springdale. 771-0757.

There are some off-price stores in the area, some well worth the time:

Government Surplus Depot (don't scoff until you've seen it!) is like Banana Republic, only much less expensive. A bare-bones store (your purchases will be wrapped in newspapers), you'll select from all-cotton goodies from over 40 countries. Close to Hyde Park. 4031 Hamilton Avenue. 541-8700.

Loehmann's, the nationwide discounter of designer and high-fashion clothes. Union Terminal. 579-9900.

Five minutes away by cab in Kentucky is the **Mill Outlet,** a large barn of a store that sells such brand names as Pierre Cardin, Gant, Evan Picone, Austin Hill, and Palm Beach at 40 to 60 percent off. Open until 6 P.M. on weekends. 606/581-7666.

CINCINNATI BY NIGHT

There are no same-day discount ticket systems in town, but you will find **Ticketron** outlets in all Shillito stores, all Sears' stores, and the Riverfront Coliseum.

The **Cincinnati Symphony,** founded in 1895, is still going strong with 48 concerts a year under the direction of Michael Gielen. In the Music Hall, 1241 Elm Street. 621-1919. During the summer, enjoy them outdoors at The Riverbend Music Center, an open-air setting in Coney Island. 232-8230.

The **Cincinnati Ballet** is ranked among the nation's top ten companies. 721-8222.

The **Cincinnati Summer Opera** is second in age only to New York's Metropolitan. 1241 Elm Street. 621-1919.

The **Cincinnati May Festival Chorus** was founded in 1880 and remains one of the oldest choral festivals in the world. Music Hall. 621-1919.

The **Cincinnati Playhouse in the Park** mounts 12 plays a year, October–June; with special summertime performances. Eden Park. 421-3888.

Taft Theater presents touring Broadway shows. 317 E. Fifth Street. 721-0411.

Showboat Majestic is a floating summer-stock-type of theater, the last of the country's original floating theaters. Docked at the foot of Broadway. 241-6550.

LATE-NIGHT CINCINNATI

Because of the large numbers of young professionals in town, the late-night scene is a lively one. A newly rising area, Second Street, is now home to several of Cincinnati's best late spots and is considered safe for women alone. Word is: things are fine up until about Seventh or Eighth streets, but don't venture north of Tenth Street.

Arnold's Grill serves lunch and dinner during the week. Traditional jazz and bluegrass take over from 9 P.M. to 1 P.M. Moderate prices. Closed Sundays. 210 E. Eighth Street. 421-6234.

Blind Lemon presents jazz and contemporary and folk music nightly in a peaceful garden setting or before a blazing fire. This "aristocrat" of Mt. Adams bars has grown elegant with age. Monday through Friday, 4 P.M. to 2:30 A.M.; Saturday and Sunday, 3 P.M. to 2:30 A.M. 946 Hatch Street, Mt. Adams. 241-3885.

Caddy's is one of Cincinnati's first nostalgic fifties bars with music and a deejay for listening and dancing. Special buffet (25 cents per person) from 4 to 8 P.M. seven days a week. Informal but classy. 230 W. Second Street. 721-3636.

Celestial Bar is expensive and elegant for after-dinner drinking and dancing. 1071 Celestial Street, Mt. Adams. 241-4455.

Dee Felice's Cafe is great for both the live jazz nightly and the Cajun and New Orleans–style cuisine. Open Sunday through Thursday until 11 P.M.; weekends until midnight. In the heart of Main Strasse Village in Covington, Kentucky. 529 Main Street. 261-2365.

Gano Alley Bar & Grill features jazz nightly along with the grill's extensive menu and wine list. One of Cincinnati's most popular places. One Bowen Place, downtown. 381-6200.

January's is a club for the sophisticate who enjoys authentic big-band entertainment and dancing to the sound of a thirteen-piece band Celebration, which performs until 2:30 A.M. Tuesday through Sunday. 411 W. Second Street (adjacent to Riverfront Stadium and the Coliseum).

Palm Court recalls the palmy days we thought we could find only in Fitzgerald novels. Try the real thing in the Omni's newly renovated jewel box of a setting. Beautiful art deco surroundings, live piano music, plus whatever beautiful people are in town. Omni Netherland Plaza. 421-9100.

Patterns is another elegant, luxuriously furnished, and intimate room. Dance or just enjoy the sounds of contemporary music. On the Skywalk in the Westin Hotel. 621-7700.

The Pavilion, on top of Mt. Adams, offers terraced outdoor decks with stunning panoramas of the Ohio River. Open seven days, 2:30 P.M. to 2:30 A.M. 949 Pavilion Street. 721-7272.

Precinct is an ideal place for combining business meetings with good times. Very popular for happy hour, too (see "Dining Out" about dining here). Delta and Columbia Parkway. 321-5454.

Under Fifth Cafe is the only Italian cafe in downtown within walking distance of the hotels. Homemade pastas, good sandwiches, warm, friendly environment. Serving until 1 A.M. on weeknights; until 2 A.M. on weekends. Even a happy hour and shrimp for a dime (from 4 to 7 P.M. on weekdays). First floor of Edwards Manufacturing Building. Under Fifth Street at Eggleston. 381-5554.

AT LEISURE

By now you know that, like it or not, Cincinnatians recognize that Kentucky is part of their Ohio lives. For visitors, short hops across the river into Covington are one thing, but to sample the real, upscale Kentucky, you'll need discretionary leisure for longer forays into the elite and horsey worlds of Lexington or Louisville. A reminder: in this part of the country, driving is done on superb roads with little or no traffic. Thus, a 90-mile trip can actually be made in around two hours.

Day-Tripping

Lexington, about a two-hour drive away, is the home of the **bluegrass horse farms** (over 300, some of which are open to the public) and beautiful **Keenland Horse Park,** one of the most elite in the country. Open fall to spring. Several groups arrange bluegrass tours: 606/252-5744 or 606/272-8954.

Keenland Raceway, open only October and April, is known as the "racers' raceway," as compared to Saratoga. Very horsey set here. This is where Queen Elizabeth brought her mare for mating. The clubhouse is for members only, but check to see if your Cincinnati company has an in. You won't want to miss this glimpse into another world: dress is elegant and formal, large-brimmed hats, ankle-length flowered skirts. It reminds us of that great scene in *My Fair Lady.*

In Lexington, the **Kentucky Horse Park** with its extraordinary museum is a must for anyone even faintly interested in thoroughbreds or racing. Man O' War is buried here; there are farm tours, antique buggies—the works. Exit 120 on Iron Works Pike. 233-4303.

About two miles south of Lexington is **Shakertown,** an authentic 19th-century village, complete with small inn for overnights and meals. Advance reservations are a must. 606/734-5411.

Louisville, home of Churchill Downs and the Kentucky Derby, is also a city full of southern charm. This is one Kentucky town that snobbish Cincinnatians love to claim. In addition to horses, Louisville also favors the arts. The **Actors Theater of Louisville** is one of the country's leading repertory companies. Every March, drama critics from around the world attend its productions. Three Pulitzer Prize–winning plays have come from here.

Wakefield Scarce Gallery, in nearby Shelbyville (502/633-4382), is something that must be experienced to be believed. But trust us: in this small town, in the middle of nowhere, is the largest collection of English antiques to be found outside London. A red brick building about half a block in size, it is literally crammed with the real thing. Georgian tea services are suspended from the ceilings to make room for the larger pieces of heirloom furniture. Every inch is bulging with authentic museum-quality pieces. As you might expect, there are lots of dealers here—but what a shopping experience it is. The Scarce Hill Restaurant (633-2825) is another don't-miss; reservations are a must.

The local hotel, the **Brown Hotel,** is open again following a decade of restoration. It is truly Old World on a grand scale, but brought up to modern-day comfort. Treat yourself. 502/583-1234.

In Town

Kings Island has something for just about every personality: a huge theme park, a Jack Nicklaus Sports Center, College Football Hall of Fame, a factory outlet mall with 25 name-brand outlets and off-price retailers, and a campground and Canoe Livery. 241-5600.

Because this is riverboat country, and because Cincinnati is known as the "Queen City," you might want to float for a few leisurely days aboard one of the **riverboat Queens**—*The Delta Queen* and *The Mississippi Queen*—which ply these waters on a regular basis, year round. There are cruises to nowhere, or you might even find one to take you to the city of your next meeting. Home port office: 511 Main Street, Cincinnati, OH 45202. Or call ahead, toll-free, 800/543-1949.

Sunday Customs

Ask anyone in Cincinnati what they like best about Sunday mornings and you'll probably hear "brunch." The local favorites are the Skywalk hotels and their individual versions of what this leisurely meal should be like. Average price is about $14 for menus that range from merely sumptuous to extravagant. And we have discovered that you can sit for as long as you like—read the entire *New York Times* if you want—and no one will try to rush you out.

Spectator Sports

Cincinnati makes it very easy to become a sports enthusiast: Riverfront Stadium is right downtown and a breeze to get to, it is clean and modern, there's plenty of parking—and their teams are winners.

The National League **Cincinnati Reds,** under the dynamic duoism of Pete Rose and Marge Schott, continue to bring baseball honor and glory to the hometown. Schott, who bought the club with her own money, is there rooting her guys on at every game, with her St. Bernard mascot Schottzie at her side. 100 Riverfront Stadium. Call 421-REDS for tickets.

The NFL **Cincinnati Bengals,** champions in their own right, play football in Riverfront Stadium. 621-3550.

There are no professional hockey or basketball teams.

Thoroughbred racing takes place at River Downs, late April through Labor Day. 6301 Kellogg Avenue. 232-8000.

Active Sports

Cincinnati is a joggers' haven, with trails in the parks and a never-ending riverbank full of scenic routes.

Dallas

9 (Hwy. 1380) Beltline
L▼

E 11

F

(I-635) LBJ Frwy.

5

A

Beltline Rd.

Loop 12

Dallas North Tollwy.

(Hwy. 75-N) Central Pkwy.

N

◄8

Airport Frwy. (Rte. 183)

Loop12

Hwy. 183

Stemmons Frwy.

N

Mockingbird Lane

7

3

4

6

Oaklawn Ave.

Fitzhugh Ave.

Ross Ave.

Lamar St.

Greenville Ave.

Turtle Creek Blvd.

C

Field St.

Turtle Creek Blvd.

M Elm St.

G Commerce St.

St.

11▶

Wood St.

Houston St.

Market St.

Griffith St.

Harry Hines Blvd.

H

K

B

J

D▶

I-30

I-30

■O
2■P■

Stemmons Frwy.

I-30 Thorton Frwy.

I-35E

I-45

10
▼

HOTELS	LANDMARKS	
1 Adolphus	A Airport	H Market Center
2 Hyatt Regency	B Convention Center	I Museum of Art
3 La Quinta	C Dallas Theater Center	J Old City Park
4 Loew's Anatole	D DeGolyer Estate/	K Reunion Tower
5 Mandalay Four Seasons	Dallas Botanical	L Southfork Ranch
6 Mansion on Turtle Creek	Gardens	M Texas Book Depository
7 Melrose	E Galleria	N Texas Stadium
8 Non-Smoker's Inn	F Highland Park	O Union Station
9 Registry Hotel	G JFK Memorial	P Visitor Information Center
10 Sheraton Park Central		
11 Westin Galleria		

DALLAS

GETTING YOUR BEARINGS

Whatever preconceived notions you may have about Dallas, we can guarantee you'll get along better if you remember this bit of information: Dallas people like their city and want you to like it and them, too. Dallas is a modern, sophisticated, prosperous city that somehow manages to combine southern friendliness and manners with hard-nosed power brokering and wealth. This dichotomy can cause problems for the uninitiated only when they fail to recognize the business fist inside the social glove.

Business is the lifeblood of Dallas, from farming and ranching to real estate, banking, and oil. One-third of the Dallas work force is in the fields of computers, electronics, and aerospace defense (the Infomart houses most computer and electronic companies; to obtain a pass, call 1-800-527-1451). Another third is involved in the wholesale/retail trade (the Dallas Market Center is the largest single-site wholesale merchandise mart in the world—eight buildings on 175 acres). Dallas is also home to the second-largest concentration of insurance company headquarters in the United States and is one of the fastest growing banking-finance centers. The city also ranks third in the nation's convention business. The Convention Center, located in the central business district, is larger than four football fields and can accommodate up to 60,000 people.

As a business traveler, you can expect a friendly and polite reception. But make no mistake, deals are driven hard here. It is merely a southern expectation that people will treat each other politely even while they are hammering out a multimillion-dollar deal.

Like many cities, Dallas has its old wealth (primarily in Highland Park, home of many of the founding families), and new wealth (primarily North Dallas, where many recent eastern transplants have moved). Any social contacts you can foster among either of these influential groups can mean good business contacts.

We must point out that the business world here is primarily male dominated, and the boardrooms remain almost exclusively the domain of white Christian males. Women have made some strides here, but not on a par with those made by counterparts in the Northeast or on the West Coast. Much of this is due to the city's conservatism, culturally and politically as well as economically. Dallas is often called the buckle of the Bible Belt, with the church community, especially the Baptists, wielding a strong influence. Minority groups (and this definitely includes women in executive positions) tend to be tolerated as long as they keep a low profile.

The four main business areas in Dallas are Far North Dallas; Dallas Central; Las Colinas; and Forth Worth (which, together with Dallas, forms the "Metroplex" that folks here seem to love to refer to). Downtown closes up by 5 P.M. when the office buildings empty for the day. If your hotel is in the downtown area, you can find some good restaurants, plus a horse-and-carriage tour of the area in the recently developed West End Historic District. But charming as this area is, it can also be dangerous—do not walk around here after dark.

Greenville is a major north-south street in the heart of town. You'll notice that many of the restaurants and clubs we've recommended are on Greenville. It is one of the few streets in town where you'll feel fairly safe walking.

WHAT TO WEAR

Keep the local Bible Belt mentality in mind when you pack for this trip. Dallas businesswomen are quite fashion-conscious (perhaps because of the strong influence of the apparel industry) but with a definite emphasis on femininity. During the day, suits and tailored dresses, in bright colors if you wish, are the best choice. In financial circles, however, the navy or gray suit still rates high, albeit with such feminine touches as soft-toned silk blouses and quality accessories. Stylish haircuts also score points for professional women.

Going out to dinner in Dallas is an occasion to dress up. When dining out with local business clients, be sure to change from your dress-for-success suit into something dressier and less severe. Just don't go overboard—your overall appearance must remain professional rather than social—perhaps a silk dress and jacket.

WEATHER WATCH

The winters here are usually mild, with temperatures in the 40s to 50s with occasional rain. Texas weather in general, however, is highly changeable, and it is not unusual for a 50-degree day to be followed by two days of snow and freezing temperatures. As always, we recommend you check the readings in your local paper daily for a week or so before arriving just to be up-to-date on what's happening in Dallas.

Summers are very hot and humid (temperatures in the 90s), but almost everything is air-conditioned—often to the point of freezing. A lightweight jacket, if you're not wearing a suit, can help ward off the chill.

GETTING THERE

Dallas–Fort Worth Airport is *big* (remember—this is Texas). Covering 17,850 acres—larger than the island of Manhattan—this giant is not especially well marked and can be very confusing to newcomers. The Airtrans shuttle system, which costs 25 cents a ride, can help speed you around this mammoth terminal. General information number is 574-6720. The airport is served by all major carriers.

The secondary airport, **Love Field,** is actually within Dallas (Mockingbird Avenue; 954-1400) and is served mainly by regional and in-state flights.

D/FW is the country's first airport to have an Air Vita facility. Air Vita, the brainchild of Bente Strong and Gayle Moeller, lets you spend your between-planes time exercising, working out, or even working in private office spaces. The walk-in fee is $15 and includes use of a weight room, locker, steam, sauna, and showers. You can also rent workout clothes. The owners expect to open in other major airports very soon.

Expect to pay about $20 for a cab into town from D/FW, a 25-minute ride except during rush hour when it can take about 45 minutes. The Link bus system leaves every 30 minutes from D/FW airport to major downtown hotels and costs about $8. However, service is not around the clock; it begins at 8 A.M. and ends at 10 P.M.

Dallas is car territory. Everything is spread out, Texas-style, often with vast distances between where you are and where you have to go. One frequent visitor describes the area as "one hundred miles of freeway searching for a town."

Car Rentals

If you rent a car at the airport, be sure to get clear instructions as to which exit and which freeway to take; it's not at all hard to get lost.

Avis	574-4100
Budget	574-4141
Dollar	256-4576
Hertz	574-2000
National	574-3400

GETTING AROUND

Don't depend on public transportation in this town. The buses aren't particularly convenient and there's no subway system. That leaves cabs and private cars. (Of course, if you want to travel in style, Texas-style, there's always "Texas Taxi," a chauffeur service that provides Eldorado Cadillacs with a pair of longhorns mounted on the hood. This bit of whimsey will cost you $50 an hour with a two-hour minimum.) At the other end of the spectrum are the show-stopping "bunny buses"—strange-looking rabbit-eared vehicles that, for a mere 25 cents, transport passengers along the major shopping routes.

There are about 1,200 cabs in town. For some reason cruising cabs can't be hailed. But you can usually find them lined up outside hotels, or they can be called for in advance (allow about 15 minutes). The companies you can rely on: Terminal Cab Co., 823-5120, or Yellow Cab, 426-6262.

Best bet of all is to rent a car. Although on-street parking in downtown is scarce, the parking lots and garages are plentiful and reasonable. And you'll be very glad you have the independence of your own wheels in this vast Metroplex city.

GETTING FAMILIAR

Dallas Convention & Visitors Bureau
Dallas Chamber of Commerce   954-1480
1507 Pacific Avenue
Dallas, TX 75201

Dallas Visitor Information Center
400 S. Houston Street
In the lobby of **Union Station,** a building that is listed in the National Register of Historic Places.

Dallas Convention Center
650 S. Griffin Street   658-7000
Dallas, TX 75202

The *Dallas Times Herald,* a morning and afternoon paper, features listings of only good to excellent restaurants in their Friday "Weekend" section, plus regular listings of clubs, movies, and upcoming events. Additional restaurant reviews may be found in the Wednesday "Taste" section. The *Dallas Morning News,* a morning paper, reviews restaurants and lists entertainment schedules in the Friday "Guide" section. *Texas Monthly* and *D* magazines are both slick publications focusing on what's happening Texas-style. *D* concerns itself mainly with Dallas, and *Texas Monthly* includes a reliable city-by-city listing of events, entertainment, and restaurants.

Note: we have found the newspapers' restaurant reviews to be more reliable than those found in the magazines, which tend to be overly kind in their critiques.

AREA CODE 214   Weather 993-2626
Time and temperature   Police emergencies 744-4444
844-6611

AT YOUR SERVICE

Dallas enjoys a wealth of excellent hotels, many of which are large and convention oriented. Local management seems pretty well tuned in to women's needs; you'll find well-trained staffs in all the following hotels.

Adolphus Hotel
1321 Commerce Street   Toll-free reservations: 800/221-9083
Dallas, TX 75202   Local number: 742-8200
                                                Telex: 84530

The beautifully renovated (435-room) historic Adolphus offers a convenient downtown location and plush facilities, including one of the city's best French restaurants. So special are the antiques and other appointments of this 1912 luxury palace built by Adolphus Busch that a booklet, "Treasures of the Adolphus," is given to guests to take along for self-guided tours of the hotel.

A must is afternoon tea, served in elegant style in the walnut-paneled main lobby. The **French Room,** a pastel-hued and chandeliered 18th-century setting, serves some very serious, very expensive haute cuisine, regarded by critics as some of Dallas's best. The **Grille** is comfortable for any meal, and the **Palm Bar,** popular with downtown executives, is open for lunch.

Hyatt Regency Dallas
300 Reunion Boulevard   Toll-free reservations: 800/228-9000
Dallas, TX 75207   Local number: 651-1234
                                                Telex: 732748

The Hyatt is huge and impersonal, but its policy of automatically upgrading single women travelers to the Regency Club's concierge floors (without extra charge) makes it worthy of consideration. Note: women traveling as part of a convention are not included in this offer. And it is wise to remind the staff of this policy when making your reservation as a single guest. Some women have complained of having missed their wake-up calls, and of long waits for room-service breakfast (possibly another reason to opt for Regency Club services).

The hotel has three restaurants, none of which is particularly distinguished. Union Station across the street has several casual eating places.

	Concierge	Executive Floor	No-Smoking Rooms	Fitness Facilities	Pool	24-Hour Room Service	Restaurant for Client Entertaining	Extra-Special Amenities	Electronic Key System	Business/Secretarial Services	Checkout Time	Frequent Guest Program	Business Traveler Program	Average Single Rate
Adolphus	●	●		●		●	French Room	●		●	1 p.m.	Adolphus Special Attention	Corp.	$129
Hyatt Regency	●	●	●	●	●		Fausto's		●	●	12 noon		Corp.	$ 95 reg. $ 90 corp. $115 Regency Club corp.
Loew's Anatole	●	●	●	●	●	●	Verandah's	●	●	●	12 noon	Gold Passport	L.A.D.S.	$100 reg. $ 90 corp. $125 ex. floor
Mandalay Four Seasons	●	●	●	●	●	●	Enjolie	●		●	1 p.m.	Self-kept Up-grades	Corp.	$135 corp. $175 reg.
Mansion on Turtle Creek	●		●		●	●	Mansion Restaurant	●		●	1 p.m.	Up-grades	Corp.	$165 reg. $125 corp.
Melrose	●	●					Garden Court	●	●	●	3 p.m.	Melrose Club	Corp.	$ 95 reg. $ 90 corp. $110 ex. floor
Sheraton Park Central	●	●	●	●	●	●	Mozart's	●		●	12 noon	Distinguished Customer Service	(America Airlines Advantage)	$100 reg. $ 85 corp. $ 95 ex. floor
Registry	●	●	●	●	●	●	La Champagne			●	1 p.m.		Registry Executive Service	$100 reg. $ 75 RES corp. $ 94 corp. $130 ex. floor
Westin Galleria	●	●	●	●	●	●	Blom's	●		●	1 p.m.	Westin Texas Preferred	Corp.	$105 reg. $ 99 corp. $175 ex. floor

Loew's Anatole

2201 Stemmons Freeway	Toll-free reservations: 800/223-0888
Dallas, TX 75207	Local number: 748-1200
	Telex: 730475

A vast, 1,620-room hotel that runs surprisingly well. A favorite with the trade show and convention crowd (it was headquarters for the 1984 Republican National Convention), it's within walking distance of the Market Center. The **Verandah Health Club** is outstanding, featuring not only excellent health facilities but a superb restaurant presided over by a talented young chef. Among the fitness classes, machines, ball courts, and other amenities is a eucalyptus room (good for treating sinus conditions).

We prefer the Verandah restaurant to the hotel's other fine choices that include the **Plum Blossom** for elegant Chinese food, **L'Entrecote** for expensive French, and the southwestern cuisine at the **Nana Grill** atop the new tower.

Mandalay Four Seasons

221 S. Las Colinas	Toll-free reservations: 800/268-6282
Irving, TX 75039	Local number: 556-0800
	Telex: 794016

A luxury hotel in a country-garden setting just 15 minutes from downtown. Las Colinas is actually a man-made landscape that includes picturesque canals lined with shops and restaurants.

The hotel offers all the special features you associate with this fine chain, including an excellent "alternative menu" (low-fat, low-salt, low-cholesterol selections in all food services), and demi-suites, called Four Seasons Rooms, with work areas separate from the bed. Also part of the hotel: the top-notch **Las Colinas Sports Club** that includes a preventive medicine clinic in addition to golf, tennis, swimming, and other athletic facilities.

Enjolie is their fine food restaurant; **Rhapsody** is more casual with a bar and dancing at night; **Cafe d'Or** is the three-meals restaurant. Afternoon tea is served in the sunny lobby lounge, **Le Jardin.**

Mansion on Turtle Creek

2821 Turtle Creek	Toll-free reservations: 800/527-5432
Dallas, TX 75219	Local number: 559-2100
	Telex: 794946

A small, 143-room, ultraluxury hotel, owned by Caroline Hunt Schoellkopf, which offers a high degree of security, privacy, and service. It is probably for these reasons that women guests are willing to pay the ultrahigh rates. Guest rooms are lavish and beautifully decorated. Security is very tight and on a personal basis.

The **Mansion Restaurant,** which is adjacent to the hotel in its own domed-top building, is extremely expensive and not all that friendly to newcomers. Ask the hotel's concierge to make your reservation; that may smooth your reception. Afternoon tea and Sunday brunches are particularly lovely in this wooded, countrylike setting.

Melrose

3015 Oak Lawn   Toll-free reservations: 800-MELROSE
Dallas, TX 75219   Local number: 521-5151

One of Dallas's lesser-known hotels, this comfortable, attractively renovated place makes an extra effort for women guests. (Jane Alexander and the princess of Sweden favor the Melrose.) Decor is Old World; rooms feature Queen Anne furniture and high four-poster beds. Security includes computerized key cards whose codes are changed daily. The location is five minutes from Market Center, five minutes from downtown, in an artsy, primarily gay area (women report feeling hassle-free here).

Sheraton Park Central

LBJ Freeway at Colt Road   Toll-free number: 800/325-3535
Dallas, TX 75251   Local number: 385-3000

A large hotel, bland-looking on the outside, that delights with its attractive interior. It also is well situated for visitors who need to travel to varying locations around the city. Women report preferring the towers, an 83-room VIP section with all the usual amenities of concierge floors.

Three in-hotel restaurants: **Mozart's** for fairly expensive Continental cuisine (when making reservations, you'll be asked if you are to be the host; if so, only you will receive the menu listing prices); **Laurel's** and the **Cafe in the Park** are less formal; we wouldn't recommend entertaining clients in either.

Registry Hotel

6350 LBJ Freeway   Toll-free reservations: 800/527-1690
Dallas, TX 75248   Local number: 386-6000
                                 Telex: 795515

If your business will be centered in North Dallas, this large, plush hotel is for you. Otherwise, the heavy traffic getting there is a strike against it. There are two concierge floors with all the usual services and amenities; good health facilities (including Jane Fonda work-out tapes and a large video screen). Some bilevel suites are available; inquire about them when you make your reservation.

Westin Galleria

13340 Dallas Parkway   Toll-free reservations: 800/228-3000
Dallas, TX 75240   Local number: 934-9494
                                 Telex: 714630182

A very popular tourist hotel, the Westin also attracts business travelers because of its proximity to great shopping, its Premiere (concierge) Floor, and its much-welcomed nonsmoking floor.

In-house restaurants include **Blom's,** with very expensive, excellent French cuisine; the **Grille,** a moderate-priced spot for all three meals; and **Zucchini's** for casual meals.

ON A BUDGET

Motels

Non-Smokers' Inn
9229 Carpenter Freeway   Local number: 631-6633
Dallas, TX 75247
We recommend this place not only for its rates (which are attractively low) but also because this 134-unit motel delivers exactly what it promises: a totally smoke-free environment. You can sleep in a room that has never known tobacco smoke; even employees must sign a no-smoking pledge in order to work here. Perhaps not the all-time best choice for a single woman—but worth it if you're an avid antismoker. There's a pool and health spa with sauna, hot tubs, and exercise machines. Two meeting rooms are available. Singles are $32 a night. The motel, located near Cowboy Stadium, is about 20 minutes northwest of downtown on Highway 183.

La Quinta
4440 N. Central Expressway   Toll-free reservations: 800/531-5900
Dallas, TX 75206   Local number: 821-4220
Near the SMU campus (a nice area) and very convenient to the expressway (three minutes into the Greenville section of town where most of the restaurants and clubs are located). Single women are given rooms near the office, which remains open 24 hours. There's an outdoor pool, free cable TV (with either HBO or Showtime), and a Denny's restaurant adjoining. Singles are $43.

Restaurants

Although there are many high-priced restaurants and quite a few ethnic spots in the inexpensive range in Dallas, it's hard to find good places in the mid-price range. However, you can rely on these:

La Cave serves bistro-type cuisine in a French setting. Dinners range from $7 to $15; lunches from $7 to $10. In the west end of town at 2019 N. Lamar. 871-2072.

The Grape features a Continental menu that changes daily. Dress is casual, and no reservations are taken. Dinners range from $6 to $15; lunches from $4 to $8. 2808 Greenville Avenue. 823-0133.

Snuffers is a restaurant and bar with great burgers, sandwiches, and nachos. Lots of lively activity here. Prices range from $3 to $5. 516 Greenville Avenue. 826-6850.

Zanzibar Deli is lots more than a deli—it's also a bar and lively meeting place for the young and casual set. The menu is more eclectic than the usual deli fare. Open for lunch only on Fridays, Saturdays, Sundays; dinners all week. 2912 Greenville Avenue. 828-2250.

DINING OUT

There's progress on the woman-as-host front, notes *Dallas Times Herald* food editor Candy Sagon in a recent column. She reports a policy change at the Adolphus Hotel's French Room, which now instructs waiters to ask who the host or hostess will be for the meal. No hassles over the check, no embarrassing mix-ups over service.

Most of Dallas's hotel restaurants are good for business meals (with the few exceptions noted in the hotel descriptions), and because hotels are accustomed to single travelers, these dining rooms are also usually a good choice for a woman dining alone as well.

For Dallas, we consider moderate any meal from $15 to $25. Above that is expensive; below, inexpensive.

Outside the hotels we can recommend these restaurants.

Panteli's, a small intimate cafe serving wine by the glass, Greek appetizers, light entrées, and good desserts. Located in an area popular for its clubs and restaurants. Open for lunch and dinner daily, and for Sunday brunch. 1928 Greenville. 823-8711.

La Cave is a wine bar serving French bistro-type food: light entrées, salads, pâté, cheese, fruit. Informal atmosphere. Closed Sundays. 2926 N. Henderson and 2019 Lamar (downtown).

Cafe Cancun serves "new" Mexico-style foods like grilled fish and chicken, as well as Tex-Mex classics. Good for nachos and appetizers, too. Informal, with friendly staff. Open daily for lunch and dinner. 4131 Lomo Alto. 559-4011.

Tong's House serves high-quality Chinese food at reasonable prices. Plain decor, informal atmosphere, located in a shopping center. About 20 minutes from downtown, but worth the trip for some dishes. Try the noodles. Open Tuesday through Sunday, closed at 10 P.M. 1910 Promenade Center, Richardson. 231-8858.

Le Boul'Mich, located in a charming old house, is a country French bistro with a friendly staff and comfortable decor. Blackboard specials are usually the best; fish is always good. Close to downtown, it is popular at lunch. Open Monday through Saturday for lunch and dinner. Closed during August. 2704 Worthington. 826-0660.

Ciao is in a predominately gay area, so single women aren't usually hassled. Good pizza and pastas. Service tends to be a bit slow but friendly, and the crowd is both diverse and casual. Good music over the sound system. 3921 Cedar Springs. 521-0110.

Chiquita, one of Dallas's best Mexican restaurants, is too noisy for a business dinner, but it is a colorful, festive place to go for a good meal. Although all the standard dishes are available, they stress the more sophisticated Mexican cuisine. Moderately priced. Closed Sunday; lunch and dinner other days. 3810 Congress and Oak Lawn. 521-0721.

Moctezuma's is friendly and informal, with outdoor dining area.

Spinach enchiladas are outstanding; all the basic Mexican dishes are good here. Inexpensive to moderate. 3202 McKinney. 559-3010.
Sonny Brian's Smokehouse is, quite simply, the best barbeque in Dallas. (Them's fightin' words in this part of the country, but we stand by our opinion.) Many business lunches are conducted at this slightly seedy, slightly tacky place where juicy barbequed brisket and ribs are sold by the carload from 10 A.M. to 5 P.M. Monday through Saturday (or until they run out of food). Pick-up trucks park next to Cadillacs and many executive types can be seen gathered around a car hood, beer in one hand and sandwich in the other. We've even seen a job interview conducted here. About 15 minutes from downtown. Inexpensive. 2202 Inwood. 357-7120.

BUSINESS BREAKFASTS
Almost any of the hotel dining rooms are ideally suited for morning business meetings, but here are some of the really outstanding ones. **The Mansion** is considered a real "power breakfast" site. The **Grille** at the **Adolphus Hotel** is another no-fail choice. The **Loew's Anatole's Terrace,** in the new tower, has a good breakfast buffet and is usually very serene in the mornings, although service can drag a bit.

BUSINESS LUNCHES
Calluaud's is convenient to downtown and therefore popular with lunch crowds. Simple, classic French cuisine prepared well. Service is attentive; decor is pleasant but not overpowering. Expensive. Also an excellent choice for business dinners. Reservations necessary. Closed Sundays. 2619 McKinney Avenue. 823-5380.

Ratcliffe's offers a good selection of fish and seafood in an attractively renovated older building near downtown. Try their San Francisco sourdough bread. Excellent wine list. Popular for both lunch and dinner. Reservations needed. 1901 McKinney. 748-7480.

Newports in the Brewery, in historic West End district. Feature is mesquite-grilled fish. Popular, so it tends to be on noisy side. 703 McKinney. 954-0220.

Ceret is a French bistro that incorporates an art exhibit in the decor. Excellent fish entrées. A $20 fixed-price dinner, and an inexpensive crepe menu (all under $5). Open daily. Next to Newport's. 720-0297.

Jozef's is a popular seafood restaurant for lunch and dinner. Comfortable atmosphere, good service. Reservations needed. 2719 McKinney Avenue. 826-5560.

BUSINESS DINNERS
If your expense account can afford $50 to $100 per person, the **French Room** in the Adolphus Hotel, **Blom's** at the Westin, or **Enjolie** at the Mandalay Four Seasons are all excellent choices. **Calluaud's** is another

(see "Business Lunches"). All have a formal atmosphere, definitely the right place for your best designer gear.

Routh Street Cafe features the creative cuisine of talented chef Stephan Pyles. Unusual is the $35 fixed-price, five-course dinner featuring American dishes made with American products. Striking modern decor; excellent service; excellent wine list. *D* magazine calls it "Dallas's number-one purveyor of restaurant chic." This restaurant has also enjoyed a nationwide press, so reserve in advance. Located near downtown, 3005 Routh Street. 871-7161.

Uncle Tai's Hunan Yuan is haute Chinese cuisine at equally haute prices (entrées from $12 to $20). Superbly prepared food, which is quite spicy unless you ask for less. Reservations needed. Closed Sundays. Galleria (near Dallas Parkway and LBJ Freeway). 934-9998.

Cafe Royal offers a fixed-price, four-course French meal for $34.50, which is expertly prepared and beautifully served. Elegant restaurant, located in hotel-shopping complex downtown. Reservations needed. Closed Sundays. Plaza of the Americas, 650 N. Pearl. 747-7222.

DALLAS BY DAY

Best place in town to see the Dallas–Fort Worth Metroplex spread out before you is from the observation deck of the 50-story **Reunion Tower.** Admission charge. Open 9:30 A.M. until midnight. 300 Reunion Boulevard. 741-3663.

Dallasites are hugely proud of their new $54 million **Museum of Art.** There are many works by 19th- and 20th-century American and European artists, Matisse, Picasso, Gauguin, and Wyeth included. Free general admission. Closed Mondays. Conveniently located downtown at 1717 N. Harwood. 922-0220.

Old City Park is an outdoor museum of some 25 authentic buildings—from cabins to elaborate Victorian mansions—that belonged to the area's early settlers. On-site restaurant, **Brent Place,** serves dishes based on recipes from 1900s cookbooks. Reservations are recommended: 421-3057. Free admission to park; tours are available. Open daily to sunset. 1717 Gano. 421-5141.

Southfork Ranch, as all you TV buffs know, is where "Dallas" is filmed. It is also an enormously popular tourist attraction, drawing 3,000 of the faithful every day. Rumor has it the place has been bought and may become a hotel—with a three-bedroom suite renting for $2,500 a night. Take I-75 north to Parker Road, turn right and go five miles to Farm Road 2551. 231-2088.

The **DeGolyer Estate/Dallas Botanical Gardens** is a Spanish colonial-style mansion with gardens built in 1939 by Texas oilman and geologist Everette DeGolyer. Among the most beautiful sights in Dallas. Free admission; house tours available. Closed Mondays. 8525 Garland Road. 324-1401.

Any day in Dallas you can find people standing still, staring up at the sixth-floor window of what used to be called the **Texas Book Depository.** There's nothing in the window to be seen now, but Americans will never forget this building that hid an assassin back in November 1963. The **JFK Memorial,** a cenotaph (empty tomb) designed by Philip Johnson, stands a few blocks east of the Book Depository on a landscaped block bordered by Commerce, Main, and Record streets.

THE SHOPPING SCENE

If you feel, as we do, that no trip is complete until the stores have all been checked out, then Dallas is your kind of town. There are branches here of just about every upscale store in the country, not to mention a wealth of small boutiques featuring everything from European to local designers. The first Bloomingdale's to be opened west of the Hudson is here, retaining its special pizzazz. As one visiting New Yorker gleefully noted, "It's just as good as the one at home but without all the crazy New Yorkers pushing and shoving."

In this town, which ranks second only to Houston nationwide in retail sales per household, shopping malls assume major status. Local blue laws used to require every retail operator to close on Sundays. With the recent repeal, it's now up to individual owners whether or not to open on that day, so it's best to check before you go.

Highland Park Shopping Village is the city's oldest mall, and is still the mall of choice for the city's old money. The architectural style is relentlessly Spanish inspired, so much so that even the Safeway is disguised as a hacienda. Favorites here include Liberty of London, Courreges, Guy LaRoche, Ralph Lauren, and Ann Taylor. Other shops include Kron chocolatier, Pierre Deux, Williams-Sonoma. There's also a two-screen movie theater and several lovely restaurants including Cafe Pacific, which is open seven days a week. The Mall is at Preston and Mockingbird Lane, in residential Highland Park.

The **Galleria** is Dallas's newest mall, built on a grand scale, with four floors terraced over the central skating rink. Attached to the Westin Hotel, the Galleria boasts Saks, Marshall Field, and Macy's, along with numerous small stores like Tiffany, F.A.O. Schwarz, Laura Ashley, Vuitton. Georgette Klinger and Elizabeth Arden both have salons here. If shopping palls, you can always sample the expensive but top-notch Chinese food at Uncle Tai's, or see movies in one of the five theaters. Dallas Parkway at LBJ Freeway.

Northpark Center is anchored by two retailing giants, Neiman-Marcus and Lord & Taylor. Noteworthy outlets here include T. Edwards, and Crate and Barrel for home and kitchenware. Located midtown (about 20 minutes from downtown or from North Dallas) at Park Lane and Central Expressway.

Valleyview, home of the Texas Bloomingdale's, also hosts Sanger-Harris and many smaller stores. This Bloomingdale's blends the New York City shopping experience with a high level of energy and busy-ness deep in the heart of wide-open-spaces country. 2040 Valley View Center (LBJ Freeway and Montford).

Prestonwood, although it has five major retail outlets—Neiman-Marcus, Lord & Taylor, Joske's, Penney's, Montgomery Ward, and even a skating rink—seems to lack the cachet of the Galleria. 5301 Belt Line Road and Preston Road.

For funky boutiques featuring trendy clothes, the lower **Greenville Avenue area** is best. Try Avant, 2716 Greenville, Pinky's, 2101 Greenville, or H.D.'s Clothing, 3018 Greenville.

The original **Neiman-Marcus** flagship store reigns supreme in the downtown area. It is an institution and one that no true shopper would want to miss. Fashion-wise, you'll do much better in the malls and designer boutiques, but you should tour the original N-M just for the experience.

While shopping Texas-style you can't pass up the chance to sample the wacky world of Western gear. **Cutter Bill's** is a good place to start. The selection is duly outrageous, extravagant, and expensive—a hoot, as they say in these parts. 5818 LBJ Freeway. 239-3742. Want to impress the folks back home? Check out **Dallas Western Wear** for cowboy boots ranging from a modest $59 to $500. 1616A Commerce. 748-0333.

DALLAS BY NIGHT

There is no half-price ticket service in town. Tickets can be purchased directly from the theater, and most are available through **Ticketron** (265-0789). Tickets for traveling Broadway shows or pre-Broadway runs should be ordered as soon as they go on sale. Smaller productions usually have good seats available a few days before a performance.

Dallas Theater Center is the biggest, most professional theater company in town. Under the leadership of noted director Adrian Hall, they present a mix of revivals and recent Broadway hits, such as *Amadeus*. In a Frank Lloyd Wright–designed building. 3636 Turtle Creek Boulevard. 526-8857.

Dallas Repertory Theater offers mostly revivals and comedies with a light family air; average age of audiences seems to be about 58. NorthPark Center, Park Lane at North Central Expressway. 369-8966.

The **New Arts Theater** is the thinking woman or man's theater; very contemporary, very British productions. 702 Ross Avenue at Market (downtown). 761-9064.

Stage One (Greenville Avenue Theater) presents contemporary American productions, including offbeat and progressive works. Usually well performed. 2914 Greenville Avenue. 760-9542.

The **Arts District Theater,** a satellite of the **Dallas Theater Center,** is located in a large contemporary building near downtown. Tends to present more hip, experimental works, plus the regular DTC schedule. 2401 Floral Street at Fairmount. 526-8857.

Theater Three presents eclectic works from lighter to experimental, off-Broadway to light dramas. 2800 Routh Street. 651-7225.

National mainstream Broadway tours are presented at the **Majestic Theater** during the fall season. Summer performances feature local dance companies and others. 1925 Elm Street. 880-0137.

The **Dallas Symphony Orchestra** is under the baton of Eduardo Mata. Fair Park Music Hall. 692-0203.

The **Dallas Opera** also usually performs at the Fair Park Music Hall. Tickets at 3200 Maple Avenue. 871-0090.

The **Dallas Ballet Association** presents mostly classics during the season. In summer it offers free Ballet in the Park performances. Majestic Theater. Box office at 1925 Elm Street. 744-4430.

Call the **Cultural Arts Information Hot Line** for 24-hour updates on events around town: 385-1155.

LATE-NIGHT DALLAS

Although essayist Jan Morris succinctly decreed "Dallas does not stay up late," we have found ample evidence to the contrary.

Poor David's, probably the safest club in town, is a friendly, casual spot featuring folk or rhythm-and-blues performers. 1924 Greenville Avenue (next door to Panteli's Restaurant). 821-9891.

Greenville Avenue Bar and Grill is a longtime neighborhood bar with light meals and good music. You're not likely to be hassled in here. Sunday regular is Hal Baker's Gloomchasers playing Dixieland jazz. 2821 Greenville. 823-6691.

Fast and Cool Club attracts the 20-to-30 fast and cool crowd. New dance club with sixties and top-40s sounds. Live groups twice a month. 3606 Greenville. 827-5544.

Strictly Tabu, an Italian restaurant, offers live jazz in the lounge Tuesday through Sunday. In the same strip of restaurants as Cafe Cancun. 4111 Lomo Alto. 528-5200.

Jazba is the lounge of Ratcliffe's restaurant and features jazz and blues. 1901 McKinney Avenue. 748-7480.

Belle Starr is a popular urban cowboy club with live entertainment nightly. Good place to see country and western action without the rowdy overtones. Dancing. Southwestern and Central Expressway. 750-4787.

No Whar But Texas, a huge club, offers lots of games, a lighted dance floor, live entertainment. Regional bands compete every Tuesday at 8 P.M. Fairly young crowd. Walnut Hill and Central Expressway. 369-3866.

In Cahoots, located in a nice area of town, draws a young executive crowd to dance. NorthPark East Shopping Center, Park Lane and Central Expressway. 692-5412.

Confetti attracts a wild crowd. If you go here alone, expect to be approached. Two dance floors and two bars. Matilda at Lovers Lane. 369-6969.

Studebaker's has a fifties theme, complete with car. Draws a 20–30-year-old dancing crowd. NorthPark East Shopping Center, Park Lane and Central Expressway. 696-2475.

Ravel's is a flashy, classy disco that attracts a lot of 20–30-year-old single women as well as the convention crowd. In the Registry Hotel, 15201 Dallas Parkway. 386-6000.

Mistral is a modernistic club with recorded and live entertainment. Frequented by young club devotees as well as hotel guests. In Loews Anatole Hotel, 2210 Stemmons Freeway. 748-1200.

Prohibition Room, in the basement of a renovated brewery, was actually a secret drinking room during Prohibition. Jazz, blues, rock, old Sinatra standards in the jukebox; pool tables. Good live rock bands on Thursday, Friday, and Saturday nights. Popular after-work place; crowded on weekends. Occasional cover charge. 703 McKinney in the Brewery. 954-4407.

Starck Club has all the trappings of a New York club: decadently appointed coed bathrooms (a scene unto themselves), sunken dance floor, and a long line waiting to get in. Packed on Saturday nights with a mix of gays, guys, punks, models, and the occasional visiting celebrity. Friday nights draw a slightly more upwardly mobile crowd. Cover charge. 703 McKinney in the Brewery. 720-0130.

AT LEISURE

Dallas's weekend hotel packages make staying over a few days after the work week very tempting. Although one visitor carped, "There's no reason to hang around for a minivacation, there's nothing to see," we don't agree. If you find you can take some time to linger in town at leisure, we can recommend the following activities.

Day-Tripping

Jefferson, Texas, is a picturesque town about a two-and-a-half-hour drive east of Dallas. You can tour stately antebellum southern mansions, ride in a horse-drawn carriage, stay in the historic **Excelsior Hotel** (famous for its hearty breakfasts) or in one of the quaint bed-and-breakfast places. Or you can tour and then return to town. Reservations must be made far in advance (especially in spring and summer). Contact the Jefferson Chamber of Commerce for information. 665-2672.

Big D Texas is a 607-acre entertainment complex that re-creates western life as it was in the wild 1880s. Over 40 buildings to tour, a western show, and much, much more. 225-8191 for details.

Six Flags Over Texas, the theme park, is in Arlington. 817/461-FLAG. Nearby is **White Water,** 35 acres of water activities. Call 264-6211.

Grand Prairie has an International Wildlife Park with a drive-through game preserve. Call 263-2201. Nearby is what locals refer to as the "Disneyland of Flea Markets," a Texas-sized spread, also in Grand Prairie. 647-2331.

Another flea market, this one in town, is the **Big D Bazaar,** at 3636 N. Bruckner. 328-6117.

If you're lucky enough to be in town in October, you won't want to miss the **State Fair of Texas.** As you've probably guessed, it's the largest in the country with everything from a 20-acre midway to shows and dances and a rodeo. Admission fee. Fair Park, Cullum Boulevard and Grand Avenue. 421-8713.

Mesquite Championship Rodeo has been holding bronco riding, calf roping, bull riding, and other such events every Friday and Saturday night for the past 30 years. It's a lot of fun, even for a city slicker. The arena is indoors. Admission fee. Just outside of town at 635 Freeway and Military Parkway. 285-8777.

Sunday Customs

Brunch and churchgoing shape the rhythms of Sundays in Dallas. If your idea of brunch is to get all dressed up and eat expensive foods with other dressed-up people, head for the **Mansion** on Turtle Creek. A very civilized place, elegant surroundings, and great people-watching possibilities. Reservations a must. Very expensive. 526-2121.

The **Grille** at the Adolphus Hotel has an à la carte menu, lovely presentation in a relaxing, subdued atmosphere. Expensive. 742-8200.

Cafe Pacific is popular with locals. Moderately priced à la carte menu of omelets and light entrées. 24 Highland Park Village. 526-1170.

Blom's provides brunch in a comfortable setting of antiques and elegant ambiance. Expensive. Westin Galleria Hotel. 934-9494.

For a funky brunch, check out the **Bronx.** An interesting, eclectic crowd; good food. 3835 Cedar Springs. 521-5821.

A leisurely Sunday is a good time to visit the DeGolyer Estate, the Dallas Museum of Art, or Old City Park (see "Dallas by Day"). You also might want to take a picnic and head out for the **Connemara Conservancy,** a 72-acre site in North Dallas. There's a shuttle bus into the park from the parking lot. Recent events have included a sculpture exhibit and dance program. Drive north on Highway 75 to exit 32 and follow signs west to Breezeway Farms. Free admission. Call 720-0098 for tour and shuttle-bus information.

Another nearby area worth a visit is **Las Colinas,** a manmade Venice-style development about halfway between town and the airport. There are canals banked with cobblestoned walks and lined with restaurants, shops, and cafes. The Four Seasons Hotel is here with its beautiful public rooms. Stop in for afternoon tea in Le Jardin.

Call the **Recreation Activity Hot Line,** 670-7070, for 24-hour taped updates of activities and events.

Spectator Sports

One might say Dallasites take their football seriously. They maintain that there are two principal sports in town: spring football and fall football. One local legend tells of a loyal fan who, forced to attend a wedding on a home-game day, took a tiny TV into the church with her. When the minister headed her way, she thought she was in for a lecture. Turned out all he wanted to know was the score. In case you're not a fan, but want to pass as one, you should know that the legendary Cowboys quarterback, Roger Staubach, was inducted into the Football Hall of Fame in August 1985.

Dallas Cowboys football games are played in Texas Stadium, 2401 E. Airport Freeway, Irving. Tickets cost about $18. General information and tickets: 369-3211. **SMU Mustangs** football games are also played in Texas Stadium. Tickets from $7 to $14. Call 692-2902. Texas versus Oklahoma is the annual football classic between these two archrivals held in mid-October. Fans fill up virtually every hotel in town, and Commerce Street downtown is the scene of wild partying, drinking, and hell-raising the night before the game. If you plan to be here on business around this time, be sure to make and confirm your hotel, flight, and restaurant reservations well in advance.

Active Sports

There is a three-mile **jogging track** around Bachman Lake (NW Highway and Bachman). But we feel safer getting advice from the hotel concierge as to which areas to avoid and which are OK near our own hotel.

Municipal **golf** at the Cedar Crest Course. 1800 Southerland. 943-1004. Municipal **tennis** at the Samuell Grand Tennis Center. Twenty lighted outdoor courts, pro shop. 6200 E. Grand Avenue. 821-3811.

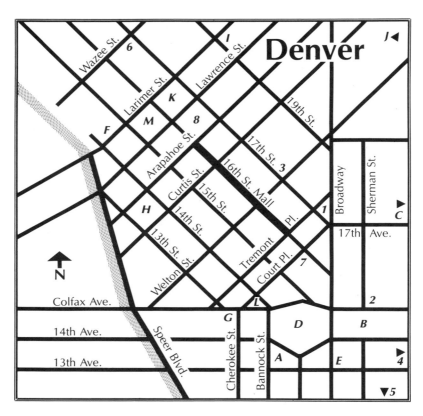

Denver

HOTELS

1 Brown Palace
2 Cambridge Club
3 Fairmont Hotel
4 Many Mansions
5 Marriott Southeast Hotel
6 Oxford Hotel
7 Radisson
8 Westin Tabor Center

LANDMARKS

A Art Museum
B Capitol
C City Park
D Civic Center
E Colorado Historical Society
F Larimer Square
G Mint

H Performing Arts Center
I Sakura Square
J Stapleton International
  Airport
K Tabor Center
L Visitor's Center
M Writer Square

DENVER

GETTING YOUR BEARINGS

In the social register of American cities, Denver is a sort of nouveau riche dinner-party crasher: not likely to hold the consommé spoon at the proper angle, but still plenty of fun to let your hair down with after the snobs go home. But there's a place for both the high-heeled evening pump encrusted with rhinestones and the spur-spangled Tony Lama boot encrusted with—well, let's just say encrusted.

On one hand, Denver is so crowded with young people making good money we feel it deserves to be tagged "the Yuppie Capital of the World." On the other hand, once there we are constantly reminded of the western heritage of Denver, which rose from a squalid little mining camp. Many of the chic buildings being renovated with yuppie capital in "LoDo," as lower downtown is known, started out as 19th-century brothels and gambling halls. This is Denver's latest frontier, in which Union Station plays a role as the place where the local live rock music scene holds court.

To get your bearings, keep in mind that downtown runs from roughly 14th Avenue across to 18th, and from Broadway (a key north-south artery) northwest to Wazee Street. After that, you end up in a warehouse train-yard district along the South Platte River Valley.

Sixteenth Street, long Denver's premier shopping avenue, died during the sixties and seventies, only to be reborn as a really nice pedestrian mall. The mall runs in front of the new Tabor Center, a three-story, two-block stacked shopping mall right across 16th and Lawrence from another tony shopping block, Writer Square.

Another beautifully reclaimed urban restoration, Larimer Square, is nearby at 15th and Larimer streets, and the lovely shopping and dining block Sakura Square, evidence of Colorado's strong Japanese presence, is at 19th and Larimer.

Seventeenth Street is Denver's answer to Wall Street, and many office and federal buildings are on Capitol Hill—18th and 19th streets.

Colorado's population of roughly 3 million includes numerous former residents of other states. But many of the powerful here—males, especially—have western or rural ties that make formal behavior on a woman's part the best bet for openers.

Sometimes Denver men seem old-fashioned, even a little sexist—but most of the time it's not meant that way. Before you take offense at an honest compliment or a man who still opens doors for women, remember: lots of these guys were reared to stand up straight, touch that hat brim, and say "Yes, Ma'am" and "No, Ma'am" if a woman approaches.

Many business travelers make use of Denver as a springboard to Rocky Mountain skiing, and that's not a bad idea. But Denver itself affords a pleasant stay and a fine business environment. We have found this city to be accessible in every way, made even more so if you have a car. And although it cannot offer a new world every six blocks, as New York City can, Denver has warmth, hospitality, and entertainment to suit a variety of tastes.

WHAT TO WEAR

Looking appropriate can be a challenge in Denver because the Rockies make the weather unpredictable. Summer clothes will see you through from mid-April to mid-September; from Halloween to March, pack winter wools, sturdy coats, and boots for good footing. In general, when in doubt as to what to wear, do as the natives do and dress in conservative clothing, worn by Denverites at the heart of the action in this conservative state.

WEATHER WATCH

You're never likely to get too hot in Denver. In fact, showers are frequent during the spring and summer even if the morning looks sunshiny. Humungous blizzards are *not* the rule in this Rocky Mountain city, but temperatures can get into the 20s and teens during the average winter storm. The snow is likely to fall as early as late autumn and as late as early spring. Evenings year-round tend to be on the cool side.

GETTING THERE

The biggest drawback at **Stapleton International Airport,** Denver's major airport, is the length of its concourses. For example, "D" is nearly half a mile long. Another drawback is its crowds, so if it's ski season or holiday time, give yourself an hour and a half to get to the airport and down that concourse. A shlep-cart for luggage or a suitcase with wheels gives your shoulders a break.

Seventeen major airlines serve Stapleton, including Frontier, Continental, Republic, and United. Six regional airlines also serve the city's major airport, including Air Midwest, Rocky Mountain Airways, and Pioneer.

Several hotel drop-off and other van and limousine services operate out of the pick-up area at Stapleton. Some run only during ski season, others year-round. Check with Ground Transportation outside Door 6 of the baggage area, or call 398-2147.

Two regional airports serve Denver's suburbs with small-plane and executive-flight service: **Jefferson County Airport** (466-2314) and **Centennial** (790-0598).

Car Rentals

Car rental firms with desks in Stapleton's baggage-claim area include:

Avis	398-3725
Budget	399-0444
Dollar	398-2323
Hertz	398-3693
National	321-7990
Alamo	321-1176
Thrifty	388-4634

GETTING AROUND

If you're planning any kind of an extended stay in Denver, rent a car. Chances are, you'll want to get out of the city for a while. But if you just need to pop in and out for a night or so, you'll be happy to know that Stapleton International is close to downtown Denver—only six miles, or 15 to 20 minutes away. Cab fare should run around $10 or less, plus tip, and cab sharing can sometimes be arranged.

Once in Denver, keep in mind that as a rule, hailing cabs doesn't work. At the airport or outside hotels are about the only places in Denver where cabs stand idle, waiting for fares. If you need a cab and you're not near a stand, phone Yellow Cab (292-1212), Zone Cab (861-2323), or Metro Taxi (333-3333). The usual cab wait is about 15 to 20 minutes.

If you have a car, keep in mind that although parking downtown is not impossible, it isn't easy to come by either. The city has metered spaces practically everywhere it's legal to park, usually good from one to two hours. The meters take nickels, dimes, and quarters. Meter maids and men are unfortunately good at their jobs, but if they nail you, you can mail in your payment. Denver has plenty of parking garages.

The Regional Transportation District is Denver's public transit system. Translation: buses. RTD generally is safe to ride, but also widely

Hotel	Average Rate	Business Traveler Program	Frequent Guest Program	Check Out Time	Business/ Secretarial Services	Electronic Key System	Extra-Special Amenities	Restaurant for Client Entertaining	24-Hour Room Service	Pool	Fitness Facilities	No-Smoking Rooms	Executive Floor	Concierge
Brown Palace	$100–$185 $115 corp.			1 p.m.	•		•	Ellyington's	•				•	•
Cambridge Club	$135 $108 corp.		1986—Play Cambridge Club Monopoly	1 p.m.	•		•	Le Profil	•			•		•
Fairmont Hotel	$120–$170	Fairmont Circle	USA Plus	1 p.m.	•		•	The Marquis	•	•	•	•	•	•
Marriott Southeast Hotel	$ 94 $ 87 corp. $125 exec. floor	Preference Plus Honored Guest		1 p.m.	•		•	The Chapparal The Wellshire Inn		•	•		•	•
Oxford Hotel	$115 $105 corp.	Corporate Rates		2 p.m.	•		•	The Sage	•		•			•
Westin Tabor Center	$105 $120 $ 94 corp. local $101 corp. national	Westin Preferred	Mileage Plus	1 p.m.	•		•	Augusta	•	•	•	•	•	•

regarded as inconvenient. However, it does operate two excellent services. One is the free 16th Street Mall shuttles, which take about 15 to 20 minutes to run from the southeast terminus at 16th and Broadway near the gold-domed State Capitol to the northwest terminal at 16th and Market streets near Tabor Center, Writer Square, and Larimer Square. The other is RTD service to and from Boulder, which is about an hour northwest of Denver. Call RTD at 628-9000.

GETTING FAMILIAR

Denver Metro Convention and Visitors Bureau
225 W. Colfax Avenue   892-1112
Denver, CO 80202
Write or call ahead for a packet of information, including the Official Visitor's Guide to Denver and Colorado, listing hotels, motels, attractions, restaurants, services, and events. Or, stop by the Visitor's Center, located at the address above, catty-corner to the U.S. Mint.

Forget the Chamber of Commerce in Denver. They offer nothing to the visitor and will only refer you to the visitor's bureau.

For up-to-the-minute listings of city happenings, buy a copy of either the *Rocky Mountain News* or the *Denver Post.* Friday editions of both papers include a pull-out, listing events for the following week. Another option is to pick up *Westword,* Denver's alternative weekly paper. It comes out on Wednesdays and is available free from red newsstands on the street, as well as in bars, restaurants, and stores. Bright and irreverent, *Westword* is widely read by locals.

Quick Calls

AREA CODE 303   Time 639-1311
Weather 639-1212   Emergencies 911

AT YOUR SERVICE

Where you choose to stay in Denver depends on which Denver you want to experience. Is it the flashy new "Dynasty" Denver? Then try one of downtown's glossy new glass-tower hotels. Or perhaps you want legendary, Old West Denver. Then we recommend hostelries such as the Brown Palace or the Oxford. Whatever style suits your fancy, we believe you'll find what you want in this sophisticated city that borders the Rockies.

Brown Palace

321 17th Street at Tremont Place   Toll-free reservations: 800/321-2599
Denver, CO 80202   Local number: 297-3111
                                          Telex: 454416

The Brown is easily Denver's most famous hotel. In fact, there's no higher-brow place to attend a party or reception here. Opened in 1892, the historic Brown's fantastic lobby is ringed by ornate balconies reaching up ten floors to a stupendous stained-glass ceiling. The 231-room brownstone is built on a triangular plot, with room prices based on size. Some, wedged into the corners, can be pretty tiny, so take a look before deciding if that's where you want to sleep. Most rooms offer Victorian decor, although a few on the top two occupied floors are done in art deco. Try to book in the old hotel (not the new addition) if possible.

Restaurants in the Brown include the **Palace Arms,** an award-winning formal dining room, and **Ellyington's,** a pretty, dressy restaurant offering live music Friday and Saturday nights. Guests also have access to the exclusive, expensive and delightful **Brown Palace Club,** where one of the memorable culinary delights is a killer black-bottom pie. The bars— **Henry C's** and the **Ships Tavern**—are cozy. The Ships Tavern is noted for its prime rib and Rocky Mountain trout; Henry C's sticks to hors d'oeuvres. The latter features a piano and small clusters of upholstered chairs and loveseats; it's a place to enjoy a quiet drink in privacy. Drinks are also served in the Brown's **lobby** Monday through Friday evenings, with a pianist for accompaniment.

Fairmont Hotel

1750 Welton Street   Toll-free reservations: 800/527-4727
Denver, CO 80202   Local number: 295-1200
                                          Telex: 9109312669

This is one of Denver's glass-tower, oil-era hotels, offering pleasing modern accommodations. It's handy both to the financial district on 17th and to shopping on 16th. The Fairmont has its own shopping pavilion as well, with a ladies' clothing store, a men's store, a shoe store, a jewelry shop, an art gallery, and a florist. Although the hotel is a high rise, the view isn't all that stunning, because other skyscrapers in the neighborhood lie between the Fairmont and the Front Range of the Rockies. Rooms in this 550-room property are large; the suites are among the largest we've ever seen. The pool is on the roof, and there's also an indoor tennis court and outdoor running tracks. Guests can also use the nearby International Athletic Club for a $10 fee.

For eating any time of the day or night, there's **McGuire's.** But formal dining with a client is best at the **Marquis.** Special gourmet meals have been designed for diet-conscious diners. The **Moulin Rouge** is a club attracting big-name Las Vegas–style talent. Al la carte dinner here is on the pricey side. An elevated **Cocktail Terrace** in the lobby is a fun place to people-watch.

Oxford Hotel

1600 17th Street
Denver, CO 80202

Toll-free reservations: 800/228-5838
Local number: 628-5400
Telex: 9109310413

The Oxford, built in 1891, and renovated and reopened in 1983, bills itself as "Denver's Grand Small Hotel." Like the Brown, it has that delightfully snooty, old-money feeling. It was the kind of place in its earlier incarnation where rich easterners came to stay when they had to check out their financial affairs on the frontier. The decor in this 82-room hotel impresses us. Floors are tiled and marbled, with Oriental rugs. Rooms are furnished with antiques, mostly Victorian, brought from France and England. The hallways—dark and gloomy in so many hotels—are spacious and brightly lit. Each floor has a hallway alcove sitting area where guests are invited to socialize over complimentary sherry and cookies at 5 P.M. daily.

Guests can dine at the **Oxford Club,** which is members-only during lunch. Two lounges here are perhaps the nicest aspect of the hotel. The **Cruise Room,** listed in the National Register as an example of art deco, is a narrow bar with recessed lighting and sculptured wall panels that make us feel like we're on board ship. The drink prices are as stiff as the drinks themselves. The **Corner Room** is a real island of cool, where a person feels with-it whether they're with anyone or not. If your mood is private, the seating around the edges where lights are low should render you reasonably inconspicuous to enjoy the jazz entertainment.

Cambridge Club

1560 Sherman Street
Denver, CO 80203

Toll-free reservations: 800/621-8385,
x917
Local number: 831-1252
Telex: 450711

This tiny hotel doesn't even look like a hotel, but rather more like an apartment building. It offers only suites, 27 in all, divided between parlor and executive suites. The latter are a bit larger and perfect for conducting meetings. The clubby atmosphere at the Cambridge Club is complemented by tight security. The building itself is locked betwen 11 P.M. and 7 A.M. and access to the elevator leading to suites is allowed only when a key is presented. A complimentary limousine takes guests to downtown appointments in style. The lobby is wood paneled with leaded glass windows and green marble floors. A large number of the suites are done in English traditional. Turn-down service is accompanied by Swiss truffles and cognac and Continental breakfast is complimentary.

Dining is elegant at **Le Profil,** Denver's oldest French restaurant.

Westin Hotel Tabor Center

1672 Lawrence Street
Denver, CO 80202

Toll-free reservations: 800/228-3000
Local number: 572-9100
Telex: 497 0844

Located on the 16th Street Mall with a great view of Skyline Park, this

420-room hotel opened in 1985 with extensive meeting facilities and some fine touches, like original art. The architectural style is traditional, with a color scheme of rose, beige, and executive gray. Extensive health facilities include two indoor racquet courts, an outdoor hot tub, an indoor/outdoor pool, and elaborate exercise rooms.

Fine dining at **Augusta Restaurant,** set against an art deco decor of ebony and peach furnishings and original Erte art. The restaurant serves new American cuisine and was named for the first wife of legendary Colorado figure Horace Tabor. The **Tabor Grille** serves three cosmopolitan meals. The bar in this eatery is okay but the one in the **Lobby Lounge** is more conducive to women who want to relax in a casual yet elegant environment.

Denver Marriott Southeast Hotel

I-25 at 6363 E. Hampden Avenue	Toll-free reservations: 800/228-9290
Denver, CO 80222	Local number: 758-7000
	Telex: 9109312595

This hotel is not to be mistaken for the Marriott City Center in downtown Denver. The Denver Marriott Southeast is listed here because of its access to I-25 and would be a likely choice if your business takes you to the Denver Technological Center, a grouping of firms south of the city, or to Colorado Springs. This 595-room high rise offers cheery, southwestern-decorated public areas and good-looking indoor and outdoor pools. Classy clothing can be found in stock at the hotel gift shop. A notable feature here is the tenth-floor concierge level, reachable only by use of an elevator key. The exercise room in the hotel has a whirlpool.

This hotel houses one of Denver's best restaurants, the **Wellshire Inn,** a Shakespearean-inspired eatery that always serves fine food. The coffee shop is called the **Fairfield Inn.** The **Chaparral** is a good place for client dining. There are also three taverns.

ON A BUDGET

Hotels

Radisson

1550 Court Place	Toll-free reservations: 800/654-1550
Denver, CO 80202	Local number: 893-3333

This hotel, right on the 16th Street Mall, offers acceptable accommodations at a lower rate than newer downtown hotels. The Radisson organization took over the high-rise, 750-room hotel from Hilton in 1985. Since then the sixth floor has become a concierge floor. There's a coffee shop and pleasant bar on the premises, and the hotel is close to good downtown restaurants for a choice of luncheon and dinner spots. A new fire system was installed in 1985.

For those who need to stay in Denver for a long period of time, it may pay to check out **Many Mansions** (1313 Steele Street, Denver, CO 80206; 303/355-1313). Located on 13th Avenue and Steele Street, Many Mansions is a mid-rise condominium-style building that's been converted into a spacious hotel. With 36 units and a minimum stay of seven days (rates go down dramatically if you're committed to 30 days or more), you'll have plenty of room in the one- and two-bedroom suites. A penthouse clubroom at Many Mansions has entertainment facilities, and guests are given complimentary passes to the Sporting Club in Cherry Creek, an athletic club with a mostly young, upwardly mobile clientele.

Restaurant

For dining, choose **Goodfriends,** which offers a wide selection of mid-priced suppers, sandwiches, and huge, satisfying salads. Wine is served in goblets big enough to house a pair of goldfish. This is a bit of a singles hangout, though, so ask the host to seat you in the restaurant—not the bar—if you're entertaining a business client or if you just want to be left alone. 3100 E. Colfax. 399-1751.

DINING OUT

Eating out is getting more interesting in Denver all the time. Having all those yuppies around, with their cosmopolitan tastes, has proven beneficial for the population at large with more restaurants emerging that serve an alternative to enormous slabs of beef accompanied by the to-be-expected side of potatoes.

Even breakfast is better than ever. For that meal, it's hard to top the **Egg Shell,** open seven days. Generous portions here of eggs, home fries, pancakes. Blueberry muffins and fresh juices are specialties. Service is prompt so you won't be late to business appointments, and if you want to breakfast without anyone you know, there's a big family-style table at which you can sit and share with others. 1520 Blake in Lower Denver. 623-7555. Handy to the Oxford. Also located in Cherry Creek at Third and Josephine.

Another great breakfast is at the **Blue Bird Cafe,** right across the street from the Cherry Creek Egg Shell. The Blue Bird serves a mean huevos rancheros plate—eggs with tortillas, refried beans, hot sauce, and sour cream. Open seven days; moderate prices. 2406 E. Third Avenue. 333-4714.

For lunch, the burger joint of choice is **My Brother's Bar.** Not only do the hamburgers come with a variety of toppings, but My Brother's—a tavern where classical music is played in the background—is also a good place for meeting friends and for low-key business meetings. It's at the other end of the 15th Street viaduct from lower downtown. 2376 15th. 455-9991.

Another good lunch spot is the **Walnut Cafe** where you can get something reasonably healthful—they often have a fish special—but you can also order great huevos, too. A standard side option is banana bread. Be aware, this restaurant can be very crowded at noon with State Capitol workers. Moderate. 338 E. Colfax. 832-5108.

The **Broadway Grill** is a bit pricier, but a nice place to take yourself or a business associate for lunch. The architecture is an openwork of girders and glass, and the grill has a lovely terrace to enjoy on a balmy day. It's only about a block from the Brown Palace. Expensive. 1670 Broadway. 830-1670.

Denver is known for Mexican food, although some of the best spots are three-stool chili bars tucked away in tough or hard-to-find neighborhoods. But the **Blue Bonnet Cafe & Lounge** is right there on a main drag in an area you don't have to worry about. It's closed Sunday and deservedly crowded the rest of the time. 457 S. Broadway. 778-0147.

If you're staying out south at the Marriott or your business takes you toward Hampden Avenue, two spots in the Tamarac Square Shopping Center mall in the 7500 block of East Hampden are fine for lunch:

One is **Houlihan's,** with good food and service that doesn't feel like the chain operation it is. Houlihan's has a menu telling you the caloric content of the offerings. Moderate. 750-0100.

The other place, on the east side of the mall, is **Chili's.** The hamburgers are great and the French fries are perfect—cut thin, with the skins left on. A Texas-style chili aficionado we know says the chili there is the best of its kind in Denver. Inexpensive. 755-6668.

Dinner in Denver can be as formal or informal as you please. Some tried-and-true spots:

The **Normandy** is an expensive formal dining place with superb French cuisine. Many Denverites cite it as their favorite dinner experience in the city. Reservations necessary. 1515 Madison at Colfax. 321-3311.

The **Broker** makes a good setting for a serious business dinner. Start off with a free bowl of shrimp before choosing something American from the menu. Expensive. In an old bank building at 821 17th Street. 292-5065.

Chez Thoa is another dressy place that serves a relatively costly meal of intermingled French and Vietnamese cuisines. Presentation is as delightful as the food's flavor. Save room for the magnifique dessert menu. Reservations advised. 158 Filmore, Cherry Creek. 355-2323.

Cafe Promenade is a particularly good choice if you're used to dining late, as the chef stays until midnight. The Continental cuisine leans toward Italian. Moderate–expensive. 1424 Larimer Square. 893-2692.

Of the hotel restaurants mentioned earlier, we particularly favor **Le Profil** (in the Cambridge Club, 839-1704), the **Marquis** (in the Fairmont, 295-5825), and the **Palace Arms** (in the Brown Palace, 297-3111) for client entertaining during the dinner hour.

DENVER BY DAY

For a daytime view of the city, the best place to go is the **Colorado Capitol.** It's one of the most prominent structures on Denver's skyline, located between Colfax and 14th and Lincoln and Sherman streets. The view from the dome is striking, and the scaffoldlike staircase to the dome walkways, accessible from the third floor of the Capitol, is open from 9 A.M. until 4:30 P.M. on days when the building is open. The Colorado Capitol is open for rambling and tours Monday through Friday from 7 A.M. to 5:30 P.M. The legislature is in session there between January and March or April, although sometimes it meets as late as June or July, depending on how the issues are going.

If you're in town with a few hours to spare, take in any of the following attractions:

The **Denver Art Museum,** with both traveling art shows and a standing collection, is well worth visiting. This museum is particularly noted for its American Indian art and artifacts, but also features modern, Oriental, medieval-Renaissance, and textile collections. There's also a well-stocked gift shop. Tours of the highlights of the museum's collections begin at the information desk daily at 10:30 A.M. and 1:30 P.M. Closed Mondays. Admission charge. 14th at Bannock. 575-2793.

The **Denver Mint** offers free tours of its money-making operations at 15-minute intervals between 8 A.M. and 3 P.M. Monday through Friday. Tours take about 20 minutes, and often there's a wait. There's also a coin shop for numismatists on the premises with an entrance on Delaware Street. 320 Colfax at Cherokee Street. 844-3582.

The **Molly Brown House** is open seven days in the summer and closed Mondays in the winter. This museum is the restored and forever opulent home of the Unsinkable Molly Brown, a Colorado folk heroine, mining heiress, and survivor of the sinking of the *Titanic.* Admission charge. Free parking one block west at 13th and Logan. 1340 Pennsylvania Street. 832-1421.

The **Denver Zoo,** pretty respectable as far as zoos go, and getting better as some of the older cramped quarters for various animals are expanded and improved. Of special interest: a bird house, which has some rooms where birds fly freely, but are prevented from escaping by chains hanging bead-curtain-style in the doorways. Admission charge. East 23rd Avenue at Steel Street, northern side of City Park. 575-2754.

The **Denver Museum of Natural History** is for those who get the urge to see dinosaur bones reassembled or a well-done diorama depicting blue-footed boobies. This is also the site of Gates Planetarium (370-6351) and the IMAX Theater (370-6300), where specially made films show the wonders of the Grand Canyon or supply incredible camera angles from aircraft. The museum is open seven days, 9 A.M. to 5 P.M. 2001 Colorado Boulevard, eastern side of City Park. 370-6363.

Look in at the **Museum of Western Art,** which opened in 1984, to

see the western culture you'd expect to find in Denver. Artists represented include Frederic Remington and Georgia O'Keeffe. Admission
charge. 1727 Tremont Place. 296-1880.

THE SHOPPING SCENE

Although city boosters are agitating to bring in a big-name, nationally
known department store like Saks Fifth Avenue or Neiman-Marcus, shopping is not bad in Denver the way it is. There are plenty of places to
purchase any type of merchandise you need or want in both downtown
stores and at the various malls in the city's suburbs.

Tabor Center, near the northwestern terminus of the 16th Street
Mall, opened late in 1984, with a wide array of shops. Offerings range
from clothing stores like Brooks Brothers and Perkins-Shearer to vendors
of blue jeans, from furniture and records to cosmetics and shoes. The
third level has a bazaarlike food area with booths offering everything
from quick sushi to Italian ice cream. And the Bridge Market, an enclosed
bridge over the street spanned by the two-block complex, has stalls and
booths selling everything from art and jewelry to the delicate, intricate
textile items handmade by Southeast Asian Hmong refugees.

Writer Square, across 16th Street, is best for clothes and shoes
shopping in several stores, notably the Aspen Leaf. There's a Haagen-
Dazs ice-cream shop, too, if you can't do without your vanilla Swiss
almond fix.

Larimer Square, a block beyond Writer Square, is one of the first
ten areas to be reclaimed in Denver's renewal drive of the sixties and
seventies. Larimer Street was the city's skid row for years, but now it's
home to such stores as Ann Taylor and Laura Ashley, several art and
jewelry shops, various restaurants, and one of the finest fabric shops
we've found anywhere called Elfriede-Swan. Don't leave the area without
stopping at the Market for a spot of cappuccino and a couple of biscotti.
It's worthwhile to know that the early bird who gets to the Market when
it opens at 7 A.M. will get still-warm-from-the-oven croisssants.

Heading southeast up the 16th Street Mall, you'll find Denver's
most consistently high-quality big department store, the **Denver,** at 16th
and California. It started out as the Denver Dry Goods Co.

Farther up the mall, you'll find **Fashion Bar** at 16th and Tremont
Place, and catty-corner from it, the **May D&F Department Store.** They're
both worth a browse; Fashion Bar has some remarkable sales.

Denver's other reasonably close-in shopping area is **Cherry Creek,**
reachable by taking Speer Boulevard southeast until it turns into 1st
Avenue and continuing to the intersection of University, or taking Colorado Boulevard south and turning west on 1st, 2nd, 3rd, or 4th.

Cherry Creek's a good place just to park and stroll for the afternoon. Again, the variety of stores and range of prices are wide. Carrick's

clearly caters to big money, while across the street at **Mr. Bud's Pappagallo** it's possible to get a fine silk dress on sale for around $50. No one in Cherry Creek should miss the **Tattered Cover**, a well-stocked bookstore.

Tamarac Square, a shopping center on Hampden mentioned earlier, also has a variety of good stores.

Old South Gaylord Street is a notable place to spend a quiet afternoon shopping. It may be reached by driving south of University Boulevard to Mississippi and turning west two blocks to Gaylord.

DENVER BY NIGHT

Denver is not much of a theater town, but if you crave this kind of an experience while you're here, check out the activity at the **Denver Center for the Performing Arts** on the west side at 14th and Curtis streets. The **Denver Center Theater Company** on the premises schedules about a dozen plays from December through March. 893-4100.

Also at the Denver Center, the **Denver Symphony**—with Philippe Entremont coming as chief conductor in 1986–87—plays at Boettcher Concert Hall. Season is roughly from mid-September to mid-Arpil. Pops concerts continue until June. The symphony also gives free concerts in city parks in the summer and sometimes during the winter at Boettcher. 592-7777.

Tickets are also available through **Datatix**. 988-6712.

For a concert-style setting, go to the **Rainbow Music Hall**. At Monaco and Evans. 753-1800. They use **Selec-a-Seat** as their telephone ticket outlet. 778-6691.

Denver's **movie houses** include a double theater in Cherry Creek and a multiplex in Tamarac Square. Reprise and art film houses include the Denver Center Cinema in the Denver Center for the Performing Arts (892-0983); the Ogden (935 E. Colfax, 832-4500; be careful in this neighborhood and try to park close to the theater); the Esquire (6th at Downing, 733-5757), and the Vogue (1465 S. Pearl Street, 777-2544).

LATE-NIGHT DENVER

Jaded Denverites sometimes complain they can hear the crunching of concrete as the sidewalks are rolled up at night. But if you know where to go, you'll find that Denver boogies until 2 A.M., when by-the-drink liquor sales end—and in some cases, even after.

Wazee Supper Club and Lounge is known as an in spot and is so crowded Friday or Saturday nights you won't want to stick it out too long in a solo stop-off. Wazee Street under the 15th Avenue viaduct. 623-9518.

The **Comedy Works** features stand-up comics. It's a good place to go alone and still blend in. Cover charge. Reservations necessary. In the basement of the Granite Building, 15th at 1460 Larimer. 595-3637.

The **Chrysler** is a dressy, classy night spot, atop the Neusteters Building. The bar is packed most nights with suit-and-tied men and sparkling-dressed women. This is a good place to finish off an evening that begins at Chez Thoa (see "Dining Out"). Dinner served Saturday and Sunday; open seven days. 2955 E. First Avenue in Cherry Creek. 355-2955.

The **Corner Room** at the Oxford Hotel (see "At Your Service") is a stylish and comfortable setting for jazz.

If you feel like dancing, check out Glendale, an enclave surrounded by Denver that's exclusively rooted in the pursuit of youthful partying. Just drive the roads in the area and you'll easily spot several large-scale nightclubs like **Thrills** (333-5855), **Confetti** (320-0117), and **Journey South** (377-2701).

Feeling bohemian? Head over to **Union Station** where the fare is usually rock and ranges from the inspired nuttiness of Robin and the Bedouins to the jazz-rock fusion music of the Bruce Odland Big Band. Cover charge. 1701 Wynkoop Street. 623-5806.

AT LEISURE

Denver is one of the most sophisticated, yet earthly, cities in the country, so take advantage of it on your off time. Discover the city, or take a day or weekend trip into the nearby mountains and ski, hike, or just relax.

Day-Tripping

Central City is a mining town where curio shops thrive and the lovely old Opera House still presents opera each summer. It is accessible on Highway 6 west of Denver, about an hour away.

Boulder, an hour northwest of Denver on Highway 36, is a bustling college city, home of the University of Colorado. The downtown mall has unique shops and it is a great place to stroll.

Colorado Springs is a little over an hour from Denver to the south, on Interstate 25. This high tech center is the site of the U.S. Air Force Academy, some great hotels (such as the exclusive Broadmoor), and the **Cheyenne Mountain Zoo,** where the giraffes chew peaceably a few hundred feet above NORAD, the United States' underground command center for defense against nuclear attack.

And of course there are the **ski slopes;** Colorado has more than 32 of them. For complete information on skiing, contact Colorado Ski Country USA at 1410 Grant St., Suite A-201, Denver, CO 80203, 837-0793. Keystone is the closest ski resort to Denver, only two hours away.

Want to relax your tired aching body? Try **Glenwood Springs,** near Aspen, about four hours from Denver. This small town, not known to many outside of Colorado, has the nation's largest hot springs pool. A tube-shaped slide is an added attraction.

During the summer, outdoor concerts are held at a natural rock amphitheater, **Red Rocks,** near the town of Morrison. Red Rocks can be reached via the I-70 exit off of Highway 6 westbound. Tickets to Red Rocks events are available, at this writing, through Select-a-Seat at 778-6691.

Around Town

There is also plenty to do in Denver proper. The new **16th Street Mall** is a mile-long, tree-lined pedestrian path with department stores, boutiques, and restaurants.

Nearby, between 17th and 26th streets, **City Park** includes 314 acres of lawns, lakes and gardens, the Denver Zoo, the Museum of Natural History with the huge IMAX theater.

Larimer Square is a restored section of one of the city's oldest streets, the 1400 block of Larimer. A free walking-tour map is available to this collection of arcades, courtyards, gas lamps, art galleries, and shops. Carriage rides can also be arranged. (See "The Shopping Scene.")

And if history is to your liking, try the **Colorado Historical Society** at 1300 Broadway. This $22 million facility traces the history of the Indians, the gold rush, and settlers of Colorado. Admission is $2.50; call 866-3682 for more information.

Sunday Customs

One of Denver's finest restaurants, the **Wellshire Inn,** is renowned for its Sunday brunch. It looks like it is right out of a Shakespeare play. Be sure to make reservations at least three or four days in advance by calling 759-3333.

Other good brunch choices include: **The Moulin Rouge** at the Fairmont Hotel, 1450 Welton St., 295-1200; and the **Viceroy India Restaurant,** 901 Larimer St., 629-7420, where authentic Indian food is mixed with the natural flavor of mesquite cooking. The Viceroy is located in the Tivoli, a restored brewery, and has a spectacular view of the city.

Spectator Sports

Denver has the **Broncos,** a perennial favorite in the AFC West. When at home, they play at Mile High Stadium; but don't be disappointed if you can't get tickets—the stadium is usually booked solid by season ticket holders. No wonder, when their defense is known as "The Orange Crush." For ticket information call 433-7466.

In basketball, the Denver **Nuggets** shoot their home hoops in McNichols Sports Arena. Call 893-6700 for ticket information.

Active Sports

Denverites like to spend a great deal of time outdoors, and hiking in the nearby mountains is a favorite pastime. We don't, however, recommend going alone. Try the **Colorado Mountain Club,** 922-8315; this organization sponsors hikes and white-water rafting. And they will also give you the lowdown about exercising in the high altitude.

In the city **Cheesman Park,** on 13th Street, is a good place to run or saunter during daylight hours. It is a hangout for gays, mostly male, both day and night.

The John F. Kennedy Golf Course, at 10500 E. Hampden, is a public course. The fee is $6 for nine holes. Call 751-0311 for information.

HOTELS

1 Dearborn Inn
2 Hyatt Regency Dearborn
3 Michigan Inn
4 Omni International
5 Hotel Pontchartrain
6 Hotel St. Regis
7 Shorecrest Motor Inn
8 Somerset Inn
9 Southfield Hilton
10 Westin Hotel

LANDMARKS

A Bus Terminal
B Civic Center
C Detroit Institute of Arts
D Greek Town
E Greenfield Village/
   Henry Ford Museum
F Hart Plaza
G Historical Museum

H Millender Center
I New Center
J Police Dept.
K Renaissance Center
L Medical Center
M Science Center
N Union Station
O Visitor Information Center

DETROIT

GETTING YOUR BEARINGS

Detroit has a distorted national image. Don't let it put you off. Like new-model cars of older editions that roll off Motown's assembly lines, America's sixth largest city is in the midst of an ambitious makeover. Major developments in recent years have infused a once-dying downtown with new vitality. First-time visitors as well as those of us returning after an absence are amazed at the city's new look and feel.

Detroit's resurgence began in the late seventies with the Renaissance Center, a $365 million hotel/office/shopping complex. In the shadows of this gleaming signature on the riverfront, whole new neighborhoods have sprung up while old ones are revitalizing.

To the east of RenCen is Rivertown, also known as the Warehouse District, where funky taverns and trendy eateries are blooming among old buildings and railroad tracks. Across Jefferson Avenue is Bricktown, a growing collection of restaurants and shops in turn-of-the-century buildings.

A few blocks away, Greektown, an area long the nerve center of Detroit night life, grew even livelier in the summer of 1985 with the opening of Trappers Alley, a festival marketplace à la Baltimore's Harborplace and Boston's Quincy Market. Housed in five buildings dating back more than a century (including its namesake, an 1853 fur trading establishment), five skylit levels house more than sixty eateries, fashion boutiques, and gift shops. Nearby, however, Detroit's business and financial district still clears out by 6 P.M.; we hardly ever see anyone strolling the deserted streets.

A late addition to Detroit's new face is the $81 million Millender Center, a two-square-block complex of apartments, offices and shops linked by skywalk to the RenCen across the street. Its centerpiece: the Omni International Hotel, new in 1985 and geared to corporate travelers.

Whether coincidental or not, at least a half dozen other Detroit and suburban hotels are sprucing themselves up, undergoing multi-million-dollar renovations to keep up with the new kid on the block. Hart Plaza is between the city's massive convention center (Metro Detroit ranks ninth nationally in attracting convention business) and the RenCen. It's a multilevel urban park and people place, perfect on weekdays for brown-bag lunches.

Logistically, Detroit is something like Los Angeles—everything tends to be spread out and scattered, but within about a half-hour's drive of downtown. A word to the wise: references to Detroit usually mean both the city and its suburbs, so be sure to find out exactly where in the metropolitan area your business will be conducted. For instance, if your work is with Ford Motor Company, you'll probably head straight for the firm's headquarters in Dearborn, about 20 minutes from downtown. Southfield, another outlying area, also draws its share of corporate business.

Motown in total is very much a family town. Some 72 percent of its homes are owner occupied, more than anywhere else in the nation. That means most business is conducted over lunch or breakfast. Top honchos in Detroit are almost all men; women are breaking into the ranks, but they are yet to be included in the power clique of movers and shakers. We have found, however, that women in the upper echelon who come into town to conduct business are taken seriously as long as they remain professional.

When it comes to safety, we must emphasize that this city's comeback hasn't been easy, and is certainly far from complete. Crime remains a problem, just as in any large metropolitan area, so stay away from places off the beaten track. Some say the compact downtown business district is an okay place to walk, but others warn that it is not. We say to walk in areas that feel right for you, with common sense your constant companion. Be aware, though, that since the suburbs play an active role to many coming here for business, you can't expect to make walking a high priority once you've left downtown. In suburban Detroit there's really no place to stroll.

In the last few years, the city has been hit by some body blows from which the collective psyche is still reeling. Downtown's premier shopping emporium, J. L. Hudson, a store that was as much a part of Detroiters' Christmas as Santa Claus and snow, closed its doors and left the central business district without a major department store. Two other Detroit institutions also left town: Stroh's Brewery, bottlers of a beloved hometown beer, and Vernor's, makers of a gingery sweet pop used to sooth the sore throats of generations of Michigan youngsters.

And, even as spirits soared to euphoric levels with the Detroit Tigers' World Series victory in 1984, disturbances afterward by rowdy fans marred the celebration and once again dragged down the city's national image. Those developments left Detroiters down but not out. For like its native son, Joe Louis, this is a tough town with a fighting spirit.

WHAT TO WEAR

Detroit women are not as fashion conscious as New Yorkers or Bostonians. High-style dressers mix with come-as-you-are types at many public gatherings. Individuality is okay here. Generally, however, corporate business calls for conservative dress: your basic skirted suits and tailored shirts or blouses, perhaps a scarf or bow at the neck, and pumps. A softer look—traditional classic dress with jacket—is also acceptable. Just remember—in Detroit, quality is the byword. If your clothing looks expensive but understated, you can't go wrong. In jewelry, less is more—perhaps a strand of pearls or simple pieces in gold.

WEATHER WATCH

If you don't like the weather, wait a minute because it'll change. That old adage about Michigan's volatile weather, though exaggerated, is telling. Best bet is to come prepared for anything. Rainstorms can blow up suddenly in Detroit, though there's usually ample warning (often wrong) from a pack of local meteorologists. Bring a raincoat and layered clothing, and you'll be all set. Michigan has short but sweet three-month summers and long, blustery winters. Temperatures are not as extreme as in many places. In the summer it's generally comfortable and in the low 80s. Winter temperatures often dip to the teens; be prepared for cold and snow.

GETTING THERE

Detroit Metropolitan Airport, the nation's 17th largest, is among the more convenient and accessible. It is located midway between Detroit and Ann Arbor along I-94. The airport (942-3685) has two domestic terminals serving 22 scheduled carriers and one international terminal serving 3 carriers and several charters. The leading carrier is Republic (283-8910), which has made Detroit its major hub. Other major airlines include American (965-1000), Northwest (962-2002), Delta (355-3200), and United (336-9000).

Ground transportation booths are in both north and south terminals where buses, vans, and charters are available to take you anywhere from Windsor, Canada, to Lansing. The cheapest, most expedient transportation is Shortway Jetport Express (357-5800) for $6. Leaves every half hour for downtown, several suburban hotels, and points beyond. No reservations required.

Taxi service is about $22 and 20 minutes in light traffic to downtown, a few dollars more or less to suburban locations. Best bet is Southfield Cab Service (356-1090). Call as soon as you leave the plane and before you get your luggage. Make reservations before arrival with Pacific Cab, 541-6880, or Somerset Cab, 689-9090.

Car Rentals

Five rental car agencies are based at the airport:

Hertz	729-5200
Avis	942-3450
Budget	258-5877
Dollar	942-1905
National	941-5030

Other nearby agencies include Thrifty, 946-7830; Sears, 258-6160; and Holiday/Payless, 772-2700.

GETTING AROUND

Unfortunately, Detroit's public transportation leaves a lot to be desired. There is no subway system, and city buses tend to run behind schedule. But this is, after all, Motown, and Detroiters are used to hopping in their cars and driving; we feel it's wise in most cases to do as the natives do. A rental is especially the way to go if your business takes you suburb-hopping (see "Getting There").

The freeway system can be jammed for an hour or so each morning and evening, but nowhere near the impossible gridlock develops here as in Los Angeles and other major cities. Delays won't be long— the coast is usually clear by 9:30 A.M. and 5:45 P.M.

If you're based downtown or in the New Center area, where General Motors and Burroughs are headquartered, taxis are your best bet. They're generally available at the Hotel Pontchartrain, Westin Hotel, Omni, or around the Greyhound Bus Terminal (963-9840). Otherwise, call Checker, 963-7000; American, 833-3800; Detroit Cab, 898-0600; City, 833-7060; or Radio, 491-2600. Citywide, fares are 90 cents to get in the cab, and 90 cents each additional mile.

Providing bus transportation is a Three Center minibus, which links the Cultural Center, New Center, and Medical Center areas. Phone DOT, 933-1300. Regular buses are operated by SEMTA (Southeastern Michigan Transportation Authority), 962-5515, 800/462-5161, providing service to the suburbs.

GETTING FAMILIAR

Metropolitan Detroit Convention & Visitors Bureau
100 Renaissance Center   Detroit, MI 48243
Suite 1950   313/259-4333

If you're already in town, stop by the **Visitor Information Center** at 2 E. Jefferson Avenue. Detroit, MI 48226, 313/567-1170.

For recorded information on what's happening in Detroit, call the **What's Line,** 313/298-6262, and get the lowdown for the week.

Current attractions are listed in the Friday section of the *Detroit News* and the *Detroit Free Press. Monthly Detroit* and *Metropolitan Detroit* are city magazines competing for the upscale crowd. They offer extensive restaurant as well as entertainment listings.

Quick Calls

AREA CODE 313	Time 472-1212
Weather 1-976-1212	Police 224-4000

AT YOUR SERVICE

Westin Hotel

Renaissance Center   Toll-free reservations: 800/228-3000
Jefferson at St. Antoine   Local number: 568-8000
Detroit, MI 48243   Telex: 755156

You can't miss this hotel. The biggest in town, this 73-story contemporary property is the centerpiece of the Renaissance Center, Detroit's signature on the riverfront. A bustling downtown hub for corporate and convention travelers, the hotel, built in 1978, features 1,400 modern rooms, freshly redone in mauves and blues. Double locks and safety chains on all doors plus a battalion of security guards posted throughout the RenCen complex make this a secure place for women to stay. It's convenient, too: word processing facilities are available and typewriters may be rented for a nominal fee. In fact, the hotel bills itself as "a city within a city" and boasts that guests need not go outside the RenCen complex, which will complete a $22 million renovation by 1988 that we hope will make the labyrinthine floor plan easier to negotiate. Some 70 retail outlets include beauty salons, a copy center, movie theaters, and other services.

Cocktail pods around the hotel are good places to sip drinks and people-watch. Restaurants in the hotel are **LaFontaine,** one of Detroit's leading dining rooms, and **The Summit,** whose revolving roof-top vantage point makes it a good place for drinks. **Cafe Renaissance** offers moderately priced Continental fare under huge yellow umbrellas and features a large salad bar and dinner music. Bars include **D.J.'s,** a loud disco with a deejay, and **The Galleria,** a more secluded spot.

Hotel	Concierge	Executive Floor	No-Smoking Rooms	Fitness Facilities	Pool	24-Hour Room Service	Restaurant for Client Entertaining	Extra-Special Amenities	Electronic Key System	Business/Secretarial Services	Checkout Time	Frequent Guest Program	Business Traveler Program	Average Single Rate
Dearborn Inn	●		●		●	●	Early American Room				12 noon		Corporate program	$ 70–$73 / $ 62–$70 corp.
Hyatt Regency Dearborn	●	●		●	●	●	Giulio's & Sons			●	12 noon	Gold Passport program	Corporate program	$ 95
Michigan Inn	●	●	●	●	●		Bistro				1 p.m.			$104–$109 / $ 99 corp.
Omni International	●	●		●	●	●	333 East	●	●	●	1 p.m.		ESP	$110 / $100 corp.
Hotel Pontchartrain	●			●	●	●	Elaine's	●	●	●	1 p.m.	Pontchartrain Plus		$ 99 / $104
Hotel St. Regis	●					●	Restaurant St. Regis	●		●	1 p.m.			$135 / $109 corp.
Somerset Inn		●		●	●		West End				12 noon		Somerset Club	$ 86 / $ 73 corp.
Southfield Hilton		●	●		●		Loopholes				12 noon			$ 84 / $ 94
Westin Hotel		●	●	●	●	●	Summit			●	1 p.m.	Romance Package		$120

Hotel Pontchartrain
2 Washington Boulevard   Toll-free reservations: outside Michigan
Detroit, MI 48226   800/537-6624
Local number: 965-0200
Telex: 8102215227

A top pick for those conducting business in downtown Detroit, this towering glass-walled hotel has 420 contemporary rooms offering views of the Detroit River. More personal than the Westin Hotel down the block, the Pontch offers attentive service with aristocratic panache. Expect such touches as twice daily maid service, turn-down service, pre-registration and complimentary early-riser coffee service in the lobby. Secretarial services, interpreters for French, German, and Spanish, typewriter rentals with advance notice, and telex are available.

Drinks and afternoon tea are served in the lobby bar and the airy lobby lounge. The main-level dining room serves fine Continental cuisine.

Hotel St. Regis
3071 W. Grand Boulevard   Toll-free reservations: outside Michigan
Detroit, MI 48202   800/223-5560
Local number: 873-3000
Telex: 235500

A $3.2 million renovation in 1982 transformed this small hotel into one that fits the classic European mold. The 117 rooms are pleasant and comfortable, done in peach, navy, and beige with loveseats and floral draperies. Geared to the corporate traveler and located in the New Center area next to the General Motors Building, rooms are great for women conducting business with sleeping areas separate from the lounge/work area. Many amenities topped by a house physician on call.

The **Restaurant St. Regis** features French/Continental cuisine with a Cordon Bleu–trained chef. Very good for a classy business breakfast and Sunday brunch. Outdoor cafe pleasant but noisy for lunch. Bar is very discreet, tucked away in a lobby/lounge area that looks like a living room. Afternoon tea is served there, followed by a caviar bar during cocktail hour.

Omni International Hotel
333 E. Jefferson at Brush   Toll-free reservations: 800/THE-OMNI
Detroit, MI 48226   Local number: 222-7700

Opened in 1985, this 20-story downtown hotel offers 258 spacious rooms (including 18 suites) with personalized state-of-the-art service for the corporate traveler. Linked by skywalk to the RenCen across the street, this first-rate hotel is part of an ambitious two-square-block, $81 million development (including apartments, shops, and restaurants) that is part of Detroit's efforts to revitalize downtown. Small and intimate, almost residential in character, the Omni features such amenities as concierge, credit card locks, full-length mirror, valet stand, scale, makeup mirror, and a tiny TV and telephone in the bathroom.

Tastefully decorated in shades of mauve with a mirrored ceiling, the lobby features a bar with grand piano. Light snacks are available. The restaurant, **333 East,** is decidedly upscale and stylish, featuring new American cuisine.

Suburbs

Southfield Hilton

17017 W. 9 Mile Road	Toll-free reservations: 800/445-8667
Southfield, MI 48075	Local number: 557-4800

Formerly the Sheraton Southfield, this 400-room contemporary hotel attracts corporate clients and is located across from Northland Shopping Center. A $3.3 million renovation transformed the hotel; it's now decorated in burgundy and light gray. Very soothing.

Both the restaurant, **L. J. Loopholes,** and bar, the **Little Bar,** are patronized by newscasters and technicians from a television station across the street. **Yesterday's,** its nightclub, tends to be a singles mating place.

Michigan Inn

16400 J. L. Hudson Drive	Toll-free reservations: in Michigan 800/
Southfield, MI 48075	482-3440; outside Michigan 800/
	521-1709
	Local number: 559-6500
	Telex: 234058

A bit quieter and more distinctive than its neighbor, the Hilton. The lobby and restaurants in the hotel, built in 1975, have been completely remodeled. A complete health club here is so complete there's even a putting green.

The **Bistro Inn** is a coffee shop on the property; **The Benchmark** features French gourmet cuisine and has a quiet bar. Don't try to conduct business in the **Red Parrot Lounge,** a high-energy, top-40 disco with deejay, clowns, and mimes.

Dearborn Inn

20301 Oakwood Boulevard	Toll-free numbers: in Michigan 800/221-
Dearborn, MI 48124	7237; outside Michigan 800/221-7236
	Local number: 271-2700

Located across from Greenfield Village, this elegant Georgian colonial-style inn has 179 comfortable rooms of which no two are alike. Furnishings and decor are tasteful early American reproductions; colors are Wedgwood blue and muted peach. Guests can use the Dearborn Athletic Club for $3, and tee times can be arranged at the Warren Valley Golf Course nearby.

Formal dining in the **Early American Room** where a harpist plays on week nights. Dinner dancing on Saturday under crystal chandeliers. Also featured are a Seafood Fantasy on Friday and a brunch Sunday.

Good coffee shop, the **Ten Eyck Tavern**. **The Snug** is a cozy wood-paneled bar, and the **Golden Eagle Lounge** offers nightly piano entertainment.

Hyatt Regency Dearborn

2 Fairlane Town Center
Dearborn, MI 48126

Toll-free reservations: 800/228-9000
Local number: 593-1234
Telex: 235613

A crescent-shaped contemporary hotel with bronze mirrored walls just a hubcap's throw from Ford Motor Company. Centered by a 16-story atrium foyer with lighted glass elevators, this attractive inn, built in 1975, has been redone in sea-mist green with mauve highlights and neutral accents. The Hyatt's 768 rooms are connected by a monorail to the Fairlane Town Center shopping mall, whose nearly 200 shops include beauty salons, drug stores, department and high fashion stores. Perhaps because many of the fashion executives, consultants, and buyers are frequent guests, the Hyatt is attentive to women travelers, who may preregister without a lot of fuss at the desk. Amenities include Crabtree and Evelyn toiletries, hair dryers, makeup mirrors. The hotel has an indoor heated swimming pool, sauna, whirlpool, and lobby concierge. Telex, light typing, and other business services can be arranged and personal computers obtained. Security is good in this hotel, which utilizes a key system on room doors.

Kafay's is the hotel's moderately priced coffee shop on the second level. **Guilio & Sons** does a booming lunch and dinner business with its homemade pastas, meat dishes, and incredibly lavish salad and dessert bars that provide meals in themselves. The award-winning **La Rotisserie** offers fine gourmet dining and gracious service in an elegant atmosphere; good place for Sunday brunch. Reservations suggested. Bars: **LePrelude,** adjoining La Rotisserie, offers drinks in a subdued, low-key atmosphere. **Guilio's,** an after-work spot for Ford Motor Company types and other nearby office workers, is a bit more preppy. The top floor **Rotunda** boasts good views and live music and dancing in the late evening.

Somerset Inn

2601 W. Big Beaver
Troy, MI 48084

Local number: 643-7800

Done up in black and gray art deco style, a black glass facade leads you through an oversized lobby. The 250 rooms include an executive wing with slightly larger rooms overlooking an outdoor pool. Guests have privileges at an executive Vic Tanny next door. The inn is next to Somerset Mall, the Detroit area's most fashionable shopping mall, anchored by Saks and Bonwit Teller, and includes Bally, Mark Cross, Godiva Chocolatier, Claire Pearone, and other chi-chi shops.

The hotel's art deco theme is carried through in the **Bar and Grill,** a moderately priced Continental restaurant with striking pink lights around the bar. The **West End** serves fresh seafood and pasta dishes in a fine dining atmosphere.

ON A BUDGET

Hotel

Shorecrest Motor Inn
1316 E. Jefferson   Toll-free reservations: 800/992-9616
Detroit, MI 48207   Local number: 568-3000
Affordable and accessible, this two-story lodging facility (faintly reminiscent of a Days Inn) is just two blocks east of the RenCen. 54 rooms, airport shuttle, Clique restaurant, outdoor parking. The motel generally has a 90 percent occupancy, so book early. Crisply decorated in basic grays, reds and blacks. Singles start at $36.

Restaurants

For a nice business meal that won't break your bank, head for Greektown, the few spreading blocks on Monroe Street between Beaubien and St. Antoine.

One favorite is the **New Hellas.** Unfortunately, because this Greek eaterie is so good, it attracts crowds. Tell your associates to expect to stand in line.

A quieter atmosphere, more conducive to making deals, can be found at the **Old Parthenon,** next door. The food's slightly better here too.

The **Pegasus Taverna** at Trappers Alley across the street offers trendier decor and more Greek fare.

The **Blue Nile** is another pleasant restaurant, but it's not Greek, it's Ethiopian. For adventuresome diners; you eat with your fingers.

DINING OUT

A good deal of ethnic influence shows up in metropolitan Detroit's restaurants, whose diversity, quality, and level of sophistication stack up favorably with any large city. There is enough variety and creative approach to appease even the most jaded palate, a fact that may surprise visitors with a preconceived notion that Detroit is just a meat-and-potatoes factory town.

For Detroit, we've defined moderate as any meal up to $12 for lunch, and from $20 to $30 for dinner. Above that is expensive, below is inexpensive.

Downtown

The **London Chop House** is the place we choose when we are on an unlimited expense account with the aim to impress. Superb Continental cuisine routinely draws rave reviews. Also has the area's largest wine cellar. You may spot auto magnate Henry Ford II or any of Michigan's business, political, and social elite dining in Booth 1. Bar is good place to hobnob with celebs. Phone reservations ahead; name will appear on matches. Very expensive. 155 W. Congress. 962-0278.

La Fontaine is one of the best places in town for a power lunch. Fine nouvelle cuisine, attentive service, and at dinner, a fresh red rose. Soothing, subdued lighting, marble fountain centerpiece, beveled mirrored walls, burgundy banquettes and chairs. Expensive. RenCen, Promenade level. 568-8110.

Caucus Club is the dark, clubby sister to the Chop House across the street. Light and trendy fare matches decor. Expensive. 150 W. Congress. 965-4970.

The **Money Tree** is reasonably priced, offering a quietly bustling ambience and creative Continental fare. Our pick for the best place for a business breakfast or lunch. Quiches, crepes, pastas, peasant soups, tempting salads, luscious desserts. Crowded at lunchtime. Small outdoor cafe open in the summers. Great Bloody Marys after business hours at the bar. Local journalists gather here to gripe. Moderate. 333 W. Fort. 961-2445.

Pontchartrain Wine Cellars' intimate French/European style (home of the first cold duck served in the United States) makes this our personal favorite. Soothing ambience, wonderful black bread, outstanding veal and seafood, served with pommes Delphine (lightly fried potato puffs— you'll love them). Mouth-watering oysters wrapped in bacon, and pot au chocolate for dessert. Excellent wines. Moderate. 234 Larned at Shelby. 963-1785.

At **Joe Muir's,** they line up outside. This institution, open since 1929, serves the nation's largest fresh fish selection. Expensive. 2000 Gratiot. 567-1088.

Van Dyke Place is east of downtown in a neighborhood of lovely old homes on the National Register of Historic Places. In fact, this is a restored Victorian mansion and one of Detroit's best restaurants. Your business buddies will be impressed—if you can get reservations. Valet parking. Expensive. 649 Van Dyke, in Indian Village. 821-2620.

Xochimilcho on the southwest edge of downtown in a slowly revitalizing neighborhood (becoming known as Mexican Town) is a fun and cheap place to eat. The neighborhood's not great, but the food is the best Mexican fare in town. Draws a lively crowd that spills into the parking lot sipping Margaritas while waiting for tables on busy nights. Bulging botanas with green olives and avocados. Inexpensive. 3409 Bagley. 843-0179.

New Center Area

A good bet is the **Restaurant St. Regis** in the St. Regis Hotel.
Traffic Jam and Snug (T.J.'s) draws a mixed crowd of Wayne State

University instructors, medical center professionals, artsy types, and office workers for flans, sandwiches, and creative vegetarian fare. Great desserts. A comfortable kind of place. Can be noisy at lunch. Moderate. 511 W. Canfield at 2d. 831-9470.

Suburbs

Food at the **Golden Mushroom** is by award-winning chef Milos Cihelka, and it's always wonderful. Attraction for a power lunch: health specials, made without fats, butter, or wine. Roasted free-range chicken with miniature vegetables delicious. Bustling atmosphere at lunch, a bit more subdued at dinner. Expensive. 18100 W. 10th Mile, Southfield. 559-4230.

Midtown Cafe is *the* place to see and be seen. Haughty waiters. Salads, open-face sandwiches, cappuccino, and pastries in late afternoon. Moderate-expensive. 139 S. Woodward, Birmingham. 642-1133.

Phoenicia is the place to go if you've never tried Arabic food. Chicken marinated and grilled, lamb in every form imaginable. You'll make return trips to Detroit for the rice pudding with honey, walnuts, and a hint of rose water. Moderate-expensive. 588 S. Woodward, Birmingham. 644-3122.

DETROIT BY DAY

For an overview of Motown, go to the top of the Westin Hotel; $2 for nonguests who want to look at the city below.

Metropolitan Detroit's best-known tourist attraction, drawing more than a million visitors a year, is **Greenfield Village/Henry Ford Museum** in Dearborn. Automotive pioneer Henry Ford had a penchant for collecting Americana; he bought up entire historical buildings, including Thomas Edison's Menlo Park laboratory and the Wright brothers' bicycle shop. They have been reassembled in this 260-acre historical village, where chatty craftspeople demonstrate vanishing skills. The museum— 14 acres of American technology—includes a prized collection of steam locomotives and early automobiles. Admission to museum or village: $8. Dearborn location is northeast of Metro Airport, off the Southfield Expressway. A SENTA bus from the RenCen runs directly to Greenfield Village. 271-1620.

The **Detroit Institute of Arts** celebrated its centennial in 1985; we consider this one of America's leading comprehensive art museums. Its extensive permanent collection of some 40,000 works in more than 100 galleries includes the renowned Diego Rivera murals depicting life in industrial society and the second largest Dutch-Flemish exhibit in the United States. Free admission. 5200 Woodward Avenue. 833-7000.

The **Detroit Historical Museum,** across Woodward, features changing displays and, in the basement, a reconstructed street scene that takes visitors from the 1840s to the 20th century. Admission $1. 833-1805.

The **Detroit Science Center** on John R and Farnsworth just behind the Institute of Arts features hands-on exhibits and a space theater that lifts you right off the screen. Bring Dramamine! Admission $4. 577-8400.

Belle Isle, the nation's largest urban island park, is just a few minutes from downtown. A sometime retreat for weary office workers, it is popular with jugglers, kite-flyers, and families. If you've a few hours to spare, visit the Conservatory, Aquarium, or Drossin Great Lakes Museum on Strand Drive (267-6440) for a look at shopping history and nautical artifacts. Also here: the Belle Isle Zoo, featuring an elevated walkway and, in season, lots of baby animals. Admission: $2. 398-0900.

The **Detroit Zoo** was the first in the nation to display animals in natural-looking habitats without bars. After recovering from a budget slump and other management troubles, it recently refurbished a neat penguinarium whose residents are guaranteed to put a smile on your face. First-class aviary and reptile house here, too. Admission $3.50 plus $2 for parking. 10 Mile Road, west of Woodward, Royal Oak. 398-0900.

The **Cranbrook** educational complex in Birmingham, 18 miles north of Detroit, includes a prestigious art school and museum, planetarium, and science museum. In March, maple trees are tapped for syrup on the lovely 300-acre grounds. Admission $1.50. 645-3142.

THE SHOPPING SCENE

Just so you're not disappointed, we must warn you shopping isn't anyone's key motivation for visiting Detroit. However, there certainly are places where your charge cards can get a workout.

Downtown, at 532 Brush near the RenCen, **Lynn Portnoy** has built a reputation for dressing women in smart and affordable career and casual wear in her shop of the same name.

The **World of Shops** complex in the RenCen offers everything from gourmet kitchen items to leather goods and clothing.

Trappers Alley is a fun place to browse and buy novelty items. Don't miss the singing fudgemakers at the **Fudgery.**

Eastern Market, an open-air marketplace operating in Detroit since 1892, is at the edge of downtown on Russell near Gratiot, east of the RenCen. You'll recognize it by the bright graphics of fruits and veggies on the terminal buildings. For variety, you can't beat the Rocky Peanut Company.

Values in china, crystal and porcelains are available across the river at **Shanfield's-Meyers,** 188 Ouellette Avenue, Windsor, Canada.

Suburban malls are the place to go to cover a lot of ground with limited time. Best are **Fairlane Mall** in Dearborn and **Eastland** in East Detroit, both with J. L. Hudson department stores. **Somerset Mall** in Troy is Detroit's most fashionable place to shop (see "At Your Service").

Downtown Birmingham, where ultrapunks rub shoulders with the Ralph Lauren crowd, offers the Detroit area's most pleasant shopping in upscale shops and charming cafes.

Don't overlook the museum gift shops.

DETROIT BY NIGHT

The **Detroit Symphony Orchestra,** under the baton of Gunther Herbig, performs at Ford Auditorium, 20 Auditorium Drive. 567-9000 for ticket information.

Symphony concerts and other entertainment in summer at the outdoor **Meadow Brook Music Festival.** Rochester. 377-3316.

The **Renaissance City Chamber Players,** a professional chamber orchestra, performs 12 concerts at each of three sites: Varner Hall at Oakland University in Rochester, Orchestra Hall and First Baptist Church in Ann Arbor. Call 62-MUSIC.

The **Detroit Symphony Chamber Orchestra** has a series of Friday evening and Sunday afternoon concerts in Orchestra Hall. 3711 Woodward. 833-3700.

Major stops on the Detroit-area theater scene include:

Fisher Theater is Detroit's version of Broadway, featuring Broadway-bound hits and touring Broadway shows. It's located in the Fisher Building, an Albert Kahn–designed building with three-story rotunda, arcades, and mural ceilings. 3031 W. Grand Boulevard. 872-1000.

Masonic Temple Theater also books national touring shows. 500 Temple. 832-2232; 832-6648.

Birmingham Theatre presents mainly off-Broadway shows. 211 S. Woodward. 644-3533.

Attic Theater, in the New Center Theatre across from the Fisher Building, offers the best in off-Broadway plays and works of new playwrights. Thursday through Sunday. 3d and W. Grand Boulevard. 875-8284.

LATE-NIGHT DETROIT

With its Motown roots and jazz tradition, Detroit is a hotbed for contemporary music. Crowds are so enthusiastic many performers say they would rather play here than anywhere else, according to a local Detroit newspaper critic. A few suggestions:

If you're here in the summer, do try to land tickets for **P'Jazz,** a popular series of performances with some name entertainers on the outdoor terrace of the Hotel Pontchartrain. It's a great place to mellow out.

For jazz, try **Alexander's,** a casual, bare-bones place with a changing lineup of artists, a short cab ride from downtown. 4265 Woodward at Canfield. 831-2662.

In Rivertown, the warehouse district, the **Soup Kitchen Saloon** features top-notch blues in a casual atmosphere with imported beer and ales and moderately priced food. Franklin at Orleans. 259-2643.

The Woodbridge Tavern, a few blocks over, has a pleasant rooftop deck, tasty inexpensive sandwiches and salads, and Dixieland jazz Thursday through Saturday nights. A good-natured crowd; can get rowdy. (This spot and the Soup Kitchen are also good for lunch.) 289 St. Aubin. 259-2208.

Nearby, the **Rhinoceros** offers a sophisticated piano bar and Continental cuisine at upscale prices. Reservations required.

Women travelers are advised to take taxis in most cases to most places, especially in the late-night hours.

AT LEISURE

Day-Tripping

If you're based in Dearborn, or if you find yourself with an extra day, head for **Ann Arbor,** the lovely campus town that is home to the University of Michigan. Museums, book stores, botanical gardens, superior restaurants, and people-watching are all great ways to pass the time in this college environment. Information: Ann Arbor Conference and Visitor's Bureau, 207 E. Washington Street, Ann Arbor, MI 48104. 313/995-7281.

For a foreign experience, plan a trek to **Windsor,** Detroit's Canadian neighbor. A convenient way to get to this lovely town across the Detroit River is via the Detroit–Windsor Tunnel Bus, 519/944-4111, which can be caught at both entrances to the tunnel. It runs until 12:40 A.M. from the Windsor side and 12:50 A.M. from the Detroit side. Fare: 85 cents one way. Once there, Windsor is a great place for shopping (take advantage of the favorable exchange rate), eating, and lounging in the gardens on the river. A pleasant escape. For information on Windsor, contact the Canadian Office of Tourism, 1001 Woodward Avenue, 19th floor, Detroit, MI 48226. 313/963-8686.

If your need for escape lasts longer than an afternoon, you may want to stay in Canada. The best place for traveling women is the **Hilton International** in Windsor. From its 302 rooms, you can see a panoramic view of Detroit's striking skyline. The **Park Terrace** restaurant here is drawing good reviews, too. Drinks and light snacks from 4 P.M. in the **River Runner Bar and Grill.** Dozens of amenities in the hotel. 277 Riverside Drive, Windsor. 519/973-5555 or 962-3834.

Northern Michigan, within a four- to five-hour drive of Detroit, offers beautiful rivers, lakes, resorts, and four-season fun. Contact Mich-

igan Department of Commerce, P.O. Box 30226, Lansing, MI 48909. 800/
292-2520.

In Town

Those who don't want to stray too far from Detroit proper but
want some leisure activities that will provide mental stimulation and fun,
too, may want to tour the city itself.

We particularly enjoyed the arrangements made by some Detroit
women.

Jill Demaris has a company called **Detroit Upbeat,** which puts
together tours that are historical and cultural in nature. Custom-designed
to fit your individual taste. 341-6808.

Art Tours can be arranged by Blanche Robinson. 356-7776.

Sunday Customs

Sunday in Detroit is a good day to take a drive up Lake Shore
Drive to Grosse Pointe. Besides seeing some of America's most opulent
homes, we find this community along the Detroit River a great vantage
point for watching freighters, reading along the banks of the river, and
just generally hanging out. So, as you approach Lake St. Claire (about
15 minutes from the center of town and where the most impressive homes
have been built), pull off the road and look back at the skyline.

If all this relaxing makes you hungry, we can suggest a great
place to replenish. It's called **Sparky Herbert's** (822-0266; 15117 Kercheval),
a kind of preppy pub and restaurant that's in an exclusive Grosse Pointe
shopping district. We've never tasted such wonderful quiche.

Brunch is catching on all over Detroit. In fact, the Detroit Symphony Orchestra even has a **Brunch with Bach** program. Call 567-1400.
Other places to partake of brunch on Sunday: at **LaRotisserie** in Dearborn
and at the **Restaurant St. Regis** (see "At Your Service").

Sunday's also an ideal day for taking in the **Eastern Farmer's
Market** (833-1560) and its tons and tons of fresh fruit, flowers, and goods
plus 33 retail shops with wholesale prices on cheeses, wines, and everything you can imagine.

Spectator Sports

Detroit is serious about its sports teams, and fans generally turn
out in droves regardless of how the home team is doing. Rain or shine
will find Detroiters rooting for the **Tigers** (baseball, Tiger Stadium, 963-
9944); **Lions** (football, Pontiac Silverdome, 335-4151); **Pistons** (basketball,
Pontiac Silverdome, 962-2628); and the once-proud, now lowly **Red Wings**
(hockey, Joe Louis Arena, 961-6444).

Active Sports

Those who want to do more than look should consider **jogging** in one of Detroit's beautiful parks (weather permitting, of course). We recommend Belle Isle if you're downtown, Kensington Metropolitan Park northwest of the city in Millford or in Stoney Creek Park northeast of the city in Mt. Clemens.

Biking is another way to get in a workout while seeing some of Detroit's surroundings. Call United Rental, 561-5696 or 855-3191, in Dearborn.

Detroit's **bowling** lanes are generally bulging in the winter. That's okay though, because Motown has three times the number of lanes than the average city. Check the Yellow Pages for lane listings.

If you're a snow skiier, night **skiing** is within an hour's drive north of downtown at Mt. Brighton (277-1451) and Alpine Valley, west of Pontiac (887-4183).

HOUSTON

HOTELS

1 Adam's Mark
2 Allen Park Inn
3 Four Seasons Houston
  Center
4 Guest Quarters Galleria
  West
5 Inn on the Park
6 Lancaster
7 Hotel Meridien
8 Remington on Oak Park
9 Residence Inn
10 Shamrock Hilton
11 Stouffer's
12 Warwick
13 Whitehall

LANDMARKS

A Alley Theatre
B Astrodome
C Commerce Tower
D Galleria
E Hermann Park
F Hobby Airport
G Sam Houston Park

H Intercontinental Airport
I Jones Center for the
  Performing Arts
J Memorial Park
K Museum Area
L Summit
M Texas Medical Center

HOUSTON

GETTING YOUR BEARINGS

If you've never been to Houston, you've probably conjured up an inaccurate image. That's not your fault. During the 1950s when the post–World War II oil boom was at its peak, people elsewhere in the country were led to believe that this was a sleepy, swampy little town that had suddenly awakened to find oil flowing in its streets.

That wasn't quite accurate. Houston never was all that sleepy, and the oil stayed decorously in the ground and outside the city limits. As for the swampiness, Houston juts out of a fertile, flat, but generally well-drained coastal plain. Live oaks join in arches over the city's residential streets; stately palms line the boulevards. Wild magnolias, dogwood, and azaleas bloom along the bayous that thread through the city.

This will give you some idea of the real Houston, but don't think you've got it all figured out. Because of an unparalleled economic and population boom, Houston changes almost as quickly as you can blink your eyes. This sprawling, sophisticated metropolis with its shimmering, ultramodern skyline looks different every time we visit.

Between 1970 and 1980, Houston's population grew from 2 million to 3 million, making this city the nation's fourth largest. Most of the influx continues to be Yankees (as old-line Houstonians call anyone from north of Tulsa) who moderate the city's conservative-Democrat bent and do much to broaden its social attitudes.

Women are accepted in Houston in all aspects of business—albeit grudgingly sometimes—and can even hold their own memberships in that bastion of the downtown establishment, the Houston Club. Some Old South manners and mannerisms, such as men opening doors, remain, however.

In fact, Houston's southern and Latin influences demand a certain amount of personal pleasantry before getting down to the business at hand. Coming too quickly to the point, especially if it's a sales call, is considered rude. Whether men are dealing with men, men with women, or women with women, the first five or ten minutes is usually devoted to quasi-social conversation. The opener is typically "I hope you had a nice trip" or "How was your flight?" It may even be "Where are you staying?" which is not to be taken as a sexual advance.

Yes, Houston is a friendly city. A contributing factor may be the city's rich, ethnically diverse cultural mix. In fact, large numbers of new immigrants—legal and illegal—mixed with a vast amount of international trade give the city a cosmopolitan quality.

Major building in this flourishing town focuses on a new downtown, with a sleek look. Office, hotel, condominium, and apartment space is overbuilt for years to come; even the plushest offer attractive deals. Law firms, large international banks and holding companies, major oil and gas companies, and other multinational corporations are generally located in the downtown area.

But don't think this is all there is to Houston's city limits. The truth is this town seemingly sprawls forever. The circle is about 60 miles in diameter, set 50 miles from the Gulf of Mexico. It's probably not surprising that we heartily recommend renting a car if you really want to experience the city.

Six miles west of downtown, architecture firms, advertising agencies, real estate developers, and independent oil and gas producers share an area called the Galleria with a cluster of posh specialty shops, restaurants, chic nightclubs, and glitzy hotels. But be careful if your activity is centered in the Galleria. We've been told that muggings and rapes are more frequent in this upscale area than in downtown Houston.

Three miles south of downtown, Rice University, the Texas Medical Center (which employs 30,000), the city's art museums, and many of its better galleries give the community intellectual ballast. Known as the Museum Area, the region spreads south toward the Astrodome and north toward Montrose, and is known for its ethnic restaurants, cabarets, and eclectic mix of artists, gays, and young professionals. The Astrodome may be the home of football and baseball games as well as mammoth conventions, but hookers casually stroll the streets that surround this popular venue, making the immediate neighborhood less than pleasing.

WHAT TO WEAR

Except in certain fields—the arts, the creative side of advertising, and a budding film industry—conservative is the byword for Houston business dress. Even oilmen tend to wear traditional suits in town, although handcrafted cowboy boots may peek out from under impeccable Brooks Brothers trousers. Boardroom-style business dress is de rigueur, even at the height of summer, but women can get by wearing open collars. Hose is a must, though, and sundresses, even when paired with jackets, are unacceptable. Polyester can be suffocating in the hot city, so stick to natural fabrics.

WEATHER WATCH

Houston's tropical climate can make looking businesslike difficult. It's located at the same semitropical latitude as Tampa, Florida, and from May or June into October, the daytime highs soar into the 90s. Nighttime lows, however, stay in the mid-70s and the temperature seldom rises above 100. Brief thunderstorms often wash and cool the late afternoon air. Because of the Gulf of Mexico, Houston is humid, but everything is mercifully air-conditioned. February through May and October through early December is when Houston weather is predictably perfect, but the most prudent pack for the unpredictable during winter when the weather, generally mild and wet (highs in the mid-50s), can soar as high as 80 or suddenly plummet to 30. Cold weather is almost always dry and windy, what the locals call a blue norther.

GETTING THERE

Located 22 miles north of downtown, **Houston Intercontinental Airport** is an international hub for flights throughout the United States and a convenient connecting point for international flights.

Most major U.S. carriers serve Intercontinental as do a number of foreign carriers.

Eight miles south of downtown, **Hobby Airport** provides a convenient hub for smaller commuter airlines serving the Southwest, but it also offers flights to most major U.S. cities. The airport is served by a dozen domestic airlines.

Getting from the airports to your business meeting isn't a major ordeal. From Intercontinental, 45 minutes and a $20 taxi fare will take you into the heart of the city. From Hobby, the $12 ride is just 15 minutes during rush hour with a cab driver who knows the side streets.

Most airport hotels offer free courtesy vans. Northline buses and limousines also serve the airports (644-8359). A ticket to Hobby is $4 one-way or $7.50 round-trip from downtown (Hyatt Regency) or South Main (near the Shamrock Hilton), and $5 one-way, $9.50 round-trip from Post Oak (near the Galleria) or Greenway Plaza. Limousines leave downtown every half hour, beginning at 6:05 in the morning. Every hour on the hour, a bus leaves from the same locations to Intercontinental. Another bus on the same schedule runs between the two airports. The fare for either is $10 each way.

Galveston Limousine serves the beach resort of Galveston plus NASA and the major communities south of Houston from both airports. The trip between Intercontinental and Galveston (about 75 miles) is $18.

For women who hate traffic, Air Link (230-1254) provides helicopter service to and from Intercontinental and several locations throughout the city. The one-way fare to downtown Houston is $45.

Car Rentals

Because it can take as long as one hour to get from one side of town to the other, the best way to get around Houston is by car. Most car rental agencies have locations at both airports and elsewhere in the city, but rates and selection tend to be better with the highest volume agencies like Hertz and Avis, who often offer better deals if you request them at the airport counter.

Some rental car companies are:

Avis	443-2130 Intercontinental;
	641-0531 Hobby
Hertz	443-0800 Intercontinental;
	941-6821 Hobby
National	443-8850 Intercontinental;
	641-0533 Hobby
Ashbaugh	649-2751 Hobby

The cheapest rentals in town are at Rent-a-Wreck (446-8387, near Intercontinental) or downtown (869-8144).

GETTING AROUND

Houston has no subway or rail system, and with the exception of airport transportation, ten-cent shopper specials looping through downtown, and some park-and-ride commuter lines, the city's public transportation system is uncomfortable and unreliable. We don't recommend it.

Cabs can take from 10 to 45 minutes to arrive, but they allow four passengers to travel for the price of one. Yellow Cab (236-1111), United Taxicab Company (699-0000), American Liberty Cab (522-2269), and Sky-Jack's Cab Company—no kidding—(523-6080) are all reliable.

If you rent a car, you will find that downtown is dotted with parking lots and garages, and meters line the streets. Private garages and well-located lots, though, can be phenomenally expensive. The best rates are at the underground City Center garage in the performing arts complex at Texas and Louisiana.

GETTING FAMILIAR

Houston Convention and Visitors Council
3300 Main Street   523-5050
Houston, TX 77027

Write, call ahead, or stop by for maps and brochures on the area's attractions and schedules of major events. We found this visitors' bureau especially eager to provide assistance for just about any need.

Houston Chamber of Commerce
1100 Milam Building   651-1313
25th floor
Houston, TX 77002

To find out what's happening in town, consult one of Houston's two daily newspapers. Owned by Sun Publishing of Toronto, the *Houston Post* is a morning newspaper with a spiffy layout and a full guide to local entertainment published on Wednesday and updated on Friday. Once an afternoon paper, the *Houston Chronicle* now starts with a morning edition. This paper is heavy on national and international coverage and light on local issues. *Texas Monthly* is a top-notch, award-winning statewide publication listing events and cultural amenities, as well as honest reviews of night spots and restaurants. The *Monthly's* reviewers tend to be very picky about atmosphere, service, and decor. *Houston City Magazine* carries somewhat more extensive local reviews, also critical when called for, and divides its restaurants by type of cuisine.

Quick Calls

AREA CODE 713	Time 844-7171
Weather 228-8703	Emergencies 222-3131

AT YOUR SERVICE

Downtown

Lancaster
701 Texas Avenue   Toll-free reservations: in Texas 800/392-
Houston, TX 77002   5566;
                                     outside Texas 800/231-0336
                                     Local number: 228-9500
                                     Telex: 790-506

This nearly flawless, small (93 rooms, eight suites), European-style hotel sits in the heart of the downtown business and arts district, next to the Alley Theatre and Jones Hall. The building is a landmark, and the decor is warm but elegant with imported furniture, three chintz patterns, and a choice of four color schemes—white, light yellow, deep rose or forest green. All rooms have seating areas, at least three phones, and marble baths. Fitness-conscious guests can use the Texas Club, a block and a half away, with indoor jogging track and other exercise facilities.

Business dress is appropriate at any hour in the single eating and lounge area, the **Lancaster Grille**. A limited but generally healthful menu is featured, including spa cuisine (prepared without butter, cream

Hotel	Average Rate	Business Traveler Program	Frequent Guest Program	Check Out Time	Business/Secretarial Services	Electronic Key System	Extra-Special Amenities	Restaurant for Client Entertaining	24-Hour Room Service	Pool	Fitness Facilities	No-Smoking Rooms	Executive Floor	Concierge
Adam's Mark	$ 79–$99 / $ 75 corp.			12 noon	●			The Marker	●	●	●	●		●
Four Seasons Houston Center	$145 / $130 corp.			1 p.m.	●	●	●	Maison de Ville	●	●	●	●	●	●
Guest Quarters Galleria West	$105 / $ 99 corp.			12 noon	●		●	The Quarter's Court	●	●	●	●		
Inn on the Park	$120–$175 / $ 95–$115 corp.	P.C.R.		1 p.m.			●	La Reserve	●	●	●	●		●
Lancaster	$125 / $115–$99 corp.	Preferred Corporate Program		1 p.m.	●			Lancaster Grille	●	●	●			●
Hotel Meridien	$ 99–$165 / $ 95–$105 corp.	R.S.V.P.		1 p.m.	●		●	Le Restaurant de France La Brasserie	●			●		●
Remington on Oak Park	$135–$210 / $115 corp.	Club Remington		1 p.m.	●		●	The Conservatory and Garden Room	●					●
Residence Inn	$ 50–$60			12 noon						●	●	●		
Shamrock Hilton	$ 72–$97 / $ 72 corp.	Hilton Plan		1 p.m.				Trader Vic's		●		●		●
Stouffer's	$ 95–$165 / $ 95 corp.	The Club Level	RSVP	2 p.m.		●	●	City Lights Justin's Amelia's		●	●	●		●
Warwick	$ 90 / $ 80 corp.			12 noon	●	●	●	The Warwick Club	●	●	●	●		●
Whitehall	$ 90 / $ 65 corp.	ESP		2 p.m.	●	●		The French Quarter		●	●			●

or salt); but the pièce de résistance is the sinfully rich cream of onion soup, laced with apple brandy and served in a pastry shell.

Hotel Meridien

400 Dallas Street   Toll-free reservations: 800/543-4300
Houston, TX 77002   Local number: 759-0202
                           Telex: 025 400

Owned by Air France, the Meridien has a cool, sophisticated air and contemporary soft green Eurostyle decor—a cosmopolitan oasis in the bustle of the center city. Standard rooms here are small by Texas standards, so if you're looking for space, ask for a corner room that has a sitting area. Baths come stocked with Hermes and Neutrogena soaps. The hotel has its own small gift and drugstore; arranged on the tunnel system, it is laced with shops and restaurants. There's a bookstore next door, and guests may use the Texas Club's fitness facilities.

For dining, the coffee shop, **La Brasserie,** is popular for business breakfasts, lunches, and Sunday brunch. Lunch and dinner are served in the award-winning **La Restaurant de France,** one of the finest restaurants in the city. We find it formal and pricey, but worth it. The **Bagatelle** lobby piano bar is a pleasant spot to unwind in the afternoon. Another lounge, the **Nautile,** has entertainment every night except Sunday. Both are appropriate for women alone.

Four Seasons Houston Center

1300 Lamar   Toll-free reservations: 800/268-6282
Houston, TX 77010   Local number: 650-1300
                          Telex: 794-653

Located on the east side of town near the site of a new convention center, this member of the luxury Canadian Four Seasons chain is attached by an enclosed skyway to the Park, a three-tiered shopping mall. The mall has a variety of boutiques, restaurants, and a health club, with pool, exercise machines, jogging track, and racquetball courts. In the hotel itself, you'll find 399 rooms, 135 of which are special Four Seasons Rooms, with separate sleeping alcoves attached to a small living area.

Breakfast and light lunch are available in the upstairs lobby, and the lobby bar serves great after-theater desserts. **The Maison de Ville** restaurant, with a smashing aubergine art deco, serves three meals of Continental cuisine and a low-calorie gourmet alternative menu.

Whitehall

1700 Smith Street   Toll-free reservations: 800/228-2121
Houston, TX 77002   Local number: 659-5000
                          Telex: 775 256

Perched on the southern edge of downtown, this 275-room hotel offers specially designated female traveler rooms located on lower floors toward the middle of the building for security. Along with more feminine decor than the rest of the property, these rooms have an extra vanity shelf and hair dryer in the bath, a clothesline in the shower, padded hangers in the closet, more lighting around the dressing area. The Whitehall is across the street from the coeducational downtown YMCA, probably the most complete health club in town and available free to corporate Whitehall guests. Free limousine service for guests who want to get around downtown from 7 A.M. to 11 P.M.

The hotel has three restaurants: a coffee shop for the budget-conscious; a moderately priced supper club called the **French Quarter,** with jazz entertainment at night; and **Bentley's,** serving an upscale American cuisine business lunch, featuring blackened redfish and the like.

Museum Area and Medical Center

Warwick

5701 S. Main Street   Toll-free reservations: 800/231-5701
Houston, TX 77251   Local number: 526-1991
                                        Telex: 76 2590

Looking like a Viennese wedding cake, this Old Guard hotel is the place where wealthy dowagers occupy suites on upper floors and older European guests feel at home. To one side are the Museum of Fine Arts and Mecom Fountain, to the other Hermann Park, Houston's answer to Central Park. Off the hotel's baroque lobby are a beauty salon, a drugstore, and even an Oriental rug dealer. Guests can use the Park Plaza Fitness Center across the street, and there's an outdoor pool and sauna on the premises.

Meals are served in the **Hunt Room,** the downstairs dining room; **Cafe Vienna,** a coffee shop; and the **Warwick Club,** a private club at the top of the hotel open to guests. The Warwick's lavish Sunday brunch, which includes a whole serving table piled with shrimp, crab claws, and raw oysters, is a Houston tradition, but the hotel's cuisine tends to be fussy, pricey, and free of nouvelle influences.

Shamrock Hilton

6900 S. Main Street   Toll-free reservations: 800/445-8667
Houston, TX 77030   Local number: 668-9211

If you want to be transported to the height of 1950s Oil Boom opulence, this Houston landmark built by legendary wildcatter Glen McCarthy (the inspiration for James Dean's Jett Rink character in *Giant*) is the place to stay. The pool here exemplifies the hotel's character: it's shaped like a giant Irish harp and is capable of accommodating water-skiers and speed boats. Open to Houstonians as a private club, the pool is a chic multiethnic after-work hangout. Each May, the Kelly green and gold brocade ballroom is the site of the lavish Western Heritage Sale of prize Santa Gertrudis cattle, quarterhorses, and cowboy art. Of the 735 rooms, the less expensive lanai rooms are like simple motel rooms, but open out into the tropical garden surrounding the pool, where even on the hottest evening, there's a cool breeze.

Meals are served at **Trader Vick's** and the **Terrace Restaurant.**

Astrodome

Residence Inn
7710 S. Main Street   Toll-free reservations: 800/331-3131
Houston, TX 77030   Local number: 660-7993

All rooms in this 297-unit hotel have fully equipped kitchens, but the studio units incorporate sleeping, living, and food preparation areas into one room. Only penthouse suites—split level with the sleeping area upstairs—have desks. Transportation to the Astrodome, Medical Center, and other spots within a five-mile radius (not downtown) is free.

The inn offers free breakfast and a happy hour, but no restaurant or room service.

Greenway Plaza

Stouffer's
6 Greenway Plaza East   Toll-free reservations: 800/468-3571
Houston, TX 77046   Local number: 629-1200
                                                  Telex: 775856-9810 8615719

Adjacent to the Summit basketball arena and concert hall in the middle of an office complex reminiscent of Los Angeles's Century City, this pleasantly efficient business hotel is directly connected to the offices, shops, beauty salon, drugstore, and three-screen art movie theater on the basement level. Stouffer's has its own fitness facilities—heated pool, sauna, exercise equipment—plus access to nearby tennis and racquetball courts.

The hotel offers three restaurants and a lobby lounge: **Amelia's,** an all-day restaurant; **Justin's,** a theme restaurant for lunch and dinner; a lobby bar; and **City Lights,** on the 20th floor, serving lunch and dinner, with live entertainment at night.

Galleria

Note: Some of the hotels in the Galleria—even the more expensive ones—encourage prostitutes frequenting their bars. The following don't, and they can tell the difference between a "working girl" and a businesswoman.

Remington on Oak Post Park
1919 Briar Oaks Lane   Toll-free reservations: in Texas 800/392-
Houston, TX 77027   4659;
                                                  outside Texas 800/231-9802
                                                  Local number: 840-7600
                                                  Telex: 765536

Depending on your taste, this may be Houston's finest hotel. Owned by H. L. Hunt's daughter Caroline Schoellkopf and her family, it certainly has the most cachet. This is where Houston's upper crust put their over-flow guests or stay themselves while the mansion is being reroofed. You don't even want to enter the lobby without being Dressed (note the capital D). The hotel is filled with fresh flowers, the decor is a serene toasty beige, and the gracious service will spoil you for any place else. For business travelers, the Remington has a fully equipped secretarial station (staffed on request), along with a boardroom, which has a marble table seating 20, a wide-screen TV, and a conference phone with overseas satellite hook-up.

The Remington is locally famous for its kitchen, which butchers its own meat, smokes its own fish, bakes its own bread, even dips its own chocolates. The cuisine is new American with a southwestern accent. **The Garden** serves breakfast, lunch, dinner, and Sunday brunch. The less formal, dark-paneled **Remington Bar** does lunch, dinner, and supper until 1 A.M. on weekends. Businesswomen find the high tea served in the **Living Room** to the accompaniment of a harpist a good place to meet clients and colleagues.

Inn on the Park

Four Riverway   Toll-free reservations: 800/268-6282
Houston, TX 77056   Local number: 871-8181
                                         Telex: 794510

It's hard to believe this tranquil Four Seasons hotel—popular with major corporate executives—is on the edge of the bustling Galleria. Black swans glide in the pond next to the two swimming pools. The decor is restful sea green and beige. The hotel provides free limousine service to and from the Galleria, an inexpensive shuttle bus to both airports, and bi-cycles to ride next door in Memorial Park. The health club on-property has exercise equipment, a Jacuzzi, a sauna, and four tennis courts.

La Reserve, a formal nouvelle French restaurant, serves dinner, the more casual **Cafe on the Green** all three meals. **The Palm Court** lobby bar features high tea with soothing piano music. **The Black Swan** club serves lunch by day and presents live entertainment and dancing at night.

Guest Quarters—Galleria West

5353 Westheimer Road   Toll-free reservations: 800/424-2900
Houston, TX 77056   Local number: 961-9000
                                         Telex: 79-1473

If you feel cramped and depressed after a night or two in a hotel, this is for you. The 336 suites are truly apartment-size, with separate bed-rooms, fully equipped kitchens, and living rooms, all furnished much better than most accommodations of this type.

Quarter's Court is a small, simple restaurant with a lunch buffet and brunch. A free limo takes guests to the grocery store if they want to prepare their own meal.

Far West

Adam's Mark

2900 Briarpark Drive	Toll-free reservations: 800/231-5858
Houston, TX 77042	Local number: 978-7400
	Telex: 9108815497

Catering to business travelers and small conventions, this hotel features comfortable rooms and a health club, with an indoor/outdoor pool, whirl-pool, sauna, and Nautilus equipment.

For dining, there's the **Pantry on the Plaza,** an outdoor cafe serving three meals, and the more formal **Marker,** serving French cuisine for lunch and dinner. The hotel has three lounges: **Quincy's** for drinks, dancing, and high action; **Pierre's,** a subdued piano bar; and **Fountain Court,** in the Atrium, a great place to people-watch against the reflecting pool.

ON A BUDGET
Hotel

Allen Park Inn

2121 Allen Parkway	Toll-free reservations: in Texas 800/392-
Houston, TX 77019	1499;
	outside Texas 800/231-6310
	Local number: 521-9321

The Allen Park is one of the city's great accommodation bargains. Situated across a boulevard from a lushly landscaped park of the same name that's studded with sculpture and threaded with hiking and biking trails running along Buffalo Bayou, this motel is only a mile from downtown. The rooms are small and simple, but clean and well maintained. We found the family that owns and runs the inn extremely friendly and helpful. This is the place where film crews—not the stars—bunk for weeks at a time while shooting movies, a big phenomenon in Houston. Exercise equipment, whirlpool, and sauna supplement the outdoor pool.

The 24-hour restaurant on the premises is accustomed to special dietary requests.

Restaurants

For dining, the best buys in Houston tend to be its ethnic fare, especially Mexican, Thai, Vietnamese, and Chinese. Lunch for these meals can run as low as $5 per person. Some ideas:

Tucked away in a strip shopping center along a seedy stretch of Lower Westheimer near the intersection of Montrose, **Renu's** has a delicious way with Thai dishes that are always fresh and crisp, never oily. Atmosphere is casual here; an appropriate place to eat alone provided you don't go wandering around the neighborhood. Closed Monday. 1230 Westheimer. 528-6998.

With white tablecloths and an atmosphere stylish enough to demand at least business attire, **India's** serves consistently good tandoori chicken and sag paneer. 5704 Richmond. 266-0131.

And although the fare is simple, the prices at the **cafeteria** in the basement of **City Hall Annex** are the best lunch deal in town. A full meal costs less than $3.

Entertainment

The best entertaiment value in town is the free performing arts series running from May through October at Miller Outdoor Theatre in Hermann Park (222-3576). This is top-notch stuff, from musicals through classical ballet, and from the nationally famous June 'Teenth Jazz Festival to the *Ballet Folklorico*. Tickets for reserved seats may be picked up between 11:00 and 1:00 the day of the performance, or you can simply arrive at 7:30 that evening with a towel or blanket in case you have to sit on the lawn.

DINING OUT

Especially in the evening, virtually all Houston restaurants assume, unless otherwise informed, that the man in the party is picking up the tab. Be sure to make it clear when you call for reservations that you will be the host entertaining a business associate.

Some of the best restaurants in town are found in Houston's major hotels. Anyone would be impressed by an invitation to dine at the Meridien's **Restaurant de France,** the Inn on the Park's **La Reserve,** or the Remington's **Garden.** A woman dining alone would be comfortable at any of the three, although they're all dressy and expensive.

If you really want to impress, take your client to **Tony's.** It's *the* place in town to see and be seen. National celebrities and multimillionaire oilmen crowd the stylish red dining room. We've found the food—especially the fresh fish, lamb, pasta primavera and dessert souffles—to be consistently excellent. The wine list is staggering. Wear the best dress you brought and be prepared to spend. Also, be sure to ask the maitre d' to seat you in the main section, not Siberia. He'll understand. 1801 Post Oak Boulevard. 622-6778.

Since Houston is only 25 miles from Galveston Bay, shrimp, oysters, crab, redfish, and other Gulf seafood delicacies are plentiful. Texas seafood aficionados swear by the New Orleans–style shrimp, oysters, and snapper (all fresh from the Gulf) at **Willie G's.** The surroundings are simple, the atmosphere informal and noisy. 1605 South Post Oak Boulevard. 840-7190.

Another good, informal spot for Cajun seafood is the **Blue Oyster Bar.** 8105 Gulf Freeway, northbound access road at Monroe exit south of Hobby Airport. 640-1117.

For beef lovers, **Ruth's Chris Steak House** is a consistent favorite, with fine prime beef and fresh salads. They've recently added some lighter entrées, mostly simple seafood dishes. Very few people come here alone. 6213 Richmond. 789-2333.

Damien's Cucina Italiana is to young professionals and the legal/political set as Tony's is to the glitterati. The homemade pasta and appetizers such as mussels marinara are savory and succulent, although the service is a bit relaxed for some tastes. Trendy Young Turks and their female counterparts are always running into one another and table-hopping. Au courant and/or expensive business attire is appropriate. 3011 Smith. 522-0439.

At noon, workers pour out of downtown Houston's high-rise office towers and jam the restaurants. If you want to get business done over lunch, choose a hotel dining room or plan to be at a restaurant by 11:30. **Carmen's** is popular with the courthouse crowd for Mexican food (1015 Texas, 227-0482). On Market Square—the oldest section of downtown—**Glatzmeier's** (809 Congress, 223-3331) dishes up seafood for lunch. Try **Treebeard's** Cajun seafood specialties for lunch. Their shrimp jambalaya is fabulous (315 Travis, 225-2160).

For lunch or early dinner in the Museum/Medical Center area, **Butera's** is a pleasant gourmet deli with indoor and sidewalk tables (only at the Montrose location), a fine selection of salads, imported beers, mineral waters, and the like. 5019 Montrose. 523-0722. Also at Shepherd and Alabama. 528-1500.

Chez Eddy treats doctors, patients, and health-conscious Houstonians to gourmet salt-free cuisine, light on sauces and calories. Scurlock Tower in the Medical Center, 6560 Fannin. 790-6474.

Like most of Texas, Houston has numerous restaurants that serve fresh, well-spiced Mexican food different from what you find at national franchises. Dress for any Mexican restaurant is casual. **Ninfa's** has several cheery, informal locations around town, all owned and run by the same family, and all serving both Tex-Mex food and lighter central and southern Mexican specialties such as sopa xochitl (chicken and avocado soup), chicken pachucos, and grilled shrimp. Locals think the original location is still the best and crowd it accordingly, but it's in a semiindustrial neighborhood—not the best for a woman alone. 2704 Navigation. 288-1175.

Merida, across the street from Ninfa's, specializes in Yucatan dishes and Tex-Mex. It's especially popular for weekend breakfasts. 2509 Navigation. 227-0260.

Owned and run by a woman, **Ousie's** is a very comfortable place for a woman alone in business dress, evening clothes, or jeans. This is an artsy-yuppie neighborhood hangout with a quiche-and-crepes sort of menu that changes daily. 708 Sunset. 526-2264.

HOUSTON BY DAY

Houston's answer to Los Angeles's Watts Towers is the **Orange Show,** Jeff Davis McKessick's eccentric monument to what he believed was the perfect food. A combination naive museum and performance space, this folk art environment (as art scholars call it) is a charming conglomeration of hand-laid tile homilies, cut-metal birds in brightly painted cut-metal palm trees, and oddly placed observation platforms. It's set on an otherwise ordinary street in a working-class residential neighborhood. 2401 Munger: take Telephone Road exit from Gulf Freeway, stay on the access road, and watch for Munger on the right. 552-1767.

The permanent collection of the **Museum of Fine Arts** includes a good selection of contemporary photography and a number of 19th-century western paintings by Frederic Remington. The MFA also sponsors traveling exhibits and special shows. Serves lunch six days a week and light dinner on Thursdays. 2001 Bissonnet at Montrose. 526-1361.

Catty-corner across the street, the **Contemporary Arts Museum** specializes in one-person shows, usually one upstairs and one downstairs. 5216 Montrose Boulevard. 526-3129.

The **Houston Public Library,** on Bagby at McKinney, is an airy, modern, well-stocked facility with comfortable reading areas and a competent research staff. 224-5441.

On the campus of St. Thomas University, a small Catholic liberal arts college in Montrose, the **Rothko Chapel** is a quiet nondenominational place to meditate and contemplate some of Mark Rothko's more profound (or more somber, depending on your interpretation) canvases. 1401 Sul Ross.

Private galleries line Bissonnet west of the Contemporary Arts Museum. Other good galleries (**Balene, Moody, Texas Gallery**) are clustered around the palm-shaded art deco River Oaks Shopping Center on West Gray and Peden between Shepherd and Woodhead. The **Houston Center for Photography** hangs works by Houston and national photographers (1441 W. Alabama, 529-4733; Saturday and Sunday 12:00 to 5:00, Wednesday through Friday, 11:00 to 5:00). Downtown, **Diverse Works** features exciting and sometimes outrageous exhibits, mostly by new artists (214 Travis, 223-8346; Monday through Saturday, 10:00 to 5:00). Virtually every Friday evening, several of these private galleries host packed after-work openings—great places to meet people.

Both the **Blaffer Gallery** off Cullen at the University of Houston/University Park (749-1320) and the **Rice Museum** at Rice University (University Boulevard at Stockton, 552-0886) stage enlightening exhibits, sometimes with accompanying performances.

Part of the MFA but physically separated from it by several miles, **Bayou Bend,** an elegant mansion surrounded by lavish gardens, houses one of the country's most complete and well-documented collections of American antiques. Bayou Bend is open to the public from 1:00 to 5:00

the second Sunday of every month except March and August and is available for tours Tuesday through Saturday by advance reservation only. Westcott off Memorial Drive. 529-8773.

Hermann Park (Fannin at Bissonnet/Binz), Houston's close-in park, contains an extensive rose garden, the Museum of Natural Science and Burke Baker Planetarium (526-4273), and the Houston Zoo (523-5888).

THE SHOPPING SCENE

There's good news for shoppers visiting Houston. The two best places to shop—the Galleria area and downtown—are also the centers of business activity.

The **Galleria** proper is a huge three-tiered enclosed mall that includes two twin-screen movie theaters, two hotels, about a dozen restaurants, and boutiques ranging from the Gap to Frete—with bed linens at $600 a set—and Fred Joallier. Marshall Field, Lord & Taylor, Neiman-Marcus, and Frost Brothers all have their major Houston stores there. A quarter of a mile down Post Oak, Saks Fifth Avenue has a full-scale store in its own smaller and consistently elegant mall along with Roberta di Camerino, Courreges, Ralph Lauren, and Alan Austin (beautiful but very expensive separates) boutiques.

Some of the best regional buys are just half a mile west of the Galleria. Cutter Bill Western World, the Neiman's of cowboy chic, carries ostrich-skin boots, mink cowboy hats, leather prairie skirts, desk-top models of oil wells that really pump, and an array of western shirts, blouses, and accessories (5647 Westheimer). Downtown, Stelzig's features authentic ranch 'n' rodeo gear (410 Louisiana).

In the downtown area, Foley's is a big but less upscale cousin to Bloomingdale's with everything from pantyhose to furniture.

Downtown also has its own mall: **the Park.** While there are no large anchor department stores there, boutiques, specialty shops, and the like offer a range of prices in secure, convenient surroundings. On the first level, Best Products sells discount jewelry, electronic equipment, and items for the home.

HOUSTON BY NIGHT

Where you'll want to go for an evening in Houston depends on whether you primarily want to be entertained or elevated or meet interesting men. The Houston Ballet and the Houston Grand Opera are among the best in the country outside New York. The Alley Theatre and the Houston Symphony are at least as good as you'd expect for the country's fourth largest city, and there are a number of small repertory companies, modern dance troupes, and the like.

Both the **Houston Ballet** (615 Louisiana, 523-6300) and the **Houston Grand Opera** (615 Louisiana, 546-0200) have excellent national reputations and perform exciting new works, as well as doing a good job with perennials. The sets are especially good. Although not quite on the same plane, the **Houston Symphony** (615 Louisiana, 224-4240) is certainly credible. Pending the completion of the new Lyric Theatre, which will become home to the ballet and opera in 1986, all three perform at Jones Hall— an elegant space with comfortable seats and fine acoustics. Unfortunately, however, you can't see much from the seats in the upper balcony. Orchestra and loge tickets are usually worth their price of $20 to $30.

Delia Stewart (1201 Westheimer, 522-6375) and **Farrell Dyde** (3221 Milam, 523-2679) are Houston's top modern dance companies.

The **Alley Theatre** is the city's main repertory house. Its major performances are featured on its large stage and the more experimental (and often better) works are featured downstairs on the Arena Stage. Tickets range from $10 to $14. 615 Texas Avenue. 228-8421.

Stages (3201 Allen Parkway, 527-8243), **Main Street Theatre** (2540 Times Boulevard, 524-6706), and **Chocolate Bayou Theater Company** (528-0119) are all competent and innovative.

The Ensemble is an acclaimed all-black troupe staging works by established and fledgling black playwrights. 3535 Main. 520-0055.

Over the past few years, comedy cabarets have sprouted all over town. The first and still generally the best is the **Comedy Workshop** (1904 S. Shepherd at San Felipe, 524-7333), which performs professionally produced topical skits. Two former workshop members have started another club, **Radio Music Theatre** (3613 Washington, 864-8648), doing on-stage spoofs and knock-offs of thirties and forties radio dramas.

Except in the case of major touring acts, it's not necessary to buy tickets before you get to Houston, although you should pin down reservations for Friday and Saturday evenings as soon as you arrive. Tickets for most Houston performing arts events, as well as for major rock concerts and the like, are available through **Ticketron** (526-7220) or at half-price the day of the performance through **Showtix** (227-9292), which has a booth downtown in Tranquility Park on Rusk (11:00 to 2:00 Monday, 11:00 to 7:30, Tuesday through Saturday).

Houston's scores of first-run **movie theaters** are relegated to outlying malls. In fact, for visitors staying downtown, the closest are the Galleria I and II in the Galleria, Loewe's Saks Twin in the Saks Fifth Avenue Center on Post Oak, and the Shamrock 6 across from the Shamrock Hilton on South Main. The Greenway Three in Greenway Plaza (626-0402) off the Southwest Freeway at Edloe screens foreign and American art films— John Sayles and the like. The River Oaks Theatre (2009 W. Gray in Montrose, 524-2175) is a revival house offering mostly one-night stands of everything from classics to first-run foreign films, gay cinema, and heterosexual erotica. The Museum of Fine Arts (Main at Bissonet, 526-1361) and Rice Media Center (University Boulevard at Stockton, 527-4853) both show revivals of artistically significant films.

LATE-NIGHT HOUSTON

Houston has its own indigenous jazz scene. Horace Grigsby and Arnette Cobb, both famous in Europe, live here. Saxophonist Kirk Whalum is one of the city's hot young talents.

Cody's is a rooftop Montrose bar with a smashing view of downtown. Jazz groups are featured, usually with no cover charge, and the atmosphere is appropriate for a woman alone or accompanied. 3400 Montrose. 522-9747.

Rockefeller's books national name acts—from Leon Redbone to B. B. King to Beto y los Fairlanes—in a renovated bank building. The neighborhood is transitional, but not especially dangerous if you exercise normal caution. 3620 Washington. 861-9365.

A holdover from the sixties, **Anderson Fair** features folk music and singer-songwriters, some of them national recording artists. It's comfortable for women alone, but don't stray from the immediate vicinity. 2007 Grant, one block east of Montrose. 528-8576.

If you enjoy sitting around in business clothes or jeans and listening to live chamber music and poetry readings while sipping wine and imported beer, you'll like **Munchie's.** It's a comfortable Rice University area hangout where women alone are welcomed. 2349 Bissonet. 528-3545.

Caribana pumps out live reggae to an audience of students, West Indian immigrants, and young professionals. 8220 W. Bellfort. 774-3454.

Still the choicest spot is **Boccaccio** in the Saks Center. This members-only disco and supper club enjoys Club International reciprocity with such spots as Regine's in New York. Although the club is large and has a smashing decor, it is divided into pleasantly scaled sections, where you can get away from the music and talk. This is the place to wear your dressiest, most daring clothes. The club is open from 10 P.M. to 2 A.M. Monday through Saturday. A guest pass is $20 per person, based on availability. 1800 Post Oak Boulevard. 626-7141.

Waiters serenade at the **Great Caruso.** It's a fun spot and the entertainment breaks up the conversation. It's open seven days a week from 6 P.M. to 2 A.M. 10001 Westheimer, way west of the Loop. 780-4900.

Fizz is a large, dressy disco where everyone who's club-hopping in the Galleria stops off at some time during the evening. 6400 Richmond. 789-7707.

Houston's richer, over-30 crowd tends to congregate at **La Cave,** a sophisticated restaurant and disco with good reasonable food. 1220 Augusta. 953-1000.

Most country-western clubs in Houston are faddish discos, but **Gilley's** is for real. Mickey Gilley and his house band, the Bayou City Beats, kick up a storm, just as they did before John Travolta filmed *Urban Cowboy* here. Their lively dance music fills up a space the size of a B-52 hangar from early morning (when the night shift at the refineries gets off work) to the small hours. At least half the crowd—both male and female—shows up alone in hopes of meeting partners for the Texas two-step and cotton-eyed Joe. You needn't dress western—jeans and an oxford cloth or frilly blouse will do—but no corporate clothes here. In Pasadena, a long way southeast of downtown, so call for directions; 9:00 A.M. to 2 A.M., seven days a week. 4500 Spencer Highway. 941-7990.

AT LEISURE

In Town

Public sculpture and postmodern commercial architecture make downtown a veritable outdoor gallery. Try to take an hour or two for a walking tour and take a look at some of the stunning new buildings such as Philip Johnson's cathedrallike **Republic Bank Tower,** and the observation platform on the 78th floor of the **Texas Commerce Tower,** the tallest structure in town.

Sam Houston Park, at Bagby and Allen Parkway, forms a rolling green oasis stocked with restored 19th-century structures in the shadow of downtown's futuristic skyscrapers. Across Bagby at Rusk, **Tranquility Park** is a square-block water garden erected to celebrate the landing on the moon.

Day-Tripping

Although normally listed in Houston tourist brochures, the **Johnson Space Center,** NASA headquarters, is actually located 25 miles south of town and takes a good half day to appreciate. To get there, take the Gulf Freeway to NASA Road 1, and then go left three miles. There is no way to miss the main entrance, dominated as it is by huge rockets. The space museum and flight simulators are open for public viewing seven days a week. Free.

Galveston, a favorite full-day or overnight escape, is just an hour south of Houston on the Gulf Freeway. If you want to stay on the beach, choose the luxurious new San Luis, a full resort hotel (53rd and Seawall Boulevard, 409/765-8888) or the plainer Marriott Hotel Galvel (2024 Seawall, 409/765-7721). The Tremont House at 2300 Ship's Mechanic Row (409/763-0300) captures the bygone elegance of the Gilded Isle, as does the Victorian Inn (511 17th Street, 409/762-3235), a charming bed-and-breakfast spot in a lovely old house with ornately carved woodwork. Prices for accommodations vary vastly depending on the season, but generally a room from late fall through early spring in a top hotel runs $75 to $95. For the best price, call ahead and ask for any available discounts.

Seafood—Cajun or straight—is one of the prime reasons for visiting Galveston. Shrimp, crab, oysters, red snapper, and other Gulf fish are fresh and delicious. **The Wentletrap,** in a restored ironfront at 23rd and Strand (409/765-5545, open seven days) has large portions and the most elegant atmosphere in town. It's pricey at dinner but a very good value for brunch. **Le Paysan** (2021 Strand, 409/765-7792, closed Monday) has a provincial French hand and moderate prices. **Russo's** (1228 Seawall, 409/762-1266, open seven days, moderate) make succulent scampi, fine fresh pasta, and some of the best pizza this side of New York.

Sunday Customs

On Sunday, those Houstonians who don't leave town stroll through the parks, museums, and galleries, take in bargain matinees at the art theaters listed above, and brunch over out-of-town papers. Among the favorite **brunch spots** are Brennan's (3300 Smith, 522-9711), the Warwick Hotel, Merida (2509 Navigation, 526-1991), La Brasserie at the Meridien, and Butera's, all mentioned above. Mama's Cafe (6019 Westheimer, 266-8514; also good for breakfast meetings) and Cafe Moustache (4702 Westheimer, 621-6281) are also popular. Dim sum fans head for the Silver House (1107 Chartres, east of downtown in Chinatown, 224-8091).

Spectator Sports

The name Nolan Ryan is known far and wide in the baseball world. Visitors to Houston will want to see the **Astros** play in the Astrodome just to see this pitcher, the first in his position to achieve 4,000 strikeouts. For tickets, call 799-9555. (Also available through Ticketmaster and Tele-ticket.) The **Houston Oilers** football team plays in the Astrodome, too.

To get to this famous sports arena, take the Kirby Exit off South Loop 610. For further information on events at the Astrodome, as well as tours, call 799-9544.

Active Sports

It's surprising, but even in hot, humid Houston, jogging is popular. One of the best jogging spots is in **Allen Park.** There, threading along Buffalo Bayou from downtown to the mansions of River Oaks, a greenbelt of flowering trees, modern sculpture, and jogging and bike trails segues into **Memorial Park** farther to the west. Memorial reaches all the way to the Loop and the Galleria area. It has more jogging trails, sports fields, and the Arboretum—a series of nature trails through a virgin patch of hardwood forest, wild azaleas, towering magnolias, and the like.

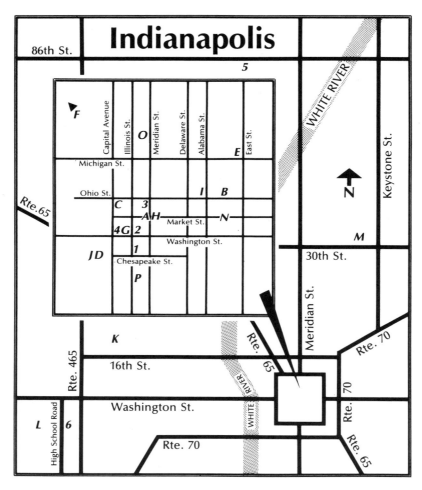

Indianapolis

86th St.

5

Capital Avenue
Illinois St.
Meridian St.
Delaware St.
Alabama St.
East St.

F

O

E

Michigan St.

Ohio St.

I *B*

C *3*

A *H*

Market St.

N

4 G *2*

Washington St.

1

J D

Chesapeake St.

P

Rte. 65

WHITE RIVER

N

Keystone St.

M

30th St.

Meridian St.

K

Rte. 465

16th St.

Rte. 65

WHITE RIVER

Rte. 70

Rte. 70

Washington St.

High School Road

L *6*

Rte. 70

WHITE RIVER

Rte. 65

HOTELS

1 Canterbury Hotel
2 Embassy Suites
3 Indianapolis Hilton
4 Holiday Inn Airport
5 Hyatt Regency
   Indianapolis
6 Sheraton Marten House

LANDMARKS

A Circle Theatre
B City Market
C Greyhound Terminal
D Hoosier Dome
E Indiana Ballet Theatre
F Indiana Museum of Art
G Indiana Repertory Theatre
H Indiana Soldiers and
   Sailors Monument
I Indiana State Museum

J Indianapolis Convention
   and Visitors Association
K Indianapolis 500 Mile
   Race
L Indianapolis International
   Airport
M Indianapolis Zoo
N Market Square Arena
O Scottish Rite Cathedral
P Union Station

INDIANAPOLIS

GETTING YOUR BEARINGS

Indianapolis acts like a prom queen in a new white formal. And for good reason. As recently as 1980, the central city was a wasteland after office doors closed at five. Today, crowds stroll the downtown streets, window shopping and stopping in at the many tiny restaurants and bars. Horse-drawn carriages pass by along brick-paved streets that surround tree-lined Monument Circle, the city's focal point.

When threatened with recession and Sunbelt defections, this town knuckled down and fought back. The result is a city alive with new development. Gleaming office towers rub shoulders with period resto-rations. A city once famous only for the annual Indy 500 now entertains with year-round attractions, including a major symphony orchestra, a resident theater, fine museums, and professional sports teams.

Fast gaining a reputation as the amateur sports capital of Amer-ica, Indianapolis has some of the finest athletic facilities in the world. When not being used for competition, they're open to residents and visitors alike. You can swim in the Olympic-sized Natatorium, bicycle in the world-class velodrome, or play tennis on the courts that annually host the U.S. Clay Court Championships.

The street plan for Indianapolis was designed by Alexander Ral-ston, an assistant to Pierre L'Enfant who planned the layout for Wash-ington, D.C. So it's not surprising that this city's broad plazas, punctuated by monuments and fountains, are reminiscent of the nation's capitol. The basic grid system, with four avenues branching at angles and Mon-ument Circle in the center, makes for easy navigating. The uninitiated should remember that Meridian Street is the dividing line between east and west, and Washington Street the divider for north and south.

Proclaimed safest of America's 50 largest cities by FBI crime reports, Indianapolis is a place where you can actually walk alone down-town at night. Although a number of women hold responsible positions here, the city is socially conservative. On first meeting, women executives still are not treated on a par with their male counterparts, but once they've proven themselves, colleagues are fiercely loyal. Integrity, diligence and punctuality are all important ingredients in doing business.

As might be expected, the pace is slower here than on the East or West Coast, but still we sense the excitement of a city on the move. Hoosiers, proud of their city and of its dazzling transformation, extend a friendly hand to all visitors.

WHAT TO WEAR

Dress conservatively—business suits or dresses, high heels, stockings. People still spruce up a little to go downtown, even if they're only shopping. Extreme fashions draw stares.

WEATHER WATCH

Indianapolis is cold and damp in the winter and hot and muggy in the summer. And sometimes there's no spring at all. But the autumns are glorious, offering vibrant fall colors and the best apple cider in the country at the Eli Lilly Orchards on North College Street. Winter's worst moments usually occur shortly after Christmas. It's been known to snow as late as April in this part of the country.

GETTING THERE

Indianapolis International Airport is 15 minutes southwest of downtown via I-70 and the Airport Expressway. Here—unlike some modern airports—you don't have to walk a marathon to get to your plane. Indianapolis International is well laid out, efficient, easy to get around.

It is eight miles from the airport to the city center; a taxi ride should cost about $7.80. AAA airport limousine service (247-7301) costs $6.80 for the same ride and can be hailed at the lower level of the airport near the TWA baggage carousel.

Several airport hotels are located nearby—Adam's Mark, Hilton, Quality Inn, Ramada Inn, Regal 8 Inn, and La Quinta—and all have 24-hour shuttle service. Some downtown hotels also offer free limo or van service.

In pioneer days, because of its central location—on the old National Road, U.S. 40—Indianapolis earned the nickname "Crossroads of America." Still eminently accessible by road, four major interstates link the city with half the nation's population in a single day's drive; I-69, I-70, I-74, and I-65 all feed directly into the city, and I-465 forms an outer beltway for easy access or bypass.

About 50 Greyhound buses arrive each day at the terminal at 127 N. Capitol Avenue (635-4501), and 40 Trailways buses pull into the station at 248 S. Illinois (632-1414).

Amtrak's Hoosier Stage leaves Union Station, 39 Jackson Place, every morning at 7:30 A.M. bound for Chicago, and returns every night at 10:45 P.M. Call 632-1905 or 800/USA-RAIL.

Union Station is an adventure unto itself. Built in 1888, the red-brick Romanesque structure with its spectacular rose windows was the first union railroad depot in the country. New here is a $48 million renovation, featuring 600,000 square feet of restaurants, shops, and a Holiday Inn with rooms in restored Pullman cars.

Car Rentals

If your business dealings are to take place mainly in the downtown area where activity is concentrated, you shouldn't require a car. But since the city extends far beyond the center to become a series of suburbs, your own transportation may become necessary. If so, try the following rental companies:

Avis	244-3307 at the airport, 243-3711 downtown
Hertz	244-2413 at the airport, 243-9321 downtown
National	243-7501 both airport and downtown
Budget	244-6858 at the airport, 634-9644 downtown
Second Hand Rose	244-4147 (one minute from the airport)

GETTING AROUND

Downtown parking is convenient and relatively inexpensive—garages and lots charge from $2 to $3.50 per day—and most hotels provide spaces for their guests. Warning: Read meters and no-parking signs carefully. Parking between 3:00 and 6:00 P.M. is often not permitted, even when there are meters, and towing often occurs 20 minutes after the posted time. Also, parking is not permitted 15 feet from fire hydrants, and curbs near the hydrants are often *not* painted yellow.

Cabs can usually be hailed on Monument Circle or in front of major hotels, but in most areas, they won't be found cruising. Call or go to a downtown cabstand. The City-County Council regulates taxi fares, which are lower than in most large cities at 80 cents for the first 1/8 mile; 10 cents for each additional. Each extra passenger older than 15 years is charged another 50 cents. Major cab companies include Yellow Cab, 637-5421; Metro Taxi, 634-1112; and Airline Taxi, 631-7521.

Indianapolis offers no adequate mass transit. Buses are generally safe to ride, but service is erratic. Besides, they're packed during rush hours. Exact fare, beginning at 60 cents, is required. If you must, call Metro Travel Center, 635-3344.

A happier option: The Trolley. Small, bright yellow, open-air

	Concierge	Executive Floor	No-Smoking Rooms	Fitness Facilities	Pool	24-Hour Room Service	Restaurant for Client Entertaining	Extra-Special Amenities	Electronic Key System	Business/Secretarial Services	Checkout Time	Frequent Guest Program	Business Traveler Program	Average Single Rate
Canterbury	●	●				●	The Restaurant	●			1 p.m.		The Club	$ 85 / $ 65 corp.
Embassy Suites	●	●	●		●		Velvet Turtle	●			1 p.m.		Attache Program	$ 79
Indianapolis Hilton	●	●	●	●	●	●	Alexander's	●	●		1 p.m.		The Executive Circle	$ 65–$85
Holiday Inn Airport	●	●		●	●		Chanteclaire / The Cafe International				12 noon	Priority Club		$ 62 / $ 59 corp.
Hyatt Regency Indianapolis	●	●	●				The Porch / The Eagle's Nest	●			12 p.m.	The Gold Passport	The Business Level	$ 84–$104 / $ 89 corp. / $115 executive
Sheraton Marten House	●	●	●	●	●		Piccard's	●			12 noon	USA Plus	Sheraton Executive Traveler	$ 65 / $ 51 corp. / $ 75 executive

buses with wooden seats shuttle passengers to various spots in the downtown area. An exact 25-cent fare is required. Also run by Metro, 635-3344.

If you're traveling due north from downtown, there's also the Jitney Express, a 15-passenger van operated by Yellow Cabs. Round-trips from Monument Circle North to 96th and Meridian streets every half hour on weekdays can be hailed anywhere along the route (241-2313).

GETTING FAMILIAR

Indianapolis Convention & Visitors Association
100 S. Capitol Avenue   635-9567
Indianapolis, IN 46225
To get acquainted with the city, pop into the **Indianapolis City Center,** right on Monument Circle, for brochures, maps, schedules, a 20-minute videotype, and a model of the city with future development indicated. Friendly attendants will answer any questions. Monday through Friday 10:00 A.M. to 5:30 P.M.; Saturday 10:00 A.M. to 4:00 P.M. 46 Monument Circle. 236-6260

The Hoosier Dome, home of the Indianapolis Colts, also includes the Indiana Convention Center and has more than 300,000 square feet of exhibit space. 100 S. Capital Avenue, 262-3452.

For a current listing of daily activities, call the 24-hour **Fun Fone** 631-1500.

The city has two daily newspapers—the *Indianapolis Star* in the morning and the *Indianapolis News* in the evening—but they're really the same, that is, both published by Star-News. The "Let's Go" section of the Sunday *Star* and the "Free Time" section of the Friday *News* will give you tips on entertainment. *Indianapolis Magazine* offers monthly features on local people, places, and things, and its Visitors Guide provides maps, emergency phone numbers, and other information. *Indiana Business* is a regional magazine that focuses on issues important to business, industry, and agricultural interests in the state. *This Week,* put out by the Convention and Visitors Association, gives current listings of events, attractions, and restaurants and is offered at hotels and the City Center.

Quick Calls

AREA CODE 317	Weather 222-2362
Time 632-1511	Emergency 911

AT YOUR SERVICE

Visitors will be amazed at the low price of hotel rooms in Indianapolis as compared with almost any other major city. Even if you lean toward the finer things in life, you'll find that a suite filled with amenities at a top property will often cost far below $100 a night. Downtown hotels are in a concentrated area so if that's where you'll be staying you'll never be farther than three blocks from Monument Circle.

Canterbury Hotel

123 S. Illinois Street   Toll-free reservations: 800/538-8186
Indianapolis, IN 46225   Local number: 634-3000
                                          Telex number: 4972551

The Canterbury is a gem of Edwardian elegance. The small (102-room) luxury hotel just south of Washington Street was restored in 1984 and radiates refinement and taste. Each room has a work area, robes, chocolates, and a refrigerator stocked with Perrier and liquor. A hair dryer is provided on request. Secretarial services available as well as a language lab, and a European-caliber concierge is on hand at all times.

The wood-paneled dining room, its walls lined with turn-of-the-century hunting prints, is one of the best restaurants in Indianapolis. Fresh blueberry muffins at breakfast are phenomenal, service, exceptional

Embassy Suites

110 W. Washington Street   Toll-free reservations: 800/EMBASSY
Indianapolis, IN 46204   Local number: 635-1000

Located on the former site of the venerable Claypool Hotel, this towering concrete and glass hotel/shopping complex in the heart of the city opened in 1985 and brought the all-suite concept to Indianapolis. Each suite has a writing table in the living room, a microwave, and a refrigerator. Women's suites have women's magazines. Every guest receives a complimentary breakfast and two hours of complimentary cocktails. Conference rooms and secretarial services are available. Also in the 360-unit hotel are an indoor pool, sauna, steam room, and two whirlpools. The Claypool shops is a two-story shopping complex that includes L. Strauss & Co and the Talbots.

The **Velvet Turtle** restaurant serves American cuisine in a semi-formal atmosphere and is a popular spot for business lunches. The **Food Court,** off the lobby, offers a variety of more casual eateries.

Indianapolis Hilton

31 W. Ohio Street   Toll-free reservations: 800/445-8667
Indianapolis, IN 46204   Local number: 635-2000

Just a block off Monument Circle, the Hilton is a popular business and convention hotel, and both visitors and locals flock to its top-floor dining room every Christmas season for the best view of the holiday lights on the Soldiers and Sailors Monument. The 370-room hotel has been completely renovated and now sports a miniballroom and a conference center. For corporate clientele there is a VIP level with its own "club," known as Club 19. Minisuites are available that include a parlor, writing table, and wet bar.

The coffee shop is open 24 hours.

Hyatt Regency Indianapolis

1 S. Capitol Avenue
Indianapolis, IN 46204

Toll-free reservations: 800/228-9000
Local number: 632-1234
Telex: 027357

With imposing red brick on the outside and a 20-story sky-lit atrium on the inside, the 496-room Hyatt Regency is Indiana's largest hotel. Its location, directly across from the Convention Center, makes it a natural for meetings and large groups. Three floors are set aside for business travelers. The Regency Club is served by a special concierge. The other two floors offer a complimentary *Wall Street Journal, USA Today,* breakfast, and shoeshine.

The hotel is actually part of a business/shopping/hotel complex and features a variety of stores and restaurants. **The Porch** is a coffee shop; **Harrison's** serves Continental cuisine in a romantic setting; and the revolving **Eagles Nest** on the roof provides panoramic views of the city and surrounding countryside.

Sheraton Marten House

1801 W. 86th Street
Indianapolis, IN 46260

Toll-free reservations: in Indiana 800/732-1375; outside Indiana 800/428-1235
Local number: 872-4111

Nestled peacefully in the northwest suburbs of Indianapolis, the Marten House offers comfort and a respite from noise and crowds. The pleasant, low-rise hotel is popular for small conferences and business meetings. Concierge rooms are available with refrigerators and the use of clubrooms. The service includes Continental breakfast. Special women's rooms have hair dryers. The hotel has a well-equipped exercise room, and an indoor pool.

There is a good coffee shop, a moderate-to-expensive dining room, and a quiet bar—the **Gondola Vista.**

Holiday Inn Airport

2501 South High School Road
Indianapolis, IN 46241

Toll-free reservations: 800/HOLIDAY
Local number: 244-6861
Telex: 15678

Not your typical Holiday Inn, this one has a five-story atrium lobby and **Chanteclaire**—one of the best restaurants in town. The hotel caters to the business traveler and offers conference rooms with audiovisual equipment, as well as a health club, sauna, and indoor pool.

The **Croissanterie** serves fresh pastries, pizza, and deli sandwiches, and the **Cafe Internationale** offers casual dining. **Chanteclaire** has a secluded lounge, **Torchies** offers live entertainment, and the **Gallery** has live piano music.

ON A BUDGET

Hotels

Indianapolis has an abundance of low-priced hotels, as previously mentioned; the rates at even the better hotels seem very affordable. Besides those listed, a Howard Johnson's and a TraveLodge are located downtown, but locals say avoid them at all costs.

Restaurants

A few ideas for those trying to keep their budget down in downtown Indianapolis:

Try **Ralf's Delicatessen** for great Reuben sandwiches and homemade desserts served cafeteria style. 7 E. Washington Street. 637-2537.

The Old Spaghetti Factory is located in a restored warehouse and specializes in pasta with four different kinds of sauces. Bar in an upper loft area. No claustrophobia here, as ceilings are high and so are windows. 210 S. Meridien Street. 635-6325.

Churchill's Pub and Eatery may not remind you of England, but you'll enjoy the ambience nevertheless. Most customers go for the gourmet pizza and burgers. Okay for client entertaining. Imported beers and wines. 27 E. Market Street. 639-6666.

Entertainment

Most Indianapolis attractions and museums don't charge, or if they do, the cost is minimal.

Tickets for performing arts programs can be purchased at half price on day of show by contacting **1/2 TIX** at 20 W. Washington Street. 636-8116.

DINING OUT

Indianapolis's renaissance is reflected in the variety and quality of good eating places. In the past few years, new discoveries have been popping up all over town while the old reliables still stick it out.

The Restaurant in the lovely Canterbury Hotel serves fine French nouvelle cuisine in its elegant, clublike dining room. Pheasant from Pennsylvania, venison from New Zealand, radicchio from Italy, all served with European graciousness. Expensive. 123 S. Illinois Street. 634-3000.

La Tour, atop the Indiana National Bank Tower, is the alma mater of trendy Los Angeles superchef Wolfgang Puck. Excellent French and Continental cuisine served in an 18th-century French Regency setting with a splendid view of downtown. Popular with business executives and theater and symphony patrons. Suit coat required for men. Expensive. 35th floor of INB building. 635-3535.

Chanteclair in the airport Holiday Inn is not the sort of restaurant you would expect to find at either an airport or a Holiday Inn. Excellent French specialties served in a romantic setting, with a strolling violinist. Exceptional wine list. Jacket required for men. Dinner only. Expensive. 2501 S. High School Road. 243-1040.

The St. Elmo Steak House, next door to the Canterbury Hotel on S. Illinois Street, is an Indiana institution. The long, ornately carved bar, wooden tables and chairs, and black and white checked flooring look much the way they must have when St. Elmo opened its doors in 1902 and began serving the best steak in the region. Moderate. 127 S. Illinois. 635-0636.

The Milano Inn, family-run by Leo La Grotte and company, serves the best Italian food in town in a warm, jovial atmosphere. People start lining up outside for lunch at 11:30 to sample Vicki Dragoo's fettuccini Alfredo with homemade egg noodles or her rich pasta e faggioli. 1930s vintage mural depicting the *Liberation of Milan.* Moderate. 231 S. College. 632-8834.

King Cole, down a flight of stairs half a block from Monument Circle, serves good American and Continental cuisine in a room decked with original 16th- and 17th-century oils. Pompano en papillote, roast duckling, and a wide selection of fresh seafoods are specialties. Jacket requested for men after 5:00. Legislators dine here; our choice for power lunching. Moderate. 7 N. Meridian Street. 638-5588.

The Majestic Oyster Bar & Grill, in a restored turn-of-the-century office building, features fresh fish, oysters, clams, mussels, and Dungeness crab. Waiters in tuxedos set a tone for the elegant setting of marble and oak, brass fittings, tile floors, and huge potted palms. Live piano music on Friday and Saturday evenings. Expensive. 47 S. Pennsylvania Street. 636-5418.

The Common Market is a country-European cafe/bistro featuring freshly baked breads and croissant sandwiches. Located on Monument Circle, it's perfect for a snack after attending the symphony in the Circle Theatre next door. Moderate. 51 Monument Circle. 636-4444.

The Cheese Cellar, in the Indiana Repertory Theatre building, serves cheese fondues, Swiss raclette, cheese boards, and chocolate fondue in a setting of bricks, stone, wood, and intimate booths. Good for lunches or after-theater snacks. Moderate. 134 W. Washington Street. 636-9052.

INDIANAPOLIS BY DAY

Walking the streets of downtown Indianapolis, with its modern high rises and beautifully restored classics, gives you a glimpse of the city's interesting past as well as its promising future. Outlines of **self-guided tours** are available at the **City Center,** and excellent **conducted tours** are offered by the **Indiana State Museum.** As you stroll the brick-paved sections near Monument Circle, you'll notice certain bricks inscribed with names. Volunteers contributed $25 to support the paving project. Some attractions are within walking distance of downtown; others require a car. **Landmark Tours** (634-0141) offers bus tours and downtown walking tours, and **Gray Line Tours** (634-4433) leave daily at 1:30 P.M. from the Indianapolis Hilton.

The **Indiana Soldiers and Sailors Monument,** a towering obelisk in the center of Monument Circle, is the focal point of the city. The 285-foot structure was built in 1887 to commemorate those who died in the Civil War. Its statues around the base depict scenes of loved ones going off to war, and on the very top is a 30-foot statue of Lady Victory. Waterfalls encircle the foot of the monument during summer months, and in the winter, there's ice skating on the frozen ponds. At holiday time, the monument becomes a giant Christmas tree. For 25 cents you can ride an elevator to the top. Open daily. Monument Circle. 631-6735.

The **Indiana World War Memorial** is another tribute to Indiana's war dead and occupies the five-block area of landscaped malls north of the circle. A 100-foot obelisk rises from the center square, and the terraced limestone Memorial Building at the south end of the plaza has an auditorium with inlaid granite floors and a memorial hall honoring the American flag. A military museum occupies the lower concourse. Open daily. 431 N. Meridian Street. 635-1964.

The **Scottish Rite Cathedral** is on one side of the war memorial plaza. Dubbed "one of the most beautiful buildings in the world" by the International Association of Architects shortly after its completion in 1929, the graceful Gothic structure has a carillon of 54 bells. Tours Monday through Friday 10 A.M. to 3 P.M. 605 N. Meridian Street.

The huge, cube-shaped and somewhat controversial LOVE sculpture by Robert Indiana graces the front of the **Indiana Museum of Art,** a building of Indiana limestone set on a magnificent bluff overlooking White River. Some 140 acres of landscaped grounds surround the museum, which contains Oriental art, 17th-century Flemish and Dutch paintings, African art, 18th-century French works, 19th-century British and American paintings, and the largest collection of Turners outside the United Kingdom. Down a winding, tree-lined path is the Lilly Pavilion, the old Eli Lilly family mansion, now housing 18th-century English and Continental furnishings. Closed Mondays. 1200 W. 38th Street. 923-1331.

Indianapolis's **Children's Museum** is the largest in the world and without a doubt one of the finest. Don't pass this up just because you're over 21. Its five floors of exhibits in a sleek modern setting fascinate all ages. If you're short on time, start on the fourth and fifth floors. You'll find a 1917 carousel, an antique doll collection, an electric train exhibit, and "Mysteries in History," where you don an archaeologist's hat to sort through clues in one exhibit. In the next room is a re-creation of the life hinted at in the first exhibit. A French fur trapper's cabin, a Conestoga wagon, and a Main Street from 1910 are among the sites you will discover. Open daily. 3000 N. Meridian Street. 924-5431.

The **Indiana State Museum** occupies the old City Hall building downtown and features exhibits tracing the state's history from prehistoric times through pioneer days and into the present. An ancient Indian artifact called a birdstone is of particular interest. The Foucault Pendulum, suspended from the stained-glass skylight in the rotunda graphically illustrates the rotation of the earth. Open daily. 202 N. Alabama Street. 232-1637.

The **Indianapolis Zoo** features Indiana animals in their natural habitats, African animals, and North American hoofed creatures. Although the current zoo is small—only about 500 animals—it's well laid out and interesting. With the completion of the new White River Park in 1990, the zoo will have a new home, and plans are to expand the animal population to 25,000. Open daily. 3120 E. 30th Street, in George Washington Park. 547-3577.

The **James Whitcomb Riley Lockerbie Street Home** is a charming memorial to the popular Hoosier poet who created "Li'l Orphan Annie" and "The Nine Little Goblins." The impeccably preserved Victorian home has many of the poet's personal possessions on display and is situated in Lockerbie Square, a restored 19th-century neighborhood with gaslights and old brick streets. Tiny wood frame cottages built at the turn of the century as employee housing for the old Lockerbie Glove Factory have been transformed into exquisite period dwellings. Open daily. 528 Lockerbie Street. 634-4474.

The **Walker Urban Life Center** is a restoration of the former headquarters of cosmetics mogul Madame C. J. Walker, the nation's first black woman millionaire. In the thirties and forties, the Walker building and Walker Theatre were the center of the nightlife and jazz that flourished in the clubs along Indiana Avenue. 617 Indiana Avenue. 635-6915.

The **Benjamin Harrison Memorial Home,** built in 1872, was the Indiana residence of the 23rd president of the United States. Much of the original furniture is here, as well as a collection of gowns worn by the first lady and her daughter. Open daily. 1230 N. Delaware Street. 631-1898.

UNIQUELY INDIANAPOLIS

The deafening roar of engines, the blinding whir of 33 internal combustion machines stretching the limits of ground speed in a seemingly endless oval pattern. From the releasing of hundreds of balloons into the air, to Speedway President Tony Hulman's "Gentlemen, start your engines," to the bottle of milk proffered to the winner at the end of Victory Lane, the **Indianapolis 500 Mile Race** is true spectacle. The annual Memorial

Day event has expanded into a month-long 500 Festival, with gala balls, a queen and court, and a grand parade. The **Hall of Fame Museum** at the **Motor Speedway** has a collection of past and present race cars as well as antique autos and memorabilia of such legendary figures as Mauri Rose, A. J. Foyt, and Bill Vukovich. Open daily. 4790 W. 16th Street. 241-2501.

Every August, the **Indiana State Fair** brings the flavor of the country to the big city. Harness racing, livestock shows, quilting exhibits, and cooking competitions remind city dwellers of our dependence on the nearby farmlands. Open year round on the grounds is Hook's Historical Drug Store and Pharmacy Museum, complete with 19th-century soda fountain. Open daily. 1202 E. 38th Street. 924-1503.

By the year 1990, 250 acres on the west side of downtown will have been transformed into **White River State Park,** which will include a 160-foot limestone water spire, a botanical garden, the Harrison Eiteljorg Museum housing western and Indian art, and the new 70-acre zoo. Currently, plans and mock-ups can be seen at the visitors' center in the 1870-era pumphouse. Open Monday through Friday. 801 W. Washington Street. 634-4567.

THE SHOPPING SCENE

Meeting "under the clock at Ayres" has been an Indianapolis tradition for decades. **L. S. Ayres,** on the corner of Washington and Meridian streets, is still a fine department store, and the Tea Room on the eighth floor is one of the nicer lunch places in the city—don't miss the chicken velvet soup. The **Wm. H. Block Co.** on Capitol Street is another large department store with fine selections. The downtown area is full of good stores, including those in the Claypool Shops arcade of the Embassy Suites hotel.

Also downtown, the **City Market** is a brick-and-wrought-iron 1886 market house that now has produce stalls, ethnic restaurants, and specialty shops. Strollers can sample Polish sausages, Persian pistachios, Greek olives, and freshly baked breads. On Market Street between Alabama and Delaware.

North of town, the current rage for trendsetting shopping for women's fashions is **Fashion Mall.** 8900 Keystone at the Crossing. 846-3283.

INDIANAPOLIS BY NIGHT

Gleaming white horse-drawn carriages carry passengers through the streets of downtown as people browse in the windows on their way to dinner or the theatre. Indianapolis sparkles at night with a wide variety of entertainments. For recorded information about current productions, call the **Entertainment Hot Line,** 639-LIVE. Tickets to many performances can be purchased at **Ticket Master** counters at Block's stores, the Natatorium, the Indiana Repertory Theatre, and Karma Record Stores. One note— these are for live performances. There are no movie theaters in the downtown area.

The **Indianapolis Symphony Orchestra,** under the direction of John Nelson, is internationally acclaimed for its renditions of works by contemporary American composers, and its new home, the completely restored Circle Theatre on Monument Circle, is a symphony itself. Built in 1916 as a grand movie palace, the theater languished for years as a porno house before being taken over by the Indianapolis Power and Light Company and returned to glory. Experts restored the exquisite Robert Adams–style moldings and duplicated the original mauve, ivory, and gray interiors. Monument Circle. 639-4300.

The **Indiana Repertory Theatre** occupies the city's other restored movie palace. The elaborate, 1920s-baroque Indiana Theatre has been divided into three stages for the IRT's October through May seasons. The professional Equity company performs on the Mainstage; the Upperstage presents more experimental productions and dance programs; and the Cabaret Theatre features musical revues in a nightclub atmosphere. 140 W. Washington Street. 635-5252.

The **Beef and Boards Dinner Theatre** offers light comedies and musicals with a buffet dinner. 9301 Michigan Road. 872-9664.

Although the IRT and the Beef and Boards are the only professional theaters in town—apart from touring companies, which usually play the 2,000-seat Clowes Hall on the Butler University campus—Indianapolis has had a long tradition of high-quality amateur and community theater groups. The **Indianapolis Civic Theatre** (1200 W. 38th Street, 923-4597), in the Showalter Pavilion at the Indianapolis Museum of Art, is the nation's oldest continuously operating community theater, and the **Repertory Theatre at the Christian Theological Seminary,** or **CTS** (1000 W. 42d Street, 923-1516), has long had a reputation of producing some of the best theater in town—amateur or professional. A relatively new group, the **Phoenix Theatre** (37 E. Ninth Street, 635-PLAY), is earning plaudits for its experimental work and programs of original plays.

The **Indianapolis Opera Company** (708 E. Michigan, 631-ARIA) performs four operas during the September through April season, and the **Indianapolis Ballet Theatre** (411 E. Michigan, 637-8979) presents five major ballets each season, which runs August through May. The imaginative young companies perform in both the Murat Theatre downtown and Clowes Hall. **Dance Kaleidoscope** (429 E. Vermont, 634-8484) is a contemporary dance troupe offering three concert series each year in March, June, and October.

Starlight Musicals (926-1581) are performed at the open air Hilton University Theatre on the Butler campus. In the summer months, audiences are entertained here by star concerts and musical comedies.

LATE-NIGHT INDIANAPOLIS

The downtown pubs and clubs have become popular after-hours hangouts.

The **Crackers Comedy Club** (8702 Keystone Crossing, 846-2500) showcases both local and national talent, and the **Indianapolis Comedy Connection** (110 S. Meridian Street, 631-3536) offers live entertainment five nights a week.

The **City Taproom** (28 S. Pennsylvania, 637-1334), in the historic Century Building, has live jazz nightly and serves over 40 different kinds of imported and domestic beer—10 on tap.

Ike & Jonesy's (17 Jackson Place, 632-4553) is a re-created fifties diner with Formica table tops and rock 'n' roll records spun by a disc jockey.

Sha-Boom's (201 S. Meridian Street, 639-1054) is more fifties ambience, with neon-lighted jukeboxes and booths cut from cars of the period—like an indoor drive-in.

Sports (231 S. Meridian Street, 631-5838) has a variety of games you can play while you sip—Skee-Ball, pinball, a free-throw net. A giant TV screen shows the current football or basketball game.

AT LEISURE

Day-Tripping

Indiana University, site of the movie *Breaking Away,* is a lovely campus of gray limestone buildings, a winding brook, and tree-lined walks. IU and its hometown of **Bloomington** make a nice day's trip. **Lake Monroe,** just minutes south of town, has sailing, swimming, fishing, and water skiing. For more information: Bloomington/Monroe County Convention and Visitors Bureau, 441 Gourley Pike, Bloomington, IN 47401. 812/334-8900.

Brown County is famous for its rich fall foliage, the quaint artists' community of Nashville, and Brown County Playhouse, where theater students at Indiana University present plays in the summer season. For more information: Brown County Convention and Visitors Bureau. 812/988-7303.

Columbus, Indiana, one hour south of Indianapolis, has become a world-famous enclave of beautiful architecture. Over 40 public and private buildings have been created by such noted designers as Harry Weese, Norman Fletcher, Cesar Pelli, and the Saarinens, father and son. For more information: 812/372-1954.

Parke County has 35 covered bridges, more than any other county in the nation, and a tour of these remnants of the past as well as glimpses of lovely old mansions and historic churches make for a refreshing getaway. Three state parks in the area have swimming, hiking, canoeing, and boating. For more information: Parke County Tourist Information Center, E. Ohio Street, Rockville, IN 47872. 317/569-5226.

In Town

Connor Prairie Pioneer Settlement, just northeast of town off I-65, is a totally re-created farm and village of 1836. You enter the past as soon as you walk through the gate. The men and women you meet will be dressed in period costume. They will be tending to their chores— spinning, weaving, milking—and will discuss with you life in the 19th century. Allisonville Road, 6 miles north of I-65, exit for Allisonville Road. 773-3633.

Sunday Customs

Sunday is relaxed and easy in Indianapolis. People go to the museums—most of which are open—play outdoor games, weather permitting, or have a leisurely brunch.

A number of the restaurants listed above serve excellent brunches, including **The Porch** at the Hyatt Regency, which has a third-floor view of the hotel's grand lobby; the **Velvet Turtle** in the Embassy Suites, which has salad and dessert buffets as well as breakfast; the **Cheese Cellar,** which features salad, pasta, fruit, and soup; and **Sir John Sexton's** at the Marten House, which offers traditional fare well prepared.

Spectator Sports

Basketball is a statewide obsession, and the NBA **Indiana Pacers** play at Market Square Arena (300 E. Market, 639-2112). The NFL **Indianapolis Colts,** lured from Baltimore in 1984, play in the 61,000-seat Hoosier Dome (200 S. Capitol Avenue, 252-COLTS). For hockey fans, there's the IHL **Indianapolis Checkers,** who skate at the State Fairgrounds Coliseum (1200 block of E. 38th Street, 872-4224). **The U.S. Clay Court Championships** are played on the tennis courts of the Indianapolis Sports Center (725 W. New York, 632-3250).

Active Sports

You couldn't be in a better place for active sports. All the facilities that make Indianapolis the amateur sports capital of the nation are open to the public when not being used in competitions. They are: **The Natatorium,** multipool complex, 901 W. New York (264-3517); **Track and Field Stadium,** 9-lane, 400-meter track, on New York Street, across from Natatorium, open 11:30 A.M. to 1:30 P.M., 4:30 to 6:00 P.M.; **Indianapolis Sports Center,** 24 tennis courts, corner of West and New York streets; and **Major Taylor Velodrome,** 3649 Cold Spring Road (926-8350), rental bikes and helmets available.

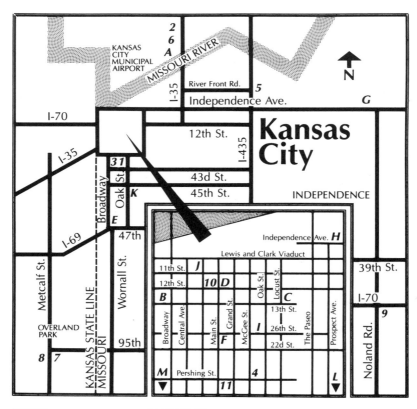

HOTELS

1 Alameda Plaza Hotel
2 Best Western Airport Hotel
3 Embassy Suites—Country Club Plaza
4 Hyatt Regency at Crown Center
5 Inn at Executive Park
6 Marriott Hotel
7 Marriott Hotel
8 Regency Park Resort and Conference Center
9 Shoney's Inn
10 Vista International Hotel
11 Westin Crown Center

LANDMARKS

A Airport
B Bartle Hall Convention Center
C City Hall
D Convention and Visitors Bureau of Greater Kansas City
E Country Club Plaza
F Crown Center

G Harry S Truman Library and Museum
H Kansas City Museum
I Liberty Memorial Museum
J Lyric Theater
K Nelson-Atkins Museum of Art
L Swope Park Zoo
M Westport Square

KANSAS CITY

GETTING YOUR BEARINGS

French essayist André Maurois once wrote, "Who in Europe, or in America for that matter, knows that Kansas City is one of the loveliest cities on earth?" Who indeed, one might echo. But with such extravagant praise—and from a Frenchman, at that—it seems we should make haste to become acquainted with this midwestern city.

Located in the heart of our nation, Kansas City excels in being the nation's number one in such diversified industries as farm equipment distribution, foreign trade zone space, hard winter wheat marketing, frozen food storage, publication of greeting cards, and manufacture of instrument landing systems. The city serves as company headquarters for Hallmark Cards, Interstate Brands, Farmland Industries, Chemagro, Cook Paints, Peterson Manufacturing, and Marion Laboratories, among many other corporations.

There are reams of other impressive statistics: Kansas City is the nation's second busiest rail center; it's second only to Detroit in automobile production; and it's among the top ten distribution, engineering, and convention centers.

But what of the heart of the city? For women, it is a city of promise and progress, a city in which a professional woman who handles herself in a professional manner is accorded the respect due her standing by the work force at large, a city in which an enlightened public awareness now makes it possible for a woman hosting a restaurant meal to host it completely—payment included—without hassle. These may sound like basic facts of life, but they represent giant steps forward for women in the Midwest.

This is a city that prides itself, too, on its beautiful surroundings. In one neighborhood alone—the Spanish-styled Country Club Plaza with its fountains, pastel-colored buildings, and wrought iron filigrees—one feels transported to old Seville, Kansas City's sister city in Spain. And the entire city has earned the nickname "the City of Fountains."

It is also a city in which shopping and dining out rank high on everyone's list of things to do. Expect to find some world-class examples of both as you become familiar with life here. Note: we learned the hard way that business entertaining in this city should be done early. Dinners at 6:30 are customary, 7 is considered starting late, and if you're the host, be sure to wrap things up by around 9:30; your motives are suspect if things go on much later than that.

Physically, the city is laid out in a classic grid pattern, making it easy to navigate once you have memorized the particulars. Numbered streets (starting with First Street) run east and west; named streets run north and south. Main Street divides the city into east and west segments. If you fail to remember these facts, however, don't despair; local people are unfailingly polite and will be delighted to give you directions.

The three main areas you will probably get to know quickly are Country Club Plaza (the "Plaza" of Seville fame, also a popular center for exclusive shops, restaurants, night spots, and strolling to admire the outdoor art); Crown Center, the "city within a city," which claims to specialize in commerce by day and entertainment by night; and Westport Square, an area of restored buildings, lovely restaurants, and shops.

About the suburbs surrounding Kansas City: the ones representing the most relative expansion sprawl to the south of downtown. They include Overland Park, with lots of new hotels, offices, and middle-class residences, and Prairie Village and Mission Hills, which are residential high-rent districts.

WHAT TO WEAR

Acceptable office-hours business wear should be unfailingly conservative; nothing too far out or avant-garde here, please. But evenings are another story. Dining out is an event, an occasion that calls for dressing up. You can even afford to err on the side of overdressing and be just fine in Kansas City. It is considered an insult to show up for a fancy evening in an outfit that is too casual.

When packing for your trip, think "layers," and include lots of pieces that can be added on or taken off as the temperatures fluctuate. And be warned: the extreme seasons (summer and winter) demand defensive dressing.

WEATHER WATCH

Blustery, icy winters and hot, humid summers are the rule rather than the exception. But the Kansas City area compensates for these extremes with lovely autumns and springs. Besides, as one loyal businesswoman puts it, "You'll remember the city for its heart, not its heat."

GETTING THERE

Kansas City International Airport is modern and large. It opened in 1972, serves 6 million passengers a year, and was designed around a multiple-terminal concept to shorten the distances between you and your flight. The designers deserve a medal—we have found this to be one of the easiest, most convenient airports to get around in the country. Some 26 airlines service KCI, with direct flights to over 90 cities in the United States, Canada, and Mexico. General information office: 243-5327.

It is about a 30-minute drive to downtown Kansas City; allow 10 minutes longer to reach Overland Park or Plaza. The KCI airport express bus costs $8.50 (243-5950). Also available is American Limo Service for $44 (421-6563), or you can take a Yellow Cab (up to five can share) for $22 (471-5000). Owing to local deregulation rulings, cabs can set their own rates—some have charged as much as $40 for the trip into town. Determine the fare *before* the trip; you do not have to take the first cab in line.

The following airport hotels operate free transportation shuttles to KCI:

Best Western	464-2525
Marriott	464-2200
Hilton	891-8900
Sheraton	741-9500

Car Rentals

Renting a car makes sense in Kansas City; in addition to the distances you may need to cover, prices are affordable and parking is generally easier than in other large cities. Rental agencies at KCI:

Avis	243-5760
Budget	243-5755
Hertz	243-5765
National	243-5770

GETTING AROUND

On-street parking downtown is available if you have the time to find it. If you're impatient, as we are, you'll probably just head for a parking lot and be done with it. Charges range from 50 cents to $5 a day.

It is more efficient and less aggravating, though, to walk or use public transportation around the downtown area. Buses in the CBD (central business district) cost only 60 cents round-trip. (Be sure to request your free return trip transfer.) Exact change is required. Buses outside the CBD run regularly from 6 A.M. to 6 P.M.; after that, less frequently. Call the Metro at 221-0660 for routes and more information.

The Johnson County Commuteride provides service between Overland Park and other Kansas locations and downtown. The cost is $1.25 one way; from 6 A.M. to 6 P.M. Call 362-2221 for more information.

For fun transportation, use the Kansas City Trolleys to negotiate the heart of downtown. For $1.00 you can ride around the downtown, City Market, Westport, and Plaza areas all day from May through October. Call 221-3399 for exact trolley schedules.

And if you're really in no hurry to get somewhere, you can hire one of K.C.'s horse-drawn carriages for a leisurely ride around the Plaza; with just a little imagination (and all those fountains and works of art out there), you could almost believe you were touring Old Spain. Carriages line up in front of Seville Square, or you can call Pride of Kansas City Carriages (931-2330) or Surreys Ltd. (764-2646).

GETTING FAMILIAR

Convention and Visitors Bureau of Greater Kansas City
City Center Square   Toll-free: 800/523-5953
1100 Main Street, Suite 2550   Recorded visitor information: 474-9600
Kansas City, MO 64105

Missouri Information Center
Truman Sports Complex   861-8800
4010 Blue Ridge Cutoff
Kansas City, MO 64133
Call ahead for printed materials and information.

Bartle Hall Convention Center
301 W. 13th Street   421-8000
Kansas City, MO 64105

Chamber of Commerce
920 Main Street   221-2424
Kansas City, MO 64105

The *Kansas City Times* includes daily entertainment listings; the *Kansas City Star* carries daily listings as well as a Sunday events calendar, a Sunday arts and entertainment section, and a Friday weekend guide. There are three *Squire* papers, look for the *Squire's Other Paper* which has weekly calendar listings. *Kansas City* magazine is a glossy monthly publication offering listings of events as well as local profiles and information.

Quick Calls

KANSAS CITY, MISSOURI,	Time and Temperature
AREA CODE 816	844-1212
KANSAS CITY, KANSAS,	Weather 531-4444
AREA CODE 913	Police and Fire Emergencies 911

AT YOUR SERVICE

Hoteliers in Kansas City are, for the most part, aware of the importance of the woman business traveler and alert to her needs. Women traveling alone will notice these attitudes reflected in the well-trained staffs. The hotels that follow all rate high in these priorities.

Airport Area

Kansas City Marriott Hotel
775 Brasilia
Kansas City, MO 64195

Toll-free reservations: 800/228-9290
Local number: 464-2200
Telex: 9107712034

A 265-room hotel that combines airport convenience with a pastoral lakeside setting. Small ponds and lakeside views outside and contemporary decor and amenities inside. Conference rooms with telex equipment are available.

The **King's Wharf Restaurant** serves three meals daily, including a Sunday brunch. The **Windjammer Lounge** has live entertainment five nights a week.

Best Western Airport Hotel
11828 Plaza Circle Drive
Kansas City, MO 64153

Toll-free reservations: 800/528-1234
Local number: 464-2525

A small property of 97 rooms that emphasizes homelike comforts. Management is on a first-name basis with many of the guests who are staunch in their loyalty to this hotel. Here you'll find such downtown-hotel comforts as a concierge, resident manager, and maintenance/troubleshooter on duty around the clock, free newspapers, morning coffee, and free champagne on weekday evenings. Business facilities are fairly extensive and include overhead projectors, movie projectors, and copy machines. Health facilities are equally extensive, including a heated pool, two saunas, and a whirlpool.

A restaurant and a lounge are on premises.

North

Inn at Executive Park
1601 N. Universal Avenue
Kansas City, MO 64120

Toll-free reservations: 800/821-8532
Local number: 483-9900

An ideal location if your business centers around the Amigo Trade Mart, which is adjacent to this hotel (and 15 minutes from the airport). The relaxing atmosphere includes fountains and a pond with some resident ducks. A vigilant security system featuring a staff of guards as well as in-room devices adds to your sense of relaxation.

Lakeside Restaurant serves three meals daily, all with views of the water.

	Concierge	Executive Floor	No-Smoking Rooms	Fitness Facilities	Pool	24-Hour Room Service	Restaurant for Client Entertaining	Extra-Special Amenities	Electronic Key System	Business/Secretarial Services	Checkout Time	Frequent Guest Program	Business Traveler Program	Average Single Rate
Alameda Plaza	•			•	•	•	Rooftop Restaurant		•	•	1 p.m.			$ 97 reg. $ 85 corp.
Best Western—Airport		•	•	•	•		Cafe Royale	•		•	12 noon		Corp.	$ 39 reg. $ 36 corp.
Embassy Suites			•		•		The Velvet Turtle				1 p.m.		Corp.	$ 95 $ 85
Hyatt—Crown Center		•	•	•	•	•	The Peppercorn Duck Club			•	12 noon	Gold Passport		$124 $109
Inn at Executive Park	•			•	•		Lakeside			•	12 noon	Ambassador Club		$ 69 $ 59
Marriott			•	•	•		The Kings Wharf		•	•	12 noon	Honored Guest	Corp.	$ 93 $ 85
Overland Park	•	•		•	•	•	Nikko's Japanese Steak House				1 p.m.			$102 $ 87
Regency Park			•		•		The Kansas Territory			•	12 noon	Regency Club		$ 49 $ 42
Vista International	•	•	•	•	•	•	American Harvest		•	•	12 noon		Executive Business Services	$ 97 $ 86
Westin Crown Center			•	•	•	•	Top of the Crown			•	1 p.m.	United Airlines (frequent flyer)		$122 $ 98

Midtown

Hyatt Regency at Crown Center

2345 McGee Street   Toll-free reservations: 800/228-9000
Kansas City, MO 64108   Local number: 421-1234
                                       Telex: 434022

If you're interested in structural safety, this is surely America's most-inspected building. Following the tragic collapse of a skywalk here in 1981 and the subsequent rebuilding of the interior, tests and inspections have become a way of life for this 732-room hotel. While we don't want to dwell on the hotel's past, we really must alert you to the extraordinarily strong feelings—pro and con—that residents have toward this Hyatt. Despite mixed reviews on a personal level, no one can deny that this is a beautiful hotel, and one with all the luxury amenities: concierge, entire no-smoking floors, well-appointed guest rooms, full-service health club and on-premises restaurants and lounges. In fact, the **Peppercorn Duck Club** is considered one of the city's choice dining spots. Renovations have resulted in what management calls an open lobby—meaning no dramatic skywalks.

Westin Crown Center

One Pershing Road   Toll-free reservations: 800/228-3000
Kansas City, MO 64108   Local number: 474-4400
                                       Telex: 426169

This 724-room hotel is built around a natural limestone formation called Signboard Hill, so that a natural five-story waterfall and an interesting midwestern rain forest dominate the lobby. In addition to the splendid health facilities, you may enjoy the unusual inclusion of a putting green, jogging track, volleyball, and shuffleboard courts.

    Top of the Crown and **Trader Vic's,** two Westin restaurants, are local favorites and enjoy the high regard of residents.

Vista International Hotel

200 W. 12th Street   Toll-free reservations: 800/445-8667
Kansas City, MO 64105   Local number: 421-6800
                                       Telex: 443454

Conveniently near the Bartle Hall Convention Center, the Municipal Auditorium, and the Lyric, Folly, and Midland theaters, the 574-room Vista provides both in-house comforts and access to what's happening in Kansas City. A dramatic nine-tier waterfall in the lobby has also become a favorite meeting place, as in "Let's meet for drinks at the waterfall." Executive floors offer 55 rooms with added amenities and security. The sports facilities are administered under the guidance of St. Luke's Hospital and include two outdoor tennis courts as well as pool and spa facilities.

    The **American Harvest Restaurant,** fast becoming an American standard of excellence, introduces the tradition to Kansas City. The **12th**

Street Rag bar offers some of the finest jazz in town (see "Late-Night Kansas City").

A new tradition is afoot here: the "Jazz Walk of Fame." Stars dedicated to jazz greats are being embedded in the hotel's 12th Street sidewalk. Each new addition is cause for much celebration.

Plaza Area

Embassy Suites—Country Club Plaza

220 W. 43d Street   Toll-free reservations: 800/EMBASSY
Kansas City, MO 64111   Local number: 756-1720

Spanish in atmosphere, this 12-story hotel is built around a 12-story atrium that highlights soaring, oversized fountains. Its proximity to the Plaza is a definite plus, as is Embassy's signature two-room-suites format.

Perks include complimentary full (as opposed to Continental) breakfasts, cooked to your order, and free two-hour cocktail get-togethers each evening.

Alameda Plaza Hotel

Wornall Road at Ward Parkway   Toll-free reservations: 800/821-5502
Kansas City, MO 64112   Local number: 756-1500
                                                            Telex: 42355

Probably the most elegant hotel in the area, the 396-room Alameda is beloved by locals and visitors alike. President Reagan set up campaign headquarters here; residents flock here weekly for the outstanding Sunday brunches. Spanish-style comfort is the byword here, with lots of overstuffed furniture and cozy little niches for informal meetings or relaxing. And literally outside the door is the world of the Plaza.

The **Alameda Rooftop Restaurant** is one of Kansas City's finest; there are also lounges and coffee shops in the hotel.

Overland Park Area

Regency Park Resort and Conference Center

9200 Metcalf Avenue   Toll-free reservations: 800/255-5030
Overland Park, KN 66212   Local number: 913/649-7000

Set on 21 acres of resort-type land, this 250-room hotel invites you to relax and go casual. Guests wander about in jogging suits or tennis whites, and nothing is high-powered (except for the athletic endeavor at hand). Lots of sports facilities, including jogging trails and heated outdoor pools.

Kansas Territory is a fireside fine-dining restaurant; **Gatsby's** is the disco.

Overland Park Marriott

10800 Metcalf Avenue   Toll-free reservations: 800/228-9290
Overland Park, KN 66212   Local number: 913/451-8000

A 402-room hotel with excellent conference facilities, a concierge level, excellent restaurants, and large-hotel services. The decor is Oriental— unexpected here in the middle of America, but restful nonetheless, with fat fish swimming in the ornamental pond, glossy marble floors, and a palette of soft colors throughout.

Nikko is the specialty restaurant where Teppanyaki chefs will prepare your dinner at tableside.

ON A BUDGET

Hotels

There's a chain of inexpensively priced, but very good quality, restaurants called Shoney's throughout the Midwest. They have added a hotel to their chain here in the Kansas City area—and we can recommend both the restaurant and the hotel as excellent value for the money.

Shoney's Inn
4048 S. Lynn Court Drive   Local number: 816/254-0100
Independence, MO 64055
Right off I-70, the main route, and near the Sports Complex, this hotel is about a 10-to-15-minute drive from downtown Kansas City. There are 116 rooms, both restaurant and coffee shop, and an outdoor pool. Singles begin at $34.

Restaurants

Shoney's restaurants (there are about 15 of them in the area) maintain the same high standards. You can count on a good steak dinner, including their top-notch salad bar, for about $6.95.

Barbeque is superspecial in Kansas City. As one local loyalist explained it, "Here, the secret ingredient is the sauce." (It seems that in Texas, the secret is in how the meat is cooked.) Whatever the secret, the end product is fiercely adored and consumed in great quantities. And it is also a bargain! Served in places deliberately called "joints," it is a folksy and casual experience that should not be missed.

At **Arthur Bryant's,** the undisputed numero uno joint in town, you can get a barbeque beef sandwich for an amazing $4.75 or a short slab of ribs for around $7 (not including the tempting side dishes, of course). A word about Bryant's: it is in a distinctly seedy part of town. Although admittedly not the greatest neighborhood, it's *not* as bad as it looks. However, we find the "joint" atmosphere a bit off-putting. We prefer to order takeout and enjoy Bryant's famous barbeque, picnic-style, in more pleasing surroundings. 1727 Brooklyn. 231-1123.

Entertainment

There are always free musical events happening in Kansas City, especially during warm-weather months. We suggest you call the Convention and Visitors Bureau (see "Getting Familiar") for schedules. You can also request their "Fun Calendar," a three-month listing of events. The general schedule includes free **concerts** on Friday and Sunday nights in outdoor settings (many of these are jazz concerts). Also, Sundays are free days at the **museums**.

Free **tours** are available, ranging from Hallmark to wineries (see "At Leisure" and "Kansas City by Day").

DINING OUT

Food writer Calvin Trillin has endeared himself in the hearts and minds of Kansas City residents by observing, "Not all the best restaurants in the world are in Kansas City—just the top four or five." We would never make so rash a statement, but we can heartily recommend the following:

Downtown Area

Golden Ox, famed for its Kansas City beef, is located between the old stockyards and the Kemper Arena. Very casual; moderate prices. 1600 Genessee Street. 842-2866.

Crystal Pavilion is glass enclosed and combines a casual atmosphere with spacious elegance. Good seafood appetizers. Expensive. 2450 Grand, Crown Center. 471-2003.

Top of the Crown offers rooftop viewing and dining. Elaborate dishes; live entertainment. Expensive. One Pershing Road, Westin Crown Center. 474-4400.

American Harvest Restaurant is the Vista International's homage to American regional cuisines. Menus change seasonally. Expensive. 200 W. 12th Street. 421-6800.

The **American Restaurant,** another celebrant of our country's regional specialties, is a multiaward winner (it has been in town longer than the American Harvest). Very formal atmosphere. Expensive. Atop Crown Center at 2450 Grand Avenue. 471-8050.

Savoy Grill is for you seafood lovers. Popular back in 1903 when Kansas City was a little cow town, the Savoy is going stronger than ever. Casual. Expensive. 9th and Central streets. 842-3890.

Lobster Pot: the historic setting enhances the entertainment value of this popular restaurant. There's a nonstop buffet of seafood favorites, and don't forget to sample the chowders. Expensive. In Union Station, 30 Pershing Road. 842-5090.

Jennie's Italian Restaurant focuses on Sicilian specialties and outstanding pizza. A casual, family-style place. Moderate prices. 511 Cherry Street. 421-3366.

Italian Gardens has been serving loyal patrons for over 60 years. Save room for dessert; the cheesecake and cannoli are made right here. Moderate prices. 1110 Baltimore Avenue. 221-9311.

Raphael's captures the delightful ambience of a French country inn, both in decor and in cuisine. Moderate prices. 325 Ward Parkway. 756-3800.

North of City

Dinner Horn Country Inn features those amazing five-course Pennsylvania Dutch–type meals. The inn is beautiful and the food is, too. Moderate prices. 2820 N.W. Barry Road. 436-8700.

East of City

Stephenson's Old Apple Farm is where country charm and country cooking get together to tempt you off your diet. Try their hickory-smoked specialties and the apple fritters. 40 Highway and Lee's Summit Road. 373-5400.

Westport

Go Jo Japanese Steak House: no Kobi beef here, just Kansas City's best. Teppanyaki specialties served with a flourish right at your table. Casual. Moderate prices. 4163 Broadway. 561-2501.

The Prospect of Westport, always trendy, *the* place for breakfast meetings with a light airy atmosphere and nouvelle cuisine. Moderate prices. 1 Westport Square. 753-2227.

South of City

E.B.T. now features a refurbished art nouveau elegance for its culinary treats. Try the Norwegian salmon and the poulet maitre d'. Expensive. I-435 and State Line, in the United Missouri Bank Building. 942-8870.

Jasper's Italian and Continental cuisine rated a place among the 75 Best Restaurants in America introduced by master chef Jacques Pepin. Expensive. 405 W. 75th Street. 363-3003.

Bristol Bar and Grill is where residents love to take visitors to impress them with the great seafood and superb service. Expensive. 4740 Jefferson (Country Club Plaza). 756-0606.

Fedora Cafe and Bar offers fine dining in European cafe ambience. A favorite of the trendier residents. Expensive. 210 West 47 Street (Country Club Plaza). 561-6565.

SPECIAL PLACES

Folks in these parts are partial to certain eating places that, over the years, have earned a special niche in their esteem. Among them: **Stroud's** and **Granny's** for K.C.-style chicken and steak dinners that come in under $10. Both have down-home atmospheres and are well worth a return visit. Stroud's is in South K.C., 1015 E. 85 Street. 333-2132. Granny's is at 1803 Baltimore. 421-1100.

And for a taste of that famous Kansas City **barbeque,** please see "On a Budget."

KANSAS CITY BY DAY

If you want to see how many fountains there are in "The City of Fountains"—or just want to get a general idea of the lay of the land—the best overview is from the 30th-floor **observation deck** at **City Hall,** a 1930s art deco building. Free admission. 414 E. 12th Street. 274-2605. Some say the best view is from atop the 217-foot **Liberty Memorial** at 100 W. 26th Street (see below).

The **Nelson-Atkins Museum of Art,** known locally as simply **The Nelson,** is internationally renowned for its Chinese treasures. So renowned, in fact, that it was one of only three U.S. sites selected by the People's Republic of China for their unprecedented archaeological exhibits in 1975. But there's more here than an Oriental treasure trove: the art of all civilizations from Sumeria in 3000 B.C. to the modern West are represented. Free admission on Sundays; closed Mondays. 4515 Oak Street. 561-4000.

The **Kansas City Museum,** on the former estate of millionaire Robert A. Long, spotlights regional history, including even an old-fashioned drugstore where ice-cream concoctions are still dished up. This museum also houses a planetarium and a natural history hall. Closed Mondays. 3218 Gladstone Boulevard. 483-8300.

The **Harry S Truman Home:** You're in Truman country now, and it is rewarding to discover this interesting president's roots. He spent his last days in this Victorian house, as did his widow, Bess. Located eight miles east of town. 219 N. Delaware Street. Independence, MO. 254-2720.

The **Harry S Truman Library and Museum** includes pieces from his White House days, a research center, a famous mural by Thomas Hart Benton, and a reproduction of his White House Oval Office where you can hear a tape of his own voice. The nearby Jackson County Courthouse offers a free 30-minute film, "The Man from Independence." U.S. 24 at Delaware Street, Independence, MO. 833-1225.

Liberty Memorial Museum, completed in 1926, is the only World War I military museum in the nation. Take the elevator to the top of the 217-foot "Torch of Liberty" tower for a panoramic view of the city. Closed

Mondays. Free admission. 100 W. 26th Street, across from Crown Center. 221-1918.

Swope Park Zoo claims to be the second largest municipal zoo in the country. Size aside, the natural habitat settings make it a pleasure to visit. Don't miss the African savannah and the tropical setting. Meyer Boulevard at Swope Park. 333-7405.

Self-guided tours offer opportunities to experience the city at your own convenience. We recommend the following free (or inexpensive) tour guides:

Plaza Walking Art Tour, Plaza Merchants Association, 4625 Wornall Road. 753-0100.

Monuments, Municipal Arts Commission, City Hall, 26th floor. 274-1555.

Battle of Westport, Westport Historical Society, Harris-Kearney House, 4000 Baltimore. 561-1821.

Harry S Truman Historic District, City of Independence, Department of Tourism, 111 East Maple, Independence, MO. 836-7111.

Hallmark Cards, 12 exhibits, short film, and crafts demonstrations. 274-3613.

Jazz district tour: see "Uniquely Kansas City."

THE SHOPPING SCENE

This town seems custom-designed for the shopper in us all: wonderful stores and shopping complexes abound, and there's not too much else to do. Kansas City ranks seventh in per capita retail sales in the nation's top 30 metro areas, so it would appear that Kansas Citians agree that shopping is also entertainment.

Country Club Plaza, referred to by locals simply as the Plaza, was modeled after Seville (Kansas City's sister city in Spain) and is an art-filled world of mosaic tiles, wrought-iron grillwork, outdoor artwork and sculpture, and fountains—fountains everywhere. Built in 1922 as this nation's first shopping center, the Plaza has held its own and remains, truly, a sight to see. Walk its Old World streets, browse through the likes of Saks, Gucci, Bonwit's, Swanson's, Macy's, and Seville Square Shops among the numerous favorites. And if you happen to be in town around the end of November, don't miss the spectacular, traditional lighting ceremonies held on Thanksgiving evening. The Plaza is in the southwest section of town, near the Nelson. 4629 Wornall Road. 753-0100.

Crown Center, although not exclusively for shopping, has its fair share of retail establishments you'll want to check out. Ranking high among the literally dozens of shops and boutiques, and the huge Halls Crown Center store, is the Heartland Market, which highlights specialty food shops and a network of markets. You also might consider buying a greeting card or two while you're here—Crown Center's parent company is Hallmark Cards. Folks around here call this center the City within a City. 2450 Grand. 274-8444.

Westport Square's origins date back to 1883, and its present-day charm is based largely on this heritage. Old-time lampposts, restored buildings, and other authentic touches enhance the shops, boutiques, galleries, restaurants, and watering holes that are so popular with both residents and visitors. Broadway at Westport Square. 931-2855.

In addition to these major centers, there are some 17 others, located in almost every area of town. As one local woman explained, "Remember—during cold Kansas City winters, shopping centers become entertainment centers for those who dare to come out of our normal hibernation." Some of these favorites include: **Bannister Mall** with about 130 stores, I-435 and Bannister Road; **Metro North,** with 115 stores, U.S. 169 and N.W. Barry Road; and **Oak Park Mall,** 140 stores, 95th and Quivira.

Two shopping areas attract residents and tourists alike with unique boutiques and specialty shops as well as artsy-craftsy stores:

Old Westport, a diverse area of shops like Pryde's, where you'll find a sort of one-stop shopping place for wedding or shower gifts. Westport at Baltimore. 531-5498.

Brookside Plaza, where Best of Kansas City sells everything made locally—including those special barbeque sauces. 6233 Brookside Plaza. 341-8186.

The **Antique and Art Center** focuses on real antiques rather than on galleries. 45th and State Line.

KANSAS CITY BY NIGHT

There's more to Kansas City night life than jazz. You'll find plenty of symphony, theater, and ballet here, too. Within a four-block area downtown are four of Kansas City's most popular cultural sites: the Folly Theater, the Midland Center for Performing Arts, the Lyric Theatre, and the Kansas City Music Hall.

The **Folly Theater,** a famous 1900s burlesque hall, was saved from demolition largely through the efforts of Joan Dillon, a self-professed "professional volunteer," whose drive to save the Folly resulted in its successful reopening in 1982 as well as its status as the first burlesque house to be listed in the National Register of Historic Places. Today's Folly productions range from one-man shows to Alvin Ailey American Dance Theater. 300 W. 12th Street. 474-4444.

The **Midland Center for Performing Arts,** a classic 1920s movie palace, serves as home to the **Theater League,** with Broadway productions offered in its main-stage gold-leaf-and-gilt opulence, and off-Broadway pieces on the more intimate Stage II. 1228 Main. 421-7500.

Lyric Theater is home to the **Lyric Opera,** the **Kansas City Sym-**

phony, and the **Kansas City Ballet** as well as various stage and ballet productions. 11th and Central. 471-7344.

Kansas City Music Hall, part of Municipal Auditorium, recently underwent a $2.25 million restoration to its former art deco splendor. A multipurpose facility for everything from concerts to presidential debates. 13th and Central. 421-8000.

The **Missouri Repertory Theatre** is in residence on the University of Missouri at Kansas City campus, Helen F. Spencer for Performing Arts Center. 4949 Cherry. 276-2704.

Dinner theaters include **Tiffany's Attic** (5028 Main) and **Waldo Astoria** (7428 Washington). Closed Mondays. Call 561-PLAY for both.

During the summer months, from mid-May through September, you can enjoy top entertainers like Elton John, Roberta Flack, and Wayne Newton at the vast outdoor **Starlight Theater** (second largest outdoor theater in the country) in Swope Park. 333-9481.

For **tickets,** call Dial-A-Tick, 753-6617; Concert Line (mostly rock or country music tickets), 931-0077; K.C. Arts Council, 842-5543; or Conservatory Concert Connection, 276-1171.

UNIQUELY KANSAS CITY

All That Jazz

If you're a jazz buff, your stay in this town will be sheer heaven—in fact, you may have come here just for the jazz.

It all began at **18th and Vine**—the unique sound that is immediately identifiable to jazz aficionados as the "Kansas City sound." Experts explain how it differs technically from New Orleans and Chicago styles, citing the distinctive two-four beat and the tendency toward more saxophones and background riffs. Whatever the musical rationales, the Kansas City jazz sound has been spellbinding audiences since the early 1900s when black musicians, migrating north from rural southern communities, arrived in town and settled in the area around 18th and Vine.

Today you can not only enjoy the sound in dozens of clubs and bars all over town (see "Late-Night Kansas City"), but you can also take a **self-guided walking tour** through the area, visiting the famous hot-pink house (now a National Historic Landmark) of the Mutual Musicians Foundation, the Gem Theater, and other significant sites in the 18th and Vine Heritage District—local jazz's road to international fame. The Kansas City Landmarks Commission publishes the walking guide. Call 474-1080 and request a free copy.

Jazz hotline, for who's playing where and information about the many special jazz festivals: 931-2888.

LATE-NIGHT KANSAS CITY

Most women who travel extensively in the nation's heartland agree that Kansas City boasts one of the liveliest nightlife scenes in the Midwest. In general, the bars in Westport draw a younger crowd; more mature revelers head for the spots in the Plaza. And because Friday nights are especially emphasized in this town, we've included a TGIF listing at the end of this section.

Jazz is king in Kansas City. Of the many places that offer the unique Kansas City sound, we especially enjoy the following three:

City Light, justifiably famous for its quality jazz performances, but also noteworthy for its great seafood and affordable prices. For about $20 you can enjoy a good dinner and some great jazz—all in comfortable surroundings. 7425 Broadway. 444-6969.

12th Street Rag offers live jazz five nights a week in an elegant lounge with a mural of jazz greats. The name comes from the piece composed by one of those musicians, Euday L. Bowman, in 1912 in a small bar just a few doors away. Vista International Hotel, 200 W. 12th Street. 421-6800.

Signboard Bar is calm and cozy, a sophisticated atmosphere for some world-class jazz performers and singers. Westin Crown Center, One Pershing Road. 474-4400.

The **Monastery** is great for quiet conversation, wine, and cheese. Sit in church pews and be served by brown-robed "monks." 6227 Brookside Plaza. 361-7319.

Stanford & Sons Comedy Shop is great for belly laughs every Wednesday through Saturday. (Wednesday is amateur night; others are strictly for the pros.) It's a very small room, so reserve in advance. 504 Westport Road. 756-1450.

Kelly's Westport Inn and Deli is very popular with Westport's younger crowd. Good for late-night munchies. 500 Westport Road. 753-9193.

Fuzzy's Sports Bar & Grill caters to sports fanatics with one-track minds; there's even a scoreboard to keep fans up-to-the-minute. 4113 Pennsylvania. 561-9191.

Checker's is the newest and hottest spot. Features a fifties theme and a tiered lounge encircling the dance floor, which is great for people-watching. 3954 Central. 561-8878.

Quincy's offers live entertainment and lively people-watching possibilities. Backgammon tables attract those who can manage to concentrate amid the commotion. Adam's Mark hotel, I-70 and Sports Complex. 737-0200.

Confetti is great if you're the type who likes New Year's Eve parties—lots of neon, bar-top dancing, nonstop noise—and, of course, confetti. 4201 Woodfield Drive. 763-9086.

TGIF

It's a local custom here to celebrate the start of the weekend with friends. Happy hours tend to expand into group dinners, and then the night life begins. The following spots are where you'll find celebrants: **Annie's Santa Fe**, 100 Ward Parkway, 753-1621; **Fred P. Ott's**, 4470 J. C. Nichols Parkway, 753-2878; **Rusty Pelican**, 8100 Ward Parkway, 523-9118; **Starker's**, 200 Nichols Road, 753-3565; **Fedora's**, 210 W. 47th, 561-6565; **Plaza III**, 4749 Pennsylvania, 753-0000; **Rusty Scupper**, 421 W. 14th, 474-4640; **Bristol Bar & Grill**, 4740 Jefferson, 756-0606; **The Prospect of Westport**, 41109 Pennsylvania, 753-2227; and **T.G.I.Friday's**, 1301 W. 86th Terrace, 361-1676.

AT LEISURE

If you find yourself with a couple of free days while you're in town, settle in a bit and enjoy Kansas City the way the locals do.

Day-Tripping

You might want to spend more time at the two **Harry S Truman** sites than a weekday visit will allow (see "Kansas City by Day"). And while you're in Truman country, which is about eight miles east of downtown K.C., continue on a bit along U.S. 24 to Sibley to visit **Fort Osage**. This is a reconstruction of the fort that served as the first outpost established by Lewis and Clark (1808–27). The entire fort—blockhouse, officers' quarters, barracks—are open for touring until 7 P.M. 795-8200.

The **James brothers**, Jesse and Frank, are two other names famous in these parts. You can visit their original homestead in nearby Kearney, MO. Call 635-6065 for directions.

Watkins Woolen Mill is a must if you are interested at all in fashion and fabrics. Established in 1860, this mill illustrates how the industry started. Visitors are also welcome to tour the family home, smokehouse, and other authentic buildings. North of Kearney, near U.S. 69 and Road. 296-3357.

Unity Village is an interesting glimpse into experimental religion at work. Established in 1889 as a nondenominational religious movement, the Unity School of Christianity now has some 6 million members in 160 countries. The village is a self-contained, self-sufficient municipality, a cluster of Mediterranean-style buildings set among the rolling hills and woodlands of Missouri. The 165-foot tower has become a mid-American landmark. Visitors are welcome, and free guided tours are offered daily. Fifteen miles southeast of downtown K.C. 524-3550.

McCormick Distilling Co. tours take you through the process involved in making bourbon. No free samples, but you can buy the product after the tour. In Weston, Platte County. 386-2276.

Winery tours, on the other hand, usually include free tastings: **Bowman Wine Cellars** (386-5235); **Pirtle's Weston Vineyards** (386-5588); **Midi Vineyards** (566-2119).

In Town

Oceans of Fun and **Worlds of Fun** are two nearby amusement parks to appeal to the kid in you. "Worlds" is huge, a 157-acre extravaganza offering over 120 rides and attractions. "Oceans" offers amazingly realistic water thrills in this landlocked location. The parks are adjacent to each other and are located about 12 minutes from downtown. Take exit 54 on I-435. 459-9283 or 454-4444.

City Market sells literally everything—from homegrown produce to clothing to potted plants. Extremely popular (an estimated 30,000 people visit on a single Saturday), this market has a festive air and is great for people-watching and browsing. Open every day except Sunday. 5th and Walnut. 274-1341.

Riverboat cruises, of all kinds and for whatever mood, are available here. Choose from sightseeing cruises, dinner cruises, even a Sunday brunch cruise. Docks at One Grand Avenue. 842-0027.

Sunday Customs

Brunch in Kansas City is a business-as-usual affair, at least as far as local dress codes are concerned. Leave the jeans and sneakers back in the room, and make your appearance in something frightfully correct, like the suit you wore on Friday, but perhaps with a more casual sweater to show it's the weekend. Of all the places in town to enjoy brunch, we like these:

Top of the Crown: the $12.50 tab includes nonalcoholic drinks. One Pershing Road. 474-4400.

Rusty Pelican offers free champagne after noon. Brunch until 3 P.M. $6 to $12. 8100 Ward Parkway. 523-9118.

Cap'n Jeremiah Tuttle charges extra for drinks. $7. Ramada Inn Southeast. I-435 and 87th Street. 765-4331.

Barney A.'s in the Radisson-Muehlebach Hotel charges $9.75 and includes nonalcoholic drinks. 12th and Baltimore. 471-1400.

Alameda Rooftop at the Alameda Plaza hotel also charges $9.75 and includes soft drinks. Ward Parkway at Wornall. 756-1500.

The Corner Restaurant serves a breakfast menu that can cost you from 70 cents to $3.75. Westport and Broadway. 931-6630.

Spectator Sports

Kansas City is a true baseball town. They adore their 1985 World Series champions, the **Royals** (owned by Muriel Kauffman, probably their number one fan).

There are excellent sports arenas in town: the **Harry S Truman Sports Complex** on the eastern edge of town features the country's only twin stadiums. Here in Royals Stadium, with its 12-story-tall electronic scoreboard, the American League team plays baseball every April through October. For information, call 921-8800; to charge tickets, call 921-4400.

The NFL **Kansas City Chiefs** play football next door in Arrowhead Stadium. An attraction here is the instant-replay action on the giant scoreboard. Call 924-9300 for ticket information.

The **Kansas City Comets** play major league indoor soccer in the Kemper Arena. The Kemper, convenient to downtown, also hosts concerts and special events, and was the site of the 1976 Republican Convention. Call 421-7770 for information.

For **sports scores,** call 234-4350. METRO runs **express bus service** to Chiefs and Royals games at the Truman Sports Complex. Call 221-0660.

Active Sports

There are tennis courts, golf courses, jogging, and other sports facilities throughout midtown, the 19,000 acres of parks, and the surrounding suburban areas. In **Swope Park,** in addition to the zoo and theater, are two golf courses, a pool, two fishing lakes, ball fields, tennis courts, a model airplane field, and a frisbee court. 444-3113.

You will find about 20 lakes nearby for all water sports. Call Kansas City Parks and Recreation at 444-3113 or Jackson County Parks and Recreation at 795-8200 for information on times, reservations (if necessary), and other information.

HOTELS

1. Hotel Bel-Air
2. Beverly Hills Hotel
3. Beverly Terrace
4. Beverly Wilshire
5. Biltmore
6. Century Plaza
7. L'Ermitage
8. Miramar Sheraton
9. Le Mondrian
10. Sheraton Premiere
11. Sheraton Grande
12. Westin Bonaventure
13. Westwood Marquis

LANDMARKS

A. Disneyland
B. Griffith Park Observatory
C. J. Paul Getty Museum
D. Hollywood Bowl
E. Huntington Art Gallery
F. LA County Museum of Art
G. Mann's Chinese Theater
H. Memorial Coliseum
I. Museum of Science and Industry
J. NBC Studio
K. Shubert Theater
L. UCLA
M. Universal Amphitheater
N. Universal Studio
O. Visitors and Convention Bureau

LOS ANGELES

GETTING YOUR BEARINGS

San Franciscans often thumb their noses, New Yorkers frequently jeer, but everyone talks about Los Angeles. You will likely hear this city denigrated with nicknames like LALA Land or Tinseltown; the bad rap takes in traffic jams, smog, and plastic people; and adjectives like mellow, laid-back, and flaky have stuck here as nowhere else.

We'd be lying if we said the jibes have no basis in truth, but they are not the whole story. Look at how Los Angeles shone under the watchful eyes of the rest of the world during the 1984 Olympics. About 625,000 people came to the City of Angels during the Games, and the event came off without a hitch. To the surprise of skeptics, there was less traffic than usual, the smog did no damage to the athletes—actually the weather was very pleasant—and no terrorists attacked. The city was totally upbeat, and visitors returned to their homes with a positive attitude.

Granted, when faced with the prospect of a business trip to the Coast, you could become intimidated. There's no doubt that Los Angeles can confound and overwhelm even the most savvy traveler with its unfathomable sprawl, but try not to overreact.

We believe the best approach is to just face facts: this city simply has no center. At least no *one* center. There is a downtown of a dozen skyscrapers, but even a panoramic view from any of their rooftops cannot encompass it all. Not even the more dazzling—and central—outlook from Hollywood's Griffith Park Observatory can quite capsulize the carpet of lights stretching to Santa Monica at the Pacific.

Los Angeles's 8 million people live in a metropolitan area of 95 incorporated cities and hamlets wrapped into one; it's almost like a patchwork quilt, each piece with a distinct identity. Taking the city as a whole is like talking about the United States as one entity. For instance, the San Fernando Valley alone (you know, that place just over the Hollywood Hills where "Valley girls" spend their teen years in vast shopping malls) is the size of Chicago. And that's just one suburb. There's Beverly Hills and Hollywood, West Hollywood and Pasadena, Marina del Rey and Venice and Santa Monica, and on and on and on.

(And, just so you don't hang on to any misconceptions about what L.A. really is, we want to point out that Disneyland and Knott's Berry Farm, often considered local attractions, are actually farther south in the county called Orange.)

Still, the sprawl of Los Angeles is not a gigantic problem if you choose a hotel convenient to your appointments, assuming they are clustered. For example, if you're in banking or in town for a convention, you'll probably be busy downtown, and if you're in the media business, there's a good chance you will be focused on Century City.

We have to admit, though, that wherever in the city your dealings take you, you really should rent a car. Locals laugh at the public transport, and taxis cost a fortune to cover the distances you'll probably end up wanting to explore. Even before you turn on the ignition, though, take our advice and get all the facts about where you're going. Always ask, "What's the cross street?" when given the address on any major boulevard. Sunset, to name one, stretches from Chinatown to the sea, about 30 miles, and Wilshire's that long, too. And pin down as many landmarks as you can, just as a safety measure. A *Thomas Guide* is the local bible for finding one's way, so do yourself a favor and pick one up upon arrival.

Except for areas you are unlikely to transit—East Los Angeles and Watts—we find L.A. to be a fairly safe city, despite its size and bad reputation. Hollywood Boulevard has fallen from its glamour days (it now draws an element of lowlife), but bright lighting and lively crowds hitting the glittery movie theaters keep it safe for accompanied women. We would say don't walk alone at night, but nobody walks in L.A. anyway.

And as to their idiosyncratic life-style, Angelenos would call their casual approach sane compared to other city dwellers' frenzied mode of operation. In fact, those who do work in this city work as hard as anyone else. Notice what time the town closes up: it's hard to find food after 11 P.M., for this is a city of early risers.

You'll notice that the city's boardrooms are still male dominated, even though women outnumber the other sex and, in some circles, carry real clout. They have made impressive inroads, considering their most visible talent has been their blonde beauty on the silver screen. That stereotype endures, since the movies perpetuate it and many young hopefuls still come to Tinseltown to sell it. We find, though, that more clever businesswomen are working their way beyond the image.

Despite its reputation as a cultural void, Los Angeles has grown up to prove Woody Allen was wrong when he cemented that image in *Annie Hall*. With a bevy of wealthy, world-class museums—spurred on by the aggressive Getty—and a new blossoming of live theater, opera, and dance, in spaces old and new, storefront and palatial, Los Angeles has become a city rich in more than just movies and television.

We know that after digesting all this—and the information to come—if you're a first-timer, you're probably sighing with disbelief and still harboring some uncertainties. But bear with us and don't get frayed because you think that you'll be put off by the city or that you won't survive comparison to the physical perfection of some Hollywood women. Los Angeles is a great place to be if you're female; it's just waiting with unlimited possibilities. Put away your fears, pack your bags, and head for the sunshine. You may not want to stay forever, but you'll be glad you put in an appearance. Anything can happen in this, the land of golden opportunity.

WHAT TO WEAR

This is not a town in which you're apt to see a proliferation of gray or navy blue tailored suits. We tend to choose our most casual clothing when packing to visit Los Angeles; even the choicest restaurants don't take offense when you arrive in jeans. In fact, of all the cities in this book, this is the only one in which we feel safe in saying that anything goes—or at least anything goes as far as you want to take it. Dressing for success in Los Angeles is as loose a concept as dressing appropriately for the privacy of your own home. You know your industry, and you know yourself, so don't dress out of character—at least too much—for either, and you'll be fine.

WEATHER WATCH

The moviemakers who first discovered Los Angeles at the turn of the century set up shop here because the sunny weather made filming possible year-round. Millions of others who have relocated here have done so first and foremost for the climate. Except for the minor winter rainy season, jaded locals will even say it is boringly sunny. Indeed, summer can be scorching, sometimes accompanied by almost unbearable Santa Ana winds, but the omnipresent air-conditioning, low humidity, and pleasantly cooled-down evenings make L.A. a comfortable scene for the most part. Even chilly winter days rarely call for more than a light jacket or sweater. And don't worry, not everybody has a tan. They are working much too hard to catch more than a few rays through the sunroofs of their cars as they drive between appointments.

GETTING THERE

Those of us who need to fly in or out of Los Angeles will be forever grateful to the 1984 Olympics for nudging city officials into a much needed renovation of **Los Angeles International Airport** (LAX). Terminal and direction signs are clearer, and the airport now has two individual roadways, the upper level for arrivals and the lower one for departures, making traffic smoother and less congested than before. For general LAX information, call 646-5252.

Nearly all major carriers, both national and international, are represented at LAX, more than 70 in all.

From the airport to downtown Los Angeles is approximately 22 miles, and depending on the amount of freeway traffic, the trip can take anywhere from a half hour to more than an hour. Rush hours occur at the conventional times, but we never try to second-guess how heavy the traffic will be. One large accident can back the freeways up for miles. Average cab fares are: to downtown, about $25 to $30; to Hollywood, about $30 to $40; and to Beverly Hills, about $22 to $25.

Another possibility—and one we recommend—is the **Super Shuttle**. This money-saving, share-the-ride service offers door-to-door pickup. Be sure to notify the company five hours prior to departure when you're leaving L.A., and allow two hours before your plane takes off for driving time. Upon arrival in the city, call Super Shuttle on the courtesy phones in the baggage claim areas after you've retrieved your luggage, and the van will usually arrive to pick you up in about five to ten minutes (except in the early morning hours when it could take longer). For most business destinations in Los Angeles, the charge is $11 per passenger. Call 777-8000, 800/554-0279 in California, or 800/554-6458 outside the state.

If you are going to be staying in Hollywood, the Valley, or anywhere in the northern part of Los Angeles, you may choose to fly into **Burbank Airport**, if possible. Call 818/840-8847 for information. If the coastal cities or the southern part of Los Angeles is your destination, you may want to land at **Long Beach Airport**. For information, call 421-8293. Burbank and Long Beach are served by a few short-haul airlines.

Car Rentals

Several other modes of transportation are available from the airport. But we recommend renting a car right there and saving yourself the bother and expense later on. Do try to find a deal that includes unlimited mileage; you're going to need it.

Car rental agencies represented at LAX include:

Alamo	649-2242
Avis	646-5600
Bob Leech's Autorental	673-2727
Budget	645-4500
Dollar	776-8100
Hertz	482-5365
National	746-3194

Rent A Wreck	478-0676
Thrifty	645-1880
General	417-3030

On the subject of rental cars, remember that in L.A., you are what you drive. So it could be a savvy business move to opt for a rental that's fancier than what you drive back home. If that's the case, and if your budget can handle it, pass up the look-alike rental counters and call one of the following: Showcase Rental Cars, offering Alfa Romeo Spider convertibles and Peugeot 505s (800/421-6808 nationwide; in California, 800/345-2277); or 7-11 Rent A Car, offering Rolls, Lamborghini, and Maserati models (714/650-1180).

GETTING AROUND

Los Angeles, with its myriad communities and long distances between business centers, can appear formidable to the novice traveler. Taxis are expensive and not very reliable. The bus system is citywide, but slow and not entirely reliable either.

Engaging a limousine is a viable alternative and, for many, a common practice. But the most effective and economical means of transportation is a car. When renting a vehicle, call in advance for current prices and availability. Most rental car agencies are represented at LAX and most offer airport pickup (see "Getting There").

Taxi fares begin at $1.90 and $1.40 for each additional mile. Aside from at the airports and some popular hotels, cabs are never seen waiting; they always have to be called. Of the major taxi companies, we trust Celebrity/Red Top (278-2500), Independent Cab (385-8294), and United Independent Cab (558-8294).

If you can, pamper yourself. You're worth it. Besides, in many instances, a limousine in Los Angeles can be more cost efficient than a taxi and without a doubt more fun. Some of the best: Paradise Limousine Service (818/891-8085), Fleetwood Limousine Ltd. (213-208-0209), and the Limousine Connection (213/277-5177).

The RTD, more formally called the Southern California Area Rapid Transit, is the only public transportation service in Los Angeles. For the uninitiated, it's difficult to figure out and not very practical. So avoid buses if at all possible. If they are your only alternative, call 213/626-4455 for information about routes and fares.

The freeway system, once comprehended, is a marvel. Just some basics:

The San Diego Freeway (405) runs parallel to the coastline from San Diego past Santa Monica and continues north to the San Fernando Valley.

The Santa Monica/San Bernardino Freeway (10) can be accessed at 405. Going east, you will travel past downtown and continue to San Bernardino. Traveling westward, you will end up in Santa Monica.

The Pasadena/Harbor Freeway (11) stretches from Pasadena past downtown and ends in San Pedro at the Los Angeles Harbor.

The Golden State Freeway (5) is one of California's main interstate highways, running the full length of the West Coast, from the Canadian to the Mexican border. Keep in mind that the Golden State travels from the San Fernando Valley to Anaheim.

For a more thorough understanding of the freeways and streets, pick up a *Thomas Guide to Los Angeles*. Few locals go out without it.

Except for major business centers, parking is convenient and inexpensive. This is the land of valet parking, available at stores, restaurants, and hotels for a nominal charge or tip. Parking rates are usually higher downtown, in Century City, and in Westwood.

GETTING FAMILIAR

Greater Los Angeles Visitors and Convention Bureau (GLAVCB)
505 S. Flower Street   213/239-0200
ARCO Plaza, Level B
Los Angeles, CA 90071

If you write ahead, the bureau will send you an in-depth visitors' guide with comprehensive information on all facets of the city. But it may be worth your while to stop in either at the above address (although it isn't that easy to find since this branch is located in the bowels of the ARCO Plaza Building; call first for directions) or at one of the others listed below. They'll offer you all kinds of brochures and advice, and in many languages.

The other bureau outlets are located at the Pacific Federal Savings Building, 6801 Hollywood Boulevard, Hollywood, 239-0290; and both the arrival and departure terminals of the Tom Bradley International Terminal at LAX, 215-0606.

If you're still not satisfied, look up the various visitors' bureaus and chambers of commerce in whatever areas interest you.

The *Los Angeles Times* is the newspaper of record in this city, but there's also the *Los Angeles Herald Examiner* and the *Los Angeles Daily News*. All three are morning newspapers. For information on what's happening in the city, pay particular attention to the *Times*'s Sunday Calendar Section and the *Herald's* Weekend Style section. *Los Angeles Magazine,* published monthly, is a thick richly produced glossy that's packed with information about people, films, stage, television, art, weekend events, and dining places. *California,* another monthly, is also worth picking up for the above information plus strict dining and film reviews. *Valley* magazine covers happenings in the San Fernando Valley. The *Los Angeles*

Weekly and the *Los Angeles Reader* are both free and available at bookstores, cafes, and the like, in tabloid format. They're worthwhile, with unbiased reporting offering an eclectic fare of reviews. *Variety* and the *Hollywood Reporter* are show business publications that appear daily. They're written in show biz lingo, though, so don't feel bad if you can't understand every word. Still, this is the most up-to-the-minute way of finding out what's going on in the industry.

You should be aware that if you are looking for a telephone number, you must know the town in which the number is listed, as each of the Los Angeles–area cities has its own telephone book. For example, if you are calling someone in Brentwood and you ask for the number in Los Angeles, the operator may not be able to help you unless he or she knows it is a West Los Angeles number.

Quick Calls

AREA CODE 213
(Los Angeles proper, Hollywood, West Hollywood, Beverly Hills, Brentwood, Bel-Air, Santa Monica, Long Beach, South Bay)

AREA CODE 818
(San Fernando Valley, Pasadena, Burbank, San Gabriel, Glendale, Pacoima)

Time 853-1212
Weather 554-1212

Emergencies 911

AT YOUR SERVICE

We can't stress too heavily the importance of selecting a Los Angeles hotel that's convenient to where you plan to conduct business. Otherwise, you could end up driving more than dealing, and that would probably defeat the purpose of your visit.

Downtown

Biltmore
515 S. Olive Street
Los Angeles, CA 90013

Toll-free reservations: in California 800/252-0175; outside California 800/421-0156
Local number: 624-1011
Telex: 677686

Since the Biltmore's opening in 1923, this venerable hotel has been the temporary home for many famous people. The birth of the Academy of

Hotel	Concierge	Executive Floor	No-Smoking Rooms	Fitness Facilities	Pool	24-Hour Room Service	Restaurant for Client Entertaining	Extra-Special Amenities	Electronic Key System	Business/ Secretarial Services	Checkout Time	Frequent Guest Program	Business Traveler Program	Average Single Rate
Hotel Bel-Air	●				●	●	Hotel Bel-Air Restaurant	●			2 p.m.			$180–$280
Beverly Hills Hotel	●			●	●		Polo Lounge The Coterie	●		●	12 noon			$140–$205
Beverly Wilshire	●			●	●	●	La Bella Fontana	●			12 noon			$105–$170 $130 corp.
Biltmore	●	●	●	●	●	●	Bernard's	●	●	●	12 noon		Business Traveler Program	$110–$160 $110 corp.
Century Plaza	●		●		●	●	La Chaumiere	●		●	1 p.m.		Century Plaza Complete	$124–$155 $118 corp.

Hotel	Restaurant	Time	Frequent Flyer Program	Corporate Program	Rates
L'Ermitage	Cafe Russe	1 p.m.		The Executive Program	$135 / $205 corp.
Miramar Sheraton	International Room / Garden Room	12 noon	Distinguished Customer Service	Sheraton Executive Traveler	$105–$145 / $110 corp.
Le Mondrian	Cafe Mondrian	1 p.m.		The Executive Program	$110–$295 / $110
Sheraton Grande	Ravel	12 noon	Mileage Plus	Sheraton Executive Traveler	$150 / $120 corp.
Sheraton Premiere	Oscars	12 noon		Sheraton Executive Traveler	$120–$160 / $125 corp.
Westin Bonaventure	Beaudrys / Top of 5	1 p.m.	Mileage Plus	Executive Circle	$89–$109 / $104–$119 corp.
Westwood Marquis	Garden Terrace / Dynasty Room	1 p.m.			$150–$190

Motion Picture Arts and Sciences took place here in 1927 through such film luminaries as Mary Pickford, King Vidor, and Jack Warner. The Biltmore is the official home for the Los Angeles Dodgers and houses its opponents. It has hosted many heads of state and royalty as well. The giant hotel—there are 1,022 guest rooms—is a landmark in California, perched on the edge of Pershing Square downtown. Renovated to the tune of $40 million, the elegance and Old World charm of this property with its high lobby ceiling and quiet atmosphere is a good choice for business and professional clientele. It pays particular attention to the woman traveler. The Biltmore Health Club has a steam room, Nautilus equipment, and a juice bar. The Club Floor features a library, wide-screen television, and an honor bar.

As for dining, **Bernard's** is a formal, award-winning, haute cuisine restaurant, popular with Angelenos and booked up well in advance. Cuisine is nouvelle with a fish specialty. The **Grand Avenue** bar is refined, one of the few downtown where a single businesswoman can feel comfortable alone.

Westin Bonaventure

404 S. Figueroa Street   Toll-free reservations: 800/228-3000
Los Angeles, CA 90071   Local number: 624-1000
     Telex: 677628

This 1,500-room hotel is as new as the Biltmore is old. It too has become a popular Los Angeles meeting spot. The mirrored towers of the complex designed by John Portman are distinctive in the city's downtown skyline. Bubble elevators rise from the lobby and then go outside the building to guest floors and a rooftop restaurant. The lobby has mirrored fountains and a meandering lagoon. Special services for business travelers include printing and copying facilities. Guests use the Los Angeles Racquet Club. Of the 94 suites, 26 are special with dining rooms and libraries.

The Bonaventure has four restaurants: the **Sidewalk Cafe,** located in the atrium lobby by the lakes, specializing in buffet and hamburgers; **Top of Five,** on the 35th floor, a dressy affair featuring New Orleans brunch; **Beaudry's,** with haute cuisine; and the **Lobby Court,** with casual fare and a seafood bar.

Sheraton Grande

333 S. Figueroa Street   Toll-free reservations: 800/325-3535
Los Angeles, CA 90071   Local number: 617-1133
     Telex: 677003

Soft pastels and a sunken lobby establish a calming ambience in this 469-room downtown hotel. A spokesperson for the hotel claims that 82 percent of those who stay here are business travelers, a large number of whom are women. So the property pampers guests with butlers on each floor who respond to the ring of a bell and four concierges, so there's rarely a wait. The Grande is connected to the Los Angeles Racquet Club, and safety is tight in this hotel with only one way in and one way out.

As for dining, **Ravel** is a *Travel/Holiday* award-winning restaurant serving California cuisine. The more casual **Back Porch** is open for all three meals, and **Tango** has nightly entertainment and a bar suited to the businesswoman on her own.

Universal City

Sheraton Premiere
555 Universal Terrace Parkway
Universal City, CA 91608

Toll-free reservations: 800/325-3535
Local number: 818/506-2500
Telex: 170738

We think that women who want to have access to all areas of the city, and who appreciate a hotel that has them in mind, should consider this lovely property. Rooms are spacious and the clientele largely professional, making for a good business environment in a nice setting. Butler services are offered in this Sheraton hotel, too. The list of guest privileges is long: jogging course, weight rooms, heated pool and spa, and, nearby, handball and racquetball courts, aerobics classes, golf—even equestrian trails. The lobby plays host to local artists' work in a changing exhibit each month.

Fine dining is on the premises, with **Oscars at the Premiere,** the hotel's formal signature dining room. The American cuisine has a New Orleans flair and is served on china with sterling silver under crystal chandeliers. **Crystal's** serves three American and Continental meals a day under a glass atrium. **Character's** is a contemporary entertainment lounge in an enclosed courtyard and the **Atrium** lounge is adjacent to the lobby, good for people-watching.

West Hollywood/Beverly Hills

Le Mondrian
8440 Sunset Boulevard
West Hollywood, CA 90069

Toll-free reservations: in California 800/343-8997; outside California 800/321-4564
Local number: 650-8999
Telex: 182570

You'll spot this all-suite hotel long before you get to it. Part of the L'Ermiate group of hotels, Le Mondrian, on the Sunset Strip, is the personification of art, inside and out. The multicolored facade was created by Israeli Yaacov Agam in the spirit of the hotel's namesake. The interiors are bold and sleek, very 1980s, with fine art by contemporary artists like Miró and Peter Max. Even the lobby floor has a Piet Mondrian motif, done in various colored marbles. The business traveler who can't go anywhere without computer in tow will be glad to know that room television sets are computer-compatible. All 188 suites have three telephones, with up to five incoming/outgoing lines. The hotel has a full European health spa, complete with indoor and outdoor whirlpools.

Cafe Mondrian offers an eclectic fare of French, American, and Japanese cuisines, all prepared with the freshest ingredients. The adjacent bar is one of the best on the Strip for a woman traveler. **La Terrase** is open for outdoor dining and drinking under the stars, with a fantastic view of the city all around.

L'Ermitage

9291 Burton Way   Toll-free reservations: in California 800/
Beverly Hills, CA 90210   282-4818; outside California 800/421-
                                         4306
                                         Local number: 278-3344
                                         Telex: 698441

Recipient of the Mobil Five-Star and AAA Five-Diamond awards, this residentially placed hotel has a reputation for excellent service and deluxe accommodations. Among the complimentary items that have made this small European-style all-suite hotel famous are Continental breakfasts, limousine service, and a minimum of three phones with two incoming/outgoing lines. The hotel's concierge is female and innovative, so depend on her if you need to set up a meeting in a hurry or want to get into an overbooked restaurant.

L'Ermitage's European panache extends to **Cafe Russe,** open only to hotel guests and their guests. Original paintings by such masters as Van Gogh, Renoir, and Dufy compliment the fine French cuisine. The adjacent bar offers nightly music, classical guitar or piano, and each afternoon serves complimentary caviar and pâté to guests.

Beverly Hills Hotel

9641 Sunset Boulevard   Local number: 276-2251
Beverly Hills, CA 90210   Telex: 691459

The Beverly Hills Hotel's pink stucco facade and flowering, palm-fringed gardens have been a signature for gracious hospitality and star-gazing since the golden days of Hollywood. In fact, so convenient are its famed pool cabanas to the adjacent tennis courts on the hotel's spacious grounds that many a movie mogul has negotiated deals in them between sets. This is a full-blown 16-acre resort set in the middle of Beverly Hills on some of the nation's prime real estate. Many of the 268 guest rooms have private patios and fireplaces, and individual bungalows on the premises offer privacy, kitchens, and full dining rooms—a good place for a mini-meeting if ever there was one. The Cinema Room is a bigger, more spectacular place to hold a meeting, as it's primarily a private screening room, with all kinds of audiovisuals.

And who wouldn't visit L.A. without stopping in at the **Polo Lounge?** It's one of the most talked about hotel restaurants in the nation, and a preferred meeting place even among local businesswomen. The **Fountain Coffee Shop** is your usual soda-fountain-type place, and the **Coterie** is the hotel's gourmet restaurant with international cuisine served in an elegant setting.

Beverly Wilshire

9500 Wilshire Boulevard
Beverly Hills, CA 90212

Toll-free reservations: in California 800/
282-4804; outside California 800/421-
4354
Local number: 275-4804
Telex: 698220

At the junction of Rodeo Drive and Wilshire Boulevard, this is the central place to stay in Beverly Hills. It is an elaborate hotel, managed by Regent International and designed in Italian Renaissance with a French influence. Italian marble is used throughout the building, which is so solid it withstood two major earthquakes. A tower was added in 1971, with its own entrance and a domed porte cochere, lighted at night with gas lamps, connecting the two wings. This is the type of hotel that encourages a sense of excitement and movement. People who work in Beverly Hills frequent it, as do representatives of the movie, law, and medical businesses. When a businesswoman checks in, she is introduced personally by the assistant manager to the maitre d's of the different restaurants, and she is roomed near the elevators to avoid long walks down the hall.

For dining, **La Bella Fontana** is a classic European-style restaurant with lace tablecloths and crystal chandeliers. The food is expensive California cuisine, and the dress is fairly formal. **El Padrino Bar–Rotisserie** is a more relaxed cafe-type establishment with an early California atmosphere. It is a very social and busy place, open for lunch and dinner daily. At **Hernando's Hideaway,** Mexican, Italian, and Continental dishes make up the menu. The coffee and sundry shop, **Cafe of the Pink Turtle,** serves fountain treats, salads, and sandwiches. El Padrino and Hernando's both have comfortable bars; Hernando's is especially relaxed. The **Zindabad** is a more romantic bar.

Century Plaza

2025 Avenue of the Stars
Century City, CA 90067

Toll-free reservations: 800/228-3000
Local number: 277-2000
Telex: 698664

This is the only hotel in Century City proper; it is also close to Beverly Hills, Westwood, and Santa Monica. The hotel added a $85 million tower in 1985, bringing the total number of rooms to over 1,000. Frequented by TV network employees and entertainment executives, the hotel is very popular with local businesspeople as well as President Reagan. Each year during the television sweeps, the hotel is crawling with out-of-town journalists covering the new shows. The main building is modern; the tower is a mixture of old and new. Fine museum pieces and antiques are used in the tower's decorations, an area specially suited for business travelers. The complex has a pool and outdoor Jacuzzi. Guests also have privileges at the Century West Club, which offers racquetball, squash, exercise equipment, massage, and whirlpool. Tennis and golf can be arranged nearby.

The **Vineyard** offers lunch and dinner in a relaxed atmosphere with an early California influence. Floor-to-ceiling wine cabinets make the diner feel as if she is in a wine-country chateau, and 220 different types of wine are offered. The **Bar,** adjacent to the Vineyard, is a very comfortable place to be alone; a harpist performs every evening. Across from the Vineyard, on the lower lobby level, is the **Cafe Plaza,** with a French sidewalk cafe feel. The **Garden Restaurant** in the lobby level, overlooks gardens, pools, and fountains. In the center of the lobby, the **Lobby Court** serves cocktails, with piano music in the late afternoon. This is a perfect place for a woman to go by herself. **La Chaumiere,** on the mezzanine level of the tower addition, is a very fancy restaurant, which serves elements of nouvelle, French, and regional cuisines for lunch and dinner. The **Club Bar,** another easy place for a woman to be alone, has the feel of a European bar. There is a private dining room for 12 people here as well. The **Terrace Room** is the tower's informal restaurant, off the lobby. The **Living Room,** lobby lounge, offers high tea seven days a week to the strains of a harpist.

West Los Angeles

Westwood Marquis
930 Hilgard Avenue
Los Angeles, CA 90024

Toll-free reservations: in California 800/ 352-7454; outside California 800/421- 2317
Local number: 208-8765
Telex: 181835

Just a block away from Westwood Village, this hotel, with its distinctive white lights and outside luggage elevators is used by those with business at UCLA, or in advertising and entertainment. The ambience of this all-suites hotel is that of a small quaint European hostelry. The management is extremely discreet about their large celebrity clientele and are known for personalized service and attention to detail. The property has six meeting and banquet rooms, and many cosmetic companies such as Lancome and Estée Lauder use these rooms for their teaching seminars. Health facilities include a hydrotherapy pool, steam bath, Jacuzzi, Universal equipment, and Life Cycles. In addition, facial consultation, and makeup and massages can be arranged.

The **Garden Terrace,** off the lobby, is graced by a white gazebo in the middle, and has one of the most talked about buffets in town. In fact, food critic Merrill Shindler in the *Herald Examiner* said that this was the best Sunday brunch he ever ate. The **Dynasty Room** offers formal dinner amid original art and porcelains from the Magnificence of China Collection of the T'ang Dynasty. Reservations are required at this restaurant, which is very popular with Los Angeles's upper crust.

Hotel Bel-Air
701 Stone Canyon Road
Los Angeles, CA 90077

Local number: 472-1211
Telex: 674151

As Richard Alleman explains in his book *The Movie Lover's Guide to Hollywood*, the main building of this elegant retreat was established in the 1920s as the real estate office for the immediate community of Bel-Air. Minority groups, including movie people, were restricted from buying within Bel-Air's prestigious gates. Then, after the depression, money began to speak. It wasn't until the 1940s that the office was converted into a hotel, filled with luminaries from the business, as it is today. In the middle of residential Bel-Air, the 92-room hotel also includes 33 suites located in Mission-style bungalows. Unhurried and elegant, it is set on 11½ acres of heavily wooded canyon. Recreation includes a heated swimming pool and a great environment for jogging or walking; tennis and golf are available nearby. The emphasis here is on personal service; as one person at the hotel put it, "We don't know the meaning of the word no."

The **Dining Room** restaurant, popular with nearby residents, is open for breakfast, lunch, and dinner; it has a particularly popular Sunday brunch. California cuisine is the fare, with French and Oriental influences. The adjoining bar is classy and attractive to women alone.

Santa Monica

Miramar Sheraton

101 Wilshire Boulevard	Toll-free reservations: 800/325-3535
Santa Monica, CA 90401	Local number: 394-3731
	Telex: 6831356

The ocean is directly across from this resort hotel and can be seen from many of the rooms. Decor is modern, and the hotel is geared toward the business traveler, especially during the week. Of the 300 rooms, some have ocean views, some have pool views, and some have mountain views. Many Hollywood stars come here to "get away," favoring the small cottages by the pool. Corporate customers can use the Santa Monica Athletic Club for a small charge. It is about five minutes away and offers racquetball, Nautilus, free weights, aerobics classes, sauna, whirlpool, and tanning equipment.

Three restaurants operate in the Miramar: The **International Room** serves breakfast and a formal dinner of Continental cuisine daily. **Cafe** is open for breakfast, lunch, and dinner, coffee shop–style. The **Garden Room** overlooks the pool area and serves lunch. The bar is a nice peaceful place where a woman can sit quietly alone.

ON A BUDGET

Hotels

Staying overnight in Los Angeles doesn't have to mean booking yourself into a gigantic convention hotel or super-high-priced luxury property. It doesn't have to mean the bottom of the barrel either, staying in a no-frills motel miles from where you plan to spend most of your time. Our choice is:

Beverly Terrace

469 N. Doheny Drive   Toll-free reservations: 800/421-7223
Beverly Hills, CA 90210   Local number: 274-8141

The location of this 37-room hotel—central Beverly Hills—is great, especially at the price. The rooms are pleasant, providing the usual double bed, color television, and direct-dial telephones. Beyond that, there aren't many frills. The decoration is simple, and service is cordial. Complimentary coffee and refreshments during the day in the hotel lobby. Rates start at $50.

Eat breakfast (often booked) or lunch at the pool or in the highly regarded **Scully's** on the premises, dished up by Englishman Phil Scully, who, according to one hotel employee, would be in show business if he weren't a chef.

If you want to break away from the norm, bed-and-breakfasts are becoming very popular and in lower price ranges. Try these: Salisbury House, in the West Adams area 737-7817; or Eastlake Inn, near Dodger Stadium 250-1620.

Restaurants

Some places we recommend if you don't want to break the bank:

The **Original Pantry** is a favorite greasy spoon among locals and is open 24 hours a day, but it's not in the best area so avoid it at night. Expect to wait in line. 877 S. Figueroa Street, Los Angeles. 213/972-9279.

Phillippe's, the Original's tagline is "Home of the Original French Dip Sandwich." Very, very casual (sawdust on the floor). Located downtown, this is a good lunch selection. 1001 N. Alameda Street, Los Angeles. 213/628-3781.

The **Cafe Casino** features quality buffet-style dining at prices averaging $6 to $10. At five locations: 9595 Wilshire Boulevard, Beverly Hills, 213/274-0201; 1299 Ocean Avenue, Santa Monica, 213/394-3717; 1145 Gayley Avenue, Westwood, 213/208-1010; 17630 Ventura Boulevard, Encino, 818/784-4872; and 3300 Bristol Street, Costa Mesa, 714/751-2737.

Entertainment

For inexpensive pleasures outdoors, go to the beaches or the many parks in L.A. We like Zuma or Malibu Beach, and Griffith Park or Hancock Park are good choices. If you like roses during the months of April and May, approximately 17,000 are in bloom at Exposition Park Rose Garden.

The best guides for free entertainment information are the *Los Angeles Weekly* or the *Los Angeles Reader.*

DINING OUT

From a culinary standpoint, Los Angeles's offerings are as diverse as the ethnic groups that populate the city. Thai and other Asian cuisines are as prevalent here as fast food is in mid-America. The following for Japanese food in the City of Angels has resulted in a proliferation of sushi bars. When we're in this town, we enjoy haute cuisine, California cuisine (some say it took off here), nouvelle, New Orleans, Mexican, Italian, French, Moroccan, German—the list is endless.

For a woman dining on business in Los Angeles, this just might be heaven. Everyone who's anyone "takes a meeting" at the chic eateries that dot this sprawling city. Below are some ideas for places in which you can do the same. One note: try not to get caught up with booking the newest in restaurant if it is miles away from your base of operation. Los Angeles boasts enough fine restaurants in which to dine that are within easy reach, so don't go out of your way because you think you'll impress your client. By the time you get there, you'll be too tired to participate in any meaningful conversation.

Also remember to keep some single dollar bills in your wallet. More often than not restaurants offer valet parking, no matter how impressive or unimpressive the establishment.

Power breakfasts are most effective when they take place in Los Angeles's hotel restaurants. If at all possible, and if your hotel contains a dining spot that's nice enough for a business meeting—as most of the better ones do—stay there for the first meal of the day.

Other suggestions for dining in the Big Orange:

Almost everyone wants to get in to **Spago** if just to see what all the hoopla is about. This trendy restaurant, located just off Sunset Strip, was star chef Wolfgang *(Good Morning America)* Puck's first endeavor after he left the legendary Ma Maison (now closed until 1987). Spago offers the diner a party atmosphere, with bright, contemporary, changing art gracing the stark walls and well-prepared California cuisine including some of the most imaginative pizzas ever invented. One hitch: it isn't easy to get in here at the spur of the moment unless you have a creative concierge or are friends with a friend of the restaurant, so plan accordingly. Surprisingly enough, the rates here are reasonable. 8795 Sunset Boulevard, Hollywood. 652-4025.

Chinois on Main is Puck's latest addition, serving a combination Chinese/French/California cuisine in a theatrical atmosphere. Interior is by Puck's wife, Barbara Lazaroff, done in an Oriental motif with a dash of new wave elegance. Not too expensive. 2709 Main Street, Santa Monica. 392-9025.

Le Chardonnay is a French bistro that's big on grilling and spit cooking. If you are celebrity hunting, eat in this lovely restaurant that's also a suitable venue for making a big deal. High-end moderate. 8284 Melrose. 655-8880.

If you're staying downtown, the **Seventh Street Bistro** is both convenient and exciting, serving French nouvelle fare. The decor of soft pastels and high columns makes the restaurant, frequented even by solitary diners, stately. Expensive. 815 W. Seventh Street. 627-1242.

Not far from downtown and worth the ten-minute ride is **La Petite Chaya,** the city's prototypical Franco/Japanese restaurant so named for the French-trained Japanese chef who is a true artist. This is an L.A. favorite. Expensive. 1930 N. Hillhurst Avenue, Los Feliz. 665-5991.

A meeting spot for businesspeople and artisans alike and convenient to both downtown and some of the television studios, **L.A. Nicola** is one of our personal favorites. Food is eclectic, once called "nouvelle friendly" by a local critic, probably because chef/owner Larry Nicola is so nice. Moderate. 4326 Sunset Boulevard. 660-7217.

Rex il Ristorante is downtown, an oasis of elegance with the feel of a luxurious ocean liner. The northern Italian fare has a nouvelle influence, served flawlessly in the art deco Oviatt Building. Extremely expensive. 617 Olive Street. 627-2300.

The **Bistro Garden** is filled with women lunching. The style is similar to a French bistro with fish, veal, and pasta specialties. Moderate. 176 N. Canon Drive, Beverly Hills. 550-3900.

Bistango's French and Italian cuisine is served in a contemporary space at lunch and dinner. 133 N. La Cienega, Beverly Hills. 652-7788.

At **Trumps** the main claim to fame is the high tea, but the cuisine is worth a try, too; it's an eclectic mix of Californian, Mexican, French, and Italian. The decor has a southwestern flavor, with pastels and subdued lighting. Expensive. 8764 Melrose Avenue, on the edge of Beverly Hills. 855-1480.

Casual but hip is the description that best suits the **Chaya Brasserie,** with its large bamboo garden and hints of Japanese style. Cuisine is Italian mixed with French. 8741 Alden, Los Angeles near Cedars Sinai Hospital. Expensive. 859-8833.

Since Ma Maison is closed until 1987, perhaps a meal at **La Toque** will do. The owner/chef Ken Frank, one of the nation's young superchefs, uses the freshest of ingredients in his French fare, and you're likely to spot a celebrity or two here. Expensive. 8171 Sunset Boulevard, Los Angeles. 656-7515.

Michael's is definitely considered the poshest restaurant in the beach area. It's fairly formal and mixes French and California contemporary cuisines. 1147 Third Street, Santa Monica. 451-0843.

We could go on and on, but we'll go just a little further by making some other can't-miss suggestions based on cuisine:

Japanese: Restaurant Katsu, 1972 N. Hillhurst Avenue, Los Feliz,

665-1891; **Mexican:** Lucy's El Adobe, 5536 Melrose Avenue, Hollywood, 462-9421; **Thai:** Tommy Tang's, 7473 Melrose, West Hollywood, 651-1810; **Continental:** Chasen's, 9039 Beverly Boulevard, Los Angeles, 271-2168; **Moroccan:** Dar Maghreb, 7651 Sunset Boulevard, Hollywood, 876-7651.

LOS ANGELES BY DAY

Although late-night life in Los Angeles is limited, daytime activities here more than make up for that lack. If you're interested in movie magic, studio tours, and television shows, see "Uniquely Los Angeles." For other attractions, read on.

Did you ever see *Rebel without a Cause?* Then you'll remember the place where James Dean went to find Sal Mineo. In real life, though, this gleaming white art deco landmark is known as the **Griffith Park Observatory and Planetarium,** where you'll now see stars of a different type—the ones in the sky—if you go there at night. During the day this is a great lookout point. If the smog stays away, you can even see the ocean miles away. 664-1191.

A myriad of museums dot the city. We think the following are especially interesting:

California Museum of Science and Industry covers computers, communications, health, energy, mathematics, agriculture, media, and aerospace. In Exposition Park. 700 State Drive. 744-7400.

Natural History Museum houses full-size dinosaurs and other, more contemporary animals in their natural settings, as well as rocks and gems. 900 Exposition Boulevard. 744-3411.

The **Los Angeles County Museum of Art** features pre-Columbian, American, and European art as well as Indian and Southeast Asian art. 5905 Wilshire Boulevard. 857-6111.

Adjacent to the County Art Museum is the **George C. Page Museum of La Brea Discoveries.** Here, dinosaur fossils are still in evidence in the tar pits on the grounds. 5801 Wilshire Boulevard. 857-6311.

Huntington Art Gallery is a mansion housing British and American paintings, most notable of which is Gainsborough's *Blue Boy.* The grounds of the estate are some of California's most spectacular botanical gardens. 1151 Oxford Road, Pasadena. 818/405-2100.

The **Norton Simon Museum of Art** contains old masters like Degas and Rembrandt, with plenty of notable sculpture on the grounds outside. 411 W. Colorado Boulevard, Pasadena. 818/449-3730.

The **Museum of Contemporary Art** mounts changing exhibits featuring innovative West Coast artists. 152 N. Central. 382-MOCA.

The **J. Paul Getty Museum,** facing the Pacific Ocean on the coast near Malibu, is a Roman-style villa with formal gardens displaying Greek and Roman antiquities and West European paintings. This is one of the richest museums in the country in one of the most beautiful settings. 17985 Pacific Coast Highway. 458-2003.

To discover the many elements of Los Angeles, do so by exploring the city's ethnic neighborhoods. Of particular note:

Olvera Street between Macy, Alameda, and Spring streets (687-4344), where the aroma of Mexican food permeates. This car-free street contains shops with homemade candies, clothes, and candles.

Nearby is the **El Pueblo de Los Angeles State Historic Park,** where you can discover the city's beginnings. At 845 N. Alameda. 625-5045.

Chinatown is between Broadway and Hill and offers numerous restaurants and fun shops.

Lining First Street, **Little Tokyo** is on the edge of Chinatown with the New Otani Hotel, pastry shops, and Japanese products sold in Japanese shops.

THE SHOPPING SCENE

Like everything else in Los Angeles, shopping possibilities are spread far and wide. People mostly think of Beverly Hills and its famous Rodeo Drive as the main, high-priced shopping areas, but Main and Montana streets in Santa Monica, Ventura Boulevard in the valley, and Melrose Avenue in West Hollywood are among other popular shopping areas.

Los Angeles is also the land of the urban shopping mall. From the Beverly Center, with its high-class European boutiques, to Del Amo, billed as the largest mall in the world, almost every town and section of Los Angeles has one or many shopping malls. Notable are the Glendale Galleria, Santa Monica Place Mall with an ocean view, Century City Shopping Center, Woodland Hills Promenade, the Topanga Canyon Mall, and the May Company Shopping Plaza in North Hollywood.

The most fashionable department stores in the city, with branches all over town are Robinson's, Nordstorms, Neiman-Marcus, and I. Magnin. Beverly Hills has Bonwit Teller and Saks Fifth Avenue on Wilshire Boulevard. In the lower priced arena, also located throughout the basin, are the May Company and the Broadway.

Beverly Hills

A stroll down the two-and-a-half block, 1,600-foot commercial center of **Rodeo Drive** defies comparison. Its sculpturally tailored Indian laurel fig trees, its valet parking, its sunshine set it more than an ocean apart from Rome's Via Condotti, London's New Bond Street, and Paris's Rue Faubourg St. Honore. Celebrities in sunglasses, tennis buffs in tans, Hollywood wives in velour sweatsuits or vicuña coats, and the tourists in awe—Rodeo Drive has become the shopping mecca of America West.

The fame of the Rodeo name in the early eighties led to its gracing the drive's first deluxe multistory shopping complex, the Rodeo Collection (which, by the way, has had trouble luring shoppers upstairs, according to a number of Rodeo veterans). The name Rodeo Collection, in turn, has been chosen by Ford Motor Company to distinguish the thirtieth-anniversary model of its luxury Thunderbird. Think luxury in Los Angeles, and you now think Rodeo.

Rodeo Drive's reputation for luxury made it a recession-proof romp of conspicuous consumption for the rich. Bijan, the Iranian owner of the sumptuous menswear store of that name—the only store on the street that requires an appointment—was only half joking when he told a reporter, "To be my customer you must have an income of $100,000—a *month.*" His neckties alone start at $75, shoes at $400, suits at $1,000.

Along with the internationally known names here, like Gucci and Cartier, there are many that are California originals. One of these is Giorgio's (205-2400) at 273 N. Rodeo, the inspiration for Judith Krantz's novel *Scruples* and clothier to the stars. This store is on the tip of everyone's tongue these days because of their popular namesake perfume.

At the end of Rodeo Boulevard, on Santa Monica Boulevard, is one of the city's trendiest athletic and casual clothing stores. Many people who visit L.A. go home with distinctive clothing from Camp Beverly Hills at 9640 Santa Monica, which bills its fare as "survival clothing" and has such items as fatigues, painters' pants, and sailors' pants.

West Hollywood

Melrose Avenue may be in the heart of **West Hollywood,** but it's on the edge of the world. It is on this boulevard of flashing neon and technicolor hairdos that you'll find the latest trends in new wave, fast forward, postmodern, and whatever's next in style. The mile and a half of intriguing, one-of-a-kind shops and splashy bistros stretching from a few blocks west of La Brea to a few blocks west of Crescent Heights has become to Los Angeles what the West Village has long been to New York City.

Farther along this stretch, to the west, Fred Segal is an old regular at 8100 Melrose (651-1800). Parachute at 8215 Melrose (651-0177) has trendy clothing inspired by its Montreal sister store. Melons at 8750 Melrose (854-7734) features clothing by up-and-coming designers.

Laise Adzer, at 8583 Melrose (655-9285) and other locations around the city, is frequented by many celebrities who take the advice of helpful saleswomen about putting together all the unique pieces of the colorful outfits here. In the same general area is the Esprit Store, at La Cienaga and Santa Monica (659-9797). This store, in a converted roller disco, has taken L.A. by storm with its innovative clothing and advertising concept.

Downtown

If it's a bargain you're after, head for **downtown.** You'll find the California Mart (620-0260) at 110 E. Ninth Street. Each month, on the last Friday, all showrooms are open to the public and offer prices below wholesale on sample items. For discount designer wear, visit the Cooper Building (622-1139) at 860 S. Los Angeles Street.

Also downtown, shopping with a Japanese flavor is fun in Little Tokyo, with modern as well as Oriental antiques—plus a branch of one of Japan's most popular department stores, Matsuzakaya, in Weller Court, near the New Otani Hotel and Garden.

Westwood

For the young—or young at heart—**Westwood** is a good localized place to shop with its villagelike atmosphere and shops standing side by side. This area became popular because of the closeby influence of UCLA, and you'll now find plenty of casual, comfortable styles as well as whimsical gifts.

To go with its emphasis on sports and health, L.A. has many super places to buy exercise clothing. A couple of suggestions: Bodywear for colorful cotton dance wear from France (2717 Main Street, 392-8651) and the Dance Center of London, in Westwood, offering a huge variety of innovative leotards, warmup clothing, and casual daywear.

LOS ANGELES BY NIGHT

Los Angeles is not the cultural wasteland that a lot of people are convinced it is. You can find within the city limits not only any kind of entertainment to suit whatever mood you happen to be in but also top-quality performances.

Live theater is hopping in the Big Orange, and although this city has no Great White Way or even a central place for stage action, there are hundreds of choices nevertheless. Houses are large and small, experimental and traditional, offering musical fare as well as comedy, the classics, and contemporary drama. One fun aspect of going to the theater in Los Angeles is the possibility that you may see your favorite movie or television star hitting the boards. Actors love the stage and frequently take the opportunity to work out in the theater even if they don't earn the big bucks there as they do on the small and large screens.

A sampling of what's available in the larger venues:

The **Music Center** downtown incorporates three theaters: the Mark Taper Forum (offering mostly new works under the direction of Gordon Davidson), the Dorothy Chandler Pavilion (mostly big-stage events like Broadway musicals), and the Ahmanson (both the classics and new plays). At 135 N. Grand. 972-7211.

The **Shubert Theater** in Century City houses large-scale Broadway musicals, usually with long runs. 202 Avenue of the Stars. 553-9000.

The **Pantages,** in an art deco building, presents mostly Broadway musicals. 6233 Hollywood Boulevard. 410-1062.

The **Westwood Playhouse** has both perfect sightlines from any-where in the house and some of the most uncomfortable seats we've ever tried to relax in. Here you'll see new plays, comedies, and musicals. 10886 Le Conte Avenue. 208-5454.

Don't overlook the smaller houses, please. You'll get the chance to experience some of the most innovative theater in the country. One of the newest is the **Los Angeles Theater Center,** which bowed in 1985 with four stages carved into a vintage bank building in the heart of Los Angeles's redeveloping downtown. The LATC presents challenging pro-ductions of contemporary and classic concerns—this place is not, as the *Wall Street Journal* noted, for the *Annie* crowd. But the fare is not so offbeat as to be off-putting. Famous American names try new works here, and there are new twists on old works as well, each for no more than $20 a ticket. As managing director Bill Bushnell put it, "I want to create the theater of the 21st century." 514 S. Spring Street. 488-1122.

Among smaller theaters, of particular note are: The **Globe The-ater** (1107 N. Kings Road, 654-5623), a smaller replica of Shakespeare's famous theater; and **Fountain Theater** (5060 Fountain Avenue, 663-1525), with contemporary comedy and drama.

As for music, anyone who's anyone eventually makes it to the Coast, not only to cut their records but to play for the locals, too. The **Universal Amphitheater** is a state-of-the-art concert facility, displaying the best in rock, pop and jazz. 100 Universal City Plaza, Universal City. 818/980-9421.

The **Los Angeles Philharmonic** uses the Dorothy Chandler Pavilion in winter months. 135 N. Grand Avenue. 972-7211.

In the summer, you really shouldn't miss taking a picnic dinner and heading for the outdoor pleasures of either the **Hollywood Bowl** (2301 N. Highland, 850-2000), summer home of the Los Angeles Philhar-monic and various visiting artists, including in June the Playboy Jazz Festival; or the **Greek Theater** (2700 N. Vermont, 216-6666), featuring the world's best popular, rock, and classical artists.

Los Angeles has no particular dance season, but several troupes make their way here every year, including the American Ballet Theater and Alvin Alley. The best way to find out who's performing where is to contact the **Los Angeles Dance Alliance** at 465-1100 or check local listings.

As for the **movies,** well, you couldn't have picked a better town. Often films are shown here before any other place in the world. Theaters dot the city, frequently showing sneak previews of upcoming releases.

Two Los Angeles theaters are of particular interest, if only for their architectural value alone. **Mann's Chinese Theater** (once known as Graumann's) is an L.A. tradition. It's done in Oriental style with lots of red and that much-photographed courtyard where stars' hand- and footprints are cemented. The second, is the **Cinerama Dome,** from the street appears to be an enormous golf ball with ultramodern interior and one of the best sound systems ever.

LATE-NIGHT LOS ANGELES

You'd think there would be a plethora of late-night activities in this town, but surprisingly enough the city on the whole tends to keep to early to bed, early to rise hours. Still, we do know of a few hot spots if you're up for the midnight hour.

Before you hit any of these places, just a friendly reminder: going out late at night alone can be dangerous in any city. Unfortunately, Los Angeles is often—perhaps unjustifiably—at the top of many lists in that department. Still, women visitors do not need to feel bound to their hotel rooms. Just be sure to do as we do: whenever valet parking is available, use it; it's convenient and safe; and before venturing out, call ahead, get directions, and discuss location and parking with proprietor.

With that in mind, here are some fun late-night places to look up when you're on the Coast:

At My Place is in a good neighborhood, near the beach. Though the food is not the drawing point of this casual cabaret, the entertainment is diverse, ranging from jazz to pop to rhythm-and-blues. 1026 Wilshire Boulevard, Santa Monica. 451-8596.

Concerts by the Sea is off the beaten path, so be careful when you go to listen to jazz at this popular club by the beach. 100 Fisherman's Wharf, Redondo Beach. 379-4998.

The **Troubador** reached the height of its popularity in the sixties and seventies, and is known for launching the Smothers Brothers and many other successful acts. This club on the Strip is now kind of touristy, but certainly crowded enough, so that a woman visiting alone wouldn't be uncomfortable. 9081 Santa Monica Boulevard, West Hollywood. 276-1158.

Sasch is a disco that attracts men and women in their twenties and thirties. It's in a safe valley location, and women alone are in good company here. 11345 Ventura Boulevard, Studio City. 818/769-5555.

Simply Blues is packed every night until 2 A.M. and is reminiscent of Harlem in the forties. Be careful in this neighborhood, it's not the safest—in fact, you shouldn't go alone. 6290 Sunset Boulevard, Hollywood. 466-5239.

The **Coconut Teazer** is a hot club on Sunset Strip playing current music. They serve food and encourage dancing. 8177 Sunset Boulevard, Hollywood. 654-4773.

McCabes Guitar Shop features folk, bluegrass, rock 'n' roll, in a wholesome atmosphere. Some of the music may be outdated in this club. It isn't a pickup place, so you won't be bothered. 3101 Pico Boulevard, Santa Monica. 828-4497.

A varied age group patronizes the more contemporary clubs, like **Club Lingerie** (6507 Sunset Boulevard, Hollywood, 466-8557) and the **Palace** (1735 N. Vine, 462-3000), but they tend to draw clients who are mostly on the youngish side. Both places are super busy on the weekends and both feature local musical groups.

Los Angeles is home to some of the nation's best comedy clubs. We like to stop in at:

The **Comedy Store,** where many famous comedians—like Robin Williams and Steve Martin—first made their mark. Three high-tech rooms provide entertainment: the Main Room, with the best of the Comedy Store; the Workshop with performances until 2 A.M.; and the Belly Headline Room, with stand-up comics. 8433 Sunset Boulevard, West Hollywood. 656-6225.

The **Improvisation**—or the Improv—is a comedy showcase for up-and-comers, of which L.A. has a full supply. You may even get to drink and dine with stars like Billy Crystal, who show up on a regular basis. 8162 Melrose Avenue, West Hollywood. 651-2583.

The **Groundling Theater** is a Los Angeles institution where zany improvisations are performed with audience participation. Late shows on some nights. 7307 Melrose Avenue, West Hollywood. 934-4747.

And, if you like country music, the queen of all the country clubs in the city—maybe even in the country—is the **Palamino.** Women will most likely be outnumbered here and will probably have a better time if they go with a friend. Talent nights are big at this club. 6907 Lankershim Boulevard, North Hollywood in the valley. 764-4010.

UNIQUELY LOS ANGELES

You can't really visit Los Angeles without at least giving a nod to the silver screens, both large and small, even if show business isn't your business. So, why not take an inside look into the worlds of television and moviemaking on your off hours?

Hollywood is a misnomer when it comes to the location of many studios in town; only a few are actually in that section of the city. Universal Studios, for instance, are stationed on the back side of the Hollywood Hills, in Universal City, and the NBC Studios are in beautiful downtown Burbank.

Although Universal Studios may be the most visible when it

comes to giving tours of the back lots, we say stay away from this commercial venture if it is the art of movie making that you're after. Instead, visit Burbank Studios, the lot where Warner Brothers and Columbia Pictures operate. They'll arrange a real behind-the-scenes tour in a small group where you can get plenty of feedback to your questions. 4000 Warner Boulevard, Burbank. 818/954-6000.

As for television, if you want to see a studio, NBC offers a one-and-one-half-hour tour of the largest facilities in the U.S. At 3000 W. Alameda Avenue, Burbank. 840-4444.

To see a television show in the making, you can obtain tickets by calling the following numbers for the following networks:

ABC: 557-4396
CBS: 852-2455
NBC: 818/840-3537

Another way of experiencing the industry is to look up *Hollywood on Location.* This company provides lists of who's filming where, with a map to the exact locations. A new listing is prepared every weekday, and you use your own transportation to get to the site in question. The company is located at 8644 Wilshire Boulevard, Beverly Hills, CA 90211. 213/659-9165.

For a good reference book on where moviemaking of old and new takes place, pick up Richard Alleman's *Movie Lover's Guide to Hollywood* (Harper & Row, $12.95), available in most major bookstores.

AT LEISURE

In Town

There's no way around it; in this town, there's a lot of ground to cover. Even if you were here ten years, you'd likely not see every nook and cranny. Still, with good advice and some of your own ideas on how you like to spend your days off, you should have a good time during your down time in Los Angeles.

One expedient way to see what you want to see is to enlist the services of a tour operator specializing in custom sightseeing. We know of two companies with women at the helm who have an excellent command of Los Angeles.

Day in LA has been in operation successfully since March 1984, thanks to two friends who put their skills together to create a firm that was "conceived for, but not limited to, the discriminating woman visitor who wishes to tour Los Angeles in a most private manner." Roxeanne Richling, a former free-lance fashion model who also worked in television production, and Vivian Goldstein, an interior designer and fashion coordinator, devise these custom packages, providing exclusive excursions about town in chauffeur-driven limousines. 1942 Westholme Avenue, Los Angeles. 470-0242. **Personally Designed Tours** is run by Judith Benjamin who doesn't specialize in any specific kind of L.A. tour. She customizes her services "for people who are not part of the herd and have seen the usual offerings. They don't wish to be regimented and want to sample the multiple choices that this city and area has to offer. The typical person who calls me is generally inappropriate because he or she wants to go to the movie stars' homes and that isn't what I do." What she does do is arrange for a variety of activities that "visitors can't arrange for the minute they get here"—so she's perfect for the business traveler. 2210 Wilshire Boulevard, #754, Santa Monica, CA 90403. 826-8810.

Day-Tripping

Traditionally, harried businesswomen who really want to get away from it all after work is done in Los Angeles head for the glamour and luxury of the desert. There's little to do in these resort communities— among them **Palm Springs, Indian Wells, Cathedral City, La Quinta, Palm Desert** and **Rancho Mirage**—except sit back, sip drinks, take a dip in the pool, get a facial and quietly pamper yourself. Palm Springs and surrounding areas are located about 100 miles from Los Angeles, a two-and-a-half-hour drive away.

For further information on Palm Springs, write the Palm Springs Convention & Visitors Bureau, Airport Park Plaza, Suite 315, 255 North El Cielo Road, Palm Springs, CA 92262. 619/327-8411.

For further information about Cathedral City, Indian Wells, Indio, La Quinta, Palm Desert, or Rancho Mirage, contact the Desert Resort Communicites Convention & Visitors Bureau, 74-284 Highway 111, Palm Desert, CA 92260. 619/568-1886.

In direct contrast to desert life, **Las Vegas** is only an hour's plane ride away. High rollers go for the day to test their luck, and curiosity seekers simply drop in for a look at what the neon is all about. For further information, contact the Las Vegas Convention Authority, 3150 Paradise Road, Las Vegas, NV 89109. 702/733-2471.

For the feel of the Côte d'Azur within a few hour's drive south of L.A., take a trek along the coast of the **American Riviera** to visit such memorable beach communities as **Huntington Beach, Newport Beach, Corona del Mar, Laguna Beach, Dana Point, San Juan Capistrano** and **San Clemente.** Each has its own flavor, plenty of sunshine year-round and direct access to the mighty Pacific. Each community has a chamber of commerce that will gladly send pertinent information; call directory assistance for the right telephone number.

And, if you can't leave the area without meeting Mickey Mouse in person, **Disneyland** is in Anaheim, less than an hour's drive from Los Angeles, 27 miles southeast of downtown. 1313 Harvor Boulevard, Anaheim. 714/999-4565.

Heading north from Los Angeles, along the coast, you'll enjoy the communities of **Ojai, Santa Barbara, Pismo Beach, Morro Bay,** and **Cambria.** Each operates a chamber of commerce or visitor's bureau with plenty of information on what's in store once you get there.

Sunday Customs

Brunch is a tradition in Los Angeles, and almost every restaurant offers some sort of Sunday specialty. This is Los Angeles, so the dress is casual, but certainly not sloppy.

The **Westwood Marquis Hotel** is legendary for its champagne brunch buffet. The Garden Terrace restaurant offers a large selection of hot and cold dishes—eggs, fruits, all kinds of breads and pastries. Dress is casual, but the Marquis gets a very elegant crowd. Hours are from 10:30 to 3:00 (see "At Your Service").

Cafe Four Oaks is a charming Victorian house. Eight unusual items grace the blackboard menu. Thirteen dollars buys freshly baked croissants, fresh fruit, choice of entree such as poached pear and brie tart, lobster and seafood casserole, eggs, and salads, most notably a roast duck salad. Two levels of outdoor seating, live entertainment. From 10:30 to 3:00. 2181 N. Beverly Glen Boulevard. 474-9317.

The **Pacific Dining Car** has been around since 1921. The brunch features eggs Florentine, as well as steak and dinner items. Served from 11:00 to 4:00. 1310 W. Sixth Street 483-6000.

West Beach Cafe, a sleek white restaurant, is a beachy artist hangout. Brunches change weekly, and feature such items as Mexican omelets, any style eggs, salmon and eggs Benedict, and Belgian waffles. Hours are 10:00 to 2:30. Dress is casual. 60 N. Venice Boulevard. 823-5396.

Cafe Reni is a charming country-style French cafe. Brunch special is any crepe or omelet with soup or salad, champagne or orange juice; also several croissant dishes. Open from 11:00 to 3:00. 2262 Wilshire Boulevard, Santa Monica. 829-5303.

After you finish eating, shopping is a perfect way to finish the day. **Main Street in Santa Monica** is a unique place to explore; many stores are in turn-of-the-century style with dark woods and brass highlights. **Heritage Square Museum,** at Ocean Park and Main, keys you in to the history of this popular beach area. The museum (392-8537) is open from 12:00 to 5:00 on Sundays.

The **Santa Monica Pier,** on Colorado Boulevard, juts into the ocean and is nonstop entertainment on Sundays, or all weekend, for that matter. Fresh fish is sold, and there are games and an antique carousel. A perfect place for people-watching.

Los Angeles beaches are pefect places to visit on a lazy Sunday in the sun. From Malibu to the Marina, at least a dozen beaches offer distinctive flavor. If you want to see some of the body builders at Muscle Beach, go to Santa Monica; for a more tranquil day, drive to the end of Ocean Boulevard in Santa Monica, where almost deserted beaches are on the Marina Peninsula; to watch surfers try their stuff, go to Malibu.

Active Sports

Any place that has a beach named Muscle has to have brawn on its brain. So we say, if you can't beat 'em, join 'em. Here are some ideas on how to do just that:

For a brisk walk or **run,** to get the best benefit, do so along the beach. If you want to run toward Malibu, just take Wilshire Boulevard west to the ocean and turn right. If you turn left, you'll be heading toward Venice and the Marina Peninsula. Public beaches dot the coastline, so take your pick. Away from the sand, joggers enjoy great scenery en route between Ocean Boulevard and San Vicente in Santa Monica.

If it's more structured recreation you want, try **windsurfing** in Marina del Rey by renting a board from **Wind Surfing West** (4947 Lincoln Boulevard, 821-5501). Boats for sailing can be rented from **Rent A Sail** (13560 Mindanao Way, Marina del Rey, 822-1868.)

Near the Santa Monica Pier, several shops rent roller skates and bicycles. **Bike paths** allow uninterrupted rides from Santa Monica to Redondo Beach.

The best spot in L.A. for **hiking** is through the many trails of the 4,000-acre Griffith Park (665-5188), with entrances on Los Feliz Boulevard, Western Avenue, and Riverside Drive. Or try Santa Monica Canyon and Will Rogers State Park, where you can also attend a polo match.

You'll find the stables for the Los Angeles Equestrian Center in Griffith Park if you'd rather explore it on **horseback** (480 Riverside Drive, Burbank, 818/840-8401).

Aerobics eat up calories fast, and seem to be a favorite Los Angeles pastime for preserving the perfect body. The following places offer classes:

Studio A, in Los Feliz, convenient to downtown, 661-8311.

The **Sports Connection,** with clubs in Encino, 818/788-1220; Santa Monica, 450-4464; and Beverly Hills, 652-7440.

Body Express, in West Hollywood, 655-5572.

Jane Fonda's Workout, in Beverly Hills, 652-9464; and in the San Fernando Valley, Encino, 818/986-1624.

The city's climate, not to mention the proliferation of public courses in Los Angeles, makes **golf** a good choice. We think you'll enjoy teeing off at Harding Golf Course (663-2555) and Rancho Park Golf Course (838-7373) where the L.A. Open used to be played.

Spectator Sports

Along with the New York City area, Los Angeles is one of the country's great sports towns, with all facets of professional sports represented here. In football, the **Rams** (714/937-6767) play at Anaheim Stadium, and one of pro sports' best teams, the **Los Angeles Raiders** (332-5901) dominate the turf at the Memorial Coliseum. You probably remember this venue from television during the 1984 Olympics.

Los Angeles also boasts two major league baseball teams: the **Dodgers** (224-1400), who play at Dodger Stadium, and the **California Angels** (714/634-2000), whose home field is in Anaheim.

In basketball, Los Angeles is well represented by the **Clippers** (748-8000) at the Sports Arena, and the **Lakers** (673-1300), who play to a fan-packed Forum in Inglewood.

In hockey, the **Kings** (419-3160) also play at the Forum, iced over for the occasion.

HOTELS

1 Grand Bay
2 Miami Airport Hilton
  & Marina
3 Holiday Inn Bricknell Point
4 Hyatt Regency
5 Biscayne Bay Marriot Hotel
  & Marina
6 Mutiny
7 Omni
8 Place St. Michel

LANDMARKS

A Art Deco District
B Bass Museum of Art
C Bayfront Park
D Gusman Concert Hall
E James L. Knight Convention
  Center
F Metro Dade Cultural Center
G Miamarina

H Miami International Airport
I Orange Bowl
J Seaquarium
K Southeast Financial Center
L Theater of the Performing
  Arts
M Villa Viscaya

MIAMI

GETTING YOUR BEARINGS

The search for the real Miami continues. Somewhere between the swaying palms romance of a forties movie and the neon sleaze of a "Miami Vice" episode exists a city on the way up—a city guided by leaders willing to sink billions into efforts to overcome a bad reputation and eager to get on with the reality of becoming an international business hub.

It's true that Miami is trying harder than almost any city in the country to clean up its image. Over $2 billion has been spent to create a downtown business area to accommodate its phenomenal international trade boom (a Miami scene that has been dubbed by some as "aggressively international"). No one can deny that the statistics are impressive: Miami is the second largest international banking city in the United States, the largest port in the world, and the third fastest growing metropolitan region in the country.

You have only to walk its streets and you'll understand the new multinational energy sparking this city. Of Miami's 1.7 million residents, more than half are Spanish speaking. Recently arrived from Cuba and other parts of Latin America, these new Miamians have brought along their wealth, customs, cuisines, and culture to spice up Miami's ethnic stew. Even a quick visit to Calle Ocho (SW 8th Street) will reveal exotic shops, restaurants offering arroz con pollo, and nightclubs that rock until dawn to the sounds of salsa. All very cultural, very desirable to a city on the way up. But unhappily for city fathers, it is the less desirable aspects—the crime, the drug dealings, the shoot-outs on the streets—that get all the press and scare off law-abiding visitors. But this aspect, too, is fading under the city's new policy.

If "Miami" is your business destination, it helps to know the territory. Greater Miami is actually a loose network of 27 individual communities, each with its own flavor and style: Coconut Grove, a laid-back, eclectic village both chic and kitschy, filled with galleries and sidewalk cafes; Coral Gables, a community of planned elegance, whose streets are lined with majestic royal palms and classic Spanish-Florida homes with jalousie windows, barrel-tiled roofs, and high-ceiling rooms cooled by paddle fans; Key Biscayne, in reality two islands, both monied and cliquish; and Miami Beach, that old showgirl of a community desperately hoping that her face-lift will help her stand up to the competition's new look of the eighties.

To save you the confusion on logistics we encountered before ever visiting the area: Miami and Miami Beach are *not* synonymous. The Beach lies seven miles to the east, a separate peninsula connected to downtown Miami by a series of four causeways over Biscayne Bay. Miami Beach is the home of the now-crumbling giant hotels most of us associate with our grandparents' visits during the cold northern winters. But despite the current ongoing shape-up, this area remains unsafe for women alone, particularly the South Beach section between 1st and 7th streets. Do your sightseeing (see "At Leisure") and then return to your mainland Miami hotel.

There's no denying the crime factor in this city, a fact of life that persists despite massive clean-up efforts. Our best advice is: don't be overly spooked by the reputation, but proceed with caution. Dust off your "street smarts," stay alert—don't daydream as you travel between appointments—and stay out of the downtown area at night.

Scheduled for sometime in 1987 is a project that should change both the face and the tone of downtown: Bayside, a Rouse Company development that will be built around the existing marina at Bayfront Park. The theme will be international, in keeping with Miami's multinational population, with two pavilions, an outdoor market, and space for some 200 international food and retail merchants.

WHAT TO WEAR

Don't make the mistake of assuming that because the temperatures are in the sticky 90s you can do business in cotton sundresses; you won't see local businesspeople in shorts and shirt-sleeves. Bare legs are a no-no, even in summer. Everything is air-conditioned—from cars to offices—and dark-colored dresses and lightweight wool suits are considered proper business wear during winter months. (In fact, because of overzealous airconditioning, we've learned to tote along a defensive cover-up to ward off the bone-chilling temperatures of some restaurants and offices.) Colors lighten up in summer, but the code remains one of strictly business. Save your Hawaiian-print trendy tropicals for after-hours when the rules dissolve and an anything-goes attitude takes over.

WEATHER WATCH

As you can guess, summers are not the best of times to visit this semi-tropical city. Air-conditioning helps. But don't be fooled—winters can produce some low temperatures. (Remember watching the snow flurries during the Orange Bowl game of 1976?) As with any new city, we suggest you check the Miami highs and lows for several days prior to your trip just to be sure you're packing the right gear.

GETTING THERE

Miami International, tenth largest airport in the world, is new, clean, and easy to navigate. The airport services 106 major airlines, and it is a major hub for southern and Latin American travel. Airport information: 871-7515.

The **Fort Lauderdale–Hollywood International Airport** lies about 40 miles north of Miami. Frequent visitors used to fly into here to avoid the crowds at Miami International. However, Lauderdale's major expansion program (due for completion in late 1986) has turned this place into a zoo. Avoid it until construction is finished.

It's about a seven-mile ride into town from Miami International, a 20-minute cab ride that should run about $11. Red Top Sedan Service runs 24-hour minibuses from the airport into town. Each holds about 12 passengers. Fare runs between $6 and $9, depending on your destination. Most hotels offer complimentary airport transfers, as do car rental agencies with offices outside the airport. Local numbers for major rental agencies:

Car Rentals

Avis	377-2531
Budget	871-3053
Dollar	887-6000
Hertz	526-5645
National	358-2334
Value	871-6760

GETTING AROUND

Miami is rather like a smaller version of Los Angeles. Taxis are expensive and public transportation is limited, so you will definitely need a car. But expect the usual, big-city driving hassles. You'll discover on-street parking is difficult to find. Best bet is to rely on your hotel's garage or private lots. Rates are relatively low. Try to avoid the expressways during peak driving times. And it will pay to plan your routes ahead to avoid having to drive through the Liberty City area (36th through 79th streets west of I-95). It makes no sense to drive through here, alone or with passengers. To keep your directional bearings: remember the ocean is always to the east. Directions down here are usually given in N-S-E-W terms, rather than "turn right," and so on.

Taxis rarely cruise and are metered at $1 on the drop and a steep climb thereafter. Sharing is not permitted. The bus system is slow and unreliable, and a transfer might mean long waits in the hot sun (fare is 75 cents). The new ballyhooed Metrorail system (638-6700), sad to say, is not the answer to everyone's transportation problems. You need a car to get from the stations to anywhere of interest, so why not drive the whole way?

GETTING FAMILIAR

Metro-Dade Department of Tourism
234 W. Flagler Street   375-4694
Miami, FL 33130
Open 9 A.M. to 5 P.M. Monday through Friday. Call ahead or stop by for city information. They publish a series of excellent brochures on specific interest areas: arts, sports and recreation, attractions. Request material about your own special interests from this group.

Greater Miami Chamber of Commerce
1601 Biscayne Boulevard   350-7700
Miami, FL 33132
Information on hotels and restaurants.

City of Miami/University of Miami/James L. Knight Convention Center
400 Southeast Second Avenue   372-0277
Miami, FL 33131

The *Miami Herald* is the daily morning paper, available citywide. Their weekend section on Friday lists "Best Bets" for activities and cultural events. Daily movie schedules appear in the "Living Today" section. *South Florida* magazine is a monthly that provides museum, gallery, theater, and restaurant information. **Kay's Corner**, 3199 Commodore Plaza, Coconut Grove, is a good place to buy those out-of-town papers and foreign publications you never thought you could find in the tropics.

Quick Calls

AREA CODE 305	Time 324-8811
Police Emergency 911	Weather 661-5065

AT YOUR SERVICE

Although Miami was once a city renowned for its hotels, times have changed. Those once-famous hotels were splashy resort complexes that catered to "snowbirds" down for the winter months. Today, Miami's visitor is more likely to be a business traveler in town for a quick trip and anxious to find a comfortable, sensible, business-oriented place to stay. The following hotels not only target this traveler but, we have discovered, also are clever enough to offer services and staffs specially trained to understand and anticipate the needs of women travelers. (You'll note that none of the hotels is on the Beach. Women who travel regularly to Miami agree with us that the Beach isn't safe enough as yet to warrant staying there.)

Biscayne Bay Marriott Hotel and Marina

1633 Bayshore Drive
Miami, FL 33132

Toll-free reservations: 800/228-9290
Local number: 374-3900
Telex: 525840

Part of the new downtown area's gentrification, this 605-room hotel offers elegance and a resortlike ambience in a location convenient to the business community. There are two concierge floors, each room with upscale amenities and special security checks. (The entire hotel is secured by 24-hour guards, but these floors employ an additional check system.)

Veroniques is their gourmet restaurant, catering to both guests and locals who consider it one of Miami's better spots. **Bay View** is a fancy waterfront coffee shop serving three meals daily. The **Oyster Bar** features a raw bar, Florida stone crab, beers from around the world, and drinks. The **Venetia Lounge** is a comfortable lobby-level cocktail lounge with a long (4 to 7 P.M.) happy hour.

Grand Bay Hotel

2669 S. Bayshore Drive
Coconut Grove, FL 33133

Toll-free reservations: 800/327-2788
800/221-2340
Local number: 858-9600
Telex: 441370

The first U.S. hotel to be built by the luxury-oriented CIGA Italian chain, Grand Bay has it all—from celebrity guests and world-class views to an on-premises Regine's nightclub. This is *not* the place to come to relax and get away from it all. The building's 181 rooms built in a Mayan step-pyramid design allow for private terraces.

The **Grande Cafe** is great for intimate dining; **Regine's** is *the* local place to see and be seen.

Hotel Mutiny

2951 South Bayshore Drive
Coconut Grove, FL 33131

Toll-free reservations: 800/327-0372
Local number: 442-2400
Telex: 519276

If you want to escape from the "real" world of downtown business into the pastel pleasures of Coconut Grove, the yacht-club life-style of the Mutiny is a great way to do it. The hotel is small, only 131 rooms, and the living is casual and easy. There's a marina (hence the emphasis on

	Concierge	Executive Floor	No-Smoking Rooms	Fitness Facilities	Pool	24-Hour Room Service	Restaurant for Client Entertaining	Extra-Special Amenities	Electronic Key System	Business/Secretarial Services	Checkout Time	Frequent Guest Program	Business Traveler Program	Average Single Rate
Grand Bay	●	●	●	●	●	●	Grande Cafe Regine's	●	●	●	12 noon			$120 $175
Miami Airport Hilton & Marina	●	●	●	●	●	●	Cove	●	●	●	12 noon		Towers Concept	$95 $135
Holiday Inn Brickell Point	●	●			●					●	12 noon	J.P. Preferred Guest	Corporate rate	$75 corp. $60–$90 reg.
Hyatt Regency	●	●			●	●	Esplanade	●	●	●	12 noon	Gold Passport	Regency Club	$83–$115 reg. $115–$125 Regency Club
Biscayne Bay Marriott Hotel & Marina	●	●			●	●	Veroniques	●	●	●	12 noon	Preference Plus	Honored Guest	$95 $120
Mutiny	●	●		●	●		Mutiny Club			●	1 p.m.		Executive Club	$68 corp. $70–$135
Omni	●	●	●		●		Signature	●		●	1 p.m.		E.S.P.	$75–$105 reg. $65 ESP including breakfast
Place St. Michel							St. Michel		I.D. required		12 noon			$60

252

things nautical in the decor) making water-related activities easy to arrange. Room rates include a Continental breakfast and daily paper *(Miami Herald* or *New York Times).*

Mutiny is both restaurant and swinging nightclub/disco, popular with members and hotel guests (who are granted limited membership for the duration of their stay). Great, status-y place to entertain clients.

Hyatt Regency

400 SE Second Avenue · Toll-free reservations: 800/228-9000
Miami, FL 33131 · Local number: 358-1234
· Telex: 5114316

Another of the new downtown hotels, this 627-room Hyatt is also adjacent to the James L. Knight Convention Center. (Handy for conventioneers, but often noisy and crowded for other guests.) Two floors—23 and 24— are set aside for business travelers and offer the usual services and perks.

The **Esplanade** restaurant offers fine food (try the poached pompano in smoked herb butter) and a decent wine list. The **River Walk** is the casual, three-meals restaurant. **Currents Lounge** is a comfortable lobby bar, ideal for sitting alone or with clients.

Miami Airport Hilton and Marina

5101 Blue Lagoon Drive · Toll-free reservations: 800/445-8667
Miami, FL 33126 · Local number: 262-1000
· Telex: 523852

Of the dozen or so airport hotels near Miami International, we like this the best. The lagoon is probably the clincher. An ideal overnighter if your business in Miami isn't anchored to a downtown location. Here, on a secluded 12-acre peninsula, is a 500-room hotel complex with its own lagoon offering all waterfront activities except ocean types. There are also jogging trails with parcours stations, lighted tennis courts, whirlpools. Concierge floors, 13 and 14 in the towers, offer the expected amenities and private lounges. You'll find beefed-up conference and meeting room facilities here because of the handy location: fly in, have your meetings, and return home.

Club Mystique is a large, late-night disco on the premises—very popular and therefore very noisy. (You might want to reserve your room at the other end of the building.)

Omni International

1601 Biscayne Boulevard · Toll-free reservations: 800/THE-OMNI
Miami, FL 33132 · Local number: 374-0000
· Telex: 152246

This 556-room hotel strives to be all things to all guests. Its location in the heart of downtown has prompted an excellent security system (guards on patrol, double locks, key checks by elevator personnel) as well as a city-within-a-city convenience contained in its 10.5-acre complex. Best are the ESP rooms, which provide business travelers with separate work areas, good reading light, and desks, in addition to upgraded in-room amenities. Adjacent to the huge Omni Shopping Mall (see "The Shopping Scene").

Signature Restaurant is an elegant dining room. The **Terrace Cafe** serves three meals daily in casual setting.

ON A BUDGET

Hotels

Hotel Place St. Michel
162 Alcazar   Local number: 444-1666
Coral Gables, FL 33134

Definitely not a business hotel, this 1926-vintage charmer has only 28 rooms, and each one is individually lavished with Victorian, art deco, and art nouveau pieces. Favorite rooms are 302 with its carved headboards and 310 with its parquet floor and oversized bath. The service and services are lavish; the atmosphere is warm and caring. A problem? The manager himself hurries to right it. Security is tight because everyone is known by sight and name. And all this for $60 for a single room. Continental breakfast (in your room or in the dining room) is included.

A first-rate restaurant, **St. Michel,** is ideal for entertaining or dining alone. A tiny deli, **Charcuterie St. Michel,** offers cuisine-to-go.

Holiday Inn Brickell Point
495 Brickell Avenue   Toll-free reservations: 800/HOLIDAY
Miami, FL 33131   Local number: 373-6000
                                                    Telex: 808693

No big surprises here, except maybe the size—595 rooms of full-service Holiday Inn. Built in 1982, the hotel affords easy access to downtown business, yet is across the river in a quiet, beautifully landscaped urban oasis. Decor is tropical, and the focus is almost entirely on the business traveler. A definite plus: there's free parking, an important factor in this prime downtown location. Corporate rates available; rooms run $60 to $90.

Fanny's by the Bay, serves three meals daily. **Fanny's Lounge** features live entertainment nightly (except Sunday) and a lively happy hour scene.

Restaurants

Granny Feelgood's offers health foods for people who like to feel good about what they eat. Inventive creations and healthy, crunchy lunches to enjoy near your downtown meetings. Total no-smoking environment. And prices are super low. 190 SE First Avenue, Miami. 358-6233.

The **S&S Restaurant** is that endangered institution—the family diner. Folks in Miami cherish this one, taking a number and waiting in line for old-fashioned American cooking. Like your grandma told you, it's filling and it's good. It's also good for the budget. 1757 NE Second Avenue, Miami.

Entertainment

Entertainment is a way of life in free-wheeling Coconut Grove And, like the song says, the best things in life are free—*all* of these festivals are fun and free: Arts Festival (February); Shakespeare Festival (February); International Artists Days at Vizcaya (February); Goombay Festival (June); Great Coconut Grove Bicycle Race (October); Banyan Festival (October); Turkey Race (November); King Mango Strut (December). Call 444-7270 for details.

DINING OUT

Wherever you go for lunch or dinner, be sure to plan ahead and make reservations well in advance. This is one town that seems to have more eager eaters than there are restaurants to feed them. Expect long lines at the nonreservation places, especially during peak season. Take advantage of Miami's multicultural scene. Sample delicious and inexpensive Cuban sandwiches, *media de noche*, sold just about anywhere along Flagler Street in tiny storefront stands. (Read further for a trio of favorite Cuban restaurants.)

Joe's Stone Crab has been a Miami classic since 1913. It's justly famous for its stone crabs, which are caught by Joe's own fleet and served in huge mounds, along with a secret mustard sauce. Other seafood is equally fresh and well prepared. No reservations accepted; expect long lines every night (lunchtime is less crowded). Open Tuesday through Saturday from 11:30 A.M. to 2 P.M. for lunch; dinner every night from 5 P.M. to 10 P.M. Closed from May to October. Moderate. Note: this neighborhood is quite rundown and unsafe. If you drive, use valet parking. Otherwise, have the doorman hail you a cab. 227 Biscayne Street, Miami Beach.

The Forge is an elegant, art deco restaurant serving Continental cuisine. Good choice for entertaining clients or for dining alone. Rumor has it that Paul Bocuse eats here when he's in town. Service is excellent, the wine list extensive. The lounge's dance scene swings until 5 A.M. Dinners from 6 P.M. to 2:30 P.M. Expensive. 432 Arthur Godfrey Road, Miami Beach. 538-8533.

Cye's Rivergate, a Continental restaurant on the Miami River, is crisp and airy, with wood floors and an illuminated bar. Good choice for hosting a business lunch or dinner. Location, too, is convenient during the work day. Open 11:30 A.M. to midnight, Monday through Friday; 5:30 P.M. to 1:30 A.M. Saturdays. Expensive. 444 Brickell Avenue (Rivergate Plaza Building, Miami. 358-9100.

Veroniques, in the Biscayne Bay Hotel, is an excellent place for business entertaining or for just pampering yourself. Elegant surroundings, formal service, dressed-up clientele. The cuisine is Continental, with an emphasis on classic razzle-dazzle flaming preparations. Open daily from 11 A.M. to 2:30 and 6 to 11 P.M. Expensive. 1633 N. Bayshore Drive, Miami. 374-3900.

The **Pavillion Grill**, in the Pavillion Hotel, is French, elegant, expensive; some say it's Florida's finest. Decor is lavish: mahogany walls, marble columns, Irish linen, Italian silver and crystal. Cuisine is nouvelle. A can't-lose place to bring clients or associates you want to impress. (Tip: lunch might be better than dinner as the area is less deserted in midday, and the lunch tab is less expensive.) Open Monday through Friday, noon to 2 P.M.; Monday through Saturday, 6:30 to 10:30 P.M. 100 Chopin Plaza, Miami. 372-4494.

Chez Vendome, in the David William Hotel, is another elegant French restaurant, popular with the international business and finance crowd. Spacious red velvet booths help make this a good place for client entertaining. Extensive wine list. Open Monday through Friday, 11:30 to 3 P.M.; Monday through Saturday, 5:30 to 11:30 P.M. 700 Biltmore Way, Coral Gables. 443-4646.

The **East Coast Fisheries** is located on the Miami River not far from downtown. This long-standing favorite has been one of the most popular, down-home seafood places in town since 1935. Supercasual, it is bright, crowded, and noisy. No problem here for women alone. Open daily 10 A.M. to 10 P.M. Moderate. 360 W. Flagler Street, Miami. 373-5515.

Monty Trainer's Bayshore Restaurant has just the atmosphere you're looking for in Coconut Grove—casual, friendly, trendy, interesting people, good food. The theme is nautical, since it overlooks Biscayne Bay. There's an outdoor raw bar or an inside dining room. Wear your jeans or your newest Rykiel here and be in good company. Open seven days. Moderate. 2560 S. Bayshore Drive, Coconut Grove. 858-1431.

Attention, all you kindred souls who believe that ice cream is nature's perfect food. Have we got a place for you—**Le Glacier**. Frenchman Jean-Claude Schacherer has brought his skills *extraordinaires* to Miami in the form of the best, richest, most seductive ice cream you'll ever taste. Try the exotic flavors or the classics. All are memorable. Le Glacier also serves salads, sandwiches, and soups. Closed Sundays. 5950 S. Dixie Highway, South Miami. 666-3120.

There are more inexpensive Cuban and Latin restaurants than you could ever have time to sample, the majority in the "Little Havana" district (SW 8th Street). Although most are good, we like the following.

Versailles features a big, bright, classic Cuban setting with lots of plants, mirrored walls, and shiny Formica tables. Cuisine—from Cuban sandwiches to roast pork dinners with rice and beans—is good and inexpensive. For the most fun, try to dine at 10 P.M. when most Cubans do. Some women have reported they prefer the large rear dining room. Open daily from 8 A.M. to 2 A.M. 3555 SW 8th Street at 36th Avenue, Miami. 444-0240.

Islas Canarias, although not in "Little Havana," is an excellent Cuban restaurant. Located in a shopping mall, it is popular with Latins and Anglos alike. Dress is casual—anything goes. Comfortable for solo dining and for small groups, but you wouldn't want to attempt a business meeting here. Try the *bistek empanizado* or shrimp creole, which come with black beans, rice, and plantains. Open daily from 7:30 A.M. to midnight. 285 NW 27th Avenue, Miami.

The most famous patron of **La Esquina de Tejas** was President Reagan, but the usual crowd here is a mix of locals, Latins, and happy out-of-towners—all enjoying authentic Cuban specialties at amazingly low prices. Open seven days, 7 A.M. to midnight. 101 SW 12th Avenue, Miami. 545-5341.

MIAMI BY DAY

Most business is conducted downtown. Some landmarks you'll need to recognize: Southeast Financial Center, overlooking Biscayne Bay, a 55-story giant; the new James L. Knight International Center, $139 million meeting, educational, sports, and entertainment complex, largest and most advanced in the Southeast; the World Trade Center office tower; the Insurance Exchange of America; and the wealth of international financial companies on Brickell Avenue.

During your leisure time don't expect to see much by wandering around the streets near your hotel—unless you're staying in Coconut Grove. Window shopping is practically nonexistent anywhere else in Miami. We have found you can enjoy the following sights in a single afternoon or part of a day. If you have more time to spend, check the suggestions in "At Leisure."

The **Villa Viscaya and Gardens** is a ten-acre extravaganza only ten minutes from downtown. This Italian Renaissance–style villa was once the winter palace of millionaire James Deering. Today 50 of its 70 ornate rooms display works by European Old Masters. Take time to wander through the manicured sculpture gardens; maybe even linger for the evening sound and light show (reservations needed for this). Villa open daily from 9:30 A.M. to 5 P.M., admission charged. (In February, the Shakespeare Festival and the Italian Renaissance Faire take place here. Call 759-6651 for details.) 3251 S. Miami Avenue, Coconut Grove. 579-2813.

Housed in an art deco building that is part of the National Register section (see "At Leisure"), the **Bass Museum of Art** features rotating exhibits as well as performing arts events, lectures, films. Permanent collection of paintings.Guided tours available. Open Tuesday through Saturday, 10 A.M. to 5 P.M.; Sunday, 1 to 5 P.M. Admission charged. 2121 Park Avenue, Miami Beach. 673-7530.

Center for the Fine Arts is part of the Philip Johnson-designed complex, the Metro Dade Cultural Center, which is located one block from the county courthouse in the heart of downtown. Drop in between appointments for a bit of culture and quiet. Exhibits, galleries. Also includes the Historical Museum of South Florida. 101 W. Flagler Street, Miami. 375-1700.

The **Metrozoo,** a zoo you can enjoy as much as the animals seem to, thanks to the state-of-the-art habitat settings. Take the monorail ride for a valuable overview of the zoo's 200-acre property. Open daily from 10 A.M. to 4 P.M. Admission charged. SW 152d Street. 251-0400.

The **Miami Seaquarium** is a tourist trap, but who cares? This is still one of the best seaquariums around. Check out Lolita the killer whale and our old friend Flipper. Open daily from 9 A.M. to 6:30 P.M. Admission charged. Rickenbacker Causeway, Key Biscayne. 361-5703.

Just a splash away from the Seaquarium is **Planet Ocean,** a quasi-scientific ocean world. Best bet: sci-fi trip to the ocean floor in a sub simulator. More than 100 marine science exhibits. Admission charged. 361-9455.

THE SHOPPING SCENE

In general, Dade County has great shopping; you can choose from the best of American retailers as well as international offerings from South American and European designers. We've found that the best shopping is usually in the malls. While it's usually too hot to trudge the streets, the malls are climate controlled, competitively beautiful, and time-saving for those of us on tight schedules.

The Falls is a state-of-the-art mall, decorated in tropical style and built around a simulated waterfall. Its anchor store is Bloomingdale's, surrounded by dozens of trendy boutiques, craft shops, and restaurants. A 20-minute drive from downtown. Open Monday through Saturday, 10 A.M. to 9 P.M.; Sundays, noon to 5 P.M. U.S. 1 at 136th Street, South Miami. 255-4570.

Adventura, a major mall, where you'll find 177 stores including Macy's, Lord & Taylor, Burdine's, Jordan Marsh, and Miami's famous Mayor's jewelry store. It's always crowded, but you can find anything you need from gourmet chocolates to South American leathers to Brazilian fashions. About 20 minutes drive from downtown. Open Monday through Saturday, 10 A.M. to 10 P.M.; Sundays, noon to 5 P.M. U.S. 1 at 199th Street, North Miami.

Omni International, a mall located in downtown Miami, lost its number one billing to Adventura and The Falls. The flavor here is decidedly Latin; you might be hampered if you don't understand Spanish. Major stores are Jordan Marsh, an upscale J. C. Penney, and smaller stores. 16th Street and Biscayne Boulevard.

Mayfair-in-the-Grove is a fancy, upscale mall that is as much a tourist attraction as it is a shopping complex. Boutiques of Ralph Lauren and Charles Jourdan, plus many fine jewelry stores and beauty salons. Here, too, you'll find the **Ginger Man** restaurant, a popular lunch and brunch spot (448-9919). The nearby streets of Coconut Grove are also fun for window shopping (an activity *not* usual in Miami). Mary and Grand streets.

Bal Harbour Shops make up an open and airy mall offering an eclectic mix of fashion—from the designer calm of Martha's to the cutting-edge chic of Parachute and Maud Frizon. Main stores are Saks, Bonwit Teller, and Neiman-Marcus. You'll enjoy lunch at Cafe Ambience, Coco's, or Tiberio's. 9700 Collins Avenue.

Dadeland is a huge suburban mall with many stores (including Burdine's and Jordan Marsh) that we find to be a bit on the dull side. Filled with local teens and bored retirees. 7535 N. Kendall Drive.

For discounts, try **Loehmann's Plaza,** which, besides Loehmann's, includes several other discount stores. Especially good for shoes. 186th Street and U.S. 1, North Miami.

Calle Ocho is more for ethnic dining than shopping. Actually SW 8th street, this is the main street through "Little Havana." Salsa sounds blare from record stores, and old Cuban men gather in Domino Park in the afternoons to smoke their hand-rolled cigars and reminisce in Spanish. Don't expect touristic goodies to buy; this is an old ethnic neighborhood, not a tourist area. Miamians come here to eat, not to shop or sightsee.

MIAMI BY NIGHT

With the exception of your hotel's lounge or club, there is no late-night life in downtown Miami that's either safe or savory enough to consider. You'll have to travel to Miami Beach, to Coconut Grove, or to other suburbs to find a night scene. At the risk of sounding like an overprotective mother, we repeat the warnings voiced by anyone who knows the city: do not go out alone at night on foot; if you drive somewhere at night alone, drive with the doors locked, and park defensively.

Tickets for most shows and concerts can be purchased at **Bass Ticket Outlets** (653-0452) or **Select-a-Seat** (call 625-5100 for nearest location). Half-price tickets are available from **TK/DISC** at Gusman Cultural Center (358-9145). These are usually for same-day performances.

Theater of the Performing Arts (TOPA) annually hosts the Miami Opera, Greater Miami Symphony, and American Ballet Theater. Presents a full calendar of music, dance, and theater, including Broadway hits past and present. A new, beautiful theater. 1700 Washington Avenue, Miami Beach. 673-8300.

The **Coconut Grove Playhouse,** located in a historic 1920s building, "The Grove" presents the best legitimate theater in South Florida. Resident director José Ferrer's tenure has been a bit stormy, but (at press time) he was still calling the cultural shots. 3500 Main Highway, Coconut Grove. 442-4000.

Designed in the ornate style of the early 1920s, the **Gusman Concert Hall** houses the Florida Philharmonic and offers concerts and dance performances. 174 East Flagler. 642-9061; performance hot line: 358-3338.

The **Greater Miami Opera** is where Luciano Pavarotti made his American debut in 1965. He returns to perform here often. 1200 Coral Way, Miami. 854-1643.

The **Grove Cinema** is the place to see foreign films and old classics. For similar film fare, also try the **Beumont Cinema** on the University of Miami campus in Coral Gables (284-2173). The Grove is at 3199 Grand Avenue. 446-5355.

Other numbers to call include the **Jazz Hot Line,** 382-3938, and the **Blues Hot Line,** 666-6656.

AT LEISURE

The Miami area didn't become the nation's number one vacation spot back in the twenties without good reason. It's still a great place for a vacation, even a minivacation. If you can manage to tack a few leisure days onto the end of your business trip, check out the hotel weekend packages and consider the following possibilities. That is, of course, if you aren't content just to enjoy the sun from a soft chaise at your hotel's pool.

Day-Tripping

John Pennekamp Coral Reef State Park, the only living coral reef in the Continental United States, is a divers' and snorklers' paradise. (Best time is early morning when it's less windy.) There are even glass-bottomed boats for non–water lovers. Scuba tours run at 9:30 A.M. and 1:30 P.M. and cost $18.50 including gear. Snorkeling costs $14. Boat rides are $6. The park is one hour's drive south of downtown on U.S. 1, Key Largo. 248-4300 or call the Florida Keys Visitors' Bureau, 1-800-FLA-KEYS.

The **Everglades National Park.** This famous nature preserve, all 1.5 million acres of it, poetically called the "River of Grass," is not a swamp, but a teeming wilderness of marshlands inhabited by alligators and exotic species of colorful birds. Pick from a variety of ways to tour it: walking tours, bike, tram, canoe. (Call 247-6211 for details.) Nearby is the Miccosukee Indian Village where you can take the famous airboat rides. (Call 223-8388.) Park entrance is 30 miles west of Miami on Tamiami Trail. Route 27. 247-6211.

Capitalizing on its tropical climate and setting, Miami offers visitors a profusion of "jungles," including **Parrot Jungle,** 666-7834; **Monkey Jungle,** 235-1611; and **Orchid Jungle,** 247-4824.

Key West is a four-hour drive or a half-hour flight away (Southern Express and PBA Airlines fly from Miami International; about $45 one way). This funky, trendy resort enjoys a history all its own. Although associated with gays, it offers uniquely beautiful vacation possibilities to everyone. It's hard not to love a town where the daily number one activity is gathering to pay tribute to the sunset. Great nightclubs and restaurants. Stay in one of the old guest houses like **La Te Da** (Duval Street, 294-8435) with clean, bright rooms surrounding a lush tropical patio with lots of handsome men in pink (wonderful brunches here); or the **Eden House** (Fleming Street, 296-6868) where your meals are served on an outdoor patio. (Area code for Key West is 305.)

Captiva Island: you've heard of Sanibel—this is the quieter sister island. The shells are just as good here, and what's even better, the atmosphere is less tourist-y. Try **'Tween Waters Hotel** (813/472-5161) for island-best resorting.

The Bahamas: Miami is a short hop from **Nassau** and **Paradise Island.** Bahamasair offers weekend packages that include airfare and hotels for as low as $150. There are also several cruise lines offering one- and two-day packages. One of the most popular is **SeaEscape** (Pier 7, Port of Miami. 379-0000).

Several charter boat companies offer short day cruises (a few hours) of **Biscayne Bay,** with narrated tours of the areas' small residential islands and their million-dollar waterfront homes.

Island Queen, Miamarina, 333 NE Miamarina Parkway, 379-5119. Every day: 10:30 A.M.; 1:30 and 3:30 P.M.

Miami Steamboat Cruise. Closed at press time. Due to reopen in mid-1986. Call 524-4501.

Haulover Beach Marina, 10880 Collins Avenue, Miami Beach, 947-6105. Dinner and luncheon cruises.

In Town

Saturday mornings, the Miami Beach Design Preservation Society hosts guided walking tours of the **Art Deco District** (about $5). You'll see some of the homes and hotels that prompted local hero Barbara Baer Capitman to fight to save this unique area, a crusade that won them National Register of Historic Places designation and protection. The streamlined geometry of the twenties and thirties in day-glo neons and etched glass doors and mirrors—best exemplified in the Carlyle and Cardoza hotels.

Call 672-2014 for tour information; or walk the area on your own and pick up a feel for the local Jewish/Cuban ethnic community.

Sunday Customs

Although Miami's typical Sunday activities include lying on the beach, sailing, or sipping piña coladas by the pool (Florida is pretty laid back), some people do rouse themselves to go out for brunch or to check out one of the area's many street fairs. (Best of the group is the Coconut Grove Arts Festival held in February.) For the best of the brunches:

Kaleidoscope: Both charming and sophisticated, this brunch is held from noon to 3:30 every Sunday. Two small dining rooms—one a glass-roofed terrace, and the other enclosed. 3312 Commodore Plaza, Coconut Grove. 446-5010.

L'Orangerie: European atmosphere with Florida art deco touches. Sunday brunch (not a buffet) is $9.95. The Falls Shopping Plaza, US 1 at 136th Street. 238-8437.

Ginger Man: brunch on Sundays from 11 A.M. A popular, busy New York saloon-type restaurant that attracts a young, trendy crowd. 3390 Mary Street, Mayfair-in-the-Grove, Coconut Grove. 448-9919.

Rusty Pelican: Right on the bay, this open air, casual restaurant provides beachside viewing for the Sunday sailboat races as you enjoy your brunch. There's a buffet as well as brunch menu. 3201 Rickenbacker Causeway, Key Biscayne. 361-5753.

Sunday afternoons, go with the local custom of jazz or reggae at the **Village Inn** (or VI, as it is known locally), where the action starts heating up about 3 P.M. If you're alone, you might feel more comfortable seated in the restaurant section. Decent menu of burgers and salads. 3131 Commodore Plaza. 445-8721.

Spectator Sports

Miami has its share of major league sports excitement, not to mention some exotic South Florida spectator sports.

DOG RACING
      Biscayne Kennel Club, 320 NW 115th Street, Miami Shores, 754-6330.
      Flagler Dog Track, 401 NW 38th Court, Miami, 649-3000.

JAI ALAI
      Miami Fronton, 3500 NW 37th Avenue, Miami, 633-9661.

HORSE RACING
      Calder, 21001 NW 27th Avenue, 625-1311.
      Hialean, 4 E. 25th Street, 885-8000.
      Gulfstream Park, U.S. 1, Hallendale, 454-7000.

(Note: Only one track is running at a time. Check which one is current during your visit.)

BASEBALL

Miami Stadium, 635-5395. Baltimore Orioles (spring training), Miami Marlins.

FOOTBALL

Orange Bowl. Tickets for Orange Bowl Classic and Festival, 642-5211; Dolphins, 643-4700. University of Miami Hurricanes, 284-2655.

Active Sports

For **golf,** the Dural Country Club is ranked among America's greatest golf courses. Also recommended are Visacaya Golf and Country Club, Miami Lakes Inn and Country Club, and the Key Biscayne Golf Course.

In addition to **tennis** courts in the public parks and hotels, you might enjoy a game at the Biltmore Tennis Center in Coral Gables (442-6565), Flamingo Park in Miami Beach (673-7761), or Coral Pine in Miami (666-1979). All have lighted courts, too.

Call the **Leisure Line** (358-PARK) for up-to-the-minute information on fishing, golf, swimming, and other activities.

HOTELS

1 Hyatt Regency
2 Marc Plaza Hotel
3 Marriot Inn
4 Midway
5 Midway
6 Midway
7 Midway
8 Milwaukee River Hilton
9 Park East Hotel
10 Pfister Hotel and Tower
11 Red Carpet Hotel

LANDMARKS

A Amtrak Station
B First Wisconsin Center
C Greater Milwaukee
Convention and Visitor's
Bureau
D Greyhound Bus Terminal
E Milwaukee Public
Museum

F Milwaukee Art Museum
G MECCA
H Performing Arts Center
I St. Joan of Arc Chapel
J Marquette University

MILWAUKEE

GETTING YOUR BEARINGS

It is not easy for a newcomer to grasp what makes Milwaukee tick, because many of its basic tenets are intangibles. For example, how's a first-timer to know that jaywalking is considered a serious offense here? (Traffic isn't especially heavy in town and the temptation is to dash across the street against the light.) Don't do it. People are arrested, and some have even been strip-searched, for this violation!

This is also a town that takes its sense of community very seriously; there are manicured parks every block or so. And you begin to grasp its overriding sense of civic pride as you notice the many well-attended cultural and performing arts centers.

Milwaukee also takes pride in its Old World influences and does much to foster them. In addition to the multinational foods and festivals you would expect from all this, one delightful surprise is the wildly diverse styles of architecture. You can spot a classical next door to a Victorian, a profusion of turrets, balconies, peaked roofs, domes all over town—a world tour of styles. Though almost every ethnic group is represented here, it is the Germans who dominate; even the word *gemutlichkeit,* often used to describe Milwaukee's easy-going cordiality, comes from the German.

Another German word to watch for is *brats.* When you see it outside places of business, you know they're advertising German sausages—not ill-mannered children. Some other uniquely Milwaukee food customs to be on the lookout for: the ubiquitous Friday night fish fry, available in almost every restaurant, an inexpensive, sometimes delicious treat; Edy's ice-cream carts around town dispensing some of the best you'll ever taste; and beer, which, although not exactly unique, is undeniably a much-beloved hometown product. There are more pubs of the small neighborhood variety per capita here than in any other U.S. city.

Physically, downtown Milwaukee is divided into two unequal parts by the Milwaukee River. The smaller, eastern segment—the part bordered by the shores of Lake Michigan—is the chic side. Here you'll find the expensive homes and most of the better hotels and shops. The western side of the river is trying very hard to catch up. Current programs involve bolstering the positive aspects of the ethnic neighborhoods (the "Old World Third Street" revitalization program is a good example of this). But we still feel that, at least for now, the west side isn't very safe, especially at night. Among other undesirables, there are lots of sailors on shore leave roaming the west side streets. (Remember, the Port of Milwaukee is an international seaport.)

The city of Milwaukee, with its population of some 636,000, is part of a larger, four-county metro area of 1.4 million. It has a substantial blue-collar population at work in the heavy industry factories (Allen-Bradley, Harnishfeger, Allis-Chalmers, Rexnord, Briggs and Stratton, Ladish, and Bucyrus-Erie to name but a few), a fair share of high-rise office buildings (the First Wisconsin Center, with 41 floors, is tallest in the state), and a sprawl of 60 major corporations and 28,000 businesses which overflow downtown and spread out into the suburbs. But you will not feel the energies of big-city life here. There's a small-town ambience—call it gemutlichkeit—that welcomes you. Just don't break any laws or try to get away with jaywalking.

WHAT TO WEAR

After reading about the city and its mores, there should be no doubt as to the appropriate dress for business or social occasions: conservative. This is not the town for your designer investment fashions; in fact, no one will even look askance at polyester.

WEATHER WATCH

Despite its snow-belt reputation, Milwaukee residents will insist that they enjoy a four-seasons climate. One definite plus is that winter snows rarely cripple traffic or commerce—everyone handles the situation with ease.

Lake Michigan helps moderate temperatures, both in summer and in winter. The coldest month is January when an entire month of subfreezing weather is not uncommon, and several of those days might feature double-digits below zero. An average July day might register 71. However, since even summer nights can be cool, we always bring along a warm blazer or jacket just in case.

GETTING THERE

General Mitchell Field Airport is Milwaukee's major airport, and a very comfortable one, too. Renovated in 1985, it is fully carpeted, making those O. J. Simpson dashes easier on the feet. Distance from town is about six miles and is usually about a 15-minute drive. Served by 16 major carriers. General airport information: 747-4635.

Cab fare into town runs about $12.50. You can expect to be charged 25 cents for sharing.

Most hotels do not offer free airport transportation. But we've heard good reports about the Oconomowoc Airport Limousine Service. Vans leave for downtown hotels every 30 minutes on the quarter hour for $4.50 per person.

Car Rentals

Avis	744-2266
Budget	481-2409
Dollar	482-1166
Hertz	747-5333
National	483-9800

GETTING AROUND

Milwaukee is a driver-friendly town. On-street parking is plentiful and garage rates are extremely reasonable ($1.75 to $5.50 for all-day parking). If your business is any distance from your hotel, you'll definitely want your own car. The expressways are good and, even during rush hour, never too crowded.

In town, Milwaukee cabs operate on metered distance rates. They do allow sharing. And, while it's true that they cruise, we've heard some negative reports on their availability. Play it safe and order your cab a couple of hours ahead—even the night before if you have a can't-be-late morning meeting. Good cab companies include Apex Cab Co., 263-4570 or 263-4555; City Veterans Taxicab Co-op, 933-2266 or 643-1212; and Yellow Cab, 271-1800 or 271-1802.

There is no subway system, but the buses are safe and fairly dependable, and cover all of Milwaukee County. Fare is 80 cents, and exact change is required. Call 344-6711 for routes or other information.

GETTING FAMILIAR

Greater Milwaukee Convention and Visitor's Bureau
756 N. Milwaukee Street 273-3950;
Milwaukee, WI 53202 Information Hot Line: 273-7222
Open Monday through Friday, 8:30 to 5:00. There are also branches of the bureau in the Grand Avenue Mall (161 W. Wisconsin Avenue, 747-4808) and at the airport, near the baggage claim area.

Metropolitan Milwaukee Chamber of Commerce
756 N. Milwaukee   273-3000
Milwaukee, WI 53202

MECCA (Milwaukee Exposition & Convention Center & Arena)
500 W. Kilbourn Avenue   Ticket office: 271-7230
Milwaukee, WI 53203   Recorded information on events and
                                tickets: 271-2750

The *Milwaukee Journal* is the daily evening paper. The Friday edition's "Accent on the Weekend" color section lists events, times, places. The Sunday entertainment section also lists activities. The *Milwaukee Sentinel* is the weekday morning paper. "Let's Go" section on Fridays gives information on music, dance, films, art. *Milwaukee Magazine*, a slick, city-trendy monthly publication, is helpful for restaurant reviews and listings, as well as for getting an idea of the tone and tempo of the town.

Quick Calls

AREA CODE 414   Weather 936-1212
Time 844-1414   Police 765-2323

Funline (recorded information on events, festivals, shows)
799-1177

AT YOUR SERVICE

You have a wide range of hotel choices in Milwaukee, ranging from downtown to suburban, ornate Victoriana to state-of-the-art functional. Rest assured—the hotels we've recommended here can be depended on for good security, service, and comfort for women traveling alone.

Downtown and Lake-front Area

Hyatt Regency
333 W. Kilbourn Avenue   Toll-free reservations: 800/228-9000
Milwaukee, WI 53203   Local number: 276-1234
                                Telex: 260369
If you're familiar with the Hyatts, then you'll know to expect the 18-story atrium, the 484-room size, and the proximity to the convention center. (An added convenience here in this town where winters can be brutal is an enclosed walkway, which connects the hotel to MECCA, the Milwaukee Exposition & Convention Center & Arena.) Of particular interest

are the rooms on the 18th-floor Regency Club level. In addition to the usual concierge-floor amenities and services, this one is reached only by a key-activated elevator. Also of interest: what the Hyatt calls "34's"— rooms closest to the elevators on every floor, suggested and outfitted for women.

The **Polaris,** on the top (22d) floor, revolves for a 360-degree view of Milwaukee, Lake Michigan, and surrounding suburbs. The **Pilsner Lounge,** lobby level, serves three meals daily. Both bars, **Pilsner Pub** and **Atrium Lounge,** offer a comfortable ambience for women alone.

Marc Plaza Hotel
509 W. Wisconsin Avenue   Toll-free reservations: 800/558-7708
Milwaukee, WI 53203   Local number: 271-7250
                           Telex: 260336

One of the city's older hotels (1927), the Marc Plaza is a good choice. It is centrally located, has lots of charm, and also lots of top-security features like the locked floors (20–24) in the tower section. These executive floors can be reached only by key-operated elevators and include the expected services and features. Call ahead to see if your company qualifies for the Marc Plaza's ETC (Elite Traveler's Club)—a corporate program that offers upgrading and extras to members at no charge. Direct line to ETC is 277-9600.

We like **Le Bistro,** the gourmet restaurant, for client entertaining. The trendy and very popular **Bombay Bicycle Club,** a jazz hideaway, is fine for women alone. **Cafe Plaza** is the casual, three-meals coffee shop.

Park East Hotel
916 E. State Street   No toll-free reservations number, but
Milwaukee, WI 53202   they invite you to call collect.
                           Local number: 276-8800

This small 160-room hotel is situated in a quiet neighborhood near Lake Michigan and somewhat away from downtown. If you're a jogger, the lake-front track is tempting, but exercise caution. Officials have thinned dense brush along the path and ordered patrols, but it's still a bit too secluded for comfort. We stick to the sidewalks.

Live music in the **Drawing Room,** the lobby bar; also big band sounds on Wednesdays. During warm weather there's an open-air bar, **Penthouse Lounge,** on the roof. The **Park Room** is the three-meals restaurant, often patronized by local business people.

Pfister Hotel and Tower
424 E. Wisconsin Avenue   Toll-free reservations: 800/558-8222
Milwaukee, WI 53202   Local number: 273-8222
                           Telex: 9102623127

The Grand Dame of Milwaukee, this 1890s landmark continues an untarnished tradition of luxury surroundings and services. New owners have kept her up-to-date, so she's as much a leader today as in the days when Enrico Caruso or seven U.S. presidents signed the guest register. The

Hotel	Concierge	Executive Floor	No-Smoking Rooms	Fitness Facilities	Pool	24-Hour Room Service	Restaurant for Client Entertaining	Extra-Special Amenities	Electronic Key System	Business/Secretarial Services	Checkout Time	Frequent Guest Program	Business Traveler Program	Average Single Rate
Milwaukee River Hilton Inn	●	●			●		The Anchorage		●	●	12 noon		Hospitality Club	$61 / $72
Hyatt Regency	●	●	●	●		●	La Rotisserie			●	12 noon			$65 / $79
Marc Plaza	●		●	●	●		Le Bistro			●	12 noon	●	E.T.C.	$70
Marriott Inn	●		●		●		Whitney's	●		●	12 noon	Honored Guest		$66
Park East			●				The Park Room				12 noon	Corporate Alliance Program		$50 / $58
Pfister & Tower	●		●	●	●	●	The English Room	●		●	12 noon	Preferred Hotels	Corp.	$75 / $70
Red Carpet		●			●		Harold's				12 noon			$57 / $67

270

attitude here is service: if they haven't anticipated your need, just ask and they'll give it their best. Another plus—concierges and guest services personnel are women. Women alone are offered rooms near elevators or in a special section opening to a second-floor lobby area. These rooms are on a grand scale, with Old World extras like illuminated bookcases and Murphy beds that fold away. Located in fashionable East Town, the hotel is adjacent to some good shopping (see "The Shopping Scene").

The **English Room** is, oddly enough, a French gourmet dining room, critically acclaimed and a safe choice for business entertaining. The **Greenery** is their three-meals restaurant. The **La Playa** bar, with its 23d floor wrap-around view, swings, Latin-style, with a deejay manning the music. The **Cafe Olé** is a bar where we feel comfortable alone.

Northwest Area

Marriott Inn

375 S. Moorland Road   Toll-free reservations: 800/228-9290
Brookfield, WI 53005   Local number: 786-1100
Located about 20 minutes west of downtown, this suburban hotel is both lively and attractive. It is surprisingly large (396 rooms), and is adjacent to Brookfield Square, a 75-store shopping center. A good choice for sports enthusiasts, the hotel offers jogging paths, indoor and outdoor pools, a fitness center, and an 18-hole golf course across the street.

Rumors is a very popular disco. Local businesspeople often dine at **Whitney's,** the Marriott's fine dining restaurant.

Northeast Area

Milwaukee River Hilton Inn

4700 N. Port Washington Road   Toll-free reservations: 800/445-8667
Milwaukee, WI 53212   Local number: 962-6040
Overlooking the Milwaukee River in the quiet suburban setting of Glendale, this inn offers peace and quiet with easy access to the business world—I-94, one block away, gets you downtown in 15 minutes. Clientele is 90 percent business travelers, but there are no special floors set aside in this 164-room inn. Some rooms have foldaway Murphy beds; others have refrigerators and separate sitting areas with a river view. There's an indoor pool. Interesting safety feature: the outdoor parking lot is checked by security guards every half hour from 11 P.M. to 7 A.M.

The **Anchorage,** a stylish, brass-nautical restaurant, is popular with local business people. Serves three meals daily.

South and Airport Area

Red Carpet Hotel

4747 S. Howell Avenue   Toll-free reservations: 800/558-3862
Milwaukee, WI 53207   Local number: 481-8000

A family-owned inn, not part of the national chain, this Red Carpet is an ideal choice if your business needn't take place in town. Located across from the airport (yet surprisingly quiet) and adjoining a convention hall, this 510-room inn seems to have grown like Topsy, with five major guestroom sections, each different in decor and atmosphere. (You may want to inquire how far your room will be from the lobby.) Good sports facilities, including indoor and outdoor pools and jogging. Also a strike away from Milwaukee's favorite sport—bowling.

Its formal restaurant, **Harold's,** is excellent and very popular with locals. **El Robbo's Disco** is also popular. The **Court Yard** coffee shop offers meals from 6 A.M. to 10 P.M.

ON A BUDGET

Hotels

There are four Midway motels around the Milwaukee area, each with excellent security, well-appointed rooms, and a pool-and-garden setting under a huge skylight bubble. A restaurant and a bar are on the premises, but no newsstand for papers or magazines. Singles are $54 (corporate) and $62 to $67 (regular). Toll-free reservations for all locations: 800/643-9291.

Airport: 5105 S. Howell Avenue, 769-2100. West: 1005 S. Moorland Road, 786-9540. West, but closer to downtown: 251 N. Mayfair Road, 774-3600. Northeast—Glendale: 7065 N. Port Washington Road, 351-6960

Restaurants

Major Goolsby's is an inexpensive lunch and dinner place that features brats, burgers, sandwiches. Its location—across from MECCA and next door to the *Sentinel* and the *Journal*—make it a meeting place for sports enthusiasts and reporters. Up-beat atmosphere, good food. 340 W. Kilbourn Avenue, corner of 4th and Kilbourn. 271-3414.

There are dozens of **George Webb** restaurants all over town serving inexpensive burgers and breakfasts—a pre–Golden Arches fast-food chain. They are clean, safe, and popular with local people.

Entertainment

There's almost continuous entertainment in this town—so many festivals take place, they tend to overlap. For a nominal admission fee you can "visit" a foreign culture—sample the foods, enjoy the music and dance, join in the fun. Check local listings or call the **Funline** (799-1177) for up-to-the-minute information on the festival of the day.

DINING OUT

Food and the entire dining experience are taken very seriously in Milwaukee. Portions are huge, service is invariably courteous, and the range of restaurants is international. To visit Milwaukee and not sample the many ethnic cuisines would be like traveling through Italy and ignoring the pasta. Be daring: sample the schnitzel at Ratzsch's one night and go for the moussaka at Kosta's the next. Whatever your culinary preference, chances are you can indulge it in this town.

John Ernst, Milwaukee's oldest (dating back to 1878) serves some of the finest German food in the United States, proclaims *Fortune* magazine. We like the live and lively music, the heavy-duty German decor, and the serious food. Lots of business lunchers, with a business and social mix at dinner. Closed Mondays. 600 E. Ogden Avenue. 273-1878.

Mader's, another upscale German restaurant, features Bavarian decor, castlelike baronial halls, and waitresses in Tyrolean costume, in addition to an excellent German menu. Open seven days. 1037 N. Third Street. 271-3377.

Karl Ratzsch's is considered by many to be Milwaukee's most celebrated restaurant. Dinners are elegant, with Viennese string trios and fashionably dressed patrons. Open since 1904, Ratzsch's also offers an extensive (450-plus) wine list. Open seven days. 320 E. Mason Street. 276-2720.

Le Bistro, at the Marc Plaza Hotel, offers classic and nouvelle French in a serene setting. Closed Sundays. 509 W. Wisconsin Avenue. 271-7250.

La Rotisserie in the Hyatt Regency overlooks the 18-story atrium. The menu is Continental and the star is the large open brass rotisserie. Draws a business crowd for lunch, a mix of couples and business for dinners. Open seven days. 333 W. Kilbourn. 276-1234.

The English Room is where the Pfister Hotel serves up its fanciest French cuisine. Lots of national food awards won here, although no one has questioned why the Gallic cuisine is served under an Anglo name. We have found the food to be uneven; if there's a large in-hotel banquet or social function, the chef's creativity is divided. But when it's good, it is very good. Very fancy here; dress up and invite your most important clients. Open seven days. 273-8222.

Grenadier's and **Fleur de Lis** are two other serious French restaurants of note. Both are good choices for business entertaining, and either welcomes women alone. At Grenadier's (747 N. Broadway; 276-0747) you can special-order your favorites with some advance notice. They also provide courtesy limousine service. Fleur de Lis, 925 E. Wells. 278-8030.

Gaetano's is a super choice for preshow dining. The Italian cuisine is bellissima, and they also offer shuttle van service to PAC, Riverside Theater, and MECCA. Good spot for business lunches, too. 272 W. Wisconsin Avenue. 289-9848.

John Byron's serves fresh seafoods in a setting that overlooks Lake Michigan. Closed Sundays. In the First Wisconsin Center, Galleria Level. 777 E. Michigan Avenue. 291-5220.

John Hawk's Pub for casual dining—burgers, salads, soups—in a traditional pub setting. No credit cards. Open seven days. 607 N. Broadway. 272-3199.

Beer Baron is another casual dining spot, with some gourmet specials to spice up the salad-and-sandwich menu. Closed Sundays. 1120 N. Broadway. 272-5200.

Cafe La Boheme is a romantic spot that adds a dollop of classical music and jazz to its exotic menu of Greek-Armenian and Middle Eastern specialties. Open until midnight seven days. 319 E. Mason Street. 224-0150.

Kosta's White Manor Inn is an intimate subterranean Greek restaurant. Live music on weekends. 1234 E. Juneau Avenue. 272-4029.

Third Ward Cafe serves northern Italian fare in the SoHo-like setting of Milwaukee's historic Commission Row. Closed Sundays. 225 E. St. Paul. 224-0895.

Toy's Sun Garden offers several regional Chinese cuisines—Szechuan, Hunan, Cantonese, Mandarin. Lunches are served cafeteria style; dinners, table service. Closed Sundays. 770 N. Jefferson St. 271-1211.

Watts Tea Shop in East Town serves light cuisine upstairs in the second-floor Tea Shop while, downstairs on the main floor, George Watts China Shop sells the china, crystal, and utensils it's served on. Breads and croissants are homemade. Nice selection of salads, desserts. Lunch or tea, Monday through Saturday. 761 N. Jefferson. 276-6352.

Benjamin's is the place when you get a craving for hot pastrami or a really good bagel. A Jewish deli open seven days, 7 A.M. to 8 P.M. 4156 N. Oakland Avenue. 332-7777.

The Anchorage serves seafood in a nautical setting overlooking the Milwaukee River. Dress is casual, and there's even a Sunday brunch. 4700 N. Port Washington Road (Hilton Inn). 962-4710.

Go to the **Old Serbian Gourmet House** when you crave the taste of burek, sarma, or goulash like mama used to make. Closed Monday. 522 W. Lincoln Avenue. 672-0206.

UNIQUELY MILWAUKEE: A CITY OF FESTIVALS

Few cities take their special festivals as seriously as Milwaukee does. Perhaps it's because of the proud ethnic heritages, perhaps it's the fun-loving spirit of the place. Whatever the reason, Milwaukee has a festival for just about anything anyone could want to celebrate. And the whole city celebrates: streets, like Old World Third Street, are closed to traffic. Our favorite is the closing of the streets around Cathedral Square Park for special Bastille Day celebrations. This, because the general manager of the nearby Pfister Hotel is French.

Summerfest, end of June/early July: billed as "The World's Greatest Music Festival," this is definitely Milawukee's largest and most celebrated. Continuous performances on ten stages for ten days. There are also water shows, foods from over 30 local restaurants, and an air show. Held on the lake-front Summerfest grounds. Admission charge. 273-2680.

Lakefront Festival of the Arts, second weekend in June: outdoor art festival. On lake front just north of the Art Museum, 750 N. Lincoln Memorial Drive. Admission charge. 271-9508.

Augtoberfest, third Friday in August: music and foods from some of Milwaukee's best ethnic restaurants. Held in Old World Third Street area. Free admission.

Oktoberfest, last three weekends in October: Old World fall festival featuring German foods, music, dance—even yodeling. Free admission. 964-4221.

And a sampler of ethnic festivals:

Greek Fest, first weekend in July. Free admission. 461-9400.

La Kermesse de la Bastille (French), weekend closest to July 14th. Free admission.

Festa Italiano, third weekend in July. Admission charge. 963-9613.

German Fest, fourth weekend in July. Admission charge. 464-9444.

Afro Fest, first weekend in August. Admission charge. 374-5850.

Irish Fest, third weekend in August. Admission charge. 466-6640.

Fiesta Mexicana, fourth weekend in August. Admission charge. 645-6740.

Polish Fest, Labor Day weekend. Admission charge. 672-4077.

MILWAUKEE BY DAY

These are some of the sights you can see in a spare hour or two. Longer day-trip activities are listed under "At Leisure."

The best overview in town is from the 41st floor Skywalk of the **First Wisconsin Center** (the state's tallest building). Free admission. Monday through Friday, 2 to 4 P.M. 777 E. Wisconsin Avenue. 765-4321.

"**Discover Milwaukee**" is a multimedia presentation that will give you some insights into the city, its history, and what makes it tick. First floor of the Plankinton Arcade of the Grand Avenue Mall. 161 W. Wisconsin Avenue. 276-8482.

At the War Memorial Center: **Milwaukee Art Museum,** housed in a 1957 Eero Saarinen–designed building, offers 19th- and 20th-century European and American art. Lake Michigan forms a striking backdrop for the outdoor sculpture collection. In summer an arts festival is held outdoors in tents on the lawn. Closed Mondays; open late Thursdays; Sundays 1 to 6 P.M. 750 N. Lincoln Memorial Drive. 271-9508.

Villa Terrace houses exhibits of the decorative arts from 1660 to 1820. Built on a high bluff overlooking Lake Michigan, this 1923 Italian-style villa's courtyards and terraces also make vista-watching a relaxing pleasure. Open Wednesday through Sunday in summer; Wednesday and weekends the rest of the year. 2220 N. Terrace Avenue. 271-3656.

Charles Allis Art Museum houses a collection of over 800 paintings and art objects ranging from the 6th to the 19th century. The museum building is an English Tudor mansion that belonged to the first president of Allis-Chalmers Co. Open Wednesday through Sunday, 1 to 5 P.M.; open 7 to 9 P.M. on Wednesdays. 1801 N. Prospect Avenue. 278-8295.

Captain Frederick Pabst Mansion, a Flemish Renaissance structure, was completed in 1893 for the man who made Pabst famous. Replete with such turn-of-the-century craft work as carved wooden cabinets, stained glass, ornamental ironwork, delicate plasterwork, this 37-room mansion exemplifies Old World wealth as enjoyed by America's first beer baron. Tours by docents. Hours vary seasonally; call for current schedule. 2000 W. Wisconsin Avenue. 931-0808.

Milwaukee County Historical Center is housed in a landmark structure built in 1913. Local history comes alive through exhibits on early settlement, business, industry, and transportation. "The Old Corner Store" is a gift shop featuring turn-of-the-century folk art. Adjacent to Pere Marquette Park on the Milwaukee River. Open weekdays, 9:30 A.M. to 5 P.M.; Saturdays, 10 A.M. to 5 P.M.; Sundays, 1 to 5 P.M. 910 N. 3d Street. 273-8288.

St. Joan of Arc Chapel is the real thing—moved stone by stone from its medieval home near Lyons, France, to a site on Long Island, New York, and finally to Milwaukee. The saint prayed here just before her death, and legends say the stone she kissed remains colder than all the others. Open daily, 10 A.M. to 4 P.M. Located on center mall of Marquette University campus, 14th Street and Wisconsin Avenue. 224-7039.

Annunciation Greek Orthodox Church is one of Frank Lloyd Wright's last works and a particularly splendid example of Byzantine architectural style with its winged, blue-domed silhouette. Tours last about an hour, but you must make an appointment in advance. 9400 W. Congress Street (about 15 minutes west of downtown area). 461-9400.

Milwaukee Public Museum houses our nation's fourth largest collection of natural history exhibits and is famous for its dioramas and walk-through settings. You'll "visit" an African water hole, a Japanese garden, and a pre-Columbian tomb, among other things. Open daily, 9 A.M. to 5 P.M. (except major holidays). 800 W. Wells Street. 278-2700.

Mitchell Park Horticultural Conservatory—"The Domes." Said to be unique in all the world, these three 85-foot glass domes house separate climates: tropical, arid, and a seasonal display—each offering visitors glimpses of exotic and often rare or endangered species growing in naturalistic settings. Hours vary seasonally; call for current hours. 524 S. Layton Boulevard (five minutes west of downtown). 278-4383.

Milwaukee County Zoo is another of our country's modern habitat zoos in which animals roam "free" in naturalistic settings. In winter, the zoo's expanse is also used for cross-country skiing. Summer hours, 9 A.M. to 5 P.M. (until 6 P.M. on weekends); 9 A.M. to 4:30 the rest of year. 10001 W. Blue Mound Road (ten minutes from downtown). 771-3040.

Rainbow Summer is not a place, but rather a series of summertime lunch-hour performances sponsored by the *Milwaukee Journal*. Events take place on the outdoor stage of the Performing Arts Center where you can sit on seats in the bandshell or in a grove of chestnut trees overlooking the river as they entertain you. Free admission. June, July, August. 929 N. Water Street. 273-7206.

Short Tours

Emerald Isle Boat Line offers narrated, ninety-minute cruises along the shoreline of Lake Michigan for just about any type of sailor. Choose from day cruises, evening dinner cruises, even a Sunday brunch cruise. You must reserve in advance. Tickets are $5.00, with additional charges for meal cruises. Boat leaves from 333 N. Water Street at St. Paul Avenue. 224-9534.

Iroquis Harbor Cruises also explore the inner and outer harbors of Milwaukee. They board at Clybourn Street bridge (one block south of Gimbel's) at 3225 N. Shepherd Avenue on the Milwaukee River just north of I-794 (use the Plankinton exit). Ninety-minute cruises, $4.00. Call 332-4194 for times.

The **Miller Brewery tour,** which lasts about two hours, includes a multimedia presentation and a visit to production areas; it ends in the Miller Inn, a restored Bavarian inn. This involves some outdoor walking, so dress accordingly. Free admission, but you "pay" by having to listen to lots of commercial messages built into the tour. Monday through Saturday, 9 A.M. to 3:30 P.M. (Saturdays during April–October only). 4251 W. State Street. 931-2153.

Historic Milwaukee Archi-Tours offer a variety of walking or bus tours that focus on different aspects of the city's diverse architecture. Appointments are necessary and schedules vary. Pick up a brochure at any major hotel, or call 332-5019 or 645-5300.

THE SHOPPING SCENE

As we have said, downtown Milwaukee is divided into east and west sections by the Milwaukee River. There are interesting places to shop on both sides of the river.

East Town, between Kilbourn and Clybourn streets, is an area filled with fine shops and restaurants. (Most area stores are open Monday through Saturday, 10 A.M. to 5 P.M. Closed Sundays.) Some that rate your special attention are:

George Watts and Son: fine china, silver, crystal and art objects in an Old World setting. A family business since 1870, through four generations. (The present George Watts is also running for governor of the state.) A tea room is on the second floor (see "Dining Out"). 712 N. Jefferson. 276-6352.

Percy's: to pamper yourself with luxury linens for bed, bath, and entertaining. 719 N. Milwaukee.

The Snow Goose boutique: for eclectic, interesting fashions. 785 N. Jefferson.

The Grand Avenue Mall is a downtown shopping complex designed by the Rouse Company to connect five historic buildings. Located on the west side of the river, it is a glass-enclosed, four-block complex of shops, gardens, restaurants, and connecting skywalks. You can begin at the Boston Store (331 W. Wisconsin Avenue; 347-4141) and end at Gimbel's (101 W. Wisconsin Avenue; 276-7050) and hit about 150 stores in between. Save time for lunch or some ethnic snacking in the "speisgarten," a parklike garden setting for the restaurants. This mall is open Sundays from noon to 5 P.M., 10 A.M. to 8 P.M. weekdays.

Old World Third Street for authentic, heritage-type gifts you won't find in many other American cities. The area is bounded by W. Wells and W. Highland Boulevard. Most stores are open from 9 A.M. to 5 P.M., Monday through Saturday; closed Sunday. Among them:

Usinger's Famous Sausages: over 75 varieties made from Old World recipes. We know one Milwaukee mother who fills an entire suitcase with Usinger's best when traveling to visit her children. They are happy to ship or pack your selections for travel. 1030 N. Third Street.

Wisconsin Cheese Mart: 215 W. Highland

The Spice Shop: huge vats of exotic spices; creative combinations to fit any cuisine. 1102 N. Third Street.

Mader's Restaurant: 1037 N. Third Street.

Also in this area: the Milwaukee County Historical Society and the Milwaukee Journal Company.

Milwaukee Antique Center. If you have any interest—even the slightest—in antiques, don't miss this three-floor center where more than 75 dealers display antiques and collectibles. (Hint: you'll be searching alongside a lot of antiques dealers.) Open Monday-Saturday, 10 A.M. to 5 P.M.; Sunday, Noon to 5 P.M. 341 N. Milwaukee St. 276-0605.

In addition to Grand Avenue, there are several suburban shopping malls with high-quality stores: Bayshore, Northridge, Southridge, Mayfair.

There are three unique shopping areas—Stonecroft Old World Village, Stonewood Village, and Cedar Creek Settlement—that are well worth your time. However, as they are some distance from town, we have included them in the "At Leisure" section.

MILWAUKEE BY NIGHT

People take their cultural arts very seriously in this town, and they lavish support and loyalty on their favorites. You can find your own interests here—from light opera to symphony, from experimental black theater to Broadway road shows.

Performing Arts Center is an entertainment complex housing a variety of companies. Located as it is right on the banks of the river, it lends itself to outdoor concerts. Some residents even arrive by boat and tie up just outside the doors. Box office is open daily, noon to 9 P.M. 929 N. Water Street. 273-7206. You'll find at the PAC:

The **Florentine Opera Company,** which celebrated its 50th anniversary in 1983, offers three programs each season. Performances are Thursdays at 7:30 P.M.; Saturdays at 8 P.M.; and Sundays at 2:30 P.M. Tickets from $11 to $47 at PAC box office. 273-7206.

The **Milwaukee Symphony,** under the direction of Lucas Foss and associate conductor JoAnn Falletta, is ranked among the nation's top ten. Offering a variety of classical and pops guest artist series from September through mid-June. Performances Fridays and Saturdays at 8 P.M.; Sundays at 7:30 P.M.; and Thursdays at 11 A.M. Tickets from $9 to $27 at PAC box office. 273-7206.

The **Milwaukee Ballet Company,** guided by Ted Kevitt, performs four series—plus *The Nutcracker*—each season. Performances on Thursdays at 7:30; Fridays at 8 P.M.; Saturdays at 2 and 8 P.M.; and Sundays at 2 P.M. Tickets from $3 to $30 at PAC box office. 723-7206.

The **Milwaukee Repertory Theater** presents six plays during the September through May season. Performances are Tuesday through Sunday at 7:30 (Saturdays at 9:30 P.M.); matinees on Wednesdays and Sundays. Tickets from $4.50 to $13.50 at PAC box office. 765-0555.

The **Skylight Theater** is used by three performing groups: Skylight Comic Opera Ltd., with operetta and musical offerings; the Chamber Theater, presenting four plays a season; the People's Theater, a black community theater group. Tickets to all three available at box office (open Monday through Friday, noon to 6 P.M.) 813 N. Jefferson Street. 271-8815.

The **Pabst Theater,** itself an 1895 landmark building, is now restored and hosts a variety of theater productions, concerts, and touring companies. The box office is open Monday through Friday, noon to 6 P.M. and before performances. 144 E. Wells Street. 271-4747.

Court Street Theater is second home to the Milwaukee Repertory Theater. It is a small house (99 seats) located in a warehouse area of town, but it does have a parking lot right next door so you won't have far to walk. 315 W. Court Street. Box office 273-7121 (evenings: 765-0555).

Riverside Theater is a newly renovated house presenting a variety of live performances. Check local listings to see what's in town. Tickets through Ticketron or box office. 116 W. Wisconsin Avenue. 271-2000.

Melody Top is fun for good old-fashioned summer theater. June through September, this domed tent theater presents seven musicals featuring Broadway stars. Performances every day or evening except Monday. Tickets from $9.75 to $12.75 available at box office. (Theater is about 25 minutes from downtown). 7201 W. Good Hope Road. 353-7700.

LATE-NIGHT MILWAUKEE

While you won't find a swinging, all-night underground in town, there are some good jazz spots and discos that don't shut down at the stroke of midnight. All the ones we mention are in safe neighborhoods and are places where a woman alone can feel comfortable.

Bombay Bicycle Club, in the Marc Plaza Hotel, features a jazz pianist. Open until 1 A.M., Tuesday through Saturday. Closed Monday. 271-7250.

The Beer Baron's, 1120 N. Broadway (just north of downtown). Open Monday through Friday until 2 A.M., Saturday until 3 A.M. 272-5200.

Two in the Red Carpet Hotel near Mitchell Field: **BJ's Saloon,** open Sunday through Friday until 2 A.M., Saturday until 3 A.M. 481-8000; and **El Robbo's,** open until 3 A.M. on Saturdays. 481-8000.

Cafe Manhattan Lounge in the Midway Motor Lodge in Glendale features live music Tuesday through Saturday. 351-6960.

Cafe Olé in the Pfister Hotel features live music. Open until 1 A.M., Sunday through Friday; until 2 A.M. on Saturday. 273-8222.

Destin's has live music on Fridays and Saturdays. Open until 2 A.M. 422 S. 2d Street. 278-7933.

La Boheme Cafe has jazz piano on Friday and Saturday, open until 1 P.M. 319 E. Mason Street (three blocks from Pfister Hotel). 224-0150.

La Playa, a South American hideaway atop the Pfister Hotel, is popular for dancing to big-band music. Often there's live music on weekends. Open until midnight during the week, until 3 A.M. on Saturdays. 273-8222.

Maxwell's, in the Midway Motor Lodge in Brookfield, features live jazz. Open Monday through Saturday until 1 A.M. 1005 S. Moorland Road.

Claiming to be Milwaukee's largest, **Papagaio** offers a variety of entertainment in its two-level lounge: live bands, deejay, dancing. 515 N. Broadway. 277-0777.

Rumors in the Marriott Inn in Brookfield is also popular for top-40s dancing. A bit younger crowd here than at Papagaio's. 786-1100.

Shepherd's Saloon and Restaurant for dancing and late dining. Open daily until 2 A.M. 1233 N. Van Buren. 224-0676.

AT LEISURE

It doesn't take long to realize just how close to nature metropolitan Milwaukee is. If you delight in scenic beauty, in outdoor sports, or in exploring local history, by all means plan to spend some free time in town (check hotels for best weekend packages); then hop into your car and enjoy Wisconsin.

Day-Tripping

Old World Wisconsin (25 miles southwest of town, about 40 minutes driving time) is a 576-acre outdoor living ethnic museum, a historic restoration of 19th-century settlements. Located in the beautiful Kettle Moraine State Forest. Admission charge. 1-594-2116.

Two nature preserves offer miles of undeveloped nature, trails, ponds—even cross-country trails in winter:

Schlitz Audubon Center in Brown Deer (about 20 minutes drive north of town); 185 acres of undisturbed wilderness; four and a half miles of nature trails. Also guided naturalist tours available. Admission charge. 352-2880.

Wehr Nature Center (about 40 minutes drive southwest of town). Free admission. 425-8550.

The **Cave of the Mounds,** with its legendary stalagmites and stalactites, offers chilly looks underground (temperatures always hover around 50 degrees). Guided tours every 15 minutes. Two hours drive west of town. Call 608/437-3038.

For old-world browsing and shopping:

Cedar Creek Settlement and **Stone Mill Winery.** Settlement dates back to 1864. Shops and restaurants are open. Winery tours available year round. There are frequent special events. Cedarburg is about a 30-minute drive north of town. 377-8020.

Stonecroft is a Tudor-style European village re-creation. Twenty-five shops and restaurants. Great crafts to buy, plus artisans-at-work to watch. Special events on most Sundays. About a 30-minute drive north of downtown in Grafton. 377-6150.

Stonewood Village is a shopping area of 28 stores and restaurants styled after a colonial New England village. Try the Proud Popover and the Loaf and Jug for dining. About a 30-minute drive west of town. 781-9703.

Johnson Wax Administration and Research Center. Tours of the building which was designed by Frank Lloyd Wright. In their theater, see the award-winning films, *To Fly, To Be Alive,* and *Living Planet.* About a one-hour drive south of town. 631-2154.

About 80 miles west of downtown is **Madison,** home of the University of Wisconsin, one of this country's most beautiful campuses. Some excellent shopping here, as well as several fine restaurants. There are beautiful northern lakes in the area (the campus runs right onto the shores of Lake Mendota), so most water sports are readily available. The trip along I-94 is postcard time—America's dairy farms abound.

In Town

If you want an idea of how the good life is lived in a midwestern high-rent district, drive north along Lake Drive and check out the mansions and estates built along the waterfront. You won't be able to see the bluffs, the private beaches, or the private views of Lake Michigan— they're hidden behind the landscaping and the fences—but all that affluence is a comforting sight.

Sunday Customs

Church and brunch share top billing as favorite Sunday activities. Among the best for brunching:

Atrium Lounge at the Hyatt Regency. An elaborate champagne buffet with homemade pastas, hot and cold entrées—the works. $13.50 a person. From 10 A.M. to 2 P.M. 276-1234.

Karl Ratzsch. Atmosphere is comfortable and tranquil. Light brunch served (no buffet). $7.95 a person. From 11 A.M. to 3 P.M. 320 Mason Street. 276-2720.

Cafe Rouge at the Pfister Hotel. Elegant buffet in the hotel's belle epoque setting. $12.50 per person. From 10 A.M. to 2 P.M. 273-8222.

SUBURBAN (NORTH):

George Pandl's in Bayside. Lovely buffet in relaxed atmosphere; picture windows for enjoying the parklike setting. Often animals will wander out of the adjacent woods in front of your window. $8.50 per person. From 10:30 A.M. to 2:30 P.M. 8825 N. Lake Drive. 352-1430.

WEST:

Whitney's in the Marriott at Brookfield. Champagne brunch; great homemade salads, desserts. $10.95 per person. From 10 A.M. to 2 P.M. 357 S. Moorland Road. 786-1100.

SOUTH:

Court Yard at the Red Carpet Hotel. Limited menu; served at table. $8.95 per person. 4747 S. Howell Avenue. 481-8000.

Sunday Events

The **Milwaukee Polo Club** hosts U.S. Polo Association games. There are bleachers, but who could resist bringing along a picnic or tailgating from your Rolls? Matches from early June to Labor Day. Sundays at 3 P.M. (from 1 P.M. if its a double header). $3 admission. 6321 W. Good Hope Road. 358-1803.

Charter fishing on Lake Michigan. Fish for trout or salmon on full- or half-day charters. All equipment supplied—they even clean your catch for you. Cost will run between $40 and $60. You must call in advance; the captain needs a few days notice to make up a party. Arjay Charters; Captain Dick Sulig. 8007 W. Meinecke Avenue. 453-3082.

Spectator Sports

Like most cities with major league home teams, Milwaukee fans are fiercely loyal to their teams. To get in on the action:

The **Milwaukee Brewers** play baseball in Milwaukee County Stadium from April through September. The stadium is just ten minutes from downtown, with plenty of public transportation and also ample parking. Tickets are from $3 to $8.50 at the box office. 201 S. 46th Street. 933-1818.

The NFL **Green Bay Packers** share their family ties, playing several home games here. Tickets are for cash only and are usually next to impossible to come by. Check with your hotel's concierge, or try in person just before the game. County Stadium, 201 S. 46th Street. Box office 342-2717.

The NBA **Milwaukee Bucks** play basketball at the downtown MECCA arena during the long October-through-April season. Tickets from $5.50 to $15.50 are available at the arena box office, 500 W. Kilbourn Avenue. Mastercard and Visa are OK. 272-8080.

Any time now, the Milwaukee hockey **Admirals** and the **Bucks** will be moving from the MECCA to a new home near the County Stadium.

Active Sports

Milwaukee County Parks: There are 14,500 acres of landscaped parks, including miles of lake front. Recreational facilities—pools, tennis, golf, ski trails, boats—available to everyone. Bradford Beach and McKinley Beach (on Lake Michigan) are within walking distance of downtown. For golf information, call 278-4345; skating, day or night, 278-4345; boating, weather, and lake conditions, 277-9272. Call 278-4345 for live, up-to-the-minute information on fees, hours, programs. Call 278-4343 for taped information hot line.

HOTELS

1 Amfac
2 Cricket Inn
3 Embassy Suites
4 Hyatt Regency
5 Marquette
6 Radisson South Hotel and Executive Towers
7 Saint Paul
8 Sofitel

LANDMARKS

A City Center
B Chimera Theater Co.
C Guthrie Theater
D Hubert H. Humphrey Metrodome
E Minneapolis Convention and Visitors Commission
F Minneapolis/St. Paul International Airport

G Minnesota Museum of Art
H Minnesota Science Museum
I Northrop Auditorium
J Salisbury Market
K St. Paul Convention Bureau Landmark Center B-100
L Town Square
M Walker Arts Center

MINNEAPOLIS/ ST. PAUL

GETTING YOUR BEARINGS

We often wonder why so many people refer to Minneapolis and St. Paul as the Twin Cities. They hardly resemble each other. We'd even go so far as to say that the two cities, roughly separated by the Mississippi River, are rivals. This sentiment goes back to the days when each had its own airport, its own athletic teams, and its own list of complaints against its neighbor.

St. Paul narrowly escaped the not-so-savory name of Pig's Eye, after one of its early founding fathers. But the state capital mercifully ended up with a more appealing title, better suited to its personality. This is a city in flux, a city of promise. It's a national leader in historic preservation of buildings; it's smaller, more stately, and perhaps more provincial than Minneapolis. St. Paul is currently trying to revitalize a sagging downtown economy. Lowertown, its latest shopping, office, and arts complex, is an exciting addition.

Minneapolis, on the other hand, is the local glass-and-steel marvel, spearheaded by the IDS Center, designed by Philip Johnson. Compared to its neighbor, the Minneapple—as the city is nicknamed—is faster paced and home to a surprising number of large companies including 3M, Honeywell, General Foods, and Pillsbury. The major league athletic teams are based in Minneapolis, and the lion's share of the University of Minnesota is here, too. Minneapolis is the more vital of the two cities and we dare say the better city to visit if you must make a choice. But the distance between the two downtown centers is short, so you can stay conveniently in one while doing business in the other.

The cities are only loosely divided into neighborhoods—people rarely get more specific than the Lakes or the Campus—and neither city is particularly well organized. Occasionally, in certain Minneapolis neighborhoods, names of the avenues are alphabetical and those of the streets are in numerical order. Downtown is essentially a grid. But St. Paul, legend has it, was laid out when its founding fathers were on a drunk. In fact, addresses that numerically are close together can be blocks apart. Most visitors—not to mention Minneapolitans—despair of ever finding their way around.

The Twin Cities do have one thing in common: they are both rife with local humor, about everything from the preponderance of carp in the nearby waters to the brevity of summer, that two-week period between winter and roadwork. But perhaps nothing is as popular a source of metroland jokes as the homogeneity of the cities' residents. The area is dominated by blond, blue-eyed Scandinavians and Germans. The ethnic population is low, but a recent influx of Vietnamese and Laotian refugees has given the city some spice. Still these two cities remain almost shockingly white and middle class.

Perhaps because of that sameness, business attitudes are a touch conservative, although Minnesotans do take pride in their tradition of liberal thinking. If we can offer any advice for conducting business here in America's heartland, we say play it straight and you'll get good results every time.

WHAT TO WEAR

The Twin Cities may appear to be conservative, but don't feel that means you can't pack your more unconventional outfits. Minneapolis—more than St. Paul—is open to new ideas in dress even though the locals may not participate with you. Of course, if gray-skirted suits worn with floppy bow ties is the business uniform of your choice, don't hesitate to wear that. You'll fit right in in most circles.

WEATHER WATCH

The hype you've heard is true: during the winter, which some of the more dour residents claim lasts from September to July, the Twin Cities are bitterly cold. The mercury often stays well below zero for days. In fact, Minnesotans get a perverse pleasure out of surviving their winters, swapping stories about the blizzard of 1981 or bragging about strolling in their shirt-sleeves when the wind chill factor was minus 70. But if business takes you to Minneapolis/St. Paul in the late spring or summer, chances are you're in for some pretty glorious weather, with fresh air (its quality gets an A plus) that hovers between 70 and 80 degrees.

GETTING THERE

The only port of call in the Twin Cities is the **Minneapolis/St. Paul International Airport** (726-1717) located in the suburb of Bloomington. You may remember the air strip from the movie *Airport,* chosen because this airport has the best emergency snow removal equipment in the country—

remember the movie's hair-raising last scene? The airport almost never shuts down.

Twelve major airlines serve the Twin Cities, offering service from anywhere in the continental United States. Best bets are Northwest Orient and Republic, both headquartered here.

Downtown Minneapolis and downtown St. Paul are each about ten miles from the airport, a ten-minute drive on Highway 494. A taxi ride should cost $15 to $18.

Probably the best way to travel to town if you choose not to rent a car is the airport limo service (726-6400). It makes runs to most of the cities' major hotels, departing from outside the lower level of the terminal on the half hour. Cost is $6.50.

Car Rentals

If you want to really see Minneapolis and St. Paul or if you're staying some distance from your meeting venue, it's best to rent a car from one of the following agencies:

National	726-5600
Hertz	726-1600
Avis	726-1723
Budget	726-5622

GETTING AROUND

If you rent a car, you'll find plentiful parking in the downtown areas, with inexpensive outdoor lots and indoor ramps, which, since they're isolated, aren't the safest places in the world. Some, however—like the LaSalle ramp and the Dayton's-Radisson ramp in Minneapolis—are monitored by hidden camera. But still, sexual assaults have occurred, so it's best to be cautious and be sure to lock your doors. On-street metered parking is available, but it's difficult to find a space.

A note about driving in downtown Minneapolis: no cars are allowed on Nicollet Mall, the city's main shopping drag.

It's not unheard of to depend on taxi service if you're visiting, but be sure to call at least a half hour in advance. We prefer the taxi services of Blue and White Cabs (333-3331), Town Taxi (331-8294), and Yellow Cab (824-4444 in Minneapolis, 222-4433 in St. Paul). Cabs are metered and fares are set by the cities they serve. St. Paul cabs are $1.10 for the first ⅛ mile and 10 cents for each additional 1/11 mile. In Minneapolis, they're $2.95 for the first mile and $1.10 for each additional mile.

The public transportation in both cities is the MTC, or Metropolitan Transit Commission city bus. There are dime zones within the downtown area, but standard fares are 75 cents during peak hours (Monday through Friday, 6 to 9 A.M. and 3:30 to 6:30 P.M.) and 60 cents other times. If you exceed the primary zone—which is unlikely—there's an additional charge, depending on how far you ride. Exact change is required for all fares.

The bus, however, is by no means the perfect mode of transport. The system is not comprehensive, particularly in outlying areas (it is adequate within and between downtown areas) and buses run infrequently at night. In fact, the system closes shop sometime between 9 P.M. and 1 A.M., depending on the line.

GETTING FAMILIAR

Minneapolis Convention & Visitor Commission
15 S. Fifth Street   612/348-4313
Minneapolis, MN 55402
For specific information on Minneapolis, write, call, or stop by at this bureau. If, however, you want to inquire about St. Paul, contact:

St. Paul Convention Bureau Landmark Center, B-100
St. Paul, MN 55102   612/292-4360
These are separate organizations, and each provides information about its namesake city only.

The daily newspaper serving Minneapolis is the *Minneapolis Star and Tribune* with variety/weekend sections providing an excellent rundown of cultural events as well as restaurant reviews. The *St. Paul Dispatch* comes out Monday through Friday evenings, and the *Pioneer Press,* Monday through Friday and Sunday mornings. Saturday the two papers combine for one morning paper. *City Pages* and the *Twin Cities Reader* are free weekly papers focusing on the arts. Both have comprehensive listings for music, theater, and movies as well as special events. *Mpls./St. Paul* is a sophisticated glossy magazine emphasizing special events and attractions around town and carrying features on local issues and personalities. *Twin Cities* magazine runs features and photography on the region, but focusing, of course, on the cities.

—————————— *Quick Calls* ——————————

| **AREA CODE 612** | Weather 725-6090 |
| Time 874-8700 | Emergencies 911 |

AT YOUR SERVICE

If at all possible, stay in Minneapolis. It's just a stone's throw from downtown St. Paul, and the pickings are much better for hotels and for cultural events. You might also check out Bloomington near the airport. The hotels on the strip often beat downtown prices, with city centers just a short jaunt on the highway. The choice is yours.

Minneapolis

Amfac

Minneapolis City Center	Toll-free reservations: 800/227-4700
30 S. Seventh Street	Local number: 349-4000
Minneapolis, MN 55402	Telex: 291116

The 600-room Amfac is built over the three-story City Center, so you can get a feel for the city's inhabitants by watching from the hotel's lobby or lounge. Part of Minneapolis's unique skyway system, a network of glass-enclosed second-level walkways that connect the business district, this hotel couldn't be more convenient, especially in inclement weather. An expanse of blond Swedish wood and restful gray and tan easy chairs set the tone for the property, which offers Guest of Honor floors including individual key access, a comfortable lounge with a sizable library and a game room and the morning papers. Health facilities on the premises are the second best in town (we like the Hyatt Regency's better) and feature a sauna, steam room, whirlpool, and Nautilus equipment. Besides the Amfac shops, the City Center shopping mall offers 60 more. It should be noted though that it's easier to get down to the latter's shops than back, as security at the hotel is polite, but tight.

All three restaurants in the hotel are excellent: **Papayas** is the most casual, similar to a coffee shop with honey-colored wood and quick service and a Friday night seafood buffet; **Gustino's,** on the sixth level, is the merriest, with singing waiters and waitresses serving northern Italian fare in bright green and white surroundings. The **Fifth Season** is the Amfac's formal dining room, accented by thick foliage and green and white decor. If you want to impress, this is the place. Order the milk-fed Wisconsin veal chops. The **Fifth Season** lounge is probably the most comfortable for women travelers. It's bright and airy, and surrounds an atrium with a spectacular waterfall. The **Cinebar** is a bit more severe, and with its low lighting, a bit daunting.

Hyatt Regency

1300 Nicollet Mall	Toll-free reservations: 800/228-9000
Minneapolis, MN 55403	Local number: 370-1234
	Telex: 290413

The Hyatt is the closest hotel to the city's cultural centers, a block from Orchestra Hall and a short walk to the Guthrie Theater and Walker Art Center. And since it's a long six blocks from the central downtown area,

Hotel	Concierge	Executive Floor	No-Smoking Rooms	Fitness Facilities	Pool	24-Hour Room Service	Restaurant for Client Entertaining	Extra-Special Amenities	Electronic Key System	Business/Secretarial Services	Check Out Time	Frequent Guest Program	Business Traveler Program	Average Rate
Amfac	•	•	•	•		•	The Fifth Season	•		•	12 noon		Amfac Express	$ 85–$225 $ 98–$150 corp.
Hyatt Regency	•	•	•	•	•		Pronto The Willows	•			12 noon	Private Line	Gold Passport	$ 89–$99 $ 91 corp.
Marquette	•		•				Marquis Gallery			•	1 p.m.			$115–$125
Sofitel	•			•	•	•	La Terrasse Chez Colette	•		•	1 p.m.	L'Avantage		$ 88
Radisson South Hotel & Executive Towers	•	•	•		•		Aurora Restaurant	•		•	3 p.m.		Plaza Club	$ 89 $ 80 corp.
St. Paul	•						L'Etoile	•		•	1 p.m.	Preferred Selection	Corporate Rate Program	$ 79–$99 $ 79–$94 corp.
Embassy Suites		•	•		•		Woolley's				1 p.m.			$ 76–$86 $ 69 corp.

van shuttle service up and down Nicollet Mall is provided. Slightly less swank than the newer Amfac, the Hyatt nevertheless was the model for that hotel, especially in terms of restaurants and amenities. The high-rise Hyatt pays special attention to the female traveler, to the point of setting aside ten businesswomen's rooms with lighted vanity mirrors on the wall, clotheslines over the tubs, and hair dryers. In addition, the hotel tries to place women in rooms nearest the elevator for safety.

The Hyatt has three restaurants, including the **Terrace**, a garden cafe for a pleasant quick bite, which offers a diet menu. **Pronto** is a popular northern Italian restaurant with branches in New York and Geneva, Switzerland. The view is classic—broad boulevards lined with stately old buildings—and so is the food, from scampi to pasta and chicken stuffed with veal. The **Willows** has a reputation as the epitome of elegance in Minneapolis. The decor is as aristocratic as the finely prepared food. Its bar is secluded and darker than the one in the Terrace. Drinks are also served in the lobby if you want to avoid altogether the unease of a bar.

Marquette

710 Marquette Avenue
Minneapolis, MN 55402

Toll-free reservations: 800 THE-OMNI
Local number: 332-2351
Telex: 9105761686

The Marquette prides itself on personal service, and as Minneapolis hotels go, it is probably the most proper. It's also the most convenient for many business travelers. Located in the heart of downtown, it's attached to the IDS Center, the nexus point of the skyway system. The 282-room property never caught up with the newer hotels in terms of frill features like health facilities. And yet the rooms are spacious, offering one of the nicest turn-down services in the Twin Cities: you'll find a small bottle of Harvey's Bristol Cream on your pillow each night.

The **Gallery** restaurant, serving burgers, salads and seafood, is perched on a vine-covered balcony overhanging the IDS Center's Crystal Court, a great spot for people-watching. The **Marquis** restaurant is for fine dining, with an extremely masculine flair, all leather and brass. The fare is nouvelle, and the dress is formal.

Bloomington

Sofitel

5601 W. 78 Street
Bloomington, MN 55435

Toll-free reservations: 800/328-6303
Local number: 835-1900
Telex: 290215

Located on the Strip near the airport, the Sofitel is less convenient for those with downtown business, but because of its more remote location, it functions as a more self-contained unit than do other area hotels. It has, besides health facilities and a beauty shop, both a doctor and a dentist on call 24 hours a day. There's nothing special about the 288 rooms, but the lighting is good, and the hotel provides skirt hangers, hair dryers, and makeup lighting. When requesting a room, you might ask for one near the elevator as the hallways are dark and it can be a long and lonely walk to your room, in spite of good security. If you're a people-watcher, ask for an inside room for a view of the hotel's garden court lobby.

Dining at the Sofitel is the pièce de résistance. **The Take Out,** boulangerie—with real French boulangiers—is one choice; another, **La Terrasse,** is a country-style coffee shop with marble tables, flowered awnings, and wicker furniture. **Chez Colette** is a lovely spot for a semicasual dinner. The menu is French with English explanations. And the **Cafe Royal** is a formal dining room with a country French entryway and mock antique appointments. The Sofitel has bars in La Terrasse and Chez Colette, but the staff recommends the lobby service to women travelers.

Radisson South Hotel and Executive Towers
7800 Normandale Boulevard   Toll-free reservations: 800/228-9822
Bloomington, MN 55435   Local number: 835-7800

The Radisson, just across the street from the Sofitel, has long been one of the town's most popular spots for business travelers. Check-in is European style; guests report to the concierge to expedite entry. A $2.6 million renovation in 1985 spruced the place up, and management added traditionally female amenities to the 163 rooms—largest in the Twin Cities.

For fine dining, try **Aurora,** with Continental American food in an intimate, elegant atmosphere. The **Shipside** serves seafood that's caught in Holland, put on ice, flown to Minneapolis via Chicago, cooked, and brought to your table within 36 hours. **Kaffestuga** is the coffee shop, with a traditional smorgasbord. The spectators' lounge features music. There's also TGI Fridays.

St. Paul

Saint Paul
350 Market Street   Toll-free reservations: in Minnesota
St. Paul, MN 55102   800/292-9292; outside Minnesota 800/
                             457-9292
                          Local number: 292-9292
                          Telex: 297008

This plush property is convenient: overlooking historic Rice Park, it is connected to the Skyway, feeding directly into the heart of downtown attractions. Part of Lincoln Hotels, the St. Paul, built in 1910, recalls an earlier era that centered on gracious living. The 255 rooms here offer a refined elegance unmatched in the city—right down to the fluffy terry cloth bathrobes and basket of luxury toiletries, all served up with a distinctly residential feel.

If you want to impress a client, make a reservation at **L'Etoile,** which serves Continental cuisine and is acclaimed as one of the city's premier four-star restaurants (the *Minneapolis Star-Tribune* called it "downtown St. Paul's dining masterpiece"). The **Cafe** is a casual place to eat, and for drinks try the **Bar,** with a great view of Rice Park, or the **Lobby Lounge.**

Embassy Suites

175 E. Tenth Street
St. Paul, MN 55101

Toll-free reservations: 800/EMBASSY
Local number: 224-5400
Telex: 4949280

Embassy Suites is located four blocks from the center of St. Paul and within walking distance of the state capitol. The hotel lobby has large hand-painted murals. Every guest stays in a two-room suite, designed with light wood furniture and a pastel color scheme of dusty rose, blue, and green. The suites, each with two telephones and two televisions, surround and open onto a lushly landscaped central atrium complete with waterfall, bridges, ponds, and pools where fish and ducks frolic. The hotel offers free transportation to and from Minneapolis/St. Paul Airport and an express checkout program. It can handle meetings for groups of 8 to 200.

Free, cooked-to-order breakfast is offered at Embassy Suites as are two hours of free beverages at the daily manager's reception.

ON A BUDGET

Hotels

For stretching your budget, we recommend staying in a **Cricket Inn,** of which there are five operating in the metropolitan area. Two of them are the best of the lot: at 2407 University Avenue, S.E., Minneapolis, MN 55414 (on the University of Minnesota campus); toll-free reservations: 800 622-3999; local number: 623-3999; or in Roseville (not convenient to downtown), on I-494, Highway 55, Minneapolis, MN 55441; local number: 559-2400.

Restaurant

For an impressive yet reasonably priced restaurant, try **Ciatti's.** The Italian food is occasionally uneven, but the decor is charming and if you are dissatisfied, the staff cheerfully changes your order. The restaurant's large space is made somehow intimate by the tables' arrangement—good if you're planning an important business meal—and dramatic beams of light cut across the floor, giving Ciatti's a dash of class. The seafood and pasta salad make an excellent lunch. For a heavier meal, try fettucine alla Ciatti's or chicken Marsala. Reservations are advisable, since this is a hot spot for the younger business crowd. 1346 LaSalle Avenue, Minneapolis. 339-7747.

DINING OUT

Once a desert for diners, the Twin Cities have responded in recent years to local palates becoming more sophisticated. Some of the cities' best food is served in the hotels—the **Fifth Season** at the Amfac, the **Willows** at the Hyatt, **Chez Colette** at the Sofitel, and **L'Etoile** at the St. Paul have some of the finest dining in the area. And for a more casual dinner or leisurely lunch, you can't beat the Hyatt's **Pronto,** the Amfac's **Gustino's,** or the Marquette's **Gallery.** Still, if you're anxious to get out and see the town, here are a few places to try:

You can be Cleopatra for a night at the **Orion Room,** decorated in neo-Nile chic, blending art deco colors with large silver sphinxes and Temple of Karnak lintels. Perched on Minneapolis's highest skyscraper in the heart of downtown, the Orion was long thought of as a "view with a restaurant"—an image changed by the new refreshing menu of regional favorites and classic American cuisine. Try the Minnesota wild rice soup and don't miss the seafood specialties. 50th floor, IDS Tower, Nicollet Mall. 349-6250.

Leeann Chin won the first annual readers' restaurant survey in *Mpls./St. Paul* magazine in 1985. Contemporary in design with clean lines and lots of wood, the restaurants feature delicately placed museum pieces. There's no menu (you choose from an ever-shifting buffet), so call in advance to see what's on for that day. Union Depot, 214 E. Fourth Street, St. Paul. 224-8814. Also at Bonaventure, Highway 12 and Plymouth Road, Minnetonka. 545-3600.

The **Blue Horse** is a local institution for the venerable business lunch with national and regional dining awards adorning the old brick entryway. If you decide to play host to a client here, be warned: this Continental cuisine restaurant has a decidedly masculine flavor. But don't let that put you off; just be sure the waiter knows who's picking up the tab. 1355 University Avenue, St. Paul. 645-8101.

In 1985, the *Minneapolis Tribune*'s food critic gave **Forepaugh's** a three and a half star—his highest rating ever. This restaurant is worth a trip if only to see its exterior, a grandly restored Victorian mansion with beautiful grounds. Inside, bric-a-brac and chandeliers add atmosphere to the traditional French fare. Service is unobtrusive here. 276 Exchange Street, St. Paul. 224-5606.

Fuji-Ya is right on the river, near the historic St. Anthony's locks. It features Japanese cuisine, including a sushi bar and the knife-wielding wonder of teppanyaki cooking. Sit upstairs in booths or at low tables in the O'Zashiki Room. Ask for a table with a view. 420 S. First Street, Minneapolis. 339-2226.

Located on Minneapolis's original main drag, **Pracna on Main** has been around for 100 years. A fairly casual restaurant, the interior is dimly lit with exposed beams and luxurious polished wood. Cocktails are served in the garden court during warm weather. 117 Main Street S.E., Minneapolis. 379-3200.

Muffuletta is a bit of a jaunt from either city, but well worth the trip. There's an open rural flavor to this nouvelle Italian grand cafe, where outdoor tables under bright Cinzano umbrellas fill up fast. Try the grilled duck with juniper berries. 2260 Como Avenue, St. Paul, near Milton Square. 664-9116. Also at 739 E. Lake Street, Wayzata. 475-3636.

If you're dining sans client, following is a quick rundown of casual spots for the single diner:

The **Good Earth,** dressed up in bright blond wood, is a chain of California-style eateries that feel nothing like a chain. Excellent vegetarian fare is featured, along with seafood and poultry dishes made with no white flour or sugar. 3460 S. 79th Street, in the Galleria, Edina, 925-1001; 5717 Xerxes Avenue N., in the West Brook Mall, Brooklyn Center, 586-0630; Highway 12 and Plymouth Road, Bonaventure, Minnetonka, 546-6432; and 1901 W. Highway 36, Roseville, 636-0956.

A combination of 19th-century elegance and California mellow, **Winfield Potter's** has the most extensive salad bar in town. 201 S.E. Second Street, St. Anthony Main, Minneapolis. 378-2660.

Annie's Parlor is a small soda fountain with wooden booths, popular with the university crowd. 406 Cedar Avenue, Minneapolis, 339-6307; and 313 14th Avenue S.E., Minneappolis, 379-0744.

Cecil's is the best deli in St. Paul (651 Cleveland Avenue S., St. Paul, 698-0334), and the **Lotus** is among the best for Vietnamese food (313 Oak Street, Minneapolis, 331-1781).

Breakfast is the low point of the cities' dining circuit. For business breakfast, your best bet is your hotel.

MINNEAPOLIS/ST. PAUL BY DAY

Three art museums dominate the metropolitan scene:

The **Walker Art Center** is exciting even by big-city standards. This is the institution that initiated such shows as the Picasso and de Stijl exhibitions. A permanent collection includes extensive examples of 20th-century painting and sculpture primarily by American artists. Vineland Place, Minneapolis, attached to the Guthrie Theater. 375-7600.

The **Minneapolis Institute of Arts** houses an encyclopedic collection of 65,000 objects from nearly all schools and periods of art as well as an ongoing series of temporary exhibits. Also here: the Minnesota Artists Exhibition Program. 2400 Third Avenue S., Minneapolis. 870-3046.

Early 20th-century American art, photography, and Asian art are on display at the main branch of the **Minnesota Museum of Art,** also host to changing exhibitions (St. Peter and Kellogg, St. Paul, 292-4355). A second location in Landmark Center (205 Landmark Center, 75 W. Fifth Street, St. Paul) features exhibitions of established regional and national artists as well as newly discovered regional artists.

The **Minnesota Science Museum** emphasizes hands-on experience for the museum-goer. You'll find an outstanding display of artifacts and history of several native American cultures here as well as the standard scientific fare: permanent and temporary exhibits on everything from dinosaurs to laser beams. One not-to-be-missed feature is the William L. McKnight 3-M Omnitheater, with a huge domed screen that makes viewers feel as if they're part of the movie.

Here are some other daytime activities for the visiting woman executive:

If you're lucky enough to catch one of the **Guthrie's** occasional Wednesday morning tours, don't hesitate. The smell of greasepaint was never like this—staff members take guests backstage, below stage, and through the dressing area for an unforgettable view of what goes on behind the scenes. 347-1111.

Avid listeners to "The Prairie Home Companion" may be disillusioned to discover there is no Lake Wobegon in Minnesota. But there *is* a real Garrison Keillor, the humorist behind the nationally broadcast two-hour radio variety show. Visitors can see the show live, but ever since Keillor appeared on the cover of *Time* in 1985, the Saturday afternoon show has been very popular; so be sure to contact Minnesota Public Radio well in advance for tickets. At St. Paul's World Theater, Exchange and Wabasha Avenues. 293-5412.

You may want to tour the historic homes on St. Paul's stately **Summit Avenue.** F. Scott Fitzgerald penned *This Side of Paradise* in the row house at 599 Summit; he was born nearby on Laurel Avenue. Summit's four-mile stretch between the Cathedral of St. Paul and the Mississippi River is one of the most exclusive areas of the cities and architecturally one of the most eclectic. Gothic, Romanesque, Renaissance, Italianate and postwar styles blend into a stunning array of houses. For a guided tour, call the **Summit Hill Association,** 928 Lincoln Avenue, St. Paul. 222-1222.

THE SHOPPING SCENE

The shopping areas in Minneapolis and St. Paul are concentrated in the two downtowns (mostly Minneapolis) and the suburban shopping centers, primarily the Dales—**Southdale** (W. 66th Street and York Avenue S., Minneapolis), **Brookdale** (N. Highway 100 and Highway 152, Minneapolis), **Ridgedale** (Highway 12 and I-494, Minneapolis), and **Rosedale** (W. Highway 36 and Fairview Avenue N., St. Paul). The Dales are anchored by **Dayton's,** which can be described as Macy's, Bloomingdale's, and the May Company rolled into one. **Donaldson's** holds down the other corner of the Dales. Donaldson's has always played Gimbel's to Dayton's Macy's: somehow the quality and service here never seemed as good.

Both downtown Minneapolis and St. Paul have a **Dayton's** (Minneapolis, Eighth Street and Nicollet Mall, 375-2200; St. Paul, Seventh Street and Cedar, 292-5222). Both also have a central mall—**City Center** in Minneapolis (Seventh Street and Nicollet Mall) and **Town Square** in St. Paul (Seventh Street between Minnesota and Cedar). Both have a standard array of women's clothing chains and specialty shops. City Center also has a Benetton (333-3673), a Laura Ashley (332-6066), and a few unique stores like Olds Pendleton (340-0771), which sells Pendleton's woolen sportswear, blankets, and yard goods. Town Square's advantage is its upper tier where shoppers can rest among ferns, palms, and a waterfall.

The biggest mall is the first closed-in mall in the country—Southdale. Both Southdale and Ridgedale have spawned satellite specialty malls. The **Galleria** (3500 W. 70th Street) near Southdale and **Bonaventure** (1501 S. Plymouth Road, Minnetonka) near Ridgedale offer small expensive shops good for those who love to browse. Bonaventure's 40 shops circle a garden courtyard and are serviced by a glass elevator. Both malls have excellent moderately priced restaurants, including Leeann Chin in Bonaventure and the Good Earth in both malls. Our favorite shops are the Lambshop in Bonaventure (545-5971), featuring gorgeous imported sweaters, and Epitome in Galleria (920-2978), a clothier specializing in dresses, suits, sportswear, and accessories for the well-dressed woman.

Restoration malls are popping up so quickly in the area that one wonders what could possibly be left to restore. The original restoration was **Butler Square** (11 N. Sixth Street, Minneapolis). Once a warehouse, this office-and-shopping complex was meticulously renovated to retain its raw look—broad wooden beams crisscross above shoppers, and an eight-story atrium makes one feel summery in the coldest Minnesota weather. Hello Minnesota (332-1755) is a whimsical shop dedicated to the warmth and frosty ironies of Minnesota life. Check out the loon slippers and the jewelry by local artisans. This is also the place to buy Minnesota wild rice (they'll tell you how to cook it). Butler Square also houses a number of small galleries, some featuring native American art.

St. Anthony Main (201 S.E. Main Street, Minneapolis) is the most hopping of all the restorations—and it's no wonder. It's located on the city's original Main Street. The former mattress company is another brick, beam, and glass affair full of specialty shops and restaurants. Recently the **Salisbury Market**—based on Boston's Faneuil Hall—opened adjacent to St. Anthony. It's full of sumptuous goodies to indulge in after a day's (or an hour's) shopping. Speaking of shopping, St. Anthony's has plenty of it. Look into the Armoire (623-0463) has lingerie—lots of little lacy numbers. And Mainstreet Outfitters (378-2228) has sportswear and shoes that the preppie in you will love.

Antique hunters should visit the row of shops near 50th Street and Xerxes Avenue S. in Minneapolis. American Classic Antiques (4944 Xerxes Avenue S., 926-2509; 10:30 to 5, Monday through Saturday, 12 to 4, Sunday), Charisma Place (3011 W. 50th Street at Xerxes, 926-5400; 10:30 to 4:30 Wednesday through Sunday), the Black Swan Country Store (3020 W. 50th Street at Xerxes, 926-9134; 10:30 to 5 Tuesday through Saturday), Fjelde & Co. Antiques (3022 W. 50th Street at Xerxes, 922-7022), and The Yankee Peddler (5008 Xerxes Avenue S., 926-1732) all have their treasures—even if sometimes they're buried treasures. Prices are higher than in the countryside, but cheaper than in other, bigger cities.

Gokey's (Fifth Street and St. Peter, St. Paul, 224-4300) is the cities' legendary, all-purpose drygoods store: men's, women's, and children's footwear, sporting goods, pajamas. This is the L. L. Bean of the Twin Cities. On the other hand, that honor may go to **Eddie Bauer** (Foshay Tower, 821 Marquette Avenue, Minneapolis, 339-9477). This is where the down-lovers flock, and where you should go if you forgot to bring your down mittens, vest, and hat. **Frank Murphy** (Fifth and St. Peter streets, St. Paul, 291-8844) sells some of the finest designer clothing in the city. If you're lucky, you'll catch their late winter sale—it's worth fighting the crowds for the bargains. For one-of-a-kind, reasonably priced jewelry, visit the **Walker Art Center** (Vineland Place, Minneapolis, 375-7633). The pieces are all handcrafted and guaranteed to be noticed.

MINNEAPOLIS/ST. PAUL BY NIGHT

If you can manage only one evening out while in the Twin Cities area, you better manage to get tickets to the **Guthrie Theater.** Otherwise, you'll never be able to show your face in town again. The Guthrie, which won a Tony for the best regional theater, offers at moderate prices classics and occasional music on a par with anything you'll see on Broadway. Call before your trip to see what's playing, and if the show's sold out, take your chances on Tuesday or Sunday when any unclaimed seat is only $5. You won't be disappointed. Vineland Place, Minneapolis. 377-2224.

Other theaters include the following:

The **Cricket Theater** is located in a renovated Romanesque land-mark, formerly a Masonic Temple, in downtown Minneapolis. The Cricket is one of the cities' most vital theater groups, concentrating on contemporary American drama. The company's performance is at times uneven, but often surprisingly on the mark. Sixth and Hennepin Avenue, Minneapolis. 333-5241.

Actor's Theater of St. Paul is this city's version of the Cricket. The company's performance runs the gamut both in the types of plays they stage and, occasionally, in quality. 2115 Summit Avenue, St. Paul. 227-0050.

Chimera Theater Company is located in the St. Paul Arts and Sciences Center and focuses on family entertainment—everything from a rollicking performance of *Guys and Dolls* to an enchanting *Johnny Appleseed.* This is one of the largest community theaters in the country, and performances are professional. During intermission be sure to browse through the museum. 30 E. Tenth Street, St. Paul. 293-1043 for tickets.

Don't be put off by the name: the **Children's Theater** is as much for adults who are young at heart as it is for kids. One of the top-ranking theaters for young people in the country, perhaps the world, the Children's Theater performs classic folktales, contemporary fantasies, and original plays developed in-house. 2400 Third Avenue S., Minneapolis. 874-0400.

The **Orpheum** is home to touring Broadway shows. 910 Hennipen Avenue, Minneapolis. 338-7968.

Mixed Blood Theater Company, located in an abandoned firehouse on the University of Minnesota's West Bank, performs pertinent new plays. 1501 S. Fourth Street, Minneapolis. 376-0937.

The **Northrop dance season** brings national and international dance talent to the cities. Northrop is a good-sized auditorium, so be careful about where you're seated. 105 Northrop Auditorium, 84 Church Street S.E., University of Minnesota, Minneapolis. 376-8378.

To see the best of local classical and contemporary ballet, go to a performance of the *Minnesota Dance Theatre.* And if you're going to be in town during the holiday season, try to get tickets to their enchanting performance of Loyce Houlton's *Nutcracker Fantasy.* Tickets sell out quickly, so call well in advance if you can. Hennipen Center for the Arts, 528 Hennipen Avenue S., Minneapolis. 339-9150.

St. Paul City Ballet is not as popular as the Minnesota Dance Theatre, but is nevertheless quite good. Classical ballet is the specialty of the house. Performances are usually during February, April, and November. 565 N. Kent Street, St. Paul. 222-4676.

If you can catch a performance of the **Nancy Hauser Dance Company,** you're in luck. Call 623-4296 for information. You might also try **Zenon Dance Inc.** for occasionally superb modern and jazz performances. 324 Fifth Ave., Minneapolis. 338-1101.

Minneapolis and St. Paul are each graced with a superlative classical music ensemble. In fact, this is the only metropolitan area with two major orchestras. The **Minnesota Orchestra,** directed by Neville Marriner, the most recorded orchestra director in history, performs in Orchestra Hall in Minneapolis and O'Shaunessy Auditorium, in St. Paul. The orchestra has a Night at the Pops series as well as free 11 A.M. Coffee Concerts on Tuesdays and Thursdays throughout the season. Tickets are available at Orchestra Hall or Dayton's. Note that the second and third balconies of Orchestra Hall have a partially obstructed view. Orchestra Hall, 1111 Nicollet Mall, Minneapolis. 371-5656.

The **St. Paul Chamber Orchestra** has just moved to the new, acoustically superior Ordway Center in downtown St. Paul. The Grammy-winning ensemble, directed by Pinchas Zuckerman, has 34 members. Their season runs from September through May and includes guest stints by some of the best artists in the world.

Movie complexes are located at all the malls, as well as other suburban shopping areas. Theaters in downtown Minneapolis and near downtown St. Paul usually cost $4.50 to $5. A comprehensive list can be found in any local paper, along with showtimes. There are also a number of art houses in the Twin Cities. They include the following:

The **Minneapolis Institute of Arts** shows classic movies. 2400 Third Avenue S., Minneapolis. 870-3046 or 870-3131 for information.

The **Minnesota Museum of Art** screens vintage and rare movies on Tuesday evenings at 8:00 in the Weyerhaeuser Auditorium. Landmark Center, 75 W. Fifth Street, St. Paul. 292-4355.

The **University Film Society** presents a variety of films—foreign, experimental, classic—year-round. Bell Museum of Natural History Auditorium, University and 17th avenues S.E., Minneapolis. 373-5397.

The **Walker Art Center** screens a variety of current, classic, and experimental films. Vineland Place, Minneapolis. 375-7600.

For the latest information about the Twin Cities' arts and cultural events, call the **Arts Resource and Information Center.** 870-3131 or 870-3132.

Tickets are often available through Dayton's or Donaldson's.

LATE-NIGHT MINNEAPOLIS/ST. PAUL

The Twin Cities don't have the night life of the bigger cities, but they do all right—especially with music. This is after all the home of the biggest rock star of the eighties, Prince. In fact, the rocker is somewhat of a local hero; Governor Perpich even declared a Prince Day in 1984. Still, there aren't a lot of places to go for a really late night out, and most available spots are filled with the very young. Jazz and comedy clubs are your best bet.

Here is a sampling:

First Avenue and Seventh Street Entry is a converted bus depot, having survived the seventies as a hard-core disco and then switching to a punk hangout. Now it's riding the wave of the eighties with new music, plain old rock-and-roll, reggae, and occasionally jazz. The movie *Purple Rain* was filmed here, where two floors of dancing are the scene of national as well as local acts. 701 First Avenue N. 332-1775.

Rupert's multitiered club is a disco with a difference—all the music is live. See as many as six acts a night. Sunday is nostalgia night—all bands play music from the forties and fifties. The suburban location gives added safety to the club, as does Rupert's attached restaurant, which has some of the best down-home southern cooking you'll find in the North. Dress up if you pick this spot. Turners Crossroad, Golden Valley. 544-5035.

Located in the basement of the Nicollet Island Inn, **Gabriel's** has some of the best jazz around. Acts, either straight from New York or on their way there, play in an intimate atmosphere. The club seats only 100 at small tables practically on top of the band. Enjoy the beautiful riverfront view. 219 Main St. S.E., 623-4223.

Classic jazz is the house specialty at the **Artist's Quarter.** You'll find the best be-bop here, and though the neighborhood is suspect, the club is fairly safe. 14 E. 26th Street, Minneapolis. 872-0405.

Coffee House Extempore features the best quality folk music in the cities. An ultracasual, fairly intimate club near the University of Minnesota, the Extempore has a natural foods cafeteria attached and live music each night. On Wednesdays, an open stage invites a variety of local talent to jam. 325 Cedar Avenue S., Minneapolis. 370-0004.

At **Night Train,** you'll find two restored Pullman cars (circa 1887) with a lounge in the center forming the hottest jazz club/restaurant in St. Paul. Stop by for a late-night dinner and stay for the show. 289 Como Avenue, St. Paul. 488-2277.

Comedy clubs have exploded in the Twin Cities, and the granddaddy of them all is **Dudley Riggs' Brave New Workshop.** The nation's oldest satirical comedy club, Dudley Riggs' has been offering on-the-nose parody and satire since 1958. Comedy clubs all over the country focus on local idiosyncracies, and Minneapolis/St. Paul clubs are no exception, but there are still plenty of laughs for the outsider. Tickets are $7; available at the box office or Dayton's. 2605 Hennepin Avenue S., Minneapolis. 332-6620.

A second club, **Dudley Riggs' E.T.C.** (Experimental Theater Company) is located on the university's West Bank. E.T.C. features cabaret-style theater and occasional visiting artists. Tickets at varying prices are available at the box office, Dayton's, or Donaldson's. 1430 Washington Avenue S., Minneapolis. 332-6620.

Other comedy clubs, and who is performing at them, are listed in the weekly newspapers.

AT LEISURE

In Town

If you're around in the warmer months, plan to take in the **Lake Harriet** series of summer concerts. The music runs the gamut from Dixieland to classical.

Free concerts are also held in **Nicollet Island Park** in Minneapolis and **Como Lakeside Pavilion** in St. Paul. But don't forget the bug spray; the mosquitoes come out en masse when the sun goes down. For more information on the Minneapolis concerts, call 348-2226. For St. Paul, call 292-7400.

TailorMaid Tours will show you around if you can't decide what to do on your own. 427 Woodlawn Avenue, St. Paul. 699-7317.

Day-Tripping

If you have a day on your hands when business is done in the Twin Cities, why not answer the call of the wild and see some of the country's prettiest countryside. More acres of water and forest land than you can fathom are located in the state's only national park, **Voyageurs;** and in the two national forests within driving distance, **Superior** and **Chippewa.** Get back to nature by camping in the countless Minnesota wilderness areas.

For free maps showing campsites, access points, and other pertinent information (like where to find portages and suitable drinking water), contact the Department of Natural Resources, Trails and Waterways Unit, Box 52, Centennial Building, St. Paul, MN 55155. 612/296-6699.

Sunday Customs

Brunch still hasn't come into its own in the Twin Cities. In fact, your best bet may be your hotel—the **Amfac** grabbed top honors in the *Mpls./St. Paul* reader's poll. Other winners were **Pronto** (in the Hyatt), **Muffuletta,** and **Winfield Potter's** (see "Dining Out"), as well as the mahogany and marble publike **Bristol Bar and Grill** (1 Main Street S.E., Riverplace, Minneapolis; 378-1338). You won't have to sing for your supper at the Bristol. A Dixieland band plays all morning long. Brunch is served from 10:30 A.M. to 2:00 P.M. For a more exotic meal, try dim sum (Chinese steamed pastries filled with a plethora of ingredients) at the **Corner House** (2800 17th Street, Minneapolis; 724-6666). Brunch is served from 11 A.M. to 2:00 P.M.

When you're ready to work off the dim sum, nouvelle, or whatever, do what the natives do and head for the lakes.

Or try one of Minnesota's biggest treats—the **zoo** (1210 Johnny Cake Ridge Road, Apple Valley; 432-9000). The animals are housed in near-natural environments rather than cages. Unfortunately, natural environments allow for more camouflage opportunities—sometimes those Siberian tigers are impossible to find. If you visit during the winter, dress warmly and rent a pair of crosscountry skis at the zoo—a number of the animals are housed outdoors (they *like* the cold) and ski trails run right by them. Be warned: even the easiest trails have difficult stretches. Summer visitors can walk the zoo's 485 acres and an all-weather monorail carries the lazy in futuristic style.

Spectator Sports

Minneapolis hosts four professional teams—the **Minnesota Vikings** football team (332-0386), the **Minnesota Twins** baseball team (332-0386), the **Minnesota Strikers** soccer team (332-0386), and the **Minnesota North Stars** hockey team (853-9300). All but the North Stars play at the Hubert H. Humphrey Metrodome downtown, 502 Chicago Avenue, Minneapolis. The North Stars play at the Met Sports Center, 7901 Cedar Avenue, Bloomington.

If you're a basketball fan, check out the action of Big Ten basketball with the **Minnesota Gophers**. 373-3181.

Active Sports

If it's active sports you want, you've come to the right place. Because of the Twin Cities' myriad of lakes and rivers, you can do everything from canoeing to paddlebiking and windsurfing. Even in the colder months, you'll see locals doing the latter, garbed in wetsuits to ward off the bitter shock of the freezing waters. We recommend seeking out **St. Croix River** and **Lake Como.**

For joggers, the chain of lakes running through central Minneapolis is a perfect place to do just that. **Lakes of the Isles, Lake Calhoun,** and **Lake Harriet** are the best of the bunch for that sport. Calhoun at 3.4 miles is the biggest, and Harriet at 2.8 miles is the smallest.

If hiking is your pleasure, take your pick: Some 38 regional parks dot the area. And if golf is your game, there are more than 100 courses from which to choose. Giving a nod to the weather factor in this area, **Edina Golf Dome** has space for indoor golfing as well as jogging, soccer, touch football, volleyball, horseshoes, and softball. 7420 Braemar Boulevard, Edina. 944-9490.

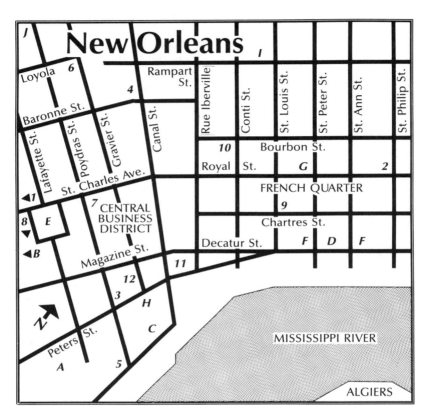

New Orleans

Loyola 6
Baronne St.
Lafayette St.
Poydras St.
Gravier St.
St. Charles Ave.
4
Rampart St.
Canal St.
Rue Iberville
Conti St.
St. Louis St.
St. Peter St.
St. Ann St.
St. Philip St.

10
Royal St.
Bourbon St. *G*
2

FRENCH QUARTER
9

7 CENTRAL BUSINESS DISTRICT
8 *E*
B
Magazine St.
1
Chartres St.
Decatur St. *F* *D* *F*

12
3
11
H
C

A
Peters St.
5

N

MISSISSIPPI RIVER

ALGIERS

HOTELS

1 Columns Hotel
2 Cornstalk Hotel
3 Crowne Plaza Holiday Inn
4 Fairmont Hotel
5 Hilton Hotel Riverside & Towers
6 Downtown Howard Johnson's
7 Hotel Inter-Continental
8 Hotel Pontchartrain
9 Royal Orleans
10 Royal Sonesta
11 Westin Canal Place
12 Windsor Court Hotel

LANDMARKS

A Convention and Exhibition Center
B Garden District
C International Trade Mart
D Jackson Square
E Lafayette Square

F Pontalba Bldgs.
G Preservation Hall
H Rivergate International Exhibition Center
I St. Louis Cemetery No. 1
J Superdome

NEW ORLEANS

GETTING YOUR BEARINGS

They call New Orleans "The Big Easy" or "The City that Care Forgot."
That says it all. This is a laid-back town that prides itself on knowing how to have a good time. We find that people here work to live, they don't live to work. In fact, the watchword for the surrounding Acadian French-speaking communities applies just as well to this Big Easy: *Laissez les bons temps rouler*—Let the good times roll.

And do they ever.

A business trip to New Orleans is one of the more enviable assignments you can snare—except perhaps in summer when the humid heat can wilt your enthusiasm. In tune with the city tempo, deals are cut over lunch and sometimes breakfast in languid and elegant restaurants and private clubs. Yet, despite the increase in the number of business-women in power positions here, we are sad to say that New Orleans is still a man's town.

The population of the city itself numbers around 500,000. Its surrounding counties (or parishes, as they are called from the area's Napoleonic legacy) bring the metropolitan count up to a million. Like most visitors, though, we tend to focus on a colorfully concentrated corner of New Orleans unmatched anywhere in the United States: the French Quarter, or *Vieux Carré.*

You are likely to approach this historic neighborhood from the high-rise Central Business District, separated from the Quarter by Canal Street, a vibrant shopping street in its own right. The French Quarter is the heart and soul of New Orleans, the center for Mardi Gras madness and everyday abandon. Originally laid out in 1718, it can be as sedate as brunch in a garden patio or as raucous as jazz and burlesque in a bevy of bars. We always feel transported to a charming corner of Europe in this neighborhood by day—and to a bawdy playground of earthly delights by night.

The busy major streets of the Quarter—Bourbon and Royal in the 200 to 900 blocks—are safe and fun to walk, day or night. Take care on the fringes, however. Like all major cities, New Orleans poses the threat—especially for women—of muggings and thievery in more isolated areas. Not only for safety's sake but for fun as well, the French Quarter is best enjoyed as a group discovery.

While quintessentially southern, New Orleans is America's most cosmopolitan southern city, thanks to its Spanish, French, and Afro-Caribbean influences. Residents and visitors alike succumb to the city's unique romance and rhythm as well as to the exotic Creole cuisine that has lately piqued national tastebuds.

Easy as it is, New Orleans may not be the easiest of cities in which a woman can do business. But it's always fun, and, with a bit of deference to old traditions that die hard, a woman can win with charm and intelligence what men here think they control by birthright.

WHAT TO WEAR

For all its ability to flaunt convention after hours, New Orleans remains a fairly conservative place when it comes to business. Keep in mind the traditional southern attitudes and dress accordingly. Preppy is the business style to emulate. You will still see members of the powerful (male) business elite sporting white linen suits and Panama hats in summer. That's not because that particular style has come back. For them, it never went out.

WEATHER WATCH

Except for the occasional cold snap in January or February, New Orleans winters are mild. Temperatures rarely fall below 40 degrees and generally hover around 50. Spring—March and April—is exceptionally beautiful with azaleas, camellias, and Japanese magnolias in flower everywhere. The temperatures in the low 70s enhance the fragrant floral air.

Summer is steaming hot. But because every place is air-conditioned, you will need a light sweater to ward off a chill once inside. Nevertheless, plan on bringing your coolest clothes—and plan on changing at least twice a day.

GETTING THERE

New Orleans has but one major airport—**New Orleans** (formerly Moisant) **International**. Given its importance as a commercial center, the city has been ill-served by air. The Mississippi River remains the lifeblood of industrial transport. But that is changing with an influx of regional airlines and the start-up of New Orleans–based Pride Air.

New Orleans International Airport lies about 20 miles west of the city center in Kenner. Seven of the 23 airlines serving the city domestically and internationally are major carriers: Delta, 529-2431; Southwest, 523-5683; Eastern, 524-4211; Continental, 581-2965; American, 523-2188; Republic, 525-0423; Pan Am, 529-5192.

For airport-city transportation information, call the airport office (464-0611). Driving time to the central city is approximately 30 minutes via highway I-10.

A 24-hour, seven-day service of shuttle vans to all major downtown hotels is available for $7 per person. The vans meet all scheduled flights and wait for you and your luggage at curbside. Call 581-7222 weekdays and 581-1590 weekends for details. This service also connects with New Orleans East (the farthest suburbs) with an $8 charge to the Chef Menteur, the Holiday Hi-Rise, or the Howard Johnson on Old Gentilly.

Taxis are always at hand. Long-haul cabs go downtown; short-haul cabs service the area around the airport. The $18 fare to downtown can be shared by up to three people going to the same location.

Cadillac limousines should be booked prior to arrival through Orleans Transportation (464-0611). Rates vary.

Public transportation includes buses from 6:30 A.M. to shortly after midnight for 90 cents exact change. It's a bargain, but luggage—except carry-on—is not allowed. The Airline bus stops only at Elk Place, one block from the French Quarter. For schedule information, call the Regional Transit Authority (569-2700).

Car Rentals

Avis	523-4317 downtown; 464-9511 airport
Budget	525-9417 downtown; 464-0311 airport
Dollar	468-3643 airport only
Hertz	568-1645 downtown; 468-3695 airport
National	525-0416 downtown; 466-4335 airport

One local rental company with good rates and service is Value Rent-a-Car. The company is located adjacent to the airport at 1700 Airline Highway. Call 468-2777.

Many hotels and motels near the airport offer complimentary airport transportation. Check the phone bank adjacent to the ground-floor baggage claim area.

GETTING AROUND

Parking is neither the hassle nor the outrageous expense here that it can be in other big cities, but a car is still more of an inconvenience if your business is all in-town. Parking meter enforcement is voracious, and driving can be a daring feat on New Orleans's narrow streets, which the locals navigate like Le Mans.

Hotel	Concierge	Executive Floor	No-Smoking Rooms	Fitness Facilities	Pool	24-Hour Room Service	Restaurant for Client Entertaining	Extra-Special Amenities	Electronic Key System	Business/Secretarial Services	Checkout Time	Frequent Guest Program	Business Traveler Program	Average Single Rate
Cornstalk Hotel		•			•						12 noon			$ 55–$75 $ 55 corp.
Crowne Plaza Holiday Inn		•	•	•	•	•	Krewe Cafe	•		•	2 p.m.		Preferred Customer Program	$ 85–$88 $ 64 corp.
Fairmont Hotel	•			•	•	•	Sazerac Blue Room	•		•	3 p.m.	Fairmont Circle	Fairmont Circle	$115–$160 $110 corp.
Hilton Hotel Riverside & Towers	•	•	•	•	•	•	The Winston	•	•	•	1 p.m.			$ 99–$134 reg. $ 89 corp.
Downtown Howard Johnson	•	•			•	•	John James Room	•		•	1 p.m.		Executive Program	$ 55–$65 $ 49 corp.
Hotel Inter-Continental	•			•		•	Le Continents	•'		•	1 p.m.	6 Continents Club	Executive Club	$110–$140 $ 95 corp.
Hotel Pontchartrain							Caribbean Room				3 p.m.		Corporate Account Club	$ 95–$125 $ 95 corp.
Royal Orleans			•		•		The Rib Room	•			3 p.m.			$125–$155 $115 corp.
Royal Sonesta	•	•			•		Begue's	•			1 p.m.		The Corporate Account	$ 90–$95 $ 85 corp.
Westin Canal Place	•		•		•	•	Le Jardin Cafe Portofino	•			1 p.m.			$120–$140 $ 90–$100 corp.
Windsor Court Hotel	•			•	•	•	The Grill Room	•			1 p.m.			$125–$175

The efficient bus system works well for the budget-minded, especially if your stops are all on or near Canal Street in the Central Business District. Minibuses connect the tinier streets of the French Quarter. The exact-change fare is 60 cents for most routes, 75 cents for the morning and evening rush hour express. Transfers cost 5 cents more.

Taxis cruise most of the major downtown streets (Canal, Poydras, North Rampart). They can be more difficult to find after dark and in less trafficked areas. Each major hotel has a taxi stand nearby as do the better restaurants. But we find cabs reliable and consistent in showing up when called by phone: Yellow-Checker, 525-3311; 943-2411; and United, 522-9771; 524-9606; they're good for package transport, too. Fares are $1.10 for the first fifth of a mile and 20 cents for each fifth of a mile thereafter. A 25-cent charge is added for each additional person.

Renting a car may be called for if you have business in New Orleans East or Metairie, the two farthest suburbs, or if you contemplate excursions to the surrounding country. In town, parking garages are reasonable—from $2 an hour to $6 for a four-hour stay. All major hotels have garages on-site or nearby.

Walking can be recommended for convenience's sake in the Central Business District and the Frenchı Quarter. Just stay on the beaten path and beware the heat. The two major taxi companies have air-conditioned cabs.

GETTING FAMILIAR

Greater New Orleans Tourist and Convention Commission
334 Royal Street   566-5011
New Orleans, LA 70130   Visitor information, 566-5031

The *Times-Picayune/States-Item,* New Orleans's daily newspaper, carries listings of events each day in its "Living" section and a comprehensive entertainment guide each Friday called "Lagniappe."

Quick Calls

AREA CODE 504	Time and
Police Emergency 911	Weather 529-2020

AT YOUR SERVICE

It's a buyer's market in hotels here, as there has been a construction boom since before the 1984 Louisiana World Exposition. New Orleans has more than 25,000 first-class hotel rooms. Some properties, while well-appointed and comfortable, are in more isolated locations less attractive to women travelers. We've listed the best-located ones.

Cornstalk Hotel

915 Royal Street   Local number: 523-1515
New Orleans, LA 70116

You'll recognize the cornstalk-motif wrought iron fence around this small and charming property in the heart of the French Quarter. Only 14 rooms in this former private home, which has been operated by the same family for the past 40 years. Advance reservations, often up to three months ahead, are necessary because of the limited accommodations. No room service here, except Continental breakfast either in bed or on your balcony.

Downtown Howard Johnson

330 Loyola Avenue   Toll-free reservations: 800/535-7830,
New Orleans, LA 70112   -7831
                                    Local number: 581-1600
                                    Telex: 6821233

Adjacent to City Hall and the state and federal court buildings, this 300-room hotel has a self-park garage and an 18th-floor executive level with concierge service. Rooms have deadbolts, latches, fire sprinklers, bed lights, and desk areas, but no full-length mirrors. The hotel is a member of the health club in the nearby Superdome. A pool, Jacuzzi, and coffee shop are on the property.

Crowne Plaza Holiday Inn

333 Poydras Street   Toll-free reservations: 800/HOLIDAY
New Orleans, LA 70130   Local Number: 525-9444

This new (1984), 450-room, upscale Holiday Inn is well located near both convention centers and a half-dozen blocks from Canal Street and the French Quarter. The concierge floor is reached by an access-key elevator. All rooms have chains, deadbolt locks, smoke detectors, and sprinklers plus bedside lights and full-length mirrors. Not all rooms have desk areas. A health facility is adjacent to the swimming pool. Valet parking costs $6 a day.

There is a full-service restaurant, the **Krewe Cafe,** and an oyster bar, **C.P.'s.** A second-floor open lounge offers nightly entertainment. The bar closes at 1 A.M. Extensive room service from 6 A.M. to midnight.

Fairmont Hotel

123 Baronne Street   Toll-free reservations: 800/527-4727
New Orleans, LA 70140   Local number: 529-7111
                                    Telex: 8109516015

One of the mellow queens of New Orleans hotels (formerly the Roosevelt), this grand old property just a block from the French Quarter is not as fresh as she once was. It is, however, loaded with European style and class. Concierges and stenographers are always available as is 24-hour room service. Amenities include shoe buffers and scales in each room along with bedside lights, desks, and full-length mirrors. A beauty shop is in the lobby.

The **Sazerac,** an elegant gourmet restaurant serving lunch weekdays is one of the city's most popular power lunch spots. Reserve your table ahead, and make arrangements with Tommy Andrade, the well-known maitre d', for your bill; otherwise, it might be offered to the wrong person. **Bailey's,** a 24-hour casual eatery, offers New Orleans–style dishes and sandwiches. The **Blue Room,** a world-famous supper club, offers two top-name shows a night (dinner show at 9 P.M. followed by the 11 P.M. show—prices vary by entertainer) and a buffet lunch from 11:30 A.M. to 2 P.M.

Hilton Hotel Riverside and Towers

2 Canal Street   Toll-free reservations: 800/445-8667
New Orleans, LA 70140   Local number: 561-0500
                                               Telex: 6821214

Large (1,602 rooms) and very well maintained, this colossus on the Mississippi (which 456 of its rooms face) is within an easy walk of both convention centers and swank shopping in Canal Place. Rooms, secured by chain locks and credit-card keys, are well appointed with desks and full-length mirrors as well as smoke detectors and sprinklers.

Among the hotel's ten eating places are **Kabby's,** a seafood restaurant overlooking the river; **Cafe Bromeliad** with a Cajun buffet on Fridays, Italian fiesta on Saturdays, and jazz brunch on Sundays; and **Winston's,** a well-regarded, highly rated gourmet restaurant. The **French Garden Bar** and the **English Garden Bar**—airy, open, and unmenacing for the single woman traveler—are the most inviting of many in the hotel.

Hotel Inter-Continental

444 St. Charles Avenue   Toll-free reservations: 800/327-0200
New Orleans, LA 70130   Local number: 525-5566
                                                Telex: 58202

Completed in 1983, this luxurious property is perfectly placed in the heart of the Central Business District. Not only are its interior furnishings of Angelo Donghia design, but its business services run the gamut from telex and secretarial service to office space for your use. Emphasis on quality artworks makes this an unusually sophisticated environment. The fifth-floor open courtyard features collaborative efforts commissioned of five major New Orleans artists—a charming sculptural oasis in the city. Rooms have bedside lights, desk areas, sprinklers, and smoke detectors plus telephone and even minitelevision in each bathroom. Health facilities open from 6 A.M. to 10 P.M. are available at One Shell Square just across the street. A pool is on the 15th floor; a beauty shop and drugstore are on the premises.

The **Veranda** is an upscale coffee shop. **Les Continents,** the gourmet restaurant, boasts a chef voted the most outstanding in all 108 Inter-Continental hotels. Dinner only, 6 to 10 P.M. nightly. Afternoon tea, cocktails, and after-dinner drinks in the striking and open **Lobby Lounge.**

Hotel Pontchartrain

2031 St. Charles Avenue   Toll-free reservations: 800/952-8092
New Orleans, LA 70140   Local number: 524-0581
                            Telex: 266068

A legendary small hotel (75 rooms), one of the Preferred Hotels World-wide, and one of America's few remaining family-owned hotels. It is near the Garden District well out of the Central Business District for those seeking a quieter area. Though the hotel is on the St. Charles Avenue streetcar line, take taxis after dark. Furnished in fine, elegant antiques, this hotel built in 1927 maintains the tradition (and safeguard) of round-the-clock elevator operators. Despite its age, the hotel is constantly updated. A beauty shop is across the avenue and a drugstore next door.

New Orleans's premiere power breakfasts are held in the impressive **Cafe Pontchartrain,** a great place to win a client or mingle among politicians and business and civic leaders meeting over blueberry muffins and scrambled eggs. Likewise, the world-renowned **Caribbean Room** makes for perfect business dinners. A word to the maitre d' will assure you any service required. New Orleans seafood tops the menu, but save room for the Mile High Ice Cream Pie, an infamous local sin of ice creams and pastry crust under rich, dark fudge sauce. One person cannot eat a whole piece.

Royal Orleans

621 St. Louis Street   Toll-free reservations: 800/228-2121
New Orleans, LA 70140   Local number: 529-5333
                            Telex: 58350

Magnificently set in the middle of the French Quarter and showered with architectural awards for being a superb 1960 re-creation of a long-gone landmark hotel. Scrupulously attentive management offering everything from clerical services to helicopter schedules. Rooms are comfortable and secure; a beauty shop is on the premises.

The rooftop pool is a grand place for summer lunches or pre-dinner drinks. For power lunching, book ahead for the **Rib Room,** a richly furnished, English-style open-rotisserie restaurant packed full from 11 A.M. to 3 P.M. You probably won't get in without a reservation. The **Cafe Royale,** small and elegantly furnished, offers casual dining. The **Touche Bar,** facing directly onto Royal Street, is popular with locals. If you are more timid and prefer an open seating arrangement, the **Esplanade Lounge** is perfect, whether for afternoon tea from 3 to 5 P.M. or cocktails, flaming coffees, desserts, and gentle jazz piano.

Royal Sonesta

300 Bourbon Street   Toll-free reservations: 800/343-7170
New Orleans, LA 70140   Local number: 586-0300
                            Telex: 58336

The magnificent, tranquil courtyard of lush, semitropical plants belies this busy convention hotel's place on one of the most bustling blocks of Bourbon Street. A mint julep on the patio is perhaps the best way to savor the romance of "Old N'Awlins," even though the hotel is but 15 years old. Well maintained and furnished, this property provides chains and deadbolts, bedside lights, desk areas, and full-length mirrors in rooms plus automatic smoke detectors and fire doors in all halls. Special VIP floor accessible only by special elevator.

The hotel has two restaurants and an oyster bar, which is open till midnight daily. All four bars are open till the wee hours of the morning. Best bet: the **Mystick Den** off the main lobby—large and comfortable with live entertainment nightly.

Westin Canal Place

100 Rue Iberville
New Orleans, LA 70130

Toll-free reservations: 800/228-3000
Local number: 566-7006
Telex: 6711201

Newly taken over by Westin (from Trust House Forte) in September 1985, this 450-room hotel used to be called Hotel Iberville. It is one of the most luxurious in the city, set as it is in the most upscale downtown shopping complex, Canal Place. Rooms have bedside lights, desk areas, dressing tables with mirrors, and bathrooms with magnifying mirrors; also mini-refrigerators with soft drinks and wines and bedside consoles with push-button connections to control room temperatures. All rooms and halls have smoke detectors and sprinklers. Rooftop lap pool.

In addition to 24-hour room service, the property has two res-taurants and bars—all on the panoramic 11th floor. **Le Jardin** offers an imaginative local menu and splendid river view, and a popular Sunday brunch with two seatings, 11 A.M. and 1 P.M. for around $19. Afternoon tea with scones, jam and Devon cream can be taken in the adjacent **Le Jardin Lounge,** also a charming and open location for cocktails or after-dinner drinks till 2 A.M. The **Cafe Portofino** serves more casual fare.

Windsor Court Hotel

300 Gravier Street
New Orleans, LA 70130

Toll-free reservations: 800/262-2662
Local number: 523-6000
Telex: 784060

One of the most elegant and best-run properties in this city or any other, this sumptuous, English-style hotel has as owner the young James Cole-man, Jr. He also serves as honorary British consul in New Orleans. The all-suite hotel has deadbolt locks, smoke detectors, and sprinklers plus in-house intercoms in each room. Each guest also enjoys a balcony and bay window with fresh plants, marble bathrooms, special soaps, and beach-size towels. The fourth floor has a pool, Jacuzzi, sauna, and work-out area with 24-hour video security. Valet parking available.

Of the two magnificent restaurants, our favorite is the **Grill Room,** open daily for breakfast, lunch, and dinner, featuring one of the city's finest wine collections. The **Saloon,** furnished like an English drawing room, offers Continental breakfast, light lunches, and afternoon tea daily plus jazz and champagne for after-dinner relaxation on Wednesday through Saturday night from 11 P.M. to 2 A.M. Flaming coffees and desserts, too.

Other commendable new hotels in the downtown area are:

Hyatt, 500 Poydras Street, New Orleans, LA 70140, 566-1234 or 800/228-9000, within walking distance of the Superdome, City Hall, and court buildings.

Hotel Meridien, 614 Canal Street, New Orleans, LA 70130, 525-6500, or 800/223-9918, a member of the prestigious French hotel chain.

Marriott Hotel, 555 Canal Street, New Orleans, LA 70140, 581-1000, or 800/228-9290, a skyscraper convention and tourist hotel.

Sheraton Hotel, 500 Canal Street, New Orleans, LA 70140, 525-2500 or 800/325-3535.

ON A BUDGET

Hotel

Columns Hotel
3811 St. Charles Avenue   Local number: 899-9308
New Orleans, LA 70115

This 18-room hotel in a restored mansion near the Garden District was the site of the filming of *Pretty Baby.* Furnished in Victorian antiques, it lies on the streetcar route to the universities and Audubon Park—but take taxis at night. Though only six of the rooms have private baths, this is a charming find, complete with concierge and Continental breakfast plus morning newspaper included.

The Columns Restaurant, the on-premise restaurant, serves weekday lunches from $6 to $11; dinner nightly from $7.00 to $16.00 and Sunday brunch from 11 A.M. to 2:30 P.M. for $15.

Restaurants

New Orleans is one of America's best budget finds. You will have no trouble finding good, cheap food in your off-hours. To discover genuine Creole food in clean surroundings at near-peasant prices (after all, high society came late to the Creole table), seek out **Eddie's,** 2119 Law Street; 945-2207 (lunch and dinner Monday through Saturday). You'll get down-home red beans and sausage, fried chicken, fried seafood and gumbo, the classic Creole stew. For more genteel but still low-priced fun, try **Gautreau's,** 1728 Soniat, uptown; 899-7397 (lunch weekdays). Tiled floor, tin ceiling, and the best crab bisque and crab au gratin in town. No credit cards at either place.

Entertainment

For amusements, the city itself is its own best asset. For colorful architecture, lively street artists and entertainers, and scenic delight, just stroll toward the river and follow your whims. The French Quarter is like a theme park with no admission charge.

Of course, the biggest bargain is **Mardi Gras.** The two weeks leading up to that pre-Lenten blowout offer 60 outrageous parades. For schedules of events, contact the Greater New Orleans Tourist and Convention Commission. It is unlikely, however, that you will be sent to New Orleans on business in this period. Hotels are too full and your local contacts are probably beyond business for the duration.

Check the *Times-Picayune/States Item* for each day's calendar of free events and activities, or call 566-5047 or 522-ARTS. The **New Orleans Museum of Art** in City Park charges no admission on Thursdays.

DINING OUT

New Orleans's reputation for fine cuisine is well deserved. Fat oysters, jumbo shrimp, and succulent crabs come from Lake Pontchartrain and the Gulf of Mexico. Locals like them spicy and hot or in classical French style. But everything tastes good in New Orleans—and good taste is de rigeur when dressing for dinner, too. Visitors are often noticeable in the better restaurants by their casual, resort–like clothing. They aren't refused entrance, but they do stand out. Except in the most casual eateries, New Orleanians tend to dress for dinner. Many establishments request jackets for men, and some still insist on ties. Our top picks for great eating experiences are listed here alphabetically and by location, not in order of cost or quality. We'll start with the French Quarter and move out to the Central Business District, St. Charles Avenue, and beyond.

The Acme Oyster House is a casual gathering place for the freshest seafood; a local tradition. No credit cards. 724 Iberville. 523-8928.

Antoine's is long established and well-known, but it has declined in quality the past few years. Still worth visiting if only for the atmosphere of an old-style New Orleans dining establishment. If you have only one night, skip it. There are better places. Closed Sundays. 713 St. Louis Street. 581-4422.

Arnaud's, a better example of an old-style New Orleans restaurant, features an eclectic mix of Creole and French specialties served in a tile-floored dining room with ceiling fans. Good for clients. Sunday jazz brunch. 813 Bienville Street. 523-5433.

At **Brennan's,** breakfast is a great way to start a business relationship—if you don't have to do any business. Bloody Marys and Milk Punches followed by Eggs Sardou, Hussarde, or any of many other ways, could finish you both off for the day. Open seven days a week for breakfast, and for dinner, with lush courtyard for perfect predinner drinks. A nice French Quarter place to bring clients. 417 Royal Street. 525-9711.

Cafe Sbisa, popular with the chic and arty set, is a wonderfully renovated French Quarter space specializing in unusual and delicately prepared seafoods from Louisiana and other parts of the country: fresh salmon, swordfish, flounder, scallops, deep-fried vegetables (including dill pickles). Chocoholics will worship the "sin" cake. Ideal for sophisticated clients. Reservations a must. 1011 Decatur Street. 561-8354.

Felix's is the spot for seafood in the simplest and most casual setting. A tradition with locals, a favorite with visitors. 739 Iberville. 524-4440.

No matter who you are, you'll have to stand in line to get into **Galatoire's,** an excellent New Orleans tradition. Local lore has it that even General de Gaulle had to wait. So bring only the most easygoing client here; otherwise, keep it for times with friends. No credit cards, so bring cash and figure about $30 per person with wine. 209 Bourbon Street. 525-2021.

Mr. B's is a charming and comfortable bistro-style restaurant in the heart of the Quarter good for a social lunch with business contacts. With friends, take a chance and walk in; otherwise, call ahead for reservations. 201 Royal Street. 523-2078.

Ralph and Kacoos is a Baton Rouge–based family seafood business that has met with great success since opening recently in New Orleans. Its casual air is good for low-key lunches with clients you don't have to impress. Fried and boiled Louisiana seafood are the specialties. Reasonable for a personal lunch or dinner, too. 519 Toulouse Street. 522-5226.

Christian's, located in a wonderfully converted old church, is one of New Orleans's best restaurants outside the Quarter. Take a taxi there and back. Mixed menu with a French touch. The smoked softshell crab (in season) is a tantalizing appetizer. No reservations taken at lunch, so not a good idea for business. Reservations are a must for dinner, however. Closed Sunday and Monday. 3835 Iberville. 482-4924.

If you're looking for a power-lunch place, **Ruth's Chris Steak House** is it. You'll see judges, politicians, and businesspeople cutting as many deals as steaks at lunch, and it's a popular place at night, too. Savvy businesswoman Ruth Fertel runs the place (now with a new counterpart on Beverly Hills' Rodeo Drive). The neighborhood's a bit shaky, so take a cab there and back or park your car in the attached lot. 711 N. Broad Street. 482-9278.

Savoire Faire French Bistro is a small and charming bistro on the first floor of the St. Charles Hotel. Small menu, too, but varied and fine. Young chef Susan Spicer is excellent and is often seen greeting guests— white chef's hat and all. Good for client lunches and dinners. Breakfast, 2203 St. Charles Avenue. 522-3966.

Bon Ton Cafe is hard to beat for some of the best and most authentic Creole food in town. Very crowded at lunchtime with lawyers, business executives, and office personnel from the surrounding Central Business District. 401 Magazine Street. 524-3386.

Commander's Palace is an outstanding restaurant with excellent New Orleans cuisine served in the grand manner under the watchful eye of Ella Brennan. A special place for business or social events. In the daytime ask for seating in the garden room, a glass-enclosed upstairs aerie that seems to float among the branches of a huge ancient oak tree outside. Jazz brunch on Saturdays at 11 A.M. and 1 P.M., Sundays at 10:30 A.M., 11 A.M., and 1 P.M. Reservations always a must. 1403 Washington Avenue. 899-8221.

Esther Carpenter opened a small and very chic establishment— called simply **Esther's**—on the fringe of the Central Business District in an area enjoying a burst of renovation. Close to the Contemporary Arts Center and next to two of the city's finest art galleries, Esther's offers nouvelle cuisine in the American style. Don't be shocked if you see some winos on the street; some of them still think this is their part of town. Lunch weekdays; dinner except Sundays. Reservations recommended. 545 Julia Street. 525-7902.

CITY BY DAY

An exquisite way to see the lay of this river delta land is to visit the 11th-floor lobby of the **Westin Canal Place,** (formerly the Hotel Iberville) in the posh Canal Place shopping mall. Enjoy an English tea, and watch Ol' Man River keep on rollin' along.

Other panoramic possibilities are (1) the **Aerial Gondola** built to link New Orleans's west bank to an east bank terminal next to the New Orleans Convention and Exhibition Center at 1984's world's fair site (the fair proved a garish bust, but it did leave some items of touristic interest, and the view from this 3½-minute cable ride, now a commuter service at $3.50 round trip, is one); and (2) the 33-story **International Trade Mart World Trade Center** (ITM Building) at the foot of Canal Street, a high-rise hive of foreign consulates and import/export firms, which is topped by a revolving bar and an observation deck with the best view of all.

We always think of the French Quarter as New Orleans's nighttime diversion, but the daytime imbues the area with an equally compelling allure. The center of the French Quarter is **Jackson Square**—named for Andrew who, in 1815, saved the city from British invasion, albeit two weeks after the War of 1812 peace treaty had already been signed. Portrait painters and artists hang their works on the iron fences surrounding General Jackson's equestrian statue. We like to get a snack at a nearby cafe or patisserie and sit on the benches to watch the street performers and the people parade.

This quaint piazza is flanked by the handsome **St. Louis Cathedral** (1794), picturesque **Pontalba Buildings** with their lacy wrought-iron galleries, the first apartment buildings in the United States (1851), and the mighty but lazy-looking **Mississippi River.** The river winds around this below-sea-level city in a crescent—the reason for New Orleans's former nickname, the Crescent City—and Lake Pontchartrain cuts off the northern side from any other land. Land is precious here, and even the posh Garden District mansions upriver from the French Quarter have small gardens relative to such upscale neighborhoods in other cities.

A 60-cent ride on the swaying, wooden St. Charles Avenue streetcar, inspiration for a famous one named Desire, will give you a leisurely look at the **Garden District.** It connects the Central Business District and French Quarter areas with Tulane University and Loyola University of the South. But you might save that jaunt for a Sunday, because the **Audubon Park and Zoological Gardens** near the colleges is worth a few leisurely hours.

Other major sights attractive to city visitors include the following:

The **Louisiana Superdome** is the world's largest covered stadium, with a diameter of 680 feet. The 27-story curved-roof stadium can house more than 90,000 people. Guided tours are conducted daily on the hour from 10 A.M. to 4 P.M. for $4. Avoid this area at night unless accompanied to an event. Poydras Street, across from the Hyatt Hotel, and diagonally opposite City Hall.

The **Louisiana State Museum** is actually a complex of quaint buildings displaying regional history and culture: the old U.S. Mint, 400 Esplanade; Presbytere and Cabildo (the old Spanish city halls), Jackson Square; 1850 House, Lower Pontalba Building (wonderfully restored). All are open Tuesday through Sunday, 10 A.M. to 6 P.M. Jackson Square (French Quarter). 568-6968.

The **Hermann-Grima House,** 818 St. Louis Street, and the **Gallier House,** 1132 Royal Street, are two excellently restored 19th-century mansions now used as house museums of that era's grand French Quarter living. They are well worth visiting. Small admission charges. 523-6722.

Historic New Orleans Collection is an important archive of 18th-, 19th-, and 20th-century materials on New Orleans and Louisiana displayed in an excellent example of a grand townhouse. Charming gift shop as well. 533 Royal Street. 523-4662.

The **New Orleans Museum of Art** is a taxi ride away from the center but worth it for fans of the visual arts—Fabergé eggs, the Billups glass collection, Cuzco Indian art from Peru plus rotating exhibits. Open Tuesday through Sunday, 10 A.M. to 5 P.M. Small admission charge. City Park. 488-2631.

Art galleries abound in New Orleans, and serious collectors will want to explore:

Aaron-Hastings, contemporary New Orleans artists. 3814 Magazine Street. 891-4665.

Arthur Rogers Gallery, contemporary art from New Orleans and elsewhere in America. 3005 Magazine Street. 895-5287.

Carmen Llewellyn, Latin American paintings, prints, and sculptures. Call ahead. 3901 Magazine Street. 891-5301.

Davis Gallery, one of America's finest galleries for African art. Unusual and precious objects. 3964 Magazine Street. 897-0780.

Galerie Simone Stern, now in an up-and-coming section of town, having moved from the French Quarter. Contemporary works; highly regarded. 518 Julia Street. 529-1118.

Nahan Galleries, one of the few really good galleries left in the French Quarter. Major artists from America and Europe. 540 Royal Street. 524-8696.

THE SHOPPING SCENE

Canal Street, separating the Central Business District from the French Quarter, is one of America's grand shopping boulevards. It has held its place as home to the city's major department and specialty stores despite massive modernization in the adjacent Central Business District. Easily accessible on foot from most major hotels, the main shopping area runs from Canal and Burgundy streets south to the foot of Canal Street at the Mississippi River. (There never was a canal, by the way—just an unimplemented plan for one.)

Canal Place is the newest indoor vertical shopping mall in the downtown area and swank home to Saks Fifth Avenue, Kreeger's, Laura Ashley, Gucci, Brooks Brothers, and New Orleans's own exceptional jewelry designer, Mignon Faget. If you did not find it already, the 11th-floor lobby of the elegant Westin Canal Place in this complex is a perfect stop for afternoon tea and a spectacular river view.

Other fine department stores downtown include Maison Blanche and D. H. Holmes, each open late on Thursdays till 7 P.M. For specialty and women's goods, head for Godchaux's and Gus Meyer, two treasured local emporia.

The **French Quarter,** too, has a myriad of shops, funky and fine, selling clothing, shoes, souvenirs, and artworks. One of the most attractive and reasonable is the Dansk Outlet, 541 Royal Street. Cut rates and excellent quality in Scandinavian woodenware, china, and flatware. No credit cards accepted but checks with I.D. are.

NEW ORLEANS BY NIGHT

New Orleans is a food city—one of America's finest—and with its French heritage has come an appreciation of eating that borders on obsession. Lose weight *before* you come, so you won't feel guilty indulging the irresistible. A large part of any night out consists of fine dining. After that, a walk in the French Quarter and a late-night drink at the Napoleon House (500 Chartres Street), a wonderfully crumbling Parisian-style bar with classical music, is probably all you'll be able to handle—and still do any business the next day.

If you dine early enough, you can catch any of many jazz club shows. Bourbon Street is still wild and raunchy with bars and jazz establishments. It is safe to walk singly or with others. Be warned, though, that many of the "clubs" are just overpriced bars. The turnover being so high, it is hard to recommend good from bad. Just use common sense. You're not in any danger here. The only thing that may get wounded is your pocketbook.

For those evenings when you'd prefer a different beat from Dixieland, here are some options. Tickets are available through **Ticketmaster,** 888-8181.

The **Saenger Theatre** offers visiting Broadway and pre-Broadway shows in fall and winter. 143 N. Rampart Street. 524-2490.

The **New Orleans Symphony** plays Wednesdays and Thursdays. Call for schedules and visiting artists. In the Orpheum Theater, University Place across from the Fairmont Hotel. 524-0404.

The **New Orleans Opera** is the oldest established opera company in America. Presents four productions each season featuring national and international singers. Call for schedule information. 529-2278.

LATE-NIGHT NEW ORLEANS

Many New Orleans clubs and coffee houses are not only safe but welcoming to the single female traveler—and not for any ulterior motives. Others will be enjoyed more in the company of another person, male or female. Those nightspots listed here are safe and inviting.

Preservation Hall is a no-frills, bare-walls jazz hall—the don't-miss, quintessential New Orleans Dixieland parlor. Wear casual clothes and bring an open heart *and* your own drinks from elsewhere; there's no bar here, but you're welcome to BYO. Simple bench seating and pillows on the floor—first come, first served. Open nightly 8:30 to 12:30 for half-hour sets with ten-minute breaks between. $1 admission is good for all evening. Check for daytime schedules. 726 St. Peter Street. 522-2238 daytime, 523-8939 at night.

Pete Fountain hangs his hat and plays his licorice stick at the **New Orleans Hilton,** a slicker version of New Orleans–style jazz on the hotel's third floor—a favorite with tourists and locals alike. One show only (10 P.M.) Tuesdays through Saturdays; $15 per person cover charge includes one drink. Poydras Street at the Mississippi River. 561-0500.

At **Dukes of Dixieland,** shows are at 9 P.M., 10:20 P.M., and 11:40 P.M. Closed Sundays. $13.75 per person includes two drinks. 214 Royal Street. 581-1567.

New Storyville Jazz Hall schedules vary with weekday, week-night, and weekend, so call ahead. Traditional jazz in the early evening hours, rhythm and blues later at night. Casual dress. 1104 Decatur Street. 525-8199.

Tyler's is the place for contemporary jazz. Open every night from 5 P.M. till 1:30 A.M. Take a taxi to the door and call one when you're ready to leave. 5234 Magazine Street. 891-4989.

For music and dancing, there are the **Blue Room** at the Fairmont Hotel (best for couples or groups) and the **Rainforest,** the Hilton's rooftop lounge. The latter features special-effects thunder, lightning, and rain, a spectacular way to watch the city through the windows. Happy hour, 5 to 7 P.M. Popular with visitors and locals.

L'Enfants is a chic, contemporary-styled restaurant whose adjacent bar acts as a disco from 9 P.M. to 1:30 A.M. Popular with the moneyed, middle-executive, Mercedes set. The crowd is dressed to kill. Expensive, glitzy, crowded. This is a $10 taxi ride from downtown north toward Lake Pontchartrain. 5236 Canal Boulevard. 486-1512.

Club 4141 is a popular disco in the uptown section. Smart, attractive people in a nice setting. Happy hour from 3 to 8 P.M. (well, this *is* New Orleans) with complimentary hors d'oeuvres. The real action starts around 10 P.M. and goes on till 3 A.M. weeknights, 5 A.M. weekends. 1613 Milan Street. 891-9873.

No matter where you find your kind of night life, the place to close out a New Orleans night is **Cafe Du Monde,** Decatur Street at Jackson Square in the French Quarter. This 24-hour, seven-day open-air cafe (covered in case of bad weather) is a Crescent City tradition for steaming cups of New Orleans–style coffee with chicory, either black or au lait, and sugar-dusted square doughnuts called *beignets.* Expect to have powdered sugar all over you when you finish, but don't be upset. Just brush it off, as New Orleanians do, whether they're in blue jeans or ball gowns.

AT LEISURE

Day-Tripping

New Orleans can easily seduce you into staying amid its urbane charm, but you will be missing one of our most charming states if you don't break the city's exotic hold. You needn't go far to get away, but in that short distance, you will travel to worlds you've only dreamed of.

PLANTATIONS

River Road is the ribbon to follow, a winding way along the path of the Mississippi River lined with elegant antebellum homes veiled by moss-hung oaks on rolling lawns. Eight miles west of the airport is **Destrehan Plantation,** the oldest such home (1781) still intact in the lower

Mississippi Valley. Open daily, the cypress-timber house is sparse of furniture but stately. Twenty minutes farther on is the lavishly restored **San Francisco Plantation,** where you will notice that most of the living space, except a dining room and service rooms, were always on the second floor.

You can keep following the River Road, have a tasty and memorable lunch at the **Cabin Restaurant**—a 145-year-old former slave dwelling in Burnside—and then cross the river by free ferry at Carville for a look at the west bank's prize, **Nottoway.** This is the South's largest plantation—64 rooms—and a splendidly restored dream estate. That will be a full day's trip.

If you are not driving your own car, book a tour with **Gray Line Tours** of New Orleans (525-0138) or check the Yellow Pages for similar reputable services.

THE COAST BEACHES

The Gulf of Mexico, dumping basin for the Mississippi, has been the salt of the Louisiana earth for centuries. But while Louisiana got marshes rich with wildlife, next-door Mississippi got the pristine white-sand beaches of **Biloxi** and **Pass Christian.** Orleanians head for those resort towns when they want to escape their own heat and humidity, but an easier escape en route there is the tiny town of **Ocean Springs**—a 90-mile drive east of the city on I-10.

Formerly a health resort, Ocean Springs (population 15,000) is now an arts and crafts community with uncrowded beaches and loads of charm. Stop in at the Chamber of Commerce in the old railroad depot at Washington Avenue and Robinson Street for free maps and information.

If you're of a mind to go the extra few miles over the bay bridge to Biloxi, the last home of Confederacy President Jefferson Davis is open daily. More lovely southern homes line the 22-mile **Scenic Route** to Bay St. Louis (Highway 90).

CAJUN COUNTRY

If you head west on I-10 instead of east (to the Gulf Coast), it will take you about three hours to come to the heart of **Cajun country.** Here is where hardy bands of French settlers in Nova Scotia (formerly called Acadia) fled when the British conquered their Canadian province in 1755. The name Cajun derived from Acadian.

St. Martinville is your goal for reaching the must-see sight of Cajun country, the **Longfellow-Evangeline State Commemorative Area.** Henry Wadsworth Longfellow's romantic heroine Evangeline (a real local lady) waited for her lover by a still-standing oak on the riverbank here. Her grave is in the little cemetery at St. Martin de Tours Church. And the **Acadian House Museum** shows how she and the Acadians lived in the early days.

New Iberia, another Acadian town about 15 miles farther, is

Louisiana's sugar cane center and home to **Shadows-on-the-Teche,** an 1830's plantation now maintained by the National Trust for Historic Preservation.

In Town

The French Quarter is likely to draw you into its alluring byways with such romantic spots as pirate Jean Lafitte's **Blacksmith Shop** (now a bar) at 941 Bourbon Street and the **St. Louis Cemeteries No. 1 and No. 2.** Don't laugh. These above ground burial lots, derived from Mediterranean tradition, double as promenades, concert sites, and parks, even if they are popularly known as "cities of the dead."

Caution: explore these historic cemeteries only with guided tours or large groups, as the adjoining neighborhood is high-crime turf. The **National Park Service** (589-2636) hosts tours daily at 1 P.M. starting at its Information Center in Jackson Square.

Walking tours of New Orleans's many historic and beautiful neighborhoods are available through a number of quality companies and nonprofit preservation groups. Inquire at the New Orleans Tourist and Convention Center for details.

But if you get tired of walking these quaint streets, relax on a river or bayou cruise. **Delta Queen Steamboat Company** makes multiday sailings upriver on authentic-styled riverboats of white lacy elegance (586-0631). The **New Orleans Steamboat Company** makes shorter excursions on beautiful old boats, including a one-hour cruise from Canal Street to the Audubon Park Zoo (586-8777). And **Cajun Bayou Cruise** uses delightful small open bateaus (French bayou boats) to float into the wilds of the Cajun Bayous (529-1669 or 891-8132).

Another exciting alternative is an air tour of the fascinating terrain on which New Orleans sits. Call **Aviation Associates** (241-9321) for fixed-wing airplane flights or **Louisiana Helicopters** (362-4500) for a whirlybird tour.

The 1984 **Louisiana World Exposition** took merciless panning for its gaudy presentation and a drubbing at the gate as well. Much of it was torn down, but for New Orleanians still paying the tab in taxes, it is not out of mind, albeit out of sight. For visitors, the riverfront world's fairground offers numerous attractions in an area now sure to develop into another lively urban center. The main on-site information center is at the Canal Gate (Girod and South Front streets).

Spectator Sports

The **New Orleans Saints,** apparently plagued with ineptitude in recent years, are nicknamed the 'Aints. Still searching for a winning season, they play their home games in the **Superdome.** This is also the venue for the Sugar Bowl played by college football teams.

The Superdome's ticket office is on Boydras Street—now called Sugar Bowl Drive—downtown. Call 587-3800.

Active Sports

Tennis anyone? Courts dot the city, many of them public. Try **Stern Tennis Center,** at 4025 S. Saratoga (891-0627); **Wisner Tennis Center** in City Park on Dreyfus (482-2230) or at the off-the-beaten-path **Joe Brown Park,** on Read Boulevard (246-5600).

Two parks in the city offer a host of activities for the athletic business woman. At **Audubon Park** (861-2537), rent canoes or boat, or choose a bike to trace the beautiful paths that meander through the park. At **City Park** (482-4888) you can also paddle a canoe through the 1,500 acres of lagoons that run through it. If you prefer dry land, ride a horse rented from the park's public stable (282-6200).

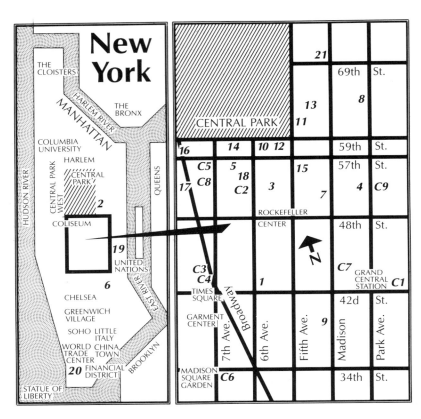

HOTELS

1 Algonquin
2 American Stanhope
3 Berkshire Place
4 Drake
5 Gorham
6 Gramercy Park
7 Helmsley Palace
8 Mayfair Regent
9 Morgans
10 Park Lane
11 Pierre

12 Plaza
13 Plaza Athenee
14 Ritz-Carlton
15 St. Regis-Sheraton
16 Salisbury
17 Sheraton City Squire
18 Shorham
19 United Nations Plaza
20 Vista International
21 Westbury

CONVENTION HOTELS

C1 Grand Hyatt
C2 New York Hilton at
Rockefeller Plaza
C3 New York Marriott Marquis
C4 Milford Plaza
C5 Omni Park Central
C6 New York Penta
C7 Roosevelt on Madison
Avenue
C8 Sheraton Centre
C9 Waldorf-Astoria

NEW YORK

GETTING YOUR BEARINGS

That ubiquitous slogan "I Love New York" just happens to sum up the way we both feel about this place—the city that some people love to hate. To set the record straight, we are both New Yorkers who are passionately in love with the city and all it has to offer. Having cleared up any notions that you'll be reading unbiased opinions of New York in this chapter, we want to share with you some of the city's unique qualities— things that make it so special.

Let's begin by exploding that old cliché about New Yorkers— when the label is used as a perjorative. You've probably heard for years that "New Yorkers are rude" or "New Yorkers talk funny" or "New Yorkers are pushy." The plain truth is that most "New Yorkers" aren't originally from New York at all—they are people who have moved here from other parts of the country. In fact, finding a born-in-the-city native is almost as hard as finding a seat on the subway during rush hour. What we're saying is simply this: if you want to get the most out of your time in New York, don't come with preconceived ideas of how you think people in this city are going to behave. For one thing, that "New Yorker" you stop to ask directions from will most likely be a visitor like yourself. New Yorkers aren't perfect people—far from it. But each is an individual and there's no telling how he or she will behave. You might be pleasantly surprised.

New York is so vast, so sprawling, that we have concentrated only on the borough of Manhattan in this chapter. There are five boroughs, or counties, that make up the greater New York metro area, but chances are your business will be in midtown Manhattan, because that's where the majority of offices are, as well as the theaters, museums, major stores and shops, and fine restaurants. So, just because we've omitted references to places in other boroughs—like the superb Brooklyn Academy of Music or Coney Island or other outlying sights to see—please don't discount their worth.

People who live in New York City must strive ceaselessly for efficiency of movement. Because one can't just hop in the car to run errands (there's too much traffic and nowhere to park once you get there), one learns to plan ahead, stockpiling things to do within a single geographic area. For example: a business meeting in the Rockefeller Center area could dictate a quick blitz through Saks for those shoes you need, a between-meetings peek at the new exhibit at the Museum of Modern Art, a dash across the street to the Donnell branch of the public library, and then perhaps lunch at one of the outdoor cafes in Rockefeller Center—all because they're in the same neighborhood. In this spirit of logistical efficiency, we've grouped most entries in this chapter into neighborhoods to help you save valuable traveling-around-town time and make the most of your visit here.

Having stressed some of its inherent hardships, it's time to introduce a particular favorite in the strictly New York cityscape—the atriums, the open-to-the-public spaces in many of the new midtown office buildings created to provide an oasis of greenery within the concrete canyons. These are quiet spots for sitting and reading a book between meetings, for eating a brown-bag lunch or a snack you buy there, or for just unwinding as you enjoy the music and entertainment. They're in buildings all over town, they're free, and they're open to everyone. Enjoy! Among the best: Citicorp Center, a minimall with a lively schedule of entertainment (53d Street and Lexington Avenue); the IBM Building, with soaring stands of live bamboo, free concerts, and a modest snack bar (Madison Avenue, entrances on 56th or 57th streets); Park Avenue Plaza, an ideal spot for a light lunch at Pasta & Cheese's Cafe Marguery where a cascade dominates one wall (55 E. 52d Street, access on 53d Street); Trump Tower, for sheer glitz with lots of pink marble and a pianist in formal dress playing dance tunes (725 Fifth Avenue, entrance through Bonwit's, through the IBM atrium, or between 56th and 57th streets).

Sometimes we love New York in spite of itself. Let's face it— not all aspects of this city can be charming. Among the more annoyingly prevalent of these are the "going-out-of-business" stores, those eyesores that blight the Fifth Avenue landscape. They're *not* going out of business, they never have and probably never will, and their wares are certainly no bargain. You should also be on your guard against the three-card monte players, those entrepreneurial young men who set up "impromptu" card games on the sidewalks and challenge passersby to bet $20 on what looks like a can't-lose game. Be warned—you can, and will, lose.

And while we're on the subject of New York City streets, a few words about "street smarts." Your best deterrent against becoming a crime statistic in this city is your own awareness. New York streets are not streets for daydreaming as you stroll along, or for tuning-out as you lose yourself in the sounds of your Walkman. You should be aware at all times of crowd movement around you as you walk, as you sit on a bus, as you hail a cab. Your instincts will tell you if something isn't quite right—but you have to be alert to pick up the signals. All the other precautions—like wearing your shoulder bag across your chest or not carrying all your valuables in one place—are excellent measures, but nothing beats simply being aware of what's going on around you.

WHAT TO WEAR

You can break out your favorite outfits for the visit to New York—literally anything goes in this town. For businesswear you should be guided by your industry's own image: women here in the more conservative fields like law, banking and finance, and insurance still adhere to ultraconservative looks. Trendier industries like communications, design and graphics, advertising, and certainly the fashion-related companies will applaud your most savvy fashion statements. Top executive women tend to avoid pants and pant suits except on the snowiest of winter days. Be sure to pack dressy boots for your winter trips.

It's a sad commentary, perhaps, but few people "dress" for the theater anymore, except, of course, for opening-night performances. So you can feel comfortable wearing whatever you wore during the day. Should you *want* to dress up, however, that's fine, too. In general, audiences dress more for performances at Lincoln Center, particularly for the opera, than for those on Broadway.

When dining out, be guided by the reputation of the restaurant. At any of the superfancy spots, you'll be in the company of New York's best-dressed women, those whose designer ensembles will be noted the next day in the pages of *WWD* and the *Times*. If, however, you're heading out for one of the "new" places, you can make whatever fashion statement pleases you most.

Even in the steamiest of Manhattan summer days, you should retain your professional look; bare legs, sandals, and low-cut cottons will never make it in the Big Apple business world.

A final fashion note: New York must take full responsibility for the current rage of pairing athletic shoes with business clothes. This practice was born of necessity during a particularly long transit strike, when one had no choice but to walk to work. We learned then to bag our ill-suited heels and lace on our sensible sneakers for the long treks between home and office. The strike is over, but the fad lingers.

WEATHER WATCH

New York is a four-season city, with wretchedly hot summers and blustery cold winters. Remember, Manhattan is an island, and the winds whipping off the surrounding rivers can be brutal. Although usually there's not much snow in midtown, the occasional blizzard can be counted on to wreak havoc with all traffic—including that at the local airports.

But New York is blessed during the other two seasons—we

always have lyrical springs and glorious blue-sky autumns. And there's Central Park—a bit of nature's own country right in the heart of the city—for watching the seasons change.

GETTING THERE

New York is serviced by three airports: Kennedy, LaGuardia, and Newark.

Kennedy International is always busy, always crowded, and seemingly always operating at peak; there's no real off time to fly into Kennedy. And there's really no off time on the overworked highways that lead into Manhattan, either, although some times (like Sunday evenings when the beach crowds are heading home) can be worse than others. Plan on the better part of an hour to travel between JFK and midtown.

LaGuardia, the domestic airport, is closer than JFK to Manhattan. A 15-to-20 minute drive is average on a good day. Eastern and New York Air operate shuttle flights to Washington and Boston from here.

Newark International, in New Jersey, is becoming the airport-of-choice for many travelers. Although the private cab fares into Manhattan are steep (about $35), there are several excellent public transportation alternatives. Three terminals and a new international arrivals facility have contributed to Newark's efficiency and its position as sixth in the nation's top ten favorite airports.

Cabs line up at various points in all airports, overseen by a uniformed dispatcher who pairs passengers with similar destinations and assigns cabs. (You can, of course, go solo if you choose.) For the journey into midtown Manhattan, figure on about $25 to $30 from Kennedy, about $15 from LaGuardia, and about $35 from Newark. Express bus service, with one stop on the west side and one on the east side, will cost about $9 from Kennedy, $6 from LaGuardia, and $5 from Newark. Nonprivate limo service, such as Fugazy's Share-A-Ride will cost about $12 from Kennedy, $9 from LaGuardia, and $15 from Newark.

You can also helicopter directly to the east side of Manhattan. Check with your airline as to whether it has an arrangement with any heli service for lower rates. Pan Am, for example, flies its first class and clipper class passengers free of charge. For general information, call 800/645-3494.

"The Train to the Plane" is one way to beat the traffic out to Kennedy. Called the JFK Express, this is a dual-transit ride, subway and then express bus, that costs only $6. Call 718/858-7272 for details.

For a complete rundown of transportation possibilities between Manhattan and the airports call 800/AIR-RIDE.

Car Rentals

Do *not* rent a car for your stay in New York. We can't imagine any situation in which it would help to have a car in this city. (Many native New Yorkers don't even know how to drive—they're never had any reason to learn.) If, however, you plan to venture out into the countryside during your leisure time, there are plenty of car rental offices in town—you don't need to rent at the airport. Among them:

Avis   800/331-1212
(nine midtown locations)
Budget   807-8700
(four midtown locations)
Hertz   800/654-3131
(twelve city locations)
National   800/328-4567
(two midtown locations)
Olins   580-6647
(ten midtown locations)

GETTING AROUND

New York City cabs (and their famous drivers) are plentiful any time of day or night in all parts of midtown. Although you might have a problem flagging a cruising cab after hours in an area like Wall Street, there are usually more than enough cabs to go around. Cabs are metered: $1.10 for the first 1/9 mile and 10 cents per 1/9 mile thereafter. Tip about 15 to 20 percent of the fare. A word about those drivers: the wisecracking cabbie of yore is almost extinct, replaced by newly arrived immigrants, many of whom barely understand either English or their way around the city. Your best bet is to know the exact address of where you want to go. Safety tip: be sure to take only yellow cabs, which have a metal medallion mounted prominently in the hood. Gypsy cabs, which come in any other color, are neither licensed nor sanctioned by the city.

The subway system in New York leaves a great deal to be desired. We strongly recommend you avoid it completely. If your business is in another borough, and you think the subway trip will save valuable time— please think again. Stay above ground while you're in this city. The bus network is extensive and fairly dependable (although they do tend to "bunch"—arriving in packs after a long irritating time of none at all). Fare is $1.00, and transfers are free. Route maps are displayed in bus shelters, or you can receive your own copy, compliments of the Convention & Visitors Bureau, by dropping by the visitors' center or calling 397-8222.

The latest transportation gimmick is call-cabs, which are cheaper than private limos and more convenient than cruising cabs; if your company has an account, you may charge your fare and tip. Among the most popular: Fone-A-Cab, 718/706-0333; All City, 796-1111; Skyline, 741-1800; and UTOG, 741-2000.

Private limousine services flourish in this city of one-upmanship. Rates average about $35 an hour. If you want to be mistaken for a diplomat or a visiting screen star, summon the following: London Towncars, 988-9700; Carey Cadillac, 599-1122; Scull, 772-1610; or Tudor, 370-LIMO (our vote for the nicest drivers anywhere). Often, drivers of private limos will moonlight while their bosses are away. A chauffeur will pull up and ask if you need a lift somewhere—a good business deal for him but very risky for you.

Having said all this, we recommend you walk whenever possible—it's faster, and you get a better feel for the city. It's easy, too. Midtown Manhattan is laid out along a classic grid system: avenues run north/south, and streets run east/west. Fifth Avenue is the dividing line; therefore 5 E. 42d Street would be just east of Fifth (between Fifth and Madison avenues); 5 W. 42d Street would be just west (between Fifth and Sixth avenues).

GETTING FAMILIAR

New York Convention & Visitors Bureau
Two Columbus Circle   Visitor information: 397-8222
New York, NY 10019
Located at 59th Street where Eighth Avenue and Broadway meet, this excellent visitors center can supply you with just about anything you need to help you learn about New York—maps, guides, brochures, listings of free entertainment. We find the city map in the "I Love New York New York City Travel Guide" brochure to be particularly easy to follow and helpful. A second center is located in Times Square (207 W. 42d Street).

Coliseum
20 W. 60th Street   757-5000
New York, NY 10019
Four exhibition floors and two mezzanines add up to 320,000 square feet of space. Four simultaneous events can be accommodated.

The **Jacob K. Javits Convention Center,** scheduled to open in April 1986 is already 80 percent booked through 1990. Designed by I. M. Pei, this "crystal palace" center is expected to boost the city's prestige convention business. 35th Street and 12th Avenue. 563-4848.

The *New York Times* is the paper of record, publishing every morning. Weekly special sections include sports (Monday), science (Tuesday), food (Wednesday), home (Thursday), weekend (Friday). The *Wall Street Journal,* published weekdays by Dow Jones, incorporates interesting, often off-beat features into its business/financial format. The *New York Daily News* publishes every day including Sunday. The *New York Post,* a tabloid belonging to Rupert Murdoch, is famous for its page 6 gossip section, sports coverage, and lurid headlines. *New York Magazine* is the slick weekly magazine famous for setting many of the standards and formats now used by city magazines all around the country. It also incorporates *Cue* magazine into the back of each issue, providing complete entertainment and restaurant listings. *Crain's New York Business* is a weekly paper that adds an extra dimension to business news. Prized also for its frequent roundups of various city services and how they stack up against one another.

Quick Calls

AREA CODES	Time 976-1616
MANHATTAN AND BRONX	Weather 976-1212
212	Emergencies 911
BROOKLYN, QUEENS, STA-	Dow Jones Report 976-4141
TEN ISLAND 718	
LONG ISLAND 516	

AT YOUR SERVICE

There are over 100,000 first-class hotel rooms in New York City, an embarrassment of riches that can be more hindrance than help—how to choose? In the face of such overwhelming numbers, we've had to be brutal in our selection of the best hotels, describing in some detail only one favorite per neighborhood and giving briefer descriptions of other outstanding hotels nearby. The accompanying chart, however, lists every hotel mentioned, highlighting the special services each one offers.

A few words of caution about the peculiarities of New York hotel accommodations. Do not think you've been shortchanged when you see the size of your "luxury" hotel room. It will be small—smaller than you've probably imagined a good hotel room could be. Space is always at a premium in this city, which is evident in the size of its offices and restaurants, as well as hotel rooms. And you should see what passes for a "five-room" apartment in this city!

Another cautionary note: although every season is "peak season" for finding available hotel space in New York City, some times of year are worse than others. The peak convention months—September/October and March/April/May—are the worst. But regardless of the season, you should book as far in advance as possible, especially if you want to stay in one of the top hotels.

Convention Hotels

New York seems to have a preponderance of big, convention-type hotels (any place with over 1,000 rooms is big, we feel). If you are

	Concierge	Executive Floor	No-Smoking Rooms	Fitness Facilities	Pool	24-Hour Room Service	Restaurant for Client Entertaining	Extra-Special Amenities	Electronic Key System	Business/Secretarial Services	Checkout Time	Frequent Guest Program	Business Traveler Program	Average Single Rate
Algonquin	●						Oak Room Rose Room Chinese Room		●	●	3 p.m.	guest history		$105
American Stanhope	●					●	The Saratoga	●		●	1 p.m.		Corp.	$180
Berkshire Place	●		●			●	Rendezvous	●		●	1 p.m.	Executive Service Plan	Corp.	$200
Drake Swissotel	●					●	La Piazzetta			●	1 p.m.		Corp.	$175 regular $155 corp.
Gramercy Park							Le Parc				1 p.m.			$ 85
Helmsley Palace	●					●	Trianon Room	●	●	●	1 p.m.		Corp.	$200
Mayfair Regent	●					●	Le Cirque	●		●	1 p.m.	●		$180

Hotel						Restaurant				Check-out	Program		Rate
Morgans	●			●		Morgans	●			1 p.m.	guest history	Corp.	$150
Park Lane	●	●		●		Park Room	●		●	1 p.m.		Corp.	$195
Plaza		●		●		Edwardian Room	●			1 p.m.	Plaza Elite	Corp.	$245 regular / $185 corp.
Plaza Athénée	●			●		Le Regence	●			1 p.m.	guest history		$225
Pierre	●	●		●		Cafe Pierre	●		●	1 p.m.	guest history	Corp.	$220 corp. / $240 regular
Ritz Carlton	●			●		The Jockey Club	●			1 p.m.			$215
St. Regis Sheraton	●			●		King Cole	●	●		12 noon	(ask reservation desk)	Sheraton Executive Traveler	$195 regular / $175 S.E.T.
				● + beepers									
Sheraton City Squire	●		●	●		Movenpick	●	●		1 p.m.	Distinguished Customer Service	Corp.	$ 99 corp. / $125 regular
U.N. Plaza	●		●	●		Ambassador Grill	●		●	1 p.m.	Gold Passport (Hyatt)	Corp.	$175 regular / $160 corp.
Vista International	●	●	●	●		American Harvest	●		●	12 noon	Vista Club	Corp.	$160 regular / $210 ex. floor / $135 corp.
Westbury	●			●		The Polo	●		●	1 p.m.		Corp.	$170 corp. / $190 regular

with a convention and are booked into one of these giants, you can expect lots of services, but impersonal service, and you may feel more like a number than a guest. We've grouped them by neighborhood.

MIDTOWN EAST
   Grand Hyatt (next to Grand Central Station). 1,407 rooms. 42d Street and Park Avenue, New York, NY 10017. 800/228-9000; 883-1234.
   Roosevelt on Madison Avenue. 1,070 rooms. 45th Street and Madison Avenue, New York, NY 10017. 800/223-1870; 661-9600.
   Waldorf-Astoria. 1,850 rooms. 301 Park Avenue, New York, NY 10022. Local Hilton Reservation Service for toll-free reservations; 355-3000.

MIDTOWN WEST
   New York Hilton at Rockefeller Plaza. 1,803 rooms in hotel, 229 rooms in executive towers. 1335 Avenue of the Americas (Sixth Avenue), New York, NY 10019. Local Hilton Reservation Service for toll-free reservations; 587-7000.
   Omni Park Central. 1,450 rooms. 870 Seventh Avenue, New York, NY 10019. 800/228-2121; 247-8000.
   Sheraton Centre. 1,850 rooms. Seventh Avenue at 52d Street, New York, NY 10019. 800/325-3535; 581-1100.

MADISON SQUARE GARDEN
   New York Penta (formerly New York Statler). 1,705 rooms. 401 Seventh Avenue, New York, NY 10001. 800/223-8585; 736-5000.

THEATER DISTRICT
   Milford Plaza (Best Western International). 1,310 rooms. 270 W. 45th Street, New York, NY 10036. 800/552-6449; 869-3600.
   New York Marriott Marquis. 1,876 rooms. 1535 Broadway, New York, NY 10036. 800/228-9290; 389-1900.

If you're in town on your own, not with a convention group, you may want to stay in a smaller hotel, one that can concentrate more on personal services and amenities. Here are our favorites by neighborhoods.

Lower Manhattan

Vista International
3 World Trade Center   Toll-free reservations: Local Hilton
New York, NY 10048   Reservations Service
                                           Local number: 938-9100
Convenient to Wall Street and the financial district. A stunning addition to the skyline of lower Manhattan, the 23-story Vista stands between the twin towers of the World Trade Center. Each of the 829 guest rooms offers the latest in comforts, such as in-room movies, interesting amenities, and a keyless electronic lock system. The two-level Executive Floor offers all the privacy and special services you've come to expect from

these areas. A superb Executive Fitness Center includes pool, jogging track, machines, racquetball, and cardiovascular fitness program—all on the top floor overlooking New York harbor.

Tops among the excellent restaurants is the **American Harvest,** winner of many national awards for its innovative salutes to American regional specialties.

OTHER LOWER MANHATTAN CHOICES
Gramercy Park

2 Lexington Avenue   Toll-free reservations: 800/221-4083
New York, NY 10010   Local number: 475-4320

Small (509 recently refurbished rooms) with lots of charm, in a quiet park area of the city.

Murray Hill

Morgans

237 Madison Avenue   Toll-free reservations: 800/334-3408
New York, NY 10016   Local number: 686-0300
                                      Telex: 288908

The eclectic brainchild of Steve Rubell (you remember him from Studio 54 and his new club, the Palladium), Morgans is like no other hotel we've ever seen. Small—only 154 rooms—the emphasis is on personal service and guests' comfort. The rooms, decorated in monochromatic grays, include hi-tech fixtures (airplane stainless sinks in bathrooms), VCRs with video libraries, and some nods to the softer life such as duvets rather than spreads on the beds and cushioned window seats. And for all it's mild-mannered quiet airs, Morgans is home to Rubell's buddies when they're in town; you'll likely encounter Liza or Cher or Calvin in the elevator. Morgans is a short walk from the garment center showrooms, near Altmans, Lord & Taylor, and the Herald Square stores (Macy's, Gimbels, Herald Center).

One of the city's most famous nouvelle American chefs, Larry Forgione, now presides over **Morgans Restaurant.**

Midtown East

Drake

440 Park Avenue   Toll-free reservations: 800/DRAKE NY
New York, NY 10022   Local number: 421-0900
                                      Telex: 147178

The new Swissotel management has shaped up this midtown classic so that everything—services, restaurants, staff—now runs like (pardon the pun) clockwork. The 640 rooms are a bit larger than the usual New York City standard-sized rooms (a plus you might not recognize until you've stayed in a really small one). The amenities are thoughtful, and we especially love the bottomless bowl of Swiss chocolates, free for the taking, on the front desk. The hotel is close to Trump Tower, Fifth Avenue shopping, and all the midtown galleries, boutiques, and museums.

La Piazzetta is the European gourmet restaurant, and the beloved **Drake Bar** is back in business.

OTHER MIDTOWN EAST FAVORITES
Helmsley Palace

455 Madison Avenue	Toll-free reservations: 800/221-4982
New York, NY 10022	Local number: 888-7000
	Telex: 640543

Jazzy, splashy, superexpensive, and loaded with status, this renovated historic mansion is Leona's crown jewel.

St. Regis–Sheraton

2 E. 55th Street	Toll-free reservations: 800/325-3535
New York, NY 10022	Local number: 753-4500

Just a few steps east of Fifth, this elegant, Old World, 521-room beauty makes an excellent choice. Free beepers to get your messages to you; and there's a valet storage service if you plan to return.

Berkshire Place

21 E. 52d Street	Toll-free reservations: 800/228-2121
New York, NY 10022	Local number: 753-5800

An Omni Classic hotel in a superb location with good service and services.

Midtown West

Sheraton City Squire

Seventh Avenue at 52d Street	Toll-free reservations: 800/325-3535
New York, NY 10019	Local number: 581-3300

This is a big-city hotel that tries harder. Not to be confused with the convention-sized Sheraton Centre across the street, this 720-room Sheraton is still small enough to remember your name, to hold your luggage when you're in a rush, and to attract a loyal following of single women in town for business in the nearby Seventh Avenue garment center. Convenient to Broadway theaters (but not a safe walk at night) and to Radio City area. Over $10 million have been spent to upgrade the guest rooms. There's a glass-enclosed pool and exercise room on the roof that allow you to work out or swim your laps while watching the bustle of New York's theater and business district 22 stories below.

Movenpick, a restaurant name well known in Europe, makes its United States debut in the hotel's main floor lobby.

OTHER HOTELS IN THE NEIGHBORHOOD
Algonquin

59 West 44th Street	Local number: 840-6800
New York, NY 10036	

Its classic reputation is a bit tarnished (reports of service falling off, and of down-at-the-heels rooms and decor), but a classic nonetheless.

East Side above 57th Street

Pierre

Fifth Avenue at 61st Street
New York, NY 10021

Toll-free reservations: 800/268-6282
Local number: 838-8000
Telex: 127426

Overlooking Central Park, this elegant 205-room Four Seasons hotel is a haven of personal service and Old World–inspired attention to detail. The rooms are furnished in Chippendale, chinoiserie, and couturier fabrics, a design scheme that makes us feel we're staying in the finely cared for home of a gracious host. Close by are the status stores of Fifth Avenue and the chic boutiques of Madison Avenue.

The famous **Cafe Pierre,** newly redesigned by Valerian Rybar, is popular with New Yorkers (a sure sign of status in this tough town) and hotel guests alike.

Westbury

Madison Avenue at 69th Street
New York, NY 10021

Toll-free reservations: 800/223-5672
Local number: 535-2000
Telex: 125388

Nestled in the rarified neighborhood of upper Madison Avenue with its designer boutiques, fine galleries and art shops, and trendy cafes and restaurants, the Westbury makes an excellent choice if you wish to escape the hubbub of midtown Manhattan. A multimillion-dollar renovation has added a sheen to this 1920s landmark hotel. The 300 rooms and 40 suites, most of which are larger sized than the New York standards, are now geared to offer more of the kind of services and amenities we're looking for.

One of the city's prestige restaurants, the **Polo,** is housed in the Westbury, its sporting club motif and fine Continental cuisine attracting both locals and guests.

Mayfair Regent

610 Park Avenue
New York, NY 10021

Toll-free reservations: 800/223-0542
Local number: 288-0800
Telex: MAYREGE

The motto of this East 65th Street beauty is "The grandeur that was, is." This sums up the changes in decor that have restored true elegance to this prestige location. If you're happy with minimalism and understatement, this hotel is not for you: guest and public rooms are replete with arches and sconces and flowering vases and chandeliers and other opulent touches. Outside, you're in patrician territory, an upscale neighborhood of elegant townhouses and their well-heeled residents. Madison Avenue's trendy boutiques are just a block away.

The hotel's fine dining restaurant, **Le Cirque,** also happens to be one of New York's top restaurants, attracting the rich and powerful on a regular basis. Ask the concierge for help here if you plan to entertain or go it alone.

OTHER UPPER EAST SIDE FAVORITES
Plaza Athénée

37 E. 64th Street	Toll-free reservations: 800/223-5672
New York, NY 10021	Local number: 734-9100

Reminiscent of the Paris hotel of the same name, this 160-room newcomer is already making big waves in the New York hotel scene.

American Stanhope

995 Fifth Avenue	Toll-free reservations: 800/847-5800
New York, NY 10028	Local number: 288-5800
	Telex: 224244

Located across from the Metropolitan Museum of Art and decorated with art and furnishings from the American Empire period.

United Nations Area

United Nations Plaza

One United Nations Plaza	Toll-free reservations: 800/228-9000
New York, NY 10017	Local number: 355-3400

Located across First Avenue from the United Nations building at 44th Street, this hotel, as you might expect, is popular with diplomats and members of foreign delegations. It is big and glittering (thanks to a skin of glass) and is handy not only to the UN complex but to such hometown concerns as the *Daily News* offices, law firms, and other East Side businesses. Guest rooms begin on the 28th floor; lower floors house businesses and offices. In-house services include a pool, tennis court, and health club facilities for guests, as well as free limo services to Wall Street, the theater district, and the garment center areas.

The **Ambassador Grill,** a big splashy affair, is best for business lunches. The cuisine is too uneven and prices too high to make for successful dinner entertaining.

Central Park South

Park Lane

36 Central Park South	Toll-free reservations: 800/221-4982
New York, NY 10019	Local number: 371-4000
	Telex: 640543

Here, as in any of the hotels that line 59th Street between Fifth Avenue and Columbus Circle, the rooms offering a view of Central Park are at a premium. A room without a park view costs around $60 less than the same sort of room on the same floor with a park view. The Park Lane is a Helmsley Hotel and Leona's much-publicized concern for guests' comfort is evident. The rooms may be small, but each one is loaded with such amenities as magnifying mirrors, scales, phones in the bathroom, small refrigerator, lots of comfortable chairs and bed pillows. Located midway between the Fifth Avenue shops and the Columbus Circle-Convention Center area.

There's a pool on the top floor, but it's for Mrs. H's private use only. (Ah, the privilege of rank!) The second-floor restaurant, the **Park Room,** has ceiling-to-floor windows to take advantage of a treetop view of the park. Lunch here is often a celebrity-studded event.

ALSO ON CENTRAL PARK SOUTH

Ritz-Carlton

112 Central Park South
New York, NY 10019

Toll-free reservations: 800/223-7990
Local number: 757-1900
Telex: 971534

A bit more masculine in feeling and decor than the Park Lane, despite the "Sister" Parish decor; more businessmen than women among the clientele. The location and rooms are fine, however, and the in-house **Jockey Club** is renowned for power entertaining.

Plaza

Fifth Avenue at 59th Street
New York, NY 10019

Toll-free reservations: 800/228-3000
Local number: 759-3000

Traditionally one of New York's best, this magnificent old landmark hotel could stand some modern upgrading in both services and decor. Women report not receiving phone messages or wake-up calls, and complain of somewhat seedy rooms.

ON A BUDGET

Does finding a trio of safe, attractively appointed, and affordable hotels right in the fashionable heart of midtown strike you as too good to be true? Read on! All three of the following hotels, which are within two blocks of one another, have all this and more, including dozens of neighborhood places to dine—from haute cuisine to fast food.

Hotels

Gorham

136 W. 55th Street
New York, NY 10019

Local number: 245-1800
(call collect for reservations)

Across the street from City Center, close to Radio City and Fifth Avenue offices and shops, the Gorham offers personalized service and security. The lobby is small, the front door is locked after 10 P.M., and a concierge is on duty from 7 A.M. until 11 P.M. All rooms and suites have equipped kitchenettes. No room service, but, as we learned, the nearby Stage Deli delivers at any hour. Singles begin at $70.

Shoreham

33 W. 55th Street
New York, NY 10019

Local number: 247-6700

Between Fifth and Sixth avenues on a street filled with excellent restaurants (the statusy La Caravelle shares ground-floor space with the Shoreham), this small hotel also offers the security of a small lobby, manned elevators, and a caring staff. Rooms here, too, have serving pantries equipped with fridges and coffeemakers. Call any neighboring deli for delivery service or bring in your own. Singles in this hotel start at $70.

Salisbury

123 W. 57th Street	Toll-free reservations: 800/223-0680
New York, NY 10019	Local number: 246-1300
	Telex: 668366

Located across the street from Carnegie Hall, the Salisbury attracts musicians and performers as well as many Fortune 500 companies' corporate travelers. The lobby is small, security is tight, and this hotel has both room service and an in-house restaurant. Singles begin at $79.

Restaurants

Outdoor food vendors are a great New York tradition. If you're new at street noshing, you may want to start with the ubiquitous hot dog sellers (heavy on the sauerkraut and mustard, please) and work your way along the culinary ladder, sampling such fare as falafel, dim sum, shish kebabs, or crêpes. You can accompany these delights with soda, of course, but why not try another New York staple, the egg cream (often called "two cents plain"), which contains neither egg nor cream, but is actually seltzer fizzed over chocolate syrup. And if you're still hungry, wander over to a neighboring pushcart and try a Dove Bar, surely one of nature's more perfect foods.

Among the ongoing **ethnic food** festivals in town, we love **South Street Seaport** (second floor of the Fulton Market building) and **Herald Center** (top floor). Both are crammed with tempting possibilities—from sushi to Tex-Mex, from New York fries to pressed duck. You can eat your fill, have fun doing it, and still have cash left over for serious shopping.

Entertainment

Not in the mood to spend $50 or $60 for a top Broadway musical? How about some of these New York entertainment possibilities:

Free **Shakespeare, New York Philharmonic, or Metropolitan Opera performances** in the park (only in summer, alas; they're outdoors).

Free TV shows: pick up same-day free tickets at the NYC Visitors Bureau.

Take advantage of **"two-fers"**—two tickets for the price of one—to selected Broadway shows. These discount tickets are available at most stores in town or at the Visitors Bureau. **New York's neighborhoods:** almost as exotic as the foreign countries themselves, ethnic neighborhoods are fun to stroll through, stopping to sample the tastes and sounds: Chinatown, Little Italy, Yorkville (German). Other interesting neighborhoods include: Greenwich Village, SoHo, TriBeCa.

Count yourself lucky if you're in town at the time of one of the city's wonderful **festivals:** Chinese New Year (February), Ninth Avenue Food Festival (May), La Festa de San Gennaro (September), Harlem Day (August), or West Indian Day (Labor Day weekend).

Free museums: on Tuesday evenings you can take advantage of the no-admission-charge policies of the Whitney, Guggenheim, Cooper-Hewitt, National Academy of Design, and the Museum of American Folk Art. The Natural History Museum is free on Friday and Saturday evenings. For an exhaustive list of what's free in New York, contact the NYC Convention & Visitors Bureau.

DINING OUT

New York is food heaven. Whether you're a gourmand or a grazer, you'll find your favorites here.

The following restaurants merely scratch the surface of what's great on the dining out scene. You would need time (about a lifetime of living in New York should do it) and the help of a library of restaurant reviews before you could sample all the best. We can't help you in the time department, but we can recommend one food guide, *The Zagat NYC Restaurant Survey,* as one of the most informative on the current scene. Its reviews are compilations of its readers' judgments. Pick it up in most bookstores, or order ahead: 55 Central Park West, New York, NY 10023 (362-1313). And afterward maybe you'll add your opinions to those already in the book.

Restaurant prices in New York are high. A dinner for two, including wine and tip, can run close to $125. However, it's also possible to lunch well for about $10 a person. In general, anything over $35 per person is "expensive," "moderate" is anything between $15 and $35, and "inexpensive" is anything less than $15.

POWER DINING

No matter how lofty the client, you can't go wrong with any of the following choices. They're recognized by everyone as the best of the best—and they're all expensive.

The Four Seasons: try for a table in the Pool Room. 99 E. 52d Street. 754-9494.

Lutece: French, considered by some to be tops in the United States. Because reservations are so hard to obtain, hosting a lunch here gets almost as many points as hosting a dinner. 249 E. 50th Street. 752-2225.

La Grenouille: classic French cuisine served in the most beautiful setting. Almost as renowned for their lavish flowers as for their food. 3 E. 52d Street. 752-1495.

La Cote Basque: another French classic that's heavy on status. 5 E. 55th Street. 688-6525.

Quilted Giraffe: nouvelle, sometimes pretentious, cuisine, served in cramped quarters. Very expensive. 955 Second Avenue, between 50th and 51st streets. 753-5355.

The Palm: an old-fashioned steak house with sawdust on the floor and no pretensions at all—just huge portions of the best ingredients available. No reservations accepted. 837 Second Avenue, between 44th and 45th streets. 687-2953. Its sibling, **The Palm Too,** just across the avenue, serves the same food and will accept reservations. 697-5198.

Il Nido: in a city that lionizes Italian cuisine, this is considered one of the very best. 251 E. 53d Street. 753-8450.

Le Cirque: top-drawer cuisine with emphasis on snob appeal. Its names-in-the-news patrons add new dimensions to the phrase "power dining." 58 E. 65th Street, in the Mayfair Regent Hotel. 794-9292.

POWER BREAKFASTING

You can count on the **Cafe Pierre** (in the Pierre Hotel, Fifth Avenue and 61st Street) and the **Trianon Room** (in the Helmsley Palace, Madison Avenue and 50th Street) to help you make your early-morning points in great style.

SOME NEW YORK CLASSICS

Maxwell's Plum: great dining-as-theater. Stained-glass ceilings, gleaming brass figures, hanging plants and ceramics, and lots of people enjoying themselves. Have a major meal or have a burger—Maxwell's is not to be missed. Moderate. 1181 First Avenue, at 64th Street. 628-2100.

The **Safari Grill** combines great grilled meats with comfortable, trendy ambience. Moderate. 1115 Third Avenue, at 65th Street. 371-9090.

Jim McMullen's (1341 Third Avenue at 75th Street; 861-4700) and **Mortimer's** (1057 Lexington Avenue at 75th Street; 861-2481) are both favorites of jet-setters, models, and other "beautiful people." Both spots offer good, simple foods and great people-watching, and both are moderately priced.

Tavern on the Green is an event; everyone celebrates something here. It's a favorite of New Yorkers and visitors alike, with its dazzling decor inside and Central Park vistas just beyond the windowed walls. No detail is overlooked—the management even creates scenic snow in winters when the weather fails to cooperate. Moderate. And don't miss the special boutique for some great gift items. Central Park West and 67th Street. 873-3200.

21 Club: without the rousing welcome accorded to regulars, we find that the "club" atmosphere fizzles. If that doesn't faze you, come for the people-watching, not for a great meal. Expensive. 21 W. 52d Street. 582-7200.

SOME NEW CLASSICS

John Clancy's is small, a bit off "restaurant row," but worth the trip. Superb grilled fish is a specialty, as are the amazing desserts. Moderate. 181 W. 10th Street, at Seventh Avenue. 691-0551.

Il Mulino: another downtown treasure. Consistently excellent northern Italian cuisine. Take a cab here. Moderate. 86 W. 3d Street, at Thompson and Sullivan streets. 673-3783.

Sistina: an elegant Italian jewel, pride of the four brothers who run it. Cuisine is innovative and excellent. Consider this one a find. Moderate to expensive. 1555 Second Avenue, at 81st Street. 861-7660.

LUNCHING SOLO IN MIDTOWN

Mme. Romaine de Lyon specializes in omelets. Period. But her menu offers hundreds of combinations and exotic fillings. 29 E. 61st Street, between Park and Madison. Inexpensive. 758-2422.

Serendipity, down the street from Bloomingdale's, serves burgers and salads—but really as a prelude to their famous ice-cream and chocolate concoctions. Budget your calories for this one. Inexpensive. 225 E. 60th Street. 838-3531.

And speaking of **Bloomingdale's,** their in-store health food restaurant, **Forty Carrots,** is great for nutritious solo snacking. Inexpensive. Lower level of store.

Oyster Bar is cavernous and noisy, and the service is harried and often annoying. But the seafood can't be topped. Try the selection of oysters or the sublime chowders. Moderate. Grand Central Station, lower level. 490-6650.

Hyo Tan Nippon, for Japanese favorites, includes a sit-down sushi bar. Nondevotees can snack on the house gourmet salad, a meal-and-a-half of slivered chicken and salad greens in an Oriental dressing. Moderate. 119 E. 59th Street, between Park and Lexington. 751-7690.

Tastings, with both East Side and West Side restaurants, offers light meals complemented by a large selection of wines by the glass. Moderate. 144 W. 55th Street, between Sixth and Seventh Avenues (757-1160) and 953 Second Avenue, at 50th Street (644-6740).

Number 1 Deli and Restaurant, an old Automat newly gussied up in art deco decor, serves classic New York deli. Sounds a bit of a mishmash, but the food is deli-perfect, prices are moderate, and the location is ideal. Moderate. 104 W. 57th Street, just west of Sixth Avenue. 541-8320.

BEFORE OR AFTER THEATER

Good restaurants in theater districts are always booked in advance. Never attempt a preshow meal in these neighborhoods without a reservation—at least, not before curtain time. After 8 P.M., they empty out until after 11 when the after-theater crowds pile in.

Cafe Un Deux Trois, a great barn of a brasserie, with bistro ambience and cuisine. Lively and fun. Moderate. 123 W. 44th Street. 345-4148.

Orso serves rustic Italian cuisine on handmade pottery. Their pizza-for-one (a pizza with pizzazz, mind you) is just enough—won't weigh you into a stupor for the performance. Moderate. 322 W. 46th Street. 489-7212.

Carolina for Creole specialties and a pretheater push to get you out in time. Moderate. 355 W. 46th Street. 245-0058.

BEFORE OR AFTER LINCOLN CENTER

Cafe des Artistes is unabashedly romantic with opulent murals and decor, and a well-heeled clientele. Moderate to expensive. 1 W. 67th Street. 877-3500.

Shun Lee, part of the Shun Lee dining dynasty, was recently renovated to reflect the trendy best in New York Chinese cuisine. Future plans call for a cafe that will serve dim sum and "country-style Chinese street food." Moderate to expensive. 43 W. 65th Street. 595-8895.

Cafe Fiorello, another West Side sibling (the East Side version, **Fiorella,** is at Third Avenue and 65th Street), serves Italian bistro food in a lively, casual setting. Moderate. 1900 Broadway, between 63d and 64th streets.

BABY-BOOMER IN SPOTS

It goes without saying that these restaurants are for the grazers— those interested less in the food than in who's at the next table, and concerned whether the place is *truly* the latest in spot. Be prepared for megadecibel noise, outrageous overcrowding, and the trendiest of trend setters.

Pig Heaven serves Chinese fare with a swine motif—the decor, the menu, even some of the patrons, we fear, are decidedly piggie. Moderate. 1540 Second Avenue, at 80th Street. 744-4887

Mezzaluna is Italian nouvelle. Moderate. 1295 Third Avenue, at 74th Street. 535-9600.

America is surely the world's largest, noisiest, trendiest. Even the menu is nonstop. Moderate. 9 E. 18th Street. 505-2110.

AFTERNOON TEA

Less confining than an after-work drinks appointment and far less time-consuming than a business lunch, afternoon tea is gaining in popularity as a classy way to do business. Among the more elegant spots: **Mayfair Regent** (288-0800), **Berkshire Place** (753-5800), **Palm Court** at the Plaza (although they serve the tea in foil packets) (759-3000), **Waldorf-Astoria** (355-3000), **Helmsley Palace** (888-7000), and **Hotel Pierre** (838-8000). Most serve afternoon tea from 3 to 6 P.M.; expect to pay about $10 per person.

NEW YORK BY DAY

The people at the New York Convention & Visitors Bureau who keep tabs on this sort of thing tell us that Manhattan's top ten attractions are the Empire State Building, Rockefeller Center, Lincoln Center, World Trade Center, United Nations, Chinatown and Little Italy, museums, theaters, houses of worship like St. Patrick's Cathedral and Trinity Church, and the New York Stock Exchange in that order. The Statue of Liberty is in a class by itself.

By all means, see them all if you have time. But before seeing any sights, top ten or otherwise, we recommend you get a **city overview** to help put things into perspective. Try the view from the **Empire State Building** (102 stories above midtown Manhattan; Fifth Avenue and 34th Street; 736-3100), or from the Observation Deck of the South Tower of the **World Trade Center** (110 stories above lower Manhattan; World Trade Center Plaza; 466-7377).

To see Manhattan Island from a different vantage point, take a **Circle Line Cruise** (particularly pleasant when the weather cooperates). Cruises last three hours and cover 35 miles of sights you've heard about. Depart from Pier 83, all the way west on 42d Street. Call 563-3200 for details and reservations.

And if the Lady has emerged from her scaffolding and is once again receiving visitors, by all means ferry out to Liberty Island, ascend the **Statue of Liberty's** inner stairs, and experience a truly breathtaking view of the harbor, lower Manhattan, New Jersey, Staten Island, and other neighboring vistas.

The New York Experience presents the city's past and present in a multimedia extravaganza. Not just for kids only, it's a lot of fun, and you'll learn some interesting things. Hourly shows from 11 A.M. daily. $4.25 admission charge. McGraw-Hill Plaza, 49th Street and Sixth Avenue. 869-0345.

There are 120 **museums** in New York, some as specialized as the **Black Fashion Museum** (666-1320), others so all-encompassing and vast they're known around the world. You won't have time for the whole lot, but we would urge you to make time for the following:

Metropolitan Museum, because it's the biggest and the best. Permanent collections include beloved art masterpieces, the most comprehensive Egyptian collection outside of Cairo, and a superb Japanese gallery. Changing exhibits are also world-class. Fifth Avenue and 82d Street. Closed Mondays. 535-7710.

Museum of Modern Art (New Yorkers call it the MoMA) presents the best of modern art, sculpture, photography, graphic design in a beautiful new setting. An outdoor sculpture garden soothes your ragged nerves, and the restaurant is handy for midtown lunch dates. The museum is closed Wednesdays. 53d Street between Fifth and Sixth avenues. 708-9480.

American Museum of Natural History: you could spend months exploring this sprawling treasure trove. For openers, start with the dinosaurs, check out the habitats, then head for the NatureMax Theater with its four-story-high screen and inventory of realistic films. Call 496-0900 for show times. The museum is at Central Park West and 79th Street. 873-4225.

The other major art museums—the **Guggenheim** (Fifth and 89th Street; 360-3500) the **Frick** (Fifth and 70th Street; 288-0700), and the **Whitney** (Madison and 75th Street; 570-3676) are equally worthy of your time.

For more eclectic museum-hopping, check out:

Museum of Broadcasting where 60 years of broadcast history are yours for the picking as you monitor your favorite TV or radio programs of the past. 1 E. 53d Street. 752-7684.

Asia Society Gallery contains John D. Rockefeller's Asian art collection, plus changing exhibits. Closed Mondays. 725 Park Avenue (at 70 Street), 288-6400.

Fraunces Tavern Museum, scene of General Washington's farewell to his officers in 1783, is now a restored 18th-century tavern filled with early American decorative arts. Short film on early city history. Closed Sundays. Pearl and Broad streets, downtown. 425-1778.

Lincoln Center for the Performing Arts offers guided tours of its theaters and performing halls: **New York State Theater, Avery Fisher Hall, Alice Tully Hall, Juilliard School, Vivian Beaumont Theater, Metropolitan Opera House.** Daily from 10 A.M. to 5 P.M. Tours last about one hour; no reservation necessary. 140 W. 65th Street. 877-1800. (For who performs where and when, see "New York by Night.") Other behind-the-scenes tours that are fun: **Rockefeller Center** (489-2947), **Radio City Music Hall** (757-3100), and **Backstage on Broadway** (575-8065).

Central Park, that swath of green in the middle of Manhattan, gets a lot of bad press. We're not pretending it's safe to romp through there after dark. But we are saying that New Yorkers (the solid citizen types, not the muggers) derive a lot of pleasure from this park. There are free concerts and free Shakespeare in the summers, rowing lakes, ice-skating rinks, jogging, biking, and bridle paths, ball fields, huge boulders for solitary contemplation, the dazzling Tavern on the Green for splendid dining, Yoko Ono's Strawberry Fields memorial to John Lennon, spaces for sunbathing, dog running, and socializing. The point is: don't write off these wonderful 840 acres of midtown Manhattan until you've tried them; exercise your best street/park smarts and enjoy yourself. Central Park runs from 59th Street to 110th Street, between Fifth Avenue and Central Park West.

The **Park Rangers,** uniformed men and women whose duties include conducting tours through various city parks, are on hand to instruct us year-round. Call 397-3080 for information about where you can join one of their free tours.

South Street Seaport, an open-air museum of the city's nautical past, is now also a restored 19th-century complex of shopping, dining, and entertainment. We suggest that, unless you're based in the area—in Wall Street or the financial district, for example—you save this for a weekend or a day when you have lots of free time to browse, nibble, and nosh your way through the complex (see "At Leisure").

Here are the addresses for the remaining top ten sights: **Rockefeller Center** (30 Rockefeller Plaza, Fifth Avenue between 49th and 50th streets; 489-2947); **United Nations** (First Avenue between 42d and 46th streets; 754-7713); **Chinatown** (a maze of streets, downtown, just west of Chatham Square); **St. Patrick's Cathedral** (Fifth Avenue and 50th Street); **Trinity Church** (Broadway and Wall Street, downtown); and **New York Stock Exchange** (20 Broad Street, downtown; 623-5167).

UNIQUELY NEW YORK

You can get it wholesale—whatever it is.

Don't laugh. One of New York's more endearing aspects is that, whatever your heart desires to buy, you can rest assured that somewhere in this remarkable city someone has it and is selling it below retail price. All you need to take advantage of this grab bag of bargains is a little know-how, some courage, and the time to pursue your goal. Here are some ideas to help you get started:

The **Lower East Side,** an area first settled by Jewish immigrants, remains an enclave of small family-owned stores offering merchandise at 20 to 50 percent below retail (see ''The Shopping Scene'' for specifics). Bargaining is very much alive here, although some of the newer stores that are trading-up their image will tag items with dollar amounts and refuse to budge. Literally everything can be found here, from designer fashions to luggage, from fine china to kids' underwear. Note: all stores are closed on Saturday, the Jewish Sabbath, but everyone shops all day Sunday. To avoid the crush, come during the week. The area runs, roughly, from Canal Street to Houston Street between Forsyth and Essex streets. Taxi in and out, or take a Second Avenue bus.

Jobbers are merchants who buy up the current season's fashion merchandise directly from designers, add on their costs, and sell to you at roughly a third less than retail store prices. Note: it's best to shop the uptown stores first and arrive knowing specific prices and style numbers. Cash or personal checks are always accepted, and sometimes credit cards, too. Ben Farber's showroom bulges with over 300 designer lines; best to shop at 9 A.M. to avoid the crowds (462 Seventh Avenue; 736-0557). Abe Geller is a similar showroom (491 Seventh Avenue; 736-8077).

Don't discount New York's well-known **off-price stores,** where bargains are an everyday way of life: perhaps the best known is **Loehmann's,** now a nationwide fashion chain, with its flagship store in the Bronx. Loehmann's remains a standard against which savvy New York shoppers pit their fashion know-how. It's a long schlepp by cab (20 to 30 minutes), but if you're serious, the savings could be well worth the fare (Fordham Road and Jerome Avenue, Bronx; (295-4100). And, of course, there's that New York institution **Crazy Eddie** (''his prices are in*sane*,'' the ads scream) for records or any stereo, electronic, or sound system. The refusal to be undersold is store policy, so come armed with an advertised price and they'll match or beat it. There are stores all over town; the number for the one near Bloomingdale's is 980-5136. **Michael C. Fina** is the place to go for wedding-gift-type items—Waterford, Baccarat, Wedgewood, hundreds of silver flatware patterns—and everything at near wholesale prices, always the lowest in the business. They also gift wrap for free and mail your purchase for you. 1 W. 47th Street, on the second floor. 869-5050.

It is often possible for civilians like us to buy direct from the insular world of designers, right from their Seventh Avenue showrooms. Not every designer allows this sort of outsider familiarity, but it's worth a try. Call your favorite, ask if they have Saturday shopping hours. If the answer is positive, then query on procedure: will they take plastic or only cash? what are the hours? can you try on the clothes?

In addition to the garment center, bargains abound in the city's **wholesale districts,** which also sell to the retail consumer: the wholesale **flower market** on Sixth Avenue in the 20s, the **button and trimmings market** in the 30s just west of Fifth, **rugs and furniture** in the 30s around Lexington, **lingerie** in the 30s near Madison, and around 47th Street between Fifth and Sixth are both the **diamond market** and several **camera and electronics stores** that will match or beat any advertised price you can show them.

If for some reason your dream item can't be found off-price, you can then shop for it in the high-rent stores with a clear conscience—knowing that you did your best to save some money.

THE SHOPPING SCENE

The problem with shopping in New York is having to deal with the volume—there's everything you could ever want and maybe too much of it. Sometimes the idea of all those stores, all that merchandise is overwhelming—even for native New Yorkers. Perhaps the most sensible way to cut the problem down to manageable size is to shop by neighborhood the way New Yorkers do:

Fifth Avenue from the 40s to 59th Street takes in the three Bs—**Bonwit's, Bergdorf's,** and **Bendel's** (although Bendel's is a few doors west of Fifth on 57th). **Saks Fifth Avenue** is here, too, at 50th Street, across from Rockefeller Center. You'll also find the serious jewelry stores like **Van Cleef & Arpels, Cartier,** and **Tiffany** on Fifth. Many big-league European names grace this street as well, names like: **Gucci, Beltrami, Valentino.** Our vote for the most pretentious shop on this or any other avenue in the world: **Bijan,** which admits no shopper into the store without an appointment. Also on Fifth is the shopping mall that could happen only in New York—the **Trump Tower.** Enter into this pink marble world, ride the escalators up through the world of haute couture and high price tags. You don't have to buy—just enjoy the spectacle of where the rich and famous come to shop and play.

Madison Avenue, especially north of 57th Street, is home to high fashion designer boutiques—**Giorgio Armani, Sonia Rykiel, Kenzo, Yves Saint Laurent, Ungaro, Pierre Balmain,** and **Missoni** are just a few of the names you'll recognize as you stroll this prestigious avenue. **West 34th Street,** an unlovely neighborhood at best, happens to be home to some retailing giants. **Macy's** and **Gimbels** are here, as well as the new **Herald Center,** an urban shopping mall for upscale shoppers. In fact, between this mall's rarified designer boutiques and Macy's recent upgrading to designer and high-fashion merchandise, scruffy old 34th Street is looking better everyday. Nearby, one or two blocks east of Macy's are two other New York retail standard-bearers: **B. Altman,** a very conservative store, and **Lord & Taylor,** long the champion of American fashions and designers.

Bloomingdale's (New Yorkers never call it "Bloomie's") is on 59th Street with entrances on Lexington Avenue and Third Avenue. Its reputation as a world-class trendsetter is deserved; love it or hate it—you must see it while you're in town.

Columbus Avenue in the 70s and 80s is one of the city's trendier shopping and dining areas. Everything is clever and "now" on Columbus. Stores are open until midnight, and sidewalks are crowded with late-night shoppers and diners. You'll feel safe there, and if you're into the latest trends, you'll also think you're in heaven.

Not everything is upscale and expensive in New York. If you're one who values a bargain over ambience, the possibilities are limitless on the **Lower East Side** (see "Uniquely New York"). Although stores in this neighborhood tend to change hands, and names, with some regularity, here are some personal favorites: **Fishkin's** for designers like Calvin Klein, Norma Kamali, Harve Benard. Good selection of designer shoes, too (314 Grand Street; 226-6538); **Lea's** for Albert Nippon designs (81 Rivington; 677-2043); **JBZ Unlimited Pret a Porter** for European designers like Fendi, Thiery Mugler, Giorgio Sant Angelo (121 Orchard Street; 473-8550); **Ezra Cohen** for linens, like Nettlecreek, and all the top sheet and towel makers (305 Grand Street; 925-7800).

SoHo is another neighborhood where wandering will net you some unique fashion finds. Nestled among the avant-garde galleries and cafes, you'll find such eclectic boutiques as **Parachute** with its architectural, clean, modern designs (121 Wooster Street; 925-8630); **Le Grand Hotel,** which showcases young American designers (471 W. Broadway; 475-7625); the **Gallery of Wearable Art** for unusual, often one-of-a-kind fashions and accessories (480 W. Broadway; GAL-LERY).

And if you want to replenish your conservative, dress-for-success wardrobe, you'll find the following stores have all the right stuff: **Alcott & Andrews** (355 Madison Avenue; 818-0606); **Streets** (914 Lexington Avenue; 517-9000); **Brooks Brothers** (346 Madison Avenue; 682-8800).

New York has two travel-related bookstores with maps, guidebooks, even fiction and essays about that exotic destination you've been dreaming about. Either store can also supply you with an abundance of

N.Y.C. guidebooks. The Complete Traveller Bookstore, 199 Madison Avenue (near Altman's at 34th Street). 685-9007. Travellers Bookstore, 22 West 52d Street (in the Rockefeller Center complex). 664-0995.

NEW YORK BY NIGHT

Although most people think "Broadway" when New York theater is mentioned, the fact is there are only about 35 Broadway theaters, but 375 other live theaters—off-Broadway, off-off-Broadway, and some nowhere near the Great White Way.

Check the theater listings in the *Times,* in *New York Magazine,* or in other entertainment-oriented publications to determine what you'd like to see. You can then order tickets by phone from **Chargit** (944-9300) or **Tele-Charge** (239-6200), charging them to your credit card (including a service fee). No refunds are given once the order is processed. **TKTS Booths** sell half-price tickets for same-day performances. Be prepared to wait in a long line, although you can call ahead to see if your choice is available (354-5800). TKTS Booths are at Times Square (47th Street and Broadway) and in lower Manhattan (2 World Trade Center). Or you can buy advance-sale or same-day tickets at regular prices at the **theater box office.**

Broadway theaters are located generally around Broadway in the forties, an area certainly not considered among New York's finest. If you're new in town, or will be going to the theater by yourself, you might want to arrange ahead of time to have a call-cab pick you up after the theater. Since most shows end at about the same time, it's virtually impossible to hail a cruising cab, and you won't want to be standing around as the crowds thin. **Off-Broadway and off-off-Broadway theaters** can be anywhere—a loft somewhere downtown or a conventional theater in a residential uptown neighborhood. One new theater district is emerging on West 42d Street, with several theaters, cafes, and restaurants bringing new life to this once-deserted section. Again we urge you to exercise caution in any of these areas at night.

Most theaters now have an 8 P.M. curtain, with performances Tuesdays through Saturdays, and matinees on Wednesdays and Saturdays. Some theaters are dark on Mondays, some on Sundays.

Lincoln Center for the Performing Arts is a jewel in New York's cultural tiara. Three dazzling buildings frame a brilliant central courtyard and fountain. Lighted at night, this area sparkles most brightly when intermission audiences spill out for a breath of air. In this prestigious enclave are: **Avery Fisher Hall,** home to the **New York Philharmonic** (874-2424); **Alice Tully Hall,** where the **Chamber Music Society** performs (362-1911); the **New York State Theater,** which hosts **NYC Opera** and **NYC Ballet** (870-5570); and the **Metropolitan Opera House,** home to the **Metropolitan Opera** and the **American Ballet Theater** (362-6000).

Carnegie Hall: Remember the old gag, "How do you get to Carnegie Hall?" "Practice, practice." You'll find it on West 57th Street. It's a beautiful old building with a fiercely loyal group of supporters. Public outcry not only helped preserve the building but was instrumental in restoring the hall's famous near-perfect acoustics. 154 W. 57th Street, at Seventh Avenue. 247-7800.

City Center Theater is the home of the Joffrey Ballet and other modern-dance troupes. In the exotic old Mecca Temple building, 131 W. 55th Street. 246-8989.

LATE-NIGHT NEW YORK

Truly, this city never sleeps. There are all-night clubs and parties, brasseries and diners serving 24 hours, even movies and TV to entertain you all through the night—right up to your breakfast meeting if you can handle the nonstop action.

Much is written about New York's **clubs.** A few years ago, the trendsetting Studio 54, with its glittering celebrities and its huddled masses of hopefuls begging to be allowed inside, literally set the standard for a new era of night life around the country. You may not want to hear this, but the truth is that aside from invitation-only private parties attended by the "beautiful people" in the VIP rooms, New York's clubs are now patronized by the very, very young. High school kids, aching to appear sophisticated and with-it, besiege the trendy spots like **Area, Visage, Limelight,** and even the new blockbuster **Palladium.** Give these night spots a try if you don't believe us. But if you go, please don't go alone; most clubs are in run-down deserted neighborhoods, and besides, they are definitely not singles' spots.

Comedy clubs are popular with New York audiences; there's a lot of talent standing up in the midtown area. Among the current hot clubs, we like these:

Catch a Rising Star, undisputed top showcase for rising—or headlining—talent. Cover charge about $10. 1487 First Avenue. 794-1906.

Improvisation, the club that introduced the likes of Bette Midler, Richard Pryor, and Joe Piscopo. Cover and minimum run about $12. 358 W. 44th Street. 765-8268.

The Comic Strip can claim the launching of Eddie Murphy. Cover and minimum come to about $10. 1568 Second Avenue. 861-9386.

Dangerfield's (yes, that's the Rodney of "I don't-get-no-respect" fame) showcases older, more established comics. Weekend cover and minimum come to about $18. 1118 First Avenue. 593-1650.

If you enjoy the unique audience-to-performer atmosphere of **cabaret,** you can get your fill in New York. A resurgence of this entertainment form is responsible for some 20 cabarets all over town. Among the best: **Don't Tell Mama,** 343 W. 46th Street (757-0788); **Upstairs at Greene**

Street, 103 Greene Street (925-2415); **Caroline's,** 332 Eighth Avenue, at 26th Street (924-3499); and **Michael's Pub,** 211 E. 55th Street (758-2272).

Hungry? The **Brasserie** is open all the time. We're not recommending it for its great food, mind you, but at 3 A.M. who cares? The French-type fare is filling, the ambience is just fine, and the midtown location is greatly appreciated. 100 E. 53d Street, between Lexington and Park avenues. 751-4840.

Call the **Jazz Line** for recorded information on who's playing where: 718/465-7500.

AT LEISURE

If you've got the time, New York's got enough to keep you amused for as long as you stay. Grab the best hotel weekend package, rent a car, and head out into the countryside. Or hang out in town and do all those things you didn't have time for during the work week.

Day-Tripping

The eastern end of **Long Island** is where many New Yorkers head for the weekends—for the world-class beaches and life-styles of the Hamptons, and of Fire Island. The Long Island Expressway is the route there (about a two-hour drive); or you can take the Long Island Railroad (718/739-4200) or the Hampton Jitney express bus service (936-0440). During the warm-weather months, as you would expect, these popular resort areas are crowded, and accommodations aren't easy to find. Best to write ahead for information on reservations and other facts to the Long Island Tourism Commission, MacArthur Airport, Ronkonkoma, NY 11779. These famous resort areas are on Long Island's legendary **south shore.**

On the less-populated and less well-known **north shore** of **Long Island,** you drive country roads bordered by acres and acres of potato farms and the old wood-frame houses of the original settlers. You can also visit some examples of the Island's newest agricultural industry, the North Shore **wine country.** You would enjoy Hargrave Vineyards, the oldest (since 1973). Call 516/734-5111 for directions and times of tours. Or stop by Lenz Vineyards, with its soaring architecture and art deco tasting room (516/734-6020), or Pindar Vineyards just down the road from Lenz (516/734-6020). Although it's not yet the Napa Valley, this section of the north shore is well worth the trip.

In the mood for a **sail?** Board the masted schooner *Appledore* for a voyage from Montauk Point (at the easternmost tip of Long Island) to Block Island, Rhode Island, an authentic whaling village that has succeeded in protecting its seafaring charms from the ravages of commercialism and progress. The sail across Long Island Sound takes about two hours, which leaves plenty of time for biking, swimming, shopping, and consuming fresh seafood on Block Island. Sleep aboard the ship that night and return to Montauk the next day. The entire trip costs about $95, including the return-trip brunch. Call 516/283-5700 for details and reservations.

The new **Bronx Zoo** is more than zoo; it is an educational experience. In addition to the African veldt habitat, the World of Darkness, the children's petting zoo, and all the other specialties, the new addition, Jungle World, is attracting worldwide attention. A re-creation of a Southeast Asian tropical rain forest, this 37,000-square-foot habitat includes waterfalls, exotic plants and animals, the world's largest flower (the red rafflesia), and an engaging family of proboscis monkeys who seem to love playing to an audience. Don't miss this zoo and its new addition. Bronx River Parkway and Fordham Road. Call 367-1010 for directions and other information.

The Cloisters, which belongs to the Metropolitan Museum of Art, is actually five medieval cloisters that house tapestries and other art treasures from the Middle Ages. The famous Unicorn Tapestries are on exhibit here. Connecting the buildings are walkways through soothing herbal gardens, where secluded benches invite you to pause and contemplate the beauties of this extraordinary complex and the surrounding Fort Tryon Park. Call 923-3700 for transportation information.

Atlantic City beckons the serious gambler and the slot player alike. It's a mere two hours or so away by special bus. Both Greyhound (635-0800) and Trailways (730-7469) have buses leaving daily from the Port Authority (42d Street and Eighth Avenue). See Philadelphia, "At Leisure," for our favorite places in this gambling town.

In Town

Now's the time to head for the **South Street Seaport** with its authentic history spiced up with such modern-day temptations as great stores and places to eat. This is another Rouse Company project, like Faneuil Hall in Boston or Harbor Place in Baltimore. At its core is New York's original harbor history—you'll hear it referred to as the South Street Seaport Museum, meaning an outdoor museum, houses, tall-masted ships, and cobbled streets, open to the public. But to spark interest, they've added a three-floor marketplace of international foodstuffs, restaurants, and specialty food shops along with dozens of other shops, some stocked with serious merchandise, others with impulse items. On weekends it's crowded, noisy, and fun. Street entertainers are out in full force, there's lots of outdoor eating and drinking, and everyone seems to be having a wonderful time. Located on the East River at South Street. Take a regular city bus marked South Street down Second Avenue, take a cab, or call 669-9424 for directions and information.

Now's the time, too, to wander the **neighborhoods** like **SoHo** where you'll share the sidewalks with fellow New Yorkers who are exploring the area's latest galleries and shops to discover what's new.

Sunday Customs

Although some New Yorkers take their Sunday mornings and its requisite armloads of newspapers very seriously, preferring to stay home, many others head for the public celebrations of brunch and fellowship. We offer a mixed bag of **brunch spots:**

El Rio Grande, Mexican with a light touch, serves great huevos and four-star frozen margaritas in your choice of venue: one side of the restaurant is "Texas," the other is "Mexico." In nice weather, you can do the whole thing on the outdoor terrace. 160 E. 38th Street. 867-0922.

Sign of the Dove, ordinary fare in a storybook setting: skylights, lacy draperies, gleaming crystal. 1110 Third Avenue, at 65th Street. 861-8080.

We have mentioned them elsewhere, but both **Tavern on the Green** and **Maxwell's Plum** are sublimely ideal spots for leisurely, festive brunches.

And, of course, any of the **"grand hotels"** of the city pride themselves on their sumptuous brunches.

For many New Yorkers, Sunday wouldn't be Sunday without a visit to **Zabar's**—that west side food emporium made famous by Woody Allen movies, the great and the near-great who shop there, and the vast array of foods from around the world. Drop by for some nova scotia (lox is the saltier version) and a bagel—and you may walk out with bags full of exotica you didn't even know existed. 2245 Broadway (at 82d street). 787-2000.

Spectator Sports

If you're a pro sports buff, New York has enough overlapping seasons to keep you happy all year long.

The football **Giants** play in nearby Giants Stadium in the New Jersey Meadowlands, about 20 minutes from midtown. Take a New Jersey Transit bus from Port Authority. However, tickets are practically impossible to find. Check with your hotel's concierge on this one. The September-December season tends to spill over at either end, giving fans almost six months of Giants action.

The **Knicks** play basketball in Madison Square Garden from fall into spring. Call 563-8000.

Also in Madison Square Garden, the **Rangers** hockey games from October through April. Tickets are scarce for these games, too. Call 563-8000.

There are two hometown baseball teams, with tickets readily available for both during the long April through October season. The amazin' **Mets** (National League) play at Shea Stadium in the borough of Queens (718/507-8499). The **Yankees** (American League) play at Yankee Stadium in the Bronx (293-6000).

There are five horse-racing tracks in the metro area, although not all are running at the same time. **Thoroughbred racing** is at Aqueduct Race Track in Queens (718/641-4700) and Belmont Park Race Track in Long Island (516/641-4700). Both are closed on Tuesdays. Nighttime **harness racing** is at Yonkers Raceway every night but Sunday (562-9500) and Roosevelt Raceway on Long Island (516/895-1246). The Meadowlands in nearby New Jersey has both flats and harness racing (201/935-8500).

Sports Phone gives up-to-the-minute scores: 976-1313.

Active Sports

Central Park has miles of trails and paths for jogging and biking (roads are closed to vehicular traffic on Sundays, which makes it a haven for bikers and runners) and horseback riding (Claremont Riding Academy, 724-5100). You can also play tennis here (call 408-0209 for free permit) and row (rental boats at boathouse on the lakeshore).

There's ice skating in Central Park at Wolman Memorial Rink, near 59th Street. If you're good, or don't mind performing for large crowds of onlookers, you can skate your stuff at Rockefeller Center's rink, from November until warm weather (757-2072).

Combine two favorites—fitness and food—when you join the Hungry Pedalers biking tours. You and your hardy fellow bikers can tour the boroughs, stopping to sample the fare of the more interesting neighborhoods. Summer weekends. Call 222-2243.

Philadelphia

Vine St.

CHINA TOWN

M

F LOGAN CIRCLE

Benjamin Franklin

25

Pkwy.

John F. Kennedy Blvd.

6

Market St.

CITY CENTER

C D

I

7th St.

Chestnut St. *H*

B

Walnut St.

4

Locust St.

A 3

SOCIETY HILL

G

SCHUYLKILL RIVER

DELAWARE RIVER

26th St.

20th St.

18th St.

17th St.

Lombard St.

South St.

Broad St.

16th St.

15th St.

5th St.

4th St.

3d St.

2d St.

E J K

N

1 L

N

HOTELS

1 Embassy Suite
2 Four Seasons Hotel
3 Hershey Philadelphia Hotel
4 Latham
5 Palace Hotel
6 Philadelphia Centre Hotel

LANDMARKS

A Academy of Music
B Amtrak
C Atwater Kent Museum
D The Bourse
E Council for International Visitors
F Franklin Institute Science Museum and Fels Planetarium
G Head House Square
H Independence National Historical Park

I Painted Bride Art Center
J Philadelphia Civic Center
K Philadelphia Convention and Visitors Bureau
L Philadelphia International Airport
M Philadelphia Museum of Art
N Sports Complex (Veterans Stadium and the Spectrum)
O United States Mint

PHILADELPHIA

GETTING YOUR BEARINGS

Philadelphia is one city in which history is an integral part of its present life. But because of the focus of this book, we can be concerned only with the present and how it relates to you, the visitor. And so, although you won't find any weighty references in this chapter to the city's role in American history, we do recommend that you save some time for the Independence National Historical Park to explore at leisure this "most historic square mile in America."

As first-time visitors we were delighted by the convenience of Center City (what Philadelphians call their downtown area)—how wonderfully handy and close by everything is to everything else. Center City radiates outward from City Hall, which happens to be in the exact center of the grid system at Broad and Market streets. For example, although the distance between City Hall and the Art Museum out along the wooded Benjamin Franklin Parkway appears, at least on a map, to be formidable, it is actually an easy and extremely pleasant walk.

In fact, your walking shoes will get a good workout here because this is, by far, the most efficient means of getting around Center City. Although cabs are abundant, so is traffic. And surely nothing is more frustrating and expensive than sitting behind a pileup of cars watching the meter ticking away.

Although we champion walking as the most efficient and pleasant means of transportation around Center City, we also urge you to employ big-city street smarts while you do it. Some parts of town leave a lot to be desired: Market Street just east of City Hall, for example, is a microcosm of truly nasty urban blight—peep shows, X-rated movie houses, litter, and loiterers. However, this is also the direct route to both the Gallery shopping mall and the Reading Terminal Market. By day, it is more menacing looking than it is dangerous. By night—forget it. In fact, after dark, you really should take cabs or drive to wherever you're going.

Historically always a city of firsts, Philadelphia continues to lead the way for many industries and professions. The first medical school

359

was founded here in 1765; there are now six major medical schools, as well as numerous teaching hospitals, research centers, and pharmaceutical companies. Starting with its first university in 1779, Philadelphia now boasts 20 colleges and universities, with an additional 30 close by. And from the founding of the first American art school, the Pennsylvania Academy of Fine Arts, has now evolved a city of cultural awareness dedicated to excellence in both the performing and the fine arts.

Although the fifth largest city in the United States, Philadelphia is also a city of small neighborhoods and landmark sections. Among those you're likely to hear locals referring to: Society Hill, a lovely section of town in the eastern part of Center City, where many streets are still cobbled and homes are lovingly restored; and Fairmont Park, the largest urban park in the United States and a haven for both athletic endeavors and cultural pursuits. The Art Museum is here, as are historic houses you can tour, the zoo, the Horticultural Center, and 8,700 acres of greenery for playing and relaxing; Rittenhouse Square, a park oasis where you can rest after a taxing bout of shopping along adjacent Walnut Street; and South "Philly," a multiethnic area usually associated with its Italian population. Here's where you'll find a wealth of superb restaurants, the famous outdoor market where "Rocky" spent so much time, the sports complex, and the South Street area with its trendy boutiques and restaurants (see "The Shopping Scene" and "At Leisure").

As for the local lingo: that river just to the west of town, the Schuylkill, is pronounced "SKOO-kul," and the city itself is called "Philly" only by those who live there—they seem to resent outsiders using the nickname.

WHAT TO WEAR

The best rule of thumb here is to pack as you would for a trip to New York or Washington, D.C.; the climates are similar, as are the fashion codes. Businesswomen here are extremely fashion-conscious and rather formal in appearance. Well-tailored suits and "important" dresses will be well regarded. As this is a northern city, boots are always part of a winter wardrobe. Summers can be sticky and very hot, but don't use that as an excuse to let down your fashion guard.

WEATHER WATCH

This is definitely a four-climate city. Winters range from the low 40s to the mid-20s; and summer days can reach the mid-80s. As always, we suggest you check the temperatures a few days prior to your arrival to avoid any unwelcome surprises.

GETTING THERE

More than 1,000 flights arrive and depart **Philadelphia International Airport** every day. Domestic, international, and commuter carriers service PHL, and although locals despair that construction facelifts will never end, the facility is well-planned and easy to navigate. Airport information: 492-3181.

Limousine/vans, express SEPTA (SouthEast Philadelphia Transit Authority) buses, taxis, and a high-speed rail line all make the eight-mile trip into Philadelphia's Center City. Cabs will run about $14 for the 25-minute trip; vans about $5; express bus about $2.50; and high-speed rail about $3.

Car Rentals

Agencies at the airport:

Avis	492-0900
Budget	492-3915
Dollar	365-1605
Hertz	492-7200
National	492-2750

Amtrak operates rail service into Philadelphia's 30th Street Station, which is about five minutes from Center City. For general information and reservations, call 824-1600; for Metroliner information, call 824-4224.

GETTING AROUND

We would expect nothing less than a logical, systematic street plan from a city like Philadelphia. In true grid fashion, the numbered streets run north and south; the named streets run east and west. The Schuylkill River borders the town on the west, the Delaware River borders it on the east, and City Hall marks the middle.

Because virtually everything in Center City is within walking distance of everything else, you won't need a car if your business is limited to this area. But if you have appointments farther out or will be staying on for a minivacation (see "At Leisure"), a car is essential. On-street parking is at a premium; plan to use lots or garages.

Cabs are readily available and reliable. They operate on the meter system: $1.32 for the first mile, $1.22 each additional mile. (These odd numbers give cabbies the chance to say magnanimously, "Forget the two cents, lady.") Sharing is legal. Cabs cruise in Center City, but to be on the safe side, we often call ahead (waiting time is about ten minutes). Some companies you can depend on: Quaker City, 728-8000; United, 854-0750; and Yellow Cab, 922-8400.

Buses are safe enough, but practical only within Center City. Fare is $1 in either coins or bills. Use the subway only to ride to the sports complex in South Philadelphia. Otherwise, it's not especially convenient, savory, or safe. SEPTA travel information: 574-7800.

GETTING FAMILIAR

Philadelphia Convention and Visitors Bureau
The Tourist Center (just behind City Hall)
1525 John F. Kennedy Boulevard   Toll-free: 800/523-2004
Philadelphia, PA 19102   Local number: 568-6599
Write or visit here for maps, brochures, and up-to-the-minute information about what's going on around town. The well-informed volunteers will even custom-design a sightseeing itinerary based on your requirements.

Council for International Visitors
Civic Center Museum   823-7261
34th and Civic Center Boulevard
Philadelphia, PA 19104
This official hospitality center for foreign visitors will arrange any itinerary or excursion, including at-home visits with Philadelphians. Interpreters and translators on duty.

Philadelphia Civic Center
34th and Civic Center Boulevard   823-7327
West Philadelphia, PA 19104

The *Philadelphia Inquirer* is published daily and Sundays in the morning. The weekend supplement on Fridays offers a comprehensive calendar of all events, and the Sunday edition includes an excellent entertainment section. The *Philadelphia Daily News* is published daily, except Sundays, in the morning. *Philadelphia Magazine,* the glossy monthly, has an extensive "Stepping Out" section listing all local events. Watch for the February "Dining Out Annual," and the August "The Best of Philly" special issue.

Call the **Philly Fun Phone** for a two-minute recording of happenings around town. This tape is updated three times every day. 568-7255.

Quick Calls

AREA CODE: 215	Weather WE6-1212
Time 846-1212	All Emergencies 911

AT YOUR SERVICE

Embassy Suites

One Gateway Center   Toll-free reservations: 800/EMBASSY
Philadelphia International Airport   Local number: 365-6600
Philadelphia, PA 19153

Opened in the spring of 1985, this airport facility aims to make you forget the location; an eight-story atrium graces the lobby, and all suites overlook a plant-filled courtyard. Each of the 250 suites includes a living room, bedroom, and bath, sofa bed, fridge and wet bar, two color TVs, and three phones.

Rates include a free full breakfast (American style) and cocktail party every afternoon, as well as courtesy airport van and free parking. The in-house restaurant is the **Ambassador Cafe.**

Four Seasons Hotel

One Logan Square   Toll-free reservations: 800/828-1188
Philadelphia, PA 19103   Local number: 963-1500
                                      Telex: 831805

This hotel is everything a woman away from home would like her real home to be. No detail has been overlooked to cosset guests in style, security, and creature comforts. The decor is muted and airy, Aubusson rugs on marble floors in the public rooms, windows that overlook fountains and lush gardens, and guest rooms outfitted with worthwhile amenities. Service, a Four Seasons trademark, includes a female concierge, twice-daily maid service, spa ("alternative") cuisine available from both restaurant and room service menus, and complimentary shoe shines. Even the health spa is designed to pamper your sensibilities—you can swim laps in a garden setting where no harsh lights glare off the water.

In this town with its serious food establishment, the **Fountain Restaurant** is recognized as one of the best. The **Swann Cafe** is popular with the local business community for both social and working get-togethers.

Hershey Philadelphia Hotel

Broad Street at Locust   Toll-free reservations: 800/533-3131
Philadelphia, PA 19107   Local number: 893-1600

Located across from the Academy of Music, and in the heart of the financial district, the Hershey offers convenience for both day and night. An unusual sawtooth architectural design ensures every one of the 450 guest rooms a dramatic view. A nice safety feature: each floor has only 22 rooms so there are no long halls or blind corners. Ask about their "female executive rooms" on the top eight floors.

Sarah's serves haute cuisine in elegant art deco surroundings; **Cafe Academie** serves three meals daily, including Sunday brunch.

	Concierge	Executive Floor	No-Smoking Rooms	Fitness Facilities	Pool	24-Hour Room Service	Restaurant for Client Entertaining	Extra-Special Amenities	Electronic Key System	Business/Secretarial Services	Check Out Time	Frequent Guest Program	Business Traveler Program	Average Rate
Embassy Suites			●	●	●		Ambassador Cafe		●	●	12 noon		Beacon Club	$ 99 $ 95
Four Seasons	●	●		●	●	●	Fountain Restaurant	●		●	1 p.m.			$170 $150
Hershey	●	●	●	●	●		Sarah's	●		●	1 p.m.			$135 $120
Latham	●						Bogart's		●	●	1 p.m.	Yes	Blue Chip Option	$125 $110
Palace	●		●		●	●	Cafe Royale			●	1 p.m.			$110 $ 95

Latham

17th at Walnut	Toll-free reservations: 800/228-0808
Philadelphia, PA 19103	Local number: 563-7474
	Telex: 831438

Here's a gem of a small hotel right in the heart of Center City. With only 150 rooms, this European-style hostelry provides elegant services and appointments: marble-topped bureaus, French writing desks, custom-designed bedspreads and draperies. The lobby is tiny—no one passes through unnoticed here. Within easy walking distance of the keystone-arched doorway lie the Walnut Street shops and fine restaurants, the museums and galleries, the landmark townhouses of Society Hill, and Independence Historic Park.

Bogart's, with its nostalgic *Casablanca* setting, serves an excellent Continental cuisine and a popular Sunday brunch; **Not Quite Crickett** is a plaid-carpeted, clubby sort of place, good for light meals and, in the evenings, for live jazz entertainment.

Palace Hotel

18th Street and Benjamin Franklin Parkway	Toll-free reservations: 800/223-5672
(at Logan Circle)	Local number: 963-2222
Philadelphia, PA 19103	Telex: 7106700218

Originally a luxury apartment house, this Trusthouse Forte hotel now incorporates European-style luxury into both its public rooms and its 244 suites and 41 guest rooms. Suites have a meeting/dining area with wet bar and a sitting area with balcony, and are furnished with reproductions of good French, English, and Chinese period pieces. Lots of fresh flowers everywhere. The location is excellent: Benjamin Franklin Parkway is near museums and prestige office buildings; its tree-lined expanses evoke feelings of the Champs Élysées.

Cafe Royal serves French cuisine and a Sunday brunch; the **Cafe Royal Bar** has live piano music.

ON A BUDGET

Hotels

There is a very active and very popular **Bed & Breakfast** organization in Philadelphia. Emphasis is placed on personalized placement geared toward your special interests—whether antiques, architecture, or whatever. Among the locations you can request are Society Hill, Rittenhouse Square, Antique Row, University City, and the Art Museum area. Call 735-1137 or 923-5459.

If you prefer the privacy of a large hotel, try the following:

Philadelphia Centre Hotel
1725 John F. Kennedy Boulevard   Toll-free reservations: 800/523-4033
Philadelphia, PA 19103   Local number: 568-3300
The location is excellent: right in Center City near tourist sites and offices, museums and shopping. The drawback is its size—850 rooms and long, winding halls. There is good security, however, and a staff of guards. Singles begin at $59 for a very small room with one twin bed or $69 for a double bed. Their largest room with a queen-sized bed is $79.

There are two restaurants in the hotel: **Crossroads,** a coffee shop, and **Pancho & Richie,** a Mexican specialty restaurant.

Restaurants

Eating can be both money-saving and fun in Philadelphia. Many of our national favorite specialty foods were born right here in town (see "Uniquely Philadelphia"). In addition to our favorite, the **Reading Terminal Market** (see "Uniquely Philadelphia"), we also like the following places for thrifty dining.

Old Original Levis, in operation since 1895, has the nation's oldest operating soda fountain (try their "champ" cherry soda)—and probably the best hot dogs around. Open every day from 10 A.M. to 11 P.M. 507 S. 6th Street, at Lombard. 627-2354.

Pat's King of Steaks is where the famous cheesesteak originated in 1930. Celebrities and blue-collar workers alike flock to this Philadelphia institution. Best to drive or cab here. It's near the Italian produce market. 1237 E. Passyunk Avenue. 339-9872.

Lee's Hoagie House, another local tradition since the 1950s. Lee's will even wrap a hoagie to go. (When they ask, "With?" they mean, "With onions?" Say yes.) 44 S. 17th Street. 564-1264.

Entertainment

One of the best deals in town is the **Trolley Tours** of the historic houses in Fairmont Park. A three-dollar ticket buys you an entire day, if you choose to stay that long, of house touring, browsing, and shuttling between the eight late-18th-century homes. Reboard the trolley whenever you wish. Tours leave from the Tourist Center near City Hall. Call 568-6599 for details.

Check local listings for free concerts and other entertainment opportunities. In summer there are free **noontime concerts** in the Lewis Triangle (at the far end of Independence National Historical Park) and a nightly **sound and light show** at Independence Hall.

Shopping

Among the many off-price retailers in the area, we find the following offer the best for the money: The **Sweater Mill** sells both designer labels and garments made by talented craftspeople (115 South York Road, Hatboro); **Brothers Shoes** for designer footwear up to 25 percent off (in the Bourse and Krewtown Shopping Center); **Dan's Shoes** is where models shop for on-the-cutting-edge styles (1733 and 1126 Chestnut Street); and **Syms** for the occasional brilliant find amid masses of so-so ready-to-wear (1865 E. Marlton Pike, Cherry Hill, N.J., if you're staying or working near the Valley Forge Convention Center).

UNIQUELY PHILADELPHIA

Favorite Foods

We're not talking haute cuisine (although Philadelphia is currently enjoying new status as a mecca for serious gourmets)—we're talking plain street foods, the kind Philadelphia has *always* been famous for. Foods like hoagies (those meal-in-a-roll grinders), cheesesteaks (indescribable treats whose not-so-secret ingredient is Cheez-Whiz), soft pretzels with or without the mustard, and the sublimely rich ice cream made by the local Bassett's.

But best of all is Philadelphia's **Reading Terminal Market,** a covered food marketplace reminiscent of those found in European towns and cities. Established in 1893, this is no chic, trendy development, but a working market where farmers come to sell their produce, where butchers go back three generations, where dedicated food people prowl the crowded aisles, serious rapture in their eyes.

Go for lunch. Join the line at **Bassett's Original Turkey** where a sandwich of moist breast meat on just-baked bread with lettuce, mayo, and tomato will cost you $4.20. Sit anywhere—there are tables set up in every available space and everyone's welcome. Stop by **Pearl's Oyster Bar** for the best New England clam chowder you're ever likely to taste. Wander the aisles. You'll discover, sandwiched between sellers of raw ingredients, dozens of sellers of ready-to-eat specialty foods—Oriental, Mexican, German, Pennsylvania Dutch, vegetarian, and health foods. On Thursdays, Fridays, and Saturdays the market is even more crowded than usual because these are the days the Amish and Mennonite families come to sell their produce and wonderful home-baked specialties.

So come for lunch (it's closed at dinnertime) or come to browse, to shop, to take in the sights and smells, or to learn. It's an experience no visitor to Philadelphia should miss. Open 8 A.M. to 6 P.M., Monday through Saturday. Enter from 12th, Arch, or Filbert streets. It's also about

one block away from the Gallery shopping mall—you can make a day of
it.

DINING OUT

Philadelphia is becoming one of this country's great restaurant cities.
Aside from the great classic traditions, which are always welcome in any
fine-dining scene, foodies are delighted with the proliferation of innovative regional and nouvelle cuisines—the lighter fun side of dining out
as exemplified by Philadelphia's own restaurateur Steven Poses whose
Commissary, Frog, and City Bites have led the way to current trendy
dining-as-theater experience.

In Philadelphia the price ranges break down as follows: "expensive" means the average entrée is over $15; "moderate" if it's around
$10; and "inexpensive" if it's around $5.

The "top three" French restaurants in town, the ones everyone
has heard about, are also very expensive, ideally suited for client entertaining, and require advance reservations: **Le Bec-Fin,** 1523 Walnut Street,
567-1000; **Déjà Vu,** 1609 Pine Street, 546-1190; and **Deux Cheminées,** 251
S. Camac Street, 985-0367.

About **Bookbinder's:** there are two here, each appearing (at least
to the newcomer) to be the real thing. So if you're meeting someone at
Bookbinder's, make sure you both understand which one you have in
mind. Both are expensive and serve excellent seafood.

Bookbinder's Seafood House, referred to by locals as "the 15th
Street Bookbinders," is run by the Bookbinder family. It is less glitzy
than the other, good for entertaining clients, and is in Center City. 215
S. 15th Street. 545-1137.

Bookbinder's Old Original is on the site of the first restaurant
(before it moved to 15th Street) and is owned by the Taxin family. It is
more elegant, more touristy, with a colonial Philadelphia decor. It is in
East Philadelphia at 125 Walnut Street. 925-7027.

Center City Area

Apropos is trendy and popular with local businesspeople; it serves
a California-inspired menu. Convenient to Center City hotels and the
Academy of Music. Open seven days, including a Sunday brunch. Moderate. 211 S. Broad Street. 546-4424.

Commissary is a gourmet cafeteria serving salads, pastas, and
light fare in an upscale setting. Everyone loves to eat here; eating solo
is fun, too, because of the great people-watching possibilities. Open
until midnight most nights. Inexpensive. 1710 Sansom Street. 569-2240.

Corned Beef Academy is another inexpensive, trendy place that's
fun if you're dining alone. Typical deli specialties with some wonderful
homemade soups. Inexpensive. 121 S. 16th Street. 665-0460.

Day by Day is fine for light meals—salads, sandwiches, and soups. Very casual atmosphere. Closed on weekends. Inexpensive. 2101 Sansom Street. 564-5540.

Frog offers a marvelous blend of American, French, and Asian cuisines. The atmosphere is elegant—it's in a lovely old townhouse—and the clientele is decidedly upscale. Open seven days, with a Sunday brunch. Moderate. 1524 Locust Street. 735-8882.

The Garden specializes in lobster, veal, and beef prepared in the Continental manner. Lovely ambience, and in summer the outdoor garden is a special bonus. Open seven days. Moderate. 1617 Spruce Street. 546-4455.

Harry's Bar and Grill: Don't let the macho name put you off—Harry's is fine for dining alone or for meeting business associates. Lots of grilled meats, seafood, Italian specialties. Popular with neighborhood stockbrokers and other businesspeople. Closed weekends. Moderate. 22 S. 18th Street. 561-5757.

Hunan serves gourmet Chinese cuisine as well as several diet specialties including the Pritikin regimen. Very popular with local people. Open seven days. Moderate. 1721 Chestnut Street. 567-5757.

Il Gallo Nero features northern Italian specialties in a sophisticated setting. Patrons are a mix of musicians and urban sophisticates, all of whom dress up for this place. Moderate. 254 S. 15th Street. 546-8065.

Marabella's is where the trendy set meets to enjoy contemporary Italian cuisine. The menu is innovative and imaginative. Equally good for dining alone and for meeting clients who would appreciate the upbeat atmosphere. Moderate. 1420 Locust Street. 545-1845.

Natural Foods Eatery serves exactly what you'd expect—good, healthy, nutritious foods. The location is good, too—across the street from the Academy of Music. Open until 1 A.M. Inexpensive. 1345 Locust Street, 2d floor. 546-1350.

Silveri's is a real neighborhood bar that serves absolutely the best burgers in town. Other specialties: Buffalo-style chicken wings and homemade pastas. Inexpensive. 315 S. 13th Street. 545-5115.

Sushi International is our choice for Japanese specialties, sushi included. Near hotels and the financial district, it attracts both tourists and the business community. Moderate. 228 S. Broad Street. 732-7300.

Top of Centre Square is popular with the young, after-work crowd from the nearby corporations. Good view, good seafood specialties, good place to meet associates. Moderate. First Pennsylvania Bank Tower, 15th and Market streets. 563-9494.

East Philadelphia, Society Hill Area

Alouette serves French with an Oriental flair. Fine for dining alone or with a friend. The neighborhood is lovely and popular with locals. Expensive. 528 S. 5th Street. 629-1126.

West Philadelphia, University City Area

La Terrase serves classical and innovative French cuisine. Located on the university campus, it attracts the academic community as well as local businesspeople. Take a cab, or drive here and back. Moderate. 3432 Sansom Street. 387-3778.

South Philadelphia Area

Don't leave town without trying at least one of the dozens of wonderful restaurants in this old **Italian neighborhood.** Everyone has his or her own favorites—it's hard to go wrong. Be sure to taxi in and out of the area. Below South Street, between the two rivers.

PHILADELPHIA BY DAY

A major cultural center, Philadelphia is home to dozens of fine museums, historically significant collections, and important galleries. We have listed only a few favorites. Please check local listings for the complete picture.

Getting an overview of this town is an experience that is historical as well as educational. The history centers around the fact that **City Hall** has always been the tallest building in town, for tradition once dictated that nothing should rise higher than William Penn's hat on the Calder statue atop this wedding-cake building (alas, mid-1980s construction is changing all that). The education? You will see how logically the city is laid out with its gridwork of streets, and you'll recognize landmarks from the observation deck of this building that is dead center in the middle of town. Open weekdays from 9 A.M. to 5 P.M. Call 686-1776. For information on 12:30 tours, call 686-4546.

Independence National Historical Park, also known as "America's most historic square mile," makes sightseeing a breeze—major sites are next door to one another. We recommend you begin with the 28-minute John Huston film, *Independence,* which is shown at the Visitors Center, and then take in any of the following: the **Liberty Bell,** in its glass-enclosed pavilion; **Independence Hall,** with narrated tours throughout the day; **Congress Hall,** the site of Congress from 1790 to 1800. There are about a dozen other sites as well. The park is in the heart of town at 3d and Chestnut streets. Call 597-8974, or 627-1776 for taped information.

Philadelphia Museum of Art is the third largest fine arts museum in the country. (And, yes, those exterior stairs are the ones Stallone's Rocky raced up in triumph.) In addition to many splendid permanent collections, the museum is known for its period rooms in which all elements—floor, ceilings, doorways—are authentic. Open Tuesday through Sunday (limited access on Tuesdays). 26th and Benjamin Franklin Parkway. Call 763-8100, or 787-5488 for recording of daily schedule.

A few blocks away from the Museum of Art is the **Rodin Museum,** which houses the largest collection of Rodin sculptures and drawings outside France. His famous *The Thinker* does his pondering outside the front door. 22d Street and Benjamin Franklin Parkway. 763-8100.

The **Atwater Kent Museum** traces 300 years of Philadelphia's history as well as the life of founder William Penn. Antiques share the spotlight with everyday objects, maps, and city-planning charts. Open daily, except Mondays, 9:30 to 5 P.M. 15 S. 7th Street. 686-3630.

The **Franklin Institute Science Museum and Fels Planetarium** is not for kids only! You're never too old to enjoy the chance to walk through a giant human heart, experience hands-on sci-fi technology, or watch the wonders of the universe under the dome in the planetarium. Open seven days. 20th Street and Benjamin Franklin Parkway. Call 448-1200, or 564-3375 for taped information.

Pennsylvania Academy of the Fine Arts is the oldest museum and art school in the nation. Tracing three centuries of American art, the collection is world-class. The Victorian building, itself a work of art, has been designated a National Historic Landmark. Closed Mondays. Broad and Cherry streets. Call 972-7600, or 972-7633 for recorded information.

The **United States Mint,** which also happens to be the world's largest, is right here in town. Self-guided tours lead you through the process, including actual coins being made. (Sorry, no samples given.) Open daily. 5th and Arch streets. 597-7350.

THE SHOPPING SCENE

You can choose your shopping pleasures in Philadelphia. There's everything here from urban malls like the Gallery to specialized areas like antiques on Pine Street and fabrics on 4th Street, from retailing giants like Wanamaker's to rows of designer boutiques along chic Walnut Street.

Center City Shopping Districts

The Bourse, a landmark Victorian building, now houses some of the city's most elegant retailers along three tiered levels: Cacharel, St. Laurent Rive Gauche, Howard Heartsfield (wearable art fashions), and Chackey & Wolpe (estate jewelry) are just a few. 21 S. 5th Street. 625-9393.

Newmarket offers several levels of shops and restaurants in a colonial-type marketplace setting. Not as exciting as some of the other complexes in town. 2d and Pine streets. 627-7500.

South Street is an emerging area—new places seem to spring up overnight. It's the "in" place to wander, especially on Friday and Saturday nights when the narrow sidewalks become nearly impassable. Shops here have everything from high fashion to vintage and punk. Interesting places to eat, too.

Antique Row, for furniture, not clothing. From 9th to 12th streets on Pine Street.

Wholesalers and retailers line both sides of the street along **Jeweler's Row.** Prices are as varied as the shops. Sansom Street between 7th and 8th.

The Gallery at Market East is a vast urban mall that stretches along Market Street from 9th to 11th. The anchor stores are J. C. Penney, Gimbel's, and Strawbridge & Clothier, with 150 shops and restaurants in between. Call 925-7162 for details.

John Wanamaker is a retailing institution. Generations have grown up knowing that "meet me at the eagle" means to meet at the large statue that marks center stage of this balconied atrium department store. Shop here for a complete spectrum of fashion, including some good designer boutiques. 13th and Market streets. 422-2000.

Because shopping is a highly personal activity, we offer some of our personal favorites:

Nan Duskin for European and American designer fashions and accessories. And **Hermès Boutique** adds further status. 1729 Walnut Street. 567-1700.

Replique for fabulous fakes—copies of jewelry and accessories. Warwick Hotel, 17th and Locust. 546-1170.

Past, Present, Future showcases unique handcrafts and gift items. Toys, too. 24 S. 18th Street. 584-0444.

Mooshka for young trendy fashions and accessories. 132 S. 17th Street. 988-0891. 510 South Street. 923-6781.

Knit Wit for fabulous, high-fashion looks. 208 S. 17th Street. 735-3642.

Strega Ltd. features expensive, unusual European-designed shoes. 1505 Walnut Street. 564-5932.

Touches is a tiny store crammed full of special jewelry, belts, and handbags. 1500 Locust Street. 546-1221.

M. Finkel and Daughter is known for quality quilts and folk art. 936 Pine Street. 627-7797.

We've listed the gigantic shopping mall out in **King of Prussia** in the "At Leisure" section of this chapter because of the time required both to travel there and to cover the hundreds of shops once you arrive. It is definitely worth a visit if you have the time.

PHILADELPHIA BY NIGHT

In 1985 Peter Davis wrote in *New York* magazine that "there isn't a doubt in my mind that Muti now presides over the country's premier orchestra." And that's not local chauvinism—*New York* has its own symphony to write about. Riccardo Muti's **Philadelphia Orchestra** performs at the Academy of Music from September through May. Broad and Locust streets. Tickets at the box office or through CHARGIT. 800/223-0120.

The venerable **Academy of Music,** oldest opera house in the United States, also hosts the **Pennsylvania Ballet** (665-8051); the **Philly Pops,** directed by Peter Nero (735-7506); and the **Opera Company of Philadelphia** (721-5811).

The **Pennsylvania Opera Theater** (known around here as "T-Pot") presents two operas in English each year. 923-8768.

Academy of Vocal Arts Opera Theater is a school that also performs at the Walnut Street Theater and in the AVA's Helen Corning Warden Theater at 1920 Spruce Street. 735-1685.

Annenberg Center at the University of Pennsylvania is a performing arts center for theater, dance, music, and film, including the **Philadelphia Drama Guild** and the **Festival Theater for New Plays.** 3680 Walnut Street. 898-6791.

Painted Bride Art Center presents experimental and professional performances in music, dance, theater, and poetry. 230 Vine Street. (Take taxis to and from this location). 925-9914.

Pennsylvania law restricts ticket agents to a maximum surcharge of $5 or 25 percent—so all charges are similar. **Ticketron** (885-2515 for recorded message) has many outlets, including Wanamaker's in Center City. **CHARGIT** is toll-free: 800/223-0120.

LATE-NIGHT PHILADELPHIA
JAZZ CLUBS

All That Jazz: until 1:30 A.M. Monday through Saturday. One block from Rittenhouse Square, 119 S. 18th Street (over Le Wine Bar). 568-5247.

Borgia Cafe: until midnight Sunday through Thursday; until 1 A.M. Friday and Saturday. 408 S. 2d Street. 574-0414.

DISCO

élan: until 2 A.M. weeknights; until 3 A.M. on weekends. In the Warwick Hotel, 17th and Locust streets. 546-8800.

Quincy's: until 1:30 A.M. on weekends. In the Adam's Mark Hotel, City Line Avenue and Monument Road. (About 15 minutes from Center City—take taxi.) 581-5000.

BARS AND PIANO BARS

Dicken's Inn Tavern: until 2 A.M., with folk music and occasional bag pipers. 2nd and Pine streets. 928-9307.

Mace's Crossing: until 11 P.M. Attracts after-work crowd for happy hour. In season the outdoor patio is very popular. 1714 Cherry Street. 854-9592.

The Piano Bar at the Frog Restaurant: 5 to 7:30 cocktail hour; call for other times. 1524 Locust Street. 735-8882.

The Piano Bar at the Commissary: features jazz piano during the week, and a vocalist on Friday and Saturday. 1710 Sansom Street. 569-2240.

Pierre's: until 2 A.M. every day except Monday. At the Adam's Mark Hotel. City Line Avenue at Monument Road. (About 15 minutes from Center City—take taxi.) 581-5000.

North Star Bar: has a cabaret on the second floor and jazz downstairs on Tuesday and Thursday. Open seven days. 27th and Poplar streets. (Art Museum area—take taxi.) 235-7827.

COMEDY CLUB
Comedy Works: open Wednesday through Saturday nights. Special guests and an amateur night. 126 Chestnut Street (third floor of Middle East Restaurant). 922-5997.

AT LEISURE

There's so much to see and do in Philadelphia that can't possibly be covered during a single business trip. If you have the time, this is certainly a worthwhile city for one of those business/pleasure minivacations.

Day-Tripping

The **Brandywine Valley,** ancestral home turf of the du Pont clan, includes a dozen or more mansions, formal gardens, and museums of great beauty. Among them are the don't-miss **Winterthur,** the **Brandywine River Museum** (three generations of Wyeths), the **Hagley Museum,** and **Longwood Gardens.** Christmas displays are especially spectacular here. In northern Delaware, about 30 miles southwest of the city. Call 800/441-8846 for information and directions.

The Barnes Foundation: one of those "best-kept secrets," the Barnes is regarded as the finest collection of early modern artists in the world. Contains 180 Renoirs, 60 Matisses, 59 Cezannes as well as works by Picasso, Seurat, Rousseau, El Greco, and others. One hundred visitors are issued reservations on Fridays and Saturdays (an equal number of nonreservation visitors are admitted as well). On Sundays, entrance is limited to 50 with and 50 without. Call 667-0290 well in advance. The Barnes is about a 15-minute drive or train ride from Center City. 300 Latches Lane, Merion, PA 19066.

While you're in Merion, you might enjoy lunch at any of the following: **Eviva,** northern Italian cuisine, Montgomery Avenue, Narberth, 667-1900; **Over the Rainbow,** health foods, vegetarian and Pritikin menus available, 856 Montgomery Avenue, Narberth, 664-8589; and **Morgan's Bistro,** contemporary European, Time Building, Ardmore, 642-5100.

New Hope, once an artists' colony, is now a quaint town of art galleries, charming shops, and historic landmarks. Despite the area's popularity with those who collect antiques there are still some wonderful buys here, but you have to be sharp to find them.

In warm-weather months, you might try a one-hour excursion on the **New Hope mule-drawn barge rides** along the Delaware Canal. 862-2842. **Mother's Restaurant** is our choice for a place to eat in town. In summer, there's garden dining. 34 N. Main Street. 862-9354.

Valley Forge National Historic Park is about a 30-minute drive away in Montgomery County. Site of the 1777–78 winter encampment of General Washington, this 20-acre park includes remnants of the original quarters and artillery, as well as a modern center that shows films and exhibits of this important part of our nation's history. Routes 363 and 23. 783-7700.

Note: Washington's Birthday is, understandably, a major event here. Call 783-7700 for tickets and information.

And while you're in the neighborhood, don't forget the **King of Prussia shopping complex**—over 300 shops and restaurants. Anchor stores include Bloomingdale's, Abraham and Straus, Bamberger's, Wanamaker's, Gimbel's, and J. C. Penney's. Route 202 in King of Prussia.

Atlantic City, the Las Vegas of the East, is about 90 minutes away by car or special bus. If you're a gambler, nothing else needs to be said. But there's also sand and ocean in this fabled resort town, not to mention some good seafood restaurants like **Knife & Fork Inn,** Atlantic and Pacific avenues, 609/344-1133; and **Dock's Oyster House** at 2405 Atlantic Avenue, 609/345-0092. For shopping, check out **Ocean One,** a mall shaped like an ocean liner. About 125 stores and specialty food shops here.

In Town

In addition to seeing the museums and historic sites you weren't able to visit during the business week, you should also try these for your leisure days in town:

Concerts and Croissants at the University Museum. Fresh coffee and croissants are served in the glass-walled Potlatch Restaurant that overlooks the Mosaic Gallery gardens during concerts that begin at 11:30 and end at 1 P.M. (just as the galleries open). Seating is limited. Call 898-3024 or 898-4000.

Biking on Kelly Drive along the Schuylkill River. Rentals along Boat House Row, at Plaisted Hall, just west of the Art Museum. Call 235-0617.

Head House Square, which runs from Pine Street to Lombard Street on 2d (adjacent to Newmarket shopping complex), is where local craftspeople, artists, and entertainers display their talents and sell their wares. Noon to midnight on Saturdays; noon to 6 P.M. on Sundays; from late June until September.

Stroll along **South Street,** where a renaissance has produced an eclectic variety of shops and restaurants. The best place in town to people-watch, it's also great for bargains, crafts, and whatever strikes your fancy. We especially like **Paper Moon,** for international publications; **The Works Gallery; Mooshka's** for eclectic fashions; **Gargoyle's** for antiques; and **Third Street Jazz** for old recordings.

You can also take an **Old City** self-guided **walking tour** that begins at Christ Church and ends at Penn's Landing. Plan on at least two hours. The tour is free, available at the Tourist Center (see "Getting Familiar"). While you're there, pick up a copy of the Official Map of Philadelphia to help you locate the sites.

And while you're at Penn's Landing, why not hop aboard a **Rainbow River Tour** out onto the Delaware River for a different perspective of the area? Cruises vary in length and leave from the Penn's Landing Boat Basin, Delaware and Lombard streets. 925-7640.

Sunday Customs

Brunch in Philadelphia can be as formal and elegant or as relaxed and casual as you want it to be. The best in town are **Apropos** (casual), 211 S. Broad Street, 546-4424; **La Terrasse** (informal), 3432 Sansom Street (on the University of Pennsylvania campus), 387-3778; **Bridget Foy's** (casual), 200 South Street, 922-1813; **Famous Delicatessen** (casual), 4th and Bainbridge streets, 922-3274; **élan** (dressy casual), **The Warwick,** 17th and Locust streets, 546-8800; **Knave of Hearts** (informal), 230 South Street, 922-3956; and **The Fountain** (elegant), Four Seasons, One Logan Square, 963-1500.

Spectator Sports

Philadelphia sports fans like the title "The City of Winners." Their pro teams have been in the running for league titles for the past 10 years.

The **Sports Complex** (Broad Street and Pattison Avenue) includes Veterans Stadium and the Spectrum (site of the 1985 LIVE-AID concert).

Basketball's NBA **Philadelphia '76ers** play at the Spectrum from October to April. For ticket information, call 339-7676.

Also in the Spectrum, the NHL **Flyers** play **hockey** October through April. 755-9700.

The **Philadelphia Phillies** play National League East **baseball** in Veterans Stadium. Call 463-1000.

Also playing in Veteran's Stadium are **football's** NFL **Eagles.** 463-5500.

Rowing regattas along the Schuylkill River offer exciting glimpses into a different sort of sporting life. Call 978-6919 for times and information.

DIAL-A-SPORT is a recording of latest scores, who's playing what and where. 976-1313.

Active Sports

Fairmont Park holds some 8,700 acres of open spaces that include jogging and bridle paths, tennis courts, golf courses, and ball fields as well as rental boats and bikes. Call 686-0053 for details.

Bikers can also take advantage of the river route (see "In Town").

Phoenix

HOTELS

1 Best Western Central Plaza
2 Arizona Biltmore
3 Camelback Inn Resort
   & Golf Club
4 Embassy Suites
5 Phoenix Hilton
6 Hyatt Regency
7 Pointe at Squaw Peak
8 Hotel Westcourt

LANDMARKS

A Art Museum
B Civic Plaza and Convention
   Center
C Desert Botanical Gardens
D Mansion Club
E Metro Center

F Pueblo Grande Museum
G Sky Harbor Airport
H Squaw Peak Park
I State Fairgrounds
J Visitors Bureau
K Zoo

PHOENIX

GETTING YOUR BEARINGS

Phoenix is a modern city that has not forsaken its past. The sophistication here is more evident to us with each subsequent visit. Innovative architecture and a thriving business atmosphere remain interwoven with traditional southwestern architecture and an emphasis on Indian culture and style.

With one of the most fertile climates for business in the United States, this city affords traveling businesswomen their due. Professional females are found in all levels of business in Phoenix, and although we have been called "honey" or "sweetie" on occasion, these familiar terms are not meant to be derogatory, just an outgrowth of the earlier wild west way of life.

The nation's ninth largest city welcomes newcomers. Entrepreneurs abound in almost every realm except heavy industry. Both ranchers and transplanted or visiting corporate executives from New York and Chicago work happily together. This is just the type of business climate we like best: open, friendly, and easy. We find that, unlike executives in other parts of the country, even people at the highest level here are easily reached by phone.

The freshness of the city is symbolized by Mayor Terry Goddard, who sees it this way: "Phoenix is an adolescent who doesn't know what he wants to be when he grows up." From the newness of the community springs a cordiality and the hope that comes with uncharted territory.

On closer inspection we find that Phoenix is not terribly well planned and is quite spread out. Despite its designation as a city, we have often noted that it does not feel like a metropolitan area. Rather it seems more like a large suburb with pockets of resort areas dotting the desert landscape. This feeling persists perhaps because Phoenix is indeed one of the nation's largest cities in terms of area with 375 square miles, up from 100 square miles in 1940.

During the winter, Phoenix and the surrounding area—dubbed the Valley of the Sun—is overrun with folks locals call "snowbirds." They are referring to the mostly older transplanted people who escape here for the sun. And although some Phoenicians deride these visitors for their slow driving and clogging already congested streets, they don't complain too loudly—the snowbirds keep Phoenix's economy fat.

Although this is not an especially dangerous city, we recommend the same precautions that apply elsewhere. Lock your doors while driving as well as when you park. Neighborhoods to avoid when alone are South Phoenix and secluded desert areas. The banks of irrigation canals are a popular place to jog or walk, but if you are going to exercise there after dark, don't do it by yourself.

WHAT TO WEAR

In Phoenix, generally, women dress according to what others in their field wear. Downtown tends to be more conservative than the adjacent cities of Scottsdale, Tempe, and Mesa where you're likely to notice the influence of southern Californian styles. Suits are appropriate everywhere, and rarely will you confront high fashion, although one woman who sits on the Superior Court bench is said to wear the most elegant clothes in town—under her robes. Women do dress for seasons here; in fact, we found that only tourists choose summer clothes in winter months. Don't make the same mistake if you want to blend in: it may be a summery 75 degrees to you, but in Phoenix it's winter.

WEATHER WATCH

Although the Chamber of Commerce calls Phoenix summers warm, we deem the 120 degrees it can reach in July—HOT. The average yearly temperature is a balmy 72 degrees. Spring and fall bring sunny warm days, usually in the 70s. Summer temperatures can be considerably warmer, but low humidity makes all but the hottest days comfortable. Winters are also warm and sunny, dipping into the 40s at night and rising to the 60s and low 70s during the day. Average rainfall is only seven inches per year.

GETTING THERE

The major airport in the Phoenix area is **Sky Harbor International Airport** (273-3300), the 16th busiest in the United States. Sky Harbor is also 99 percent operational, the highest figure in the country. The airport has more than 200 commercial flights arriving and departing every day. Sixteen major airlines are served by three terminals. Republic Airlines has more flights in and out of the city than any other.

Visitor information centers for ground information are located at terminals 2 and 3 at the airport. One very popular way to get from the airport to downtown Phoenix is the Sky Harbor Transportation shuttle service (275-8501). Call ahead of time and they will be waiting for you; a typical fare to central downtown is about $5.

Cabstands are found at the terminals. Phoenix cabs are deregulated, so determine the price before you set foot in the cab; an approximate fare to the downtown area is $7. Two cab choices are Air Courier Cab of Arizona (244-1818) and Arizona Taxi (253-TAXI).

Car Rentals

Renting a car is far and away the best bet for getting around. Some car rental agencies to choose from at the airport are:

American International	273-6181
Dollar	275-7588
Avis	273-3222
Hertz	267-8822

Leaving the airport on 24th Street is your best bet for downtown Phoenix and areas north and west. Hohokam Expressway South connects with Interstate 10 South toward Tucson, Tempe, and Mesa.

GETTING AROUND

We have found that public transportation (only buses) is greatly lacking here. The Phoenix Transit System (257-8426), however, does provide some scheduled bus service in Phoenix, Glendale, and Scottsdale on weekdays and Saturdays and Tempe and Mesa on weekends. For $2.50 an all-day pass issued by the Phoenix Transit System allows you to board and re-board as much as you like.

Taxis do not cruise, but you are likely to find them at the larger hotels. Otherwise call Air Courier (244-1818) or Arizona Taxi (253-TAXI).

If you feel like going about in high style with a matching high budget, try Carey Limousine (996-1955).

GETTING FAMILIAR

Phoenix and Valley of the Sun Convention and Visitors Bureau

505 N. Second Street, Suite 300   602/254-6500
Phoenix, AZ 85004

Out-of-town visitors can call 800/528-0483 for reservations at more than 100 area resorts as well as transportation assistance. The in-state number is 800/221-5596. Other visitor information centers are located at the north-

Hotel	Concierge	Executive Floor	No-Smoking Rooms	Fitness Facilities	Pool	24-Hour Room Service	Restaurant for Client Entertaining	Extra-Special Amenities	Electronic Key System	Business/Secretarial Services	Check Out Time	Frequent Guest Program	Business Traveler Program	Average Rate
Arizona Biltmore	●		●	●	●		Orangerie Gold Room Adobe	●			12 noon	Westin Corporate Rate	Westin Corporate Rate	$140 $112
Camelback Inn Resort & Golf Club	●			●	●	●	Navajo				12 noon		Camelback Adventures	$130–$145
Embassy Suites	●		●		●		Ellington's				12 noon			$110 $ 94–$105
Phoenix Hilton			●	●	●		Sandpainter				1 p.m.	Hilton Stars	Hilton Plan	$ 70–$130 $ 75 corp.
Hyatt Regency	●		●		●		Compass Hugos The Paris Cafe	●			12 noon	Gold Passport Program	Gold Passport Program	$ 85–$105 $ 95
Pointe at Squaw Peak	●				●		Beside the Point	●			12 noon			$120 $ 88
Hotel Westcourt	●	●			●		Trumps			●	12 noon	Inner Court	Club West	$ 92 $ 82 $112

west corner of Adams and Second streets downtown, and terminals 2 and 3 at the airport.

Phoenix is an aggressive contender for convention business. Many of the larger conventions and meetings are held at:

Phoenix Civic Plaza Convention Center
225 E. Adams Street   602/262-6225
Phoenix, AZ 85004

The *Arizona Republic* is the city's morning paper and has the largest circulation. The *Phoenix Gazette,* published by the same company, is the afternoon paper. The *New Times,* which is free and comes out on Wednesdays, is a good source of listings for cultural events and restaurants. For some insight into Valley life-styles, try *Phoenix* magazine, *Phoenix Home and Garden,* and *Arizona Living.*

Quick Calls

AREA CODE 602   Police 262-6151
Weather 273-7511 or 261-4000   Visitor information 254-6500
Time 1-976-7600

AT YOUR SERVICE

Arizona Biltmore
24th Street and Missouri   Toll-free reservations: 800/528-3696
Phoenix, AZ 85016   Local number: 955-6600
                                                   Telex: 165709

This hotel is a star in Phoenix. Although we have never seen them, we are told that everyone from Gloria Swanson to the chairman of Reynolds Metals have stayed here. The five-star, 500-room resort is located on 39 acres of beautifully landscaped grounds. The lobby is castlelike because it is all stone. It is light and airy and decorated in greens and blues with an Aztec influence. The Biltmore dates back to 1929 and has a great art deco pool to prove it. There is golf and tennis; and a lovely part of the canal bank runs through the golf course, making a great walking path. A coed fitness center offers nutritional consultation on request.

   Orangerie is the hotel's gourmet restaurant. The **Gold Room** and **Adobe** restaurants are more casual choices. Drinks are served throughout the large lobby area; entertainment accompanies cocktail hours on most evenings.

Westcourt

10220 N. Metro Parkway East
Phoenix, AZ 85051

Toll-free reservations: 800/858-1033
Local number: 997-5900
Telex: 706629

This suburban hotel is set amid a lush garden. With 300 rooms, it is a luxury property, yet reasonably priced. Located on the west side, the hotel is adjacent to the 250-story Metro Center. Honeywell and other computer corporations are nearby on the northwest side of Phoenix. The Plaza Court level is a private floor: as women business travelers, we like the convenience. It offers a private concierge, free Continental breakfast and hors d'oeuvres, an honor bar, and the *Wall Street Journal.* Secretarial and other services can be arranged through the concierge.

Trumps is the restaurant and bar. Entertainment is provided in the evenings.

Embassy Suites

2630 E. Camelback Road
Phoenix, AZ 85016

Toll-free reservations: 800/EMBASSY
Local number: 955-3992

A top pick for women who want roomy accommodations, this pink hotel is just a minute's walk from Biltmore Fashion Park with I. Magnin and Saks Fifth Avenue. The hotel opened in March of 1985, and its lobby is an atrium filled with 10,000 plants, a fountain, and a creek.

All 232 suites include a kitchen, two phone lines, and two television sets. A complimentary, made-to-order breakfast is served daily in the atrium, but it can be taken to your suite or the pool if you wish. A two-hour complimentary cocktail hour takes place in the lobby daily and is a comfortable spot for women alone since it is so busy.

The restaurant, **Ellington's,** serves both lunch and dinner in a casual atmosphere.

Marriott's Camelback Inn Resort and Golf Club

5402 E. Lincoln
Scottsdale, AZ 85253

Toll-free reservations: 800/228-9290
Local number: 948-1700
Telex: 9109501198

This is the classic Scottsdale resort; it is an adobe circa 1937. Decorated in earth tones of peach and rust, it blends right into the environment. We are especially fond of the big fireplace in the lobby, which warms everything during cool desert evenings. With 413 rooms, this is the perfect place for combining business and all types of recreation, year-round. Special services are available for business travelers.

The **Navajo Room** is for informal dining, and the **Chapparal Room** is the gourmet restaurant. The **Oasis Lounge** is not recommended for women alone—this is a very conservative place.

Pointe at Squaw Peak

7677 N. 16th Street
Phoenix, AZ 85020

Toll-free reservations: 800/528-0428
Local number: 997-2626
Telex: 4953529

Each time we approach this resort nestled in a beautiful mountain area, we get excited. Wildly popular since its opening in 1978, it offers horseback riding, golf, and tennis. Each of the 600 sleeping accommodations is either a suite or a villa. The deluxe villa section caters specifically to business travelers, with a concierge service that can arrange for any business need. Complimentary breakfast buffets and cocktails are served. The bars are casual and easygoing with many young people around. The suites have large work areas in the living rooms, and the villas have dining room tables. Washers and dryers are available as well as one-day laundry service.

The resort has four restaurants. **Aunt Chilada's** offers Mexican food; **Hole in the Wall** has western specialties; **Beside the Pointe** is potpourri; and **Pointe of View** is the deluxe dining area. All the restaurants are very casual.

Hyatt Regency Phoenix

122 N. Second Street
Phoenix, AZ 85004

Toll-free reservations: 800/228-9000
Local number: 252-1234
Telex: 668347

This striking bronze and stone building overlooks the Civic Plaza. The lobby is in Hyatt's signature atrium style, highlighted by a modern steel starlike sculpture. The 711-room property boasts the Mobil Four-Star and AAA Five-Diamond awards.

Senor Hugo's, with Mexican or American food, is decorated with handwoven Indian fabrics; the **Catina** is a popular bar. From the **Compass,** a revolving rooftop restaurant and lounge, diners can see the mountains and desert.

Phoenix Hilton

Central Avenue and Adams Street
P.O. Box 1000
Phoenix, AZ 85001

Toll-free reservations: 800/445-8667
Local number: 257-1525

Located in downtown Phoenix, this hotel has a lobby decorated in rich burgundy, forest green, mauve, and taupe with contemporary chandeliers and green plants. We are especially fond of the weaving of a southwestern landscape behind the registration desk. Another interesting work of art is the continuous hand-painted desert mural on the walls next to the escalator. The 534-room hotel is a Mobil Four-Star and AAA Four-Diamond property and has recently undergone a transformation. Meeting space spans 34,000 square feet in 19 modern rooms. The fifth floor is a recreation area with heated pool, carpeted jogging path, equipment, and free weights. We enjoy the feeling of exercising and seeing the tall buildings of the city surrounding us.

Restaurants include the gourmet **SandPainter Restaurant,** and the **Citrus Grove Coffee Shop. Clementines** is a bar that also serves an elaborate weekday buffet.

ON A BUDGET

Hotel

Best Western Central Plaza

4321 N. Central Avenue   Toll-free reservations: 800/528-1234
Phoenix, AZ 85102   Local number: 277-6671

This hotel, near all points of interest in the Phoenix area, recently added new furniture to all its rooms as well as a Jacuzzi. The 190-room property offers complimentary limousine service via a courtesy phone to and from Sky Harbor International Airport. All the rooms overlook either the garden or the pool area. A 24-hour movie channel is offered in the room at no additional cost. Be sure to ask about their corporate rate.

Whether you are staying at this hotel or not, the **Backstage Restaurant,** located at the front, is a good bet for a slim budget. We are very comfortable eating alone here, and the desserts are especially good.

DINING OUT

Phoenix is a casual, open city; as traveling businesswomen we have encountered no problems dining alone or entertaining at business meals for clients or colleagues. The following restaurants are suitable for lunch or dinner, alone or with associates. We have defined as moderate dinners costing around $15. Above that is expensive, below that, inexpensive.

The **Impeccable Pig** is a restaurant we frequent because we love the atmosphere. It is in an antique store that is well known for its quilts. Menu changes daily. Moderate. 7042 E. Indian School, Scottsdale. 941-1141.

Oscar Taylor has an old Chicago atmosphere and is one of the most popular places to eat in the history of Phoenix. Emphasis is on ribs and meat, although fresh fish and lighter fare will make nonmeat eaters happy as well. Reserve several days in advance. The bar is a popular after-work haunt for single yuppies. Moderate. 2420 E. Camelback, Phoenix. 956-5705.

The **French Corner** is especially convenient for lunch. French nouvelle cuisine is the fare here, with specials daily. Reservations are suggested. Inexpensive. 50 E. Camelback Road. 234-0245.

Orangerie at the Biltmore Hotel is very snooty and very elegant. It has won *Travel/Holiday* and Mobil awards. We like this for a splurge, and especially enjoy the garden setting. Very expensive. 24th Street and Missouri. 954-2507.

The **1895 House Restaurant** is located in the oldest Victorian house in Phoenix. It has won several Best of Phoenix awards and is a short walk from downtown hotels. The food is international. Moderate. 362 N. Second Street. 254-0338.

Josephina's is the place we go when we crave continental Italian gastronomic delights. Expensive. 2650 E. Camelback Road. 957-6888.

The **Golden Eagle Restaurant,** a downtown Phoenix favorite, is located on the 37th floor of its building, so the lights of the city glitter all around during dinner. The menu is Continental; shrimp Pernod and Caesar salad are among the specialties. Expensive. 201 N. Central. 257-7700.

Etienne's Different Pointe of View sits atop a mountain peak rather than a building. A 360-degree view of the desert is an accompaniment to dining here. The fare is French, and the restaurant has won a *Travel/ Holiday* award. Etienne's, which is very comfortable for the lone woman diner, has the most extensive wine list in Arizona. Expensive. At the Pointe at Tapatio Cliffs. 11111 N. 16th Street. 866-7500.

We go to **Steven** for the best of nouvelle cuisine with a California influence. Only the freshest of ingredients are used. This restaurant is perfect for client entertaining. Expensive. 4333 N. Brown, Scottsdale. 941-4936.

The **Petite Cafe** is a French restaurant with a separate back room that is very conducive to business meetings. The menu is innovative. Moderate. 7340 E. Shoeman Lane, Scottsdale. 947-5288.

PHOENIX BY DAY

For a great **overview** of the entire city, try lunch, dinner, or Sunday brunch at the revolving **Compass Room** restaurant at the Hyatt Regency. We love to relax and just stare out into the desert.

The **Phoenix Art Museum** has changing exhibits as well as a permanent collection that includes 18th- and 19th-century European, western American, and Asian art, and 20th-century costumes. Open Tuesday through Saturday. 1625 N. Central Avenue. 257-1222.

The **Heard Museum** has an impressive collection of southwestern cultural and ethnic artifacts. Anthropology and primitive arts are the focus. 22 E. Monte Vista Road. 252-8848.

The **Arizona Mineral Resource Museum,** at the state fairgrounds, has a beautiful array of minerals and ores, the largest collection in the state. Most are indigenous to the area, but some come from around the country. Free admission. 255-3791.

We have been known to get lost for hours among the 8,000 plants at the **Desert Botanical Garden.** Classes, workshops, lectures, and tours are offered for people who want to enhance their knowledge of the desert specimens. Admission $2.50. 1201 N. Galvin Parkway. 941-1225.

The **Phoenix Zoo** has over 1,000 animals on 125 acres. Guided safari tours are a good way to get around without getting tired. A special Arizona exhibit features native animals. Admission $4. 5810 E. Van Buren Street. 273-1341.

The **Pueblo Grande Museum** is located on Hohokam Indian ruins, which are thought to have been occupied from 200 B.C. to A.D. 1400. This is a great place to get off the treadmill for an hour. Admission 50 cents. 4619 E. Washington Street. 275-3452.

Another place to convene with nature is **Squaw Peak Park,** which has horseback-riding and walking trails in the desert. Free admission. 2701 Squaw Peak Drive.

THE SHOPPING SCENE

Phoenix and Scottsdale are perhaps best known for their wide selections of Indian jewelry, rugs, and art. The most authentic (and we have been warned time and again to beware of imitations) are found in Scottsdale shops, although **Lee's Indian Crafts** at 1833 E. Indian School in Phoenix shouldn't be missed by the serious collector.

Park and Swap will be of interest to flea market fans every Saturday and Sunday, October through May. Check the local newspaper for the exact time. You'll find a wide array of merchandise here, in the parking lot of the Greyhound Racing Park on East Washington and 40th Street. The usual will predominate however; don't expect London's Portobello Road.

There is very little shopping in the downtown area with the exception of the **Park Central shopping mall** at Osborn and Central Avenue. This mall includes major department stores, Goldwater's and Diamond's, and about 70 shops.

Another good shopping opportunity is at **Biltmore Fashion Park,** Camelback at 24th, with department stores, I. Magnin and Saks Fifth Avenue, and upscale boutiques. We have found shopping here to be a good investment of a few well-deserved shopping hours.

Metro Center, I-17 and Peoria, is a megamall with several major department stores and shops of all varieties. This mall has a massive selection of items for middle America.

The **Borgata,** 6166 N. Scottsdale Road in Scottsdale, intimidates us out of our wits. If you have to look at the price tags in these ultraexpensive shops, you can't afford to buy here!

PHOENIX BY NIGHT

For great theater you are better off heading for New York; Arizona is making great progress but Phoenix is not yet known for its great theatrical productions. There are no half-price services in town, but tickets are reasonably priced. **Ticketron** is located in Diamond's Department Store. 267-1246.

Professional theater performances are offered at the **Arizona Theater Company,** with the season running from October through May. 17 E. Thomas Road. 234-2892.

Phoenix Little Theatre is a community playhouse. 25 E. Coronado Road. 254-2151.

The **Phoenix Symphony Orchestra,** known as the southwest's finest, plays at the Civic Plaza Convention Center and Symphony Hall. The symphony is often joined by world renowned guest artists for classic, chamber, and pops performances. 225 E. Adams Street. 262-6225.

Frank Lloyd Wright designed the **Gammage Center for the Performing Arts** at Arizona State University in Tempe. It is an acoustical masterpiece and offers many different types of cultural events. 965-3434.

The **Camelback Plaza Cinema,** in Scottsdale, features foreign films. 7001 E. Highland. 945-6178.

LATE-NIGHT PHOENIX

Phoenix is not known for its late-night activity; however, a few spots may be interesting.

For information about jazz performances around the state, listen to KJJZ-FM (91.5) or call the **Arizona Jazz Hot Line** at 254-4545.

Tête-à-Tête is sharp looking and avant-garde in spirit. The French-accented bistro serves drinks until 1 A.M. 7117 E. Third Avenue, Scottsdale. 945-6888.

Casablanca comes alive at **Rick's Cafe Americana.** This hot night spot resembles the original Rick's in everyone's favorite Bogey movie. Ask Sam to play it again until 1 A.M. 8320 N. Hayden Road, Scottsdale. 991-2233.

The **Pony Express** has the city's most popular happy hour. A large video dance floor features three screens. This nightclub is big with the younger set. In Tower Plaza, 40th and Thomas. 244-2694.

AT LEISURE

In Town

If you want to stay close to town and would like someone else to do the work so you can have fun, here are a couple of tour options.

We were fascinated by the lore surrounding the old Wrigley Mansion, which is now the **Mansion Club** and is shown daily by Mansion Club Tours (955-4079). This 1929 southwestern-style adobe is being restored to its full grandeur and contains a great deal of its original furniture.

Arizona Desert Mountain Jeep Tours (948-9192) is a good choice for staying close to the city, yet getting out in nature. The Jeep picks you up at your hotel and takes you to such places as Salt River Indian Reservation, Superstition Mountain, and a cowboy ranch for horseback riding. In Tonto National Forest there is a nature walk and survival talk; such wildlife as wild mustangs and bald eagles are plentiful.

Day-tripping

After a week of business, look for some wonderful opportunities for day or weekend getaways from Phoenix. There are tremendous contrasts within this state. For example, during the winter months you can sun by the pool on a Saturday morning and ski in the afternoon on a 10,000-foot peak just three hours to the north.

The **Grand Canyon,** one of the great natural wonders of the world, is a four-hour drive from Phoenix. The South Rim is open all year and features nature walks and mule rides down the canyon trails. The North Rim is open from mid-May to October. Lodging is available for visitors who want to spend more than a day. Call for reservations. 800/528-0483.

Sedona, a cultural community of 9,000, has become a mecca for art lovers and collectors who are drawn here by more than a dozen commercial galleries featuring paintings, sculpture, and art objects. We, however, prefer to look at the deep red rock formations and multicolored buttes that make this resort area unique in the country. When NBC newsman Hugh Downs first saw pictures of the red rock country, he thought they were faked. "Rocks aren't red," he said. But now he knows better; he lives just north of Scottsdale and commutes to New York. The Sedona–Oak Creek area is only two and a half hours from Phoenix, and it's a charming community well worth visiting.

While you're in town don't miss Tlaquepaque (say: T-lockey-pockey), a tile-for-tile reproduction of a small village just outside Guadalajara, Mexico. Amid the Spanish Colonial arches, wrought-iron balconies, and courtyards of this Arizona/Mexican version are dozens of upscale shops, art galleries, and restaurants. Everything is top-of-the-line here; there's nothing schlocky in Tlaquepaque—not a tacky ashtray or an I ♥ Arizona T-shirt in sight.

If you stay over, try the Slide Rock Lodge (282-2531). And, to make this visit truly memorable, sign on for a sunset tour of the backcountry in an open jeep. Defying gravity, you will scale sheer rock face, bouncing and scrambling up and up until you're on top of one of those red-rock buttes, watching the setting sun stain the vistas even redder. Call Pink Jeep Tours at 282-5000.

The Sedona–Oak Creek Canyon Chamber of Commerce: 282-7722.

The small community of **Prescott** was founded after the discovery of gold in 1863 and was the first permanent capital of the Arizona territory. Less than two hours from Phoenix, Prescott gives the visitor a sense of the years gone by in the wild west. Wonderful hiking and camping here.

The **Apache Trail** winds through spectacular desert mountain scenery from Phoenix to the city of Globe northeast of the valley. Highlights of the trip include the dams and lakes of the Salt River. The entire trail takes about four hours round-trip and is an excellent way to see desert scenery at its finest.

The **Mogollon Rim** (pronounced Muggy-own) is a magnificent geological fault. The dramatic face of the rim, jutting up a mile, consists of a multicolored wall of rock, dotted by pine, manzanita, and oak shrubs. The Rim Country, as this area is called, was made famous by writer Zane Grey, who spent many hours writing, hunting, and fishing in this country. You can visit the cabin where he lived and see some of his memorabilia. Located about an hour and a half from Phoenix, Rim Country is cool and comfortable in the summer and serves as a mecca for cross-country skiers during winter snowfalls.

Tucson, a quieter and smaller city than its northern counterpart, is two hours from Phoenix. Tucson reflects more Spanish culture than Phoenix does and is more relaxed. Old Tucson, a wild west movie set, is interesting; it's located near the Arizona Sonora Desert Museum, a renowned natural desert habitat.

Sunday Customs

Sundays in Phoenix are low-key. It is a great time for strolling along the canal banks, visiting a museum, or picnicking at Squaw Peak Park.

Brunch is popular here, and there are several good places to partake of this meal. The best spot to catch a bit of elegance on Sunday morning is at **Palm Court.** The atmosphere is luxurious and the food plentiful. Scottsdale Conference Resort. 991-3400.

For a more casual approach, try **Munch-a-Bagel.** We go here when we are feeling a lox and bagel attack, and there are not many places to go for this food in the city. Dr. Brown's sodas are an added plus. 5111 N. Seventh Street. 264-1975.

If there is one place that is *the* Phoenix brunch tradition, it is **El Chorro Lodge.** Open from October through May, brunch served outside on a sunny winter morning can't be beat. The food is always reliable and the atmosphere of the 1930s building is interesting. Make reservations at least two days in advance. And if you want a Bloody Mary or mimosa with your meal, plan to eat at noon or later; state law prohibits the sale of liquor before 12 on Sundays. 5550 E. Lincoln Drive, Scottsdale. 948-5170.

Spectator Sports

If you would rather spectate than participate, **Arizona Downs** has thoroughbred racing from October through May. 942-1101.

The **Phoenix Suns National Basketball Association** has its home court at Veterans Memorial Coliseum. Call 263-SUNS for tickets.

Greyhounds race year-round at Greyhound Park with pari-mutuel wagering. Clubhouse dining is an added attraction. 273-7181.

Active Sports

Phoenicians are more apt to be interested in your tennis game or your golf handicap than in your career goals. On Friday evenings you may be asked to go on a twilight hike or a bike ride in lieu of indulging in the cocktail hour. So when visiting Phoenix, make sure you pack your most sporting attitude and attire.

Phoenix is so geared to **golf and tennis** that a special section in the Visitor's Guide lists over 75 golf courses and 1,000 tennis courts in all.

If **hiking** is your thing, Squaw Peak is a favorite of Phoenicians. This 2.4-mile walk takes you 2,608 feet up from the 1,400-foot base for a great view of the city. Wear your grubbiest shorts and sweatshirt; this is no place for raspberry velour. It is also no place to be without a jug of water.

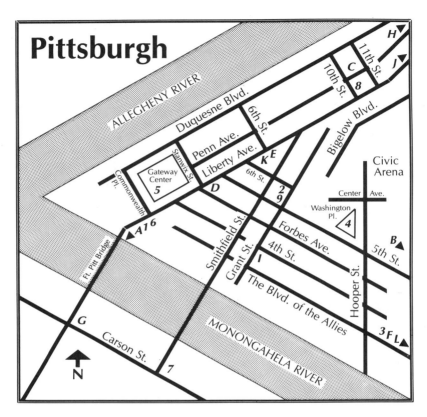

Pittsburgh

HOTELS

1 Airport Hilton
2 Bigelow
3 Harley Hotel of Pittsburgh
4 Hyatt Pittsburgh
5 Pittsburgh Hilton
and Towers
6 Pittsburg Marriott
7 Sheraton Hotel
8 Vista International
9 William Penn Hotel

LANDMARKS

A Airport
B Carnegie Institute
C Convention Center
D Convention and Visitors
Bureau
E Heinz Hall
F Frick Art Museum

G Mount Washington
H New Zoo (Highland Park)
I One Oxford Center
J Pittsburgh Ballet Theater
K Pittsburgh Symphony
L Schenley Park

PITTSBURGH

GETTING YOUR BEARINGS

From the minute you hit town until the minute you leave, expect to hear a lot about Pittsburgh's status as America's "most livable city"—a title bestowed in 1985 by Rand McNally's *Places Rated Almanac.* Residents have mixed feelings about this honor and so, probably, will you.

Although the title seems to imply that Pittsburgh is the best place to live in the United States, we all know this is pushing reality a bit. Certainly, one must admire the incredible turnaround wrought by the various urban rehabilitation projects in Pittsburgh: the air is once again breathable, rivers now run almost free of pollution, and the urban landscape has experienced a general rebirth. But you'll be hard-pressed to find anyone, particularly a local woman in business, who will insist that this city is utopia.

It is a town of contradictions: at once the "most livable city" but with pockets of hard-core urban blight; a city with a blue-collar reputation that also supports and maintains some of the country's most prestigious cultural and educational institutions; home of the third largest concentration of Fortune 500 companies with, at the same time, the largest majority of women who list their occupation as "homemaker"; the birthplace of both the AFL and N.O.W.

It is undeniably a tough town for women. "We're years behind the times," laments one local businesswoman. Progress seems to be hampered by a high-industry, ultraconservative attitude that shapes the local corporate power structure. We've heard reports of negative attitudes—even of one outrageous episode in which a visiting woman executive, unaware of the prevailing mood, was subjected to lewd (and unprintable) abuse by her male "peers."

Perhaps it is because of this prevailing good-old-boy mentality that networking among businesswomen is so effective in this town. One publication, *The Pittsburgh Woman,* targets the female manager and offers networking information; and Women in Business is a long-standing organization representing member women in 88 fields of business. See "Uniquely Pittsburgh" for details of this group's program. Out-of-town women are welcome to take advantage of its resources.

Women with a game plan seem to do all right in the Pittsburgh business community. Although it is a conservative place to do business, patience, persistence, and respect for the past can be the route to success. Old attitudes die slowly, however, and most Pittsburgh residents still believe that family life is next to godliness and a woman's place is you-know-where.

Although it began as a steel city, white-collar workers now outnumber blue collars four to one. Pittsburgh is number two in the U.S. in multinational headquarters and is the nation's third largest company-headquarter city. Thus it attracts ever-increasing numbers of yuppies and, hence, a proliferation of trendy neighborhoods replete with chic boutiques and restaurants and gentrified streets. The current "in" neighborhoods (*Pittsburgh Magazine* calls them "Yup-It-Up Neighborhoods") are Shadyside, Squirrel Hill, and Mt. Lebanon. Almost everything you, as visitor, will do—meet, eat, shop, or attend performances—will be in either downtown or in these areas that lie east of downtown.

Physically the city layout makes getting around very easy. Imagine a < shape, with the legs representing the two rivers that border the city. The point where they meet, aptly called "The Golden Triangle," is downtown Pittsburgh. You can also imagine the number of bridges necessary in a water-dominated place like this; the locals claim the city has more bridges than Venice. You'll probably find yourself heading across some of them on your way to Station Square or Mount Washington.

Downtown is an eclectic mix of old and new buildings where Gothic blends harmoniously with modern. We feel this architectural stew is at its best at night when lighting smooths the rough edges. The entire downtown area is only 1.1 square miles, so you should have little trouble finding the major landmarks: Grant Street, the "money street" (lots of flamboyant architecture here, too); One Oxford Center, a 46-story tower office building (with a 5-story atrium that houses some of the best shops in the country); One Mellon Bank Center; Warner Center; and PPG's Gothic "ice castle," a multibuilding complex made of, what else, plate glass, which also contains a winter garden and a food court.

The only part of town where we don't feel comfortable or safe is around Liberty Avenue, where prostitution and peep shows thrive. Otherwise, this is a fairly safe city. Of course, you should never let your guard down; apply the customary urban street-smart rules here as elsewhere.

WHAT TO WEAR

As you have gathered, women on the way up the corporate ladder in this town must bow to local conservativism. Skirted suits and skirts paired with jackets are safest here. You'll see very few business dresses worn— and even fewer pantsuits. Until you develop a "feel" for the attitudes of the local people you'll be working with, it's best to play it safe in the fashion department—even after working hours. Put those trendy dressy dresses on hold and opt for the classic silk shirtdress—at least until you're sure the local group is ready for your own special fashion statement.

WEATHER WATCH

To paraphrase the ever-popular *Places Rated Almanac,* Pittsburgh enjoys a better year-round climate than Phoenix, Fresno, or Fort Lauderdale. This should come as a welcome surprise as you shiver in the icy blasts coming in off Lake Erie on a winter's day. Local weatherman, Joe Dinardo of WTAE-TV describes it as, "a decent, moderate climate," but he does admit to some intense cold snaps in winter and heat waves in summer.

GETTING THERE

Greater Pittsburgh International Airport is now the hub for USAir and Allegheny Commuter. You can also take advantage of direct flights between Pittsburgh and London's Heathrow Airport, which are available via British Airways. A dozen or so major carriers service this airport. Information number: 778-2525

The airport lies about 14 miles west of the city; driving time is 30 to 40 minutes. Expect cab fare to run about $25. Best bet: we have discovered that for this same $25 we can ride into town in comfort in the white Lincoln town cars of the Limo Center. This company accepts credit cards, the drivers are dependable, and you can use the in-car phones to update your appointments. You must reserve in advance (923-1650). An Airlines Transportation Bus costs only $6 from the airport to your hotel. Catch this near the baggage claim area, but check first to be sure your hotel is on their route (471-8900).

Car Rentals

You'll need to rent a car if your business is outside the downtown area. Even if you stay at an outlying hotel to be near your appointments, you'll still want to come into town for restaurants and sightseeing. Don't expect to find on-street parking when you need it. An all-day garage or lot costs $6 or $7.

Agencies at the airport:

Avis	262-5160
Ajax (not in terminal: use courtesy phone or call 262-4020)	
Budget	262-1500
Dollar	262-1300
Hertz	262-1705
National	262-2312
Thrifty	264-1775

GETTING AROUND

Taxis in this town have a reputation for being dirty, uncomfortable, and in general disrepair; they may even break down en route. Other than that, they're great. Sometimes a cruising cab can be hailed, but it's safer to call ahead. If you call from downtown, there's almost no waiting time; from other parts of town it may take up to 15 minutes. Rides are metered: $1 on the drop and $1.40 each additional mile. We've found Yellow Cab to be the most reliable: 665-8100.

Forget about using the buses to get from appointment to appointment. The local PAT Transit system is primarily for commuting to such areas as Shadyside and Oakland. Exact fare, $1, required.

The new subway, the Light Rail Transit System, currently services only a relatively small area, but plans call for it to link downtown with the suburbs to the south someday. Known as "the world's shortest subway," it covers only three downtown stops (Gateway, Wood Street, and Steel Street), but it's free, at least until 7 P.M. when the fare goes to 60 cents. You can also use the subway to cross the river to Station Square, a trip that will cost you 60 cents.

GETTING FAMILIAR

Greater Pittsburgh Convention and Visitors Bureau
Four Gateway Center   281-7711
Pittsburgh, PA 15222
Can provide information on business services, restaurants, and hotels.

Greater Pittsburgh Chamber of Commerce
Three Gateway Center   392-4500
Suite 1400
Pittsburgh, PA 15222

David L. Lawrence Convention Center
1001 Penn Avenue   565-6000
Pittsburgh, PA 15222

The *Post-Gazette* is a morning newspaper published every day except Sunday. A special weekend section appears on Friday, and a business section on Tuesday. The *Pittsburgh Press* comes out every evening and Sunday and contains a business section on Tuesday. *Pittsburgh Magazine* includes local dining reviews, a calendar of films, theater, music, and exhibits, as well as WQED (public TV) and QED/FM listings. *The Pittsburgh Woman* offers networking information and lists events of interest to women. The *Pittsburgh Business Journal* covers the city's business scene. Call 922-2404 if you can't find it anywhere. The *Pittsburgh Business Times* also covers the city's business scene. Call 391-7111 if unavailable.

```
─────────────────── Quick Calls ───────────────────
┌─────────────────────────────────────────────────────────────┐
│                                                               │
│   AREA CODE 412                          Emergencies 911      │
│   Time 921-7272                    Recording of Daily Events  │
│   Weather 936-1212                               391-6840     │
│                                                               │
└─────────────────────────────────────────────────────────────┘
```

UNIQUELY PITTSBURGH

There's no excuse to feel alone and out-of-it while you're in Pittsburgh. You can be in immediate contact with women in your field or in other professions just by calling this number: 232-2615. That will put you in touch with Florence Hiedovitz, who has directed Pittsburgh's Women in Business program in conjunction with Kaufmann's Department Store for the past 17 years. As you can imagine, with all that experience Ms. Hiedovitz is now the best source of information for who's achieving what in which area for whatever industry in town.

Her organization is free and open to all professional women. Out-of-town visitors are invited to join Pittsburgh's professional women at lunch every Wednesday at noon at Michael's Restaurant (in Kaufmann's). Heidovitz says there's no need to call ahead, but we feel more comfortable letting her know that we're planning to attend.

The group's other functions of interest to businesswomen include advisory board meetings, lunches with editors of *Savvy* magazine (called "Savvy Tables"), ceremonies to honor outstanding women in the 88 fields represented by members, and many ongoing events.

"We're in touch with every professional group in town," says Ms. Hiedovitz. "Any woman who wants a connection should give us a call or drop by our fifth-floor offices." It's free, of course.

AT YOUR SERVICE

Airport Area

Airport Hilton

Parkway West at White Swan Park   Toll-free reservations: your local Hilton
Pittsburgh, PA 15231   Reservation Service
                                                  Local number: 262-3800

At press time this hotel was undergoing a total refurbishing. The final results—both physical and in its policies—promise to be ideal for women traveling alone. The hotel runs a 24-hour courtesy van to and from the airport and to and from the nearby Research and Development Park, a

	Concierge	Executive Floor	No-Smoking Rooms	Fitness Facilities	Pool	24-Hour Room Service	Restaurant for Client Entertaining	Extra-Special Amenities	Electronic Key System	Business/Secretarial Services	Check Out Time	Frequent Guest Program	Business Traveler Program	Average Single Rate
Airport Hilton Inn	●			●	●		Rennick's		●	●	1 p.m.	Family of Friends	Corp.	$ 75 corp. / $ 77 reg.
Hilton and Towers	●	Exec. Towers	2 floors	●			Sterling's	●	●		1 p.m.		Corp.	$ 80 corp. / $ 98 corp. in Tower / $118 Tower
Hyatt at Chatham Center		Regency Club	● floor	●	●		Hugo's			●	12 noon	Gold Passport	Private Line	$ 85 reg. / $112 Regency Club
Marriott/Greentree		●	●	●	●		Ashley's	●		●	1 p.m.	Honored Guest Awards	Corp.	$ 84 corp. / $ 91 reg. / $104 ex. floor
Sheraton at Station Square	●	Exec. Tower		●	●	●	River's Edge		●	●	12 noon	(with American Airlines)	Corp.	$ 88 corp. / $ 91 reg. / $118 Tower
Vista International	●	●	●	●	●	●	American Harvest	●	●	●	12 noon	Premium Award		hotel opening Dec. 1986
William Penn	●	Crown Service	●			●	Terrace Room		●	●	1 p.m.	Preferred	Corp.	$ 90 corp. / $105 reg. / $115 ex. floor

free-trade zone for numerous French and Italian companies, as well as corporate headquarters for important U.S. chemical companies. If your business is in this park, you may never have to leave the airport area.

The formal restaurant, **Rennick's** (formerly named the Butcher Block) with its piano bar, is suitable for client entertaining. We found **Boots Saloon** to be not particularly welcoming for a woman alone. Perhaps the newer version will offer a more updated attitude.

Downtown Area

Hyatt Pittsburgh at Chatham Center

112 Washington Place Toll-free reservations: 800/228-9000
Pittsburgh, PA 15219 Local number: 471-1234
Telex: 812364

A 404-room Hyatt with all the usual Hyatt services—Regency Club, Gold Passport, Private Line Club—you've come to expect. Not all rooms have desks or work spaces, though. If you will require these, be sure to request them when you reserve your room. The clientele here is mostly corporate people and sports teams. The health facilities are excellent, and you can work out with the pros.

A nice plus here is the **Captain's Table,** a system that offers single diners the opportunity to eat with other singles. One Hyatt regular told us this is one of the reasons she keeps returning. She recounted many tales of interesting evenings that resulted from meeting others at the Captain's Table. The gourmet restaurant is **Hugo's Rotisserie and Wine Bar** (over 60 varieties, and a free tasting). **The Whiskey Rebellion,** the in-hotel bar, is small, dark, and clique-ish with locals.

Pittsburgh Hilton and Towers

Gateway Center Toll-free reservations: your local Hilton
Pittsburgh, PA 15222 Reservation Service
Local number: 391-4600

An 800-room hotel with an 80-room Executive Tower that provides the business traveler with all the privacy, amenities, and services we've come to expect from concierge floors. The location, on the tip of the downtown peninsula, is handy to businesses and offices.

Sterling's is their formal dining room, an attractive setting of forest green, etched glass, and brass—a very comfortable place, excellent for client entertaining. Here, too, is a **Captain's Table** arrangement where singles are invited to join other solo diners and share companionship during the meal. It beats reading a book or staring into space—unless, like Garbo, you want to be left alone. The hotel bar, **Three Rivers Pub,** has a macho, superjock atmosphere that can be off-putting unless you feel like being one of the guys.

Sheraton Hotel at Station Square

Smithfield and Carson streets Toll-free reservations: 800/325-3535
Pittsburgh, PA 15219 Local number: 261-2000

Great location, with river views, and right in the heart of historic and fun Station Square. Also near Three Rivers Stadium and the Convention Center. Contemporary, with a high-tech atrium design, the hotel offers a two-floor Penthouse Tower in addition to its 293 guest rooms. We've heard conflicting reports about the tower. One guest reports she prefers a regular single to these rooms, but others prefer the built-in luxuries of a concierge floor.

Rivers Edge is their specialty restaurant; **Waterfall Terrace,** in the atrium lobby, serves casual meals. **Mr. C.'s Showplace** is a traditional lounge with live entertainment—usually singers with "dancing girls," followed by disco music. This place appears to be more popular with locals than with hotel guests.

Vista International
Liberty and Penn at 10th Street   Local number: 281-3700
Scheduled to open in December 1986, the arrival of a Vista International on the Pittsburgh scene represents several firsts: it will be the first world-class hotel in town, and its size (610 rooms) and facilities will enable Pittsburgh to host major conventions for the first time. Like its sister hotels in New York, Chicago, Los Angeles, and Washington, D.C., this Vista International will offer such services as 24-hour communications, secretarial and room service, large state-of-the-art conference and meeting facilities, full-service fitness center, and three Vista Executive Floors. An enclosed overpass will connect the hotel to the David L. Lawrence Convention Center.

The American Harvest, the signature fine-dining restaurant in all Vista Internationals, will feature creative cuisine, with the spotlight on American regional and seasonal specialties.

William Penn Hotel
530 William Penn Place   Toll-free reservations: 800/228-3000
Pittsburgh, PA 15230   Local number: 281-7100
                              Telex: 866380
This seems to be the local hotel nobody can agree on. We've talked to women who swear by it and wouldn't dream of staying anywhere else in town. We've also heard stories from women guests who were spooked by the long corridors lighted only with what were described as 15-watt bulbs. One indisputable fact: this hotel is now a Westin and it is definitely on the way up, undergoing a total revitalization that includes reducing the 840 rooms to 600. The William Penn has a style all its own: it's described as a "grand old hotel from 1916," is listed in the National Register of Historic Places, and is conveniently located right on Mellon Square. Crown Service, their concierge levels, occupy three floors. The room service menu includes a spa cuisine complete with nutritional information.

The Terrace Room, the formal dining room, is not only fine for client entertaining but also the "in" spot in town for breakfast meetings.

The Palm Court, an elegantly baroque haven complete with crystal, palms—the whole works—currently features afternoon tea. This custom is not very big in Pittsburgh, so it might be discontinued.

Southside Area

Pittsburgh Marriott/Greentree

101 Marriott Drive	Toll-free reservations: 800/228-9290
Pittsburgh, PA 15205	Local number: 922-8400
	Telex: 7106442016

Just ten minutes southeast of downtown, this 489-room hotel also offers a full-service concierge floor complete with such security features as a key for the elevator and a concierge escort to your room at check-in. You can also request cookies and milk, instead of a brandy, with your turn-down service. The decor, which was refurbished in 1985, is contemporary and appealing throughout, with rose and teal tones predominating, and accents of blonde wood and brass.

Ashley's is their fine-dining restaurant; **the Market** is for light meals. We've had nothing but good reports on **Cahoots,** the hotel bar. One frequent visitor raves, "This is the best-looking and laid-out bar in the city. Great for when you're meeting people, and singles also feel comfortable."

ON A BUDGET

Hotels

Harley Hotel of Pittsburgh

699 Rodi Road	Toll-free reservations: 800/321-2323
Monroeville, PA 15235	Local number: 244-1600

An interesting mix of excellent and not-so-great, this Helmsley hotel ("Leona should be ashamed," was one design assistant's critique) is well situated for anyone in the fashion industry, as it is located near both the Expo Mart and a heavy concentration of retail mall shops. Rooms have good reading lights, nice amenities. Indoor and outdoor pools and fitness facilities available. Average single is $56; business travelers studio with Murphy bed is $60.

Water's Edge bar offers music every night.

Bigelow

Bigelow Square	Toll-free reservations: 800/225-5858
Pittsburgh, PA 15219	Local number: 281-5800

Located downtown across from the Civic Arena, this hotel is especially ideal if your business in town will last more than a few days. The Bigelow specializes in renting newly furnished apartments on a short-term basis. On-site amenities include restaurant, maid service, 24-hour front desk, room services, health club, coin-operated laundry—plus the convenience of apartment-style living. Studios rent from $60 daily or $301 weekly.

Restaurants

Bahama Mama Cafe lets you build your own Dagwood-style sandwiches or salads from their vast array of selections. It's a casual, fun kind of place, inexpensive and open until 11 P.M. The Bank Center Shops (downtown), 414 Wood Street. 562-0889.

Almost any of the cafes and restaurants in the downtown **Kaufmann's** are ideal for casual, inexpensive meals. Open for dinner on late-store nights—Mondays and Thursdays.

Mr. K's Market Inn is lively, friendly, and casual. Steaks, shish-kebabs, Greek salads. Open for lunch and dinner, closed Sundays. Market Square (near PPG Plaza). 391-0180.

Upper Crust (Town's Home of Homemade) guarantees the "best breakfast in the city." We go along with that, and especially with their delicious lunches that range from $3 to $6. 429 Forbes Avenue (downtown, between Kaufmann's and the courthouse). 281-1600.

Colonnade Cafeteria for top-of-the-line breakfasts and lunches. We particularly like their baked goods and affordable, no-nonsense prices. There are two locations: Union Trust (281-3420) and Gateway Two (281-2482).

Books & Bread is a comforting sort of place where you can snuggle up with a good book (over 12,000 titles here) on a window seat and enjoy a free cup of coffee or tea. The atmosphere is friendly, antiques abound, and there are even homemade bread and baked goods for sale. Closed Sundays, open late Thursdays. 4284 Rte. 8 (Castle Town Square South), Alison Park. 486-7112.

DINING OUT

You will notice that most of the restaurants we've recommended are closed on Sundays. We didn't do this to complicate your weekend planning; it's hard to find any place in town that does stay open on Sunday. Local people accept this situation, explaining that the many ethnic groups in town prefer to remain close to their traditional roots—and being home with the family on Sundays is an important Old World tradition. Do not fear starvation on Sundays, however. Station Square, a two-minute subway ride away, offers dozens of restaurants, cafes, and stores that stay open every day of the week.

For Pittsburgh, we're calling anything over $45 for a dinner for two expensive.

Best bet for **power breakfasts** is the **Terrace Room** of the **William Penn Hotel** at 530 William Penn Plaza (262-3800). Best for **power lunching: de Foro's, Common Plea,** and the **Carlton**—all described below.

Downtown

De Foro's, considered to be one of the area's best, serves Continental cuisine. Fairly dressy; draws a business crowd. Closed Sunday. Expensive. In the Lawyer's Building, 428 Forbes Avenue. 391-8873.

Common Plea was voted "best moderately priced restaurant with best business lunch in town" by readers of *Pittsburgh Magazine.* Seafood and veal with an Italian focus. No dinner reservations accepted. Closed Sunday. Expensive to moderate. 308 Ross Street. 281-5140.

Garden on the Square is fairly casual, a good place both for dining alone and for entertaining clients. Italian cuisine. Reservations required for lunch. Closed Sunday. Moderate. 430 Market Street (in Market Square). 765-3185.

The Wine Restaurant offers your choice of tasters: two-ounce or six-ounce glasses or by the bottle from a large international selection. Cuisine is "new American" and light, with emphasis on presentation and nutritionally sound combinations. Trendy. Closed Sunday. Moderate to expensive. One Oxford Centre. 288-WINE.

Lawrence's serves Continental cuisine in a dressy atmosphere. Closed Sundays. Moderate. 613 Penn Avenue. 391-1414.

Lizzie Farrell's is ideal for solo dining when you don't feel like a big deal. Light cuisine—salads, pasta, baked brie—served in pretty surroundings. Casual dress. Closed Sunday. Moderate to inexpensive. 134 Sixth Street. 471-2336.

1902 Landmark Tavern is one of the most authentically restored taverns in western Pennsylvania. Noted for prime ribs, oyster bar, seafoods, and chowder. Closed Sunday. Moderate. 24 Market Square. 471-1902.

Piccolo Piccolo features an antipasto bar, seafood and pasta specialties. Attracts a business clientele. Closed Sunday. Moderate. One Wood Street. 261-7234.

Tambellini-Woods is another downtown landmark; the seafood is best. Italian cuisine. No reservations needed. Closed Sunday. Moderate to inexpensive. 213 Wood Street. 281-9956.

The **Carlton** is very posh, an "in" spot for sophisticates. Dress up for this one. American cuisine—ribs, steaks, seafood specialties. Closed Sunday. Moderate. Mellon Bank Building, Grant Street. 391-4099.

Station Square/Southside

Grand Concourse seats over 400 people and is one of the most attractive restaurants we've seen. The former waiting room of the old Pittsburgh & Lake Erie terminal, it is blessed with vaulted ceilings, Edwardian marble, stained glass, and polished woods. Varied cuisine. Mostly business crowd at lunch; dinner crowd is mixed. Also lovely for Sunday brunch. Expensive to moderate. One Station Square. 261-1717.

Guido Cartwright's Ribber City Saloon features northern Italian specialties in a clubby atmosphere. Good for hosting business dinners. Not too dressy. Moderate to inexpensive. 1805 E. Carson. 481-1805.

Mount Washington

Christopher's is *the* place if you want to dine with a view. Ride up in an exterior glass elevator for a spectacular view of the city and the junction of the three rivers. A special occasion restaurant with Continental cuisine and good wine list. Dressy. Live entertainment on Friday and Saturday nights. Closed Sunday. Moderate. 1411 Grandview Avenue. 381-4500.

Shadyside/Squirrel Hill

Jimmy Tsang's specializes in Mandarin, Hunan, Shanghai, and Cantonese dishes. Try the honey shrimp and the Mongolian beef. Casual, family-style place. Moderate. 5700 Centre Avenue, in the Kennilworth Apartment Building, Shadyside. 661-4226.

La Normande is known for serious classic French cuisine. Voted Pittsburgh's best by most food critics and writers. Dinners only. Closed Sunday. Expensive. **Le Bistro** is the casual, cafe-type version of La Normande. Good food, moderately priced. Dinners only. Closed Sunday. 5030 Centre Avenue, Shadyside. 621-0744.

Poli's is considered by many to have the best seafood in the area. (The word is: go to Grand Concourse for atmosphere—but Poli's has the best food.) Luncheon specialty is the French omelet. Closed Monday. Moderate. 2607 Murray Avenue, Squirrel Hill. 521-6400.

North Hills

Rico's offers good Italian dishes in a lovely setting with great views. Closed Sunday. Moderate. 2330 Evergreen Road (off Babcock Boulevard). 931-1989.

Strip District

Roland's introduced Pittsburgh to authentic New Orleans Cajun with a Creole sizzle. Crayfish, that beloved finger food, is the house specialty. And they're open for Sunday brunch with a Dixieland band. 1904 Penn Avenue. 261-3401.

Monroeville (East)

D'Imperio's is a dressy place, serving Continental specialties like salmon in puff pastry, shrimp with Roquefort, steak Taranto. Open seven days. Expensive. 3412 William Penn Highway. 823-4800.

West (near Airport)

Hyeholde is a delightful country inn (winner of four stars from Mobil—the only one in town). Dressy. Continental cuisine. Try the excellent local fish called Virginia spots. Closed Sunday. Expensive. 190 Hyeholde Drive, Coraopolis. 264-3116.

Dinner on the Water

Choose either the Captain's Dinner Dance Cruise or the Tropical Island Dinner Cruise aboard the Gateway Clipper Fleet. Cruises leave from Station Square Dock. 355-7980.

PITTSBURGH BY DAY

Merely walking the streets of this city is a delight to the eye. Pittsburgh's founding industrial giants like Mellon, Frick, and Carnegie wanted to be remembered also as patrons of beauty and art and spent vast sums erecting elaborate Gothic-style buildings. Today these legacies grace almost every street of the city. Great cathedrallike structures share air space with high-tech designs—stunning juxtapositions that turn even a routine walk into a architectural minitour.

Beginning, as we always prefer to do, with an overview of an unfamiliar city and its layout, we recommend the breathtaking views from atop Mount Washington. Take either the Monongahela or Duquesne Incline aboard elegant little railcars that were built back to 1870 and updated in 1963 for the five-minute ride to the top. From this vantage point you can see graphically displayed how the three rivers created the strategically located Pittsburgh. Daily until 1 A.M.; costs 60 cents each way. 381-1665.

For river-level sightseeing, we like the Gateway Clipper Riverboat Cruises with their wide range of sightseeing possibilities: lunch and dinner cruises, one-day vacations, even shopping cruises, and, of course, plain old sightseeing trips aboard their paddlewheel riverboats. Cruises leave from Station Street Dock. Call 355-7980 for times and rates.

Carnegie Institute—Museum of Art, itself an architectural work of art, houses a vast collection of French impressionists, postimpressionists, 19th-century American works. Contemporary artists are in the Scaife Gallery. The museum also exhibits ancient collections—Egyptian, Greek, Middle Eastern. This is truly a world-class museum. Closed Monday; open until 5 P.M. 4400 Forbes Avenue, Oakland. 622-3300.

Carnegie Institute—Museum of Natural History is one of this country's six largest natural history museums. Over 5 million pieces including Indian and Egyptian artifacts; entire halls of gems and botanical species. Closed Monday; open until 5 P.M. 4400 Forbes Avenue, Oakland. 622-3270.

Frick Art Museum exhibits its Italian Renaissance, Flemish, 18th-century French tapestries, Russian silver, and Chinese porcelain collections in its own precious jewellike setting. Count yourself lucky if you're in town for the special musical performances offered at Easter and Christmas time. Closed Monday and Tuesday. Free admission. 7227 Reynolds Street, Point Breeze. 371-7766.

Schenley Park Nature Museum and **Phipps Conservatory** offer free guided tours through vast tropical and subtropical settings that feature countless exotic plants and cacti. There are also four special seasonal shows. Schenley Park, Oakland Civic Center. Call for information: 255-2375.

The Store for Art in Crafts is part gallery and part store, showcasing such exhibits as Wearable Art, New Collectibles, and Year's Best Crafts. You can purchase these one-of-a-kind creations by talented artists and artisans; just think of it as investment buying. Displays change every month or so. Free admission. 719 Allegheny River Boulevard, Verona. 828-6121.

Westmoreland Museum of Art showcases American artists like Winslow Homer, Benjamin West, Mary Cassatt. Also many changing exhibits. Free admission. Closed Monday. 221 N. Main Street, Greensburg (outside city). 837-1500.

THE SHOPPING SCENE

Like most cities, Pittsburgh has its fair share of suburban malls, some of which—like Monroeville—are quite remarkable. However, Pittsburgh's renaissance has produced some excellent downtown (read "convenient for visitors") shopping areas, attractive atrium complexes with seemingly endless varieties of shops, in addition to the traditional downtown department stores.

Downtown

Kaufmann's, known as "The Everything Store," and **Horne's** are the major department stores. In addition to the range of merchandise you'd expect to find in a large department store, Kaufmann's also offers a complimentary shopping and wardrobe service (call Joni Ostrow at 232-2940) and a well-established service for businesswomen (see "Uniquely Pittsburgh" for details). Kaufmann's, located at the corner of Fifth Avenue and Smithfield, is open daily from 10 A.M. to 5:30, and until 9 P.M. Mondays and Thursdays. Horne's, at Stanwix Street and Penn Avenue near Gateway Center has the same hours. Please note: do your department store shopping during the week, because both stores are closed on Sunday.

Monroeville Mall, reputed to be the largest on the East Coast, is about a 30-minute drive east of the city on Business Route 22. Open Sunday from noon to 5 P.M.; daily from 10 A.M. to 9:30 P.M.

In-Town Malls

One Oxford Center is a five-story atrium with 30 heavy-duty designer shops: Maud Frizon, Giorgio Armani, Ferragamo, Yves St. Tropez, Charles Jourdan, Polo/Lauren, Ungaro, Kenzo, Valentino—to name-drop a few. Located at 301 Grand Street at 4th Avenue.

Molly Moses, on the 3d level of Oxford Center, is where you should head for some truly luxe European designer fashions: Versace, Rykiel, Soprani, the area's only Fendi Boutique, even a Ben Kahn Fur Salon. Lots of upscale services here, too, like the complimentary limo to and from your hotel (it will also deliver your purchases) and the pampering you receive while you ponder your high-fashion decisions. 642-6710.

The **Bank Center Mall** presents its shops in the appealing interior of five turn-of-the-century buildings that have been converted and interconnected. Saks Fifth Avenue shares space with the small boutiques. Wood Street and 4th Avenue.

PPG Place, an important item on your list of sights to see—a Gothic "ice castle," a fantasy built entirely of plate glass, of course—also offers 26 boutiques, a delightful food court, winter garden, and charming street performers throughout. In Market Square.

The Shops at Station Square, just across the river via the Smithfield Bridge, are housed in two Victorian railroad warehouses. About 70 shops offer everything from cookware to antiques and fashions. Really more for gift/impulse items than for serious shopping.

If you need to augment your dress-for-success wardrobe while in town, we can recommend the following: **Professional Woman,** One Oxford Center, 301 Grant Street (765-1220), and also in the Monroeville Mall, Business Route 22 (856-7555); **Brooks Brothers,** 600 Smithfield Street at Mellon Square (471-2300); and **Larrimor's,** 522 William Penn Plaza at Mellon Square (471-5727). **Post Horn,** a division of J. G. Hook, offers fashions at discounts of 33 to 60 percent at The Shops at Station Square, 3 Freight House Shop (765-1800).

For fun shopping and browsing, wander **Walnut Street** in **Shadyville.** Imagine a tiny version of Union Street in San Francisco and you've got the picture.

UNUSUAL BOOKSTORES IN TOWN

Owner Shirley Stark's goal is to make **Travel Bound** the best such bookstore anywhere. Her selection includes over 2,000 titles covering traveling basics as well as books for special interest travelers and hard-to-find maps. Stark also keeps an up-to-date file of *New York Times* travel articles. Closed Sunday. 2020 Smallman Street, Strip District. 281-2665.

The Tuckers stocks more than 10,000 out-of-print and rare books. Great browsing here; you can even find publications from the 1700s. Open from 1 to 5 P.M. (call ahead just to be sure). Closed Sunday. 2236 Murray Street, Squirrel Hill. 521-1049.

PITTSBURGH BY NIGHT

Despite all the talk of a renaissance, Pittsburgh remains an urban center and, as such, should be approached with your usual good judgment and common sense. Specifically: do not walk the downtown areas alone at night—take cabs, hire a limo service, drive your rental car, whatever. We heartily urge you to walk no farther than from the doorway to a waiting vehicle, even when you are just going from the theater to your hotel.

There is no Ticketron service in town, but the **TIX Booth** sells both advance-sale tickets and half-price tickets on the same day of a performance. Oliver Street near Sixth Avenue (391-8368). We've learned the hard way that the smart move is to buy tickets in advance for surefire sellouts like certain operas and Broadway subscription series.

Newcomers to town usually admit they consider the **Pittsburgh Symphony** to be synonymous with its native-son conductor, the gifted and high-profile André Previn. The season for this world-class orchestra is September through May. Thursday and Saturday at 8 P.M., Friday at 8:30 P.M.; Sunday at 2:30 P.M. Permanent home is Heinz Hall, an ornate theater dating back to 1926. 600 Penn Avenue. 281-5000.

Pittsburgh Ballet Theater is a double delight: both for the grace of the company and for its new home, the Benedum, created from the grand old Stanley movie theater. Restored to its former grandeur, the Stanley also received a state-of-the-art acoustical renovation. Ballet performances October through December; March through June. Thursday and Saturday at 8 P.M.; Sunday at 2 P.M. 281-0360.

Pittsburgh Dance Council hosts visiting companies and therefore has no regular schedule. Call 355-0330 for times and information.

Pittsburgh Opera is under the direction of Tito Capobianco, who has directed at both La Scala and the Met. He is quoted as believing the city's cultural potential to be "a sleeping lion"—and he is out to awaken it. Season is October through April (excluding March). Thursday and Saturday at 8 P.M. 281-0912.

Civic Light Opera has no regular schedule. Call 281-0912 for performance information.

Broadway shows and concerts are often held at the **Syria Mosque.** Call 355-0983 for information, or check local listings.

The City Theater Company offers stage shows October through April. Thursday through Saturday at 8 P.M.; Sunday at 2 and 7 P.M..

Pittsburgh Public Theater performances are Tuesday through Saturday at 8 P.M.; Sunday at 7 P.M. Closed the month of August. 321-9800.

Broadway Subscription Series produces a constantly changing schedule. Call 355-0983 for updated information.

We can recommend the **Pittsburgh Playhouse** as one of the best movie theaters in town, showing everything from recent releases to favorite classics. Two shows nightly; $2.95. 222 Craft Avenue, Oakland. 621-4445.

LATE-NIGHT PITTSBURGH

Chauncy's is probably the most popular night spot in town, with all the "hot-spot" inconveniences like long lines. Conveniently located in The Shops at Station Square, it serves dinner until 11 P.M., and then dancing takes over until 2 A.M. Draws an interesting mix of people—young professionals, blue-collar workers, all ages. Commerce Court. 232-0601.

Celebrity is a traditional disco, rocking every night except Sunday. Open Monday until midnight; Tuesday through Saturday until 2 A.M. In the Kossman Building (downtown). 391-0924.

Mirage (formerly called Heaven!) is a multimedia happening fashioned after the big-hit discos of the eighties. Several dance floors, lots of action. Open only on Fridays and Saturdays until 1 A.M. Sixth Avenue near Fulton (downtown). 281-0349.

Gandy Dancer Saloon is part of the elegant Grand Concourse restaurant. Open Sunday through Thursday until 11 P.M.; Friday and Saturday until 1 A.M. One Station Square. 261-1717.

Houlihan's Old Place is a combination restaurant, bar, dancing spot. Draws a friendly crowd. Open Sundays until 11 P.M.; later other nights. In the Freight House Shops at Station Square. 232-0302.

Froggy's is another good-times bar that stays open until 1 A.M. on weekends. This one is closed on Sunday. Attracts young professionals. 100 Market Street (downtown) in a safe neighborhood. 471-3764.

FOR DRINKS ONLY

Top of the Triangle on the 62d floor of the U.S. Steel Building offers a sweeping panorama of the city and miles beyond. Open until 1 A.M. 600 Grant Street (downtown). 471-4100.

Arthur's boasts "the largest Scotch bar in the world," and owner Chuck Liberatore isn't exaggerating. He offers a selection of 195 single malt Scotch whiskies at varying prices. Atmosphere is cozy colonial, complete with 16 working fireplaces. Open until 11 P.M. 209 Fourth Avenue (downtown). 566-1735.

JAZZ CLUBS

Harper's serves up dinners and the great jazz sounds of Walt Harper and All That Jazz as well as other headliners. Cover charge. Open until 1 A.M. on weeknights; until 2 A.M. on weekends. One Oxford Centre (downtown). 391-1494.

The Balcony attracts a trendy crowd, especially on Wednesdays, the big night in Shadyville. Don't be misled, however—weekends also swing at this jazzy jazz club. Open until 1 A.M. on weekends; midnight during the week. 5520 Walnut Street, Shadyville. 687-0110.

AT LEISURE

Perhaps the best way to appreciate the scope of Pittsburgh's renaissance is to stay around for a day or two after your work here is finished. Wander about at your leisure, explore the various ethnic neighborhoods, or drive into the countryside. As in most American cities, the downtown hotels offer excellent weekend packages. Check around, find the best deal, and then enjoy Pittsburgh and western Pennsylvania.

Day-Tripping

The **National Pike Region** and **Laurel Highlands** area is located about 50 miles southeast of town (a 90-minute drive). Could be a day trip or extended into one or two overnights. Best time: April through October. Some places to see in this region:

Fallingwater, Frank Lloyd Wright's 1936 masterpiece, is built over a waterfall. Off Route 381. Open April to mid-November; hourly tours 10 A.M. to 4 P.M. Call 329-8501.

Laurel Caverns is the largest natural cave in North America north of the Mason-Dixon line. Route 40. Open weekends all year; daily from April 15 to November 15. 329-5968.

Nemacolin Castle is a 22-room structure begun in 1787 as a fort, and then made into a trading post. Today it commands a spectacular overview of the Monongahela River (locals call it simply the Mon River) valley. Open Tuesday through Sunday; 1 to 5 P.M.

Fort Necessity National Battlefield: a landmark of the French and Indian War.

Friendship Hill: the Albert Gallatin estate.

Hanna's Town: a re-created 18th-century county seat.

Mt. Washington Tavern: remnants of the National Road, established by Albert Gallatin.

There are several delightful lodgings in this bucolic area. Among them:

Nemacolin Woodlands with 3,000 acres in the Laurel Woodlands. An English Tudor inn offering golf, fishing, riding. Carriage or sleigh rides at dusk.

Century Inn on the National Road, c. 1794, registered as a National Landmark. Furnished in antiques, noted for its excellent cuisine.

Linden Hall, a 1913 English Tudor mansion with 35 rooms, 13 baths. Opulent furnishings include signed Tiffany windows, an Aeolian pipe organ (one of three in the world), baroque woodwork, gold-leaf fireplaces. Some 785 acres for swimming, golf, fishing.

Contact Fayette County Visitors Information for reservations and further details. 439-5610.

In winter, call **Hartwood Acres** and reserve a seat in one of their horse-drawn sleighs; it's a trip straight out of a Currier and Ives painting.

215 Saxonburg Boulevard, about 12 miles north of Pittsburgh. 767-9200. **Delta Queen Steamboat Cruises** get you away from it all—and you can decide how long you want to be away. Leisurely cruises along the Ohio River—if your next business destination is Cincinnati, for example. this could be a delightful commute. Depart from Monongahela Wharf, foot of Wood Street, downtown. Call 800/543-1949 for details.

Sunday Customs

Of all the **brunch** spots in town for enjoying this leisurely Sunday tradition, we like the following:

Grand Concourse for its elegant ambience and its upbeat mix of patrons. 10 A.M. to 2:30 P.M. One Station Square. 261-1717.

Hugo's Rotisserie in the Hyatt Hotel. Probably the most lavish brunch in town. Nice mix of hotel guests and locals all dressed up for a special occasion. 11 A.M. to 2 P.M. 288-9326.

Houlihan's is a bit contrived, with its nostalgic theme. But it's well meaning and the brunch is good. 10:30 A.M. to 3 P.M. Freight House Shops, Station Square. 232-0302.

Ashley's in the Marriott Greentree is a bit more formal than the others. Contemporary decor. Brunch from 10 A.M. to 2 P.M. 101 Marriott Drive, Greentree. 922-8400.

Cafe Azure serves French country cuisine in classic bistro setting. Outdoor cafe in season. 11 A.M. to 3 P.M. 317 Craig Street, Oakland. 681-3533.

Le Petite Cafe is casual and chic. French brunch with great desserts. Noon to 2:30 P.M. Belleffonte Shops, Shadyside. 621-9000.

Golden Trout is for serious brunchers. It's a long drive (65 miles southeast of the city), it's dressy, and it's expensive. But the setting is a Tudor mansion in wooded seclusion and it's idyllic. Reservations are a must. Brunch from 10 A.M. to 2 P.M. Nemacolin Woodlands, Farmington. 329-8555.

In Town

The **New Zoo** in Highland Park is all spruced up with new habitat settings for its residents. (Helps make for guilt-free viewing.) Don't miss the AquaZoo and the Twilight Zoo. Open weekends until 6 P.M. 441-6262.

Flea Markets: **Common Market,** across from Allegheny Center in Northside (322-0443) or **Keystone State Grand Flea Market** in Penn Avenue Strip district, downtown.

There are **farmers' markets** at Penn Avenue, downtown Strip District, and various other locations around town. Call 322-0443 for information.

The **Fabulous Fun Free Fairgrounds Festival** offers arts, crafts, antiques, collectibles, and homemade items every Saturday and Sunday from 9 to 5 P.M. South Park Fairgrounds.

For Sunday shopping, try the **Monroeville Mall** or **Station Square** (see "The Shopping Scene" for details).

Nationality Classrooms re-create the period classrooms—architecture and art—of the 18 ethnic groups who settled Allegheny County. University of Pittsburgh, Fifth Avenue, Commons Room, Cathedral of Learning. 624-6000.

Fort Pitt Museum and Blockhouse is the only remnant of the original settlement of Pittsburgh around the time of the French and Indian War. In Point State Park (tip of Golden Triangle)—a great place to visit on a beautiful day.

The Three Rivers Shakespeare Festival is held during the summer. If you're in town then, don't miss this annual event. Held at the University of Pittsburgh campus. Call 624-6805.

Spectator Sports

The **Pittsburgh Steelers,** the only NFL team with four Super Bowl victories, play in the 55,000-seat Three Rivers Stadium. You can walk there easily from downtown. 323-1200.

The **Pittsburgh Pirates,** who last won the World Series in 1979, also play in Three Rivers Stadium. 323-1150.

And while you are at the stadium, you might visit their Sports Hall of Fame. 400 Stadium Circle. 321-0650.

The **Pittsburgh Penguins** haven't made the hockey playoffs in the last few years, but they're in the toughest division. Civic Arena, Washington Place, Center and Bedford avenues. 642-1800.

Note: the Civic Arena is a 15,000-seat, indoor/outdoor arena with a state-of-the-art retractable roof. Everything from conventions to rock concerts to sporting events are held here. Downtown near Bigelow Boulevard.

Active Sports

Runners and joggers head for **Schenley Park** or **Highland Park.** Schenley provides 456 acres of sporting challenges for the athlete: golf, tennis (13 lighted courts), swimming, fishing, cross-country skiing. All this in the heart of downtown Pittsburgh. The city also has 92 public golf courses.

Other skiing possibilities include the waters surrounding downtown in summer or Laurel Highlands for downhill or cross-country skiing in winter. The Youghiogheny River is the site of whitewater rafting. Call 255-2350 for information.

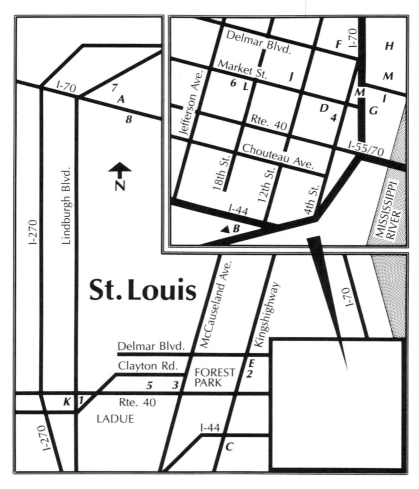

St. Louis

HOTELS

1 Breckenridge
2 Chase-Park Plaza
3 Cheshire Inn & Lodge
4 Clarion
5 Clayton Inn
6 Omni International
7 Park Terrace Airport Hilton
8 Stouffer Concourse Hotel

LANDMARKS

A Airport
B Anheuser-Busch Brewery
C Botanical Gardens
D Busch Memorial Stadium
E Central West End
F Convention Center
G Gateway Arch

H Laclede's Landing
I The Levee
J Memorial Plaza
K Plaza Frontenac
L Union Station
M Visitors Centers

ST. LOUIS

GETTING YOUR BEARINGS

It's difficult to pigeonhole St. Louis in terms of geographical persuasion: it's a town known as the "Gateway to the West," but it serves grits with breakfast. Even longtime residents have trouble pinpointing their town's leanings: some think of themselves as carrying on southern traditions; others pride themselves on their midwestern sensibilities.

But whether midwestern or southern, the city's conservatism is a fact of life, evidencing itself in the way business is conducted, in the dress codes, and in the way people entertain. As a visiting business-woman you can expect to be entertained in private clubs (as opposed to restaurants) and in the homes of business associates. In fact, after you have been doing business here for any length of time, you'll know you have arrived when you are invited home. And when this happens, be sure to stick to the local formula: follow up with a written note on personal stationery (a thank-you call will not do) and a gift of flowers the next day.

Local customs aside, we find this a surprisingly comfortable town to visit. While corporate structures are conservative, they are also open-minded; hotels and restaurants are plentiful and managed by up-to-date, savvy policies; and even the urban sprawl is easy to navigate, thanks to a well-planned network of highways. Even in the commercial heart of downtown the streets are broad and lined with spacious parks. The absence of wall-to-wall towering buildings adds to the feeling of being in a city blessed with lots of wide-open spaces. Another oddity most city dwellers will mark is the lack of pedestrians; very few people walk the sidewalks of downtown or the suburbs.

St. Louis's downtown business district is compact, filling up the rounded area that bulges out into the Mississippi River. Here you'll find a concentration of offices and government buildings, many hotels and restaurants, Busch Stadium, and the tourist areas around the Gateway Arch and the levee.

Just west of downtown is midtown and the Forest Park area with its sites and amenities inherited from the 1904 World's Fair. Another neighborhood you'll likely be visiting is the Central West End, with Euclid

and Maryland streets at its center, a funky, trendy, fun area a bit like
New York's Greenwich Village or Washington's Georgetown. And farther
to the west stretch the dozens of communities of St. Louis County (suburbs), among them the chic bedroom communities of Clayton, Ladue,
and Frontenac.

Long gone are the days when poor St. Louis had to contend
with the unwanted title of "first in booze, first in shoes, and last in the
American League." Today it ranks sixth among the nation's corporate
headquarters for Fortune 500 companies. Among them: Monsanto, Ral-
ston Purina, Emerson Electric, Anheuser-Busch, General Dynamics,
McDonnell Douglas, Kellwood, Interco, and Chromalloy American. If the
aerospace industry can be considered the chief employer in St. Louis,
the second largest is certainly the medical/health care industry. There
are two major medical schools, schools of dentistry and orthodontics,
the world-famous children's hospital and the Shriner's Hospital for crip-
pled children, and several fine nursing schools and specialty hospitals,
not to mention the research and private practices—all of which make St.
Louis one of the major medical centers in the country.

This is a wealthy town, a place that enjoys the creature comforts
of world-class opera and symphony and an abundance of excellent places
for dining and shopping. St. Louis is, in the final analysis, both southern
and midwestern in the attitude of its business community toward women:
independent women are fine, just as long as they are charming at the
same time.

A final insight: despite the words to that old World's Fair standard, "Meet Me in St. Louis, Louis," folks in the know never say "St.
Louie." The Americanized "St. Louis" is definitely preferred.

WHAT TO WEAR

As if you haven't already guessed, conservative is the word in fashion as
well as everything else around St. Louis. Taking one's business success
too seriously doesn't play well in this town. So go easy on the "dress
for success" look of man-tailoring; opt instead for a middle-of-
the-fashion-road look—add some feminine touches to your less-severe
business wear. For evenings, you can dress up. Dining is a favorite pursuit
in this town, and it is considered a compliment to your host to dress
accordingly.

WEATHER WATCH

In a word: humid. Especially in summer when muggy heat rolls off the
Mississippi and hangs around, wreaking havoc with your hairdo. Winters
can be cold, with January temperatures logging in at around the freezing

point (and it does snow here, too), and summers are hot, but seem hotter because of the humidity. We strongly suggest you check the local temperatures for a week or so before packing for this trip.

GETTING THERE

Lambert International Airport, in northwest St. Louis County, is served by most major airlines. And because St. Louis is a hub city for TWA and Ozark, you can take advantage of increased direct-flight service.

It takes about 25 minutes to reach downtown from the airport. If you're planning to take a cab into town, you should be aware of the following situation: because of airport politics only certain taxi companies are allowed to maintain cabstands at the terminals. These cabs cost about $18 one-way into town. Less expensive cabs are available, but you must call them; expect to wait about 15 minutes for one to arrive. Their fare into town will be only about $12.50. We recommend calling the Laclede Cab Company (652-3456) or St. Louis Cab Company (991-5300), both of which are also reliable for in-town transportation.

Airport Limousine, another reliable service, connects between airport and most hotels for $5.90 one-way (429-4940).

Car Rentals

Agencies at the airport:

Avis	426-7766
Budget Rent-A-Car	423-3000
Dollar Rent-A-Car	434-4004
Hertz	426-7555
National	426-6272

Plan ahead. We have learned the hard way to allow more than ample time to return rental cars. The lines are unusually long at this airport.

GETTING AROUND

St. Louis is another car town. Unless your business is confined to downtown, you'll want some mobility for trips into St. Louis County or any of the 92 municipalities. FYI: the downtown area covers only about a 12-block area—good for walking to and from appointments.

Happily for drivers, there's plenty of on-street, metered parking available throughout the downtown area. Five cents buys you 15 minutes; the maximum two-hour limit costs 75 cents. Beware the ticket-happy squads of meter maids who ply their trade with zeal; tickets run about

$10, and scofflaws come away with criminal records in this town. If in doubt, use the parking garages, which are plentiful and relatively inexpensive.

Driving routes are well planned and are crowded only at peak hours. A series of highways connects downtown to outlying plants and company headquarters. Radio station KMOX (1120 AM), the local CBS affiliate, gives excellent traffic reports for drivers. A bit of local trivia: in 1960 KMOX originated the nation's first all-talk radio format.

Taxis are plentiful but must be called or picked up at a cabstand (located primarily at major hotels); don't waste time trying to flag a cruising cab. Allow about 15 minutes if you call a taxi, and longer if the weather is bad (see "Getting There" for our favorites). The Laclede Cab Company also runs a package delivery service, guaranteeing delivery of a package within the hour or the delivery charge is on them.

Forget about using buses in this town unless the weather is so bad nothing else is running. The system is slow, inadequate, and unsafe for women alone. It is rarely used by local women. There is no subway system in St. Louis.

GETTING FAMILIAR

St. Louis Convention and Visitors Bureau

10 S. Broadway, Suite 300   Toll-free: 800/325-7962
St. Louis, MO 63102   421-1023

Write or call ahead for metropolitan area maps, which are vital. The city's streets can be confusing; they run spokelike rather than on the conventional grid system. Also available are excellent brochures and local information guides. In town, you can also stop by the two **Visitors' Centers:** Levee branch, which is docked next to the Goldenrod Showboat (421-1799); Mansion House, 330 N. Fourth Street (241-1764).

St. Louis Chamber of Commerce

10 S. Broadway   Tourist information: 421-1023
St. Louis, MO 63102   231-5555

Alfonso J. Cervantes Convention & Exhibition Center

801 Convention Plaza   342-5000

The *St. Louis Post-Dispatch* is the newspaper of record, published every morning. The Thursday edition has a calendar section offering complete guides to goings-on around town for the next ten days. Its Sunday TV listings are the most extensive in the area. The *St. Louis Globe-Democrat* publishes daily except Sunday and carries a regular feature on St. Louis history. *TravelHost, Key,* and *Where* magazines are in most hotels, featuring information for out-of-towners. *Riverfront Times,* given away near the riverfront, has excellent tourist information as well as some interesting features. *St. Louis* magazine, a slick city monthly, publishes excellent features and profiles, in addition to entertainment and events listings.

──────── *Quick Calls* ────────

AREA CODE 314	Time 321-2522
Recorded 24-Hour Tourist	Weather 321-2222
Information 421-2100	All Emergencies 911

AT YOUR SERVICE

Strange but true: because several of the top hotels in town have similar-looking names (Clarion, Clayton, Cheshire), we have had reports of women who booked in haste, only to discover they had booked in the wrong hotel.

Airport Area

Stouffer Concourse Hotel

9801 Natural Bridge   Toll-free reservations: 800/HOTELS 1
St. Louis, MO 63134   Local number: 429-1100
                              Telex: 709107

Adjacent to airport, government offices and courthouse, and about 20 minutes from downtown. The Stouffer is a 393-room hotel with Club Level concierge floor providing, in addition to the complimentary breakfast and other expected perks, a VIP lounge with pool table, large-screen TV, and meeting rooms. The health club also has two pools. All guest rooms have good security, with adequate reading lights and work space and HBO.

Tivoli is the top-floor gourmet restaurant; **Flight Ninety-Nine** lounge provides live entertainment and dance bands. (Hotel staff, alert to the welfare of its single women guests, will help ward off aggressive men who can't take no for an answer.) **Faraday's** is the three-meals coffee shop.

Park Terrace Airport Hilton

10330 Natural Bridge   Toll-free reservations: 800/345-5500
St. Louis County, MO 63134   Local number: 426-5500

Part owner of this hotel is local baseball hero Stan Musial, who, with his partners, has spruced up the existing property, adding nearly five acres of landscaped gardens dotted with 17th-century French statuary. The grounds include even a separate guest chalet. As you might expect, the health facilities here are excellent, including everything from weight rooms to lighted tennis courts. The eighth and ninth floors are concierge floors

	Concierge	Executive Floor	No-Smoking Rooms	Fitness Facilities	Pool	24-Hour Room Service	Restaurant for Client Entertaining	Extra-Special Amenities	Electronic Key System	Business/Secretarial Services	Checkout Time	Frequent Guest Program	Business Traveler Program	Average Single Rate
Breckenridge Frontenac	•	•	•	•	•		Provinces			•	12 noon	Breckenridge Bonus	Le Club	$ 85 $ 95 ex. floor
Chase-Park Plaza	•	•					Tenderloin Room			•	1 p.m.	Chase Club		$ 60
Cheshire Inn & Lodge				•	•		Cheshire Inn				2 p.m.			$ 65
Clarion	•	•		•	•		Top of the Riverfront			•	12 noon		Crown Club	$ 78 $ 74 corp.
Clayton Inn			•	•	•		Top of the Sevens, Velvet Turtle				1 p.m.		Corp.	$ 68 $ 54 b.t. $ 65 corp.
Omni International	•					•	American Rotisserie	•		•	12 noon		E.S.P. ESP	$ 90 Garden $115 headhouse $ 80 Garden $ 95 headhouse
Park Terrace Airport Hilton	•	•	•	•	•	•	Posh's	•		•	12 noon		Corp.	$115 $ 78 corp.
Stouffer Concourse Hotel	•	•	•	•	•	•	Tivoli		•	•	1 p.m.	Club Express (w/Am Ex)	Club Express	$ 88

with all the usual amenities and a welcome extra: a secretary on call from 7 A.M. to 11 P.M.

Veranda's at the Park serves standard meals and includes a pasta bar. **Posh's** restaurant serves nouvelle cuisine with emphasis on natural and light. Background piano music and the beautiful presentation of food help make this an impressive place to entertian clients.

Downtown Area

Clarion Hotel

200 S. Fourth Street	Toll-free reservations: 800/325-7353
St. Louis, MO 63101	Local number: 241-9500
	Telex: 2911010

A good address in the downtown area: great views of the Mississippi River, the Arch, and cityscape; and just a short walk to financial district offices and to Laclede's Landing entertainment area. Has 830 rooms in twin 22-story circular towers; South Tower is best for view and privacy (no nearby high-rises); North Tower has lower-priced rooms with identical in-room amenities. Two floors of the hotel are concierge levels.

Top of the Riverfront restaurant revolves for spectacular panoramic views. Also has a wine-tasting bar. The **Coffee Grove** features soups and salads; **Zelda's** is a deli. The **Dug-Out Bar,** a hangout for sports fans, tends to get crazy after a game, so be on your guard.

Omni International

St. Louis Union Station	Toll-free reservations: 800/THE-OMNI
1820 Market Street	Local number: 241-6664
St. Louis, MO 63103	Telex: 510800387

A major part of the extraordinary Union Station restoration, this 550-room hotel puts you right in the heart of where everyone wants to be. Some guest rooms are in the original building (the "headhouse"), and others are in the newly built garden section. All are charming and provide such amenities as robes and a second TV and phone in the bathroom. Plans call for a health club and a pool to be built on the premises. Until then, there's exercise galore in just wandering the 11 acres of this complex.

The Grand Hall, with its vast barrel-vaulted ceiling, Romanesque arches, and intricate detailing, now serves as the hotel's main lobby. Light meals are served here in an open cafe. The **American Rotisserie** (see "Dining Out") is another showcase for the beauty of the original decor.

Midtown/Forest Park Area

Chase-Park Plaza Hotel

212 N. Kingshighway	Toll-free reservations: 800/325-8989
St. Louis, MO 63108	Local number: 361-2500

A 385-room landmark hotel in the heart of St. Louis's fashionable Central

West End. The neighborhood, in addition to being Old World beautiful, is also chic, trendy, and safe. Celebrities and visiting dignitaries stay here; and the hotel ballroom, the Khorassan Room, is traditionally the scene of the city's classier charity events. Management is interested in attracting business travelers, so services are geared accordingly. The only lapse we see is the lack of health facilities, although hotel guests are welcomed at the West End Health Club two blocks away.

The **Tenderloin Room** is the gourmet spot favored by locals; good for entertaining. Ask for Hack. The **Hunt Room** is the traditional Sunday brunch place, although unaccompanied women should steer clear at other times. Altogether, there are three lounges, a coffee shop, and three good restaurants.

Cheshire Inn and Lodge

6306 Clayton Road   Toll-free reservations: 800/325-7378
Clayton, MO 63105   Local number: 647-7300

A 110-room hotel (the inn and lodge, open for 21 years, are contiguous) in aggressively English Tudor style. Along with its proximity to pastoral Forest Park, the hotel's decor, food, and service combine to create the ambience of an English countryside experience. Rooms are decorated with antiques and have work spaces and good security.

Although free Continental breakfasts are available for all, don't let this deter you from the breakfast feasts set forth in **Miss Hulling's** dining room. A London-style double-decker bus provides diners at the Inn with transportation to most sporting and theatrical events. Be sure to reserve a spot in advance.

West St. Louis County Area

(about 25 minutes drive from downtown)

Breckenridge Frontenac

1335 S. Lindberg   Toll-free reservations: 800/325-7800
St. Louis, MO 63131   Local number: 993-1100
                                      Telex: 434383

If your business is out this way (IBM, Citicorp, Monsanto, and Maritz Motivation/Travel are in the area, along with many others), you'll appreciate the relaxed, safe atmosphere of this 310-room hotel. You can walk across the street to Plaza Frontenac, the best shopping in St. Louis (see "The Shopping Scene"). The second and third floors are executive floors with all the privacy and amenities you expect from special sections. The health club features both Universal and Nautilus equipment; the pool is outdoors.

The **Provinces** is the fine-dining restaurant; **Le Rendezvous** bar is so nonthreatening that working women from all over drop by to unwind after work.

Clayton Inn

7750 Carondelet Avenue   Toll-free reservations: 800/325-6130
Clayton, MO 63105   Local number: 726-5400

A homey, comfortable 212-room hotel in this homey, comfortable sub-urb. One local told us she recommends it to women friends from out of town because she feels its small size ensures top service and safety. And statistics do indeed show Clayton to be the lowest crime area in town. (Local legend tells of Clayton's lone lawbreaker—a flasher who departed in shock after a Clayton matron laughed at his performance.) The Clayton Inn's health club facilities (and two pools) are so good the local residents use them as a sort of country club. Security is tight and includes closed-circuit cameras in the hallways. Rooms have work spaces and good lighting.

Top of the Sevens restaurant offers both good food and a great view from the 24th floor; the **Velvet Turtle,** reopened in the fall of 1985 after extensive renovations, vies for the honor of being the best in the area.

ON A BUDGET

Restaurants

On the south side of downtown, off Kingshighway, is an area known informally as "The Hill." Here is the largest concentration of Italian and other ethnic restaurants, either fancy or family style. We especially like **Crusoe's** (3152-4 Osceola, 351-0620) and **Del Pietro's House of Pasta** (5625 Hampton, 351-1700), but it's hard to go wrong in this neighborhood if you're looking for an inexpensive (under $6 for lunch; under $10 for dinner), enjoyable eating experience.

Entertainment

In summer, free or inexpensive concerts abound in the St. Louis parks. Check the local listings and be alert to events in Queenie Park out in the county suburbs.

The annual Fourth of July celebration lasts four or five days in this town—a nonstop series of free festivities including an air show, fireworks, parades, and performances that take place on and around the levee.

DINING OUT

St. Louis, as any resident will tell you, is an eating-out town. And, because of this predilection, there are lots of interesting choices even if you're dining alone. But for business entertaining, be prepared: this town still harbors chauvinistic strongholds when it comes to fine dining. One businesswoman, aware of potential problems, called ahead to one of the more stellar French restaurants to alert them that she would be the host that evening at dinner. The maitre d' informed her sternly, "Madame, it is against our policy ever to present a check to a woman."

Some of the best areas of town for women dining alone are the Central West End, some parts of downtown, and Clayton. We strongly recommend you send ahead for a free booklet called, *St. Louis: The Wine 'n' Dine Place,* put out by the Convention and Visitors Bureau. In addition to giving complete information, it also keys each restaurant on a detailed map and indicates location by color-coded zones.

Midtown and Central West End

Dressels, for informal dining with the ambience of a Welsh pub. Taped music and live string quartets celebrate classical composers' birthdays. Good burgers and stews of the day for moderate prices. Open seven days. 419 N. Euclid Avenue. 361-1060.

Duff's, another spot that appeals to the intellectual, features monthly poetry readings. Moderate prices for chicken or seafood specialties, huge salads, hot sandwiches. Open seven days. 392 N. Euclid Avenue. 361-0522.

Cafe Balaban (or just **Balaban's**), offers an ambience once described as "left bank, turn-of-the-century." One of the city's favorite dining spots, featuring fresh seafood and Continental cuisine. Draws an upscale clientele to its glassed-in outdoor cafe and enclosed dining room. Closed for Sunday dinner. 405 N. Euclid Avenue. 361-8085.

Palm Beach Cafe is a comfortable, moderately priced Italian restaurant with a Florida beach decor. The family dining scene begins early, and then switches to trendy about 9 P.M. when live music begins at the piano bar. Good place for a nightcap, too. No dinner reservations accepted; open seven days. 4755 McPherson. 361-6190.

Downtown

Cafe de France is a most impressive place to take anyone who understands good food. Some nouvelle, some classic French cuisine. Lunch and dinner served; reservations recommended. 410 Olive Street. 231-2204.

Tony's wins all the food honors in town year after year, including the big five-star award from Mobil. Everything is ideal here—food, service, ambience—except for one major detail: no reservations. Expect a long wait at the bar, no matter who you are. Expensive. (One enterprising writer discovered it is possible to eat only pasta at Tony's and keep the check low. Her good sense convinced her, however, that it's practically a sin to ignore the rest of Tony's menu—no matter what the cost.) 826 N. Broadway. 231-7007.

Anthony's belongs to Tony's younger brother (remember that you are in St. Louis where everyone is related to almost everyone else). Anthony's menu is Continental and fairly expensive. The supermodern decor favors almost pitch darkness, relieved by pin spots over each table. Your fellow diners will likely be the local elite or those on lavish expense accounts, but you won't be able to see them through the gloom. 10 S. Broadway, in the Equitable Building. 231-2434.

The **American Rotisserie** is a beautiful room, resplendent with restored oak ceilings, columns, and panels, and one entire wall that showcases a rotisserie unit imported from France. American cuisine is featured, with emphasis on meats you can watch being cooked. Staff is trained to give priority seating to solo women. Expensive. In the Omni International at Union Station. 1820 Market Street. 241-6644.

Mid-County

Top of the Sevens offers both good food and some dazzling vistas. Cuisine leans heavily to at-table flaming dishes and attracts a mature expense-account crowd. Piano player and singer perform Thursday through Saturday. Closed Sunday. 7777 Bonhomme Avenue. 725-7777.

At **Chez Louis** the food's the thing: classic French and nouvelle served in surroundings decorated with contemporary art. Good wine list; reservations advised. Moderate to expensive. Closed all day Sunday and Saturday lunch. 26 N. Meramec, Clayton. 863-8400.

Fio's La Fourchette, in the west side of Westroads Shopping Center, is the pride and joy of an owner-chef who studied his culinary art in Switzerland. Particularly notable is the "tastings" menu—six courses of the chef's daily best at $31.75. Regular menus change every few weeks. Expect to spend $25 to $35 a person, exclusive of wine. 863-6866.

SPECIAL ATTRACTIONS

This is, after all, Mississippi country and what's a good river without a riverboat? The local mustn't-miss showboat-dining experience is the **Goldenrod** (see "St. Louis by Night"). But you might also want to check out the fleet: **Robert E. Lee** and the **River Club** feature interesting cuisine, and there's even a **McDonald's Riverboat** serving you-know-what. Whatever the fare, hurry on board and enjoy.

POWER BREAKFASTS

Cheshire Inn in Clayton serves a buffet-style breakfast every weekday morning from 7 to 10. Reservations are accepted. Very popular for breakfast meetings. 647-7300.

West End Cafe, 2 N. Euclid, known for its huge omelets. Open from 6 A.M. 361-2020.

Miss Hulling's Cafeteria, 1105 Locust Street, is very popular with locals and enjoys an upscale reputation we don't usually associate with the word *cafeteria*. (Miss Hulling's son, Steven Apted, bought the Cheshire Inn and Lodge and incorporated his mom's lavish pastry-and-biscuit breakfasts into his hotel's menu—remember we told you everyone in St. Louis is related to almost everyone else.) Private rooms available for business groups. 436-0840.

POWER LUNCHES
    Catfish and Crystal is another of Miss Hulling's enterprises. This one offers Missouri-style home cooking with emphasis on fresh vegetables. Some vegetarian plates available. Moderately priced and very popular—reserve well in advance. 231-7703.

ST. LOUIS BY DAY

The famous **Gateway Arch** is a site both to see and to see from. For an overview of the city you can't beat the 30-mile panorama from atop this 630-foot landmark. The five-minute ride to the top is aboard tiny "capsules" that travel inside the arch's curve. If you're the slightest bit claustrophobic, or are nervous about heights, you might want to consider passing up this experience. Most people don't seem to mind, though; the lines are endless. Plan to arrive early in the day.
    Underground, beneath Eero Saarinen's world-famous Arch, is the **Museum of Westward Expansion,** focusing on the period 1800–1890 when names like Lewis and Clark and Thomas Jefferson were making their mark on our nation.
    While you're near the Arch, get in touch with St. Louis and its roots—there aren't too many cities where you can still wander along something like the **Mississippi's levee,** watching riverboats and cargo freighters ply the broad river much the same as they did more than a hundred years ago. In addition to the dozens of pleasure boats tied up along the levee, today's riverfront includes **Laclede's Landing,** a nine-block restored historic district of shops, restaurants, and offices.
    Forest Park, west of downtown, is 1,400 acres of grasslands and cultural and entertainment sites, legacies of the 1904 World's Fair. Parking is a breeze here. Among the places you'll want to visit in Forest Park:
    St. Louis Art Museum is a superb fine arts museum with several world-class collections including French impressionists, and works by Max Beckmann, who lived in St. Louis during the 1940s. Save some time for the oceanic and pre-Columbian art. You can lunch at the Cafe de Beaux Arts and enjoy the sculpture garden. Free admission to museum. 721-0067.
    St. Louis Zoo is one of the country's finest. Don't miss Big Cat Country, a new addition. The Flight Cage, a walk-through aviary, is the world's largest. Free admission. Some women avoid the zoo when alone, except on weekends when crowds are large.

The Jefferson Memorial, in the north side of the park, exhibits Lindbergh memorabilia and other local history collections.

The new **St. Louis Science Center** combines the McDonnell Planetarium and the Museum of Science. Lots of hands-on, visitor-activated exhibits. Join in the fun or enjoy watching the kids as they get a kick out of learning. 535-5810.

Jewel Box is a floral conservatory complete with electric carillon for background music. Free admission. 534-9433.

Forest Park also houses **MUNY,** the world's largest outdoor theater, and the **Steinberg Skating Rink.** Nearby is the **St. Louis Arena,** home of the St. Louis Blues Hockey Club and the indoor soccer league.

The **Missouri Botanical Garden** is a National Historic Landmark and a botanical collection second only to Kew Gardens. Nature's wonders include a Climatron, Japanese gardens and teahouse, Mediterranean house, and rose gardens, to name just a few. The gift shop here is packed with items perfect for take-home presents or local house gifts. Small admission fee. 4344 Shaw Boulevard, about ten minutes south of the riverfront. 577-5122.

Laumeier Sculpture Park is a 96-acre landscaped park studded with works of 50 contemporary artists including Louise Nevelson, Richard Serra, and Ernest Trova. A beautiful, peaceful place to unwind after a stressful meeting. Open year round. Free admission. Geyer and Rott roads. 821-1209.

Union Station is a Rouse Company re-creation of one of the city's landmark areas. There's an Omni International hotel here, along with shopping, boutiques, food stalls, restaurants, and nonstop entertainment.

Anheuser-Busch Brewery Tours. You can't be in St. Louis and ignore everyone's favorite beverage. The building itself is a National Historic Landmark. Tour lasts one hour, with a rest stop for some tastings. Free admission. Closed Sundays and holidays. Broadway and Pestalozzi. 577-2626.

THE SHOPPING SCENE

We marvel that any single city can support the heavy retail concentration that exists in St. Louis. Malls, long the trademark of big-city suburbs, are now taking over downtown St. Louis, offering stiff competiton to their country cousins. And all this competition creates ideal conditions for us; what's tough for the retailer is great for the shopper. At least for the next few years or so, St. Louis should continue to be a true shopper's market.

You'll want to explore two areas: downtown, and the county, out along Clayton Road. More than a mere commute, Clayton Road is also a scenic drive, affording you glimpses into the high-rent districts while you pursue your shopping quests.

Plaza Frontenac has long been synonymous with St. Louis shopping excellence, a high-income, low-key complex with a very ladylike image. Saks and Neiman-Marcus anchor this brick and white-pillared complex, with the likes of Gucci, Polo, Laura Ashley, and Caché in between. Some St. Louis classics include Karl Bissinger confectioners, Helen Wolff's, and Montaldo's. About 30 minutes from downtown, but worth the trip if you're looking for serious shopping. Lindbergh Boulevard and Clayton Road. Call 432-5800 for hours.

Not quite five minutes away is the new **Galleria** shopping complex, which will take over the old West Roads Mall when it opens in the spring of 1986. Dillard's will anchor, with over 100 stores to fill the three-story enclosed mall. Local observers feel this is retail overkill, but it will be interesting to compare the shopping in both. Clayton Road and Brentwood Boulevard.

Just east of Plaza Frontenac on Clayton Road are several small but noteworthy boutiques: Lily Pulitzer, Belinda's, Post Horn, Pappagallo, and others. For bargains, we like Good Buys, a store specializing in seconds and overbuys from the nearby boutiques on Clayton Road. However, these are strictly off-the-rack fashions—don't look for designer bargains.

West Port Plaza considers itself a city within a city with business and shopping by day, dining and entertainment by night. Some good European-style boutiques here. I-270 and Page Boulevard in West County.

Downtown, two giant retail complexes compete for your browsing/shopping business: the **St. Louis Centre** and **Union Station.** The **Centre,** billed as the largest downtown mall in the United States, is anchored by Famous-Barr and Dillard's Styx, Baer & Fuller, with 150 smaller stores and "Taste of St. Louis" food court. 611 Olive Street. 231-5522. Without question, the most exciting newcomer to town is the Rouse Company's renovation of **Union Station**—a gloriously beautiful and faithful restoration of a beloved St. Louis landmark. Entirely climate controlled, with a soaring superstructure to lend an outdoor feeling, this complex is marble and gleaming brass and fun to shop; about 50 stores, 30 food outlets, and 10 restaurants. Don't expect a serious shopping experience; come here to enjoy and to share in the excitement.

Downtown is also where you'll find Brooks Brothers (in case your wardrobe is a bit too avant-garde for the local business scene). 2 South Broadway. 421-3600. Another dress-for-success place is Boyd's, with locations downtown (425-0793) and on Clayton (727-8204).

Antiques abound. Try the shops along Laclede's Landing or in the Central West End. If your eye is good, stalk the shops along Lower Cherokee Street in South St. Louis. Some of these shops are open on Sundays, too.

And if all this isn't enough, you might want to join the **Shopper's Shuttle,** a service run by two local women to introduce dedicated shoppers to St. Louis's more interesting stores. ("We don't do malls," says owner Pat Schaumann.) Their five-hour, $22 tours follow themes, like

"Putting on the Ritz" with entree into the city's five most expensive stores, or "Bargains," which explores off-price outlets. Drinks and snacks are served aboard these shuttle excursion buses. Alas, no Sunday tours. Call 752-5234.

ST. LOUIS BY NIGHT

Entertainment possibilities in this city range from black-tie openings at the opera to hiss-the-villain "mellerdramas" presented aboard old-fashioned riverboats.

Musical performances alone are in such abundance that Pulitzer Prize–winning critic Frank Peters of the *St. Louis Post-Dispatch* has written that there is almost too much good music in St. Louis to be adequately supported.

The **St. Louis Symphony,** a world-class orchestra, under the direction of Leonard Slatkin, is this country's second-oldest symphony. The season runs from September through May; some tickets are usually available at the last minute because season subscribers will generally turn in their unwanted tickets to the box office. The symphony goes pops in the summer, performing light classics in the parks. Powell Symphony Hall, 718 N. Grand Boulevard, midtown. 533-2500.

The **Fabulous Fox** is a restored theater in the opulent style (some call it gaudy, others "Siamese Byzantine") of the 1920s. The decor alone is worth a visit, and daytime tours are offered (call 534-1678 for times and reservations). Performances include musical comedies, Broadway road shows, Las Vegas-style revues. 527 N. Grand Boulevard, downtown. 534-1111.

MUNY, a 12,000-seat outdoor theater in beautiful Forest Park also offers popular musical theater. Some 1,500 seats are offered free on a first-come, first-served basis just prior to the performance. Season runs June through August. Call 361-1600.

The **Opera Theater of St. Louis** is considered to be the finest regional opera theater in the country. Begun by the formidable Richard Gaddes, it is now under the direction of Charles McKay. Season runs May through June in the Loretto Hilton Center on the campus of Webster University in the nearby suburb of Webster Groves. All performances in English. Bring along a box lunch and some wine, and enjoy a preperformance picnic on the manicured lawn. Later, go to the pavilion to meet the cast and staff. Opening night is usually black tie; other nights, anything goes. Tickets are at a premium. Best to write ahead: St. Louis Opera Theater, Box 13148, St. Louis, MO 63119. Call 961-0644.

The **Repertory Theater,** also held in the Loretto Hilton Center, offers a range of Shakespeare to contemporary. 968-4288.

Goldenrod Showboat is just plain fun. As one frequent visitor said, "Sure, it's for tourists—but it's also for locals. If you haven't been there at least once, you haven't really been to St. Louis." No serious theater here, just dinner, some campy shows (here's where you get to hiss the villain), incorporating ragtime and vaudeville, presented on a real, old-time showboat. Open Tuesday through Sunday, shows at 8 on weeknights, 7 and 10 P.M. on Saturday, and Sunday matinee. Tickets cost about $20 and include the meal. Lenore K. Sullivan Boulevard (more often called Wharf Street or the Levee by natives). Reservations a must: 621-3311.

Westport Playhouse can be a complete evening of entertainment. The theater is in the West Port Plaza, so there are lots of good restaurants and some popular singles bars. (These bars are definitely for pick-up, so if the play's the only thing on your mind, head home as soon as the curtain falls.) Theater offerings include such stars as Pearl Bailey and David Brenner. 600 West Port Plaza, St. Louis County. 878-2424.

Dance St. Louis offers a small ballet season during the fall and winter, bringing top troupes into the city. Box office is at 8338 Big Bend Boulevard; phone orders: 968-3770. Place of performance will be announced.

For **tickets,** call Ticketmaster, 421-1701; Dialatix, 421-1400; or Charge-A-Tic, 231-1234. Ticket hot line, 421-1554.

LATE-NIGHT ST. LOUIS

In terms of late-night bars, discos, and clubs, St. Louis is simply not that great a town for women alone. Some areas are rowdy and unsafe; some management policies make it clear that single women alone are literally on their own. So unless you are in the mood for what could become a major adventure (or misadventure), we recommend staying in your own hotel and limiting your late-night scene to its bar or disco. As one local woman laments, "After hearing the stories from my daughters who are in their twenties and from co-workers in their thirties, I really can't say this town after dark is great for a single woman."

Having said all that, we must tell you that there are three main entertainment areas in town, each with an occasional oasis of charm and welcome tucked away: **Laclede's Landing,** with its quaint Old World aura is alive at night with partying throngs, is well policed, and offers over 50 restaurants and night spots along its gaslit streets; the **Central West End,** bastion of gentrification and chic, is fairly safe and savory. The **West Port Plaza,** with its discos and singles bars, is where singles go to meet people; expect to be approached in these places.

AT LEISURE

As we mentioned earlier, the lure of the mighty Mississippi is so great it almost seems to dictate some leisure-time exploring and enjoyment—whether just walking along the levee or relaxing aboard an old paddlewheeler on the river. If you can find the time, St. Louis offers a peaceful mix of self-indulgent pleasures along with a sense of history.

Your rental car will come in handy, as some of the sights are in the outlying county or in neighboring Illinois.

In Town

Hop aboard the festive little blue and white **tour trams** that make the rounds of all the major sites (or catch up on those you couldn't squeeze in during the work week). You can get off and reboard at your leisure. Tours are narrated, and one ticket ($10) is good for all day. Saturdays, 9 to 6 P.M.; Sundays, 11 to 6 P.M.; weekdays, 9 to 4 P.M. Call 241-1400.

Day-Tripping

Those authentic-looking **riverboats** on the Mississippi are there for your pleasure. Want a short cruise? A weekend trip? Take your pick from one-hour narrated daytime harbor cruises aboard the *Tom Sawyer* or *Huck Finn* (about $5 per person) to evening dinner and dance cruises (about $21 per person). 621-4040. Board the *Delta Queen* or the *Mississippi Queen* for authentic paddlewheel or sternwheeler nostalgia cruises. Call 800/543-1949.

The **August A. Busch estate** is open to visitors and offers two-hour tours that include an animal exhibit in the Tier Garden, trained bird shows, and a train ride through a game preserve to Grant's cabin (home of President U. S. Grant) and the stables of the world-famous Clydesdale stallions. Admission and tours are free but you *must* call ahead for a reservation. 843-1700.

St. Charles, across the Mississippi River, is a bedroom community whose riverfront area is fairly exploding with charming little restaurants and antique shops. Well worth a leisurely visit.

Neighboring Illinois offers a scenic river road that leads to **Pere Marquette State Park,** passing the legendary piasa bird painted on the rock cliff by Indians hundreds of years ago.

About 85 miles south of town is **Ste. Genevieve,** a riverfront town with a decidedly French accent. Some of the authentically restored 18th-century homes are open for touring.

There are some 25 **wineries** in the St. Louis area, centered primarily around Hermann and Augusta, Missouri. We particularly like the Mt. Pleasant winery in Augusta (314/228-4419). En route to the wine country, stop off at local shops for bread, sausage, and cheese to complete a great country picnic.

Interested in archaeology? There are **Indian mounds** in Cahokia, Illinois, that date back hundreds of years, and are currently being established as the richest archaeological treasure in the United States.

The **Wolf Sanctuary,** founded by Carole and Marlin Perkins (remember "Wild Kingdom" on TV?) attempts to preserve these misunderstood animals in natural settings. Not exactly life in the real wilds, but fascinating to see all the same. Located at the Washington University Tyson Research Center in Eureka, Missouri, about 30 miles southwest of town on I-44.

While you're in Eureka, and if you feel like cutting loose and being a kid again, head for **Six Flags over America,** the huge theme park with enough rides, games, and junk food to refuel anyone's childhood memories.

Sunday Customs

St. Louis is a town that takes its **Sunday brunch** very seriously. In fact, around here, only churchgoing surpasses this pleasant meal as a popular Sunday activity. **Balaban's** (405 N. Euclid Street, 361-8085), the **Chase-Park Plaza's Hunt Room,** and the **Cheshire Inn and Lodge** are the best places to brunch and check out the local scene.

Union Station adds shopping and entertainment to your Sunday scene. No formal brunch here, but lots of snacking at the **Picnic Express.** Reserve a seat at the Omni's **American Rotisserie** for more formal brunching amidst beautifully restored history.

Spectator Sports

You no doubt are familiar with the **St. Louis Cardinals**—a name that seems to work so well they use it for both major league teams. All Cardinal games are played in the 50,000-seat Busch Stadium. You'll find the **St. Louis Sports Hall of Fame** here, too. And there's plenty of parking available, even though the stadium is located in the center of town at Walnut, Broadway, Spruce, and 7th streets. Call 421-6790 for general information; 421-3060 for baseball tickets; 421-1600 for football tickets.

St. Louis Blues hockey is NHL action at its iciest. Held at the Arena, 5700 Oakland, the 40-game season runs from October through April. 781-5300.

St. Louis Soccer Steamers also play at the Arena. Specializing in hard-playing major indoor soccer league action, the Steamers barely missed the championship and are coming back strong.

Active Sports

Tennis, anyone? Bring along your racket and play at the Dwight Davis Tennis Center (a local champ, he was the founder of the Davis Cup). Call 367-0220 for permits and information.

Forest Park, a municipal park, offers tennis, 9- and 18-hole golf courses, bike and jogging paths, fields for ball games, handball and racketball courts, casting docks, an archery range, and dozens of picnic facilities. This park is very popular and much used by local residents. Everything is free and open to everyone. Call 535-1503.

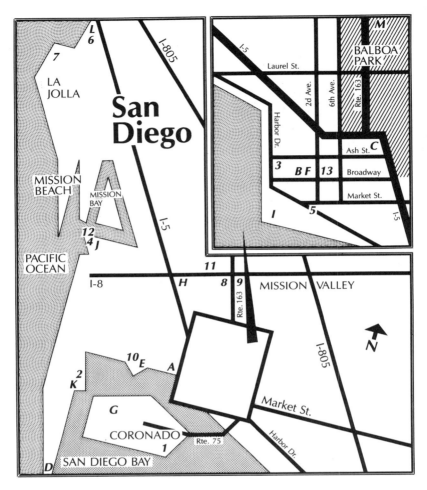

San Diego

HOTELS

1 Del Coronado
2 Half Moon Inn
3 Holiday Inn at
  the Embarcadero
4 Hyatt Islandia
5 Inter-Continental
6 La Jolla Village Inn
7 La Valencia Hotel
8 Mission Valley Inn
9 Radisson
10 Sheraton Harbor
   Island East
11 Town and Country
12 Vacation Village Resort
13 Westgate

LANDMARKS

A Airport
B Amtrak station
C Balboa Stadium
D Cabrillo National
  Monument/Pt. Loma
E Harbor Island
F Horton Plaza
G North Island/U.S. Naval
  Station

H Old Town
I Seaport Village
J Sea World
K Shelter Island
L University of California
M Zoo

SAN DIEGO

GETTING YOUR BEARINGS

Some of San Diego's romance has faded with the roar of traffic on the new highways bisecting the city's still beautiful communities. As the city grows, excitement flourishes. And a little excitement proved to be just what this city—once known strictly as a retirement town—needed. Not too long ago, San Diego had a reputation for being a cultural wasteland and a conservative mecca. But even in these areas, times are changing.

The theater and arts community has never been so strong. The restaurant scene bears little resemblance to its former self; formal, boring Continental cuisine palaces of yesterday having mostly been replaced with bright, lively little restaurants headed by young, enthusiastic, and imaginative California chefs, several making names for themselves across the country. The nightlife, though still tame compared to what you'll find in New York or Los Angeles, is at least now in evidence. And, amazingly, while all these changes have been transpiring over the last decade, San Diegans haven't lost sight of the lovely old city that is theirs to preserve and restore. In fact, the revitalization of downtown, we think, is the reason behind the city's new look and attitude.

Women traveling to California's second largest city should be aware that San Diego has more than one business center. Downtown is the legal, financial, and government center.

Shelter Island and Harbor Island, two manmade islands designed as resort areas with large, luxury hotels, are just ten minutes away. Both offer a nice respite from the noise and activity of the inner city.

Connected to the mainland by the sweeping arc of the Coronado Bridge, Coronado Island is about ten minutes southwest of downtown. This is a community unto itself, with a beautiful beach, parks, jogging trails, and lovingly restored historic homes.

Mission Valley is the retail service industry area, with two major shopping malls and scores of new office buildings. Hotel Circle, in the center of the valley, is what its name implies. There are large convention facilities, small budget hotels, and everything in between. The valley is

437

far from scenic, but it is centrally located and affords easy access to the city's major attractions.

Also centrally located is Mission Bay, a 4,600-acre manmade aquatic park with playgrounds, picnic areas, and every form of water recreation you could want. The bay is lined with first-class hotels and many luxurious resorts.

La Jolla is a research/high-tech center, where the University of California, San Diego, the Scripps Institute of Oceanography, and the Salk Institute are located. Just outside La Jolla is the Golden Triangle, where developers are building state-of-the-art industrial centers to attract research and light industry corporations. As of yet, there are no hotels within the Golden Triangle. The closest place to stay is La Jolla, about 15 minutes from downtown San Diego when the traffic is light.

Although San Diego is no longer the quiet little town we used to think it was, it is still one of the safest big cities we know. There are few places, if any, where we would hesitate to walk alone, except possibly downtown Tijuana at night. Although it certainly never does any harm to keep your wits about you, for the most part, you need not worry about getting from your car to a restaurant. And, by all means, feel free to take a lone sunset stroll on one of the city's seventy miles of breathtaking beaches. It's the perfect place to forget the stresses of a long working day.

WHAT TO WEAR

San Diego thinks of itself more as a beach town than a big city, so dress here tends to be on the casual side. You won't see a lot of high fashion in the boardrooms or ballrooms; what you will see are carefully but conservatively dressed women, often in the rather straitlaced two-piece business suits that have become something of a uniform. Add pantyhose (yes, even if you are planning a walk on the beach at lunch) and pumps and you will fit right in.

WEATHER WATCH

Possibly the biggest thing San Diego has going for it is its climate. Without exaggerating, meteorologists say it is the only area in the country with perfect weather. Perfect! The temperatures average a balmy 70 degrees, with the ocean climbing above that in the summer months and dropping closer to 60 degrees in the winter. It is usually rainy off and on in January and February, and June is often socked in with fog, but that is about as serious as the weather gets. If you are planning a winter or early spring trip, we'd suggest packing a lightweight raincoat. Even in summer, you will probably need a sweater for the evenings, since it can be cool and breezy near the water.

GETTING THERE

The **San Diego International Airport,** also known as **Lindbergh Field,** is the city's only major airport. It's centrally located at the edge of downtown, making it one of the most convenient city airports we've ever come across. There are two terminals, east and west, so it is a good idea to ask where your flight departs from when confirming reservations. It's served by most major airlines.

Many major hotels offer free or low-cost shuttles to and from Lindbergh Field, and if you are not planning to rent a car, this is the best way to go.

Plenty of taxis wait outside the baggage claim areas. Average rate to any downtown hotel is $3; the trip to Mission Valley and Hotel Circle runs around $10; and for a ride to the beach areas, expect to pay upwards from $7. Some of the most reputable cab companies: Airport Taxi, 280-9381; Checker Cab, 234-4477; Independent Cab, 291-3333; and Yellow Cab, 234-6161.

Car Rentals

Unless your time in the city is limited with meetings confined to one area, such as downtown or Mission Valley, we would strongly recommend renting a car. Without one, it is virtually impossible to reach even a sampling of all the city has to offer. Car rental companies abound in San Diego, with competitive rates. Since mileage can add up (the county comprises some 4,261 square miles), it is best to get some kind of unlimited mileage package. Most major companies have offices at the airport:

Avis	231-7171
Budget	297-3851
Hertz	231-7000
National	231-7100
Sears	297-1917

GETTING AROUND

As we've already mentioned, a car is by far the best means of getting around San Diego, which is mercifully free of the volume of traffic that turns freeways into parking lots. For now, even rush hour is manageable without serious delays. But like other California motorists, San Diegans can be ruthless on the freeway, so it's a good idea to plan your route and memorize your exit before heading up the on-ramp.

San Diego Transit operates buses throughout the county, but traveling time can be frustratingly slow, and some routes run infrequently. Many hotels and tourist information centers have bus schedules and route maps, or you can call 233-3004 from 5:30 A.M. to 8:30 P.M. Be prepared to redial often as the exchange is frequently busy. The fare is 80 cents (exact change only) for regular routes and $1 (no bills) for express routes.

If your work requires that you spend a day or two in Los Angeles, consider taking the train. Amtrak runs daily from San Diego to L.A. from 5:15 A.M. to 7:45 P.M. The route traces the coast much of the way, making the ride scenic and soothing. If possible, avoid peak commuter hours and weekends, when trains can get crowded. All depart from the recently refurbished Spanish-style Santa Fe Depot on Kettner and C Street downtown. One-way fare: $17.85. For taped schedule information, call 239-9021; for reservations and information, call 800/872-7245.

GETTING FAMILIAR

San Diego Convention and Visitors Bureau

1200 Third Avenue
Suite 824
San Diego, CA 92101

24-hour information recording: 239-9696
24-hour arts and entertainment hot line: 234-2787, 232-3101

The bureau publishes a brochure on San Diego available in several languages, as well as maps and pamphlets, including the monthly *What's Doing in San Diego,* which lists special activities and information on major tourist attractions. A very accommodating staff willing to help with specific questions. Open Monday through Friday 9 A.M. to 4:30 P.M.

San Diego has two daily newspapers—the morning *San Diego Union* and the *Evening Tribune.* Both carry complete movie and entertainment listings daily, with Thursday local events supplements. The *San Diego Reader,* a free weekly paper distributed every Thursday, covers the local entertainment scene extensively. *San Diego Woman,* a free monthly paper, features articles on women's concerns and activities. *San Diego Magazine* runs a monthly column called "What's Doing" that covers arts, entertainment, and nightlife and a guide to dining out.

Quick Calls

AREA CODE 619
Police and Fire
Emergencies 911

Police 236-6566
Time 853-1111
Weather 289-1212

AT YOUR SERVICE

Each San Diego business center has its own crop of hotels. You may want to stay close to where you will be working; then again, there is a lot to be said for booking a room at one of the city's resort hotels and using your free evenings to take advantage of their fitness facilities. We know one businesswoman who regularly does just that and, despite a heavy work load, always returns home feeling energized and refreshed. Some hotels offer unabashed elegance; others provide superior business services.

Downtown, Coronado, Shelter Island, Harbor Island

Half Moon Inn
2303 Shelter Island Drive   Toll-free reservations: 800/542-7401;
San Diego, CA 92106   in California 800/542-7400
     Local number: 224-3411
Low-rise garden rooms and suites with patios or decks right on the water, lush tropical landscaping, and a lovely pool all make for a kind of barefoot vacation atmosphere here. Most of the rooms have kitchenettes. Referrals to business and personal services are available through the front desk.

     The restaurant at the hotel is called **Humphrey's,** and the decor, fittingly, is reminiscent of Casablanca, with an abundance of ferns and white ceiling fans. The view of the marina and Point Loma is breathtaking, especially at night. And although the food is usually acceptable at best, the elaborate Sunday brunch can be fun.

Holiday Inn at the Embarcadero
1355 N. Harbor Drive   Toll-free reservations: 800/238-8000
San Diego, CA 92101   Local number: 232-3861
Of the two Holiday Inns downtown, this is the one to ask for. There is nothing outstanding about this hotel other than its very convenient location, though a remodeling effort has created two luxurious concierge floors. Two towers, one topped with a sun deck, swimming pool, and whirlpool bath. Currently, the Holiday Inn has the largest meeting and convention facilities in central downtown. Business service available.

Hotel Del Coronado
1500 Orange Avenue   Local number: 435-6611
Coronado, CA 92118
The Del, as the locals call it, is one of San Diego's most famous landmarks and surely its most famous hotel. This rambling white Victorian palace with its red-roofed turrets and cupolas is steeped in tradition and history. Built in 1888, the Del has played host to princesses and presidents, movie stars and foreign ambassadors. Rooms in the main building can be charming and quaint or rather awkward and confining, depending on the lo-

	Concierge	Executive Floor	No-Smoking Rooms	Fitness Facilities	Pool	24-Hour Room Service	Restaurant for Client Entertaining	Extra-Special Amenities	Electronic Key System	Business/Secretarial Services	Checkout Time	Frequent Guest Program	Business Traveler Program	Average Single Rate
Del Coronado	●			●	●		Prince of Wales			●	12 noon			$ 99–$600 $135 corp.
Half Moon Inn					●		Humphrey's	●		●	12 noon			$ 85 $ 65–$75 $140
Holiday Inn at the Embarcadero	●	●	●	●	●		Embarcadero Room	●		●	12 noon	Priority Club	Corporate Rate Program	$ 81–$101 $ 71 corp.
Hyatt Islandia	●	●	●		●	●	Islandia Restaurant	●		●	12 noon		Gold Passport	$ 90–$145
Inter-Continental	●			●	●	●	Lael's	●		●	12 noon	Six Continents Club USA Plus	Preferred Executive Plan	$115
La Jolla Village Inn					●		Visions			●	12 noon		La Jolla Village Inn #504	$ 85–$121 $ 62 corp.

Hotel					Restaurant			Check-out		Frequent Guest Program	Rates
La Valencia Hotel	•		•	•	Sky Room	•		12 noon	•		$ 83–$103
Radisson	•	•	•	•	Alfresco's	•		12 noon	•	Radisson Hospitality Club	$ 85–$115 $ 74 corp.
Sheraton Harbor Island East (The Towers)	•	•	•	•	Sheppard's	•	•	12 noon Distinguished Customer Service	•	Sheraton Executive Traveler	$ 99–$135 $120 corp.
Town and Country	•		•	•	Le Pavillion Gourmet Room	•		12 noon	•	Sunset Club	$ 72–$106
Vacation Village Resort	•		•	•	Dockside Broiler	•		12 noon	•	Princess Preferred Corporate	$ 98
Westgate	•				Le Fountainbleu	•		12 noon	•	Executive Club	$104 $ 84 corp.

cation. The adjoining towers contain multiroom suites and apartments suitable for business entertaining but without much of the ambience.

Edward, prince of Wales, met Wallis Warfield Simpson here in 1920, and this history-changing moment is commemorated in the **Prince of Wales** restaurant, where the menu is traditional and the service solicitous.

Hotel Inter-Continental

333 W. Harbor Drive   Toll-free reservations: 800/327-0200
San Diego, CA 92101   Local number: 234-1500
                             Telex: 695425

Rising like a mirrored parabola above the downtown waterfront, the dramatic new Inter-Continental offers European elegance in the form of marble, antiques, and elaborate flower arrangements. The central court-yard, with its waterfalls, sinuous pool that winds around rocky coves, and bubbling whirlpool, is more water than walkway. The fitness facilities here are extensive and include an on-site health club and lighted tennis courts. Business services can be arranged through the concierge.

There are four restaurants to choose from—**Maison Ann Marie** for elegant Continental dining; **Lael's** for seafood; **La Cascadas** for Mexican food; and **Molly's Pub,** casual and lively.

Sheraton Harbor Island East

1380 Harbor Island   Toll-free reservations: 800/325-3535
San Diego, CA 92101   Local number: 291-2900
                            Telex: 697877SDGUN

Businesswomen will want to choose this Sheraton over the one next door. The Towers level, with its own concierge, boardrooms, and private lounge where cocktails and hors d'oeuvres are served in the evening and complimentary Continental breakfast in the morning, is something of a business traveler's dream come true. In addition to meeting and convention facilities, there is a complete business center with secretarial services and teleconferencing. And when you are not working, take advantage of the fully staffed Nautilus club, with its five-mile jogging path, lighted tennis courts, and pool.

Cindy Black, one of the hottest young chefs in the country right now, is the chef at **Sheppard's,** a sophisticated restaurant with outstanding food. Cindy's cooking combines French techniques with the freshest local ingredients available, and the results are memorable. **Reflections** disco is popular with the locals.

Westgate Hotel

1055 Second Avenue   Toll-free reservations: 800/221-3802;
San Diego, CA 92101   in California 800/522-1564
                            Local number: 238-1818
                            Telex: 695046

The Westgate, with an opulent French provincial lobby, profusion of fine art, guest rooms in period styles, and bathrooms in Italian marble, is San

Diego's most elegant hotel. Salima Din, the concierge, is known as Lady Westgate, a woman famous for her ability to meet any request a guest might have. Business services are readily available through the Executive Club, which provides express check-in, discount rates, and access to meeting rooms.

Le Fontainbleu Room offers rich and classic Continental dishes in style, with piano music and white-gloved waiters. **The Plaza** bar is a quiet refuge in the early evening.

Mission Valley/Hotel Circle

Radisson Hotel
1433 Camino Del Rio South   Local number: 260-0111
San Diego, CA 92108

The top two floors of this relatively new high rise make up the Plaza Club with a full-time concierge and luxury suites. Business services are available through the concierge, and there are meeting rooms on the property.

Alfresco's specializes in northern Italian fare, and the **Encounters** nightclub has live sixties music and dancing.

Town and Country
North Hotel Circle   Toll-free reservations: 800/854-2608,
San Diego, CA 92138   800/542-6082 in California
                                       Local number: 291-7131

This hotel/motel complex is currently the largest convention and exhibit facility in San Diego, dealing in high-volume turnover. Beautifully landscaped; resort atmosphere has four pools with whirlpools, and guests have privileges at a nearby health club.

There is a restaurant here for every dining whim—six of them all told, including **La Pavillon,** a French restaurant and lounge, the **Gourmet Room,** and **Kelly's Steak House. Crystal T's Emporium** is both disco and dining room.

Mission Bay and Beaches

Hyatt Islandia
1441 Quivira Road   Toll-free reservations: 800/228-9000
San Diego, CA 92109   Local number: 224-1234
                                     Telex: 697844

A deluxe hotel on Mission Bay, just across from Sea World, the Islandia accommodates women traveling alone by giving them rooms on floors with special security and providing extra amenities, such as hair dryers, complimentary cosmetics, and bathtubs along with showers. A full-time concierge assists with business and personal needs. Most high-rise rooms have views of either the ocean or the marina; low-rise buildings by the pool area are surrounded with lush landscaping.

The **Islandia Restaurant** serves one of the most lavish Sunday brunches in town. There are two cocktail lounges: the **Mermaid,** with wide-screen TV, and **Circe,** with live entertainment.

Vacation Village Resort

1404 W. Vacation Road   Toll-free reservations: 800/542-6275
San Diego, CA 92109   Local number: 274-4630

Situated on its own manmade island, this full-scale resort—reminiscent of a Polynesian Disneyland—has something for everyone. Families with children like to vacation here, but it is also popular with businesspeople who want to combine work and play. Large meeting rooms and business facilities are available through the front desk. And when that five o'clock bell rings, there is just about every outdoor activity you could want—five pools, boat and bike rentals, tennis, and a bay-front beach.

Restaurants include the **Dockside Broiler,** a good steak and sea-food spot overlooking the bay, and the **Polynesian Princess,** with South Seas cuisine and a good Sunday brunch.

La Jolla

La Jolla Village Inn

3299 Holiday Court   Toll-free reservations: 800/854-2900;
La Jolla, CA 92037   in California 800/532-3737
                                       Local number: 453-5500

Situated outside the village of La Jolla near the university campus, the inn is convenient to the Golden Triangle, the beach, and central San Diego. It does a heavy corporate group business and has access to business services.

Visions does a fine job with what has come to be called California cuisine. The dishes are imaginative and often beautifully presented, with the emphasis on fresh, locally available products. **Shooters,** the lobby piano bar, is popular with locals for the happy hour.

La Valencia Hotel

1132 Prospect Street   Local number: 454-0771
La Jolla, CA 92037

This beautiful old roseate Spanish-style hotel is in many ways the centerpiece of La Jolla. Perched high on a hill above the beautiful little La Jolla cove, the utterly charming La Valencia, with its elegant furnishings and gracious staff (who, by the way, will be happy to arrange business services for you), seems to set the tone for the rest of the town. To really get the feel of this legendary place, linger over a drink at sunset in the grand lobby with its huge arched window.

The **Whaling Bar** is a popular gathering spot for local VIPs. The hotel's restaurants are good, but not great. Patio dining in the courtyard.

ON A BUDGET

Hotels

Mission Valley Inn
875 Hotel Circle South   Toll-free reservations: 800/854-2608
San Diego, CA 92108   Local number: 298-8281
A modest low-rise hotel that's quiet and comfortable by Hotel Circle standards. Business and personal services arranged at front desk. Guest privileges at nearby Atlas Health Club.
   Hacienda restaurant on the premises is a good Mexican eaterie with friendly cocktail lounge.

Restaurants

   There's at least one—if not many—restaurant in each section of town designed to be easy on the pocketbook. To cut costs, stop in at some of the country's best Mexican restaurants, scattered around town.
   Downtown in the waterfront area is **McDini's.** It's the oldest bar in San Diego—heavy on nostalgia, neighborhood characters, and Irish music. Menu includes first-rate corned beef and cabbage. Great gumbo. Neighborhood a bit seedy and bar a tad run down, but worth a visit. Lunch and dinner. 647 Market Street. 232-1795.
   In Hillcrest is **City Deli.** With pink art deco decor, New York attitude, this is the only traditional deli in town. Breakfast, lunch, and dinner. 535 University Avenue. 295-2747.
   In Balboa Park is the **San Diego Museum of Art Sculpture Garden Cafe.** Light lunches and dinners artfully served in indoor sculpture garden. Pleasant place to relax. In Prado area. 232-7931.
   In Mission Bay is the **Firehouse Beach Cafe.** Large selection of omelets and freshly baked breads and rolls, fresh seafood, and chicken served on an outdoor sundeck. Good boardwalk view. All three meals. 722 Grand Avenue. 272-1999.
   In La Jolla is **Alfonso's.** Great margaritas and excellent meals are the fare at this La Jolla landmark. Outdoor patio fun for people-watching. A good place to dine alone without feeling bored. Lunch, dinner. 1251 Prospect Street. 454-2232.

Transportation

   Rather than flying directly into San Diego, many major airlines offer better rates on flights into Los Angeles International Airport. If you take that route, then utilize one of the smaller carriers for reasonable commuter rates from LAX to San Diego International.

DINING OUT

It used to be that the diner in San Diego had limited options. There were the typical Continental establishments, the trendy fern-bar chains, and the steak-and-potatoes family restaurants. No more. Today's San Diegan, when confronted with having to decide where to eat dinner, has a difficult choice to make. And that's good news for travelers, too.

New restaurants seem to open here everyday; and we are not talking about just your average "let's get a bite to eat" kind of place. These are serious establishments run by young enthusiastic chefs, many thoroughly trained in culinary academies, some succeeding on sheer talent alone. Their menus are exciting, full of dishes based on indigenous foods and locally grown products. Their restaurants are bright, cheerful, and fun.

In addition to these new and very contemporary restaurants is a wide variety of ethnic eateries, including, as you might well imagine, excellent little Mexican restaurants. Look for the Greek, Vietnamese, and Japanese places, too, and don't miss the mom-and-pop type cafes serving great yet cheap breakfasts.

Downtown and the Waterfront

Anthony's Star of the Sea Room is one of the city's older establishments, but still very popular. The setting is inspiring, the furnishings elegant, and the service consistently good. The seafood preparations, though somewhat predictable, are always excellent. Dinner. Deluxe. Foot of Ash and Harbor Drive. 232-3085.

Though the **Chart House** at the San Diego Rowing Club is one of a chain, with another location in La Jolla, you wouldn't know it from its lively atmosphere, cheery staff, and good food. The fresh fish dishes are consistently well prepared. Dinner. Expensive. 525 E. Harbor Drive. 233-7391.

Ciao Bella, a little restaurant situated in a remodeled Victorian cottage, is exactly what a neighborhood bistro should be: friendly and cozy (there's a fireplace in one of the rooms), with good, innovative California-style specialties. Lunch and dinner. Moderate. 1409 Fourth Avenue. 239-9077.

Dobson's is a restored turn-of-the-century pub popular with business, political, and arts heavyweights. The international menu includes a memorable mussel bisque. Reservations are essential at lunch, and while you're on the phone, ask for the upstairs table overlooking the bustling downstairs bar. Lunch and dinner. Expensive. 956 Second Avenue. 231-6771.

Fat City is as trendy as the pink neon Cadillac that lines one wall, and the menu is varied enough to satisfy most anyone. **China Camp** is designed to resemble an early California Chinese mining camp and serves adequate Chinese dishes. The long antique teak and rosewood bar that separates the two restaurants is a friendly place where a woman could feel comfortable alone. Lunch and Dinner. Moderate. 2137 Pacific Highway. 232-0686 (Fat City). 232-1367 (China Camp).

The San Diego old guard headquarters for over 30 years, **Lubach's** is a see-and-be-seen kind of place where serious deals are made over serious meals of steaks, grilled fish, and hamburgers. Men decidedly outnumber women here, so you will want to let the maitre d' know in advance if you'll be paying the bill. Lunch and dinner. Expensive. 2101 N. Harbor Drive. 232-5129.

Pacifica Grill is a magnificent new restaurant built around a giant atrium in a completely remodeled historic building. The menu features fresh fish, ribs, and steaks grilled over mesquite or smoked, and hot Cajun specialties. The location is unusual, right off the railroad tracks beside the Santa Fe Depot, and is in easy and relatively safe walking distance from the waterfront hotels. The tables lining the atrium edge are good spots for dining alone. Lunch and dinner. Moderate to expensive. 1202 Kettner Boulevard. 696-9226.

Papagayo is one of the best fish restaurants in town, serving seafood with an elegant Mexican touch and great margaritas—straight up, not the more usual frozen slushes. Pretty bay-front setting. Lunch and dinner. Expensive. Pacific Highway at Harbor Drive. Seaport Village. 232-7581.

Piret's has modern country French cooking in a sophisticated cafe setting, with charcuterie, boulangerie, and patisserie. The service is attentive, and the selection ranges from simple cheese and pâté plates to unusual pizzas. Good place to dine and drink alone and a great spot for people-watching. Breakfast, lunch, and dinner. Hours vary in other locations. 701 B Street. Imperial Bank Tower. 696-0225. Also at 8657 Villa La Jolla Drive, 455-7955, and at 902 West Washington, 297-2993.

Harbor Island and Point Loma

Sheppard's in the Sheraton Harbor Island East Hotel has had much to do with San Diego's culinary coming of age. Chef Cindy Black describes her cuisine as "uncontrived cooking with the freshest local ingredients, using French techniques." The setting is lovely: soft colors, impeccable china, fresh flowers everywhere, and a view of the marina. Lots of private corner seating partially hidden by towering palms. Dinner. Deluxe. 1380 Harbor Island Drive. 692-2255.

Mission Valley

Adam's Steak and Eggs serves up what could be the best breakfast in town, with massive portions of home fries, grits, corn fritters, and egg dishes. Always crowded and fairly noisy. The wait can be rather long, but if you're hungry for a real breakfast, this is the place. Open 7 A.M. to 11 A.M. weekdays, 8 A.M. to 1 P.M. weekends. Inexpensive. 1201 Hotel Circle South. 291-1103.

Old Town and Vicinity

Cafe Pacifica has a stylish open dining room and outdoor cafe serving fresh fish grilled over mesquite, steamed, sauteed, or baked. The menu changes daily. You'll see media types here; the crowd is typically young and upscale. Lunch and dinner. Moderate–expensive. San Diego Avenue. 291-6666.

Impress a native San Diegan with a meal at **Old Trieste,** an out-of-the-way spot favored by old-line VIPs for its excellent northern Italian cooking (particularly the veal and fish dishes) and experienced, conscientious service. Reservations required. Lunch and dinner. Expensive. 2335 Morena Boulevard. 276-1841.

Mission Bay and Beaches

Diego's Cafe y Cantina is an enormously popular spot for the youthful beach crowd. The selection of traditional Mexican offerings is extensive and the portions are ample. Patio dining and a crowded bar. Lunch and dinner. Inexpensive. 860 Garnet Avenue. 272-1241.

Giulio's is one of the best Italian restaurants in town, with unusual homemade pastas and seafood and veal preparations. The decor is classic red and white checks; the ambience is noisy and friendly. Dinner. Moderate–expensive. 809 Thomas Avenue. 483-7726.

926 offers French cuisine with a California influence. The menu includes grilled meats and fish, unusual fresh vegetables and fruits, pastries and breads made on the premises. The decor is elegant but low key. Dinner. Deluxe. 926 Turquoise Street. 488-7500.

La Jolla

Bully's serves up the best burger in town, as well as great steaks and prime rib. The drinks are generous and the singles scene active. Lunch and dinner. Moderate. 5755 La Jolla Boulevard. 459-2768. Also **Bully's East** at 2401 Camino Del Rio South in Mission Valley. 291-2665.

One of the most exciting restaurants to appear in recent years, **Gustaf Anders** is for many San Diego's premier dining experience. The two young owners have created a menu that combines Scandinavian influences with classic European preparations. A separate caviar bar and lounge serves cold seafood appetizers and champagnes and wines by the glass. The clientele is interesting and sophisticated, and although you might feel uncomfortable dining alone here, you would be fine at the bar. Expensive–deluxe. 2182 Avenida de la Playa. 459-4499.

SAN DIEGO BY DAY

There is no doubt about it: San Diego is a daytime town, what with its 70 miles of beaches, acres of parkland, and that famous zoo. We wouldn't hesitate to schedule an extra day here just to take in a few of the in-town sights.

Beaches

Each beach has its own character and crowd. At **Mission Beach,** for example, the long boardwalk attracts bicyclists, roller skaters, and skateboarders, not to mention folks out for a stroll—great people-watching. North of La Jolla is the infamous **Black's Beach,** where swimwear is optional.

Parks

Most famous of San Diego's many parks is **Balboa Park,** the cultural and recreational heart of the city. Don't miss its cluster of Spanish- and Moorish-style buildings, constructed in 1915 and 1935 for two world's fairs and now housing most of the city's finest museums. Other pleasures include the glorious botanical garden, the Spreckels Organ Pavilion and the performing musicians, mimes, and jugglers scattered across the park's grassy lawns.

Other of the city's parks are **Cabrillo National Monument, Presidio Park,** and **Torrey Pines State Reserve.**

Animal Attractions

Sea World is a 100-acre marine park featuring marine life exhibits, including enormous salt-water aquariums, a large shark exhibit, and, newest and best of all, the Penguin Encounter, where hundreds of penguins in a simulated antarctic environment do a clever job of imitating the human gawkers. And Shamu, the killer whale, puts on quite a show. Open daily 9 A.M. to dusk. Admission charge. Sea World Drive. 222-6363.

The San Diego Zoo is one of the city's biggest tourist draws, and rightly so. The setting and sculpturing of the land into jungles, forests, and arid planes is as fascinating as the 3,000 animals themselves. Skip the double-decker tour bus and opt for strolling the winding paths over bridges, past waterfalls, and in and out of aviaries. Open daily 9 A.M. to dusk. Admission charge. Balboa Park. 234-3153.

Endangered and nearly extinct breeds of wild animals roam free in the **San Diego Wild Animal Park,** a 1,800-acre animal preserve, where the settings are designed to resemble native habitats. An electric monorail winds through the exhibits. Open 9 A.M. to 5 P.M. in summer and to 4 P.M. in winter. Admission charge. Located 30 miles northeast on I-15, exit on Via Rancho Parkway. 480-0100.

Museums

All the following museums are located in **Balboa Park.** You might take in two or three during an afternoon's stroll.

Museum of Man has exhibits of the anthropology and archaeology of the western Americas and artifacts from Indian and Mexican cultures. Open daily 10 A.M. to 4:30 P.M. 239-2001.

San Diego Museum of Art has a permanent collection of old master paintings and American and Asian arts, as well as popular traveling exhibits. Open Tuesday through Sunday, 10 A.M. to 5 P.M. 232-7931.

The **Timken Art Gallery** boasts a fabulous collection of European paintings and Russian icons. Open Tuesday through Saturday, 10 A.M. to 4:30 P.M. 239-5548.

San Diego Art Institute has monthly shows by local artists. Open Tuesday through Saturday 10 A.M. to 4:30 P.M. 234-5946.

Museum of Photographic Arts mounts prestigious exhibits. Open Tuesday through Sunday 10 A.M. to 5 P.M. 239-5262.

Also worth visiting is the **La Jolla Museum of Contemporary Art** for its collection of post-1950s art and design and the rotating exhibits by major modern artists. An International Film Festival is held here in the fall. Call for hours. 700 Prospect Street. 454-3541.

Historical Sites

Gaslamp Quarter Association is located in the historic William Heath Davis house. The association offers guided tours of historic buildings and neighborhoods in the Gaslamp Quarter, site of the original downtown settlement. 410 Island Avenue. 233-5227.

Mission San Diego de Alcala was established by Padre Junipero Serra in 1769. Museum features relics of early mission days. Open daily 9 A.M. to 5 P.M. 10818 San Diego Mission Road. 281-8449.

THE SHOPPING SCENE

San Diego isn't a shopper's paradise if you are looking for high fashion or big-city funk, but you won't find better beachwear or casual clothing anywhere. You will also discover an excellent selection of Mexican crafts and artifacts, particularly in Old Town, where the items are of higher quality than those you might barter for on Tijuana streets.

Old Town is not only a national historic park with exhibits and tours; it's also a cluster of shops selling items of Mexican origin. The Bazaar Del Mundo is a pseudo-Mexican marketplace selling ethnic clothing, jewelry, pottery, rugs, and crafts. Better prices are to be found in some of Old Town's smaller shopping centers, including the Galleria. On weekends, the historical section along San Diego Avenue is lined with artisans selling blankets, pottery, jewelry, and crafts, usually priced lower than in the shops.

Seaport Village offers a fairly new collection of shops, many one of a kind, at the south end of the downtown waterfront. This reproduction of an early California fishing town makes for a pleasant stroll, if not bargain shopping.

Horton Plaza is the newest thing to say about shopping in San Diego. Considered the fulcrum of downtown's revitalization, this elaborate, pastel-colored, postmodern structure rambles over six city blocks with its four major department stores, dozens of specialty shops, a large farmers' market, and indoor/outdoor restaurants. Broadway and First Avenue. 238-8181.

At **University Towne Centre,** there is more than meets the eye. In addition to its wide range of shops and department stores, there is a fine crafts museum, a day-care center, an indoor ice-skating rink, a fitness club, and a hospital wellness center. 4545 La Jolla Village Drive.

The most interesting shopping in San Diego is in its **neighborhoods,** where little shops reflect local character. Mission, Pacific and Ocean beaches all have the latest in swimwear. In La Jolla, Prospect and Girard streets are lined with elegant shops and galleries. Hillcrest Hill and Mission Hill are older neighborhoods that have been rediscovered and transformed into fashionable centers populated by young professionals and artists.

The gift shops in the museums in **Balboa Park** carry unusual clothing, jewelry, books, and gifts, usually reasonably priced. The park's **Spanish Village** (233-9050) brings artists and craftspeople together in small studios spread around a central lawn. Over 100 artists work in over 40 mediums, and their works are for sale daily until dusk.

SAN DIEGO BY NIGHT

San Diego is experiencing something of a cultural awakening. Performance artists finally have supporters and followers in town. The city's live theaters are gaining international attention, and in music, dance, stage, and opera, there is much worth seeing. Add to that the fact that tickets here tend to be less expensive than in other big cities and you have the makings for a lovely evening on the town.

In addition to the box offices, tickets are often available through **Ticketron** and **TicketMaster,** with many locations. **COMBO,** an organization that oversees arts events and calendars has an arts hot line (234-ARTS) listing each week's events.

A sampling of what's available:

The San Diego Civic Light Opera Association presents the Starlight Opera summer series of musical plays in Balboa Park's outdoor Starlight Bowl (283-7827). You'll see the old favorites as well as more current hits. 4408 Twain Avenue. 280-9111.

The **San Diego Opera** season starts in September and runs into the winter. House of Hospitality. Balboa Park. 232-7636.

The **San Diego Symphony** was resurrected from a bankrupt, floundering organization in the past couple of years under the direction of David Atherton. Now it's a first-rate company. Winter series of performances runs from the traditional to the offbeat; in the summer the symphony takes on the pops, with an enormously successful 12-week series of concerts and fireworks. House of Hospitality. Balboa Park. 699-4200; 283-SEAT for 24-hour concert info.

On the legitimate theater scene, **La Jolla Playhouse** has an excellent reputation, showcasing productions that are always unusual and meticulous. On the UCSD Campus. 452-3960.

Mandell-Weiss Center for the Performing Arts (452-4574), **Mandeville Center Auditorium** (452-2380), and **Mandeville Recital Hall** (452-2559) are all UCSD campus venues offering a variety of concerts, lectures, and performances. The university is noted for its avant-garde faculty and student body.

The **San Diego State Open Air Theater** is the best place for outdoor concerts. Top rock, pop, folk, classical, and comedy performances appear during the summer. College Avenue. 265-6947.

The **San Diego Repertory Theater** is a local troupe with a good reputation. 1620 Sixth Avenue. 235-8025.

Simon Edison Centre in Balboa Park includes the **Old Globe Theater, Cassius Carter Center Stage,** and **Old Globe Festival Stage.** The Old Globe celebrated its fiftieth anniversary in 1985. It has gained international acclaim for its annual Shakespearean series, some played on the outdoor Festival Stage. The summer and winter repertory series of contemporary and classic plays draws big name actors. 239-2255.

As for dance, the **San Diego Arts Foundation** (234-5855) sponsors an annual series of guest performances by top-notch companies. The winter-spring series is usually very popular.

Three's Company is an innovative troup with a critical yet loyal following. It also sponsors appearances by other dance companies. 3255 Fifth Avenue. 296-9523.

In the mood for a film? Among the best of the old San Diego theaters with comfortable seats, good sound systems, and big screens are the **Loma** (3150 Rosecrans, 224-3344); the **Cinerama** (5889 University Avenue, 583-6201); **Cinema 21** (1140 Hotel Circle North, 291-2121); and the **Valley Circle** (Mission Valley Center West, 297-3931).

Neighborhood theaters showing cult and foreign films and series include the **Fine Arts** (1818 Garnet Avenue, Pacific Beach, 274-4000); the

Cove (7730 Girard Avenue, La Jolla, 459-5404), and the **Strand** (4950 Newport Avenue, Ocean Beach, 223-3141).

LATE-NIGHT SAN DIEGO

San Diego, as much as we love it, is not much for late nightlife. The big draws are the sun and the beach, and when the first goes down and the other turns chilly, the local folk tend to pack up and head inside for the evening. There are, of course, coffeehouses, music places, and clubs, just not to the extent that there are in, say, Los Angeles.

Upstart Crow & Company is a good browsing bookstore at two locations, each with an espresso bar serving pastries and other desserts. The Seaport Village location (835 W. Harbor Drive, 232-4855) has an upstairs that's comfortable for working or relaxing. The Pacific Beach location (4475 Mission Boulevard, 272-8990) has a more extensive menu with light meals and a wine bar. Both open until 10 P.M. Sunday through Thursday, and until 11 P.M. Friday and Saturday.

JAZZ

Jazz greats appear at **Elario's** regularly, interspersed with appearances by local groups. 7955 La Jolla Shores Drive, La Jolla. 459-0541.

For years the King Biscuit Blues Band has perfected their rock and blues act at the **Mandolin Wind.** Their weekend shows are always packed. Other local bands appear during the week. The crowd is friendly and casual, and there is no problem going alone. 380 University Avenue, Hillcrest. 297-3017.

COMEDY

At the **Comedy Store,** top local and national comedians appear nightly, with Mondays reserved for amateurs. You will see more groups here than singles. 916 Pearl Street, La Jolla. 454-9176.

The **Improv** is a new addition to these clubs from New York and L.A. High-caliber live comedians in a cabaret setting, with meals served during the first show. 832 Garnet Avenue, Pacific Beach. 483-4520.

ROCK AND DISCO

An outrageously popular disco, **Club Diego's** is packed on weekends. Top 40 and New Wave dancing. You could go alone—it's so noisy and crowded no one would notice. 860 Garnet Avenue, Pacific Beach. 272-5171.

Halcyon is the premier spot for singles into dancing, with live rock and roll nightly. 4258 West Point Loma Boulevard, Point Loma. 225-9559.

Though there's nothing classy about **Spirit,** most of the area's top bands start out here. The live music is experimental, New Wave, and rock, and the crowd is as offbeat as San Diego gets. 1130 Buenos Avenue, Bay Park. 276-3993.

AT LEISURE

Day-Tripping

Say you wind up with an extra day in San Diego. Rather than pack up your towel and suntan lotion and head for the beach or take in a few of the sights, why not head for the open road and see a bit of southern California? You could, of course, point yourself in the direction of **Los Angeles** or **Disneyland,** or even quaint **Laguna Beach,** a little over an hour north. But by far the most popular day-trip from San Diego is **Tijuana,** just a hop, skip, and jump over the Mexican border.

MEXICO

Visitors are always struck by how foreign Tijuana seems. It may be a border town, but it is thoroughly Mexican and nothing like San Diego. You can, however, get by with English and a smattering of Spanish phrases, and it is not necessary to exchange your dollars for pesos.

In planning a trip to Tijuana, keep in mind that most rental companies will not allow you to take their cars into Mexico, but there are plenty of large parking lots on the U.S. side of the border. Cabs line up just inside the border; the fare to town should cost about $5. If you do drive into Mexico, be sure to get Mexican auto insurance at one of the many stands at the last few exits before the border. The bright red Tijuana trolley runs through downtown San Diego to the border. It's a convenient way to get there, and the fare is only $1 (231-1466).

Once there, you will find that **Avenida Revolucion,** the center of downtown, is lined with stores selling souvenirs. Bartering here is the name of the game. Some of the best restaurants in town are close by, among them **Tijuana Tilly's, Tilly's Fifth Avenue, Bol Corona,** and **La Costa.**

Attractions include the **Agua Caliente Racetrack,** with year-round racing of greyhounds during the week and horses on weekends (706/ 686-2002). You can also take in **jai alai** at the Palacio on Avenida Revolucion. Games are played daily except Thursdays.

For more information, contact the **Mexican Consulate,** 1333 Front Street, San Diego, CA 92101 (231-8414). Or the **Tijuana Convention and Visitors Bureau** offers information and reservations for Tijuana hotels, restaurants, and attractions. Open Monday through Friday 9 A.M. to 5 P.M. 7860 Mission Center Court, Suite 100, San Diego, CA 92108 (299-8518).

Sunday Customs

To the typical San Diegan, the ideal Sunday would probably begin with brunch at a favorite little spot, segueing into an afternoon at the beach, where she might play a little volleyball, take a dip, or just perfect her tan. Those with energy to spare might take in a museum (all the major tourist attractions are open on Sunday) or plan a picnic (popular spots include Mission Bay and Balboa and Presidio parks).

Brunch starts early at many places and the dress is usually casual. Most of the beach restaurants along the Mission Beach boardwalk serve breakfast or brunch—it's a good way to get to the beach early enough to get a parking space. Following are some of the more popular spots serving brunch.

At **Atlantis,** you can enjoy a nice champagne brunch while admiring a beautiful view of Mission Bay. 2595 Ingraham Street. 226-3888.

The white-washed walls and framed tapestries in **Calliopes** give this Greek cafe a sophisticated yet comfortable atmosphere. The fresh-baked bread and homemade Greek specialties are delicious. 3958 Fifth Avenue. 291-5588.

There is a lovely view of the city from the open-air patio of **Casa Vallarta** in Old Town. Good Mexican breakfasts. 2457 Juan Street. 260-8124.

Frenchy Marseilles is a cheery sidewalk bistro and indoor restaurant offering Continental cafe fare. Eighth Avenue and C Street. 233-3413.

During the week, many a downtown businessperson starts his or her day at **Hob Nob Hill,** a friendly family-owned restaurant featuring home-style cooking. Closed on Saturdays and packed on Sundays. Reservations recommended. 2271 First Avenue. 239-8176.

Spectator Sports

The three items a sports enthusiast in San Diego might need are a sun visor, binoculars, and the capacity to yell. At **Jack Murphy Stadium,** the **San Diego Chargers** (280-2111) charge for touchdowns; the **San Diego Padres** (283-4494) bat for homeruns; and the **San Diego Sockers** (280-GOAL) try for the most goals.

If horses are your game, head for **Del Mar Racetrack.** The 43-day racing season begins in late July, with nine races daily except Tuesdays. 299-1340; 755-1141.

Active Sports

With 70 miles of shoreline and an amazingly pleasant year-round average temperature, San Diego lends itself to outdoor sports. The coast is the place for **surfing** (body and board); Mission Bay, for **water skiing;** and the La Jolla Shores Ecological Reserve, for **skin diving and snorkling** (call local dive shops like the Diving Locker at 272-1120 for information). Other popular water sports here include **sailing and windsurfing** (call the Mission Bay Aquatics Center for rental information at 488-1036 or check the yellow pages), and deep-sea or freshwater **fishing** at local lakes (236-5532).

If the water is not your game, there's volleyball, tennis, golf, cycling, and jogging. **Volleyball** nets are usually set up at Ocean Beach or North Mission Beach. For **tennis,** call the Parks and Recreation Department (236-5717 or 236-7083), or try Morley Field (295-7665), known for having the city's finest courts. San Diego has as many **golf** courses as it has beaches. There's Balboa Park Municipal, 9 holes (232-2717) or 18 holes (232-2470) and Torrey Pines (453-3530), just to name a couple. For **cyclists,** along the beach seems to be the best choice (for rentals, try California Bicycles at 454-0316).

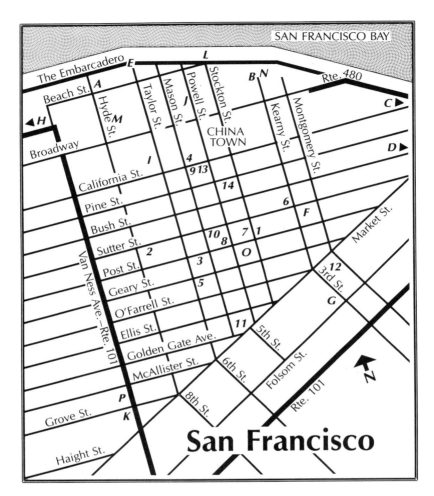

San Francisco

HOTELS

1 Campton Place
2 Bedford
3 Donatello
4 The Fairmont Hotel
  & Tower
5 Four Seasons Clift
6 Galleria Park
7 Hyatt on Union Square
8 Kensington Park Hotel
9 Mark Hopkins
  Intercontinental
10 Orchard
11 Ramada Renaissance
12 Sheraton Palace
13 Stanford Court
14 Vintage Court
15 York Hotel

LANDMARKS

A Cannery
B Coit Tower
C Embarcadero Center
D Financial District
E Fisherman's Wharf
F Galleria at Crocker Center
G George F. Moscone
  Convention Center
H Golden Gate Bridge

I Nob Hill
J North Beach
K Performing Arts Center
L Pier 39
M Russian Hill
N Telegraph Hill
O Union Square
P Veteran's Bldg.

SAN FRANCISCO

GETTING YOUR BEARINGS

San Francisco calls itself "the city that knows how," and it *does*. Most of all it knows how to charm you into wanting a corporate transfer. We have left our heart in this hilly city enough times to warn you that this is a place that will lure you from your business all too easily. Its stunning scenery, tantalizing shops, and funky night life are so tempting that you'll not want to stay cooped up in your hotel—even though some of the hostelries here are the most historic and beautiful in America.

Women have fared well in San Francisco from the gold-rush years. More than many cities, San Francisco has provided women the opportunity to win male respect by sharing hardships during the rough pioneer days and the 1906 earthquake, to name two biggies. It may have been Isaac Magnin's name on the city's most famous native department store, but his wife, Anna, ran the retail empire. And when popular mayor George Moscone was assassinated in 1979, it was City Supervisor Dianne Feinstein who set about, in her words, to "sweep up the glass and put the city back together again."

The pervading tolerance, the live-and-let-live tenor of San Francisco, fits its naturally awesome beauty. Prejudice, though present, seems to dissipate against the spectacular setting of the city. Thus, individualism flourishes, sometimes to the consternation of people from other places. But life is too wonderful by their bay for San Franciscans to care and all these people knowing they are here more for the place than for profit lightens the work environment.

We have one friend who forsook Manhattan for San Francisco. She loved it, but the lure of greater career opportunities and better pay diverted her to Los Angeles for a year. Her move, indeed her *flight,* back to San Francisco came down to a quality-of-life decision. The difference shows in her face and in her subsequent career success.

Who can knock it? In 46 square miles of densely packed humanity, San Francisco is like a jewel box of delights, a necklace of neighborhoods strung across the hills ranged against the sparkling backdrop of San Francisco Bay and beyond. Gingerbread Victorian houses share the turf with striking skyscrapers, Chinese pagodas, and stately *belle-époque* public buildings. This is *not* "just another city."

Of course, San Francisco has been a rough-and-tumble town since the days of the original forty-niners; it can still get that way if today's football 49ers win a big one at Candlestick Park (you'll pass it coming in from the airport). The area around the new George F. Moscone Convention Center, though coming on strong with new hotels, still betrays its shabbier skid row origins; don't walk alone here. The waterfront, too, though touristy with the lively restaurants and shops of Fisherman's Wharf and Pier 39, has its share of hard-drinking teens and light-fingered pickpockets; you'd do well to go with a friend. But the Tenderloin, formerly a sleazy district of cheap bars and shady characters, has been transformed into an upwardly mobile boutique paradise, thanks to the lordly Ramada Renaissance Hotel. In fact, the area has been retitled the Renaissance District.

We love strolling the streets of the Marina (upscale residential), the Haight (only by day, though, a persistent drug scene makes it dangerous at night), and the Hills—Nob, Russian and Telegraph. From Coit Tower, a 1934 landmark atop Telegraph Hill, you can see the whole city from the Golden Gate to Twin Peaks and quaint Sausalito across the bay. That tiny island in the middle of the water is Alcatraz, and the National Park Service gives one of the most fascinating tours there of any place we know.

But you are here on business, remember? The concentrated downtown includes the financial district with its towering banks abutting high-rise Embarcadero Center. Locals consider this the symbol of a Manhattanization of their city (not a compliment). Future development has been severely limited to preserve a lower scale for the place.

Fortunately, the compact nature of San Francisco puts the shopping meccas within an easy walk of the business areas. The Galleria at Crocker Center, a glass-domed corridor of fine shops and foods, is closest at hand. Union Square, the heart of great stores (Neiman-Marcus, Macy's, Saks, and the ever-strong I. Magnin), connects to arteries of streets with dazzling local specialty shops from chocolatiers to jewelers. Take tea at the venerable Westin St. Francis Hotel overlooking Union Square; its lavishly restored Compass Rose drawing room is one of America's most romantic retreats.

Whether you catch a cable car from the St. Francis to the top of Nob Hill and another down the other side to the financial district (San Franciscans do ride them to work) or experience the ultramodern BART train under the bay to Oakland, you will find the thrill of the city old and new.

And even if you leave your heart here, San Francisco will always, as its other theme song says, open its Golden Gate for you to come back again.

WHAT TO WEAR

The trick of dressing for San Francisco success—and comfort—is to wear layers. You may be surprised how often you find yourself taking off or putting on a light jacket or sweater or vest. Just remember: this is a fashion-conscious and relatively dressy city, not to be confused with the lighter and more casual look of Los Angeles. High fashion goes here, as does the next trend in ready-to-wear—as long as that trend isn't *too* trendy.

WEATHER WATCH

Sure, it gets foggy in San Francisco. You can watch the clouds billow through the Golden Gate and hear boats blasting their foghorns on a gray day. The fog can make it damp and depressing in winter, but it also acts as natural air-conditioning in summer. No matter what the season, San Francisco weather can turn damp, chilly, or briskly windy at a moment's notice. So be sure to carry a jacket or sweater despite the local weatherperson's cheery predictions, which, more often than not, will be the mild 60s in the summer and a few degrees lower in the winter. Any heat wave likely to hit the city will do so in September or October.

GETTING THERE

San Francisco International Airport (761-0800) is the world's sixth busiest. Located 15 miles south of San Francisco, SFO serves 41 airlines and is port of call for 32,000 flights per month. The airport's bilevel, easy access, compact terminal consists of three buildings: the South, International, and North terminals. Bufano sculptures (native to northern California) in the North Terminal's boarding area F, nicely displayed folk art, photographs, and historical objects showcased in the terminal connectors offer a visual respite from travel's hectic dashing. Electronic "You Are Here" systems provide an assist to first time arrivals.

Transportation time from SFO to downtown is about 30 minutes; another 15 to 30 minutes during rush hours. Bus and shuttle stops, taxi stands, limousines and hotel/motel courtesy van pickup points are primarily located on the lower level roadway in front of all terminals.

Airporter is a regularly scheduled, convenient form of transportation between SFO and several downtown hotels or Airporter's downtown terminal at Taylor and Ellis streets. This is one of the least expensive methods of transport to the city. Keep in mind that unless the Airporter drops you at your hotel, you'll have to grab a cab to your final destination. 673-2432.

Lorrie's Travel & Tourism, Inc., between SFO and several San Francisco hotels, is inexpensive; Lorrie's will also drop you at nonhotel destinations for a small extra charge. 826-5950.

Taxis are possibly the speediest, though most expensive, way to get into S.F. besides a limousine. Plan on $20 to $30 (depending on your final destination and ensuing traffic) plus tip. Only taxis displaying a gold San Francisco International Airport seal are authorized to pick up passengers at the airport. Limousines are an expensive, though decidedly luxurious way to enter the city. Plan on $40 to $100, though some companies offer a ride-sharing plan for substantially less. Several limousine firms are found in the airport's baggage claim area, or you can plan ahead by calling Airport Connection, Inc., 872-2552; P & F Limo, 824-6767; Associate Limousines of San Francisco, 563-1000 (ask about their ride-sharing to and from the airport); or Regency Limousine Service, 922-0123.

Several hotels and motels offer complimentary shuttle service to and from the airport. This is not, however, standard practice, so be sure to ask about the service when making your travel reservations.

Car Rentals

The hilly terrain, one-way streets, slip-and-slide cable car tracks, sometimes maniacal cab drivers, and lumbering buses make driving here seem like San Francisco's version of the Grand Prix. And if driving isn't scary enough, you'll shriek at outrageous parking costs and nearly impossible-to-find parking spaces. San Francisco is not a city for rental cars unless you're a one-time resident well-versed in the city's unconventional defensive driving and parking techniques.

But if you're planning a trip outside the city, a rental car is the best way to see beautiful northern California. Rental car companies are centrally located in downtown San Francisco. Call direct and ask about weekend packages, special rates or promotions.

AVCAR	440 O'Farrell St., 441-4779
Avis	675 Post St., 885-5011
Budget	321 Mason St., 928-7863
Dollar	333 Taylor St., 673-2137
Hertz	433 Mason St., 771-2200
Thrifty-Rent-a-Car	435 Taylor St., 673-6675

GETTING AROUND

If your hectic itinerary plays havoc with your regular excercise schedule, stop moaning when you reach San Francisco. This is one city where you get your daily aerobics without donning a leotard. Just start walking and climbing—up and down hills, in and out of cabs, buses, BART, cable cars, ferryboats, pedicabs, and limousines.

San Francisco Municipal Railway (MUNI)

Dubbed "Hallidie's Folly" in 1873 after their inventor, Andrew S. Hallidie, San Francisco's celebrated **cable cars** are not only a national landmark but a vital link in the Municipal Railway's 700-mile public transportation network. Fresh from a $60 million systemwide refurbishing, the 40-car fleet crisscrosses the city's hills on three routes carrying more than 12 1/2 million passengers yearly.

A cable car ride, whether strictly for pleasure or as transport between appointments, is a must. Block out an extra 20 or 30 minutes and ride an entire route, or hop on (after the car comes to a complete stop) at any corner along the three lines. Your reward is a trolley tour de force complete with spectacular vistas. Cost for this chic conveyance is $1; transfers are free.

These boxy treasures operate along the following routes: The Powell-Mason line begins at the corner of Powell and Market streets, climbs Nob Hill, and descends gently into Fisherman's Wharf. The most scenic line—Powell-Hyde—starts from the same downtown intersection and ascends Nob and Russian hills. Its 20-minute journey ends at the waterfront turntable in Victorian Park, across from the famous Buena Vista Cafe where Irish coffee became popular in the United States as a potent warmer-upper. The midtown route originates at the foot of California Street, lurches through the financial district, along the edge of Chinatown, and out to Van Ness Avenue, one of the city's main thoroughfares.

San Francisco's **electric buses and motor coaches** blanket the city. You're never more than two or three blocks from a stop. When it runs on time, it's probably the best transportation bargain in town. But as with similar systems in other major metropolitan areas, when it falls off the mark, it falls hard. Fortunately, for the millions of commuters each year who depend on it, the MUNI doesn't trip too often.

Exact change is required, and free transfers are good in any direction for 90 minutes. Your best route information source is found by calling 673-MUNI. Tell the courteous operators where you want to go, and they'll tell you the precise bus or buses to take from your point of origin to your destination. Be sure to follow some general (and, we hope, obvious) safety rules: sit at the front of the coach near the driver; keep an eye on your purse, briefcase, and wallet; and don't ride MUNI in an area you wouldn't want to walk through.

Taxis

San Francisco taxis are moderately priced, usually clean, and generally hailable from any corner except in residential areas. Fares are about $2.50 for the first mile and $1.20 for each additional mile. As in most cities, the fleet seems to shrink mysteriously in wet weather. You can, however, call the cab companies direct and get one in 10 to 20 minutes. Some companies are DeSoto Cab, 673-1414; Luxor Cab, 552-4040; Veteran's Taxicab, 552-1300; Yellow Cab, 626-2345; and Sunshine Cab, 776-7755.

Bay Area Rapid Transit (BART)

The 71-mile, oft-praised, and sometimes cursed BART system links eight San Francisco stations with Daly City (south) and 25 stations in the East Bay. These sleek, silent, usually efficient trains zip under the San Francisco Bay, providing an underwater link between the city and its transbay neighbors. Trains run every three and a half minutes during peak hours, seven days a week. Ticket machines are at every station, and you don't need exact change. Huge color-keyed wall maps, depicting routes and destinations, and change machines are also located in the stations. BART stations are clean and cordial, and security guards are strategically located at each stop. Call 788-BART for schedule and fare information.

Ferry Service

Until the 1937 opening of the Golden Gate Bridge, ferries were the only way to cross the San Francisco Harbor. Today, as in Hong Kong, they still ply the bay as part of San Francisco's public transportation system. The short seagoing journeys start or end the day for thousands of commuters with a touch of romance and nautical adventure. **Golden Gate Ferries** depart several times daily from the south end of the ferry building at the foot of Market Street to Sausalito and Larkspur. Count on a 30-minute crossing to quaint Sausalito, while high-speed service to urban Larkspur in Marin County cuts that lengthy commute to 15 minutes. Call 332-6600 for fare and schedule information.

A boat-tour concessionaire, the jaunty **Red & White Fleet** provides ferry service to and from Tiburon, a classy shopping and dining village, and Angel Island, a beautiful reserve for day picnicking and limited overnight camping. Tiburon ferry service operates weekdays only during commuting hours from the ferry building. The Angel Island ferry sails from Pier 43½ near Fisherman's Wharf on weekends and holidays only; no service is available November, December, or January. For fare and schedule information about both services, call 788-1880 or 546-2815.

GETTING FAMILIAR

San Francisco Convention & Visitors Bureau
201 Third Street, Suite 900   974-6900
San Francisco, CA 94103
Write or call for just about any kind of information you could possibly

need about the city. This bureau is one of the best in the nation. It also provides information on San Francisco's Moscone Center, a high-tech convention center that for the most part has been built underground.

If you're already in town and in need of visitor aids, stop by the **Visitors Information Center,** located in Hallidie Plaza at Market and Powell streets, lower level. Or for an up-to-the-minute report on what's happening, call 391-2001 for a taped two-minute summary of cultural, sports, and sightseeing events.

San Francisco still has morning and evening newspapers: The *San Francisco Chronicle* (morning) and the *San Francisco Examiner* (afternoon) combine forces on weekends to put out the Sunday paper. The Calendar Section—known to natives as the Pink—offers a complete overview of cultural activities from theater to rock 'n' roll clubs and museums. The *Examiner's* TGIF section published each Friday offers a look at weekend activities. To learn of neighborhood happenings, pick up the *Nob Hill Gazette, CenterVoice, San Francisco Progress,* or the *Bay Guardian.* There's no charge for any of them, and they're available at cafes, shopping areas, and the like. As for monthly city magazines, *San Francisco* and *Focus* profile Bay Area people and activities and offer restaurant and theater reviews.

Quick Calls

AREA CODE 415
Time 767-8900

Weather 936-1212
Emergencies 911

AT YOUR SERVICE

Four Seasons Clift
495 Geary at Taylor
San Francisco, CA 94102

Toll-free reservations: 800/268-6282
Local number: 775-4700
Telex: 00340647

Fortune magazine once dubbed the Clift one of the "eight great small hotels in the world." We tend to agree. The hotel, located on the edge of Union Square, is the only one in northern California to have garnered both the AAA Five-Diamond and Mobil Five-Star awards of excellence. You couldn't ask for more from a hotel: appointments are elegant yet comfortable and the services plentiful and prompt, including one of the city's best concierges. Powder blue and soft peach room decor soothes the spirit after a harried day conducting business in the city.

	Concierge	Executive Floor	No-Smoking Rooms	Fitness Facilities	Pool	24-Hour Room Service	Restaurant for Client Entertaining	Extra-Special Amenities	Electronic Key System	Business/Secretarial Services	Check Out Time	Frequent Guest Program	Business Traveler Program	Average Rate
Campton Place	•						Campton Place Restaurant	•		•	2 p.m.			$160–$220
Donatello	•	•					Donatello	•		•	12 noon		Club Gracie	$135–$170
The Fairmont Hotel & Tower	•			•		•	The Squire	•			1 p.m.		Gold Circle	$130–$185
Four Seasons Clift	•		•			•	The French Room	•			1 p.m.		Clift Club	$135–$235 $140 corp.
Galleria Park				•			Brasserie Chambord				12 noon	Park Preferred Club		$ 89 $ 84 corp.
Hyatt on Union Square	•	•	•	•		•	Hugos	•	•		12 noon	Gold Passport	•	$135–$175

468

Hotel				Restaurant				Check-out		P.E.T.	Rate
Kensington Park Hotel	•					•		12 noon		P.E.T.	$ 85–$115 $ 75 corp.
Mark Hopkins Inter-Continental	•		•	Nob Hill Restaurant	•		•	12 noon	Advantage Club	#1 Nob Hill Club	$130–$205 $154 corp.
Orchard	•	•	•	Annabels	•	•		12 noon		Business Traveler Program	$ 85–$105 $ 75 corp.
Ramada Renaissance	•	•	•	Corintia	•	•		12 noon			$105–$160
Sheraton Palace				The Signature	•	•	•	12 noon		Red Phone	$105 $ 90 corp.
Stanford Court	•			Fournou's Ovens	•			2 p.m.			$135–$210
York Hotel	•	•	•				•	1 p.m.		Club 940	$ 74–$84 $ 70 corp.

Dining is supreme in the **French Room,** where executive chef Werner Albrecht draws raves for his medallions of veal, poached fresh salmon, and cassoulet of Maine lobster. Dieters will appreciate the Four Seasons alternative gourmet cuisine, low in calories, cholesterol, and sodium. Redwood burl paneling surrounding art deco decor in the **Redwood Room** makes this one of San Francisco's most distinctive bars. It's been around for 50 years, offering afternoon tea as well as providing a pleasant respite for evening cocktails.

Campton

340 Stockton	Toll-free reservations: outside
San Francisco, CA 94108	California 800/647-4007; in California
	800/235-4300
	Local number: 781-5555
	Telex: 677-1185

The luxurious Campton Place, a quiet oasis in the midst of bustling Union Square, was once the Drake-Wiltshire, a small European hotel that rose like a phoenix from the ashes after a $18 million renovation. Each of the 123 unpretentious rooms are now decorated to offer the warmth of a private residence with handsome furnishings like Henredon armoires housing color televisions. Resplendent baths are adorned with travertine marble and brass fixtures. Original and limited edition art and stylish accessories add a personalized flair. An attentive professional attitude permeates the hotel; a valet will even pack and unpack for you. For the harried business traveler, secretarial services include typing and copying, messengers and multilingual translators.

Fine dining suitable to a city like San Francisco may be experienced in the **Campton Place** restaurant. Chef Bradley Ogden's nationally acclaimed American cuisine is prepared through French cooking techniques. Weary travelers will be pleased to know one of the hotel's most delightful secrets—you can order anything from the restaurant's menu through room service. The cheery **lobby bar** is great for sipping martinis, people-watching, and eavesdropping.

Ramada Renaissance

55 Cyril Magnin, Market at Fifth	Toll-free reservations: 800/228-9898
streets	Local number: 392-8000
San Francisco, CA 94102	Telex: 755-982

Opened in late 1984, the Ramada Renaissance is part of an extensive renovation project near Market Street, the area that surrounds Moscone Center, San Francisco's underground convention complex. This 1,015-room hotel pierces San Francisco's skyline at 32 stories and contains more than a million dollars worth of fine art—traditional and modern—including an imposing six-ton sculpture by San Francisco artist Ruth Asawa. Accommodations are stylish, protected by one of the city's most stringent security and life safety systems and graced by a sparkling view of San Francisco outside each bay window. A piazza overlooks a spacious three-story atrium filled with a verdant garden of fresh flowers and trees.

Pianists caress the keys of a gleaming ebony grand piano as hotel life bustles below.

The hotel has two restaurants.

Galleria Park

191 Sutter Street
San Francisco, CA
94104-4595

Toll-free reservations: 800/792-9855
Local number: 781-3060
Telex: 470733

Once known as the Sutter Hotel, this newly renovated 177-room hotel is located in the heart of the city's financial district. Because of its downtown locale, close attention was given to soundproofing rooms during the refurbishing, with special glass installed in all windows to silence outside traffic. The hotel has a second-floor conference center, with three rooms for groups from 12 to 60.

Bentley's Restaurant for seafood and the **Oyster Bar** occupies the mezzanine floor and are part of the hotel's art nouveau lobby. The bar has become a popular respite for financial district habitués who stop for a drink on their way home.

Hyatt on Union Square

345 Stockton
San Francisco, CA 94108

Toll-free reservations: 800/228-9000
Local number: 398-1234
Telex: 340592

Soaring 36 stories, the Hyatt on Union Square is a few steps from one of San Francisco's most elegant shopping districts. This stately 694-room hotel offers personal attention and grand lodging. Mozambique wood graces the central lobby and mezzanine; warm salmon, caramel brown, mint green, and brass decor and furnishings create a quiet, relaxing atmosphere. A subtle Oriental influence softens the lobby. Sunny, spacious guest rooms provide sweeping views of the San Francisco Bay area and are furnished with custom rattan and cane accoutrements and commissioned lithographed and original art. Besides the expected amenities, this hotel provides some innovative surprises: a free limousine ride early each weekday morning to and from the Embarcadero's parcourse, gratis guest membership during your stay at the highly ranked San Francisco Tennis Club, and access to the swank Telegraph Hill Club.

This spacious hotel boasts four restaurants and lounges that run the gamut from elegant to deli dining. The rooftop **One Up** restaurant and piano bar overlooks some of the city's most stunning vistas. Ride the elevator up 36 floors for a nightcap here, accompanied by the romantic tones of a Bosendoerfer concert grand piano.

Orchard

562 Sutter Street
San Francisco, CA 94102

Toll-free reservations: in California 800/433-4434; outside California 800/433-4343
Local number: 433-4434
Telex: 171500

Constructed 12 months after the great 1906 earthquake, the Orchard is now in full bloom after an extensive facelift. This 96-room hotel is nestled amid fine shops, boutiques, and theaters on posh Sutter Street, with exemplary hospitality and personal service traditionally found in small European inns. Pleasant guest rooms are decorated in peach tones with traditional Old World furnishings and are equipped with the latest safety devices. Armoires with full-length mirrors and a variety of personal care items grace each room, along with minibars and telephones with call waiting.

The seven-story hostelry houses **Annabel's,** an informal brasserie with frequently changing menu to feature seasonal seafoods, fowl, and grilled meats. The adjacent lounge comes alive at night as a pianist/singer entertains from her extensive repertoire.

Donatello

501 Post Street
San Francisco, CA 94102

Toll-free reservations: in California 800/792-9837; outside California 800/227-3184
Local number: 441-7100
Telex: 172875

This hotel brings a regal touch of northern Italy to the heart of San Francisco, one block from Union Square. It warms you with the civilized, stately ambience, exquisite dining, and attentive service usually found in better European hotels. Large guest rooms are tastefully appointed as is the elegant lobby. Extralength double and king-sized beds, soft lambsdown blankets, two telephones, complimentary local telephone calls, remote control color TV, plus full-length terry robes, skirt hangers, and fine soaps and linens grace each room.

In the hotel, **Donatello's** is one of San Francisco's finer restaurants, specializing in the classics of northern Italy. Prices here are steep, but worth it. The same experience surprisingly is available through room service.

Kensington Park

450 Post Street
San Francisco, CA 94102

Toll-free reservations: 800/553-1900
Local number: 788-6400
Telex: 470429

Recently joining the ranks of San Francisco's small sumptuous hotels, this neoclassic building has reawakened after a $4.5 million restoration completed in 1984. The hotel, originally built in 1924 to house the Elks Club, is located on tony Post Street, steps from Union Square. Each of the 81 rooms is faithfully furnished in authentic Queen Anne and Chippendale styles. You'll be surrounded by mahogany furniture accented with damask fabrics, Chippendale armoires housing color TV, and Chinese vases designed into bedside lamps. Enjoy the French-milled soaps and terry robes.

A hotel restaurant is expected to open in spring 1986. Tea and sherry are served in the chic lobby every afternoon as a pianist serenades in the living-room-like atmosphere under beautiful Spanish-Gothic wood beam ceilings.

Sheraton Palace

639 Market Street at New
Montgomery
San Francisco, CA 94105

Toll-free reservations: 800/325-3535
Local number: 392-8600
Telex: 340947

Once upon a time, San Francisco's social set flocked to the Palace to play host to the wealthy, powerful, and famous who stayed here. American presidents U. S. Grant, Teddy Roosevelt, and Franklin D. Roosevelt checked in frequently as did literary and stage notables Rudyard Kipling and Sarah Bernhardt. The latter had a suite for herself, her pet tiger, and her parrot. San Francisco literally grew up around the Palace. Today, as part of the Sheraton group, the centrally located hotel is just a few blocks from Moscone Center and the financial district. (The Palace is located on the somewhat seedy side of Market Street; daytime walking is fine, but nighttime strolling is not advised.) The 500 guest rooms are furnished to reflect the hotel's turn-of-the-century heritage.

The elegant hostelry boasts three restaurants and four lounges, including the legendary **Garden Court,** which opened in 1909. Meals are served under a magnificent high-ceilinged lead-glass dome with crystal chandeliers. Sunday buffet is accompanied by the San Francisco String Quartet, completing the ambience echoing the city's golden past. The **Happy Valley Lounge** was named for a long-ago mining camp. **Lotta's Coffeeshop** is another link with the past; it was named for Lotta Crabtree, a singer/dancer who captured San Francisco's heart over a century ago. The **Pied Piper Room** houses an original Maxfield Parrish mural and is a favorite venue for business lunches or informal dinners.

York

940 Sutter Street
San Francisco, CA 94109

Toll-free reservations: in California 800/
327-3608; outside California 800/227-
3608
Local number: 885-6800
Telex: 6972047

The York, built in 1922 at the height of Prohibition, has an underground passageway. That's just a hint of the secrets you'll find in this renovated hotel treasure located near Chinatown and Russian Hill. Once known as the Glen Royale Hotel (you may remember seeing it in Hitchcock's *Vertigo* as the Empire), this soothing retreat is decorated in soft pastels and features wet bars, walk-in closets, and window seats in the 100 guest rooms.

This lovely hotel has no restaurant, but a terrific night spot, the **Plush Room,** once a speakeasy (for details, see "Late-Night San Francisco").

Fairmont Hotel and Tower

950 Mason   Toll-free reservations: in Texas 800/492-
San Francisco, CA 94108   6622; outside Texas 800/527-4727
                                             Local number: 772-5000
                                             Telex: 9103726002

Perched atop Nob Hill, the Fairmont Hotel is perhaps the grande dame
of San Francisco hostelries. Built in 1905, the main building survived the
Great Earthquake a year later. Today the 700-room hotel comprises two
buildings, with a commanding front entrance and expansive lobby (you'll
recognize it if you watch "Hotel"; a facsimile was created for the television show). Although cavernous (the hotel houses 9 restaurants and
lounges, a sleek health club, and 23 meeting rooms), it offers superb
personal accommodations. A courteous, detail-oriented staff, often carefully supervised by exemplary owner, Richard L. Swig, quickly puts the
novice traveler at ease. Fairmont guest rooms are tastefully decorated,
many have stunning views, and all are stocked with an impressive array
of amenities like cotton terry cloth bathrobes, electric shoe polisher,
goosedown pillows, and incredibly soft sheets. Twice-daily maid service
is a busy executive's dream.

Once at the Fairmont you may never leave. A typical evening's
entertainment can begin with cocktails in the grand **Cirque** lounge, and
continue with an exquisite, attentively served dinner in the **Squire.** Then,
retire to the **Venetian Room** to listen to the likes of Tina Turner, Joel Grey,
or Kenny Rankin, and wind it all up with a nightcap in the **New Orleans
Room** or the **Crown Room** towering 24 stories over the city. Most of the
restaurants offer a fitness menu, tasty recipes prepared under American
Heart Association guidelines.

Mark Hopkins Inter-Continental

#1 Nob Hill (999 California Street)   Toll-free reservations: 800/327-0200
San Francisco, CA 94108   Local number: 392-3434
                                             Telex: 340809

This is one of the oldest buildings on esteemed Nob Hill. It was elabo-
rately designed by Mark Hopkins, a cofounder of the Central Pacific
Railroad, and was completed after his death in 1878. Like many other
homes built on the area's solid rock, the Hopkins house fell victim to
the raging fires following the 1906 earthquake. A more utilitarian structure
was then built, serving as a school until 1921. In mid-1926, the grand
hotel opened, graciously serving area residents as well as visitors. Today
part of the worldwide Inter-Continental hotel group, the Mark—as it's
affectionately called—particularly caters to the business traveler. You
could practically set up your office in the hotel with every type of service
available from word processing to access to a well-stocked business publication library. A house physician is on call.

The hotel has two restaurants and two lounges. The famed **Top
of the Mark** is still magical for late-night cocktails and panoramic views.
The gourmet **Nob Hill Restaurant** serves grills, roasts, poultry, and seafood.

Stanford Court

Nob Hill (905 California Street)
San Francisco, CA 94108

Toll-free reservations: in California 800/
622-0957; outside California 800/227-
4736
Local number: 989-3500
Telex: 34-0899

At first glance, the Stanford Court feels like a private club, not a hotel. The wood-paneled lobby is warmly furnished for privacy (thus providing a good business environment in a public space) with finely upholstered Empire settees and armchairs. The 402 rooms and suites are serene, many with canopied beds, marble bedside tables, heated towel racks, and old San Francisco etchings. Throughout the hotel, San Francisco designer Andrew Delfino has mixed modern design with period pieces for a residential flavor. Special touches include Baccarat chandeliers, Carrara marble, and oak armoires.

For dining in the hotel, try **Cafe Potpourri,** actually three cafes in one, for casual breakfast and lunch; and **Fournou's Ovens,** a unique restaurant with massive open-hearth ovens that produce roasts of every description. The award-winning eatery features one of the country's largest collections of California fine wine.

ON A BUDGET

Hotels

Vintage Court

650 Bush Street
San Francisco, CA 94108

Toll-free reservations: in California 800/
654-7266; outside California 800/654-
1100
Local number: 392-4666
Telex: 470733 (goes to the Bedford
first—see next entry—then here)

Built in 1913, this charming, eight-story 106-room hotel was revitalized in 1983. Its approximately $75-a-night rooms make this one of the city's best values. Its location (two blocks from Union Square) and tasteful decoration offset the fact that there's no room service. California wines are celebrated here with guest rooms named for Domain Chandon, Stag's Lap, and Chateau Montelena. Besides complimentary California wines served in front of the lobby's cozy fireplace each weekday evening, a fully stocked refrigerator, and overnight valet, amenities include complimentary limousine service to the financial district.

The Vintage Court is home to one of the city's finest restaurants, **Masa's,** described by *San Francisco Examiner* restaurant critic Stan Sesser as "arguably one of the best French restaurants in the United States." This is not a budget find, however—dinner is about $35 per person.

Bedford

761 Post Street   Toll-free reservations: in California 800/
San Francisco, CA 94109   652-1889; outside California 800/227-
                                   5642
                                   Local number: 673-6040
                                   Telex: 470733

This 17-story hotel was renovated in 1983 on the premise that today's travelers demand stylish accommodations at reasonable prices. This cozy, European-style hotel hits the mark, radiating San Francisco charm at a comfortable price. Located in the heart of the theater district and four blocks from Union Square, the 144-room hostelry offers sparkling views of Pacific Heights, Nob Hill, the city's busy port, and bustling East Bay. Snug rooms are warmly furnished with English country chintz bedspreads and draperies in coordinated colors ranging from soothing salmon to vibrant sky blue. The hotel caters to the business traveler with quiet, well-lighted conference facilities, an efficient meeting planning staff, and free limousine service to the financial district twice each weekday morning.

Downstairs, the popular **Cafe Bedford** specializes in innovative California cuisine. Vegetables are fresh from the cafe's own garden. Located off the lobby, the **Wedgewood Bar** is worth a visit, if only to see some of Lord Wedgewood's own collection that hangs on the walnut-paneled walls of this intimate lounge.

Restaurants

If your budget can't handle the usual San Francisco restaurant prices, here are some suggestions:

For breakfast, try **Doidges** for hearty American breakfasts in a fashionable setting. Creative menus are offered for lunch and dinner, too. 2217 Union Street, in Cow Hollow. 921-2149.

Savory hamburgers are served amid loud new-wave tunes and wacky furnishings at **Hamburger Mary's** by a friendly crew sporting the latest in street apparel. Full bar; breakfast, lunch, and dinner until 1:30 A.M. 1582 Folsom, south of Market. 626-5767.

The superb Vietnamese dishes at **Mai's Restaurant** make this a popular lunch or dinner stop. Outside seating and a chic Union Street location contribute to its popularity. 1838 Union Street, in Cow Hollow. 921-2861. Also in the Richmond district at 316 Clement. 221-3046.

DINING OUT

Dining in San Francisco is a treasure hunt of mythological proportions. What Italian cucina prepares the best linguini pesto? What cavernous dining room cooks up the best dim sum? Who will do what to California cuisine next, and how to find it before the crowd? In a city of some 5,000 restaurants, the search is unmercifully endless. Here chefs become celebrities by performing culinary wizardry with the oddest ingredients meticulously combined. To save you anguish, here are some San Francisco restaurants we enjoy:

At the **Blue Boar Inn,** woodsy, clubby, romantic English decor and elegant service are the backdrop for excellent French and California cuisine. 1713 Lombard. 567-8424.

L'Olivier offers wonderful French cooking in both the country-style dining room and the glass-enclosed terrace. 465 Davis Court, in the financial district. 981-7824.

Sutter 500 is multifaceted. Located on the ground floor of the building, adjacent to the Powell Street cable car line, is a moderately priced cafe, an international bookstore, a bar, and an extravagantly priced restaurant. The cafe is great for breakfast or a midmorning espresso, and the restaurant features French nouvelle meals. Downtown at 500 Sutter. 362-3346.

Cafe Riggio is a cheery restaurant serving exquisite Italian cuisine, fresh fish, and several chicken and veal dishes. Try the cheese sauté as an appetizer. Friendly, helpful service is a plus here, although the restaurant is very crowded during prime dining hours. 4112 Geary, in the Richmond district. 221-2114.

Gold Street Restaurant & Bar serves up Italian specialties in a historic building topped with a glittering stained-glass dome. Jazz piano accompanies lunch and dinner. 56 Gold Street, in the financial district. 397-4653.

The theme of busy **Little Joe's** restaurant is "rain or shine, there's always a line," testifying to the terrific Italian meals served up in hearty portions. Sandwiched between strip joints and new wave–rock 'n' roll clubs, the cafe hums with activity, so this isn't a good place to conduct business. You can sit at the counter for a quick bite and watch your meal being prepared over open-flame stoves. Be sure to bring cash; no credit cards accepted here. 523 Broadway, in North Beach. 433-4343.

Frothy Irish coffee was introduced to the United States at **Buena Vista,** and that's probably the reason this corner restaurant/saloon overlooking Victorian Park, the cable car turnaround, and the bay is constantly jammed. Inexpensive dining, big breakfasts, and of course, steaming Irish coffee are good reasons to join the crowd. 2765 Hyde Street, on Fisherman's Wharf. 474-5044.

At **Harris's,** beef, beef, beef is the tradition. This early San Francisco steak house has heavy carpets and drapes, sumptuous booths, and a piano bar. 2100 Van Ness Avenue. 673-1888.

Set in the thriving Marina district, **Mulhern's** is a pleasant saloon specializing in gourmet hamburgers, onion soup, and lamb chops. A friendly bar crowd makes this a good place to patronize. 3653 Buchanan Street. 346-5549.

Once a huge warehouse, the **Cadillac** has been converted to an expansive Mexican restaurant and cantina serving margaritas, seafood, and steaks grilled over mesquite. Be prepared for a lengthy but fun wait during prime dining hours. 1 Holland Court. 543-8226.

The **Balboa Cafe** does double duty: the attractive bar is one of the city's busiest single scenes, while the restaurant serves delicious California cooking. Fresh fish, warm salads, pastas, and special hamburgers are all moderately priced, making this corner eatery a favorite with locals. 3199 Fillmore Street, in Cow Hollow. 921-3944.

Camargue has a French bistro motif and serves grilled meats, seafood, and spit-roasted fowl accompanied by light, simple sauces. The creative menu and revolving list of daily specials are moderately priced. 2316 Polk Street. 776-5577.

Chez Michelle is the place to woo a new client or consummate a deal. This chic, intimate restaurant blends classic French cooking with the latest culinary innovations and seasonal specialties. Under owner Michelle's watchful eye, meals are prepared and served impeccably. Also great for late-night dining. (By the way, the chocolate soufflé is divine.) Very expensive, 804 Northpoint, on Fisherman's Wharf. 771-6077.

Gaylord Restaurant serves elegant Indian food—prawns, chicken, lamb from the fiery tandoori oven, several varieties of baked breads, curry dishes, and delicious vegetarian options. The stylish, calming decor overlooks the bay. In Ghiradelli Square at Fisherman's Wharf. 771-8822.

Operated by the Tassajara Zen Center, **Green's** is a strictly vegetarian establishment that grows its own vegetables and concocts delicious meals. The location affords tremendous bay views. Reservations for dinner are taken several months in advance, but don't despair—just call for cancellations. Fort Mason, Building A, in the Marina district. 771-6222.

Red hot Chinese delicacies served at modest prices and without MSG has made cavernous **Hunan** restaurant an institution. The tasty, but heavily spiced food more than makes up for the gymnasiumlike atmosphere. 924 Sansome, in Chinatown. 956-7727.

High-priced classic French cuisine is found at **Le Castel**, dished up in large portions. The softly lit, restful decor and gracious service make for an appropriate, low-key business environment. 3235 Sacramento Street. 921-7115.

The California cuisine at **Cafe Americain** is served straight from oak ovens and mesquite grills. Moderately priced, imaginative pasta dishes, fresh fish, grilled meats are all carefully prepared and nicely presented. Windows on busy Columbus Avenue—which runs through the heart of North Beach—make this a great vantage point for wine or espresso sipping and people-watching. 317 Columbus Avenue, in North Beach. 981-8266.

Clinging to the tip of Pier 39, **Neptune's Seafood Palace** cooks up some of San Francisco's best seafood. Special menus honor seasonal specialties like salmon and crab. Panoramic views are seen from all tables, though a call to secure a window table is worthwhile. Shoe-saving hint: if it's raining, ask your cab driver to take you down to the restaurant, rather than braving the long wet hike from the entrance to the pier. 434-2260.

Alejandro's offers exceptional Spanish, Peruvian, and Mexican fare. Creative appetizers and hearty portions are served in a warm, lively atmosphere. Try the delicious paella. This place can get very crowded. 1840 Clement, in the Richmond district. 668-1184.

The owner of **Square One** is an alum of Berkeley's Chez Panisse, said to be the birthplace of California cuisine. The menu here changes daily with a focus on pastas and Mediterranean specialties, all made with incredibly fresh ingredients. 190 Pacific Avenue, in the financial district. 788-1110.

SAN FRANCISCO BY DAY

The best orientation to the city we can recommend is to take a trek over to Pier 39 for the **San Francisco Experience.** This multimedia presentation will provide an overview of the city that should whet your appetite for discovering the many attractions that make San Francisco what it is. 982-7394.

While you're discovering San Francisco's roots, why not take in **Jackson Square?** Bounded by Sansome, Washington, and Pacific streets, and Columbus Avenue, the Barbary Coast of the 1860s has emerged as a collection of tiny shops and cafes with much brick-laden charm.

Museums in the city not to be missed include:

M.H. de Young Memorial Museum, for its 64 galleries packed with Western world artifacts from early Egypt to the 20th century. Many masterpieces in the collection of sculpture, painting, and furniture, and the Cafe de Young for relaxing. In Golden Gate Park. 221-4811.

Also in Golden Gate Park, the **California Academy of Science** is excellent, boasting both an aquarium and a planetarium. The latter's exciting laser shows are some of the best we've seen. 750-7145.

Rodin's *The Thinker* holds court in front of the **Palace of the Legion of Honor,** setting the tone for the French art here, including works of Manet, Degas, and Fragonard. Visit if only to enjoy the building itself, an architectural wonder inspired by Napoleon's Palais de la Legion d'Honneur. Lincoln Park. 221-4811.

The **Museum of Modern Art** has a collection of works by Calder, Klee, Pollack, Rauschenberg, and Motherwell. Bay area artists are showcased here as well, and traveling exhibits cover the gamut, from photography to sculpture and painting. At Van Ness and McAllister, in the Veteran's Building. 863-8800.

Three historic homes worth taking a look at are the **Whittier Mansion** (2090 Jackson, 567-1848), the **Haas-Lilienthal House** (2007 Franklin, 441-3004), and the **Octagon House** (2645 Gough Street, 885-9796).

THE SHOPPING SCENE

Deciding where to shop in San Francisco will probably be as difficult as choosing what to buy. Whether you're just peering into windows or testing your credit card limit, you'll find this city to be a veritable shopper's Babylon. A word to the wise: as for nearly every other event, San Francisco dresses up to shop, so don't wear your jeans and tennis shoes. Here's a closer look at S.F. shopping:

Embarcadero Center now stands on what was once the Long Wharf of the Barbary Coast and later the site of San Francisco's produce market. Shoes, clothing, books, luggage, cards, specialty soaps, gourmet confections, and kitchenware are available in 175 shops that share space with numerous restaurants, bars, and dance spots.

Modeled after Milan's vast Galleria Vittorio Emanuele, the **Galleria at Crocker Center** is capped with a huge glass vault that lets in natural light. The stunning architecture embraces 60 shops and several restaurants. Signature stores include American and European designers plus several one-of-a-kind boutiques. Two neoclassic clocks keep time at the Post Street and Sutter Street entrances of this two-story shopping pavilion.

Built in 1894 as Del Monte's fruit canning operation, the **Cannery** was lavishly remodeled into a delightful three-story complex offering a kaleidoscope of more than 50 shops, galleries, restaurants, cafes, and a movie theater. A labyrinth of balconies, bridges, and walkways guide you through Old World charm and contemporary shopping. Located on Leavenworth and Beach near Fisherman's Wharf.

The red brick buildings housing the elaborate and enticing **Ghirardelli Square** date back to 1864 when Civil War uniforms were made in the Woolen Building. In 1893 the world-famous confection-producing family purchased the site to concoct their delicious chocolates until some time in the 1960s when the complex was renovated to house 80 shops and restaurants. The square occupies 21 acres, bounded by North Point, Polk, Beach, and Larkin streets.

Once an abandoned cargo pier, **Pier 39** was transformed in the late 1970s into a thriving $5.4 million entertainment, dining, and shopping complex. Nearly 120 shops purvey everything from clothing to kites. One of our favorite shops is devoted to chocolate. The 45-acre weathered-wood village is also home to San Francisco's street performers, an eclectic, highly talented group of roving performers.

Union Square offers San Francisco shopping at its finest. Elegant stores and richly appointed shops stylishly cater to every taste. Neiman-Marcus, Macy's, Saks Fifth Avenue, Gump's, Wilkes Bashford, Anne Taylor, Yves St. Laurent—these are just some of the names you'll pass in this citified shopping area. Serious shoppers should concentrate on the blocks bounded by Geary, Powel, Post, and Stockton streets and surrounding blocks between Market and Sutter streets and Kearny to Mason.

If you want to get off the beaten path, check out some of the city's neighborhood shopping, usually a more casual approach to that age-old sport of spending money. (You can get by in jeans in some of these areas.) Usually a five- to ten-block section in each area is devoted to chic apparel shops that are local success stories interspersed with cafes, bookstores, and gourmet food shops. You can easily devote half a day to any of the following:

Union Street, between Gough and Sutter (not to be confused with Union Square); **Chestnut Street,** between Fillmore and Pierce; **Fillmore Street,** between Jackson and Pine, Union and Lombard; **Sacramento,** between Presidio and Cherry; **Clement Street,** between Arguello and 25th Avenue; **24th Street,** between Diamond and Delores; **Haight Street,** between Masonic and Stanyan; and **Polk Street,** between Union and Sutter.

SAN FRANCISCO BY NIGHT

Many San Franciscans consider their city to be the cultural capital of the West. We can't be sure we totally agree, but we do promise you won't be disappointed at the diversity of entertainment to be found here. A beautiful performing arts complex, two long-running, uniquely San Francisco stage shows, some of the nation's finest theater, and an enthusiastic, supportive patronage give the city its cultural heartbeat.

Ticket agencies that handle most theater, music, and dance events are Bass, 893-2277; Ticketron, 392-7469; and STBS, with day-of-performance tickets for selected events at half price (also handles advance, full-price tickets). Cash sales only and no reservations or telephone orders accepted. Located on the Stockton Street side of Union Square. Call 433-STBS for recorded information.

The **San Francisco War Memorial and Performing Arts Center** is located just west of City Hall in the civic center area of town. Louise M. Davies Hall, War Memorial Opera House, Zellerbach Rehearsal Hall, and the Veteran's Building compose the second largest performing arts complex in the United States. Tours offered: call 431-5400 for more information.

The **San Francisco Symphony Orchestra,** its home in the stunning $27.5 million Louise M. Davies Symphony Hall, performs throughout the year. Symphony box office, 431-5400.

The **War Memorial Building,** built by the WPA, is the venue for touring opera, dance, and performing arts groups. 864-3330.

The **Veteran's Building** houses both the recently refurbished Herbst Theatre and the San Francisco Museum of Modern Art (see "San Francisco by Day"). The theater was the site of the signing of the United Nations Charter in 1945. Today it features chamber groups, special films, and guest lecturers. 750-3636. Tickets available at City Box Office, 392-4400.

A $10 million ballet building is the center's newest addition and home to the celebrated **San Francisco Ballet.** 621-3838.

For **theater,** you've got quite a choice. Long-running *Beach Blanket Babylon* (a song-and-dance tribute to S.F., at Club Fugazi, 421-4222) and *Dance between the Lines* (a lively cabaret at the Music Hall Theater, 931 Larkin Street, 776-8996) will probably still be running when you hit town. Or for more traditional fare, try:

The **American Conservatory Theatre** (ACT), acclaimed as North America's finest resident theater, with classic and modern drama. Geary Theater. 415 Geary, Union Square. 673-6440.

The **Curran** (445 Geary) and the **Golden Gate** (25 Taylor Street) share the honors of hosting touring musicals and dramas. For information on both: 473-4400.

The **Orpheum** includes large-scale musicals in its repertoire. 1192 Market Street. 474-3800.

LATE-NIGHT SAN FRANCISCO

This is a late-night town, but it's also during the wee hours that the underside of humanity comes out in San Francisco. Still, we shouldn't be sheltered—just safe.

North Beach along Broadway is where most of the city's vibrant bars and clubs gyrate with nighttime sounds. It's also a bit sleazy here. Although it's not necessarily walking distance from your hotel, if you do choose to check out the scene, don't drive—you'll spend half the night looking for a place to park.

A tamer way to be entertained after the theater or dinner is to check out the city's stunning views, equally beautiful at midnight. Good spots for this are in a number of skyscrapers scattered throughout the city, great places to capture and savor the panoramic vistas.

Equinox, Hyatt Regency Hotel, 18th floor, Five Embarcadero Center. Lunch and dinner daily until 10 P.M.; cocktails until 1:30 A.M. Platform makes one revolution each 45 minutes for a gentle journey and 360-degree view.

Oz, in the Westin St. Frances, 32nd floor, Geary at Powell. Cocktails from 4:30 P.M.; dancing nightly 9 P.M. to 2 A.M. and 4 A.M. on Friday and Saturday. Hefty cover charge for nonmembers. Strict dress code.

One Up, in the Hyatt on Union Square, 36th floor, Stockton at Sutter. Lunch Monday through Friday; dinner nightly until 10:30 P.M.; Sunday brunch 10:30 A.M. to 2 P.M.; piano lounge from 4 P.M. to midnight daily.

Henri's Room at the Top, 46th floor, 333 O'Farrell. Buffet lunch daily; dinner until 10 P.M., Sunday brunch from 11 A.M. to 2:30 P.M. Live entertainment and dancing from 9 P.M. to 1 A.M.

Carnelian Room, in the Bank of America Building, 52nd floor, 555

California. Dinner until 10:30 P.M.; Sunday brunch 10 A.M. to 2:30 P.M.; cocktails until 1:30 weekends. Centrally located for business executives.

S. Holmes, Esq., in the Holiday Inn Union Square, 30th floor, Sutter at Powell. Buffet lunch Monday through Friday; cocktails until 1:30 A.M. daily.

Crown Room, in the Fairmont Hotel, 24th floor, 950 Mason. Buffet lunch Monday through Saturday; dinner until 10 P.M.; cocktails daily until 1:30 P.M.; Sunday brunch 10:30 A.M. to 2:30 P.M.

Starlight Room, in the Sir Francis Drake Hotel, 21st floor, Sutter at Powell. Sunday brunch 10 A.M. to 2 P.M.; cocktails from 4 P.M. Monday through Saturday; dancing until 1 A.M. daily.

Top of the Mark, in the Mark Hopkins Hotel, 19th floor, California at Mason. Cocktails nightly until 1:30 P.M.; Sunday buffet brunch 11 A.M. to 3 P.M.

AT LEISURE

In Town

If you're fortunate enough to spend a weekend in San Francisco, budget your time carefully, because you'll not have enough of it to enjoy all the city offers. Grab a bus, cable car, taxi, or a good pair of walking shoes, and start exploring.

Get a different perspective on San Francisco from the water. Hop aboard the **Blue and Gold Fleet's yachts** for an hour-and-a-quarter cruise of San Francisco Bay. The fully narrated tour passes under both the Bay and Golden Gate bridges, around Alcatraz, and past many historical sites. Cruises run daily and year-round with frequent departures. The sleek 400-passenger boats shove off from Pier 39's west marina. Call 781-7877 for schedule information.

Day-Tripping

Want to get out of town for a day or so? That's simple. Go in practically any direction: over the Golden Gate, under the water via BART, or down the peninsula for a variety of day trips just outside San Francisco.

North of the city, across the bay in Marin County, is **Sausalito,** a charming hillside community populated with trees, city views, fine restaurants and specialty shops. From the city, take the ferry across the bay or drive over the Golden Gate Bridge. Adjacent to Sausalito is the city of **Tiberon,** similar but smaller and less touristy than its neighbor. For further information call the Marin County Chamber of Commerce, 415/472-7470.

If you're traveling by car, take U.S. 101 just north of Sausalito, and you'll pass the **San Rafael Civic Center,** a unique gift of architecture from Frank Lloyd Wright. Above Marin are Napa, Sonoma, and Mendocino counties—known for the **California wine** that is produced there. Wine lovers should leave San Francisco early in the day, as there are many hours of tasting in store. The majority of the best wineries are east of Highway 101 on Highways 29 and 12. For further information, contact the Sonoma County Chamber of Commerce at 707/996-1034; Saint Helena Chamber of Commerce, 707/963-4456 (for Napa information); or the Wine Institute at 415/986-0878.

Continuing up Route 101, you'll find yourself in **redwood country,** shaded by the tallest trees on earth, the sequoias. Another way to reach the redwoods is along the coast via Highway 1, past fine beaches and charming restaurants.

East of San Francisco across the bay, spend a day in **Berkeley.** Take the San Francisco–Oakland Bay Bridge by car to U.S. 80 or under the water on BART (call 788-2278) to the campus. The University of California at Berkeley offers museums, galleries, and outstanding architecture. At the hub is Sproul Plaza with musicians, mimes, and public debates on almost any subject. In the Student Union Building, visit the Visitor's Center (642-5215) for information and tours of the campus.

Up the hill from the university is **Strawberry Canyon,** featuring the world's largest botanical garden. Don't forget your camera for some great shots of San Francisco and the Golden Gate Bridge with the sun setting behind.

South along the coast, San Francisco U.S. 1 will take you through Santa Cruz to Monterey, Carmel, and Big Sur. **Santa Cruz's** college town atmosphere is enriched by sweeping beaches and Victorian architecture. Farther down the coast, in **Monterey** and **Carmel,** you'll find museums, boutiques, art galleries, five-star restaurants, and antique stores. Call the Monterey Peninsula Chamber of Commerce for more information. 408/649-3200.

Carmel marks the beginning of the **17-Mile Drive,** California's most beautiful coastal stretch of land. Chances are you'll see whales or seals or sea lions lining the rocks. **Carmel Mission** is one of California's oldest. For information on 17-Mile Drive, call 408/624-3811 or 408/375-5687.

South of Carmel at **Big Sur,** a forest borders the sea, separated only by high cliffs. If you like hiking, this is the place. It's also one of the most romantic spots on earth.

Sunday Customs

You could easily spend several days in **Golden Gate Park,** but Sunday's a good day to explore the three-mile lush garden developed more than 100 years ago on a site once covered with shifting sand dunes. In 1894, the park was the site of the Midwinter International Exposition, a world's fair of sorts attended by more than 2.5 million people. Tent cities were erected in the park to provide shelter and medical aid to the over 200,000 people left homeless by the 1906 earthquake. Today, the park is a recreational and cultural haven. Within its colorful confines you can find archery, baseball, basketball, bicycling, boating, picnicking and more. The park also houses the Asian Art Museum, the M.H. de Young Museum, the California Academy of Sciences (see "San Francisco by Day"), plus the Japanese Tea Garden, and the Conservatory of Flowers. All are open to the public year-round and charge an admission fee. You can also explore Golden Gate Park through a guided walking tour, offered free on weekends from May through December. Call park headquarters (558-3706) for further information about walking tours and other park activities.

Spectator Sports

The **San Francisco 49ers** (468-2249 or 771-1149), play all their home games at Candlestick Park, also the summertime home of baseball's **Giants** (467-8000). In 1985, the 49ers won the Super Bowl behind Joe Montana at quarterback.

The **A's** (for athletics) from Oakland (638-0500) play baseball at the Oakland–Alameda County Coliseum. They're an average team in the American League West.

Active Sports

Believe it or not, **bike riding** is a popular pastime in this hilly city. To make it easy on the knees, call Cal-Trans (557-1840) for a bicycle path map.

For those who like to exercise inside, you can sweat it out at **In Shape,** a no-frills exercise studio offering invigorating one-hour aerobics classes, gentler hour-long stretch classes, and challenging one-and-a-half-hour advanced classes. Six dollars buys you a competent instructor who'll keep an eye on you during the up-tempo, enervating workouts. Two locations: 2328 Fillmore Street, 346-5660, or 3214 Fillmore Street, 922-3700. Classes from 6 A.M. to 7:30 P.M. daily. Limited shower facilities.

UNIQUELY SAN FRANCISCO

Although we've given you plenty of ideas of where to stay in San Francisco, we'd still like to offer a unique alternative. The inner city, unlike any other in the country, is packed with charming, reliable, and decidedly unpretentious bed-and-breakfast inns in convenient locations. All exude the kind of charm you can't hope to get from large convention hotels or even small European-style hotels. So, if B-and-Bs are for you, we'll gladly point you in the right direction with the following:

Petite Auberge is in the heart of downtown, a 26-room French country inn with cheery wood-burning fireplaces and vases of fresh flowers. 863 Bush. 928-6000.

The **Queen Anne,** located on the edge of Pacific Heights, takes you back to Victorian S.F. with turret towers, gable roof, and marquetry wood floors. American and English antiques dot the 49 rooms and suites; this establishment even has meeting rooms. 1590 Sutter. 441-2828 or toll-free 800/262-ANNE.

The **Mansion** is San Francisco's most unusual bed-and-breakfast, the home of the late Claudia Chambers, daughter of Senator Chambers and one of the most remarkable piano players of our time. Every night, Claudia's ghost gives a piano recital in the sitting room; requests are honored. Victorian-era antiques decorate the mansion, where such luminaries as Barbra Streisand, songwriter Paul Simon, and Liberace have stayed in the past. Make Reservations as early as possible for this popular inn. 2220 Sacramento. 929-9444.

The **Sherman House** is a 15-room sanctuary for frazzled travelers, built in 1876 by Leander Sherman, founder and owner of the Sherman Clay Music Company, who added a three-story recital hall in 1901 so that great divas and stage stars could perform. A historical landmark, rooms and suites are individually designed and furnished in French Second Empire, Biedermeier, or English Jacobean motifs and antiques. Some rooms have marbeled wood-burning fireplaces and canopied beds draped with rich tapestry fabrics and covered with feather down comforters. 2160 Green Street. 563-3600.

Stanyan Park Hotel is the oldest hotel near Golden Gate Park. Built in 1904 by saloon owner Harry P. Heagerty, this 36-room Queen Anne–style Victorian is not only a national landmark but an inexpensive place to stay with prices starting at $55 a night. 750 Stanyan Street. 751-1000.

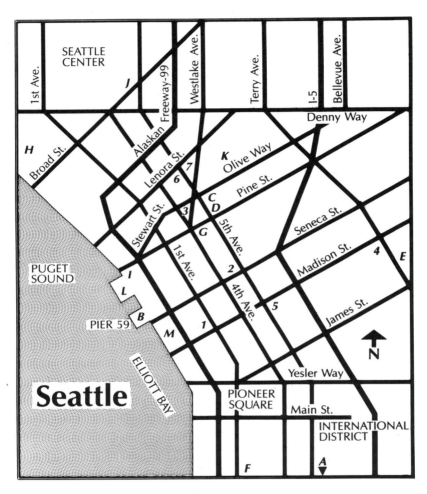

HOTELS

1 Alexis
2 Four Seasons Olympic
3 Mayflower Park
4 Sorrento
5 Stouffer Madison
6 Warwick
7 Westin

LANDMARKS

A Airport
B Aquarium
C Fifth Avenue Theatre
D Frederick & Nelson
E Frye Art Museum
F Kingdome
G Monorail terminal

H Myrtle Edwards Park
I Pike Place Market
J Space Needle
K Visitors Bureau
L Waterfront Park
M Waterfront Place

SEATTLE

GETTING YOUR BEARINGS

Everyone told us we'd love doing business in Seattle. They were right. This is one relaxed city, where life satisfaction is measured not in money but in the quality of life. When *Harper's* called this metropolis a dream, the magazine was on the mark. It wouldn't be hard to live and work in the Emerald City. Seattle got that title by holding a contest to find a suitable nickname, so we guess the residents, too, knew they had a real gem.

For anyone interested in outdoor life, this is the best of all worlds. Built on seven hills between expansive Puget Sound and Lake Washington, the city is dominated by Mount Rainier, with spectacular scenery all around. Because of this environment, most Seattleites are into something or other outdoorsy. The air is clean, the climate is invigorating, and you really feel like *doing* something—if only walking to business appointments rather than taking a cab or bus.

This is a city on the move. It's innovative. It's cultured. It's a great place to be if you're young and ambitious. We encounter women living here who fit that mold and who have an open entrepreneurial attitude to boot—so we don't hesitate to be real in our business dealings with either sex.

The downtown business district is edged by a well-developed waterfront, its focal point being Pike Place Market with its open-air stalls and shopkeepers who sell everything from flowers to antiques. Other attractions, like the Seattle Center, home of the 605-foot Space Needle, and the Kingdome, are very close by.

Perhaps because of the convenience of it all, people in Seattle truly use their city. They explore it. They enjoy it. The trolley system actually works. Locals use it to commute and to travel around town. Downtown in the Magic Carpet area, bus travel is free, but if you choose to walk the steep city street hills, good for you. The locals would approve.

The Boeing Company is Seattle's largest employer located in the South End, with Lockheed Shipbuilding and Todd Shipyards sharing the spotlight. The bio-engineering and aerospace industries play a big role

here, making this one of the nation's most important high-tech centers—
a lot of that activity taking place in Bellevue, east of Lake Washington.

By contributing to these fields, Seattle is carrying on a tradition
started long ago. An interesting mix of achievements and contributions
has emerged from this hub of the Pacific Northwest. Not only did Jimi
Hendrix and Gypsy Rose Lee come from Seattle, but also the floating
bridge, the B-29, and the 747. The first labor strike in history took place
here, and the city boasts the purest drinking water in the nation.

WHAT TO WEAR

No one ever blamed Seattle for being too chic. Rather, this is a down-
to-earth city, even in the clothes women wear for business. They dress
in appropriate fashion, though, often in tailored suits in natural fabrics
topped by a Burberry or London Fog. In the less constricting professions,
dress is not so regimented, however.

WEATHER WATCH

Everyone knows it rains in Seattle—and rains and rains and rains. But
actually there are times when the clouds clear away; in fact, more than
80 percent of the rain occurs between October and April. Summers are
lovely; there's rarely a time when the temperature tops 80. It's usually
more like the mid-60s, dry and comfortable. And as for Seattle winters,
well, they're comparatively warm if you look at the rest of the country,
usually hanging in there at over the freezing point. So it's worth it to
endure some rain once in a while.

GETTING THERE

The **Seattle-Tacoma International Airport** is equidistant between the two
cities. It's operated by the Port of Seattle and is one of the most modern
and efficient facilities of its kind in the United States. In 1981, Sea-Tac
was awarded the FAA's Aviation Environmental Award for planning and
was ranked among the five best U.S. airports by the Airline Passengers
Association.

At the main terminal, you purchase tickets, claim baggage, buy
gifts, and exchange money, but you leave from one of two satellite terminals. A one-and-a-half-mile computer-controlled subway reached by
a series of escalators connects the terminals and transports up to 4,500
passengers per hour. It's claimed that you don't have to walk more than
600 feet once you're inside the terminal, but we suggest not carrying
anything too heavy just in case.

More than two dozen national and international carriers serve Sea-Tac.

The Sea-Tac Airport Information Center is located in the central baggage claim area across from carousel 10. Here you can get information on transportation, hotels, restaurants, current events, the works, before you even hit town. Call 433-5217.

Sea-Tac is 13 miles south of Seattle, a 20- to 25-minute ride on the freeway. Taxis going the distance cost around $20.

To get to and from the airport, you've got your choice:

The Grayline Downtown Airporter (343-2070) operates daily every 30 minutes. The cost is $4.75; the trip takes 20 minutes. You can be picked up at the Madison, Holiday Inn Crowne Plaza, Four Seasons Olympic, Sheraton, and Westin hotels.

Metro Transit (447-4800) is good if you don't have heavy bags. Bus 174 leaves Second and Pike roughly every half hour for a 40-minute ride to Sea-Tac. Cost is 75 to 90 cents, depending on the time of day. Service from the airport is every half hour.

Graves Limousine Service (329-6090) picks up from any point in the city and carries a full limousine for a flat rate of $20.

Some hotels operate courtesy vans; check via the courtesy telephones in the baggage claim area.

Car Rentals

Although having a car is not always necessary when visiting Seattle (see "Getting Around"), we suggest the following agencies at the airport if you decide you want to rent one:

Avis	433-5231
Budget	433-5243
Dollar	433-5825
Hertz	433-5264
National	433-5501
Sears	244-5454

GETTING AROUND

This is a city that offers many viable options when it comes to getting from one place to the other. One option, of course, is to rent a car (see "Getting There"). It's not necessarily the best choice, though, unless you have suburban business connections. Downtown Seattle is very compact and most of the attractions can be reached either by walking—if you don't mind a few hills—or by taking the free Magic Carpet bus that runs between Battery Street on the north, South Jackson Street on the south, Interstate 5 and Eighth Avenue on the east, and the waterfront on the west. When riding this free bus, be careful not to board one marked "express," or you could find yourself on the freeway heading for some distant suburb.

If you decide to rent a car, you will find that ample, if expensive, parking is available in numerous lots and office buildings. Street parking meters require 60 cents an hour, and parking is prohibited on many downtown streets between 7 A.M. and 9 A.M. and 4 P.M. and 6 P.M.

Seattle's bus system, run by METRO (447-4800), is safe to ride and very efficient. The exact fare is 50 cents within the city limits (60 cents during morning and afternoon rush hours) and 75 cents beyond the city limits (90 cents during rush hours). Drivers don't carry change.

Although Seattle has no subway system, the city is one of the few in the world that has a functional **monorail** serving its transportation needs. Run by METRO, the system was built for the 1962 Seattle World's Fair. The monorail connects the Westlake Mall—which is downtown in the heart of the department store district—with Seattle Center, 1.2 miles to the north. Seattleites use the monorail often as a way out to the Seattle Center for lunch or to beat the evening parking crush for events at the center. They drive downtown, park, have a drink at a hotel bar, and then hop onto the monorail for an easy ride and short walk to the Opera House. The 90-second trip zips along at 45 mph, although the system was originally designed to do 60 mph. Fare is 50 cents. Departures are every 15 minutes during hours of operation, with more frequent departures during lunch hour. Call 447-4800 for further information.

Another option is to take Seattle's waterfront streetcar, which first started rolling in June 1982 and has been immensely popular. The three handsome mahogany cars are 1927-vintage Australian and run on rails next to Alaska Way, from Myrtle Edwards Park South to Pioneer Square. The system is also operated by METRO (447-4800), costs 60 cents, and runs every 15 to 30 minutes daily until 6 P.M. in the winter and 11 P.M. in the summer. With a transfer you can get on and off at various points along the waterfront. A round-trip takes 60 minutes.

If you're going to depend on taxis and you haven't been to Seattle in the past several years, you'll be happy to know that the June 1979 deregulation of the city's taxi system saw a vast number of much-needed additional taxis hit the road. We have unfortunately heard some complaints of indifferent service and uncontrolled prices. Best to stick with standard, long-time cab companies that offer consistent pricing and courteous service. Try Farwest (622-1717), Yellow (622-6500), Graytop (622-4949), or Hansom (323-0365). You can hail a cab, but it's best to telephone one of the companies we've just mentioned, as they'll usually dispatch a car by radio within a matter of minutes. During the rush hour in bad weather, you can wait upward to an hour. Flag costs tend to range between $1 and $2, with from $1.20 to $1.50 for each additional mile. Cabstands are located at or near the major hotels as well as at various corners throughout downtown.

GETTING FAMILIAR

Emerald City Seattle–King County Convention and Visitors Bureau
1815 Seventh Avenue   447-4200
Seattle, WA 98101
This bureau offers good regional information, lots of brochures and guides, and personal assistance to both tourists and business travelers. They also operate at Sea-Tac (see "Getting There") and, in the summer, at the Seattle Center at the base of the Space Needle (447-7280).

Newspapers in town are the *Seattle Post-Intelligencer,* a morning daily with a Friday "What's Happening" section and the *Seattle Times,* an evening daily with a Friday "Tempo" section listing coming events in the arts and entertainment. The *Seattle Daily Journal of Commerce's* editorial format is limited to business reports and is published daily except Sunday. The *Weekly* comes out on Wednesday, serving as the authoritative calendar of Seattle's goings-on each week. You'll find lively reviews of restaurants, films, and the arts, and the latest on state and city politics. The *Seattle Business Journal* is just that, published weekly and available on Monday. The *Seattle Business Magazine* is published by the Seattle Chamber of Commerce every month. *Seattle Woman* is a monthly glossy with interesting features about the city on topics like local fashion designers and area health spas.

─────────────── *Quick Calls* ───────────────

AREA CODE 206	Weather 382-7246
Time 844-1111	Emergencies 911

AT YOUR SERVICE

Warwick
Fourth and Lenora   Toll-free reservations: 800/426-9280
Seattle, WA 98121   Local number: 443-4300
                           Telex: 152331
The wood-burning fireplace in the Warwick's lobby sets the tone for this downtown hotel that opened in May 1981 to cater mainly to business travelers. An executive boardroom on the 18th floor of this medium-sized hotel (there are 230 rooms) is luxuriously appointed, with a dramatic Seattle view. Suites also have panoramic views of the city and whirlpool spas adjacent to the master bedrooms. One woman traveler noted that an outstanding service of this hotel is the excellence of the housekeeping staff. She'd never seen a cleaner hotel. Health facilities include a sauna, exercise room, and indoor swimming pool. In addition, guests are invited

Hotel	Concierge	Executive Floor	No-Smoking Rooms	Fitness Facilities	Pool	24-Hour Room Service	Restaurant for Client Entertaining	Extra-Special Amenities	Electronic Key System	Business/Secretarial Services	Checkout Time	Frequent Guest Program	Business Traveler Program	Average Single Rate
Alexis Hotel	●					●	Alexis Restaurant	●		●	1 p.m.	Guest History Program		$115–260 / $96–$204 corp.
Four Seasons Olympic	●		●	●	●	●	The Georgian	●		●	1 p.m.			$135–$190 / $145 corp.
Stouffer Madison	●	●	●	●	●	●	Prego	●			1 p.m.	RSVP	Court Express	$115–$155 / $98–$128 corp.
Sorrento	●						The Hunt Club	●		●	1 p.m.	Return Guest Program	Fireside Corporate Club	$95–$120
Warwick Hotel	●	●	●	●	●	●	The Liaison	●		●	1 p.m.			$90–$105 / $86 corp.
Westin	●		●	●	●	●	Palm Court	●			1 p.m.		Mileage Plus	$110 / $90 corp.

494

to use at a minimal charge the Seattle Club, which is close to the hotel and offers racquetball and other facilities.

The polished brass, black glass, and exotic plant atmosphere of the **Liaison Restaurant** makes for an elegant seafood meal. The **Liaison Lounge** is comfortable and not intimidating.

Sorrento

900 Madison Street   Toll-free reservations: 800/426-1265
Seattle, WA 98104   Local number: 622-6400
                                       Telex: 244206

This hotel is European in look and attitude with all the services you could possibly want, not least of which is very special attention. The owners used to do a lot of business traveling themselves, and they compiled a list of anything they found lacking in hotels they stayed in. Then they made sure their own hotel remedied the problem. Although the Sorrento is only *almost* downtown, its location on First Hill is positioned so that the view is terrific. The feel inside is a tad masculine. It was modeled after a castle in Sorrento with Renaissance architecture and expensive touches such as Honduras mahogany throughout. The 76 rooms are uniquely designed to give a distinctive character. Some say the rooms have an Oriental touch, others that they're more art deco. Whatever you call them, they reflect the good taste of owner Michael Malone and his wife. Some rooms have antique furnishings and original art.

For a power lunch, even if you're not staying in the hotel, make reservations at the **Hunt Club**. All mahogany paneled, it offers first-class dining; seafood is the specialty of the nouvelle cuisine. The **Hunt Lounge,** English in feel and comfort, is a classy place so it tends to attract classy barflies. Drinks are also served in the **Fireside Room** in the lobby, with comfortable chairs, a super fireplace, and a clublike atmosphere.

Alexis

1007 First Avenue   Toll-free reservations: 800/426-7033
Seattle, WA 98104   Local number: 624-4844

This 54-room gem, part of the downtown renewal project, is close to everything. It has a decidedly feminine appeal with art deco decor and a female general manager. The hotel is elegant and European, and the renovators made the most of the turn-of-the-century building. One unusual feature: no tipping is permitted here. The trappings are done with immense good taste—in dusty roses, deep blues, and grays. Lots of brass and marble and vases filled with exotic flowers are found everywhere. The hotel attracts the same kind of crowd as New York City's Pierre or San Francisco's Stanford Court. The concierge at the Alexis speaks seven languages, so he'll honor any request no matter how it's put to him.

The **Alexis Restaurant** has garnered rave reviews. *Travel/Holiday* called it "one of the outstanding restaurants in the world." Small and elegant with a European flair, the restaurant features a seasonal menu with fresh ingredients, many of them locally grown. This is an excellent place for a power meal. The **Alexis Hotel Bar** is intimate but not threatening, focused around a fireplace and run so that even the most timid of women could enter without qualms.

Four Seasons Olympic

411 University Street
Seattle, WA 98101

Toll-free reservations: 800/268-6282
Local number: 621-1700
Telex: 152477

The hotel was originally built in 1923–24 in an ornate, modified Italian Renaissance style; at the time it was called the grandest hotel west of Chicago. Declared a historic landmark in 1979, the Four Seasons began renovation the next year. The result is fabulous and particularly inviting to the woman business traveler. About 50 percent of the 451 guest rooms are now alcove rooms, with sleeping areas divided from sitting areas by French doors. Amenities include everything, from plush terry cloth robes to one of the classiest health clubs we've ever tried out. In fact, the staff goes so far as to invite frequent business travelers who stay at the Olympic to leave their luggage, take off, return to Seattle, pick up their keys, and find their cleaned and pressed clothing waiting for them.

As for dining, the **Garden Court Lounge,** packed with lots of plants and skylights, serves breakfast, lunch, English tea, and cocktails. To say the **Georgian Room** is elegant is an understatement. It's a truly imposing room in pastel blue against white with crystal chandeliers from the original hotel. This is the place to really impress an associate. The **Georgian Terrace** serves cocktails and lunch. **Shukers,** the hotel's fish restaurant, serves lunch, dinner, and cocktails.

Stouffer Madison

515 Madison
Seattle, WA 98104

Toll-free reservations: 800/HOTELS-1
Local number: 583-0300
Telex: 888730

For a 28-story, 557-room property, this hotel feels much smaller. The Madison in midtown Seattle mixes classic elegance with contemporary flair, and offers as many amenities as more massive places. Among them is a beautiful health club. Where else can you work out while gazing at Puget Sound and the Cascade Mountains through floor-to-ceiling windows?

We recommend booking one of the 86 spacious corner suites if you intend to meet clients in your room. Otherwise, the hotel has ten regular meeting rooms.

As for dining, look to **Maxwells** on the second floor for casual American fare in a cafe setting; **Prego** for northern Italian cuisine and stunning views; **Visions** on the 28th floor for cocktails; the **The Lobby Bar** for a quiet drink alone.

Westin, Seattle

1900 Fifth Avenue
Seattle, WA 98101

Toll-free reservations: 800/228-3000
Local number: 728-1000
Telex: 152900

Rising from the Seattle skyline, the Westin's two circular towers jut 47 stories into the sky. This is a massive hotel: 875 guest rooms, 47 suites, 24 meeting rooms, 4 lounges, 3 restaurants. It's a convention hotel in the conventional sense, but it's also a good hotel for women who want to be in the heart of things when in Seattle as it's probably the best located of all the city's properties. Contemporary decor and furnishings are clean and inviting.

The restaurants are the **Palm Court,** fine dining featuring nouvelle and Continental cuisine, and a lovely decor of four glass dining pavilions, crystal chandeliers, rich brocade fabric, brass and travertine marble trim, and large potted palms; the **Market Cafe,** resembling historic Pike Place Market, an all-day dining room with seafood specials and more than 50 brands of domestic and imported beer; and **Trader Vic's,** with Chinese and Polynesian dishes, the former prepared in authentic Chinese ovens. Lounges include the **Lobby Court,** for people-watching, surrounded by a glass atrium in the main lobby; **Fitzgerald's on Fifth,** where drinks are served around a 65-foot curved green marble bar; and **Shampers Wine Bar,** up the stairwell from the Palm Court, and the most intimate of the three.

ON A BUDGET

Hotel

Mayflower Park
405 Olive Way at Fourth   Toll-free reservations: 800/426-5100
Seattle, WA 98101   Local number: 623-8700
This is a small, intimate hotel with a central location right in the department store and theater district. The 200 moderately priced rooms have a soft, feminine quality and are done in warm tones like peach and dusty rose. The hotel was originally built in 1927 and boasts marble and brass fixtures and crystal chandeliers. The manager, Marie Dempcy, is personally involved in everything that goes on here. She is apparently a very artistic woman (there are flowers everywhere, beautifully arranged) who instinctively focuses on what women need.

The hotel restaurant, **Clippers,** is an award winner for its classic northwestern fare. It opened in 1983 and is a very popular lunch spot for the Seattle business community, but be sure to go here on an expense account—it's not a bargain. The hotel's lounge, **Olivers,** is comfortable and not intimidating with large windows, lots of green plants, and understated beige decor.

Restaurants

For northwestern fare that's moderately priced, visit Pioneer Square's **Washington Post Restaurant.** The brick-and-plant decor draws an interesting professional crowd, especially at lunch. 88 Yesler Way. 623-8100.

For a power dinner that won't cost you an arm and a leg, go to **Triples,** offering just about the best fresh fish selection in town and a splendid view of Lake Huron. For health-conscious diners, this eatery creates dishes low in sodium and high in fresh and healthful ingredients. 1200 Westlake N. 284-2535.

Entertainment

As for events, **Seafair** is a long-standing tradition in Seattle and the biggest happening of the year. It is a three-week affair held usually in July and offers plenty of free activity including a torchlight parade through downtown. The party begins with the landing of the Seafair pirates. Call 623-7100 for information.

Beyond that there are scores of festivals, fairs, and annual events in Seattle. Call the Convention and Visitors Bureau for a lengthy list, 447-7273.

DINING OUT

If giving a business breakfast is a task you must face while visiting Seattle, we offer a few places that should work well.

Athenian Inn, if you like the hustle and bustle of a market with European flavor. In Pike Place Market. 624-7166.

Eggs Cetera has the best selection of omelets in town, as well as delicious and unusual waffles—try the ones with macadamia nuts. Three locations: 220 Broadway E., 325-3447; 4220 E. Madison, 324-4140; 5001 California S.W., 932-3307.

Having breakfast at **Julia's 14-Carrot Cafe** is like having breakfast in mother's kitchen with a warm friendly atmosphere and great plain cooking featuring homemade breads and baked goods. 2305 Eastlake E. 324-1442.

As for lunch, we've got some suggestions, too. They are:

Andy and Jemmy's Wok for good Chinese food, imaginatively prepared and light on the calories. This is a good place to go when putting on the dog isn't the main objective. 11030 Eighth N.E. 364-6898.

For lunch with a view, go to **Benjamin's.** It's perched on top of one of Bellevue's tallest buildings; Lake Washington, the Olympic Mountains, Mt. Rainier, and the city skyline all stretch out before you. The food consists of salads, pastas, steaks, and fresh seafood prepared in an open kitchen. 10655 N.E. Fourth, Bellevue. 454-8255.

Located on Pioneer Square downtown, **Brasserie Pittsbourg** is Seattle's oldest continuously operating restaurant and a popular luncheon spot. It's a great setting—a basement eatery lined in white tile and filled with flowers, antiques, and old kitchen utensils. Soups, pastas, and omelets are the big hits here. 602 First. 623-4167.

For distinctive South American dishes, try **Copacabana** on the second floor of the Triangle Building with a balcony where diners can munch and people-watch on a warm day. In Pike Place Market. 622-6359.

For young professionals, a popular downtown watering hole is **Duke's,** offering light lunches and suppers as well as a small cafe deli that serves sandwiches and salads. 236 First W. 283-4400.

You could take your business client to **Mirabeau** in the Seafirst Building. This is one of the city's tallest buildings, and the restaurant is at the top, serving French cuisine. 1001 Fourth. 624-4550.

For dinner, we like:

Adriatica, a restaurant in a converted house that serves excellent Greek, Italian, and Yugoslavian dishes and a famous dessert made of dates and walnuts baked in filo with cognac and served hot with thick cream. 1107 Dexter N. 285-5000.

The **Alexis Restaurant** (see "At Your Service") is good for a true power meal.

Canlis is a dressy place with starched linens, sterling and fine china, and fine northwestern fare. If you want a steak, this is the place to eat. 2576 Aurora N. 283-3313.

Cutters Bay House, a favorite haunt for professionals, is conveniently located on the north edge of Pike Place Market overlooking Elliot Bay. Stylish decor and a huge and eclectic menu with seafood and Oriental dishes are the draw. 2001 Western. 622-7711.

Try the **Green Lake Grill** for an informal setting with a simple menu that integrates fresh ingredients. Try the fettuccine with smoked trout and capers or the linguine with chicken and tarragon. 7200 E. Green Lake Drive N. 524-0365.

Henry's Off Broadway reminds us of the grand elegance of New York dining in the thirties. Soft piano music, mirrors, and chandeliers lend a classy touch to a showy display of appetizers. House specialities are scampi, roast rack of lamb, and premium aged steaks. A large oyster bar serves succulent northwestern morsels. 1705 E. Olive Way. 329-8063.

The **Hunt Club** is in the Sorrento Hotel (see "At Your Service").

The **Palm Court** is in the Westin Hotel (see "At Your Service").

Rosellini's Four-10, on the edge of downtown, has an Old World feeling of easy elegance. Good service, and a menu that offers fish and poultry prepared in the French or Italian style. Fourth and Wall. 728-0410.

SEATTLE BY DAY

Seattle Center, site of the 1962 World's Fair, is now a 74-acre park with a number of standing attractions, not the least of which is the **Space Needle,** Seattle's official symbol. If you take a ride up this sleek tower you can get a good bird's-eye view of the city from 605 feet for $3—or free if you dine at the Space Needle.

Also here is the **Pacific Science Center,** with hands-on displays, volcano exhibits, a planetarium, and films, and the **Seattle Art Museum Pavilion** (for details, see below) located at Fifth Avenue North and First Avenue North, Mercer Street, and Denny Way. Parking can be a problem; your best bet is to park downtown and take the monorail. 625-4234.

The **Seattle Aquarium** is one of the city's most popular draws, having won numerous awards for its outstanding display of marine life. A big attraction here is the Underwater Dome where you "descend like Captain Nemo" into the aquatic world, surrounded on all sides by water and fishy life. There's a touch tank where you can handle starfish and sea anemones and a Museum of Sea and Ships (628-0860) displaying an assortment of ship models, charts, paintings, instruments, and other nautical equipment. Pier 59, Waterfront Park. 625-4358.

Woodland Park Zoo is considered one of the best in the country, with its strong emphasis on natural environments that allow animals to live in surroundings closely resembling their native habitat. The zoo has a tropical forest zone, a wide-open African savannah, a desert, a tundra, and a swamp. The savannah is our particular favorite; its barriers separating lions, giraffes, and zebras are carefully concealed, so you have the impression you see the animals in a native African setting. 5500 Phinney N. and Aurora Avenue. 782-1265 or 625-2244.

Museums worth visiting include the following:

The **Museum of Flight** features the historic Red Barn, a turn-of-the-century wooden building in which William E. Boeing, Sr., founded the famous airplane company. The museum covers the history of flight from the days of Wilbur and Orville Wright through the late thirties. 9404 E. Marginal Way S. 767-7373.

The **Bellevue Art Museum** displays a series of changing exhibits and a permanent collection of northwestern art including crafts. Great samurai swords and a bonsai collection. 301 Bellevue Square, Bellevue. 454-3322.

The **Burke Memorial Museum** has a good collection of Pacific northwestern art and artifacts, including such specialties as a 12,500-year-old giant ground sloth, found at the northern end of Sea-Tac Airport, and the cast of a rhino buried in lava in ancient eastern Washington. 17th Avenue and N.E. 45th Street, University of Washington. 543-5590.

Frye Art Museum is a conservative place with watercolors, oils, etchings, sculpture, 19th- and 20th-century art, and Alaskan art. 704 Terry and Cherry. 622-9250.

Henry Art Gallery has a small permanent collection, but mounts some very good specialized loan exhibitions such as "No, Dada in America." University of Washington. 543-2280.

Seattle Art Museum has great African art, Asian art, and photography collections. Seattle Center. 447-4796. The Capitol Hill branch of the museum has a good permanent collection plus exhibits including Rembrandt prints and Russian decorative arts.

Museum of Science and Industry features Seattle artifacts and an old Boeing mail plane. 2162 E. Hamlin. 324-1125.

THE SHOPPING SCENE

Seattle is known as the leading commercial center in the Pacific Northwest and to complement this reputation, centers have been so arranged that shopping is a joy. Because of Seattle's proximity to the Orient, wonderful Asian goods in great variety are available, like lacquer and rattan furniture. And because Seattleites are such fanatics for the outdoors, this is the place to buy any kind of recreational equipment and clothing.

Northwest Indian art is also abundant here and is always a wise investment. You can find the good stuff at the following locations:

Seattle Indian Arts and Crafts (617 Second, 623-2252); **Daybreak Star Gallery** (in the Daybreak Star Cultural Center in Discovery Park, 285-4425); the **Legacy** (in the Alexis Hotel, 1003 First, 624-6340); and **Sacred Circle Gallery of American Indian Art** (607 First, 223-0072).

For general shopping, here are some suggestions:

In downtown Seattle, all the major department stores and many of the city's most elegant retailers are not only within a few blocks of one another but also within walking distance of all major downtown hotels. To make things even easier, downtown has a free-zone bus service, so you can bop around and buy until your credit runs out with minimal wear and tear on your feet.

Downtown, the larger department stores are on Pine between Third and Sixth. You'll run into **Frederick & Nelson** at Fifth and Pine (682-5500), considered the only world-class department store in Seattle; **Nordstrom** on Fifth between Pike and Pine (628-2111), with great fashions plus such services as delivery to your hotel and personal shoppers to help out with that business wardrobe; and the **Bon** at Fourth and Pine (344-2121), with quality fashion and home furnishings and six dining spots.

Most of the department stores are open seven days a week and Monday and Friday evenings.

You'll locate **Pike Place Market** on First between Pike and Virginia, a great place to wander through and pretend you're in Europe. A lot of specialty stores sit side by side with stands packed with seafood on ice, as well as vegetables and fruit, all fresh. Look for good buys on second-hand clothes here and quality handicrafts.

Pioneer Square is a revamped area around First and Yesler that abounds in specialty shops—one just selling kites—as well as galleries, bookstores, antique shops, clothing, and gifts.

Another refreshed and revitalized area near the waterfront just west of First Avenue between Madison and Seneca is appropriately called **Waterfront Place.** Here you'll find a good selection of nifty shops showing sports equipment and furnishings as well as small specialty boutiques, restaurants, a bakery, and a pub.

Pier 70 has great little shops showing off the best the area has to offer in specialty items plus places to nosh. It's on Seattle's downtown waterfront.

And now for something different: a shopping center located in turn-of-the-century homes. **Gilman Village** has lots of housewares and gift shops plus restaurants that are nearly all operated by women.

SEATTLE BY NIGHT

It may come as a bit of a surprise that Seattle, with its outdoor-recreation enthusiasts, also has culture—but it does, and lots of it. Theater is hot in Seattle. A good number of companies perform both new and innovative material as well as Broadway musicals and classics. Among them:

The **Seattle Repertory Theater** is the oldest and biggest show in town. It has a six-play season, running from October to June in the 860-seat Bagley Wright Theater, Seattle Center. 447-2222.

The **Contemporary Theater** does the summer season until November in a 430-seat facility with a thrust stage. This theater presents Broadway and regional hits. 100 W. Roy. 285-5110.

Intiman Theater features an ensemble company that stages the classic works of Chekhov, Ibsen, and the like. 624-2992.

5th Avenue Theater is worth the time if only for a look at the theater itself, an architectural monument. Once an old-time movie palace, it was decorated in a dazzling imperial Chinese style with gilt and dragons everywhere. It takes a big show to fill this space, so the huge Broadway musicals and big production numbers are an event in Seattle when they come here. 1308 Fifth. 625-1900.

The **Group** offers good productions often with a political cast. Ethnic Cultural Theater. 3940 Brooklyn N.E. 543-4327.

The **Bathhouse Theater** is one of those amateur groups that's so good you'd swap for a lot of professionals. Plays are staged in a remodeled Parks Department building with verve and originality. Has 130 seats. 7312 W. Greenlake Drive N. 524-9110.

New City Theater has a varied program of plays, cabaret acts, improv, comedy troupes, and other special shows. The big yearly event is the director's festival of one-act plays each spring. 1634 11th Street. 323-6800.

The **Gilbert and Sullivan Society** does, obviously, Gilbert and Sullivan on an occasional basis. The Playhouse, Seattle Center. 782-5466.

If opera's your thing, you'll be pleased to know that the **Seattle Opera Association** mounts five full-scale operas each season, drawing international casts in well-known pieces in the original language. Opera House, Seattle Center. 447-4711.

There is also a program of more innovative operas staged by the **University of Washington School of Music** in Meany Hall at the university. Critics applaud the acoustics in this arena. 543-4880.

The **Seattle Symphony Orchestra** plays in the Opera House. Information on current programs is available on the fourth floor, Center House, 305 Harrison Street, Seattle. 447-4736.

Pacific Northwest Ballet at the Opera House is a classical company with a Balanchine bias. Its season runs from January to May. 447-4655.

On the Boards presents about six modern dance evenings a month. Washington Hall Performance Gallery. 153 14th. 325-7901.

Tickets for all of the above performances are available at the **Bon Ticket Office**, Third and Pine, 344-7271; **Fidelity Lane,** 1622 Fourth, 624-4971; **Ticketmaster,** 201 King, 628-0888; or **U District Ticket Center,** 4530 University Way N.E., 632-7272.

As for the **movies,** they are very popular here, with possibly more filmgoers per capita in Seattle than anywhere else in America. Some of the theaters even have fireplaces in the lobbies or waiting areas to keep you warm and cozy until the movie begins. Check the local papers for current offerings.

LATE-NIGHT SEATTLE

If you're not yawning after a long day and evening in Seattle, try some of the following night spots to put you in the mood for a good night's sleep. We feel they're all appropriate for women who want to venture out on their own.

Central Tavern is a funky place, popular with the young and the single. It features local rock and rhythm-and-blues. Conveniently located on Pioneer Square. 207 First S. 622-0209.

Chiyoko adds amateur entertainment in the back room to a popular sushi bar. 610 S. Jackson. 623-9347.

Comedy Underground is another Pioneer Square establishment, located under Swannie's Bar. The draw here is national and local comedy with lots of audience participation. 222 S. Main. 628-0303.

Greens in the Seattle Sheraton Hotel features top local acts and is a good bet for safety late at night. Sixth and Union. 621-9000.

If you can imagine an intimate jazz club in a rambunctuous Italian restaurant, you have **Jazz Alley,** featuring the best jazz available in this city. This place often draws top names like guitarist Charlie Byrd. 2033 6th Ave. 441-9729.

Jolly Roger Roadhouse, once a speakeasy in the 1920s, now brings in the best in national and local blues groups. Some of the past remains: check the lookout turret and prostitution cribs (no longer in use). 8721 Lake City Way. 524-7479.

Matzoh Momma looks like a Jewish deli by day but then becomes a hopping night spot for comedy and light jazz; this is a singer's showcase. 509 15th E. 324-6262.

AT LEISURE

In Town

You'll never want for things to do in Seattle should you decide to hang around a day or two before or after your business takes place. You may even learn to love the city as we do. Seattle has so many surprises.

Take **Pioneer Square,** for instance. You've heard of skid row? This is the original. It was the heart of town until the 1920s and was the place where loggers used to skid logs downhill along Yesler Way to the waterfront. The handsome brick buildings were built after the Great Fire of 1889 but became very run down and were only in recent years recognized as a historical district that should be preserved. Today it's considered one of the few extensive and stylistically consistent old towns in the nation. There are one-of-a-kind shops, bookstores, restaurants, lots of art galleries, bars, and nightclubs.

One of the best ways to get a feeling for what the square is and was is to take **Bill Speidel's Seattle Underground Tour,** which leaves about every two hours starting at 11 A.M. The guide's running commentary is enthusiastic and amusing. At 610 First on Pioneer Square. 682-1511.

Hidden away in a storefront at 117 S. Main Street in Pioneer Square is the **Klondike Gold Rush National Historic Park.** It tells the story of the great Klondike rush and Seattle's role as a gateway to the gold. Exhibits include gold-mining artifacts and equipment, photographic murals, and slides. Charlie Chaplin's *The Gold Rush* is shown free at 3 and 4:30 P.M. on weekends.

Pike Place Market deserves a few hours; it's one of the oldest continuously operating farmers' markets in the United States and has been called the biggest mom-and-pop store in town. Get there early in the morning and explore all the nooks and crannies. Call 625-4764 for tours of the area.

The **International District** just east of the Kingdome is another historic area, home of the city's Asian communities. Visit Uwajimaya, a large Japanese supermarket, bazaar, and delicatessen; the Chinese pavilion in Hing Hay Park; the Wing Like Museum; Kobe Park; and the community gardens. The Nippon Kan Theater, a national historic site, features Japanese performing arts. Unlike other Chinatowns, this is not really a touristy kind of place. Walking tours available; call 624-6342.

Seattle's waterfront, once known as the Gold Rush Strip, stretches from Pier 51 on the south to Pier 70 on the north. The best way to survey this area is from a seat on the vintage trolley that shuttles from Pier 70 and Myrtle Edwards Park on the north to Pioneer Square on the south. Handsome mahogany 1927-vintage streetcars run every 15 to 30 minutes and cost 60 cents. The waterfront is a great place for strolling, shopping, dining, and exploring. Waterfront Park is a hive of activity at Pier 57 with fishing, fish-and-chips bars, and lots of places selling goodies from around the world.

For a view from the waterside, hop aboard a tour boat at Pier 56 for a survey of the harbor or a visit to **Blake Island** to the south. Seattle Harbor Tours also goes to **Tillicum Village** (623-1445), which holds an authentic Indian salmon bake on Blake Island. North Coast Indian culture is highlighted through presentation of interpretive native dances, artifacts, and craft displays in a spectacular cedar longhouse.

The **Chittenden Locks** has rising and falling boats, an underwater observatory showing salmon fighting their way up the fish ladder, and the Carl English Gardens.

For garden buffs, there are 200 acres of carefully groomed plants, trees and shrubs at the **Washington Park Arboretum and Japanese Garden,** proving that Seattle offers a great climate for greenery. Growing here are more than 5,500 species from all over the world. The arboretum is both a botanical research center for the University of Washington and a public park. Call 543-8800.

The **Japanese Tea Garden** is a favorite place with the color, symbolism, and tradition of its lakes, forests, bridges, and orchards. The teahouse itself, a work of art, is made of cypress and cedar with a copper roof. Call 625-2635.

Green Lake was once a glacial lake that the city has spruced up as a recreational setting (see "Active Sports").

Day Tripping

Seattle's greatest assets are its mountains, its ocean, its islands—and its ferry system. This is probably the biggest fleet in the nation; it can take you and a picnic lunch to the most wonderful places. On the Washington State Ferries (464-6400), you can discover Puget Sound, the San Juan Islands, Hood Canal, Hurricane Ridge, or Victoria, British Columbia. Special walk-on excursion fares are available. For information, call 464-6400.

The **San Juan Islands** (which change their name to the Gulf Islands as you cross into Canada) lie under a rain shadow—which means lots more sunshine and lots less rain, a great place to escape to for the tranquility of ocean and island. The 172-island archipelago is about a 45-minute to 2-hour ferry ride, depending on which island you choose. The ferries in the summer tend to be crowded, and there can be a long line if you come by car. So a lot of people just walk on after parking at the nearest convenient lot, or they bring along a bicycle, a good way to tour an island.

Besides the ferries, you can also get to the islands via San Juan Airlines (800/438-3880), and Seattle area seaplane charter companies also offer flights.

Some island highlights: on **San Juan Island,** Friday Harbor has restaurants and galleries, as well as little hotels, a bed-and-breakfast, and a charming little hostel. Check out the Duck Soup Inn in the twenties-style Roche Harbor Boatel Resort (1-378-2155). **Coras Island** has the very popular Rosario Resort (1-376-2222) and the dramatic 2,409-foot Mount Constitution which provides a spectacular 360-degree panorama of the islands from its lookout point. Camping and fishing are available at the Moran State Park on **Orcas** and also in a county park on **Shaw Island.** For more information, contact the San Juan Chamber of Commerce at 206/378-4600.

Victoria is, and has always been, Canada's English museum piece—a town that hangs stubbornly onto its royal connection. For a day trip or overnight, you can take the *Princess Marguerite,* an old-time cruise ship that leaves Seattle's Pier 69 each summer morning at 8 A.M. and arrives back in Seattle at 9:45 P.M. You can also take a seaplane from Lake Union (1838 Westlake N.) from Kenmore Air Harbor (486-1257 or 364-6990).

Highlights in Victoria: in addition to all the Englishness—the wee fish-and-chips shops, double-decker buses, lamp posts decked in flowers, cricket matches, woolen and china shops—there's the **Provincial Museum** (604/387-3014), one of the finest in Canada with reconstructed historic street scenes, lots of good Northwest Indian trappings, and gold rush lore. **Butchard Gardens** (604/652-2066) is usually crowded, but it is internationally renowned for its varying garden displays. For shoppers, there are lots of woolens and china and antiques shops in the city. The **Empress Hotel** (604/384-8111) has become legendary for its afternoon tea, and so there are always lots of tourists and a long line. Unless you're into very old and very quaint, avoid stying there overnight.

To get more than a vista view of **Mount Saint Helens**—you know, the one that erupted May 18, 1980—you can charter with either Columbia Air Services at Kelso Airport (1-577-8550) or General Aviation at Chehalis (1-748-0035) for an into-the-crater experience. The mountain is about a two-hour drive south of Seattle off I-5. For a list of good viewing spots, call the National Forest Service Mount St. Helens Visitors Center (1-864-6699) or the Kelso Chamber of Commerce Visitors Center (1-577-8058).

For Seattleites, **Mount Rainier** is the ultimate presence; they've even named a beer after it. The mountain rises 14,410 feet and is the second highest peak in the continental United States. If you want to get close, there's a visitors' center at Sunrise at 6,400 feet; the road's open only in the summer. Spectacular views may be had also at the lodge and visitors' center at Paradise at 5,400 feet. The mountain is 110 miles southeast of Seattle, and there are camping facilities and inns at Longmire (1-569-2565) and Paradise (1-569-2291). People say that if you have time for only one minivacation, make it a trip to Mount Rainier. Call 569-2343 for a recorded message.

If you're into wine, Seattle is a good place to sip and savor. Until fairly recently, **Washington wines** meant sweet syrupy Mogen David stuff, but that's a thing of the past. In October 1974, a Chateau Ste. Michelle Riesling beat out 14 California wineries, 3 German, and 1 Australian in an international tasting—and it's been award after award ever since. Seattle now has 31 wineries; most offer tours and tastings. Call the Washington Wine Institute (281-7156) for more details.

Sunday Customs

What better day to get out to shop than on the day of rest? At least three Seattle shopping centers are open on Sunday afternoons, just waiting to take your money.

Northgate was the first planned regional shopping center in the area and is now modernized with four major department stores (the Bon, Nordstrom, Lamonts, and J. C. Penney) plus a bunch of specialty shops and a movie theater. Located just off I-5 on N.E. Northgate Way and First N.E.

Bellevue Square offers a full range of goods in stores like Nordstrom, Fredrick & Nelson and J. C. Penney. Located at N.E. Eighth Street and Bellevue Way.

Southcenter is a biggie with shopping among soaring columns, interior plantings, fountains, and dramatic hanging mobiles. Located a mere five minutes from Sea-Tac Airport, just off I-5 at the Renton-Southcenter exit, it's an enclosed, climate-controlled mall packed with just about every kind of store you can imagine. 447-4800.

If you'd rather spend your money eating instead of buying, check out the following places for **brunch:**

Our favorite is the Sorrento's **Hunt Room** (see "At Your Service") for one of Seattle's most civilized brunches.

The **Hi-Spot Cafe,** a laid-back cozy little place in a refurbished Madrona House and storefront, features hearty brunch fare. 1410 34th Street. 325-7905.

Raison d'etre, very much its own place with dramatic, ever-changing decor, attracts a fascinating cosmopolitan mix of patrons. Try the butter brioche and caramel cinnamon rolls. 113 Virginia. 624-4622.

Active Sports

If you want to stay active while away from home, this is the place to be. Seattleites are about as outdoorsy as you can get, and so the town is packed with sports organizations and activities. Sailboat racing, bicycling, salmon fishing, road racing, and gaming of all types go on constantly in Seattle. To get the dope on exactly what's going on when, call the **Seattle Parks and Recreation Department** (625-4671).

If **bicycling** is your game, you'll be glad to know there's a Bicycle Hot Line (522-BIKE) with a recorded message to tell you what's up and coming in the bicycling arena. If you leave your name and number, they'll call back with information, too. There's a bicycle racing track at the Marymoor Park Velodrome (329-7381) and several local bicycling clubs. Bike rentals are available in the city from stores such as the Bicycle Center (523-8300), Gregg's Greenlake Cycle (532-2822 or 462-1900), and Alki Bike 'n' Boats (938-3322).

For **boating** enthusiasts, rentals are available in every size and style, from a canoe to a full-crewed yacht, at the various marinas and boathouses around Seattle. With all the lakes, rivers, and Puget Sound, this is a popular sport. Many canoeing and kayaking clubs offer tours and excursions, and rafting companies will take you on white-water rafting trips. Because of all the possibilities here, it's best to get in touch with the Seattle Parks and Recreation Department for suggestions about boat rentals.

To tee off for a game of **golf,** visit any of the following golf courses: Bellevue Municipal Golf Course, 5500 140th N.E., Bellevue, 885-6009; Mont Si Golf Course, 9010 Meadowbrook, North Bend Road S.E., 888-1541; Snohomish Golf Club, 7806 147th S.E., Snohomish, 1-568-2676; or West Seattle Golf Course, 4470 35th S.W., 932-9792.

Two of our favorite spots for **jogging** and **running** are the Seattle waterfront and the three-mile trail around Green Lake. Runners also enjoy the numerous paths in the arboretum and the trails and parcourse in Discovery Park, 36th W. and West Government Way. There's an 880-yard dirt path winding around small Laurelhurst Park (N.E. 45th and 48th N.E.) and lots of trees and paths in Lincoln Park (Fauntleroy Way S.W. and S.W. Trenton). Magnolia Bluff/Discovery Park (along Magnolia Boulevard) has a great view of the Olympic Mountains across Puget Sound. For detailed infromation on trails, runs, parcourse locations, and mileages of various runs, call the Seattle Parks and Recreation Department.

Spectator Sports

Only a decade ago, many sports enthusiasts passed Seattle by as a bush-league town, but today the city shines in professional sports. In football, the **Seahawks'** (827-9766) famous "blue wave" (a routine the fans have created to show their support) still rolls in the Kingdome, while during the summer months, the **Mariners** (628-0888) aren't quite so successful playing baseball under the same dome. In basketball, the **SuperSonics** (281-5850) have long been a major NBA attraction also at the Kingdome. For further information on Kingdome events, call 628-3663.

Washington, D.C.

HOTELS

1 Admiral Fell Inn
2 Belvedere
3 Comfort Inn
4 Days Inn
5 Holiday Inn Inner Harbor
6 Hyatt Regency
7 Omni International
8 Society Hill
9 Tremont Hotel
10 Tremont Plaza

LANDMARKS

A Arlington National Cemetery
B Convention Center
C Corcoran Art Gallery
D Hirshorn Museum
E Jefferson Memorial
F John F. Kennedy Center
G Library of Congress
H Lincoln Memorial
I Museum of American History
J National Air and Space Museum

K National Archives
L National Gallery
M National Portrait Gallery
N Natural History Museum
O Smithsonian Institution
P Supreme Court
Q Tourist Information Center
R Union Station
S U.S. Capitol
T Vietnam Veterans Memorial
U Washington Monument
V White House

WASHINGTON, D.C.

GETTING YOUR BEARINGS

Washington, D.C., is more than just the U.S. capital—it's a world capital. It's a city of power and power brokers, a city where the elite is determined by political status rather than bloodlines.

It has been called the world's largest company town, the company being, of course, the U.S. government. Fully 21 percent of D.C.'s work force is employed by the federal government, and 83 percent of these jobs are white collar.

Although not many of the nation's major corporations are headquartered in D.C., industrial America has nevertheless had to establish outposts here to be near the seat of power. Hundreds of large corporations from Xerox to American Express maintain Washington offices as listening and lobbying posts. For other businesses there are trade associations that represent an entire industry. Downtown K Street is known as "influence alley" because of all the meetings, lobbying, trading of intelligence, planning, and strategy making that goes on in the office buildings and expensive restaurants in the area. Lawyers form another large block of the downtown business scene, many of them earning large incomes and national fame by helping corporate clients gain access to the powerful or navigate the legislative and regulatory mazes in the capital.

Washington also has several universities and internationally important centers of thought and research. The Smithsonian, for example, is home to a large number of scholars and curators working in a wide variety of disciplines. The National Institutes of Health in nearby Bethesda form a major center for health research. There are think tanks such as the Brookings Institution, the American Enterprise Institute, and the Georgetown University Center for Strategic and International Studies, not to mention the Library of Congress.

According to *Washingtonian* magazine, the city leads the country in opportunities for women: "D.C. is the Best Big City for Women." They base this judgment on the fact that 26.3 percent of the professional, managerial, and technical workers in Washington (the job-holding elite) are women. The statistics auger well for visiting women, too. The city's excellent hotels, restaurants, and cultural centers and events are stimulating and sophisticated, offering an unqualified welcome to women who travel alone.

Finding your way around town is easy once you learn the rules. Basically, everything falls into four quadrants that radiate out from the Capitol Building: NW, NE, SW, SE. Most of your downtown business will probably take place in the NW section of town. Although NW is generally considered the "nice" section, you should be aware that there are lovely areas in other sections *and* that there are some parts of NW (like 14th Street) you should avoid at all costs.

Some neighborhoods, frequented primarily by locals, are interesting and merit your perusal if you have the time: Adams-Morgan is the most concentrated ethnic neighborhood in downtown D.C. and, as such, is fun to explore (located around 18th and Columbia Road). You can browse the shops, eat in inexpensive restaurants serving exotic cuisines, and be relatively safe (taxi back to your hotel after dark). The waterfront, in the SW section, offers some pleasant strolls, inexpensive restaurants, and a great park. DuPont Circle is trendy, upscale, and fun to browse.

You can feel completely safe on the Metro, Washington's utopian subway system. It gets you where you want to go quickly and hassle-free.

WHAT TO WEAR

Let the city's size and location be your guide; a large eastern city calls for the best your wardrobe has to offer. Go conservative if your business dictates or on the cutting edge of fashion if your industry appreciates that sort of statement. The only mistake you can make is to be overly casual. Even in summer when the humidity wilts the starchiest of white collars you should continue to dress for success—and pray for air-conditioning.

WEATHER WATCH

Summers can be outrageously hot and humid, and winters can chill your bones. Spring, with the blossoming of Washington's famous cherry trees, is definitely the city's finest season—although anyone who visits in the fall, with its clear, blue-sky days that offset the changing leaves, might argue convincingly that that season is best. Some summer days can be ideal, however, with blue skies and kind temperatures, and winters can be mild. We recommend you check temperatures in your local paper a few days before deciding what to pack for your trip to D.C.

GETTING THERE

Three major airports serve Washington, D.C. **Washington National** is located directly across the Potomac River from downtown. Handles domestic and some Canadian flights. Call 892-0721 for airport information. Only three and a half miles from downtown, it is 15 minutes driving time in non-rush-hour traffic and, surprisingly, not much worse during peak time. About $7 by cab; 80 cents on the Metro's Blue Line.

    Dulles International Airport is located in the Virginia countryside with dual-lane expressways leading directly into the terminal. One of the world's most modern terminals, it was voted second-most-admired U.S. airport by travelers in an *Ad Age* poll in 1985. Handles transcontinental and intercontinental flights. Call 703/471-7838 for airport information. It is situated 23 miles west of the city; count on about 40 minutes driving time. Cab fare is $35. No Metro service.

    Baltimore-Washington International (BWI) serves both cities with domestic and international flights. Call BWI at 301/261-1000. This airport is 31 miles northeast of the city, or 45 minutes driving time. Cab fare is around $40, but be sure to negotiate the fee with your driver before leaving. Amtrak (Union Station) connects with BWI about five times a day ($7.75 one way). Call 484-7540 or 800/USA-RAIL for times and information.

    Bus Service to all three airports is available on the hour during the day, an abbreviated schedule at night. Call Washington Flyer, 685-1400, for information. There is a helicopter shuttle with regular departures and arrivals between all three airports. Costs about $60 one way. Call Capital Helicopter, 620-6551.

Car Rentals

Ajax	979-3700
Avis	800/331-1212
Budget	628-2750
Hertz	800/654-3131
Holiday/Pay Less	530-3610
National	800/328-4567
Thrifty	548-1600

GETTING AROUND

Although mass transportation in Washington is about as good as you're likely to find anywhere in this country, you still may need a car for getting to far-flung appointments.

    Be warned that traffic police here are diligent, and casual overparkers will find their cars towed away. Many streets have only two-hour parking limits. Women who travel here frequently recommend parking in your hotel's garage and using mass transit around immediate areas.

Taxis are abundant (9,000 in the D.C. area) and work on the zone system. The fare in a nonrush hour is $1.70 for one zone and $2.45 for two zones, and rises 75 cents for each zone crossed. Into Maryland or Virginia, expect to pay a per-mile charge. Sharing is the norm. Don't be alarmed if the cab that picks you up already has one or more passengers. It's accepted here. Besides, you can meet some interesting people this way. For more information or complaints, call 727-5401.

The good news is the Metro, Washington's interlinked bus and subway system. It is efficient, clean, safe, and cheap. If your destination is remote from the Metrorail (subway) station, rest assured there's a Metrobus to get you there. Metrobus fares in D.C. run 80 cents during rush hour, 75 cents other times; in Maryland, between 80 cents and $1.65; and in Virginia, between 80 cents and $2.20. Metrorail is virtually crime-free and is so well designed and well maintained that it has been compared to a museum rather than a subway system. Lines are color coded: Blue, Red, Yellow, Orange. Its computerized ticket card system is fast once you figure it out. Transit information is available at 637-2437, seven days a week, 6 A.M. to 11:30 P.M. For an all-inclusive route map, call 367-1261.

Limos are always present in this status-conscious town. There are about 60 companies, so shop for a good price; it should run between $50 and $80 for two to three hours. We've found the following to be dependable: Admiral (554-1000); Executive Transportation, with Rolls-Royce (467-6355); and Watergate (333-0383).

GETTING FAMILIAR

Washington Tourist Information Center

Between 14th and 15th streets on Pennsylvania Avenue, NW

Located one block from the White House, this center offers walk-in information, free maps, guides, brochures.

Washington Convention and Visitors Association

Suite 250, 1575 I Street, NW   789-7000
Washington, DC 20005

Call or write ahead for information on hotels, restaurants, transportation, leisure activities.

The *Washington Post,* a daily, is the paper of record. Has an excellent Friday section called "Weekend," with reviews and listings of all entertainment options. Check page 3 for "Weekend Best." The *Washington*

Times, a daily, carries an arts and entertainment section on Friday. In the fall and winter, it includes a dining guide tabloid. The *Washington Monthly* has a "Where and When" section on entertainment. Available at newsstands. The *Washington Dossier* is a monthly magazine with features on general-interest subjects; also the "Sophisticate's Itinerary" for wining and dining recommendations. *Where,* available in hotels and tourist offices, is a weekly handout. The *Hill Rag,* a weekly, reports on what's happening in government, film, world events. The *Washington Weekly* is popular for "our town" gossip and features.

The *Washingtonian,* a monthly magazine, carries hard-ball features, profiles. *Survivor's Guide to Washington,* a monthly, is a handout detailing what's happening. Recommended reading: *The Walker Washington Guide,* a standby and good general all-around source of information.

Quick Calls

AREA CODE 202	Weather 936-1212
Time 844-2525	All emergencies 911

Numbers to call for information on upcoming events include Dial-An-Event, 737-8866; Dial-A-Park, 426-6975; Dial-A-Museum, 357-2020; and National Archives Events, 523-3000.

AT YOUR SERVICE

In this supertransient city, where large crowds and hectic numbers are the norm, we take comfort (literally) in the small hotels—those whose rooms number around 100 and whose service and personal attention both soothe and pamper. However, if you prefer to be where the action is, we've included the best of those as well.

The Watergate Hotel

2650 Virginia Avenue, NW   Toll-free reservations: 800/424-2736
Washington, DC 20037   Local number: 965-2300
    Telex: 904994

Considered by some to be D.C.'s finest hotel, the 238-room Watergate has a lot going for it: excellent location (steps away from the Kennedy Center, walking distance from the White House and the State Department); top-drawer clientele (heads of state, ambassadors, performers, and film personalities); some of the best health club facilities in town. Security is tight. Business services include electronic equipment and audiovisual facilities. The hotel adjoins the Watergate Shopping Mall and Les Champs, an international dining and shopping area (Valentino, La

	Concierge	Executive Floor	No-Smoking Rooms	Fitness Facilities	Pool	24-Hour Room Service	Restaurant for Client Entertaining	Extra-Special Amenities	Electronic Key System	Business/Secretarial Services	Checkout Time	Frequent Guest Program	Business Traveler Program	Average Single Rate
Canterbury	front desk						Chaucer's	•		•	12 noon	Garfinkel's gift cert.		$110
Four Seasons	•		•	•		•	Aux Beaux Champs	•		•	12 noon	Connections		$175
Grand	•				•	•	Mayfair	•		•	1 p.m.		Corp. rates	$165 $145 corp.
Hay Adams	•					• butler service	John Hay Room	•		•	1 p.m.		Corp. rates	$150 $115 corp.
Jefferson	•		•			•	Hunt Club	•		•	1 p.m.	by request	Corp. rates	$135 $100 corp.
Phoenix Park	front desk						Powerscourt	•	•	•	1 p.m.		Corp. rates	$137 $ 99 corp.
Vista	•	•	by advance request	•		•	American Harvest	•		•	12 noon	Premium Award	Corp. rates	$110 $170 corp. on Vista floor
Watergate Hotel	•		•	•	•		Jean-Louis				12 noon	Delta Airlines Program	Personal Valet Service	$170

Roche, Gucci, YSL). Unique to the Watergate is their Personal Valet Service, which allows departing guests to leave behind any clothing they wish. By their next return visit, it will have been cleaned, pressed, and hung in the closet.

Hotel dining includes the **Wintergarden Restaurant and Terrace** offering candlelight dining, live piano music, and **Jean-Louis,** rated by Henri Gault as the "best French restaurant outside France" (see "Dining Out"). Bars include the **Saddle Bar** and the **Potomac Lounge** (Potomac is the favorite of most women who've tried both).

Hay Adams

One Lafayette Square   Toll-free reservations: 800/424-5054
16 and H Streets, NW   Local number: 638-2260
Washington, DC 20006   Telex: 7108229543

This elegant small (165 rooms) hotel reflects the taste of legendary hotel woman, Rose Narva. A $3 million renovation recently upgraded this 1927 classic to its present English Tudor manor-house ambience. An eclectic mix of periods (two huge Medici carpets, dating from 1610 and 1620, share space with 18th-century English Regency commodes) adds to the English country-house charm. A bit of history trivia: John Hay, secretary of state under Theodore Roosevelt and Henry Adams, began his career as personal secretary to Abraham Lincoln. Hay originally lived in homes on the hotel site.

Dining within the hotel: the **John Hay Room,** serious French cuisine in a small, oak-paneled room; the **Adams Room,** sunny, airy, overlooking Lafayette Square; breakfast, lunch, and Sunday brunch; the **Tea Room,** daily from 3 to 5 P.M., in a richly appointed alcove; the **English Grill Room,** typical English fare. The **John Hay Lounge** for evening cocktails features Peter Duchin as music director.

Four Seasons

2800 Pennsylvania Avenue, NW   Toll-free reservations: 800/828-1188
Washington, DC 20007   Local number: 342-0444
     Telex: 904008

The excellence of service and ambience of this superb group of hotels is well known, and their Washington property is no exception. Designed to blend with its historic Georgetown neighbors, the building is a handsome six-story brick structure with a landmark clock tower. Inside, the design stresses simplicity of line embellished with quality furnishings: plush sofas, Carrara marble, handwoven carpets, fine antiques, lush indoor gardens of some 2,300 plants. Quiet elegance is the byword here, from check-in at an antique reception desk to personalized service by all staff members. The setting is oddly bucolic—many guest rooms overlook the C&O Canal and Rock Creek Park—yet the hotel is in the heart of Georgetown's boutiques and bustle.

Hotel dining includes: **Aux Beaux Champs,** sunlit by day, candles at night in a three-meals-a-day setting; lunch features a light cuisine; the

Garden Terrace, an airy indoor garden serving lunch, dinner, and traditional afternoon tea; **Le Petit Champ,** a private dining room; and the **Plaza Cafe,** an open-air courtyard restaurant serving light lunches and drinks. The **Garden Terrace Lounge** is serene and totally comfortable for meeting clients for drinks or tea. **Desiree** is a private nightclub which extends temporary membership to hotel guests for late-night entertaining.

Canterbury

1733 N Street, NW	Toll-free reservations: 800/424-2950
Washington, DC 20036	Local number: 393-3000

A little gem of a hotel, this 99-room townhouse is on one of Washington's most residential streets, a tree-lined street just off the bustle of busy Connecticut Avenue. Reflecting the taste of General Manager Lanny Lewis, the rooms are decorated in antiques, some with four-postered canopied beds, and a wealth of small collectibles, unusual in hotel decor. Each room also has a kitchenette, complete with coffeemaker. Guests are invited daily to the library-lounge for free drinks, and later for free champagne; a free Continental breakfast is served in the restaurant. The staff is friendly, and service is highly personalized; everyone knows your name almost immediately.

   Chaucer's is their small but excellent restaurant (see "Dining Out"). This is also the brunch spot-of-choice for many local women.

   An indoor garage is attached to the hotel.

Grand Hotel

2350 M Street, NW	Toll-free reservations: 800/848-0016
Washington, DC 20037	Local number: 429-0100
	Telex: 904282

In 1984, when it was The Regent, this hotel received lots of really good press—*Travel & Leisure* named it "hotel of the month" (November 1984); and *Fortune* magazine singled out its business center for praise. (There's even a daily wire service in addition to state-of-the-art everything else, including seven meeting rooms with capacities ranging from 200 to board-meeting size).

   Today it has changed hands, and changed names, but remains a medium-sized hotel, 265 rooms, in a location midway between the business district and Georgetown, making it extremely convenient. The exterior is that of a lovingly restored old building. It's actually a new luxury structure—$64 million worth of planning for perfection (although some feel it's a bit too sterile). The bathrooms alone are worth the tarrif—floor to ceiling Portuguese marble with sunken tubs and separate glassed-in showers. The clientele is a mixed bag of top-management business traveler, politician, and entertainer (Michael Jackson was one of the first; he took over an entire floor).

   In-House dining: the **Mayfair Restaurant and Bar** serves on Wedgewood plates. Expect dressy, pricey, but comfortable. **Mayfair Court** is for private dining. **Promenade Lounge,** which overlooks a landscaped courtyard, serves breakfast, lunch, tea. String and piano music during the cocktail hour. The **Mayfair Bar** is stand-up. Excellent service and courtesy shown by staff, especially to women alone.

Jefferson

1200 15th Street, NW   Toll-free reservations: 800/368-5966
Washington, DC 20036   Local number: 347-2200

This is a super-deluxe, small hotel, comprising 102 rooms with no two alike. Recent renovations, under the direction of manager Rose Narva, have produced a cozy, intimate atmosphere: four-poster beds, mahogany furniture, crystal lamps, grandfather clocks—all touches that reflect her hospitality genius. It's been nicknamed "White House North" because of its heavy-duty clientele (Lee Annenberg, William French Smith, Caspar Weinberger). Popular with film stars and entertainers as well. The quote we like best from management, "We don't say no to any request; we get anything a guest wants." We also like the security measures: the front door is locked after 1 A.M., and it's the only entrance. All guests are known and called by name. Strangers can't get past the desk unless they're expected.

In-house dining: the newly refurbished **Hunt Club** (formerly Bennett's) is a restaurant with the atmosphere of a fine club. Excellent food, with seasonal specialties. The bar is equally clubby and comfortable, attracting a very classy crowd.

Phoenix Park Hotel

520 N. Capitol Street, NW   Toll-free reservations: 800/824-5419
Washington, DC 20001   Local number: 638-6900
        Telex: 904104

Another small hotel, this one with only 87 rooms in a setting reminiscent of baronial Ireland. Antiques throughout, in both public and guest rooms. The location, a bit off "hotel row," can actually be a plus: just across the street from Union Station (handy to both Amtrak and the Metro) and close to the Capitol.

Adjacent to the hotel is the **Dubliner,** the city's best Irish pub (see "Late-Night Washington"). **Powerscourt,** their fine dining restaurant, features Continental cuisine with a focus on Irish specialties.

Vista International Hotel

1400 M Street, NW   Toll-free reservations: your local HRS
Washington, DC 20005   number
        Local number: 429-1700
        Telex: 440237

A large (413 rooms) hotel that manages to personalize its guest services, making it comfortable for women to stay here alone. The interior design is open and airy, with many guest rooms overlooking the interior courtyard's Tower Lounge (women like these overview windows that let them preview the scene in the Lounge before they arrive). Designer rooms—by couturier Givenchy—are located in the interior tower. Individual histories are kept, so returning guests enjoy a personalized welcome.

Executive Fitness Menus are available (complete with calorie counts) in the **American Harvest** at lunchtime. And a Vista Breakfast—an expanded version of the Continental—is included, no matter what the rate. The **Federal Bar** is like a neighborhood pub: friendly bartender, saloon piano, spontaneous sing-alongs.

SOMETHING SPECIAL:
Executive Club
1317 Connecticut Avenue, NW   Local number: 955-6090
Washington, DC 20036
A membership club, open to senior-level women executives. Facilities include private dining and entertaining, library, and a health spa that offers classes, massage, and skin treatments. You can discuss possible membership with Jody Murphy, president.

The **Hotel Association of Washington** publishes a brochure in which all accommodations are listed by price range on a map marking all hotels by location. Send for one: 1219 Connecticut Avenue, NW, Suite 300, Washington, DC 20036. Or call 833-3350. A toll-free call to 800/554-2220 puts you in touch with **Central Reservations Center,** a service that suggests lodgings to meet your specific requirements and will then book reservations for you.

ON A BUDGET

Hotels

Each of the following hotels is located in the heart of downtown:

Holiday Inn—Capitol Hill
550 C Street, SW   Toll-free reservations: 800/465-4329
Washington, DC 20024   Local number: 479-4000
Single rooms for $87 a night, regardless of season.

Quality Inn—Capitol Hill
415 New Jersey Avenue, NW   Toll-free reservations: 800/228-5151
Washington, DC 20001   Local number: 638-1616
Single rooms for $70 a night, regardless of season.

Hotel Washington
15th Street and Pennsylvania   Toll-free reservations: 800/424-9450
   Avenue, NW   Local number: 638-5900
Washington, DC 20004
Women who stay here report, "nothing fancy, but it's safe, and the staff is very nice." And you can't beat the location for convenience. Singles from $72.

Restaurants

Millie and Al's Pizza, in the ethnic Adams-Morgan neighborhood, is casual, fun, and inexpensive. 2440 18th Street, NW. 387-8131.

Most restaurants in **Adams-Morgan** are ethnic in cuisine, and are relatively inexpensive. There are more Ethiopian restaurants here than in Ethiopia. Take care leaving the area at night.

Georgetown, too, has a good number of inexpensive ethnic restaurants. (We especially like the Vietnamese places.) Our advice is to walk along M Street between Foggy Bottom and Key Bridge, reading menus and trying whatever appeals. It's a lovely neighborhood for walking, and you're bound to find someplace you'll like.

Entertainment

See a movie *before* dinner—many D.C. movie theaters offer half-price tickets during daylight hours. Check listings in local newspapers.

DINING OUT

POWER BREAKFASTS

Working breakfasts have become very popular in Washington, particularly among government officials, lobbyists, journalists, and local professionals. Lots of politics are discussed over morning coffee. Hotel dining rooms like the following are the best bets for early-morning power grabbing:

Bennett's (Jefferson Hotel), 347-2200

Montpelier (Madison Hotel), 862-1600

The Adams Room (Hay Adams hotel), 638-6600

Aux Beaux Champs (Four Seasons Hotel), 342-0444

The Jockey Club (Ritz Carlton Hotel), 659-8000. This one opens at 6:30 A.M.—great if you have to squeeze in two meetings before the day begins.

The Bread Oven, at two locations, is considered one of the best French cafes in town. 1201 Pennsylvania Avenue, NW (favorite hangout of lobbyists and government folk) 737-7772; 1220 19th Street, 466-4264.

WHEN YOU'RE HOSTING

Whether the goal is to land the account, impress the client, or merely do a little business, the following places are proven winners.

Jean-Louis (Watergate Hotel) is number one if you want to impress with your impeccable taste. Considered by some to be America's premier French restaurant. Very classy, exclusive atmosphere. Only 12 tables, fine service, excellent wine list. Very expensive. Reservations a must. 2650 Virginia Avenue, NW. 298-4488.

L'Auberge Chez François is quite far out of town and you'll need to call for directions, but it's worth the trip. Lots of charm (voted "best restaurant of the year" in a 1984 reader's poll by *Washingtonian* magazine). Moderate.

Iron Gate Inn serves Middle Eastern cuisine outdoors under a grape arbor during summer. In winter, the converted stable with its comforting fireplace is the setting. 1734 N Street, NW. 737-1370.

House of Hunan is a favorite for lovers of Szechuan and Hunan cuisine in an elegant atmosphere. Central location a plus. 1900 K Street, NW. 293-9111.

Old Ebbitt Grill recently won kudos as the best new restaurant in town. Clublike atmosphere, traditional American fare. 657 15th Street. 347-4800.

Morton's of Chicago has great dry-aged beef, barbeque ribs, and lobster. About eight blocks north of the White House, so the location is ideal. 3251 Prospect Street, NW. 483-2000.

Dominique's is the place if your client loves the exotic. Order the rattlesnake, buffalo, ostrich, or camel salad. 1900 Pennsylvania Avenue, NW. 452-1126.

Maison Blanche, called by the *Washington Post* "the hot shot's hot spot." Also won a four-star Mobil rating for classic French cuisine. 1725 F Street, NW. 842-0070.

Duke Zeibert's is famous for table-hopping Washington power brokers and sports figures. Crowded, but a good place to go, to be seen. Don't expect a quiet, elegant meal. 1050 Connecticut Avenue, NW. 466-3730.

Lion d'Or is one of the city's finest. Impressive clientele, excellent cuisine. Expensive. 1150 Connecticut Avenue, NW. 296-7972.

Marrakesh, an up-scale Moroccan restaurant, is a bit offbeat, but could be perfect for the right client. One devotee observed, "It's the woman's answer to spending the day on the golf course with the guys. You can sit for hours, relax, really get to know someone. A marvelous alternative." And the food is an ice-breaker, too; you eat with your fingers. 617 New York Avenue, NW, at 6th Street. 393-9393. (There's no sign outside, just a brass knocker.)

TABLE FOR ONE

You can feel at ease in any of the hotel dining rooms mentioned in "At Your Service." In addition, women who travel frequently to D.C. agree with us that single women can feel at home in the following restaurants.

American Cafe, in several locations around town. Trendy California-style menu, with emphasis on fresh produce. Sidewalk cafe in nice weather. Georgetown (1211 Wisconsin Avenue, NW, 337-3600) open until 4 A.M. Capitol Hill (227 Massachusetts Avenue, NE, 547-8504) open till 3 A.M. National Place (between Pennsylvania Avenue and F Street, on 13th, 737-5153).

Captain Days Seafood. Moderately priced seafood in a converted warehouse. Very cozy once you're inside; a bit hard to find. It's in an alley off 18th Street. 1130 Rear 18th Street, NW. 296-1133.

Food for Thought offers alternatives to the red-meat rut; vegetable burgers, lots of pita pocket fillers, even old-fashioned ice cream sundaes. Place becomes a coffee house with entertainment on Friday and Saturday nights. Inexpensive. 1738 Connecticut Avenue, NW. 797-1095.

1789 Restaurant offers French cuisine and an impressive array of fellow diners. Despite the Gallic atmosphere, service is friendly, even for women alone. Closed Sunday. 1226 36th Street, NW (near Georgetown University). 965-1789.

La Nicoise has an interesting menu, but the big draws are the waiters on rollerskates and the general good-times atmosphere. There's even a slapstick, if slightly raunchy, show around 10:30 P.M. 1721 Wisconsin Avenue, NW (Georgetown). 965-9300.

Twigs is good for light fare, perhaps lunchtime entertaining. Known for butternut pancakes and Belgian waffles as well as seafood and veal. In the Capital Hilton, 16th and K streets, NW. 393-1000.

Cafe Mozart is small, unpretentious, and charming. Celebrates Oktoberfest all year with wide selection of German specialties, and music while you dine. Closed Sunday. 1331 H Street, NW. 347-5732.

Bacchus serves Lebanese cuisine in an atmosphere comfortable for single diners. Excellent appetizers. 1827 Jefferson Place, NW (duPont Circle). 785-0734.

Charlie Chiang's is inexpensive Chinese food in an attractive setting. 1912 I Street, NW. 293-6000.

Chaucer's, recently named "best new discovery," is in the Canterbury Hotel on a quiet street just off the business district. Dignified, comfortable place for dining alone; it's also a superb choice for entertaining a friend or client. Good service, food, and wine list. 1733 N Street, NW. 393-3000.

WASHINGTON BY DAY

Washington is a city as rich in things to do and see as you're likely to find anywhere. The following list is not intended to be definitive; for that, you should contact the Convention and Visitors Association. Rather, we suggest some don't-miss favorites.

For some spectacular overviews of the city:

Top of the **Washington Monument.**

Sky Terrace Bar atop the Hotel Washington, 15th Street, NW. 638-5900.

Balcony at Library of Congress in the new James Madison Memorial Building, 101 Independence Ave., SE.

Scenic overlooks along the **George Washington Memorial Parkway,** particularly the bluff overlooking Georgetown between Key Bridge and the Spout Run exit.

Clock Tower in the Old Post Office Building. Much easier to get to than the Washington Monument, and at 315 feet, it's high enough to afford a helpful idea of the city's layout.

Seeing the Monuments

Most of what visitors want to see is located on or near the Mall. The Tourmobile is an ideal way to get around to the Mall sites and beyond, but because of its laid-back pace, we prefer it when we have all day (see "At Leisure" for details).

THE MEMORIALS

The **Lincoln Memorial,** as majestic in real life as in pictures, with the familiar 19-foot statue housed in a classic Greek temple. Open 24 hours a day, with a Park Ranger on duty until midnight. Call 426-6842 for tour information.

The **Washington Monument** is to Washington what the Eiffel Tower is to Paris—symbol of the city. Also, at 555 feet, the tallest masonry structure in the world. Take the free ride to the top for a truly monumental view of the city. Open until 5 P.M. On the Mall at 15th Street, NW. Call 426-6839.

The **Jefferson Memorial** is housed in a rotunda, our third president's favorite design. On the south bank of the Tidal Basin, a fairyland site during cherry blossom time. Call 426-6822.

The **U.S. Capitol** is Washington's most prominent site, covering three and a half acres. Guided tours every 15 minutes from 9 A.M. to 3:45 P.M. (building open until 4:30 P.M.). Call 225-6827.

The **White House:** We're not alone in feeling the "standard tour" is the biggest disappointment in town. VIP tours are far more inspiring; contact your state representatives to get on the list. To walk through, pick up a free ticket from the booth on the Ellipse. Summer lines can be never ending; in winter, you'll breeze through. Call 456-7041.

Arlington National Cemetery: JFK's gravesite, with its eternal flame, is the premier draw; he's buried between his two infant children. Nearby, Robert Kennedy's grave is marked by a simple white wooden cross. Arlington is our largest national burial ground—500 acres of landscaped hills. Open 8 A.M. to 5 P.M.

The **Vietnam Veterans' Memorial,** a poignant black granite wall, lists the names of 57, 939 Americans who died or were lost in Vietnam. Near the Lincoln Memorial in Constitutional Gardens; open 24 hours a day. Call 426-6700.

The Smithsonian Museums

Some statistics whiz has calculated that if one were to spend one minute at every item exhibited in the **Smithsonian Museums**, it would take 72 years to see all of them. Lining both sides of the Mall, any of the 11 museums is an absolute must. Because it would take so long to see them all properly, your best bet is to select your area of interest and do one museum well. Most are open from 10 A.M. until 5:30 P.M. in winter; until 7:30 P.M. in summer. They are located in a horseshoe configuration on the Mall, which stretches from the Capitol to the Lincoln Memorial.

The **National Air and Space Museum** is recognized as the world's most popular museum. Covering three city blocks, this behemoth houses reminders of some of aviation's finest moments: the Wright brothers' first plane, Lindbergh's *Spirit of St. Louis,* Chuck Yeager's Bell X-1, the Apollo 11 command module *Columbia,* and much more. Free guided tours; fine films on five-story-high screens (don't miss the film *To Fly).*

The **National Museum of American History,** a.k.a. the "nation's attic," is a collection of Americana that includes George Washington's teeth, Thomas Edison's phonographs, and the original Star-Spangled Banner.

The **National Museum of Natural History** has it all, including the infamous 45-carat Hope diamond, an Easter Island stone head, a 92-foot blue whale—you name it.

The **Arts and Industries Building** is a must for anyone who loves Victoriana. Also has a fine gift shop.

The **Freer Gallery of Art** houses the finest private collection of Far and Near Eastern art outside the Orient. Donated by industrialist Charles L. Freer.

The **Joseph H. Hirshorn Museum and Sculpture Garden** exhibits more than 6,000 19th- and 20th-century paintings and sculptures, donated by financier J. H. Hirshorn. The sunken garden has magnificent pieces, including some by Rodin and Matisse.

The **Museum of African Art** traces the history and heritage of African art.

The **National Museum of American Art** and the **National Portrait Gallery** include works from medieval to modern. Titian, Rembrandt, El Greco, Gainsborough, Renoir, and da Vinci works are part of the collections.

The **Renwick Gallery** displays American design, crafts, and decorative arts.

The **Castle,** the Smithsonian's first building, of Gothic Revival architecture, is resplendent with spires, towers, turrets, and crenellated parapets. Stop by for a slide show of the complex's best-known treasures.

Call **Dial-a-Museum,** 357-2020, for current special events and shows.

Other Major Sites to See

The **National Zoo** is a must, if only to see Washington's most charming couple, giant pandas Hsing-Hsing and Ling-Ling. They're in fine company, among lots of other charmers. Free admission. Open daily, 10 A.M. to 6 P.M. Entrance in the 3000 block of Connecticut Avenue, NW. 673-4800.

Try the **Botanic Gardens** (1st and Maryland Avenue, SW), the **National Arboretum** (3501 New York Avenue, NE), or the **Kenilworth Aquatic Gardens** (Kenilworth Avenue and Douglas Street, NE) for exotic plants, trees, marsh settings.

Hillwood is how you might choose to live if you were heiress to a cereal fortune. This residence of the late Marjorie Merriweather Post includes a 40-room mansion with Faberge jeweled Easter eggs and a dinner service used by Catherine the Great. Outdoors, there is a Japanese garden, a formal French garden, a hothouse with 5,000 rare orchids. Call well in advance for reservations. Open daily except Sunday and Tuesday. Tours from 9 A.M. to 1:30 P.M. Admission charge.

The **National Archives** is the permanent depository for the nation's most valuable documents. On display: the original Declaration of Independence, Bill of Rights, Constitution. Want to hear the Watergate tapes? Call 523-3099 to make an appointment. Open daily from 10 A.M. to 9 P.M. 8th Street and Constitution Avenue, NW.

The **Supreme Court of the United States:** Monday is best day to attend a session because that's when decisions are usually handed down. The yearly schedule begins the first Monday of October and adjourns in June; cases are usually heard from 10 A.M. to 3 P.M. Located at the corner of First and East Capitol streets. 252-3000.

Art Treasures

The **National Gallery,** not part of the Smithsonian although it is on the Mall, is one of the world's great art museums. Two wings: East, designed by I. M. Pei, for contemporary works; West, designed by J. R. Pope, for Old Masters. Open seven days. Call 737-4215 for hours. 4th Street and Constitution Avenue.

Phillips Collection, housed in a beautiful renovated building, contains a small, but charming, group of modern works as well as French impressionists. Most famous here is Renoir's *Luncheon of the Boating Party.* Open Tuesday to Saturday, 10 A.M. to 5 P.M.; Sunday, 2 to 7 P.M. Free admission. 1600 21st Street, NW. 387-0961.

The **Corcoran Gallery of Art** is the capital's oldest art gallery and is known for its collection of American art. Also has some European Old Masters, including Rubens and Rembrandt. 17th Street and New York Avenue. 638-3211.

THE SHOPPING SCENE

The suburbs of this cosmopolitan city are thick with state-of-the-art shopping malls, but the big news here is that the downtown area is being revitalized into a super-shopping area that's convenient as well.

Downtown: The old retail guard—**Garfinkel's, Woodward & Lothrop** (called Woodie's), and **Hecht's**—are here on F Street, NW, between Seventh and 14th streets. New shopping activity forms a triangle, each of the three sides being five blocks long: Woodie's is one leg of the triangle, Garfinkel's and the Old Post Office, the others.

The Shops at **National Place** (between Pennsylvania Avenue and F Street at 13th) is a Rouse Company project consisting of 51 shops and restaurants. Great for a quick lunch at one of the fast-food gourmet shops or for unusual impulse gift buying.

The Pavilion at the Old Post Office (1100 Pennsylvania Avenue, NW) was, in fact, the old post office. Its new incarnation is gussied up and elegant, boasting 60 shops and restaurants. Forget greasy french fries here. There's Indian quick food, Texas barbeque, ice cream-in-waffles, and classy french fries. Among the unique boutiques: **Modigliana** (exquisite lingerie), **Upper Duck** (anything with a waterfowl theme), an all-Christmas boutique.

Connecticut Avenue, considered by many serious shoppers to be D.C.'s premier hunting ground, starts downtown and stretches five miles, changing character several times along the route. Beginning at H Street across from Lafayette Square (a great place for an al fresco sandwich at lunchtime) are trendy boutiques and sophisticated old-line shops. Good men's shops are here as well, favorites of busy congressmen, senators, and judges. Further along Connecticut (at L Street), the shops take on a European flavor. Wonderful antique stores, hand-knits shops, and antique jewelry stores like the Tiny Jewel Box at 1143 Connecticut Avenue.

Dupont Circle features status designer wear. (**Rizik Brothers** and **Claire Dratch** specialize in better fashions.) The Circle area is relaxed, European with sidewalk cafes and bookstores (try Afterwords or the Newsroom for international periodicals).

Georgetown, *the* choice place to live, is also *the* place to shop or browse. Georgetown Park, an exquisitely restored Victorian area, offers carefully edited shops and tony boutiques. Begin shopping Georgetown at M Street and Wisconsin and you'll find Laura Ashley, the French Kitchen, Martin's Cheese Shop, Tootsie's (1519 Wisconsin), which, despite its silly name, offers an excellent selection of businesswear.

Chevy Chase/Bethesda, an area way up on Wisconsin, includes distinguished retailers like **Lord & Taylor, Saks Fifth Avenue,** and **Woodie's.** Best stop: **Mazza Galerie,** a three-story mall (Wisconsin at Western) that reeks with chic. Head here for name European and American designers, Mic Mac, Emmanuelle Khan, Pierre D'Alby. A couple of blocks from

Mazza, is the tiny Status II, a discounter of such European biggies as YSL, Valentino, Courrèges, Rykiel. They deduct anywhere from 50 to 80 percent off the ticket, depending on the season. 4405 Willard Avenue. 301/652-4541.

White Flint Mall offers some of the best suburban mall shopping. Bloomingdale's, I. Magnin, plus lots of small outlets. The usual mall—but classy. Bars, theaters, and a disco. 11301 Rockville Pike, N. Bethesda. 301/468-5777.

Les Champs offers shopping in a great location—the Watergate Complex between the hotel and the Kennedy Center. Has more than 30 specialty shops, even a deli so you can nosh while you shop before theater. 600 New Hampshire Avenue, NW.

Old Town Alexandria is just across the Potomac in Virginia. This is a shopping mall with a touch of colonial history. Fashion, antiques, craft shops. Don't miss the Torpedo Factory Art Center, a remodeled 1918 munitions factory now housing about 200 artisans and artists who work and sell their crafts here.

WASHINGTON BY NIGHT

We've learned the hard way that it is advisable to make reservations for the Kennedy Center performances (or for any other major performance) as far in advance as possible. All major theaters, however, hold a certain number of seats for last-minute VIP guests. To get one of these plums, use your connections. Try the concierge of your hotel, or call someone who knows someone. You can also call Barbara Kleine, president of Premiere Theater Seats at 703/963-6161. She buys up blocks of top-sellers and resells them for an $8 premium. Call in advance and she'll hold your tickets until you arrive. The Talbert Ticket Agency in the Hotel Washington (628-5575) is another good source, frequent visitors tell us.

The Ticketron number is 659-2601. You might also try TICKET-place, which sells half-price day-of-the-show tickets (for cash only) on a first-come, first-served basis. 12th and F Streets, NW. 842-5387 (TIC-KETS).

One final word on safety. Darkness changes any city's character. Avoid areas like the Mall that, although completely safe during the day, become deserted and dangerous at night.

Kennedy Center for the Performing Arts

2700 F Street, NW   Toll-free: 800/424-8504
Washington, DC 20566   Ticket information: 254-3600

There are four performance halls in the Kennedy Center: The Eisenhower Theater, Concert Hall, Opera House, and Terrace Theater. Check daily newspapers for current productions. Charge by phone through Instant Charge 857-0900. Credit cards. You can reach Kennedy Center by cab or Metro. Exit Foggy Bottom/GWU Station and walk about seven minutes along New Hampshire Avenue. It's safe enough.

Kennedy Center has four restaurants: the Roof Terrace for lunch, dinner, midnight supper, reservations required, 833-8870; the Hors d'Oeuvrerie, drinks and snacks; Curtain Call Cafe; Encore Cafeteria. For more elegant dining, try the Wintergarden at the Watergate Hotel and then walk to the center through the underground passage.

The **Arena Stage,** famous as a theater-in-the-round, won the first Tony Award given outside New York City. One of D.C.'s pride and joys. 6th and Maine Avenue, SW. 488-3300.

The **Folger Theater** presents Elizabethan and contemporary theater. 201 E. Capitol Street, SW. 546-4000.

Ford's Theater offers legitimate theater and tours that point out Lincoln's Presidential Box. 511 10th Street, NW. 347-4833.

The **Lisner Auditorium** presents experimental shows and dance, ballet, and concerts. At George Washington University, 21st and H streets, NW. 676-6800.

The **Library of Congress's Coolidge Auditorium** is the scene of regular Friday concerts at 8 P.M. A nominal charge for such ensembles as the Juilliard String Quartet, Academy Trio. 101 Independence Avenue, SE. 257-0547.

The **National Theater,** the oldest in America, was built in 1835. Hosts top touring shows such as *Cats.* Some free performances (in Helen Hayes Gallery; Saturday morning children's shows). You can visit its library of theater history by requesting an appointment in advance. 1321 E. Street, NW. 544-1900.

The **New Playwright's Theater** showcases new works, followed by discussions with cast, director, playwright. 1742 Church Street, NW. 232-2151.

The **Warner Theater** is a spot for Broadway-bound shows still in try-outs. 513 13 Street, NW. 626-1050.

Wolf Trap Farm Park is the first national park for the performing arts. Located about 30 miles outside town (see "At Leisure").

DINNER THEATERS

Brook Farm Inn of Magic. 7101 Brookville Road, Chevy Chase, Md. 652-8820.

Burn Brae Dinner Theater. Route 29 and Blackburn Road, Burtonsville, Md. 384-5800.

Harlequin Dinner Theater. 1330 Gude Drive, Rockville, Md. 301/340-8515.

Hayloft Dinner Theater. Has a great buffet. 10501 Bullsford Road, Manassas, Va. 368-3666.

Lazy Susan Dinner Theater. Pennsylvania Dutch buffet. Woodbridge, Va. 703/550-7384.

West End Dinner Theater. 4615 Duke Street, Alexandria, Va. 703/370-2500.

CONCERTS

Many of the best concerts are free. The **National Gallery of Art** presents concerts from September to June on Sundays at 7 P.M. 537-6247. There's chamber music at 5 P.M. on Sundays at the **Phillips Collection** as well as at the **Library of Congress** (the latter charges a nominal fee of 25 cents). The Smithsonian Chamber Players also give free evening concerts. 357-3030.

Check weekend papers or the *Washington Post Weekly* entertainment section for current information.

LATE-NIGHT WASHINGTON

To those who insist Washington is an early-to-bed town, we wish a hearty "sleep well." To those who search for life after dark, we offer the following suggestions.

Long hours of pub-crawling have gone into researching this list. If you're heading out alone, we can recommend **F. Scott's, Sign of the Whale, Rumor's,** and **Bullfeather's** as safe singles spots. Local women regard the area around 19th and M as singles' heaven—a cluster of bars and restaurants with upscale clienteles and safe atmospheres.

Local professional women agree that one place—**Mike Baker's**— is their favorite. Mike is a very popular personality around town, charismatic and generous, hosting events in his club like "celebrity bartenders" in which customers get a chance to tend bar and the proceeds go to charity. 1716 H Street, NW. 342-6433.

PIANO BARS AND CABARETS
Every place listed here is classy and fine for women alone.

The Federal Bar. Vista International Hotel, 1400 M Street, NW. 429-1700.

Fairfax Bar. Ritz Carlton Hotel, 2100 Massachusetts Avenue, NW. 293-2100.

The Garden Terrace. Four Seasons Hotel, 2800 Pennsylvania Avenue, NW. 342-0444.

Capitol View Lounge. Hyatt Regency Washington, 400 New Jersey Avenue, NW. 737-1234.

Hay Room. Hay-Adams Hotel, 800 16th Street, NW. 638-2260.

Bennett's. Jefferson Hotel, 1200 16th Street, NW. 467-4849.

The Fire Escape Cabaret. 105 N. Alfred Street, Alexandria. 548-0076. Comedienne Joan Cushing entertains with show tunes, monologues, and satirical take-offs on political foibles. Popular club, all ages. You actually climb a fire escape to get in.

JAZZ

Jazz is big in Washington. The city has a long history as a center for good jazz.

Blues Alley is one of the top spots in the country. Expect top performers, celebrity clientele. The cover charge varies with the importance of the talent. Open nightly until 2 A.M. 1073 Wisconsin Avenue, NW (Georgetown). 337-4141.

One Step Down features a more casual setting. Jazz combo or the club's amazing all-jazz jukebox that features vintage Billie Holiday, Charlie Parker, Dizzy Gillespie. Burger and deli-type menu available. Top (weekend) cover is $7.50. No reservations. 2517 Pennsylvania Avenue, NW. 331-8863.

Mr. Henry Adams Morgan is popular with jazz musicians. Also has a jazz brunch. 1836 Columbia Road, NW. 797-8882.

AFTER-HOURS BARS

Clyde's. Once *the* spot, maybe a bit too popular now. 3236 M Street, NW, Georgetown. 333-0294.

Bullfeather's. You can rub elbows with and eavesdrop on Capitol Hill's best here. 410 1st Street, SE. 543-5005.

Bojangles. Sidewalk cafe and background of new wave, rock, top-40 music. 2100 M Street, NW. 659-3536.

Beowulf. This spot attracts newspaper and media types. 1112 20th Street, NW. 296-4111.

The Dubliner. Handsomest Irish bar in town. Live entertainment; sing-alongs. Eavesdrop on some big-name political gossip in the making. In Phoenix Park Hotel. 520 N. Capitol Street, NE. 737-3773.

F. Scott's, an art deco, trendy spot. Draws film stars, upscale crowd. Height of Georgetown chic; dress up to go here. 1232 36th Street, NW, Georgetown. 965-1789. Just across the street is the renovated **Biograph Theater,** which features art and foreign films, old Hollywood classics.

Mr. Henry's of Georgetown. Casual neighborhood place serving light foods until 12:30 A.M. Popular with gays and straights. 1225 Wisconsin Avenue, NW. 337-4334.

Numbers. This is big with folks who like the strobe lights–video type of disco. Closed Mondays. 1330 19th Street, NW. 463-8888.

Jenkins Hill. Popular with media and Hill types. Canned music, dancing. 223 Pennsylvania Avenue, SE. 544-6600.

Rumors. Features enclosed sidewalk cafe, dancing. 1900 M Street, NW. 466-7378.

Sign of the Whale. A favorite of lawyers and paralegals. More dressy than casual. 1825 M Street, NW. 223-4152.

Tabard Inn. A medieval honeycomb of small nooks and crannies. Summer outdoor cafe, winter by blazing fireplace. 1739 N Street, NW. 785-1277.

The Nightclub 9:30. Go with friends, not alone, to this frenetic new wave spot. Lots of punk trendies slam-dancing and modeling the latest in spiked hair fashions. 930 F Street, NW. 393-0930.

AT LEISURE

You've worked hard. Now can you squeeze in some well-deserved fun time, even a one- or two-day minivacation tacked onto the end of your business trip? If you can, be sure to save yourself some money by checking various hotel weekend packages.

Day-Tripping

Wolf Trap Farm Park is our only national park dedicated to the performing arts—jazz to dance, musicals to symphonies. The shelter holds about 3,500 while others sprawl on blankets and enjoy picnics. Performances also in the Barns. Send for free calendar and schedule. 1624 Trap Road, Vienna, VA 22180. 703/255-1916.

Old Town Alexandria, a charming colonial city, was once George Washington's hometown. Founded by Scots in the 18th century as a seaport, it retains much of the original ambience. Best way to get acquainted with the area is on foot. Take the self-guided walking tour that starts at Ramsay House, the oldest home in the district and also the site of the Alexandria Tourist Council. Don't miss the Torpedo Factory Art Center (also some good shopping here), Gadsby's Tavern Museum, Robert E. Lee's house. A 13-minute film is shown twice daily. Ramsay House is open daily, 9 A.M. to 5 P.M., except on major holidays. Located six miles south of downtown; take Metro Yellow line. If you drive, a free 72-hour parking pass is available. 221 King Street, Alexandria, Va. 703/549-0205 or 549-SCOT.

C&O Canal Historic Park has a wide towpath along both sides of the canal, a favorite for joggers, bikers, or hikers. In summer there are mule-drawn barge trips from Georgetown to Great Falls, Maryland. The park is at 11710 MacArthur Boulevard, Potomac, Md. 472-4376 or 301/299-2026.

Great Falls Park is a beautiful setting where the Potomac River plunges over huge boulders through the Stephen Mather Gorge. Wooded park is great for hiking, picnicking, even bird watching. Free admission. Open daily 8 A.M. to dusk. 9200 Old Dominion Drive, Great Falls, Va 703/759-2925.

Luray Caverns are the largest and most popular caverns in the East. On-site museum, too. Less than two hours southwest of town (take I-66 west to U.S. 211 west). Call 703/743-6551 for hours.

At the **NASA Goddard Space Flight Center,** you can see full-scale displays of rockets and satellites with film clips of recent flights. A model rocket launch occurs the first and third Sunday of every month. Free admission. Greenbelt, Md. 301/344-8101.

Mount Vernon, most popular of the nation's shrines, draws a million visitors a year. Here you can feel the presence of George Washington, the man, in his stately home, and see trees he planted himself, his herb and vegetable garden. Guides are present to answer questions. Open every day of the year, from 9 A.M. to 5 P.M. Best time to visit: during the week, if possible, when crowds are lighter. Gray Line and other operators run scheduled tours. For maximum enjoyment, take the boat trip down the Potomac on a paddle wheeler (Washington Boat Lines, 554-8000). Mount Vernon, Va. 703/780-2000.

You might visit **Woodlawn Plantation,** while you're in the Mount Vernon neighborhood. Designed by Dr. William Thornton, first architect of U.S. Capitol. On grounds, the Frank Lloyd Wright–designed Pope-Leighey House. 703/557-7880.

Around Town

Here is your chance to visit those Smithsonian Museums you didn't have time for between appointments during the week.

The **Tourmobile,** a shuttle bus provided by the National Park Service, runs between all the major sites and allows you to see them at your own pace. For one price ($6.50), you can board and reboard buses all day long within the scheduled route that covers 18 sites from the Mall to Arlington National Cemetery.

Tours are narrated, and because of the group dynamics on board, they are a great way to meet people. Begin the tour anywhere you see a red and white Tourmobile stop sign. Hint: be prepared for long lines at reboarding sites. For more details and a route map, write to 1000 Ohio Drive, SW, Washington, DC 20024, or call 554-7950.

In nice weather, take advantage of D.C.'s waters. Try **paddleboating in the Tidal Basin** for a relaxing and pleasant experience. Boat rentals are $4.50 for 30 minutes. Consider bringing along a picnic lunch to really get away from it all.

A bit more lavish: dinner aboard the **Dandy,** a cruising restaurant. Both luncheon and dinner cruises are offered. Leave from Old Town Alexandria. Call 703/683-6076 for reservations.

Spectator Sports

Super Bowl champs, the **Washington Redskins,** knock heads from August through the end of the season. RFK Memorial Stadium. 546-2222.

The Capital Centre in Landover, Md. (301/350-3400), is home to Washington's hockey and basketball teams. The NBA **Bullets** hit the courts from October through April; tickets at Ticketron. The **Capitals** of the National Hockey League also play October to April; for tickets, call 202/432-0220 (outside the Washington area, 800/448-9009).

Active Sports

Free golf courses, tennis courts, jogging trails, and other out-door pursuits are enjoyed at both **Rock Creek Park** (Washington's largest municipal park) and **East Potomac Park** at Hain's Point. You can also hire horses at Rock Creek Park. Jogging is safe in either park—Rock Creek is patrolled by mounted Park Service Police. We feel safe in the early morning hours, but wouldn't recommend dusk-to-dark jogging here. The same advice for jogging along the Mall, another D.C. favorite jogging path.